# When a Great Tradition Modernizes

# When a Great Tradition Modernizes

*An Anthropological Approach to Indian Civilization*

Milton Singer

FOREWORD BY M. N. SRINIVAS

The University of Chicago Press
Chicago and London

For Helen—
with love and gratitude

The University of Chicago Press, Chicago 60637
The University of Chicago Press, Ltd., London


Midway Reprint 1980
Printed in the United States of America

ISBN: 0-226-76102-9
LCN: 79-26490

# Contents

# *Foreword*

Professor Milton Singer is too well-known an anthropologist for his book to need an introduction from anyone, and I consider his request that I write a foreword for it one more instance of his regard for me and of his generous acknowledgment of such stimulation as he may have received from my writings. It is only fair to add here that my own thinking has been influenced in recent years by Singer, as my *Social Change in Modern India** will show. It gives me particular pleasure to acknowledge that his writings continue to stimulate me in a variety of ways. The present work, for instance, is uniformly thought-provoking, and I find Singer's comments on the adaptive strategies of Indian culture to new forces and circumstances particularly insightful. He rejects, and rightly, the view that traditional Indian society was resistant to change; he shows that the adaptive strategies evolved over several centuries prior to the establishment of British rule continue to function today.

The course of anthropological theory has been deeply influenced by the work of such scholars as Sir Henry Maine, Robertson Smith, and Fustel de Coulanges, whose primary interest was in the older civilizations or in the ancient periods of modern civilizations. Subsequent generations of anthropologists, including such renowned scholars as Sir James Frazer, Marcel Mauss, and A. L. Kroeber, have moved freely from the consideration of ethnographic data bearing on primitives to literary and historical data on the ancient and medieval periods of the "civilizations." In short, though cultural and social anthropology did concentrate until the end of World War II on primitive peoples, it occasionally went beyond its self-imposed boundaries to consider parallels and linkages between the "civilized" and the "primitives."

There is, however, a difference between reliance on literary, archaeological, and historical material on the civilizations of the Old World and carrying out field work in them. If field work, especially intensive field work, is an important diacritical sign of cultural and social anthropology, then field work in civilized countries is an appropriate way of indicating their formal inclusion in the discipline. The Department of Anthropology of the University of Chicago played a leading role in this enterprise in the

* Berkeley and Los Angeles: University of California Press, 1966. See especially Chapter I.

1930's, when, under the leadership of Robert Redfield, field studies began to be carried out in Mexico, Guatemala, Canada, and Japan. As a result of his field work, Redfield formulated in the 1950's his project on the "Comparative Study of Civilizations," and Singer was intimately associated with Redfield in that project. Indeed, Singer's first visit to India came about in connection with the establishment of a suitable "base" from which he and Redfield could conduct field studies. That visit led to Singer's involvement in India, an involvement that has paid rich dividends for Indian studies in the United States and elsewhere. This book is also a happy outcome of that involvement.

The 1930's were also important for the development of anthropology and sociology in India. Indian scholars, in particular G. S. Ghurye at Bombay, encouraged their students to do field work among tribal or other sections of the population, ignoring the conventional barriers between cultural and social anthropology and sociology.

Understandably, the extension of anthropology to include civilizations has profound consequences for the discipline. For one thing, no single discipline can hope to subsume within itself the study of all aspects of a civilization. The need for collaboration with scholars from a variety of other fields is the first thing that impresses itself upon the anthropologist when he is confronted with the study of a civilization. Finally, the richness and diversity of the culture and the abundance of the historical and other data available require from him long and patient study. Students may well find that it is even more difficult to apply the comparative method to the study of civilizations than it is to the study of "primitive societies." Perhaps they should begin by applying the comparative method within that civilization and consider applying it across civilizations only subsequently.

The extension of the scope of social and cultural anthropology to include civilizations means, among other things, that theories that have emerged essentially from the study of primitive societies will have to be tested against the vastly more complex data about civilizations, with the likelihood that they will need to be radically modified. (See in this connection the introduction to Part Three, with Singer's fruitful comments on the contribution of the study of the Krishna myth to anthropological theory.) The availability of data of sufficient richness on selected periods of a civilization might prove crucial for the understanding of social change. Anthropology will have to move closer to history, especially social, economic, religious, legal, literary, and art history. Anthropologists will have to work in collaboration with other social scientists and with scholars who have specialized in the study of the relevant classical languages. Such cooperation will, it is hoped, increase the relevance of anthropology to the problems of the modern world.

Singer points out that the classical structural-functional approach to anthropology subordinates culture to social structure and that this greatly limits its heuristic value in the study of civilizations. A student of civilizations can ignore culture only at his peril. One of the characteristics of a civilization is a class of literati whose business it is to study, comment upon, interpret, and even elaborate ideology, myth, and ritual. Its existence and functioning are crucial to the understanding of the patterned behavior of ordinary members of the civilization. Hence, attempts to abstract social structural elements from culture are hazardous.

Singer finds the concept of "Sanskritic Hinduism" complex, inasmuch as each devotee perceives the phenomenon only through his sectarian, caste, and other affiliations. In other words, a multitude of perceptions find expression in differing rituals, myths, dogmas, and even world views. The problem for the anthropologist is to relate the various perceptions to each other and to trace out the elements common to all. The ways in which these perceptions have altered during the last hundred years or so of nationalism and cultural and social change ought to provide a fascinating subject for study.

In his introduction to Part Four, Singer writes that his Chapter 7, on social organization, "raises the question whether, in view of the existence in India of variant models for 'Sanskritic Hinduism' as well as of non- and anti-Sanskritic models, a more general conception of the Indian Great Tradition should be defined, perhaps in terms of S. K. Chatterjee's 'Indianism.'" It is, however, very difficult, as Singer recognizes, to put salt on the tail of this "Indianism," for the one institution common to all Indians, irrespective of religion, sect, language, and region, is caste, which, according to the reformers at least, is notoriously divisive. Other widespread features of Indian society are the extended family and the general idiom of hierarchical social relationships based on caste and also ownership of land. It must be recognized here that a common cultural idiom, while it does provide a *basis* for unity, is not the same thing as unity. Common values uniting the entire country, or at least a large majority of its inhabitants, are probably still emerging. The fact that this observation also applies to several "developed" countries does not make it less true.*

Parts Four and Five, which bear on the popular theme of "Tradition and Modernity," are among the most stimulating parts of the book and deserve a wide audience. Singer brings a truly anthropological perspective to the discussion when he states that an "adequate theory of modernization will articulate much more closely with a general theory of cultural change than does the classical theory of 'traditional' and 'modern' societies." Equally significant is his point that it is wrong to equate the "traditional" with the stagnant and unchanging, as is usually done. Indian society, for instance, has been adjusting itself to new forces and circumstances throughout its recorded history and has evolved certain strategies of adaptation which continue to serve it well. In Part Four, Singer has identified some of these strategies and he stresses the need for more study and analysis in order to identify others: "The particular kinds of adaptations, such as compartmentalization, ritual neutralization of the work sphere, vicarious ritualization, and the others used by the [Madras] industrialists may not be the only kinds involved. And the nature and interrelations of these adaptive strategies need a good deal more study and analysis."

* I am not considering here the phenomenon whereby nationalism splinters into lesser loyalties—an occurrence in a few developed countries.

It is a fascinating paradox that the "cultural ideology of 'traditionalism' is one of the major instruments of modernization." Movements that progressive intellectuals in developing countries would castigate as revivalist frequently contain elements of modernization. Often such "revivalism" is the best means for introducing new ideas and practices. The process of modernization is complicated enough in any society but far more so in the historic civilizations.

In short, the present book is indispensable not only to anyone who wishes to understand the forces operating beneath the surface in modern India but also to all students of social and cultural change and, in particular, of the modernization process in developing countries. Finally, I will be failing in my duty if I do not call the reader's attention to Singer's informal and lucid style, which makes the book a pleasure to read.

M. N. SRINIVAS

*Delhi*
*January, 1972*

# *Preface*

This book is a record of one traveler's passage to India, begun in 1953 and still not finished after three trips and continuing study. The passage has been a journey of discovery about India, its people, problems, and civilization. It has also brought discovery about America and Europe, oneself, and human culture—a passage to more than India, in Whitman's words.

The method of discovery has been the anthropological one, getting to know another culture in its own terms. India, however, was not just out there waiting to be understood. It had already been discovered and rediscovered many times in other people's terms. India has been struggling to free herself from these foreign terms since Independence. The foreign visitor must struggle to understand India through and beyond these terms.

No traveler to India goes with pure eyes or an untouched mind. He is lured by the fabulous or exotic and spiritual images that have passed over India like the mist of her hills. These are the private goals and the childhood dreams of that journey to the East which Herman Hesse says also aims at lofty public goals.

This book is not a report of intensive field studies. The well-rounded ethnographic study and the small community study have not proved sufficient for the discovery of a historic and living civilization. These methods of social and cultural anthropology need extension and modification to deal with the social structure and culture patterns of such a civilization. The three field trips reported in this volume are explorations of an extended method for a social anthropological study of civilizations. They should be read in this spirit and in the context of the more general issues discussed in the theoretical papers. Between these discussions and the field studies there is an interplay. The movement of thought in the general discussions tends to be deductive, from general concepts and assumptions to probable particular facts. In the reports of the field studies, the movement is reversed; we begin with particular facts of observation and pass to general ideas and explanations suggested by these facts. At least one of the chapters, "The Social Organization of Sanskritic Hinduism in Madras City," begins with the particular observations from transcribed field notes and goes on to a more abstract level of analysis suggested by these observations. A roughly chronological sequence is retained in the volume as a whole to make it possible for the reader to retrace the order of discovery.

No claim is made that the theoretical papers dovetail perfectly with the field reports; the particular facts disclosed in the latter provide observational tests for the general hypotheses of the former, and the results of the field tests in turn furnish new ideas for theoretical elaboration. Even in the most rigorous natural science studies, the dialectical interplay between theory and observation is not quite so logical. Contexts of people and "accidental" events, as well as contexts of ideas and observations, have to be reckoned with. The introductions to each major part of the book give some of the biographical and historical information about the contexts of time, place, and person in which the theoretical papers were written and the field trips conducted. If a reader chose to read through these introductions in rapid sequence, he might discern the dialectic of thought and observation stimulated by the author's passage to India.

No one can claim accurately to reconstruct the movements of his thought over a seventeen-year period, and this claim is not made here. Whatever the autobiographical accuracy of the reconstruction, the reader will find a set of leading ideas winding through the following pages as the creeper or *latā* curves through Indian art. Some of these ideas are Robert Redfield's, especially the conception of a civilization as at once a set of cultural products, of cultural processes, and of communities. The cultural products embrace the "great tradition" of intellectual and aesthetic achievements as well as the "little tradition" of folk and popular culture. Cultural products of a civilization are not created in a vacuum; they flourish in the primary and secondary processes of urbanization that organize and transform little and great communities as well as cultural traditions. The details of Redfield's theory of the growth and transformation of civilizational structures are given in several papers in this volume. The relevance of the present volume to this theory is that it explores field methods for testing Redfield's ideas in a metropolitan urban setting.

In the late 1940's and early 1950's, when, in collaboration with Robert Redfield, I first started to work on an extended method for a social anthropology of civilizations, there was little interest in the project among anthropologists. National character studies using the personality and culture approach had a certain vogue then; Alfred Kroeber's *Configurations of Culture Growth* stood as a lonely monument to a culture-historical approach to civilizations, and a number of small community studies had been undertaken in India, Japan, China, and several other civilizational areas. But the suggestion that the field methods and concepts of social anthropology might be extended to a study of the social organization of Great Traditions of these civilizations was greeted with skepticism. Some Sinologists, Indologists, and Islamicists expressed more confidence in the desirability and feasibility of such a development than did anthropologists. In this climate of opinion the appearance of M. N. Srinivas's

*Religion and Society Among the Coorgs of South India* in 1952 was a decisive event. It was the first anthropological monograph to show us how a Great Tradition (of Sanskritic Hinduism) could be analyzed within a social anthropological framework, and it set going much of what follows in this volume. I am gratified that Professor Srinivas recognizes the family resemblance in the distant descendant of his monograph, and I thank him for his Foreword. There were of course a few other anthropologists who had started to work along similar lines at that time—David Mandelbaum, Louis Dumont, Clifford Geertz—but their monographs had not yet appeared, and Srinivas's Coorg study stood as the model for us all. Since then the interest among anthropologists in a social anthropology of civilizations has grown. Recent publications by Bernard Cohn and McKim Marriott on India, Melford Spiro on Burma, Jack Goody on literacy in traditional societies, and Edmund Leach on dialectics in practical religion testify to this growing interest and provide good company for the present volume.

Chapters 3, 4, 5, 6, and 8 frequently make use of the present and historical present although the observations and interviews on which they were based were made over a ten-year period, from 1954 through 1964, and the analysis and writing extended over a sixteen-year period, from 1955 to 1971. I hope that the introductions and contexts will make the temporal references clear. In those cases where it seemed important to update references I have done so in appropriate footnotes.

In and around Madras City, and especially in Mylapore, the author found India's Great Tradition of Sanskritic Hinduism still a pervasive force in the lives of ordinary people. Jean Renoir has said that "in India one could make a full-length picture just by following someone through the day. A grandmother, say, getting up in the morning, cooking, washing clothes. Everything noble." He has made such a film, and Satyajit Ray has made several. The nobility of these ordinary people, however, is to be found not only in what immediately strikes the visitor—the women's colorful grace, the dignified faces and bearing of the men, the slow rhythms of a folklike culture. Their lives also take their form and color from an imposing corpus of epics, legends, philosophies and religions, arts and sciences. The rounds of life and ceremonies move through an ancient ritual calendar; they still worship the gods of the Vedas, the *Mahābhārata,* the *Rāmāyaṇa,* the *Bhāgavatapurāṇa,* as well as numerous local deities; their world view may be drawn from the Upaniṣads, their ethics from the *Bhagavadgītā,* the *Dharmaśāstra,* and the *Tirukkuṟaḷ;* their rules of art from the *Śilpaśāstra,* and their rules of medicine from *Āyurvedic* texts. Their worldly ambitions are guided into practice by the *Arthaśāstra,* and their spiritual inspiration is drawn from the lives and songs of poet-saints.

Life in India, of course, is not all governed by ancient religion, philosophy, and ethics. Times are changing in Madras as everywhere else. The demands of modern living and work are felt in the most orthodox Hindu homes and institutions. A vigorous political movement has made Sanskritic Hinduism a target and is promoting a more purely Dravidian cultural nationalism. How some Madras Hindus adapt their cultural traditions as they acquire modern literary and scientific educations, move into a metropolitan center, and go into industry is a major theme of this volume. These adaptations have something to say, the author believes, about the structure and change of Indian civilization and perhaps of other civilizations as well.

# *Acknowledgments*

The obligations incurred in the preparation of this volume are far too many to acknowledge adequately in a brief note. A general expression of gratitude to all those who have helped will not repay these obligations but will at least express my feeling of indebtedness. A few individuals and institutions must, however, be singled out for their special contributions to my work.

Among the individuals to be thanked are Robert Redfield for his personal inspiration and the framework of ideas for a social anthropology of civilizations; Fred Eggan for an unfailingly sympathetic interest in and encouragement of a maverick anthropological project; W. Norman Brown for introducing me to the Great Tradition of Indian civilization and of Indological scholarship, which he represents; David Mandelbaum for his lucid and humane teaching and writing in Indian anthropology; M. N. Srinivas, whose *Religion and Society Among the Coorgs of South India* first showed me how to extend the methods and concepts of social anthropology to a complex historic civilization.

Also, Dr. V. Raghavan, Sanskritist, who was my chief cultural guide on the first trip to Madras and whose specialized knowledge of Hinduism and Indian culture has continued to be generously available to me and to other visitors to Madras; T. S. Krishnaswami and his son, Professor T. K. Venkateswaran, for welcoming a foreigner to the Rādhā-Krishna *bhajanas* and patiently expounding their devotional and theological significance; Dr. K. A. N. Nilakantha Sastri; R. Venkataraman, the enlightened Madras State Minister of Industries in 1964; Mr. Chitty-Baboo; and Marie Buck, all of whom helped me find and understand the successful industrial leaders of Madras City. To former and present colleagues and students in the University of Chicago Committee on Southern Asian Studies, especially J. A. B. Van Buitenen, Edward C. Dimock, Jr., and A. K. Ramanujan, who have helped to create a community of scholarship from which I have greatly benefited I owe a special debt of gratitude; their help is more specifically acknowledged in the book.

My wife Helen has shared the Indian passage with me and has read the manuscript more than once. Her humanity, wit, and intelligence have, I hope, in some measure been incorporated into it.

I am indebted to my colleague Donald Nelson, a scholar of Sanskrit and Tamil, for standardizing the transcription of Indian words and for preparing the index and glossary. Jacqueline Peterson has given expert secretarial assistance with the preparation of the manuscript, Maureen Patterson, Alice Kniskern, Phyllis Wilson, and Hervé Varenne with the checking of the bibliographical information. Miss Mervyn Adams, editor for Praeger Publishers, has been unsparing of her time and editorial skills to bring the manuscript into shape. I am also grateful to Stella Kramrisch for permission to use in the jacket design the plate of Durgā killing the Buffalo Demon from her book, *The Art of India Through the Ages* (Lonson: Phaidon Press, 1965). To all these and the others not mentioned here, my heartfelt thanks.

My first two trips to India in 1954–55 and 1960–61 were financed from a Ford Foundation grant to the University of Chicago for a project on comparative civilizations organized by Robert Redfield in 1951. The third trip was made possible by a Faculty Research Fellowship from the American Institute of Indian Studies in 1964.

Released time and facilities for analysis, library research, and the writing of various parts of the manuscript were made available to me by the Institute of Far Eastern Studies, University of California, January-June, 1956; the Center for Advanced Studies, Stanford, California, 1957–58 and January-March, 1965; and through the University of Chicago's cooperation with these institutions. The Committee on Southern Asian Studies and the Department of Anthropology of the University of Chicago have funded secretarial and research assistance for the preparation of the manuscript.

For permission to reproduce in somewhat revised form those portions of the volume previously published, the author is indebted to the following publishers in whose publications the material first appeared:

The University of Chicago Press, for "Passage to More than India," published in *Essays in Honor of George Bobrinskoy* (Chicago, 1968).

The Adyar Library and Research Center, Madras, for "Text and Context in the Study of Contemporary Hinduism," published in *Brahmavidyā,* Commemoration Number, 1961.

*The Journal of Asian Studies,* for "The Cultural Pattern of Indian Civilization," published in the *Far Eastern Quarterly* 15, No. 1 (November, 1955): 23–36.

The American Folklore Society, for "The Great Tradition in a Metropolitan Center: Madras," published in M. Singer, ed., *Traditional India: Structure and Change* (Philadelphia, 1959).

The University of Chicago Press, for "The Radha-Krishna Bhajans of Madras City," published in *History of Religions* 2 (1963): 183–226.

*Diogène,* for "The Social Organization of Indian Civilization," No. 45 (1964), pp. 84–119.

Viking Fund Publications, for "The Role of the Joint Family in Modern Industry," in M. Singer and B. Cohn, eds., *Structure and Change in Indian Society* (New York, 1968).

*Comparative Studies in Society and History,* for "Beyond Tradition and Modernity in Madras," Vol. 13, No. 2 (April, 1971), pp. 160–95.

# *A Note on Transcription and Pronunciation*

The current scholarly conventions for transcription of literary forms have been employed for the Indian languages in this volume. For Tamil, the system of the Madras Lexicon has been used with two modifications. First, voiced consonants have been so indicated—thus, *aṟiyādavan* instead of *aṟiyātavan, vaḍa* instead of *vaṭa.* Second, final *n,* since it is always and only alveolar, is not so marked—thus *aṟiyādavan* instead of the hypercorrect *aṟiyādavaṉ.* A consistent effort has been made to standardize spelling throughout the volume by adhering to the Sanskrit model and sacrificing regional, dialectical, and some Anglicized forms. Thus, Hindi *bhajan,* Tamil *upanayanam,* and Anglicized acharya have given way to the Sanskrit forms, *bhajana, upanayana,* and *ācārya.* Further, following this principle, Tamilized Sanskrit, especially in titles, has usually been re-Sanskritized—thus, *Divyaprabandham* rather than the Tamil spelling *Divviyapirabandam.* Words that are found in Webster's International Dictionary (Fourth Edition) are generally given with their Anglicized spelling (but often with diacritics) except where context demanded otherwise. Thus, Krishna usually appears in its Anglicized form but not in the title *Kṛṣṇalīlātaraṅgiṇī.* Where regional or dialectical spelling seemed relevant in context, it has been left intact—thus, the frequent Tamil spelling *bhāgavatar* for Sanskrit *bhāgavata.* Geographical names and the proper names of contemporaries have been left with their "popular" or dialectical spelling—thus, Triplicane, not Tiruvallikkēṇi; Gandhi, not Gāṃdhī.

My overriding principle has been to transliterate directly from the written form, just as it would appear in Devanāgarī or Tamil script. For this reason, compounds rarely occur with splits or hypens between words. Capitalization has been avoided except for proper names—e.g., Yoga, the name of a system—and titles of works. When a word is used in the plural, it has been given the English *-s* ending (which is italicized with the rest of the word). Virtually all declined forms of Sanskrit words have been sacrificed to undeclined forms, in the interests of consistency—thus, *karman* for *karma,* Tvaṣṭṛ for Tvaṣṭā. The names of castes, places, sects, months, gods, and *varṇas* are consistently romanized, while the names of festivals and rites are italicized. Nasalization of a preceding vowel, variously indicated by other writers, is here marked by *ṃ,* but for Sanskrit the preferable system of homorganic nasals has been employed—thus, Śaṅkara instead of Śaṃkara.

These transcription systems are graphic, not phonetic, and not based on English vowel and consonant values. Therefore, we add here a brief note on pronunciation. Vowel length is indicated by macrons above the letter, except for *e* and *o* in Sanskrit which are only long. The letter *a* is pronounced as the vowel in "but," *i* as in "pit," *u* as in "pull"; *ā, ī,* and *ū* are as in "call," "routine," and "tune"; *e* and *o* as in "hey" and "go"; *ai* and *au* as in "time" and "cow." Vocalic *r* (*ṛ*) is pronounced as the *ri* in "rich"; *c* and *g* are as in "church" and "gate," never as in "coat" and "page." Sub-dotted consonants are retroflexed. Consonants followed by *h* are aspirated—thus, *th* and *ph,* for example, as in "hothouse" and "uphill." *Ś* and *ṣ* may both be pronounced as *sh,* with the latter more retroflexed. *S* is as in "muss," never as in "muse." The Tamil *ḻ* is a voiced, retroflexed, frictionless continuant. Intervocalic *k* in Tamil is pronounced as *h*. The points and manners of articulation of the remaining Tamil sounds are similar to those described for Sanskrit. Tamil has short *e* and *o* as well as long, and an additional liquid (*ṟ*) which, like the other Tamil *r,* is similar in pronunciation to the Sanskrit single-flap *r*.

# PART ONE / *INDIA AND THE COMPARATIVE STUDY OF CIVILIZATIONS*

# *Introduction*

The understanding of another culture or civilization, as social and cultural anthropology rightly teaches, requires that the foreign traveler rid himself of ethnocentrism and look at another culture in its own terms. Malinowski's axiom that a major aim of ethnology is to understand the "native" from his own point of view, *his* relation to *his* world, has been accepted by anthropologists since the 1920's. Practical application of this axiom is another matter. Anthropologists have come to realize that ridding oneself of ethnocentric bias in the study of another culture is more difficult, even for anthropologists, than it was assumed to be at the dawn of field work. They are now willing to regard such cleansing as a desirable outcome of comparative cultural studies rather than as a necessary starting point. The difficulty arises not only from the strangeness of other cultures but also from one's own ignorance of ethnocentric biases. To become aware of these biases requires more than a desire to make them explicit and to eliminate them. It requires comparison and contrast with other cultures. The process of getting to understand another culture, it appears, brings greater understanding of one's own, and this increased self-knowledge in turn leads to greater awareness of the ethnocentric and personal screen through which we peer.

The mutual interaction between the understanding of other cultures and the knowledge of one's own is strikingly illustrated by European and American images of India. The changing history of these images, briefly sketched in the essay "Passage to More than India," suggests not only that Westerners have been lured to India by fabulous projective imagery but also that, as they travel there in greater numbers and stay longer, they reach a deeper understanding of both the Indians' and their own cultures.

The essay "Passage to More than India" is a preliminary historical sketch of two Western images of India—the "white man's burden" and "spirituality" images—that reflect the changing economic and political relations between the subcontinent and the West. Harold Isaacs's study *Scratches on Their Minds: American Images of China and India* shows on the basis of direct interviews that many "experts" and leaders of U.S. public opinion are still influenced by such images. Those of us who have been teaching an introductory course on Indian civilization at the University of Chicago since 1956 have also found the same "scratches" on the minds of our students. We have tried to counter this ethnocentrism by bringing it to conscious awareness and placing it in historical perspective. Our purpose has been to help students recognize and take account of such images, not to polish their minds clear of all "scratches." In the last three or four years, we have seen some of our students bring to the Indian civilization course a set of images derived from the "pop Hinduism" stimulated by the Beatles, Allen Ginsberg, and the music of Ravi Shankar. These images in part continue the older romantic belief in Indian "spirituality" of Thoreau, Emerson, and Whitman; they also include a strong interest in communal ecstasy and love, in learning the practical arts of Yoga, drumming the *tablā,* playing the sitār, and chanting *bhajanas.* While some students have a desire to go out to help India's "starving and teeming millions," more are now convinced that India has much to teach them.

"Text and Context in the Study of Contemporary Hinduism" is a plea for collaboration between humanistic scholars who make literary, historical studies of religious texts and social and cultural anthropologists who make direct observational studies of religious beliefs, attitudes, and practices. The chapter originated as a paper prepared for a conference on religion and culture in which most of the participants were historians of religion. It was written before my second trip to India and the Rādhā-Krishna *bhajana* study and presents a methodological rationale for that study and for the Krishna symposium that followed.

The distinction between "textual" and "contextual" is not equivalent to Redfield's distinction between Great Tradition and Little Tradition. The terms "textual" and "contextual" refer to two different *methodological* approaches that various disciplines adopt in the study of culture, while the terms Great Tradition and Little Tradition distinguish the *cultural content* of those aspects of a culture that are regarded as "higher" from those that are considered "lower." The "higher" aspects are usually more reflective and more systematically presented and embody the greatest intellectual and aesthetic achievements of the culture. As such, they tend to be stored in "texts" of various kinds—oral, written, inscribed, carved and painted, sung and acted. In the Indian Great Tradition, these texts include the Vedas and Upaniṣads, the *Dharmaśāstra,* the *Mahābhārata* and *Rāmāyaṇa* epics, the *Bhāgavatapurāṇa,* and a good many others.

A whole cluster of humanistic disciplines developed very early in Indian civilization, as in other civilizations with Great Traditions, to transmit, codify, analyze, and interpret the "sacred" texts. These disciplines include grammar and phonetics, semantics and logic, linguistics, rhetoric, philosophy, the history and criticism of art, and literature and music. Many of these disciplines are still taught as appendages (Vedāṅga) to the study of sacred scriptures in the Madras Sanskrit College and at Śrīperumbudūr (see pp. 108–11). They are also still applied in practical life by a wide range of specialists—pandit, priest, astrologer, *Āyurvedic* doctor, image-maker, diviner and healer, dancer, musician, reciter, and storyteller. Practical knowledge of these disciplines has been transmitted through family inheritance, the teaching of renowned specialists, and schools organized for the purpose. This practical knowledge of the textual disciplines and its transmission have felt the competition of "modern" schools and universities and have responded to this competition (see Chapters 4 and 5).

In the history of Western scholarship, the textual disciplines were at first closely bound to a single corpus of classical texts—those of ancient Greece and Rome—which provided the subject matter, methods, and normative models for the humanistic disciplines. By the end of the eighteenth century, the horizons of the humanities were grudgingly enlarged to include classics of Hebrew, Islamic, Persian, Hindu, Buddhist, and Confucian literature and culture. This development, which is sometimes called the "Oriental renaissance," generated a whole new set of disciplines in comparative humanities—comparative religion, mythology, folklore, literature, philology and linguistics, philosophy, and art. These comparative studies were at first dominated by the normative models of Greek and Roman works; their exponents would not admit an Oriental work into the pantheon of classics unless close affinities with Western models could be demonstrated. Many such affinities were spurious, but occasionally a genuine and productive one was found. A notable genuine affinity was that found by Sir William Jones in the resemblances between Sanskrit and European languages. His discovery stimulated the development of Indo-European linguistic and cultural studies, creating enthusiasm and curiosity in the West about the spiritual treasures of the East, which were considered to be the source of Western religions, philosophies, arts, and languages.[1]

Eventually, the view gained acceptance that the "Oriental humanities" should be studied as classics in their own right, even if they did not resemble European classics and were not the archaic prototypes of European culture and civilization. This approach is now recognized as the appropriate method for the comparative humanities, including cultural and social history. The approach is also followed in contemporary social and cultural anthropology, where it is known as "cultural relativity." Its reincarnation in anthropology, however, was at first divorced from the study of the classics or texts of the Great Traditions. Until quite recently, in fact, most social and cultural anthropologists deliberately eschewed the study of the classics or texts of the Great Traditions. There are good reasons for the antitextual bias. It represents, in the first place, a reaction to the excesses of nineteenth-century anthropologists who, in their zeal to extend the humanists' comparative method, sought to relate all civilizations and cultures by premature universal theories of cultural evolution or cultural diffusion. Second, there is a desire to avoid ethnocentric bias in judgment, especially such bias as may be imposed by the classical norms and standards of Western high culture. Finally, the antitextual bias expresses the anthropologist's methodological commitment to direct personal observations of living communities of people. As a result, social and cultural anthropologists tend to restrict their work to intensive studies of preliterate and simple societies and cultures and nonliterate groups in civilized societies. A major aim of these studies is to demonstrate on the basis of field work how such a society operates as a functionally interdependent social and cultural "system." Such systems were treated as "primitive isolates," to be observed and analyzed in abstraction from any wider culture or society in which they might be embedded.

Such methodological isolationism, populism, and radical empiricism were not well suited to a comparative study of civilizations.[2] As a result, that field of study was neglected by social and cultural anthropologists until after 1945. It was kept alive by the work of a few archaeologists, culture historians, philosophers and historians of civilization, and Orientalists.

Robert Redfield was one of the first social and cultural anthropologists to move in the direction of a "social anthropology of civilizations" by combining the sociological and humanistic approaches. His Tepoztlán and Yucatan studies of the 1930's extended the functional and systemic methods of social anthropology to communities of different size, ecological zones, and levels of cultural development—tribal, peasant, and urban. These communities were not treated as "primitive isolates" but as points on a folk-to-urban continuum, as "gradients of civilization." Degrees of isolation from, or contact with, a civilization center became major independent variables in the study.

The time perspective in these earlier comparative studies was synchronic; the communities were observed and analyzed more or less simultaneously. Conclusions about change and history were based on the comparison of similarities and differences and the assumption that they represented different stages of historical development. Redfield introduced a more directly diachronic time perspective in his lectures on *The Primitive World and Its Transformations.* In this work, the folk-urban continuum is given a long time perspective and is used to chronicle the itinerary of "the human career." Peasantry is traced as a distinctive type of society and culture which emerges from precivilized folk societies when agricultural communities become symbiotically linked to urban centers. These primary urban centers and their satellite peasant and tribal peoples represent an *indigenous civilization* in which literati and other full-time specialists play key roles, including the creation and cultivation of a Great Tradition. The foreign contacts of an indigenous civilization lead to further transformations. "Intelligentsia" who adjust conflicts between the indigenous and foreign cultures play the key role in this secondary urbanization, superseding the literati.

Redfield's application of the folk-urban transformations to a theory of civilization was further extended in our joint paper, "The Cultural Role of Cities."[3] This paper, written for a 1954 conference on urbanization organized by Bert Hoselitz, developed some of Redfield's ideas in *The Primitive World and Its Transformations* toward a comparative study of civilizations. On the basis of that work's explorations in the long-run time perspective of "the human career," the paper sets forth a framework of ideas and hypotheses for studying the role of cities in cultural change within the middle-run time perspective of individual civilizations. This framework also includes links with the short-run "functionalist" studies of the urban geographer, sociologist, and anthropologist. Although the paper opens with a classification of types of cities, the classification is not a major aim or result of the analysis. The classification and illustration of types of cities are introduced in order to identify and illustrate two basically different roles that cities play in processes of cultural change: the "orthogenetic" role of carrying forward and systematically elaborating long-established local cultures, and the "heterogenetic" role of introducing or creating modes of thought and behavior that go beyond or conflict with the established local cultures. The same city may and usually does perform both roles to some extent and will be classified as "orthogenetic" or "heterogenetic" only when one or the other role predominates at a particular period. The paper argues that the "functional" roles and types of cities are best understood if particular cities are seen not as isolated "givens" but as historical growths from underlying patterns of urbanization and culture-change in the orbit of a civilization. It postulates two hypothetical patterns of urbanization, one "primary" and the other "secondary," and traces their social, cultural, and psychological consequences. Special emphasis is given to the ways in which urban-rural cultural integration depends on the formation of a Great Tradition:

> Embodied in "sacred books" or "classics," sanctified by a cult, expressed in monuments, sculpture, painting, and architecture, served by the arts and sciences, the Great Tradition becomes the core culture of an indigenous civilization and a source, consciously examined, for defining its moral, legal, esthetic and other cultural norms. A Great Tradition describes a way of life and as such is a vehicle and standard for those who share it to identify with one another as members of a common civilization.[4]

Political, economic, social, intellectual, and aesthetic activities and institutions tend to be coordinated and understood by reference to the norms of the Great Tradition. These norms are interpreted and implemented by literati, rulers, chiefs, and other agents. Consciousness of a common culture is both a condition for and a consequence of the functional integration of city and country and of the different spheres of society. It provides the source for the communication between Little and Great cultural traditions and for the formation of a world view, value system, and personality type characteristic of the civilization as a whole, in spite of the many internal differences and changes.

Secondary urbanization corrodes the unity and continuity of a primary civilization by introducing conflicting cultural traditions and social groups that cannot be smoothly assimilated to the primary social and cultural structure. Indeed, these new traditions and groups sometimes displace the old by conquest or rapid change. Internal differentiation under these conditions leads to the autonomous development of separate social institutions and spheres of culture held together only by a consensus on the technical order, whose accelerated rate of change tends to outrun the moral order. In metropolitan and colonial cities and in other "secondary" urban centers, the intelligentsia and reformers serve both as agents of cultural innovation and as the "cultural brokers" who try to reconcile and rationalize these innovations with the Great and Little Traditions of their primary civilizations.

The framework of ideas developed in "The Cultural Role of Cities" and in Redfield's *The Primitive World and Its Transformations* extends Redfield's folk-urban continuum theory in two directions. It adds the dimensions of history and archaeology to the spatial-ecological one, and it interposes a "primary civilization" between the folk society and culture, on the one hand, and modern, urban, Western civilization, on the other. Mayan civilization also went through a primary phase of development, according to Redfield, but its Great Tradition and literati were decapitated by the Spanish conquest. By the time he came to study it in the 1930's, it was well into a secondary and even tertiary phase.

> I think what needs to be pointed out is that in Yucatan the old "orthogenetic" changes had been erased by the Conquest, and that, like other students of Latin-America, I happened to come upon the civilizational dimensions of culture and society at a place where things were historically very confused: a folk culture (indigenous) had begun to develop its orthogenetic civilization only to be 'decapitated,' the surviving folk culture then becoming modified into a folk culture of mixed historical origin while, and subsequently, it was being heterogenetically transformed by a very mixed civilization indeed. It is not until the student comes upon the Oriental civilizations that he sees clearly the problems of interrelation of great and little tradition, of folk and civilized components. Merida looked like an "abattoir" of folk culture because it had few orthogenetic features, especially with respect to a largely Mayan peasant-like community.[5]

Other civilizations, such as those of Japan, China, India, and perhaps some of those in Southeast Asia and the Middle East, were in this respect more fortunate, since their Great Traditions appear to have survived foreign intrusions, although with many changes. Redfield decided about 1950 that a cooperative and comparative series of studies of these living civilizations with respect to the ways in which they integrate their Great and Little Traditions would be a useful and important direction for anthropology to take and would also contribute to greater understanding among the peoples of the world.

In 1951, Redfield proposed to Robert Hutchins, who had just resigned as Chancellor of the University of Chicago to become an Associate Director of the Ford Foundation, that a continuing international scholarly effort be mounted to describe and compare the great and enduring cultural traditions of mankind. The foundation made the first of several grants in 1951, to Redfield as director, in support of the project at the University of Chicago. Redfield asked me to serve as associate director. We quickly enlisted the cooperation of Gustave von Grunebaum for studies of Islamic civilization, Arthur Wright and John Fairbank for studies of Chinese thought, Harry Hoijer for research on language and world view, and a number of other scholars for work in history, linguistics, and anthropology. The continuing discussion and planning for the project were centered in the Comparison of Cultures seminar, which we held several times a year at Chicago with student and faculty participation. The seminar concentrated on the problems of method and theory in the comparative study of civilizations. Reports of research were introduced as they became available. The directors of the project also sought to acquaint themselves with scholars and scholarly organizations that were working in these fields in the United States, Europe, and Asia. Special conferences and seminars were sponsored on Chinese, Islamic, and Indian studies and on the relation of language to culture and world view. Promising individual research was supported. With the help of Sol Tax, who was then editor of the *American Anthropologist,* and Morton Grodzins, then editor of the University of Chicago Press, publication was arranged for a memoir series. Plans were made for both Redfield and the author to go to India in order to enlist Indian scholars and undertake field research.[6]

At the time we wrote "The Cultural Role of Cities," neither Redfield nor I had yet visited India. Only one extended reference to India occurs in the paper, the illustration toward the end of how the Great Tradition of Indian civilization is expressed and functions in cultural integration. We had already decided, however, to take Indian civilization as a good field in which to explore the relations of Great and Little Traditions in the context of a living world civilization with a rich historic past. To prepare for the trip to India, I spent about seven months during 1953 and 1954 attending classes at the University of Pennsylvania in W. Norman Brown's South Asia program and at Berkeley in David Mandelbaum's classes. On returning to Chicago in the spring of 1954, I further extended my knowledge of Indian civilization by discussions with a group of specialists on Indian studies whom we had invited to Chicago and from participation in the seminar on Village India, to which we brought eight social anthropologists who had just completed field studies in India. This latter seminar was particularly crucial, for it ended with an unusual consensus that the Indian village is not a self-contained "primitive isolate" but depends on extensive networks of social and cultural relations with other villages and with towns, cities, and local and national political units. While most members of the seminar still regarded a village field study as a useful point of entry to India, they did not think it was the only possible point of entry or even the best. This conclusion gave me the courage to undertake something other than the customary village study on my first trip and to consider some other possibilities for a social anthropological field study of Indian civilization.[7]

## Notes

Works that appear with full publication data in the Selected Bibliography are cited in an abbreviated reference in the notes following each chapter.

1. Raymond Schwab, *La renaissance orientale* (Paris: Payot, 1950), and G. T. Garratt, ed., *The Legacy of India* (Oxford: The Clarendon Press, 1937).

2. Problems of developing method in an anthropology of literate civilizations with textual Great Traditions are discussed in Redfield, *Peasant Society and Culture;* Singer, ed., *Traditional India* (hereafter: *TI*); *idem,* "Social Anthropology and the Comparative Study of Civilizations," in Ward Morehouse, ed., *The Comparative Approach in Area Studies and the Disciplines* (New York: Foreign Area Materials Center, 1966); and throughout the present volume.

3. Redfield, *The Primitive World and Its Transformations;* and Robert Redfield and

Milton Singer, "The Cultural Role of Cities," *Economic Development and Cultural Change* (hereafter: *EDCC*) 3, No. 1 (October, 1954): 53–73, reprinted in M. P. Redfield, ed., *Human Nature and the Study of Society,* and in *Man in India* 36 (July-September, 1956): 161–94.

4. Redfield and Singer, "Cultural Role of Cities," p. 63.

5. From a personal communication written in May, 1956, by Robert Redfield. Redfield also emphatically denies that he thinks of the distinction between Great and Little Traditions as ideal-types or polarities:

> I think of the two traditions not as ideal-types, because I cannot characterize them as possible but non-existent extreme forms of something; I think of them as concepts for separating out, in any old-established civilization with important orthogenetic features, the content, roles and offices, media and process of one system that cultivates a reflective component with other unreflective systems in local communities. It would not have occurred to me to refer to these conceptions as ideal-types. Nor as "polarities."

6. An early account of the project is David G. Mandelbaum, "The Study of Complex Civilizations," in W. H. Thomas, ed., *Current Anthropology* (Chicago: University of Chicago Press, 1956), pp. 203–25. Major publications supported by the project include Wright, ed., *Studies in Chinese Thought;* Fairbank, ed., *Chinese Thought and Institutions;* von Grunebaum, ed., *Unity and Variety in Muslim Civilization;* Harry Hoijer, ed., *Language in Culture* (Chicago: University of Chicago Press, 1954); Marriott, ed., *Village India* (hereafter: *VI*); Singer, ed., *TI;* Leslie, *Now We Are Civilized;* Guiteras-Holmes, *Perils of the Soul.*

7. India specialists attending the 1954 Chicago meeting included W. Norman Brown, Robert Crane, Chadbourne Gilpatrick, Daniel Ingalls, S. M. Katre, Richard Park, Gitel P. Steed, and Phillips Talbot. This group canvassed the needs and trends in Indian studies and made plans for organizing a professional association of all South Asia specialists in the United States. The association was formed and later was incorporated into the Association for Asian Studies. Social anthropologists who participated in the 1951 "Village India" seminar included Alan R. Beals, Bernard S. Cohn, E. Kathleen Gough, Oscar Lewis, David G. Mandelbaum, McKim Marriott, M. N. Srinivas, and Gitel P. Steed.

# *1 / Passage to More than India: A Sketch of Changing European and American Images*

## Introduction

Harold Isaacs's study[1] of the underlying attitudes, feelings, and impressions that 181 American leaders of opinion have regarding China and India reveals sharp "scratches" on their minds about the two countries and their inhabitants. These leaders come from many different fields and professions: universities and colleges, newspapers and magazines, government, business, church and mission groups, and voluntary organizations concerned with education and public opinion. Since we shall be dealing only with images of India, let us see what kind of mental "scratches" Isaacs found among his interviewees relating to India. The images are familiar enough—of a fabulous land of glittering wealth and wild animals, a land of religion and philosophers, a land of benighted heathen and lesser breeds, of Gandhi the saintly statesman and Nehru the intellectual world leader. Some of these are predominantly positive and favorable images: the fabulous, the religious and philosophical, and Gandhi; others are predominantly unfavorable: the benighted heathen and the lesser breeds. In the case of Jawaharlal Nehru, the then Prime Minister, a favorable image was held (in 1958) by more than twice as many as held the unfavorable image.

Isaacs expresses some surprise that leaders of American opinion, many of them "experts," should have such "scratches" on their minds. He probes the sources for these in personal contact, travel, what people read in books and newspapers, see in movies, and learn in school. He also attempts to assess the influence of such images on politics and international relations.

The Isaacs study is a cross-sectional one, probing the images held by a sample of contemporary American leaders. It would also be useful to have a longitudinal study that traces the history of these images as they appear and fade in the encounters of Europeans and Americans with India and Indians. This longitudinal study would be an essential complement to the cross-sectional study, for—as Isaacs indicates—the sources of his interviewees' images are rooted in the past, in the history of their own lives, as well as in the social and cultural history of their country. They are not as individuals entirely free to take or leave the prevailing images and stereotypes, although each may add something personal and eccentric to them.

In this chapter, I propose to sketch the "natural" history of European and American images of India. The history is rather complex, for there are several different dialogues going on simultaneously. There is the dialogue between image and reality. An image always contains some element of truth and is responsive to changes in reality. Events in Goa, for example, not long after Isaacs's book appeared, forced a revision in the image of Indian nonviolence. A second dialogue takes place between the Western image of India and the Indians' self-image. Self-conscious nations, like self-conscious individuals, quickly become aware not only of how they look to themselves but of how others look at them, and then the two sets of images may begin to influence each other. "It was very gratifying to see now what a fine image of India there was before Goa and what an unusually great man Mr. Nehru was and how he has fallen," Nehru said on December 28, 1961, in New Delhi. A third conversation takes place between the images one country holds of another and the psychological needs, fears, and hopes projected onto these images. An image may sometimes reflect more about the psychology of its holder than about any reality to which it purportedly refers. Finally, there is the dialogue between what society and culture contribute to an image and what an individual brings to it. The variety and eccentricity of personal backgrounds need not block intercultural understanding, for this individuality may motivate us to a voyage of discovery we might not otherwise take. The American chicken-farmer in Burma who is described in *The Ugly American* went out to Asia lured by the sound of such words as "cinnamon" and "Rangoon." Herman Hesse expresses in his strange little parable of a "Journey to the East" a good deal of wisdom about this individual and social dialogue:

> One of the characteristics of the Journey to the East was that although the League aimed at quite definite, very lofty goals during this journey . . . yet every single participant could have his own private goals. Indeed, he had to have them; for no one was included who did not have such private goals, and every single one of us, while appearing to share common ideals and goals . . . carried his own fond childhood dream within his heart as a source of inner strength and comfort.[2]

These various conversations of images have made up an important part of the communication that has gone on between India and the West. They have also influenced international policy and behavior. Perhaps the relations between different nations will never be completely free of the dialogue of image and self-image. Yet, as each nation becomes aware of how it looks to others and to itself, and of how it looks upon others, and comes to recognize the distortion, bias, and incompleteness in these different views, the chances for misunderstanding are lessened, and the opportunities for mutual understanding increased. At least that is my assumption and my reason for sketching the character, sources, and changes of some of the images Europe and the United States have held about India.

## Opulent and Fabulous India

The image of India as a land of great wealth, natural marvels, and strange customs prevailed in the ancient world, in the Far East as well as around the Mediterranean.[3] Strabo refers to India as "a nation greater and more flourishing than any other," and Horace called it "opulent India." Dionysius of Periegetes wrote a poem in which he said, "India enriches her sons with wealth in every form," and listed as the country's major occupations the mining of gold, the sawing and polishing of elephant tusks, the weaving of linen, and searching for precious stones in mountain torrents.

Herodotus says that all Indian animals are bigger than those in Europe, except horses. He and other early writers describe eels in the Ganges 300 feet long, ferocious dogs that fight lions, monkeys that roll rocks on their pursuers, one-horned horses with heads like deer, and serpents 80 and 140 cubits long. Among the fabulous races described in these early accounts are a wild tribe with heels in front and toes turned backward, who have no mouths and live on the smell of roast beef and the odors of flowers and fruits; a tribe with ears that hang down to their feet and are used as covers at night; and another whose women conceive at the age of five and are old at eight. Many Indian customs and traits are recorded: a love of finery and ornament paired with a love of simplicity, the marrying of many wives, the burning of wives upon the death of the husband, and exercising by passing smooth ebony rollers over the surface of the body. At that time, Indians had a reputation for seldom going to law to settle disputes.

So strong is the sense of the marvelous in the classical reports of India that one is tempted to conclude that the early Europeans found India interesting because of the wonders it purportedly contained. Its land, animals, plants, and people were in some respects strange and astonishing. Its wealth of gold, silver, precious stones, and spices also took on these qualities of the wonderful and must have owed much of their importance in the "luxury trade" to these qualities. Even its philosophers were distinguished, in the eyes of Greek and Roman writers, for the unusual character of their doctrines and the still more astonishing rigors of their conduct.

I shall give two examples of how this image of a land of wonders merges with the images of opulence and wisdom. The first is Herodotus's description of how the Indians obtained the large amounts of gold they paid as tribute to Darius; it is the first account of the gold-digging ants:

> In this desert . . . and in the sand, there are ants in size somewhat less indeed than dogs, but larger than foxes. . . . These ants, forming their habitations underground, heap up the sand, as the ants in Greece do, and in the same manner; and they are very like them in shape. The sand that is heaped up is mixed with gold. The Indians therefore go to the desert to get this sand, each man having three camels, on either side a male one harnessed to draw by the side, and a female in the middle. . . . The Indians then adopting such a plan and such a method of harnessing, set out for the gold, having before

calculated the time, so as to be engaged in their plunder during the hottest part of the day, for during the heat the ants hide themselves under the ground. When the Indians arrive at the spot, having sacks with them, they fill them with the sand, and return with all possible expedition. For the ants, as the Persians say, immediately discovering them by the smell pursue them, and they are equalled in swiftness by no other animal, so that the Indians, if they do not get the start of them while the ants were assembling, not a man of them could be saved. Now the male camels . . . slacken their pace, dragging on, . . . but the females, mindful of the young they have left, do not slacken their pace. Thus the Indians, as the Persians say, obtain the greatest part of their gold; and they have some small quantity more that is dug in the country.[4]

This story is repeated with embellishments by other ancient and medieval writers. One reports that he saw the skins of the gold-digging ants in India. These reports seem to be based on an Indian tradition. There is a passage in the *Mahābhārata* that mentions "gold dug up by ants (Pippilikas) and therefore called ant-gold (Pippilikas)." [5] Because Megasthenes states that the gold was carried away from the Derdai, modern scholars have concluded that the "ants" were Tibetan miners.[6]

My second example is the story of the Indian embassy to Augustus Caesar. This embassy included eight naked servants who presented gifts consisting of a man born without arms, large snakes, a serpent ten cubits long, a river tortoise three cubits long, and a partridge larger than a vulture. These were accompanied by an ascetic who burned himself at Athens.

Strabo explains the ascetic's self-immolation: "As everything had gone well with him up to this time, he thought it necessary to depart, lest if he tarried longer in the world some unexpected calamity should befall him. . . . On his tomb was the inscription 'Zarmanochegas, an Indian from Bargosa, having immortalized himself according to the custom of his country, lies here.' " [7] Of this custom, one early writer remarked that no Sophist has yet appeared among the Indians, as among the Greeks, to perplex them by asking, "If everybody did this, what would become of the world?" The early sources do not indicate, however, whether this custom and the other marvels that astonished the Greeks were equally astonishing to the Indians themselves.

The chief sources of the early European image of India were the luxury trade through the Middle East and the accounts of travelers. The objects in the luxury trade—pepper, cinnamon, nutmeg, cloves, gold, diamonds, pearls, precious stones, ivory, silks, and cottons—spoke for themselves. Many of the European words for these objects are loan words from Indian languages. The English word "India" itself carries the traces of the old trade routes, for it comes from the Latin *India* which can be traced from the Greek *Indikē* through the Persian *Hindu* back to the Sanskrit *Sindhu,* the name the ancient Indians gave to the Indus River. Pliny complained that the trade with India was draining Rome's treasury. In some cases, India was not the original source of the luxuries but only an entrepôt, for some of the spices, precious stones, and gold came from Ceylon, Indonesia, and the Malay Peninsula.

The travelers who wrote accounts based on personal observation were merchants, soldiers, and ambassadors. The most detailed were written by some of Alexander's scholarly officers and by Megasthenes, who was sent as an ambassador to the Maurya Court in Pāṭaliputra. Strabo, the Roman geographer, is highly critical of Megasthenes and the early Greek writers, although he draws heavily on their accounts. Everything about Megasthenes' account, he says, is "exaggerated and represented as marvelous." In another place, he concludes that "the men who have hitherto written on the affairs of India are a set of liars" who have coined fables. He prefers Roman sources: "The entrance of a Roman army into Arabia Felix under the command of my friend and companion Aelius Gallus and the traffic of the Alexandrian merchants, whose vessels pass up the Nile and Arabian Gulf to India, have rendered us much better acquainted with these countries than our predecessors were." [8]

A story that seems to have impressed both the Greeks and the Romans concerns two Indian ascetics, called in Greek accounts "philosophers" and named Kalanos and Mandanis. The story is derived from Onêsikritos, one of Alexander's officers, who was sent to find the sages. Alexander had heard that they went about naked, were inured to hardships and held in highest honor, but would not go to others when invited. Onêsikritos found some outside of the city (Takṣaśilā) sitting or lying naked in the hot sun and talked with two of them. Kalanos, the younger, told Onêsikritos that if he wished to hear him he should strip off his clothes and lie down naked on the stones to listen. Mandanis, the older and wiser, rebuked Kalanos for his insolence and said he would talk with Onêsikritos. He praised Alexander for desiring wisdom and for being the only philosopher in arms he had ever seen.

"I am entitled," he added, "to indulgence, if while conversing by means of three interpreters, who, except for the language, understand nothing we say any more than the vulgar, I am unable to demonstrate the utility of philosophy. One might as well expect water to flow pure through mud."

Mandanis said that the best doctrine was that which removed pleasure and grief from the mind, and that grief differed from labor, which was a friend to man. He said they would unite in advising Taxilês (the King) to receive Alexander as a friend, for if he received a person better than himself, he would be benefited, and if one worse, he would dispose him to be good.

Mandanis asked whether such doctrines were current among the Greeks and was told that Pythagoras, Socrates, and Diogenes held similar views. Mandanis replied that in other respects he thought they entertained sound notions, but erred on one point by preferring custom to nature, for otherwise they would not be ashamed to go naked like himself and to subsist on frugal fare—"for that was the best house which required least repairs."

Both ascetics were invited to accompany Alexander. Kalanos went, changed his mode of life, became an adviser, and went to Persis, where he died on a funeral pyre. Mandanis refused to go, saying he wanted none of the gifts of a man whose desires nothing could satisfy; while he lived he had food enough, and when he died he would be delivered from the flesh and would be translated to a better and a purer state of existence. Alexander praised him and excused him from coming.[9]

## From the Land of Desire to a White Man's Burden

There were during the Middle Ages a number of events that may have increased Europe's knowledge of Asia and of India in particular—the Muslim invasions, the Crusades, and the Mongol invasions. While European merchants, soldiers, slaves, diplomatic embassies, and missionaries traveled to the East, the amount of new knowledge brought back was meager. Marco Polo's travel records and those of a few Franciscan friars gave Europeans their most detailed knowledge of Asia until the end of the fifteenth century, when the Portuguese discoveries began. It is not surprising, therefore, that when religious and political conflict during the fourteenth century cut off the Middle Eastern trade routes to India, the efforts to find a direct sea route should have been guided by the ancient geographies and travel accounts. Nor is it surprising that European explorers, being dependent on these accounts, should continue to be lured by the image of India as a land of fabulous wealth and wonders. In one of the medieval digests of world geography probably used by Columbus, *Imago Mundi,* there is a chapter on "the marvels of India," which repeats the stories of the Greek and Roman authors.

For medieval Europe, as for ancient Greece and Rome, the image of India continued to be that of marvels and great wealth, an image which must have acted as a strong lure for the explorers. As one historian of the explorations writes:

> The information gathered by travellers pictured farthest Asia, with all the enchantment that distance lends, as a land of vast wealth, rich in the commodities which formed the luxuries of Europe, a land of gold and silver, of silks and spices, a land of cities that dwarfed the proudest towns of Europe. And thus the lure of the East became a potent incentive to the explorations of da Gama and Columbus, and later to those of English adventurers who attempted to find the route around the North American continent.[10]

The same idea is stated more abstractly by the German philosopher Hegel:

> India as a land of desire formed an essential element in general history. From the most ancient times downwards, all nations have directed their wishes and longings to gaining access to the treasures of this land of marvels, the most costly which the earth presents, treasures of nature—pearls, diamonds, perfumes, rose essences, lions, elephants, etc.—as also treasures of wisdom.[11]

As the explorations succeed, however, and the Portuguese, Dutch, English, French, and other European nations establish colonial settlements in India (and elsewhere in Asia), a significant transformation takes place in the European image of India. The change does not take place suddenly or all in one place. Rather, new images gradually supersede the old. As more Europeans travel and work in India, the sense of the fabulous fades. By the middle of the nineteenth century, the British scholar and colonial administrator Sir Henry Maine chides his countrymen because they find

Indian topics dull, while the continental Europeans still look upon India as "the most exciting, as the freshest, as the fullest of new problems and the promise of discoveries." For the British, Maine thinks, India is in some respects too near:

> It has none of the interest of a country barely unveiled to geographers, like the valley of the Oxus or the basin of Lake Tanganyika. It is mixed up with the ordinary transactions of life, with the business of government, with debates in Parliament, not too well attended, with the stock exchange, the cotton market, and the annual relief of regiments. Nor do I doubt that the curse of the evil reputation of India which extends most widely is the constant and frequent complaints which almost everybody receives from relatives settled there, of the monotony of life which it entails upon Europeans.[12]

In other respects, he thinks, India's political and moral institutions were too far from the experience of the Englishman, who had not yet seen in them the challenge to his own premises about the universality of his political maxims and moral principles.

This is one side of the transformation—the "land of desire" becomes the white man's burdensome colony. Maine might have added, as further explanation of the change, colonial policy and the relative spurt in manufactures that took place in England in the nineteenth century. Well into the eighteenth century, the products and processes of Indian craftsmen were sought after and imitated by European craftsmen. But as the industrial revolution made headway in Europe, and was simultaneously inhibited in Europe's colonies as a matter of deliberate policy, India began to fall behind in technical and economic development.

The "white man's burden" image does not crystallize on a particular day to displace the older medieval and ancient images. In the popular poem *Lalla Rookh* (1817) by Moore, and in the poetry and prose of the nineteenth-century romantics, the magic of the older images is renewed to entertain and to lure even a "nation of shopkeepers" to India. Some of the magic was also enshrined in the "Indian Gothic" architecture of the Brighton Pavilion.

The foundation for the image of India as a land of dark-skinned, benighted heathen who need the blessings of Christianity and European civilization was laid several hundred years before England's industrial revolution and the establishment of the British Rāj in India. It goes back to the conflict of Christian Europe with Islam. The Portuguese and other early explorers looked upon the Muslims as their hated enemies and rivals. They expected to find in India the Nestorian Christians and the fabled Christian monarch Prester John, about whom Marco Polo and other medieval travelers wrote. When Vasco da Gama was asked at Calicut what he had come for, he replied, "Christians and spices." He found the spices, but many more Hindus and Muslims than Christians.

When the Portuguese (and other Europeans) learned that the Hindus were not Christians, their hatred of Muslims was expanded to include these new "heathen." The Portuguese epic of empire in Asia, *The Lusiads,* as translated by Sir Richard Fanshawe, tells the story of this transformation, of how da Gama's search for Christian allies and spices also discovers the "barbarous sect" worshiping "man-beasts" and "monsters deified," whose ruler is without "shame or worth."

In another stanza (7.31) the new arrivals are told:

> God, God hath brought you: He hath (sure) some grand
> And special buis'ness *here* for *you* to do.

The "special business" is to extend the Christian faith (7.3). Portugal calls upon Germany, England, France, and Italy to unite "to scourge the arrogant Mahumetan."

> Against the Turke let Bootie league you all,
> If not to see the Holy City Thrall [7.11].

But, seeing that these other Christian nations are diverted by fighting with one another, Portugal assumes the burden alone. The history and customs of the people of Malabar are described to da Gama by a Spanish-speaking Moor (7:30–41) in a relatively objective manner, except for the lines

> The natives' manners (poor, as well as rich)
> Are made up of all Lyes and Vanitie [7.37].

Da Gama was impressed by what he saw in the city, especially in the royal palace. But when he passes a Hindu temple, the words of the poem convey revulsion. The worshippers are described as "barbrous people of that sect" and their worship as "superstition" (7.49).

Da Gama is represented as offering the local ruler a treaty of peace and friendship with the King of Portugal, if he will

> Allow commerce of superfluities
> Which bounteous Nature gave *his Realms* and *Thine,*
> (For *Trade* brings *Opulence* and *Rarieties,*
> For which the *Poor* doe *sweat,* and *Rich* doe *Pine*)
> Of two *great* fruits, which will from thence redound,
> *His* shall the *glory, thine,* the *Gain* be found [7.66].

His mind poisoned by local Muslim advisers, the Zamorin rejects this offer and seeks to imprison da Gama. By bribing his captors with European merchandise, the captain gets back to his ship to sail home with some "Malabars," "burning pepper," nutmegs, black clove, and cinnamon (9.14). Sailing away he reflects on the unworthy moral character of the ruler and his advisers.

> At leisure *then* he walks upon his *Decks*
> To see what *Time* and *Patience* will bring forth.
> No *Ruler* hath he *there* to make him vex,
> Imperious, brib'd, without or *shame* or *worth.*
> *Now* let the judging *Reader* mark what *Rex*
> The *Idol Gold* (which all the World ador'th)

Plays both in *Poor* and *Rich:* by *Money's* Thurst
All *Laws* and *Tyes* (Divine, and Humane) burst.[13]

Against this high-minded judgment should be set that of Saint Francis Xavier on the Portuguese officials he observed in India and the East not very many years after da Gama's first trip, in a private letter to Simon Rodriguez: "All go the same road of 'I plunder, thou plunderest,' and it terrifies me to witness how many moods and tenses and participles of that miserable verb 'to rob,' those who come to India discover." [14]

For the Portuguese, the image of India as a Christian's burden persisted right down to the occupation of Goa. On November 30, 1954, Dr. Salazar said: "The preservation of Portuguese Goa is an indispensable base for the conservation and spread of Christianity in India." This claim was rejected by representatives of Indian Christians meeting in New Delhi on August 21, 1955. They pointed out that there were more Christians in India than in Portugal.

There were many missionaries from Europe and the United States who observed, disapproved, and even tried to rectify the unjust conduct of their countrymen in India and who contributed the first scholarly works on the languages and religions of the Orient. Through their schools they introduced science, medicine, agriculture, and much else. Yet it probably remains true that more of them assumed the "white man's burden" toward the Indians, and it was their letters home and the books they wrote to raise funds which made this a sharp and vivid image in the popular imagination. "The Heathen Mother," a verse in a nineteenth-century children's book, expresses the dominant attitude of some missionaries:

See that heathen mother stand
Where the sacred current flows;
With her own maternal hand
Mid the waves her babe she throws.

Hark! I hear the piteous scream;
Frightful monsters seize their prey,
Or the dark and bloody stream
Bears the struggling child away.

Fainter now, and fainter still,
Breaks the cry upon the ear;
But the mother's heart is steel
She unmoved that cry can hear.

Send, oh send the Bible there,
Let its precepts reach the heart;
She may then her children spare—
Act the tender mother's part.[15]

The verse is illustrated with two pictures, one showing the heathen mother standing on the banks of a river as a crocodile approaches the shore where an infant lies. The other is called "Saugor Island," which is described as "inhabited only by wild beasts," and is said to be a place where "thousands of Hindu mothers have thrown their children into the Ganges to be devoured by alligators."

The "white man's burden" image was, of course, not limited to missionaries. Rudyard Kipling gave us the phrase, as also its sister epithet, "the lesser breeds without the law." Whatever Kipling himself may have meant by them, these two phrases quickly came to symbolize the European's stance of arrogant superiority toward the colonial peoples he considered inferior to him socially, morally, and culturally. There is a statement attributed to Kipling by a missionary official indicating that he shared this stance. The Reverend R. A. Hume quotes Kipling as having said: "What's the matter with this country (India) is not in the least political, but an all-round entanglement of physical, social, and moral evils and corruptions, all more or less due to the unnatural treatment of women. . . . The foundations of their life are rotten—utterly rotten." [16]

It remained for an American writer, a woman named Katherine Mayo, to write the classic epitome of the "white man's burden" in a book called *Mother India,* published in 1927 in the United States. It ran through twenty-seven editions and sold about a quarter of a million copies. Compared to the righteous moral indignation of this work, Kipling and the missionaries appear morally lax. In her book, based on a six-month trip, Miss Mayo collected a gallery of horrors to haunt the most tolerant reader: child-marriage, subordination of wives to husbands, low status of widows, unsanitary and unskilled midwives, purdah, *devadāsī,* worship of idols at Kālīghaṭ, and sickness (cholera and malaria, plague, hookworm); Indian medicine, discussed in a chapter called "Quacks Whom We Know"; dirty water and unsanitary conditions in Benares the Holy City, in village tanks and wells, and in Madras City; untouchables; Brahmans as seen by Southern non-Brahmans; high marriage costs, rapacious moneylenders, unproductive hoarding, and shameless begging; the sacred cow, sick dogs, cruelty to animals; lies without shame; trappings of parliamentary government without the reality; Hindu-Muslim quarrels; the educated unemployed, with their calling cards engraved "B.A. failed" and "B.A. plucked," their unwillingness to work with their hands in agriculture, their remoteness from villages and villagers; and opposition to education of women and untouchables. "The Home of Stark Want," in short, was produced not by the "drain" of British rule but by Indian bad habits.

She says her motives are friendly and humanitarian: "Some few Indians will take plain speech as it is meant—as the faithful words of a friend; far more will be hurt at heart. Would that this task of truth-telling might prove so radically performed that all shock of resentment were finally absorbed in it, and that there need be no further waste of life and time for lack of a challenge and a declaration!" [17]

It is quite possible that Miss Mayo's profession of humanitarian motivation for harsh criticism was sincere, as sincere as was the motivation of missionaries, soldiers, merchants, politicians, and liberal reformers who shared the image of India as "the white man's burden," although they may have differed on the best means for lifting that burden. A judgment of total inferiority passed on another civilization can justify a wide range of attitudes and policies toward that civilization.[18]

When Miss Mayo is compared with Megasthenes and other classical writers on India, one is struck by a singular contrast. For Miss Mayo, India and Indians are objects for moral judgment and censure, while for the ancient Greeks and Romans they are objects of curiosity and wonder. Judgments occur in the early accounts—as when Megasthenes remarks that it would be better for social life if Indians ate together at fixed times —but these judgments are infrequent, unimpassioned, and incidental to the descriptive account. Although many of the same institutions and practices are dealt with—such as caste and suttee—there is not the same quick disposition to indignation on religious or humanitarian grounds, or the same complacent confidence that one's own religion and moral standards are the only possible and correct ones. Even the Brahmans, who as a class are not noted for their humility, were struck by the arrogance of the early Europeans.[19]

## America, the Road to India

Although the United States developed no colonial interest in India, Americans tended to take over and exaggerate, as in the case of some missionaries and Katherine Mayo, the prevailing European images of India. India was one of the great fields for American Protestant missionaries throughout the nineteenth and early twentieth centuries. There were other contacts also. Before this, a modest trade was carried in United States ships, which took ice, coal, flax, candles, medicines, and Madeira wine to Madras and Calcutta and brought back pepper, ginger, sugar, blue cloth, camboy, pulicate handkerchiefs, and a great variety of Indian cottons. Samuel Eliot Morison relates that on the brig *Caravan* of Salem, early in 1812, Captain Augustine Heard took several thousand dollars to invest in East Indian goods for his relatives. Friends also commissioned him to buy for them shawls, necklaces, thin muslins, straw rugs, bedspreads, and pots of ginger. Henry Pickering asked Captain Heard to bring him a "Sanskrit bible," and three children gave him a dollar each to invest in Calcutta.[20]

In 1845, three-fourths of the ships that docked in the port of Calcutta were U.S. vessels. From about 1859, British restrictions, the United States tariff on cloth, and new ice machines caused American trade with India to dwindle. After this the missionaries and a small number of consular officials, travelers, and scholars kept the contact alive.

That these prosaic contacts did not extinguish the image of India as a fabulous land of marvels and ancient wisdom may be gathered from visiting the East India Marine Hall in Salem, Massachusetts, and recalling the Indian influences on Emerson, Thoreau, Whitman, Melville, and Hawthorne. The Salem Hall, now called the Peabody Maritime Museum, was built in 1824 by the Salem East India Marine Society. The Society was founded in 1799 by an association of sea captains, factors, and supercargoes engaged in the East India trade. Every member kept journals of each voyage and collected articles of curiosity. The Society held meetings and issued publications.

The Catalogue of the Museum listed a "pregnant queen ant," "the tail of an African elephant," "a flying dragon," "lava from Java," "a ball of hair from the stomach of a cow from Madagascar," "vocabulary of the Cochin-Chinese language, with a Latin translation," "a very elegant hubble-bubble," "a medal of the Pope and the Devil," "a cigar from Manilla, used by females," and so on. Hawthorne's essay "The Virtuoso's Collection" is probably based on the museum and these lists.[21]

At Walden, Thoreau mused on a highly poetic exchange—the exchange of ice, taken from his pond and shipped to India, for Hindu philosophy:

> Thus it appears that the sweltering inhabitants of Madras and Bombay and Calcutta, drink at my well. In the morning I bathe my intellect in the stupendous and cosmogonal philosophy of the Bhagavat-Geeta . . . I lay down the book and go to my well for water, and lo! I meet the servant of the Brahmin, priest of Brahma and Vishnu and Indra, who still sits in his temple on the Ganges reading the Vedas, or dwells at the root of a tree with his crust and water jug. I meet his servant come to draw water for his master, and our buckets as it were grate together in the same well. The pure Walden water is mingled with the sacred water of the Ganges. With the favoring winds, it is wafted past the site of the fabulous islands of Atlantis . . . melts in the tropic gales of the Indian seas, and is landed in ports of which Alexander only heard the names.[22]

Thoreau, writing of the value of history, also said: "I do not wonder that men read history, for I am as nearly related to the men of history as to my contemporary. Farthest India is nearer to me than Concord and Lexington."

A distinctive note entered the United States image with the belief that America was the "passage to India." This belief undoubtedly goes back to Columbus's mistake, and the belief held by many explorers of his day, that North America was just a group of islands through which a passage to the "Indies" existed. Much of the early exploration of North and South America was spurred by the search for a "northwest passage." One sixteenth-century globe (1531) showed a land connection between Mexico and the peninsula of Hindustan and placed the province of "Cathay" in the western part of Mexico.[23]

Long after it was recognized that America was a wide continent separated from Asia by a vast ocean, the idea of America as the "passage to India" continued to fascinate the imagination of Americans. Senator Thomas Hart Benton, who tried in the 1840's to arouse interest in a railroad from St. Louis to the Pacific, called the railroad "the American Road to India." Of the American West, Benton said, "There lies the East, there lies the road to India." His perspective was historical:

> The impassable mountain has become passable—the uninhabited desert has become inhabitable—the Siberia of America has become a promised land! and the exalting fact stands revealed that, from the Father of Floods, to the Mother

of Oceans, the rolling tide of American population may go on spreading its wide and lofty wave; and, from San Francisco to St. Louis, in a straight line with Canton and London, the rich stream of oriental commerce, after wandering for forty centuries upon unstable and devious routes, is to find its last, its greatest and its everlasting channel. These great facts are now revealed—established—fixed and all that we have to do is to act upon them. . . . The knowledge is acquired—the means are at hand—the spirits of the people are up. All that is lacking is the action of the government; and that, as always, needs stimulating.[24]

This was more than high-flown senatorial rhetoric, for when the Union Pacific, starting from Omaha, joined the Central Pacific, starting from San Francisco, the event was hailed as symbolizing the westward march of civilization and as the meeting of East and West. *Harper's Weekly* published a picture of the two roads joining, each flanked by a panorama of Western and Oriental peoples climbing to the light. To sing this and two other "achievements of the present"—the laying of the Atlantic cable in 1866 and the completion of the Suez Canal in 1869—Walt Whitman wrote *Passage to India,* perhaps the closest thing to an American epic. In one verse he salutes Columbus:

Ah Genoese thy dream! thy dream!
Centuries after thou art laid in thy grave,
The shore thou foundest verifies thy dream!

He speaks of America as:

Bridging the three or four thousand miles of land travel
Tying the Eastern to the Western sun,
The road between Europe and Asia.

In the three "modern wonders" he sees "God's purpose from the first":

The earth to be spann'd, connected by network,
The people to become brothers and sisters,
The races, neighbors, to marry and be given in marriage,
The oceans to be cross'd, the distant brought near,
The lands to be welded together.

The American's passage to India Whitman sees as a return to the "soothing cradle of man," "the past lit up again." In "a retrospect brought forward" he reviews the history of

The old, most populous, wealthiest of Earth's lands,
The streams of the Indus and the Ganges, and their many affluents;

by a stirring recital of the "passages" to India from Alexander on. It is "a passage indeed," not to lands and seas alone but to "primal thought," "to reason's early paradise," "to wisdom's birth," "to innocent intuitions," to "the flowing literatures, tremendous epics, religions, castes." It *is* "a passage to more than India," "a circumnavigation of the world" which takes the soul through "the regions infinite."

> Bathe me, O God, in thee—mounting to thee,
> I and my soul to range in range of thee.[25]

This, too, is a characteristically Indian devotional sentiment! America, the road between Europe and Asia, the passage to India, is seen as the road to the brotherhood of man and also to man's self-discovery in the universe.

## The Treasures of Ancient Wisdom

The belief of Thoreau, Whitman, and the New England transcendentalists that India is a land of ancient wisdom was not a peculiarly American notion. Fortunately for Europe and for its relation to India, this image developed there too from the end of the eighteenth through the nineteenth century, at the very time when the "benighted heathen" image was displacing the older image of the "fabulous land of wealth." The source of the favorable view of India's religion, philosophy, and culture can be traced to the work of a handful of students, among missionaries, administrators, and scholars, who discovered and appreciated the great intellectual and aesthetic achievements of Indian civilization and made them available to the West. This work began with the translation into European languages of many classics from Sanskrit literature—*Śakuntalā,* the *Bhagavadgītā,* the Upaniṣads, the *Ṛgveda*—and extended to translations from Pali Buddhist scriptures and tales and Hindu codes of law, as well as research in the fields of archaeology, art, history, linguistics, dance, music, medicine, mathematics, the game of chess, and many other aspects of Indian civilization.

The movement of discovery set in motion by these scholars has still not lost its momentum. When the first results were published in Europe and the United States, they started something like a second renaissance, an "Oriental renaissance," Raymond Schwab has called it.[26] Writers, poets, and philosophers found inspiration in the Oriental classics and modeled some of their work on the new forms. Goethe's poetic tribute to *Śakuntalā,* written after he read the German translation, gives the flavor of the romantic enthusiasm aroused:

> Willst du die Blüthe des frühen, die Früchte des späteren Jahres,
> Willst du was reizt und entzückt, willst du was sättigt und nährt,
> Willst du den Himmel, die Erde, mit Einem Namen begreifen;
> Nenn' ich, Sakontala, Dich, und so ist Alles gesagt.
>
> Wouldst thou the young year's blossoms and the fruits of its decline,
> And all by which the soul is charmed, enraptured, feasted, fed,
> Wouldst thou the earth and Heaven itself in one sole name combine?
> I name thee, O Sakontala, and all at once is said.[27]

Goethe also modeled the prologue to *Faust* on a feature of Sanskrit drama.

The romantic movement in Germany (the Schlegels, Schiller, Schopenhauer, Fichte, Nietzsche), as well as in England (Shelley, Wordsworth, Coleridge, Byron, Tennyson), was influenced by these Indian sources. And this influence has continued to be effective in our own day on writers and poets who are not all "romantics" (for example, Yeats, Eliot, A. E., Thomas Mann, Aldous Huxley, Hermann Hesse).

The strong interest in Oriental literature led to the establishment of European and American chairs in Sanskrit and Oriental languages during the nineteenth century. How the knowledge of Sanskrit was first brought to France, Germany, and England is an interesting story: An English East India Company servant, Alexander Hamilton, who was in Paris in 1802, where he was detained for three years, taught his fellow prisoners Sanskrit; he met A. L. de Chézy, self-taught first professor of Sanskrit at the Collège de France. They taught the brothers Schlegel, who took it to Germany. Chézy's successor was Eugène Burnouf, who studied Avesta hymns, Buddhist scriptures, and translated the *Bhāgavatapurāṇa*. F. Max Müller, a German student of Burnouf, went to Oxford, revived Sanskrit studies, translated the *Ṛgveda,* and edited *The Sacred Books of the East.*

Indeed the effects of the "Oriental renaissance" in Europe went far beyond romantic poetry and philosophy and the study of Sanskrit, Pali, Persian, and Arabic. They helped to generate, besides, a cluster of new branches of scholarship—comparative philology, comparative mythology, comparative religion and folklore, comparative law and anthropology.

This unexpected series of developments grew from the discovery that Sanskrit was closely related to Greek, Latin, and other European languages. One of the first scholars to notice this relationship was Sir William Jones, a pioneer of the "Oriental renaissance." In 1786, Jones, who was then sitting as a Supreme Court Judge on the Calcutta bench and studying Sanskrit in his spare time, announced to the Asiatic Society a most unusual observation:

> The *Sanskrit* Language, whatever be its antiquity, is a wonderful structure; more perfect than the Greek, more copious than the Latin, and more exquisitely refined than either. Yet bearing to both of them a stronger affinity, both in the roots of the verbs and the forms of the grammar, than could possibly have been produced by accident; so strong, indeed, that no philosopher could examine them all without believing them to have sprung from some common source, which perhaps no longer exists. There is a similar reason, though not quite so forcible, for supposing that both the *Gothick* and the *Celtick,* though blended with a very different idiom, had the same origin with the Sanskrit; and *Old Persian* might be added to the same family.[28]

This observation was the basis for the beginning of comparative Indo-European studies developed by Bopp, Müller, Grimm, and others.

"If I were asked," Müller once said, "what I considered the most important discovery of the nineteenth century with respect to the ancient history of mankind, I should answer by the following short line: 'Sanskrit Dyaus Pitar—Greek Zeùs patêr—Latin Juppiter—Old Norse Tyr.' "[29]

Overarching the literary and scholarly ramifications of the "Oriental renaissance" in nineteenth-century Europe and America was the firm conviction that the "sacred books of the East" contained an ancient and profound wisdom of great value to the modern Western mind. Friedrich Schlegel, who introduced the new learning into Germany, called his first book on the subject *On the Language and Wisdom [Weisheit] of the Indians: An Essay on the Foundations of Antiquity* (1808).

Consider also Schopenhauer on the Upaniṣads: "That incomparable book," he declares in *The World Considered as Will and as Idea,*

> stirs the spirit to the very depths of the soul. From every sentence deep, original, and sublime thoughts arise, and the whole is pervaded by a high and holy and earnest spirit. Indian air surrounds us, and original thoughts of kindred spirits. And oh, how thoroughly is the mind here washed clean of all early engrafted Jewish superstitions, and of all philosophy that cringes before these superstitions! In the whole world there is no study, except that of the originals, so beneficial and so elevating as that of the *Oupnekhat*. It has been the solace of my life, it will be the solace of my death.[30]

This conviction created an avid market for translations from the Oriental classics. Sir Edwin Arnold's translations of the *Bhagavadgītā* (*The Song Celestial*) and of the *Dhammapada* (*The Light of Asia*) (1879) went through sixty editions in England and eighty in the United States, and were translated into many European languages.[31]

The poet A. E. sums up the feeling about the ancient Indian wisdom:

> Goethe, Wordsworth, Emerson, and Thoreau among moderns have something of this vitality and wisdom, but we can find all they have said and much more in the grand sacred books of the East. The *Bhagavad-Gītā* and the Upanishads contain such godlike fulness of wisdom on all things that I feel the authors must have looked with calm remembrance back through a thousand passionate lives, full of feverish strife for and with shadows, ere they could have written with such certainty of things which the soul feels to be sure.[32]

The desire for the "treasures of wisdom" may seem out of place among the more mundane pleasures. Arthur Christy follows the neo-Humanists Irving Babbitt and Paul Elmer More in trying to separate the two kinds of treasures, material and spiritual, sought in the East:

> Clearly, at the end of the nineteenth century and continuing into our own day, the Occidental imagination created for itself two worlds which are romantically "oriental." One was a world of untrammeled nature, exotic mystery, and unchecked passions. The other consisted of the mysticism of the Sufis, Buddha, the Upaniṣadic seers, and Lao-tzü. It remained for the Neo-Humanists of the twentieth century, particularly Irving Babbitt and Paul Elmer More, to point out that the popular imagination of the West could not consistently live in both worlds. "If the temple bells are calling the British private to 'raise a thirst,'" wrote Babbitt in an essay on "Buddha and the Occident," published together with his translation of the *Dhammapada,* "to what, one may enquire, are they calling the native Burman?" Babbitt answers: "Certainly not to be 'lazy' and irresponsible . . . a central admonition of Buddha may be summed up in the phrase: 'Do not raise a thirst.'"[33]

## The Spiritual East and the Materialistic West

We are now at the threshold of the modern image of India as a land of surpassing spirituality, an image that also implies the contrast with Western "materialism." Before we cross this threshold let us briefly review how the dialogue of images has brought us to this contrast.

Ancient and medieval Europe, whose knowledge of India depended on the Eastern luxury trade and the accounts of a few travelers, formed the image of India as a civilized country, endowed with glittering wealth, fabulous marvels of nature, and wise philosophers. This image lured the European explorers to India in the fifteenth and sixteenth centuries. As the European nations turned India into a colony, however, the older image was transformed in two opposed directions. On the one hand, Indians became "benighted heathen," a "burden" of conscience for white Christians prepared to serve their captives' need for peace, food, medicine, education, roads, and ports and to bring them Western morality and ethics. It was conveniently overlooked that colonial policy was deliberately inhibiting the spread to the European colonies of the commercial and industrial revolutions, which were the source of the materal benefits of European civilization.

On the other hand, there were some colonial administrators, missionaries, and scholars who rediscovered the ancient glories of Indian civilization in its Sanskrit scriptures and architectural monuments. As these glories became known in Europe from the end of the eighteenth century on, they were hailed as treasures of an ancient wisdom by orientalist scholars and other humanists, including poets and philosophers. By the end of the nineteenth century, some circles of popular interest had been so stimulated by the "Oriental renaissance" that they were ready to look upon modern India as a civilization animated by a spirituality far superior to the materialistic civilization of the European powers.

Leading Indian reformers, exposed to the harsh criticisms of Christian missionaries, the superior technical and economic development of nineteenth-century Europe, and the liberal philosophy of late-nineteenth-century British liberalism, were also encouraged by the European appreciation of Indian culture to launch an Indian renaissance in many different fields. Whatever the fields, however, they too made the spiritual-material contrast between India and the West a dogmatic principle of their thinking.

While the United States did not join the European powers in establishing colonies in India, it did share the dominant European images of India as a never-never land, a white man's burden, and a land of surpassing spirituality. These were derived in part from European sources and in part from direct American contacts with India through trade, missionary activity, and travel. A special ingredient of the American image of India has been the belief in America as the "passage to India" and as a bridge between East and West. This belief, given a transcendental interpretation in Whitman's *Passage to India,* complemented the belief in India's spiritual mission to the West.

There is a striking contrast between the orientalists' approach to ancient Indian wisdom and that of the early Greek and Roman writers, which calls for a word of explanation. The orientalists find the wisdom in ancient texts and inscriptions; the Greek and Roman writers find it in philosophers with whom they converse. Perhaps there were fewer texts and more sages in the ancient period, but the predominance of the personal approach in the classical accounts and of the textual one in the modern orientalist suggests an active principle of selection. The basic difference, I believe, is that the Greek and Roman writers looked upon India as a living civilization with philosophers in it who reminded them of Socrates and Diogenes, whose opinions and way of life they found interesting enough to report. The orientalists, on the other hand, looked upon India as a dead civilization whose achievements are to be discovered in ancient texts and monuments. Paradoxically, they came to this view because of their own classical education in Greek and Latin.[34] India was for them another ancient civilization, such as that of Greece and Rome, and Sanskrit and Persian were new-found "classics," to be placed on a par with the old. The living civilization surrounding them, as they lived and worked in India, was considered no more related to their "classical" studies than, say, the life of modern Greece would be for a scholar of ancient Greece. Some of the orientalists, such as Sir William Jones, learned their Sanskrit with the help of Indian pandits, whom they looked upon as walking libraries, as living fossils, not as individual thinkers or scholars with a life of their own.

The attitude of these orientalists, especially those who were colonial administrators, toward *contemporary* Indians was dominated by the image of the white man's burden, as was that of the scholarly missionaries. This ambivalence between respect and admiration for the past and mistrust and disdain for the present is most dramatically expressed in Sir William Jones's request to Cornwallis for support of his grand project to translate Hindu and Muslim law books:

> If we had a complete digest of Hindu and Mohammedan laws, after the model of Justinian's inestimable Pandects, compiled by the most learned of the native lawyers, with an accurate verbal translation of it into English . . . we should rarely be at a loss for principles, at least, and rules of law applicable to the cases before us, and should never perhaps be led astray by the Pandits or Maulavis, who would hardly venture to impose on us, when their imposition might so easily be detected.[35]

This well-intentioned effort to entomb a living civilization did not, fortunately, succeed. Nor could it, for as the "treasures of ancient wisdom" became available to a wider audience without a classical education, they aroused a great curiosity about the people and the land that had produced them. From the latter half of the nineteenth century to the present, the pilgrimage to the wise men of the East became a popular reason for a trip to India or Ceylon. Europeans and Americans sat at the feet of sages and holy men and recorded their conversations, modes of life, and unusual powers. In some cases the Westerner was converted. Among the latest of these conversions is that of the Austrian Leopold Fischer, who became a Hindu monk, Svāmī Agehananda Bharati, and who has published a most interesting account of his experience in *The Ochre Robe.*

One of the earliest and best-organized movements in the West to popularize "Eastern Wisdom" was the Theosophical Society, founded about 1875 by Madame Blavatsky, a Russian lady, and Colonel Olcott, an American, and later directed in India by Annie Besant, a British reformer. The objects of the Society were various:

> It influences its fellows to acquire an intimate knowledge of the natural law, especially its occult manifestations. . . . The Society teaches and expects its fellows to personally exemplify the highest morality and religious aspiration; to oppose the materialism of science and every form of dogmatic theology . . . to make known among Western Nations the long suppressed facts about Oriental religious philosophies, their ethics, chronology, esoterism, symbolism; to counteract as far as possible the efforts of Missionaries to delude the so-called "Heathen" and "Pagans" as to the real origin and dogmas of Christianity . . . to disseminate a knowledge of the sublime teachings of that pure esoteric system of the archaic period which are mirrored in the oldest Vedas, and in the philosophy of Gautama Buddha, Zoroaster and Confucius; finally and chiefly, to aid in the institution of a brotherhood of Humanity, wherein all good and pure men, of every race, shall recognize each other as the equal effects (upon this planet) of one Uncreated, Universal, Infinite and Everlasting Cause.[36]

The Theosophical doctrines were drawn chiefly from Hinduism and Buddhism combined with admixtures of nineteenth-century spiritualism, occultism, and humanitarianism. The movement attracted wide attention and followers in India, where it set up headquarters at Adyar near Madras, as well as in Europe and the United States. Its popularity in India was, no doubt, a result of its defense of Hinduism against the attacks of Christian missionaries and the inroads of skepticism that Western education brought. The new pride and interest in Hinduism that the movement stimulated among Indians became part of a revival (or renascence) of Hinduism, as it has been called. This revival expressed itself in organized form through the activities of several Indian Societies, the most important of which were the Brāhmo Samāj, Ārya Samāj, and the Rāmakrishna Movement.[37] In specific objectives and programs these movements differed, but they all tended to agree on one general conclusion: that while the civilization of the West was superior in material techniques and comforts of life, the civilization of the East was superior in spiritual techniques and standards. This materialism-spiritualism contrast became the standard message, not only of Western Theosophists and seekers after Eastern wisdom, but of the speeches of distinguished Indian visitors to Europe and America, among them Svāmī Vivekānanda and Rabindranath Tagore. The following excerpt from the Svāmī's letters is characteristic: "As our country is poor in social virtues, so this country [the United States] is lacking in Spirituality. I give them spirituality, and they give me money." [38]

Tagore's conception of the meeting of the spiritual East and the materialistic West was expressed as early as 1878 in an essay he wrote when he was only sixteen. Stephen Hay thinks this was written just after his arrival in England for a study tour of eighteen months:

> That the remnants of Indian civilization should be the foundation on which European civilization is to be built, what a beautiful sight that will be! The European idea in which freedom predominates, and the Indian idea in which welfare predominates; the profound thought of the Eastern countries and the active thought of the Western countries; European acquisitiveness and Indian conservatism, the imagination of the Eastern countries and the practical intelligence of the West—what a full character will be formed from a synthesis between these two.[39]

These claims to a superior spirituality did not go unchallenged. They were attacked by missionaries, rationalists, and skeptics, and by all those who were reluctant to give up their image of the "benighted heathen." An editorial in a Detroit newspaper on the occasion of Svāmī Vivekānanda's visit there in the 1890's expresses the hard-headed American attitude at the time. The editorial was called "Give Us Some Miracles."

> It may sound vulgar, but it is not improper for Detroit to insist, now that it has gotten one of these wonderful East Indian mahatmas or priests, or whatever they are called, that he either "put up or shut up." During the past 10 or 15 years the people of Christian lands have been asked to believe that there exists among some of the upper castes of India a profundity of esoteric wisdom and a knowledge of the laws of nature which, in comparison with our occidental ignorance, borders on the infinite. The mystifying tricks of the eastern fakirs have been long recognized as the best specimens of sleight-of-hand work that exists anywhere in the world, and these tricks have been used as the foundation for stories of wonder-working that places the doings of the adepts of India on a par with the miracles of Jesus of Nazareth.
>
> Swami Vive Kananda will talk at the Unitarian church, but will he do nothing but talk? There are thousands of Americans who can talk better and longer than he can. They can say sweeter things and say them in more elegant form, but they cannot grow a pine tree before the eyes of 10,000 people. They cannot pick up Belle Isle and sink it in Lake St. Clair and then put it back again. If Swami Vive Kananda declines to do some of these things in addition to saying sweet things, he will injure his boasted religion of superiority more than he will help it. If his religion is better than ours, it surely does not show among the millions of people of India. It does not show in any wonders seen by Western eyes. Where, then, does it show? Answer: As yet only in sensational stories of travelers which thousands of Americans have swallowed. Will Kananda do something handsome while in Detroit? [40]

The same paper then ran an interview with the Svāmī headed: "Only Wonders Worked. No Miracles in the Pure Hindoo Religion," in which Vivekānanda disclaimed miracles:

> "I cannot comply with the request of The News to work a miracle in proof of my religion," said Vive Kananda to a representative of this paper, after being shown The News editorial on the subject. "In the first place, I am no miracle worker, and in the second place the pure Hindoo religion I profess is not based on miracles. We do not recognize such a thing as miracles. There are

wonders wrought beyond our five senses, but they are operated by some law. Our religion has nothing to do with them. Most of the strange things which are done in India and reported in the foreign papers are sleight-of-hand tricks or hypnotic illusions. They are not the performances of the wise men. These do not go about the country performing their wonders in the market place for pay. They can be seen and known only by those who seek to know the truth, and are not moved by childish curiosity." [41]

The Detroit newspaper's challenge to Svāmī Vivekānanda to perform some miracles in demonstration of the superiority of his religion[42] recalls Marco Polo's plea to the Pope to send several priests to the Court of Kubla Khan who could compete with two Indian ascetics at the Court. These ascetics, according to Marco Polo, by their ability to make goblets of wine pass through the air from a buffet to the Emperor's dining table and to bring or avert rain, were winning his allegiance to their religion. Marco Polo was sure Kubla Khan could be won to Christianity if the Pope sent the clever priests quickly. There is no record of the Pope's response.

## After Nonviolence, What?

Higher ground for criticizing the claims for India's superior spirituality has been taken by some Western thinkers. These generally appreciate the development of Indian thought and religion at its highest level, but tend to characterize it as predominantly otherworldly and nonsocial, if not antisocial. In *Indian Thought and Its Development,* Albert Schweitzer, for example, argues that the distinctive Indian world view is based on a world- and life-negating world view, which makes individual salvation consist in withdrawal from the world. From such a world view it is not logically possible, Schweitzer said, to derive an active social ethic inspired by world- and life-affirmation. He recognizes in modern Indian thought the striving for such an ethic and finds some expressions of it in Vivekānanda, Gandhi, and Tagore, among others. But this is, he contends, a very late direction of development in Indian thought and one in which Western thought is farther advanced. It cannot logically be reconciled with the otherworldly trend of Indian thought, even if it coexists with it.

> By a magnificent paradox Gandhi brings the idea of activity and the idea of world and life negation into relationship in such a way that he can regard activity in the world as the highest form of renunciation of the world. In a letter to the Brahmin ascetic he says, "My service to my people is part of the discipline to which I subject myself in order to free my soul from the bonds of the flesh. . . . For me the path to salvation leads through unceasing tribulation in the service of my fellow-countrymen and humanity." [43]

A sociological counterpart to Schweitzer's analysis had been given a little earlier by the German sociologist Max Weber. In his studies of Hinduism and Buddhism, recently translated into English as *The Religion of India,* Weber argues that Hinduism and Buddhism are otherworldly and irrational in their "inner spirit" and are incapable of producing the positive social ethic required for the development of industrial capitalism and social progress. He contrasts Indian religion with the positive role that he believes "the Protestant ethic" played in the rise of capitalism in Europe. Not many Indians seem to take either the Schweitzer or the Weber position very seriously. The distinction these European scholars draw between an other-worldly spirituality and a this-worldly spirituality seems to Indians overly sharp, overlooking as it does a long-standing coexistence of both kinds of spirituality. And is not Gandhi's "magnificent paradox" also the same paradox involved in the transformation of Protestantism's other-worldly asceticism into a this-worldly asceticism? [44] Upon popular thought in Europe and the United States the Weber-Schweitzer analysis has not been very effective. Western popular thought sees India as "spiritual" and does not bother about distinguishing an other-worldly from a this-worldly variety of spirituality. The educational and social services of the Rāmakrishna missions; Gandhi's nonviolent campaigns on behalf of spinning, untouchables, and independence; and Tagore's cosmopolitan aestheticism are all caught up in the popular image as modern expressions of India's ancient spirituality. Since the modern reformers are ascetic in their personal habits, self-sacrificing and high-minded in their work, and conversant with the ancient scriptural texts, there is some justification for looking upon them as following in the tradition of Indian saints and sages, as Romain Rolland does in his tribute to Gandhi published in 1924:

> His principle of *Ahiṃsā* [nonviolence] has been inscribed in the spirit of India for more than two thousand years. Mahavira, Buddha, and the cult of Vishnu have made it the substance of millions of souls. Gandhi has merely transfused heroic blood into it. He called upon the great shadows, the forces of the past, plunged in mortal lethargy, and at the sound of his voice they came to life. In him they found themselves. Gandhi is more than a word; he is an example. He incarnates the spirit of his people. Blessed the man who is a people, his people, entombed, and then resuscitated in him! But such resurrections are never haphazard. If the spirit of India now surges forth from temples and forests, it is because it holds the message for which the world is sighing.
>
> This message carries far beyond the boundaries of India. India alone could formulate it, but it consecrates the nation's greatness as much as its sacrifice. It may become its cross.[45]

Over the last thirty to forty years, the image of India as a "spiritual" land, dedicated to peace and democracy, has become worldwide and has gradually gained ascendancy over the competing image of a land of benighted heathens. For this change and its worldwide dissemination, Gandhi's nonviolent campaigns are chiefly responsible. Not everyone, to be sure, accepted the image at its face value. There have been many realists, skeptics, and rivals for righteousness who have resented the notion that India was assuming a moral burden for them and was becoming the conscience of the world. And they have been quick to point out discrepancies between the image and realities. Even they, however, were temporarily silenced when Great Britain granted India independence and commonwealth status. This was a most spectacular demonstration of the effectiveness of nonviolence. If Gandhi and his disciples were performing rope tricks, the tricks worked, and no one knew how or why. So impressed was the world with this triumph of the weak and virtuous that not even the partition riots, the "police action" in Hyderabad, or the fighting with Pakistan over Kashmir could dim the luster of India's spiritual effulgence. Idealists, pacifists, and liberals looked to India as a model of successful morality and began to apply the methods of nonviolence and "spiritual" techniques in other parts of the world to other problems. Nehru's consistent championing of the cause of peace and nonviolence in international affairs brightened the image still further, in spite of the irritations that India's nonalignment policy aroused in the West.

The continuous growth of India's reputation for spirituality was suddenly interrupted on December 18, 1961, with India's military action in Goa. The universal condemnation of this action in Europe and the United States was no doubt motivated by a complex constellation of circumstances. But the one circumstance which best seems to explain the intensity of the indignation is the shattering of the image of India's spirituality. In the realists' response there was a note of gloating. The Indian rope trick had at last been exposed. Goa had liberated them from the nagging superego that, speaking with an Indian accent, has condemned every Western effort in *realpolitik*. On December 19, a Laborite MP, the only Member of the House of Commons to support India's action on Goa, asked Prime Minister Macmillan to "restrain his delight because he thinks he has caught out somebody much more virtuous than himself in doing something naughty, and ask himself and the Government to consider the facts." [46]

The idealists were dismayed and saddened by the Goa action. India could no longer be looked to as the world's leader in the practice of nonviolence. Adlai Stevenson put the idealists' predicament most starkly in his speech at the Security Council: "Prime Minister Nehru himself has often said that no right end can be served by a wrong means. The Indian tradition of non-violence has inspired the whole world, but this act of force mocks India's own professions of faith." [47]

The effect of the Goa incident on India's self-image was not completely unequivocal. During the first few days there was almost universal enthusiasm. All major Indian political parties and newspapers supported the action. One newspaper called it "Nehru's finest hour." Getting rid of the last, and first, colonial foothold in India overshadowed in the minds of Indians any concern about India's reputation for nonviolence. As the strong Western criticism of the action became known in India, there were, however, some second thoughts. The leader of the opposition Swatantra Party, C. Rajagopalachari, stated that by the Goa action India "has totally lost the moral power to raise her voice against the use of military power." He invoked Gandhi's doctrine of not using "bad means to end bad things" and added, "our nationalism has, I fear, led us into impatience at the wrong moment, when in the international world there is trouble brewing everywhere, and we have a mission for promoting peace and a special qualification for fulfilling that mission." [48]

Prime Minister Nehru was amazed and disturbed by the criticism and defended himself against it by declaring that India "remained firmly and fully committed to her traditional policy of nonalignment and of trying to encourage the forces of peace, to settle problems peacefully." He added: "In spite of the fact that I have been called a hypocrite, I might say I work for peace."

He said it was gratifying to be told "what a fine image of India there was before the Goa action" and what an unusually fine man Nehru was. "It is good to know that a man was great even if he is not now." The Goa action, he said, was "entirely in keeping" with Gandhi's principles and Gandhi's closest followers supported it. Gandhi himself, Nehru said, "definitely and clearly approved" of India's 1947 action against Pakistani tribesmen in Kashmir.[49]

Whether Gandhi would have approved the action in Goa, or a military response against China, or even the Five-Year Plans, I do not know. These questions will continue to be debated. In these debates, it will be increasingly difficult to assume that Gandhi's distinctive contribution consisted in his personal asceticism and loyalty to Hinduism. That contribution appears more and more to spring from the way he brought elements of Indian religious traditions into the service of political, social, and economic reform. Precisely because Gandhi did harness his "spirituality" to a philosophy and program of social reform was he forced to break with the more orthodox interpretations of Hinduism. As I have written elsewhere:

> His philosophy of non-violence (*ahiṃsā*), of the simple life in self-sufficient villages, of the necessity of work and the dignity of manual labor, of service to neighbors, of social justice in the distribution of power and wealth, has breathed a vitality into traditional Indian asceticism which animated India's successful struggle for independence and which shapes much of the present government's domestic program.[50]

While Gandhi was opposed to unbridled industrialism and the "craze for machines" that put men out of work and led to irresponsible concentrations of power and wealth, he was not opposed to programs of moderate industrialization and modernization. In 1944, he endosed S. N. Agarwal's *The Gandhian Plan of Economic Development for India*, which proposed a national economic plan essentially similar to the Second Five-Year Plan. Many heavy industries, including defense industries, were in the Agarwal plan. And about the defense industries he added the following footnote: "Although Gandhiji is an uncompromising pacifist and a staunch believer in nonviolence he is practical enough to concede that a free India may require an armed defence." [51]

The impression that India is so "spiritual" that it is opposed to the use of force in the defense of its national interests has been rapidly corrected by other events, and perhaps the correction is even more rapid in India than elsewhere.

A few days after the Chinese attacks, Nehru called upon the people and the government to awake from their undogmatic slumbers. Speaking of Congress Party members, he said, "We were getting out of touch with reality in the modern world and we were living in an artificial atmosphere of our own creation. We have been shocked out of it, all of us whether it is the Government or the people." [52]

On the same day Dr. Rajendra Prasad, the former President of India, in a stirring call to Indians asking them to drive out the Chinese invaders from Indian soil, said that "there was no conflict between India's traditional faith in non-violence and resisting Chinese aggression with force. It was open for everybody to act according to his belief in meeting force with force and meeting force with non-violent means." [53]

Even Gandhi, who practically identified nonviolence with the golden rule, conceded the necessity of a military establishment to defend Indian territory. In a famous article written in 1920 on "The Doctrine of the Sword," Gandhi argued for nonviolence but stated conditions under which violence would be justifiable:

> I do believe that when there is only a choice between cowardice and violence, I would advise violence. . . . I would rather have India resort to arms in order to defend her honour than that she should in a cowardly manner become or remain a helpless victim to her own dishonour. But I believe that nonviolence is infinitely superior to violence, forgiveness is more manly than punishment.[54]

Gandhi interpreted nonviolence as a religious principle applied to politics; for most of his followers in the freedom struggle it was simply a practical political weapon, to be judged by its effectiveness. Nehru's autobiographical statement on this point expresses the general Indian position:

> For us and for the National Congress as a whole the nonviolent method was not, and could not be a religion or an unchallengeable creed or dogma. It could only be a policy and a method promising certain results, and by those results it would have to be finally judged. Individuals might make of it a religion or incontrovertible creed. But no political organization, so long as it remained political, could do so.[55]

In retrospect, the exaggerated modern contrast of Eastern spirituality with Western materialism recalls the fanciful ideas of the ancient and medieval images, but with one important difference. The splendor of the ancient and medieval images was as much material as spiritual—deriving from the gems, spices, and silks of the luxury trade. No attempt was made to segregate in moral or intellectual principle these "material treasures" from the "spiritual treasures" of Indian civilization. Such segregation is a legacy of European colonial rule and attitudes. As an object of the "white man's burden," India was stripped, at least in image, of both material and spiritual treasures, and was left as the abode of naked and benighted heathen. As if to compensate for such an uncharitable view and for the activities with which they were associated, the orientalists rediscovered the ancient spiritual wisdom. This inspired a romantic enthusiasm for Indian philosophy and religion in the West and a new-found pride among Indians in their spirituality. Unfortunately, this compensatory movement did little to restore respect for the material arts and achievements of Indian civilization. At best, "material India" came to be considered a field for Western improvements and for humanitarian endeavor. This cleavage between a "spiritual" and "material" India has been of the greatest consequence, not only for Western understanding but India's self-understanding as well. For Indians, too, were lulled by this half-flattering Western attitude to develop a one-sided image of their civilization.

Now that India is completely free of colonial rule, with an army, navy, and air force of its own, and in its Fifth Five-Year Plan for social and economic reform, its attitude toward the relative merits of "soul force" and "material force" may change. Perhaps it will now want to be a nation like other nations, rather than a topic of marvelous fables, or an object for self-righteous pity and charity, or the last home of occult mysteries. As India takes the path of modern nationalism, it will undoubtedly become less fascinating to the rest of the world, but it will also become less of an "image" and more of a reality in that world.

When he looked on the first atomic explosion at Los Alamos, J. Robert Oppenheimer memorialized the event by reciting a Sanskrit verse from the *Bhagavadgītā:*

> If there should rise suddenly within the skies
> Sunburst of a thousand suns
> Flooding earth with rays undreamed of,
> Then might be that holy one's
> Majesty and glory dreamed of.

(Alternate translation by J. A. B. van Buitenen:

> If the light of a thousand suns suddenly
> arose in the sky, that splendor might be
> compared to the radiance of the
> Supreme Spirit.) [56]

Near Bombay, Indian scientists have successfully established a nuclear reactor. If this work has reminded them of Sanskrit *ślokas,* they have not, as far as I know, expressed themselves to that effect in public. Their attitude more likely is that expressed by Nehru at the end of his *Discovery of India,* when he observed that while the Westerner's "passage" to India is a search for humanity's past, the Indian travels abroad in search of the present and future:

> We in India do not have to go abroad in search of the Past and Distant. We have them here in abundance. If we go to foreign countries it is in search of the Present. That search is necessary, for isolation from it means backwardness and decay. . . .
>
> [For] we march to the One World of tomorrow where national cultures will be intermingled with the international culture of the human race. We

shall therefore seek wisdom and knowledge and friendship and comradeship wherever we can find them, and co-operate with others in common tasks, but we are no suppliants for others' favors and patronage. Thus we shall remain true Indians and Asiatics, and become at the same time good internationalists and world citizens.[57]

## Notes

1. Harold Isaacs, *Scratches on Our Minds: American Images of China and India* (New York: John Day, 1958).

2. Hermann Hesse, *The Journey to the East,* trans. by Hilda Rosner (New York: Farrar, Straus & Giroux, 1968).

3. For sources, see J. W. McCrindle, *Ancient India as Described in Classical Literature* (Westminster: Archibald Constable, 1901), and Wheatley, *Golden Khersonese.*

4. J. W. McCrindle, *Ancient India in Classical Literature,* pp. 3–4.

5. *Ibid.,* p. 3, n. 2.

6. J. W. McCrindle, *The Invasion of India by Alexander the Great* (Westminster: Archibald Constable, 1893), p. 342.

7. McCrindle, *Ancient India in Classical Literature,* p. 72.

8. *Ibid.,* p. 98.

9. *Ibid.,* p. 74.

10. N. M. Crouse, *In Quest of the Western Ocean* (New York: W. Morrow & Co., 1928), pp. 22–23.

11. Georg Wilhelm Friedrich Hegel, *The Philosophy of History* (New York: Dover Publications, 1956), p. 142.

12. Sir Henry Maine, "The Effect of Observation of India on Modern European Thought," in *idem, Village Communities in the East and West* (New York: Henry Holt, 1876).

13. De Camões, Luis, *The Lusiad,* trans. by Richard Fanshawe (Carbondale: Southern Illinois University Press, 1963).

14. Quoted in J. Correia-Afonso, *Jesuit Letters and Indian History* (Bombay: Indian Historical Research Institute, Saint Xavier College, 1955), p. 27.

15. Quoted in M. L. Burke, *Swami Vivekananda in America* (Calcutta: Advaita Ashrama, 1958), p. 131.

16. *Ibid.,* p. 321.

17. Katherine Mayo, *Mother India* (New York: Harcourt Brace, 1927), p. 409.

18. See, e.g., George D. Bearce, *British Attitudes Toward India, 1784–1858* (London: Oxford University Press, 1961).

19. Cf. J. T. Phillips, trans., *Thirty-four Conferences Between the Danish Missionaries and the Malabarian Brahmans or Heathen Priests in the East Indies, Concerning the Truth of the Christian Religion, Together with Some Letters Written by the Heathens to the Said Missionaries* (translated from High Dutch) (London, 1719).

20. Samuel Eliot Morison, *Maritime History of Massachusetts, 1783–1860* (Boston: Houghton Mifflin, 1941).

21. C. E. Goodspeed, *Nathaniel Hawthorne and the Museum of the Salem East India Marine Society* (Salem, Mass.: Marine Society, Peabody Museum, 1946).

22. From *Walden,* end of Chapter 16, quoted in Morison, *Maritime History,* p. 284.

23. Crouse, *In Quest of the Western Ocean,* p. 80.

24. Letter from Thos. H. Benton to Messrs. Rice, Howard, Haight *et al.,* in the Chicago *Daily Democrat,* May 17, 1849. I am indebted to my colleague William T. Hutchinson for this reference.

25. Walt Whitman, "A Passage to India," in Emory Holloway, ed., *Walt Whitman: Complete Poetry and Selected Prose and Letters* (London: The None-Such Press, 1938), pp. 372–81.

26. Schwab, *La renaissance orientale* (note 1, Introduction to Part One, above).

27. Quoted by H. G. Rawlinson in Garratt, ed., *Legacy of India* (note 1, Introduction to Part One, above).

28. Sir William Jones, quoted in Garland Cannon, *Oriental Jones* (Delhi: Indian Council for Cultural Relations, 1964), p. 141.

29. Quoted by Rawlinson in Garratt, ed., *Legacy of India,* p. 35.
30. *Ibid.,* p. 32.
31. Arthur E. Christy, "A Sense of the Past," in Arthur E. Christy *et al., The Asian Legacy and American Life* (New York: Greenwood Press, 1968), p. 43.
32. H. G. Rawlinson, "Indian Influence on the West," in L. S. S. O'Malley, ed., *Modern India and the West* (London: Oxford University Press, 1941), p. 551.
33. Christy *et al., Asian Legacy and American Life,* p. 49.
34. S. K. De, "Western Contributions to Sanscrit Scholarship" (ms.); A. J. Arberry, *Oriental Essays* (London: George Allen & Unwin, 1960); and, by way of contrast, V. Raghavan, *Indological Studies in India* (Delhi: n.d., 1964).
35. Quoted in Cannon, *Oriental Jones,* p. 152.
36. *Golden Book of the Theosophical Society,* p. 26, quoted in D. S. Sarma, *Studies in the Renaissance of Hinduism in the Nineteenth and Twentieth Centuries* (Benares: n.p., 1944), p. 195.
37. An excellent account of these movements appears in Sarma, *Studies in Renaissance of Hinduism.*
38. Swāmī Vivekānanda, *Complete Works* 4 (Almura: Advaita Ashrama Mayavati, 1926–36): 254–55.
39. Quoted in Stephen Hay, "The Origins of Tagore's Message to the World," *Quest,* May, 1961, pp. 50–54.
40. Quoted in Burke, *Swami Vivekananda in America,* pp. 211–13.
41. *Ibid.,* p. 216.
42. *Ibid.,* pp. 211–13.
43. Albert Schweitzer, *Indian Thought and Its Development* (Boston: Beacon Press, 1936), pp. 237–38.
44. Milton Singer, "The Religion of India: The Sociology of Hinduism and Buddhism (Max Weber)," *American Anthropologist* (hereafter: *AA*) 63, No. 1 (1961): 143–151; *idem,* "Cultural Values in India's Economic Development," *The Annals of the American Academy of Political Science and Social Science* (hereafter: *The Annals*) 305 (May, 1956): 81–91; Hajime Nakamura, "The Vitality of Religion in Asia," in Congress for Cultural Freedom, *Cultural Freedom in Asia* (Rutland, Vt., and Tokyo: Charles E. Tuttle Co., 1956); John Goheen, M. N. Srinivas, and D. G. Karve, "India's Cultural Values and Economic Development: A Discussion," *EDCC,* Vol. 7 (1958), Nos. 1–12; and Milton Singer, "Religion and Social Change in India: The Weber Thesis, Phase Three," *EDCC,* 14, No. 4 (July, 1966): 497–505.
45. Romain Rolland, *Mahatma Gandhi: The Man Who Became One with the Universal Being* (New York and London: The Century Co., 1924), pp. 237–39.
46. *The Times* (London), December 20, 1961, p. 4.
47. *New York Times,* December 19, 1961, p. 19.
48. *New York Times,* December 26, 1961, p. 2.
49. *New York Times,* December 29, 1961, p. 3.
50. Singer, "Cultural Values," p. 84.
51. Shriman Narayan Agarwal, *The Gandhian Plan of Economic Development for India* (Bombay, 1944), p. 41. See also *idem, The Gandhian Plan Reaffirmed* (Bombay: Padma Publications, 1948).
52. *The Hindu* (Madras), October 26, 1962, p. 7.
53. *Ibid.*
54. M. K. Gandhi, "The Doctrine of the Sword," in *Collected Works of Mahatma Gandhi* 17 (Ahmedabad: Government of India, Publications Division, November, 1965): 132.
55. Jawaharlal Nehru, *Toward Freedom: The Autobiography of Jawaharlal Nehru* (New York: John Day, 1941), p. 84.
56. *Bhagavadgītā,* 11.12.
57. Nehru, *Discovery of India,* pp. 578 and 579.

# 2 / *Text and Context in the Study of Contemporary Hinduism*

## Introduction

There is no royal road to the "meaning" and function of a complex religion such as Hinduism. One reason for the development of anthropological studies of world religions has been the incompleteness of purely textual studies. These tell much about what is transmitted but very little about how, and to or for whom. The result tends to be a collection of disembodied "ideas" logically manipulable into a systematic "philosophy." By adding the information supplied from anthropological interviews with representatives of the religion, and from the observation of the incidence of religious beliefs and practices in the context of daily life, we are able to find for these ideas a local habitation and learn how they operate in the lives of ordinary people. The contextual studies of the anthropologist thus help in essential ways to locate and specify the meaningful content of a religious system depicted by the textual studies of the historian of religion, the philosopher, and the philologist.

The articulation of textual and contextual studies has been most successful in cases of "primitive" religions, where the small scale of the society and the oral nature of the texts make it relatively easy for the anthropologist to trace the web of functional connections.[1] In the case of the world religions, however, with their complex traditions of literary development, frequently cultivated by specialized literati who are interested in logical consistency and standards of universal truth, the articulation is more difficult to bring off. The "cosmology" constructed by the intellectual frequently seems quite remote from the "world view" implicit in the conduct and beliefs of every man.[2] Robert Redfield's conception of a civilization as a compound structure of Little and Great Traditions and M. N. Srinivas's concept of "Sanskritization" are both designed to deal with this problem. The application of these conceptions by anthropologists to the study of Hinduism has so far not incorporated in any direct fashion a coordinate textual analysis. Because they are not usually Sanskritists and cannot often obtain the collaboration of Sanskritists, anthropologists must perforce bypass the textual corpus and content themselves with noting the references to it that turn up in their interviews and observations.

The Hinduism that emerges from such studies will more closely approximate the "world view" of popular Hinduism than the systematic "cosmology" of any school of Sanskritic Hinduism.

The problem is equally formidable on the other side: The knowledgeable scholar of the philosophical and religious literature will appear casual in his references to the social and cultural context of the literature by comparison with his thorough and systematic analysis of the texts themselves.[3] The literary scholar who is willing and able to incorporate interviews and observations of the living religion into his work is as rare as is the anthropologist who employs textual studies.[4]

The cleavage between the textual and contextual studies of religion, which is but a special instance of the cleavage between the humanities and the social sciences, is bred in part by the differences in the disciplines involved and in part by the different kinds of interests and activities that the practice of these disciplines engenders. Whatever its source, this cleavage must be transcended if our understanding of religion is to be advanced. There are some encouraging signs that many scholars on both sides of the great divide of text and context now recognize this and are making fresh and vigorous efforts at interdisciplinary communication.[5]

In this chapter I shall try to show how contemporary Hinduism can be clarified by bringing textual and contextual studies closer together.

## The Influence of Religion on Daily Conduct: Limitations of Textual Interpretation

Although the pace of social change in Asian countries is accelerating, it is not yet fast enough to give these countries the standard of living they would like to have. In the discussions of obstacles to more rapid social change, particularly by Western writers, there is a recurrent reference to religion—religion understood not only as a creed but as an important source of values, mental attitudes, and practices of daily life. Such writers usually assume that the social transformations brought about by modern science and industry in the West were preceded, or at least accompanied, by transformations in religious beliefs and practices and the social, political, and cultural institutions through which these were expressed.[6] India particularly has been singled out in these discussions as one of those countries beset by a religious syndrome of "backwardness"—sacred cows, wandering ascetics, a caste society, and a passive and otherworldly attitude to life. Indian writers, on the other hand, have sometimes traded on these stigmata as signs of a "spirituality" superior to the "materialism" of the West. This issue has also been debated by serious students of Indian religion and philosophy with copious references to the appropriate texts. In one of the best of these debates, that between Schweitzer and Radhakrishnan, the argument about whether Hinduism is life-negating and without an active social ethic seems to depend on selection and interpretation of particular texts from Christian and Hindu scriptures.[7]

The outcome of such textual debates cannot, for several reasons, settle the question of Hinduism's compatibility with social change. Where the interpretation of Hindu texts is made by Westerners, there is a common risk of construing basic terms according to familiar categories of Western thought or of failing to recognize in Asian thought ideas essentially similar to those in the West because they have a different place and setting. An example of the first pitfall is the interpretation of the "otherworldliness" of Hinduism and Buddhism in terms of the Western dualism of heaven and earth. This interpretation leads to a misreading of the Eastern contrast between the transitory and the eternal in this world. Whether one thinks of the next birth in a cycle of rebirths or of the final release from the cycle of rebirths by fusion with the Absolute, there is no need to think of another world. Both states are in theory attainable in this world through appropriate training and discipline. It is not necessary, therefore, to escape from this world in order to be "otherworldly" in the Hindu or Buddhist sense. It is rather more a question of striving to perceive what is permanent and to order one's conduct accordingly.

The second kind of pitfall is illustrated by the failure to recognize the role of individualism in Asian religions. Not only is the Western form of church organization missing in these religions, but the ultimate religious quest has meaning only to and for the individual seeker. He alone must choose the path appropriate to him and the disciplines that go with it. Spiritual advisers and other religious functionaries are there to help him, but his is the choice, the effort, and the judgment of consummation. The outward traditionalism of Eastern religions masks a wide latitude for individual choice and inner development. Gandhi's autobiography, *My Experiments with Truth,* vividly shows this highly individualized do-it-yourself spirit of Hinduism functioning in a modern context. Within the limits of the traditional framework, this spirit can be highly pragmatic and experimental. Gandhi experimented with diet, cooking, hair-cutting, medical treatment, celibacy, and nonviolence in his quest for "truth."

### *Extra-textual Factors: Belief-Intensity, Function, and Functionaries*

A more important reason for the inconclusiveness of textual debates on the "philosophy" of Hinduism lies in another direction. Suppose that the Western student has a thorough knowledge of the canonical scriptures and of the commentaries of Hinduism and is not likely to fall into the obvious pitfalls. Such knowledge would still leave him unable to assess the effects of the scriptural philosophy on daily conduct without the knowledge of some extra-textual considerations. One of these considerations would be the intensity of belief of the adherents of Hinduism whose conduct is in question. In a very lively article on "The Indian Spirit: Past and Present," the Indian philosopher K. Satchidananda Murty writes that "to think that the average Hindu of the modern world cares more for his religion than the average Christian or Jew of England or the U.S.A. for what is literally said in the Bible is a gratuitous assumption." [8] The assumption may well be gratuitous; the truth is, we simply do not have the studies on which to base a nongratuitous judgment. The American anthropologist Morris Opler comes to the conclusion, after analyzing data gathered over a ten-year period in one Indian village, that religion does play an important part in Indian village life.[9] Opler is careful, however, not to commit himself on whether Indian villagers are *more* religious than their European counterparts. Murty's question remains unanswered.

Opler's concluding comments, however, turn the problem in another and more fruitful direction. He suggests that the important role religion does play in the Indian villager's life "may be due less to any innate religiosity than to the links between all aspects of the culture which Hinduism has come to provide." These links are manifest in all phases of the villager's life:

> To live a very full and estimable life, a villager has to partipate in the religious round. Religion justifies the existence of his line, the tie between his ancestors and his sons. It holds his kin together in family rituals. It provides travel, adventure, and new experience, and connects his village with others. It makes possible the rewarding of servants and dependents, facilitates property exchange, and points to family status. It offers a means of keeping in touch with married daughters. The presence of the protective godlings of the villages strengthens group consciousness. The agricultural rites, the worship of the disease goddesses, and the life-cycle ceremonies awake courage and hope in areas of life where uncertainty and anxiety are most prevalent. The important place of religion in village India will not be banished by denying it. If village Hinduism weakens, it will be because of the development of functional equivalents for the purposes it now serves.[10]

In the towns and cities, the links provided by religious beliefs and activities are neither so pervasive nor so strong as in the village Opler describes. Urban conditions have not, however, destroyed them altogether. The scattered evidence shows religion to be a still potent force, which trade unions, political parties, and Indian intellectuals may neglect at their own risk.[11]

An extra-textual question about the intensity or degree of religiosity of Hindus very quickly takes us into studies of the functional relations between Hinduism and all aspects of social life in village, town, and city. A very similar road will have to be followed in order to take account of the other extra-textual considerations that need to be known to assess the impact of Hinduism on daily life. In Hinduism, for example, as in other world religions, there exists a specialization of functionaries to interpret the scriptures and apply them to cases. Obviously, a knowledge of the organization of these functionaries and of their role as conservators and innovators of the tradition becomes crucial for connecting scripture with the problems of everyday life. It was presumably the interpretations of some of these functionaries that purified the hands and workshops of the "unclean" craftsmen, thus neutralizing the caste contamination that might otherwise arise. Today the guru, the pandit, the spiritual adviser, has, as I have written elsewhere,

> a comfortable scope for interpretation and reconciliation of scriptural sanctions. He freely invokes considerations of logic, experience, the convenience or inconvenience of a particular circumstance, and local usages in coming to his decision. In this process the wise men and particularly the learned literati are an institutionalized agency for changing tradition, so long as they regard the change as primarily preservative of the tradition's essentials.[12]

This process, in fact, is not very different from the application of legal principles in common law. And perhaps what Justice Holmes said of the latter also applies to the former—that it is not logic but experience that is its heart.

## The Unity and Diversity of Religious Traditions in India

So far the discussion has assumed a single authoritative tradition of Hinduism. This is, of course, a gross oversimplification, the removal of which requires the introduction of another set of extra-textual considerations. Indeed, even a cursory comparison of some of the texts—the Vedas, the Upaniṣads, the *Bhagavadgītā*, the *Mahābhārata*, the *Rāmāyaṇa*, and the *Bhāgavatapurāṇa*, to name only the best known of the Hindu scriptures—calls for a reconciliation of very different, and sometimes contrary, positions on such fundamental questions as monism, theism, vegetarianism, and caste. Much of the history of Hinduism reflects the efforts to make this reconciliation. But it is a history of the formations of schools and sects, of timely political support of one orthodoxy and the elimination of some heterodoxy, and of ever new syntheses. It is not in any case a process of purely intellectual analysis, which yields a logically consistent common denominator. More accurate is Sir Charles Eliot's characterization of Hinduism as a great reservoir of beliefs and practices from which different sects have at different times drawn different positions.[13]

In this respect, Hinduism is perhaps not very different from other world religions, including Christianity. The example of Roman Catholicism, with a single universal church and a single head, is really atypical. Hinduism does not have a single church organization with a single spiritual head. When recently the head of the Hindu *maṭha* at Puri visited the United States and was announced in some cities as "the spiritual head of Hindu India," letters from Indians appeared in the papers protesting against this title and denying that there was any such person in Indian religion. If an Anglican archbishop touring India were advertised as "the spiritual head of Protestant Christianity," there is no doubt that similar letters of protest from Christians would appear in the papers.

### *The Spread of Sanskritic Hinduism*

The multiplicity of sects and the absence of a single church organization within Hinduism has not prevented scholars from postulating an underlying unity and continuity.[14] The demonstration of such unity is a formidable task if justice is to be done to the diversities of region, tribe, caste, village, town, and city and of levels of education and sophistication. One of the most fruitful ways of conceiving this unity amidst diversity has been proposed by the Indian anthropologist M. N. Srinivas in his study *Religion and Society Among the Coorgs of South India*.[15] In this work, Srinivas distinguishes variations in Hinduism according to degree of geographical spread. "All-India Hinduism" is Hinduism with an all-India spread, "Peninsular Hinduism" spreads over the entire peninsular part of India, "Regional Hinduism" is restricted to particular regions, and "Local Hinduism" has a spread confined to local areas within a region. In a very broad sense, Srinivas believes that, as the area of spread decreases, the number of ritual and cultural forms shared increases; as the area increases, the common forms decrease.

This conception of spread would make the unity of Hinduism consist in a rather thin geographical common denominator of ritual and cultural forms. Srinivas's thinking, however, goes beyond this. He adds a notion of "horizontal spread," which includes the ritual forms shared by the same or similar castes in different parts of India (Brahmans everywhere, for example, have much Sanskritic ritual in common), and a notion of "vertical spread," which includes the cultural and ritual forms shared by different castes in a single homogeneous linguistic and cultural region. What really carries these conceptions beyond the notion of geographical distribution is Srinivas's identification of All-India Hinduism with the corpus of Sanskrit scriptures and the ritual practices of the Brahmans. This identification sets up an ideal standard for Hinduism and a yardstick for measuring its spread to different regions and groups. Srinivas calls the process of spread of Sanskritic Hinduism "Sanskritization," since he thinks of it as occurring in the following two ways: "by the extension of Sanskritic deities and ritual forms to an outlying group, as well as by the greater Sanskritization of the ritual and beliefs of groups inside Hinduism." [16] Through Sanskritization, lower castes and tribal groups are brought into the Hindu fold.[17]

There are certain general characteristics of Hinduism, Srinivas observes, that facilitate its spread through the process of Sanskritization. Among these are a vast and growing mythology; the worship of rivers, trees, and mountains; and the association of deities and epic heroes with local spots. The caste hierarchy is another such characteristic; a new group signalizes its entry into the Hindu fold by becoming a caste, and the adoption by a lower caste of the customs and habits of a high caste is motivated by the desire to raise the group's status in the caste hierarchy. The "pantheistic bias" also makes it easy to absorb tribal and low-caste gods. "The village deity who wants the sacrifice of animals and toddy is also one of the myriad manifestations of the formless Brahma whom the philosophers contemplate." [18]

Because the Sanskritizing process has been a matter of spontaneous growth, Srinivas sees it as producing some inconsistencies in ritual and belief. He would probably accept, however, the characterization of the process suggested by Dr. V. Raghavan, who sees it as on the whole consolidative and systematizing, with a tendency to universalize selected local and regional elements.[19]

Srinivas's ideas on "Sanskritization" and "All-India spread" offer one approach to the problem of the unity of Hinduism. This approach locates the unity in a set of normative standards in belief and ritual and suggests a process whereby these standards have been adopted by an ever increasing number of groups. More recent studies have suggested several important revisions in this formulation. For example, a study by Bernard Cohn of low-caste Camārs in one village shows that, as the Camārs have "Sanskritized" their customs, their high-caste models, the *ṭhākurs,* have been Westernizing theirs.[20] Srinivas, in turn, has taken account of this kind of change in "Sanskritic" norms by observing that "Sanskritization" and "Westernization" may occur simultaneously and sometimes within the same social group.[21] This possibility has been further confirmed for Brahman groups.[22] Still other studies have shown that different groups have different normative standards and that these may change with the changing prestige of different groups. In a study by A. M. Shah and R. G. Shroff, directed by Srinivas, it was found that one Gujaraṭ caste that had formerly claimed to be warrior Rājpūts now aspired to be Bāṇiyas, because the merchants in Gujarat now enjoy greater prestige.[23] Differences in the rituals and beliefs of Rājpūts, merchants, Brahmans, and craftsmen are of long standing and well established.[24] These differences tend to drive a wedge between Srinivas's conception of "All-India Hinduism" and his conception of "Sanskritic Hinduism." They suggest instead a plurality of standards for an All-India Hinduism, a plurality that includes Sanskritic Hinduism as one set. There is in the Sanskritic scriptures a theory of four classes or *varṇas*—Brahmans, warriors, common people, and serfs—which seeks to rationalize the caste structure into a single functional hierarchy.[25] In another paper, Srinivas discusses this theory as contributing to the spread of an All-India Hinduism by encouraging the assimilation of local and regional caste differentiation to the simpler *varṇa* scheme.[26] It is not clear from his discussion, however, how far he would be willing to accept the *varṇa* theory, itself a construct of Sanskritic Hinduism, as an objective theory.

### *Popular Hinduism and Its Relations to Sanskritic Hinduism*

To identify All-India Hinduism with "Sanskritic Hinduism" raises another series of questions. Many beliefs and practices have been observed among tribal, village, and even urban Indians that seem to have an all-India spread and yet are not sanctioned in Sanskritic Hinduism. These include the worship of numerous godlings, animal sacrifice, witchcraft and magic, and widow remarriage. On the other hand, the popular cults frequently do not include the Sanskritic belief in the ethical qualities of the deities worshiped or the notion of ethical retribution for "right" and "wrong" conduct, even where there may be a belief in transmigrating souls.[27] The existence of this widespread "popular Hinduism" suggests that there may be more than one kind, or at least more than one level, of All-India Hinduism. This "lower-level" Hinduism cannot simply be regarded as another layer of "horizontal spread," for it is not linked with any particular caste or other agency responsible for its spread. Nor is there any obvious incentive, as there is in the case of Sanskritic Hinduism, for its adoption by groups that do not already share its traits.

There are two likely explanations for "popular Hinduism": Either it is a diluted form of Sanskritic Hinduism or it is an independent form, existing prior to Sanskritic Hinduism and absorbed by it at different times and places. To determine which of these explanations is the more adequate and to ascertain the precise characteristics of "popular Hinduism," anthropologists have embarked on a series of comparative studies of the religion of particular villages, particular castes and tribes, and other groups.[28] An examination of these studies makes it plain that the sources and nature of "popular Hinduism" cannot be derived simply by summing up the results of the individual studies. The published studies represent only a tiny fraction of India's villages, castes, and tribes. Moreover, a comparison of the several studies cannot dispense with some knowledge of Sanskritic Hinduism as embodied in the sacred texts and in the beliefs and rituals of the special classes who claim adherence to it. To interpret these empirical studies properly, in other words, it becomes necessary to relate them to some construct of Indian civilization as a whole. Such a construct will have to make a place for both the "higher-level" Sanskritic Hinduism and the "lower-level" popular Hinduism, allow for their reciprocal interaction, and trace their relation to characteristics of the social order and its changes.

### *Peasant Hinduism as an Evolutionary Emergent*

One of the few systematic efforts to develop the required construct of Indian civilization is that of Surajit Sinha.[29] Applying Redfield's concepts of Great and Little Traditions, Sinha distinguishes a "primitive" or "folk Hinduism," a "peasant Hinduism," and an "urban Hinduism." These are envisaged as different dimensions of Indian culture and are said by Sinha to "represent a series of increasingly complex levels of socio-cultural integration with evidence of continuity in core pattern." [30] The economy, social structure, and ideological systems of these different dimensions are characterized in their distinctive aspects as well as in their shared traits. For example, Sinha contrasts the equalitarianism and hedonism of the tribal "primitive" world view with the superordination-subordination hierarchy and ethical "puritanism" of the Hindu peasant outlook. Since he favors an evolutionary interpretation, he sees the distinctive features of Hindu peasantry as "emergent," and the "primitive" features of tribal cultures as a "relatively untransformed section of the original primitive culture, arrested in its development mainly as a result of ecological factors of isolation and also perhaps because of some unknown series of historical accidents." [31] This "evolutionary" interpretation, however, must remain a hypothesis, since the evidential data to which Sinha appeals are chiefly contemporary studies of tribal and peasant Hindu communities. These studies are sufficient, nevertheless, to support the major conclusions of Sinha's analysis: that the culture of tribal India represents a "folk" dimension of the Little Traditions of Hinduism, while the culture of Hindu peasantry represents a mixture of folk elements with elements from the greater and Sanskritic tradition of Hinduism.

### *The Social Organization and Communication of Hindu Traditions*

It may be plausibly supposed that the process of mixture of elements in Hindu traditions has been going on from the earliest times and has resulted in a form of society and culture in which the interaction of Little and Great Traditions has become endemic and relatively stable.[32] If this is so, contemporary observation should disclose the pattern of interaction and the media through which it is sustained. Several studies of Indian villages have identified these media in the networks set up by marriage, trade, religious pilgrimages and festivals, public administration, and the activities of itinerant entertainers, genealogists, and holy men. Even within rural areas these networks are so extensive as to produce a "rural cosmopolitanism." [33]

The flow of reciprocal influence between "higher" and "lower" levels of Hinduism is largely channeled through such media and can be traced in concrete studies. Using festivals and deities as "tracers" within one Indian village, Marriott has analyzed in detail the process of "parochialization" or downward spread into the parochial village culture of elements from Sanskritic Hinduism, as well as the converse upward spread, or "universalization," of elements of village culture into Sanskritic Hinduism.[34]

Hinduism conceived as a structure and organization of tradition transmitted through a network of social and cultural media may also be studied in towns and large cities. In these places, the structure is more complex, the pace of change faster, and the influence of "foreign" cultures more evident. The degree of contrast with the Hinduism of the tribal or peasant village will depend on the size and kind of urban center. Small towns and sacred cities will naturally show less contrast with village Hinduism than large metropolitan centers. But it is striking that even a modern urban center such as Madras retains a social and cultural structure of Hinduism recognizably continuous with the structure of a smaller city such as Surat, of a sacred town such as Gayā, and of a small village such as the one studied by Marriott.[35]

This result is perhaps the most important conclusion of recent anthropological studies of Hinduism. It suggests that the unity of Hinduism does not exclusively reside in an exemplary set of norms and scriptures, such as those defined by Sanskritic Hinduism, or in an alternative "lower-level" popular Hinduism of the uncultivated masses. The unity is to be found rather in the continuities that can be traced in the concrete media of song, dance, play, sculpture, painting, religious story, and rite that connect the rituals and beliefs of the villager with those of the townsman and urbanite, one region with another, and the educated with the uneducated. Even the sects lose some of their exclusiveness when one looks at the media that they use to communicate their particular version of Hinduism.[36]

The commercial mass media of film, radio, and print bring elements of a modern, secular culture with them into the cities and eventually into the towns and villages. Yet this trend has not displaced the traditional media or the traditional culture. On the contrary, it is common to find such traditional institutions as temples adopting the tape recorder, the public address system, the radio, and the printing press for the popularization of prayers, devotional songs, and religious discourses. Traditional media are also employed to spread the "modern" messages of community development, sanitation, and industrialization. Perhaps the only recent movements that have been outspokenly antireligious are Communism and the Southern "Drāviḍa" Leagues. Yet they too have used mythological themes and devotional songs, sometimes in satirical form, as the very vehicles of their propaganda.

The introduction of the mass media forms but a part of the modernization that all of Indian civilization is now undergoing. In this process, some political leaders and intellectuals actively seek to create a modern national culture that is "democratic" and "secular." Nehru has written that "Hindi" rather than "Hindu" is the correct word for the Indian country and culture, because "Hindi has nothing to do with religion, and a Moslem or Christian Indian is as much a Hindi as a person who follows Hinduism as a religion." [37] To the non-Indian observer, however, it is striking to find how far the modern national culture depends on the idea-contents and media of traditional Hinduism, both popular and Sanskritic.[38] This dependency is quite understandable in a civilization where religion and culture have been practically coextensive for thousands of years. In a society in which what and where one eats and drinks; whom one marries; where one lives and travels; and what occupation one follows have all been influenced by religious belief and practice, it should be easy enough to trace the functional links between the most abstract religious ideas and social life. A Brahman friend of the author is fond of pointing out that his mother will not allow a "non-dualist" Brahman in her kitchen, since her own family belongs to a "qualified dualist" sect. In this kind of society, it may be more problematic to find the autonomous, "secular" sector that is the modernist's desideratum.

## The Contribution of Textual Studies

The emphasis in the discussion so far has been on the extra-textual studies of the anthropologist and sociologist. The balance will now be redressed in favor of textual studies and their connection with the nontextual. It is not easier, however, to characterize Hinduism as a unified whole with the help of textual studies than it is to do so with nontextual. There are simply too many varied and difficult texts. Hinduism does not have a single canon with a single dogma attributed to a single founder. Its primary textual sources are vast, the languages in which they occur are many, and the distinction between "religious" and nonreligious works is difficult to make. In view of this situation, the textual scholar who devotes his life to a single text, or to a basic term in several texts, will naturally be reluctant to generalize about Hinduism as a whole. And when some of the textual scholars occasionally venture to make such generalizations, they offer them not as conclusions following directly from their textual studies but rather as a characterization of salient themes drawn from general knowledge or special experience.[39]

Indeed, extra-textual criteria and sources of knowledge must be invoked, even when the analysis of particular texts is in question. For these usually form part of the tradition or canon of a particular sect, school, caste, or community. As the Indologist Louis Renou has written, "Religious books can be defined as books written for the use of a sect. . . ." [40] The study of such texts is guided in part by knowledge of the character, history, and influence of particular sects and schools. Or when a sectarian text has become widely popular, as has the *Bhagavadgītā,* its analysis, together with other knowledge, may suggest "dominant ideas" in Hinduism.[41]

While some criteria for selecting and interpreting texts must frequently be looked for outside of the texts, it is equally true that the texts are a major source of information about the history and character of the different schools and sects, as well as about social life generally. This is especially likely to be the case for the ancient and medieval periods, where independent historical and sociological writing is very scarce; it is less pertinent for the later periods, where such writing does exist or where the methods of direct observation and interview are available. Histories of Buddhism, of Jainism, of Vedic and Classical Hinduism must depend in large measure for their sources on the sacred texts of these movements. The histories of the modern *bhakti* movements and of reform sects such as the Ārya Samāj, on the other hand, can draw upon biographies and reminiscences, upon public documents and legal cases, and upon the observation and testimony of outsiders.

Quite apart, then, from their contribution to our knowledge of religious doctrines and beliefs, textual studies of Hinduism also can make important contributions to religious and social history, the history of science and philosophy, and our knowledge of earlier forms of social and economic organization. E. W. Hopkins's studies of the conflict between priestly and martial classes, Jean Filliozat on the history of medicine, G. J. Held on Vedic ethnology, A. S. Altekar on ancient political and village organization, Étienne Lamotte on the history of Buddhism, and K. A. N. Sastri on the history of South India are but a few examples of such contributions made by textual scholars to fields far removed from philology and theology.[42]

The literary evidence of the texts cannot, of course, be taken at face value. It must be sifted and critically appraised, just as any other kind of evidence must be. The "traditional history" of the Epics and Purāṇas may contain many grains of historical truth, but the critical apparatus of modern scholarship is required to find them. Since so many of the religious texts tend to be normative and didactic, it would be unrealistic to regard them as accurate reflections of life. As Renou observes, "We should know little of the position of women in India if we had nothing but the idealized representations of Sītā, Draupadī, and Sāvitrī. The idealization of woman is as great as her social and religious status was low." [43] The literary evidence also will be more cogent for the study of some aspects of Hinduism than for others; more for a study of the religion of the intellectuals than for that of the illiterate masses; more for a study of the *Mīmāṃsā* schools, who attach great importance to textual exegesis, than for a study of antischolastic schools such as Yoga or the *bhakti* movements. There is no doubt that the literary evidence furnished by textual studies, used critically and with discrimination, is indispensable for an understanding of religious doctrines and practices and their relation to social change.

As the social anthropologist extends his contextual approach to the study of the great civilized traditions, he must increasingly rely on the literary evidence of textual studies, because so much of these traditions is expressed in texts. How he should apply the contextual approach to the texts is a problem of method that remains to be solved. He is not disposed to treat the texts as "classics," if a "classic" is a book that can be read in a vacuum, as George Burch wittily defined it. The anthropologist wants to understand a text in relation to the culture and society in which it is found, or at least in relation to segments of that society and culture. The fact that certain texts may be regarded as "literary classics," or as sacred and canonical in a particular society, is a significant fact about them that must be taken into account in interpreting their contextual role. The official interpretations of such pre-eminent texts cultivated by the literati of a culture are not, on the other hand, the answer to the anthropologist's need for a new art of textual interpretation. The literati's interpretations give important clues to the self-image of a culture and possibly to its normative principles, but, as Arthur Wright has shown, they do not usually give an accurate history of the culture or a realistic description of behavior.[44] And as evidence for self-image and normative ideas, these interpretations are not unequivocal, for in any particular context of place and time, there are always lesser literati to give alternative interpretations of the same or of lesser texts.

The question that the anthropologist is disposed to ask both of the texts and of the literati's interpretations is how they relate functionally to the rites, behavior, and attitudes of everyday life. No doubt different civilizations differ in the degree to which their philosophies—religious or secular—are embedded in the contexts of everyday life, and therefore discoverable in such contexts. But the precise character of these differences in different civilizations is a project for a kind of inquiry that will unite the sociological approach of the anthropologist with the textual approach of the humanistic scholar. In this kind of inquiry, the cleavage between the contextual and the textual approaches will be progressively closed as the texts of different kinds—written, seen, and heard—come to be regarded as the media of cultural transmission cultivated by intellectuals, modern as well as traditional, to link different groups of people into a single and differentiated network of communication.

## Notes

1. E.g., Clyde Kluckhohn and Dorothea Leighton, "The Navaho View of Life," in *idem, The Navaho* (Cambridge, Mass.: Harvard University Press, 1948); and E. E. Evans-Pritchard, *Nuer Religion* (New York and London: Oxford University Press, 1956).

2. Robert Redfield, "Primitive World View and Civilization," in *idem, The Primitive World and Its Transformations* (Ithaca, N.Y.: Cornell University Press, 1953).

3. See, e.g., Renou and Filliozat, *L'Inde Classique;* J. N. Farquhar, *An Outline of the Religious Literature of India* (London: H. Milford, Oxford University Press, 1920, 1929); and Diehl, *Instrument and Purpose.*

4. Norvin Hein, "The Rām Līlā," in Singer, ed., *TI,* pp. 73–98, and M. B. Emenau, "Oral Poets of South India: The Todas," in *TI,* pp. 106–18.

5. See, e.g., Wright, ed., *Studies in Chinese Thought;* Wright and Nivison, *Confucianism in Action;* Fairbank, ed., *Chinese Thought and Institutions;* von Grunebaum, ed., *Unity and Diversity in Muslim Civilization;* and Singer, ed., *TI.*

6. See, e.g., Gunnar Myrdal, *An International Economy* (New York: Harper, 1956),

and W. W. Rostow, *The Stages of Economic Growth* (Cambridge and New York: Cambridge University Press, 1960).

7. Albert Schweitzer, *Indian Thought and Its Development* (Boston: Beacon Press, 1936), and S. Radhakrishnan, *Eastern Religions and Western Thought* (New York and London: Oxford University Press, 1939, 1940), esp. Chapter 3, "Mysticism and Ethics in Hindu Thought."

8. K. Satchidananda Murty, "The Indian Spirit: Past and Present," *Comprendre*, No. 20 (Société Européenne de Culture, Venice, 1959), p. 107.

9. Morris E. Opler, "The Place of Religion in a North Indian Village," *Southwestern Journal of Anthropology* (*SWJA*) 15, No. 3 (Autumn, 1959): 219–26.

10. *Ibid.*, p. 226.

11. T. B. Naik, "Religion of the Anāvils of Surat," *TI*, pp. 183–90; Milton Singer, "The Great Tradition in a Metropolitan Center: Madras," *TI*, pp. 141–82; and Edward Shils, "The Culture of the Indian Intellectual," *Sewanee Review* 67, No. 2 (Spring-Summer, 1959): 239–61.

12. Singer, "Great Tradition in Madras," pp. 179–80. See also Chapter 5, below.

13. Sir Charles N. E. Eliot, *Hinduism and Buddhism*, 3 vols. (London: E. Arnold & Co., 1921).

14. Franklin Edgerton, "Dominant Ideas in the Formation of Indian Culture," *Journal of the American Oriental Society* (*JAOS*) 62 (1942): 151–56, and V. Raghavan, "Some Leading Ideas of Hindu Thought," *The Vedanta Kesari* 16, No. 10 (February, 1955): 344–49.

15. Srinivas, *Religion and Society Among Coorgs* (hereafter: *Coorgs*).

16. *Ibid.*, p. 214.

17. See also Nirmal Kumar Bose, "The Hindu Method of Tribal Absorption," in *idem*, *Cultural Anthropology and Other Essays* (Calcutta: Indian Associated Publishing Co., 1953), pp. 156–70.

18. Srinivas, *Coorgs*, p. 226.

19. V. Raghavan, "Variety and Integration in the Pattern of Indian Culture," *Far Eastern Quarterly* (*FEQ*) 15, No. 4 (August, 1956): 497–505.

20. Bernard S. Cohn, "The Changing Status of a Depressed Class," in Marriott, ed., *VI*, pp. 53–77.

21. M. N. Srinivas, "A Note on Sanskritization and Westernization, *FEQ* 15, No. 4 (August, 1956): 481–96.

22. Shils, "Culture of Indian Intellectual" (note 11, *supra*), and Parts Two, Four, and Five of this volume.

23. A. M. Shah and R. G. Shroff, "The Vahīvancā Bāroṭs of Gujarat: A Caste of Genealogists and Mythographers," *TI*, pp. 40–70.

24. John T. Hitchcock, "The Idea of the Martial Rājpūt," *TI*, pp. 10–17; Helen Lamb, "The Indian Merchant," *TI*, pp. 25–34; Daniel Ingalls, "The Brahman Tradition," *TI*, pp. 3–9; Stella Kramrisch, "Traditions of the Indian Craftsman," *TI*, pp. 18–24; and W. Norman Brown, "Class and Cultural Traditions in India," *TI*, pp. 35–39.

25. Brown, "Class and Cultural Traditions."

26. M. N. Srinivas, "Varna and Caste," in S. Radhakrishnan *et al.*, *Essays in Philosophy* (presented in honor of A. R. Wadia) (Bangalore: University of Baroda, 1954).

27. C. Fürer-Haimendorf, "The After-Life in Indian Tribal Belief," *Journal of the Royal Anthropological Institute* 83, Part I (1953): 37–49; Henry Whitehead, *The Village Gods of South India* (London: Cambridge University Press, 1916); L. S. S. O'Malley, *Popular Hinduism* (New York and Cambridge: Cambridge University Press, 1935); and Louis Dumont and D. Pocock, eds., *Contributions to Indian Sociology*, Vol. I (Paris and The Hague: Mouton, 1957).

28. Marriott, ed., *VI;* Srinivas, ed., *India's Villages;* Dube, *India's Changing Villages;* Dumont, *Une sous-caste de l'Inde du sud;* V. Elwin, *Religion of an Indian Tribe* (Bombay: Oxford University Press, 1955); C. Fürer-Haimendorf, *The Raj Gonds of Adilabad* (London: Macmillan, 1948); E. B. Harper, "A Hindu Village Pantheon," *SWJA* 15 (Autumn, 1959): 227–34; E. Kathleen Gough, "Cults of the Dead Among the Nayars," *TI*, pp. 240–72; and David G. Mandelbaum, "Form, Variation, and Meaning of a Ceremony," in Robert F. Spencer, ed., *Methods and Perspective in Anthropology: Papers in Honor of Wilson D. Wallis* (Minneapolis: University of Minnesota Press, 1954), pp. 60–102.

29. Surajit Sinha, "Tribal Cultures of Peninsular India as a Dimension of the Little Tradition: A Preliminary Statement," *TI,* pp. 298–312.

30. *Ibid.,* p. 311.

31. *Ibid.,* p. 300.

32. Redfield, *Peasant Society and Culture.*

33. Oscar Lewis, "Peasant Culture in India and Mexico: A Comparative Analysis," *VI,* pp. 145–70; McKim Marriott, "Little Communities in an Indigenous Civilization," *VI,* pp. 171–222; Morris E. Opler, "The Extension of an Indian Village," *Journal of Asian Studies* (*JAS*) 16, No. 1 (November, 1956): 5–10; Rudra Datt Singh, "The Unity of an Indian Village," *JAS* 16, No. 1: 10–19; and Surajit Sinha, "The Media and Nature of Hindu-Bhumij Interactions," *Journal of the Asiatic Society of Bengal: Letters and Science* 23, No. 1 (1957): 23–37.

34. Marriott, "Little Communities."

35. Cf. Singer, "Great Tradition in Madras"; Naik, "Religion of the Anāvils"; Vidyarthi, *Sacred Gayawal;* and Marriott, "Little Communities."

36. V. Raghavan, "Methods of Popular Religious Instruction in South India," *TI,* pp. 130–38; William McCormack, "The Forms of Communications in Vīraśaiva Religion," *TI,* pp. 119–28; and Y. B. Damle, "Harikathā: A Study in Communication," *Bulletin of the Deccan College Research Institute* 20 (S. K. De Felicitation Volume), Part I (October, 1960): 63–107.

37. Nehru, *Discovery of India,* pp. 63–65.

38. McKim Marriott, "Changing Channels of Cultural Transmission in Indian Civilization," in Verne F. Ray, ed., *Intermediate Societies: Social Mobility and Communication: Proceedings of the 1959 Annual Spring Meeting of the American Ethnological Society* (Seattle, Wash.: American Ethnological Society, 1959), p. 72, and Singer, ed., *TI, passim.*

39. Raghavan, "Some Leading Ideas" (note 14, *supra*), is a good example.

40. Louis Renou, *Religions of Ancient India* (London: University of London Press, 1953).

41. This is essentially what Edgerton does in "Dominant Ideas" (note 14, *supra*).

42. Jean Filliozat, *La Doctrine Classique de la Médecine Indienne: Ses Origines et Ses Parallels Grecs* (Paris: Imprimerie Nationale, 1949); Étienne Lamotte, *Histoire de Bouddhisme Indien,* Vol. 1: *Des Origines à l'Ère Saka* (Louvaine: Publications Universitaires, 1958); K. A. Nilakantha Sastri, *A History of South India* (London: Oxford University Press, 1958); A. S. Altekar, *A History of Village Communities in Western India* (Bombay: H. Milford, Oxford University Press, 1927); Edward W. Hopkins, *The Social and Military Position of the Ruling Caste in Ancient India, as Represented by the Sanskrit Epic* (New Haven, Conn.: Tuttle, Morehouse & Taylor, 1889); and Gerrit Jan Held, *The Mahabharata: An Ethnological Study* (Amsterdam: Uitgeversmaatschippij, 1935).

43. Renou, *Religions of Ancient India,* p. 52.

44. Arthur Wright, "The Study of Chinese Civilization," *Journal of the History of Ideas* 21, No. 2 (April-June, 1960): 233–55.

# PART TWO / *STRUCTURE AND TRANSFORMATION OF A GREAT TRADITION*

# *Introduction*

In his earlier characterizations of the Great Tradition of a civilization, Redfield emphasized "those aspects of the cultural heritage of the folk" that "have been there developed by a self-perpetuating intellectual group into highly specialized and systematized thought, often esoteric, commonly connected with religion, and in many (but not all) cases dependent on writing for its continuance and development." This characterization of a Great Tradition implies that it is a *learned* and *literate* tradition, preserving and developing the dominant systems of thought and value of a civilization. When he first began to work in this field of comparative civilizations in the early 1950's, he found that the humanistic scholars and orientalists were by and large students of the Great Traditions and the anthropologists and the field sociologists of the Little Traditions. The former studied "the written documents and the artistic products of the literate few of the great civilizations," and the latter studied the small communities of people who live by Little Traditions. Redfield wanted to bring these two kinds of study together in order to gain a fresh view of the Great Traditions of civilization from the grassroots perspective of the "little community." In this perspective, the anthropologist becomes interested in how the Great Tradition emerges from the culture of the folk and in how the two kinds of cultural traditions and two kinds of community, little and great, interrelate.[1]

India presented an opportunity to study these problems firsthand. Social anthropologists had begun to make intensive field studies of small village communities there, while the well-established fields of Indology and culture history had been disclosing to the West, at least since the end of the eighteenth century, the great intellectual and aesthetic achievements of Indian civilization. The time seemed ripe to bring the two approaches together. How to do an anthropological field study of a Great Tradition, was not, however, described in any manual of anthropology. Nor was there at that time any exemplary study to serve as a model.

M. N. Srinivas's conception of "Sanskritization" and "Sanskritic Hinduism," which he introduced in his Coorg study, provided a promising point of departure. Social anthropological studies of Indian and other Great Traditions were not then considered a feasible or desirable direction of research. Although we had discussed some of the problems of field method in the study of Great Traditions at the 1954 Chicago seminar on Village India, McKim Marriott was the only participant who concentrated on elements of the Great Tradition at the village level.

One implication of Redfield's conception of a Great Tradition was that it was socially embedded in a context of specific social relations, statuses, roles, and institutions. This meant that a field study of India's Great Tradition would not simply be a journey to the wise men of the East or a search for collections of ancient manuscripts and monuments. The wise men, the manuscripts, and the monuments are all there and are ingredients of the Great Tradition, and those who find and study them contribute to its understanding. An anthropological field study, however, needs to demonstrate how these and other ingredients operate in the living context of social life; it seeks to describe the concrete context of the "texts."

Before my first trip to India, I attempted to identify the underlying institutional and cultural representations of India's "Great Tradition" that would explain how a Great Tradition is formed, as well as its relation to Little Traditions. In a preliminary formulation, I listed them as follows:

1. A body of sacred scriptures and texts in which the Great Tradition is embodied and expressed
2. A class of literati who have the authority to read and interpret the sacred scriptures
3. Leading personalities, such as Nehru and Gandhi, who convey their vision of the Great Tradition to the masses of the people
4. A "sacred geography" of holy places—rivers, holy places of saints, temples, and shrine centers—defining a set of "sacred centers" that provide the forum, media, and vehicle for expressing the Great Tradition
5. A "sacred calendar" of rites and ceremonies marking the important occasions of the individual life cycle and of the seasons.[2]

A direct field study of any of these representations, with the possible exception of the first—the scriptural texts—would lead one to find the social embeddedness of the Great Tradition. Even a direct study of the scriptural texts would lead into their social contexts if one did not insist, as some textual scholars do, on a method of reading and translating texts that tries to abstract them from the social context. Conversely, in a civilization as "scripturalist" as that of India, a field study that begins with any of the other components is bound to find scriptural texts deeply embedded in social life.[3]

On my first trip to Madras I began with a study of the literati representatives of the Great Tradition and their social organization and discovered in the course of it the importance of analyzing rites, ceremonies, and cultural performances for discovering the structure and transformations of a Great Tradition in a metropolitan center. I also encountered the scriptural texts, leading personalities, and sacred geography and have referred to them in the contexts where they occurred.

Part Two contains the reports of the first trip. Chapter 3, "Search for a Great Tradition," describes in a preliminary way the abortive search for all-India units of field study and observation and the discovery of cultural performances in Madras City. Chapter 4, "The Social Organization of Sanskritic Hinduism in Madras City," reports detailed interviews with the literati specialists of Sanskritic Hinduism and attempts on this basis to construct the social organization and structure of Sanskritic Hinduism. The specialists' move to an urban center initiates or intensifies processes of change in the social organization and the structure of Sanskritic Hinduism. These are briefly summarized in the last section of the chapter.

Chapter 5, "Urbanization and Cultural Change," continues the discussion of change but concentrates on an analysis of cultural performances and cultural media as a source of evidence for inferring the effects of urbanization on the emergence of a new cultural structure.

A preliminary report of the first Madras study was presented in the spring of 1955 to a joint seminar on social change conducted by Robert Redfield and Raymond Firth at the University of Chicago and was published as "The Cultural Pattern of Indian Civilization" in the November 1955 issue of the *Far Eastern Quarterly,* together with a companion piece by Robert Redfield, "The Social Organization of Tradition." Two other closely related papers were submitted and were published in the same journal in August, 1956. One was M. N. Srinivas's "A Note on Sanskritization and Westernization." After becoming acquainted with Srinivas in Madras, I had suggested to him that it would be helpful to have a clarification of the relations between "Sanskritization" and "Westernization." The other paper, by V. Raghavan, "Variety and Integration in the Pattern of Indian Culture," had been presented to the 1954 seminar on Indian studies held at the Deccan College, Poona.

After my return from my first trip to the University of Chicago in the spring of 1955, India dominated my academic life more and more. Six of my colleagues and I organized an interdisciplinary faculty committee to develop the university's research and teaching activities on South Asia. Members of this committee were responsible for planning and teaching general introductions to Indian and Islamic civilizations, which became part of a College non-Western civilizations program in the autumn of 1956. Younger faculty with specialized training in the South Asia field were recruited. A conference, "Introducing India in Liberal Education," met in 1957 to discuss alternative undergraduate programs on Indian civilization. The university's graduate program was also gradually expanded to add modern South Asian languages and literatures. After 1959, when the Ford Foundation and the U.S. Office of Education awarded the university grants for the support of South and Southeast Asian studies, the development of the field rapidly accelerated.[4]

The Redfield project on comparative civilizations also continued. In the autumn of 1955, Professor and Mrs. Redfield went to India to participate in a conference in Madras and to undertake field research in Orissa and Bihar. In Calcutta, where they had gone to purchase field equipment, Professor Redfield became seriously ill and returned home to find that he had lymphatic leukemia. He continued to teach and write during the next three years as brilliantly and productively as ever. His lectures on peasant society and culture and on civilization during this period reflect his great and increasing interest in India.

In the spring of 1958, he presented three papers to a seminar on comparative civilizations organized by David Mandelbaum and me at the Center for Advanced Studies in the Behavioral Sciences at Stanford. A. L. Kroeber, N. K. Bose, Gustave von Grunebaum, Arthur Wright, Charles Wagley, and Ethel Albert also contributed papers.

The full report of my first Madras study was drafted in 1957–58, when I was a Fellow at the Center. About half of it was first published in the symposium *Traditional India: Structure and Change* under the title "The Great Tradition in a Metropolitan Center: Madras." It is reprinted in Part Two of this volume along with the other half of the report, "The Social Organization of Sanskritic Hinduism in Madras City," which has not been published before.

Thomas Sebeok, also a Center Fellow and then editor of the *Journal of American Folklore,* invited me to serve as guest editor of the *Journal* for a special issue on India. Since I had been in touch with scholars in India and in the United States about their research on Indian cultural traditions and change, I accepted Sebeok's invitation, and the symposium *Traditional India: Structure and Change* appeared in a special issue of the *Journal* in 1958 and as a volume in its bibliographic series in 1959. The symposium was dedicated to Robert Redfield, who did not live to see its final publication but had read most of the manuscript copy.[5]

Redfield's concepts of the structure and organization of tradition were used as the framework for the *Traditional India* symposium. The four major social classes or *varṇas*—Brahman, warrior, merchant, and craftsman—were discussed as living cultural traditions in Indian civilization. The social organization and culture of each *varṇa* were analyzed as distinctive variants of India's Great Tradition by a Sanskritist, an art historian, an economic historian, and an anthropologist, respectively. The functional relations among the *varṇas* were analyzed by a Sanskritist.

Redfield had not explicitly included cultural performances within his concept of the "social organization of tradition." After their importance emerged in the Madras study, it seemed useful to take them as observable units of cultural organization from which a "cultural structure of tradition" could be abstracted, much as a "social structure of tradition" could be abstracted from concrete instances of its social organization. The *Traditional India* symposium included studies of the *Rāmalīlā,* Toda songs, Lingāyat media of communication, and methods of popular religious instruction in ancient India as examples of the analysis of cultural performances. Two Sanskritists, a historian of religion and a social anthropologist, respectively, undertook these analyses.

The discussion of change in cultural traditions was divided between an analysis of the effects of urbanization, including a portion of the Madras study, and studies of recurrent processes linking tribal and peasant traditions to those of the Great Tradition as well as to the changes that come with modernization. The role of the professional caste of genealogists and mythographers, and of religious sects as agents of "traditionalization" and of modernization was emphasized in several of these latter studies, all of which were written by anthropologists.

The symposium *Traditional India* was the first interdisciplinary demonstration of the viability and fruitfulness of Redfield's approach to the study of a civilization as a social organization of Great and Little Traditions. The number and variety of studies showed some of the complexity of the approach as well. Such complexity, however, reflects the complexity of India and, perhaps, any civilization. Strands of unity were also revealed in the symposium—some derived from ancient Great Traditions, some from Little Traditions, and some from modern innovations. The weaving of these many strands into a unified national culture is a highly selective process that creates new traditions and that preserves some old ones in the search for a cultural identity that will be both "modern" and "traditional."

> The movement of modern nationalism in India, as in most other countries, has always shown a strong interest in the recovery or reinterpretation of India's traditional culture. With the achievement of national independence, this interest has received an official definition. Language, national history, archeological monuments, folk arts and crafts, classical music, dance, and drama have become symbols of a modern Indian identity alongside the national emblem, Five-Year Plans, parliamentary institutions, and atomic installations.
>
> The definition is selective and creative. A traditional culture, notably that of India, is far too varied and rich a growth to be displayed adequately in Republic Day celebrations. And not all cultural traditions will be thought suitable for display; some are perhaps thought best left to grow or wither in provincial obscurity. Those cultural traditions that become symbols of national identity undergo, by virtue of their new role, a sea change; they take on a life of their own, quite different from their life as regional and local traditions. They have become the chosen representatives of a national tradition.
>
> Theoretically, any element of traditional culture is a potential candidate for selection, but in fact only a small number are so chosen at any given time. In this selective and creative process, cultural traditions take on a fluidity and self-consciousness that reflect constantly changing moods and aspirations, and changing conceptions of national identity. They reflect, too, the fact that a civilization is a process of becoming, as well as a state of being, as Nirmal Kumar Bose has remarked apropos the modern history of Bengal. Now this is not the way we ordinarily think of traditions; they are, ordinarily, the things that we take for granted, the unquestioned assumptions and the handed-down ways of our ancestors. But it has become a commonplace of modern history that even the most traditional societies are no longer sure of what it is they can take for granted. Confronted by swift currents of internal and external change, they have been compelled to restate themselves to themselves in order to discover what they have been and what it is they are to become. Their cultural traditions have become problematic hypotheses in an inquiry into the design for a meaningful and worthwhile life.[6]

## The Great Tradition in a Metropolitan Center

To readers of "The Cultural Role of Cities" by Robert Redfield and myself, the linkage of a great cultural tradition with a modern metropolitan center may appear puzzling if not incongruous.[7] For in that earlier study it was suggested that Great Traditions get fashioned out of local folk cultures, or Little Traditions, through a process of continuous development by professional literati centered in orthogenetic towns and cities. We also said there that in metropolitan centers, ancient and modern, another process—heterogenetic transformation—operates to destroy or supersede the great cultural traditions of an indigenous civilization. This transformation is carried on with the help of professional intellectuals of a new social type—the intelligentsia—who stand astride the boundaries of the cultural encounter, mediating the alien cultural influences to the natives and interpreting the indigenous culture to the foreigners.

We also suggested in that article, however, that the two processes—that of primary urbanization leading to the growth of a Great Tradition in orthogenetic centers and that of secondary urbanization leading to a heterogenetic transformation of that tradition—are not always discontinuous. There seem to be civilizations, or at least particular historical phases during which some civilizations undergo imperial and colonial expansion, in which we can almost see how one process is succeeded by the other and how a new social type, the intelligentsia, takes over from the old, the literati. Indic civilization appeared to us to be particularly well characterized by such lines of continuity, and the communities of western Guatemala, with their well-established institutions of trade and travel, may even represent a simpler preurban phase of the process.

The details of the subsequent fate of a Great Tradition as it undergoes secondary urbanization have, we must confess, remained shadowy because there have been too few intensive case studies to give a detailed picture. In the general literature on cultural and civilizational history, this kind of change is usually presented as a sharp one and a change for the worse, representing a decadence, fossilization, or secularization of the great cultural traditions. Because I suspected that this common view of the matter is, in part, influenced by a particular kind of cultural analysis—the textual study of the outstanding products of art and learning, abstracted from social and cultural context and the matrix of little and popular cultural traditions—I undertook in a preliminary way a functional and contextual study of what happens to a Great Tradition and its literati in a metropolitan urban center in South India.[8]

## Madras as a Heterogenetic and a Colonial City

Because Madras is a heterogenetic and was a colonial city, it is a good place to investigate the effects of urbanization on cultural traditions.

The urban characteristics that go with large metropolitan centers are to be found in this capital city—a large population, rapid growth, predominance of males over females, a high proportion of immigrants, high literacy rates, a highly specialized nonagricultural occupational structure, an abundance of social and cultural facilities and organizations, and a heterogeneity of linguistic, religious, ethnic, and social groups. These characteristics do not always have the same high absolute values in Madras that they have in other metropolitan centers of the world, but the degree of urbanization is high if compared with the city's hinterland in the State or with India's present degree of urbanization. The city's hinterland is about 80 per cent agricultural villages and small towns. It includes a predominantly Telugu-speaking north as well as a predominantly Tamil-speaking south.

Located on the coastal plains of the Bay of Bengal in southeastern India, Madras is India's third largest city, with a 1951 population of 1,416,056. Its population is exceeded only by Bombay, which has more than 2.8 million inhabitants, and by Calcutta, with more than 2.5 million. The year 1921 marks an important change in Madras's population growth. For at least thirty years before that date, the rate of growth was fairly steady; after that, there is a series of spurts probably induced by immigration to escape famine or to take advantage of opportunities in employment or of the city's medical and educational services and cultural amenities. The population figures in round numbers for these periods are: 1891, 450,000; 1901, 500,000; 1911, 518,000; 1921, 526,000; 1931, 645,000; 1941, 776,000; 1951, 1,416,000.[9]

Before 1891, the population figures are less reliable; the earliest accurate figure is probably that of the 1871 census, which gives 399,552 as the population of the city.

The steady and slow growth of Madras until very recent years has permitted the survival of many parts of the villages and small towns, which have become incorporated into its limits as it has expanded. As late as 1908, the *Imperial Gazetteer* describes Madras as "a collection of villages." And even today, many of the preurban characteristics are visible: large tracts of unused land with palms growing on them, paddy fields and irrigation tanks, buffalo and washermen in the city's rivers and lagoons, fishermen's thatched huts and catamarans on the beach. The accelerated growth of the last twenty years is, however, quickly filling up the vacant land and sending an increasing number of daily commuters farther and farther out of the city on the electric trains.

In its origin, Madras City resembles many other pre-European towns in India and some medieval European towns: It began in 1640 as a settlement of traders around a fort and several villages. But because the fort was one of the trading factories of the English East India Company, the settlement soon developed a character and career distinctive of the British colonial city in Asia. These cities, like Madras, Surat, Bombay, and Calcutta, at first entrepôts for European trade with Asia, later became bases for the spread of European political and military control over the entire country. Their history is the story of the encounter of differing civilizations and of their mutual transformations.

As early as 1688, the East India Company's directors in London were so impressed with the prosperity and growth of Madras that they decided to call it a city rather than a town. In 1752 it became the seat of the Madras Presidency and, from 1774 on, it was subject, through the Bengal Government, to the control of the British Parliament.

The city's importance as an administrative center has continued to the present, with a concentration of state and union government offices. It is, however, also a prominent commercial, transportation, and cultural center. With 98 per cent of its population depending on nonagricultural employments—production other than cultivation (25 per cent), commerce (22 per cent), transport (9 per cent), government and professional services (42 per cent)—and only 2 per cent on agriculture, Madras is a highly urbanized metropolitan center.[10]

## The Great Tradition in Sacred Geography and Social Structure

Where in a metropolitan center shall we find the Great Tradition of Hinduism? It is natural for a Westerner to assume that a large modern city is not a very likely place to look for it, but in India this assumption does not hold. It is true that the full-blown "classic" version of the tradition as it might be constructed from selected texts is not evident in the city today. In fact, there is not a single unequivocal version of the Great Tradition in Madras, but several overlapping and competing versions with varying degrees of admixture of regional and local traditions. This is not surprising in a study that begins with a contextual analysis in a limited region. Only as the accumulation of studies in different regions and in different historical periods permits an extension of comparisons will we be able to say with some confidence what is common and pervasive and what is local and episodic in Indian civilization as a whole.

There are three general methods for localizing a Great Tradition within a limited area: through a study of its sacred geography, of its professional representatives and their social organization, and of its cultural performances (including religious rites and ceremonies).

Although modern Madras is not a major temple city or pilgrimage center, its relation to the sacred geography of Hinduism is not insignificant. For the modern city grew up around historic temple villages like Mylapore and Triplicane, whose large Śiva and Viṣṇu temples, respectively, continue to be actively patronized today. And even as the city developed under the East India Company, the local merchants and landlords continued to build new temples and to patronize Sanskrit scholars, traditional poets, musicians, and dancers.[11] It would be interesting to trace the continuity of the historical cultural associations of the city with the neighboring religious and cultural centers like Kāñcīpuram (Conjeeveram, the present residence of the head of the Śaṅkara *maṭha*), Śrīperumbudūr, and Tiruppati, and with the many other temples and *maṭhas* in South India, as well as with the modern temples and religious seats within the city, e.g., the Rāmakrishna Mission, the Divine Life Society, a Śiva-Viṣṇu temple, and a Sāī Bābā temple in honor of a Hindu-Muslim saint, among others.

Contemporary residents not only visit the major and minor temples (of which there are hundreds) within the city but also make frequent pilgrimages to other shrine centers in South India and in North India. This practice has been helped by modern improvements in transportation. Automobiles and buses, planes and trains now take large numbers of pilgrims on organized tours of the major temple and shrine centers. The pilgrimages now tend to merge with patriotic sightseeing, which has become popular even with the secular-minded.

The 1951 census tells us that 81.62 per cent of Madras residents declared themselves as Hindus, 9.91 per cent as Muslims, and 7.72 per cent as Christians. But we cannot assume without further evidence that every Hindu is a representative of the Great Tradition, or even an active participant in it, or that there is a single system of Hinduism.

Hindus in Madras city are subdivided into a number of sect-like groups. The most important of these are the Smārta Brahmans, followers of Śaṅkara (A.D. 788–820), believers in monistic or Advaitavedānta who are supposed to conform to *smṛti* traditions; the Śrīvaiṣṇava Brahmans and non-Brahmans, followers of Rāmānuja (A.D. 1017?–1137), and believers in a qualified monism; the Mādhvas, predominantly Brahman followers of a dualistic Vaiṣṇavite system developed by Madhva, a Canarese theologian of the thirteenth century; and the predominantly non-Brahman Śaivasiddhāntins, followers of a dualistic and monotheistic system of Tamil Śaivism. Each of these groups has its distinctive theology and philosophy, canonical scriptures, ritual practices, shrines, and centers of religious teaching and leadership, known as *maṭhas,* in different parts of the South. They do not generally intermarry.

In addition to these major Hindu groups, there are also in Madras City small numbers of Sikhs, Jains, Buddhists, and Zoroastrians. Of these, only the Jains exceed 1,000, numbering about 6,000 in 1961. The 1951 census returned 1,267 self-declared atheists for Madras City and a very few members of the Ārya Samāj, the Brāhmo Samāj, and the Rationalists. The increase in atheism in Madras City and State (the 1921 census listed four for the state as a whole) is generally attributed to the active antireligious propaganda of two non-Brahman organizations, the Dravidian Federation and the Dravidian Progressive Federation.[12]

The second method that I used to identify the Great Tradition in Madras City was essentially an application of Robert Redfield's suggestion that a Great Tradition is cultivated and transmitted by a class of learned specialists, the literati, who have a definite social structure and organization.[13] This idea is very apt for India, where for thousands of years a special learned and priestly class, the Brahmans, have had almost a monopoly as officiants, teachers, and scholars of Hinduism. And in Madras City, I was able to locate many different kinds of Brahman literati: temple priests, domestic priests, gurus, and pandits specializing in sacred law, in logic, in poetics, in Vedic exegesis; astrologers, *Āyurvedic* doctors, and others. But I also found that not all Brahmans are literati; they are also lawyers and high court judges, businessmen, physicians, movie producers, authors and journalists, professors and architects, cooks and chauffeurs. Many of those in the higher professions have been trained abroad and have been agents of Westernization and modernization in India. Some of the literati, on the other hand, are non-Brahmans.

These findings raise the question whether the Brahman literati in Madras are changing their social role, giving up their traditional role as cultivators of the Great Tradition (and agents of Sanskritization, as M. N. Srinivas would say)[14] to become intelligentsia, that is, agents of Westernization and modernization. To some extent, I believe this is occurring, but it is difficult to give a clear-cut answer to the question because there have always been important social and status differences between priestly Brahmans (*vaidikas*) and worldly Brahmans (*laukikas*), because some Brahmans are traditionalizing and Westernizing at the same time, and because new forms of Sanskritization have been developing under urban conditions. A detailed study of how the worldly Brahmans have been recruited into modern professions, of their family histories, of the statistics of changes in traditional occupations, of how they relate themselves to Hinduism, and of the ancient parallels and precedents is necessary before definite answers can be given.

These sociological studies are just beginning to be made in different parts of India, and I shall not report them at this time. There is some evidence from Madras, however, to suggest that the Brahmans are relating themselves in new and constructive ways to the changes affecting Indian traditions and are not schizophrenically split down the middle into traditional Indian and modern Western halves. This evidence is indirect and comes chiefly from observation of cultural changes. I should like to present some of it because it is intrinsically interesting and also because it illustrates a third method of approach to the problem of urbanization and culture change.

## The Great Tradition in Cultural Structure: Comparative Analysis of Cultural Performances

This third method emerged naturally in the application of the second method. Whenever Madras Brahmans (and non-Brahmans, too, for that matter) wished to exhibit to me some feature of Hinduism, they always referred to, or invited me to see, a particular rite or ceremony in the life cycle, in a temple festival, or in the general sphere of religious and cultural performances. Reflecting on this in the course of my interviews and observations, I found that the more abstract generalizations about Hinduism (my own as well as those I had heard) could generally be checked, directly or indirectly, against observable performances. The idea then occurred to me that these performances could be regarded as the most concrete observable units of Indian culture, the analysis of which might lead to more abstract structures within a comprehensive cultural system. Looking at performances from this point of view, it soon became evident that the rites and ceremonies performed as ritual obligations, usually by domestic or temple priests, had many elements in common with the more secular cultural performances in the theater, concert hall, radio programs, and films, and that these linkages revealed not only the outlines of a cultural structure but also many indications of the trend and process of change in that structure.

Through an analysis and comparison of cultural performances and their constituents—e.g., the media and themes, the place and occasion of performance, the performers, the audience—it is possible to infer the structure and organization of particular kinds of performances. Then, by tracing the linkages among these structures and organizations, it is possible to arrive at the more comprehensive and abstract constructs of cultural structure, cultural value system, and a Great Tradition. To the extent that exact dates or relative temporal orderings are available for the different performances or their constituents, it is also possible to analyze continuities, trends, and processes of change in these structures and organizations. Given such data about the persistences and transformations of cultural traditions, it is then possible to relate these continuities and changes to urbanization and other relevant causal conditions.

The method is operational: It begins with concrete units that can be directly observed, the cultural performances, and proceeds, through analysis and abstraction, to constructions that are not directly observable at all or only indirectly so. It thus makes up two methodological deficiencies in holistic concepts of culture—directly observable units and a "ladder of abstraction" that leads from these units to the holistic constructs. In studies of the relations of urbanization to culture change, it is more usual to begin at the societal end—with particular social groupings; their structure, organization, and interrelationships; and the impingement on them of economic, demographic, geographical, and other changes. This, too, is a legitimate procedure and is required in a complete analysis of the problem to complement the procedure that begins with cultural traditions.

## Notes

1. Quotations are from Robert Redfield, "The Natural History of the Folk Society," *Social Forces* 30, No. 3 (March, 1953): 224–28, and *idem,* "Community Studies in Japan and China: A Symposium," *FEQ* 15, No. 1 (November, 1954): 3–10. The rise of civilization from a natural history of the folk society is developed in Redfield, *Primitive World and Its Transformations.* See also the foreword by Robert Redfield and Milton Singer to Wright, ed., *Studies in Chinese Thought.*

2. Robert Redfield and Milton Singer, "The Cultural Role of Cities," *EDCC* 3, No. 1 (October, 1954): 66–70, and Srinivas, *Coorgs* (see note 15 to Chapter 2, above). At the Cambridge meeting of the International Congress of Orientalists in 1954, we found Dr. Arnold Bake and Dr. T. N. Dave of the School of Oriental and African Studies and Dr. Morris Carstairs especially helpful. Members of the 1954 seminar on Indian studies who had been invited to the Deccan College in Poona through the courtesy of its director, Dr. S. M. Katre, included A. S. Altekar, W. Norman Brown, S. K. Chatterjee, Y. B. Damle, V. M. Dandekar, Roger Evans, D. R Gadgil, Chadbourne Gilpatric, John Gumperz, R. Wade Jones, D. G. Karve, Irawati Karve, S. V. Kogekar, V. K. Kothurkar, D. N. Majumdar, V. Raghavan, H. D. Sankalia, Milton Singer, Merrill Goodall, and M. N. Srinivas.

3. The difference between textual and contextual analysis is also an issue among textual scholars. See, e.g., Chapter 2 in this volume and Edwin Gerow, "Renou's Place in Vedic Exegetical Tradition," *JAOS* 88, No. 2 (April-June, 1968): 310–33. The term "scripturalist" as an attribute of a civilization is borrowed from Geertz, *Islam Observed.*

4. See Singer, ed., *South and Southeast Asian Studies,* for details. See also *idem,* ed., *Introducing India in Liberal Education; idem, Introduction to Civilization of India;* and *idem,* "The Social Sciences in Non-Western Studies," *The Annals* 356 (November, 1964): 30–44.

5. Singer, ed., *TI* (see note 2, Introduction to Part One, above). Papers presented at the 1958 seminar on comparative civilization were later published in the following forms: Robert Redfield's in M. P. Redfield, ed., *Human Nature and Study of Society;* Kroeber's in Kroeber, *Anthropologist Looks at History;* Bose's in N. K. Bose, *Culture and Society in India;* von Grunebaum's as "An Analysis of Islamic Civilization and Cultural Anthropology," in Gustave von Grunebaum, ed., *Modern Islam* (Berkeley and Los Angeles: University of California Press, 1962); Wright's "Study of Chinese Civilization" in *Journal of the History of Ideas* 21, No. 2 (April-June, 1960): 233–55;

Wagley's in Wagley, *Latin American Tradition;* and E. Albert's as "Une Étude de Valeurs en Urundi," *Cahiers d'Études Africaines* 1, No. 2 (Paris, May, 1960): 148–60, and as "Rhetoric, Logic, and Poetics in Burundi: Culture Patterns of Speech Behavior," in John Gumperz and Dell H. Hymes, eds., *The Ethnography of Communication,* special issue of *AA* 66, No. 6, Part 2 (December, 1964): 35–54 (reprinted by Committee for African Studies, University of California, Berkeley, African Series, No. 173).

6. See editor's preface to *TI.*

7. Redfield and Singer, "Cultural Role of Cities" (see note 3, Introduction to Part One).

8. A preliminary report of this study was published as "The Cultural Pattern of Indian Civilization," *FEQ* 15, No. 1 (November, 1955): 23–36.

9. In 1961, the population was 1,729,141. Statistical data are available in *Census of India, 1951,* III: *Madras and Coorg* (Part I: Report; Part II-B: Tables by S. Venkateswaran, I.C.S.) (Madras, 1953). George Kuriyan, "The Distribution of Population in the City of Madras," *Indian Geographical Journal* 16, No. 1 (1941): 58–70, and N. Subrahmanyam, "Regional Distribution and Relative Growth of the Cities of Tamil," *Indian Geographical Journal* 16, No. 1 (1941): 71–83, contain useful material on growth and topography. H. D. Love, *Vestiges of Old Madras, 1640–1800,* 4 vols. (London: John Murray, 1913), is valuable for early maps and records. For a recent summary, see John E. Brush, "The Growth of the Presidency Towns," in Fox, ed., *Urban India.*

10. The 1961 census showed increases for production to 34 per cent and transportation to 13 per cent, and decreases for commerce to 20 per cent and for services to 33 per cent. *Census of India, 1961* 9, Part X, 13C (Delhi, 1964): 11.

11. V. Raghavan, "Some Musicians and Their Patrons About 1800 A.D. in Madras City," *Journal of the Music Academy* 16, i–iv (Madras, 1945): 127–36.

12. The 1961 census gives the corresponding percentages as 84 per cent, 7 per cent, and 6.5 per cent, respectively. Atheists have decreased to 1,017, and seventeen have declared themselves Rationalists. *Census of India, 1961* 9, Part X, C1, "Cultural Table for Madras State" (Delhi, 1964): 627.

13. Redfield, "Social Organization of Tradition" (see note 1, Chapter 3, below), and Redfield, *Peasant Society and Culture.*

14. Srinivas, "Sanskritization and Westernization" (see note 21, Chapter 2, above).

# 3 / *Search for a Great Tradition in Cultural Performances*

During a visit to India in 1954–55, I had an opportunity to do a methodological field study in South India. The purpose of this study was to chart an intellectual map of some of the researchable territory that lies between the culture of a village or small community and the culture of a total civilization. This study is not easy to classify in terms of prevailing conceptions about "research," since it falls between the intensive anthropological field study and the purely conceptual types of methodological analysis. But despite its unorthodox character, it seemed an appropriate study to undertake in a new and not-well-known field. Although the study was primarily designed to serve the methodological purpose of giving an empirical content to some very general ideas and to suggest concrete hypotheses for further research, it also turned up some substantive findings that have importance on their own account. In this report, I shall mention some of these in passing but will in the main confine myself to the problems of method posed by the study.

Before I went to India I already had a fairly explicit framework of ideas for the study of civilizations. Most important of these was the view of a civilization, suggested by Redfield, as a complex structure of a Little Tradition and a Great Tradition.[1] Using these ideas, as well as another distinction of Redfield's between "orthogenetic" and "heterogenetic" cities, I had tried to formulate several broad hypotheses concerning the relation of Little and Great Traditions in Indian civilization.[2] These were:

1. that because India had a "primary" or "indigenous" civilization which had been fashioned out of pre-existing folk and regional cultures, its Great Tradition was culturally continuous with the Little Traditions to be found in its diverse regions, villages, castes and tribes
2. that this cultural continuity was product and cause of a common cultural consciousness shared by most Indians and expressed in essential similarities of mental outlook and ethos
3. that this common cultural consciousness has been formed in India with the help of certain processes and factors that also play an impor-

tant role in other primary civilizations: i.e., sacred books and sacred objects as a fixed point of worship, a special class of literati (Brahmans) who have the authority to recite and interpret the sacred scriptures, professional storytellers, a sacred geography of sacred centers—temples, pilgrimage places, and shrines—and leading personalities who by their identification with the Great Tradition and with the masses mediate the one to the other

4. that in a primary civilization like India's, cultural continuity with the past is so great that even the acceptance of "modernizing" and "progress" ideologies does not result in linear forms of social and cultural change but may result in the "traditionalizing" of apparently "modern" innovations.

In considering how such broad hypotheses might be tested by a field study in India, I got some help and encouragement from several other quarters. One of these was M. N. Srinivas's study, *Religion and Society Among the Coorgs of South India.*[3] From this work I learned that the Great Tradition of Indian civilization might be approximately identified with what Srinivas called "Sanskritic Hinduism" and what previous writers like Monier-Williams called "Brahmanism" in contrast to popular Hinduism. As Srinivas defines it, Sanskritic Hinduism is the generalized pattern of Brahman practices and beliefs that have an all-India spread, in contrast to those forms of Hinduism with a local, regional, or peninsular spread. From Srinivas's work, too, I learned that Sanskritic Hinduism was not confined to the Brahmans but, as in the case of the Coorgs, might be taken over by non-Brahman groups as part of an effort to raise their status. To this process Srinivas has given the name "Sanskritization," and it is obviously an important way in which the Great Tradition spreads from one group and region to another group and region.

Other ways of conceiving the relationship of the great Indic civilization to the culture and social structure of a particular Indian village were suggested by McKim Marriott in a seminar that we held in Chicago during the spring of 1954.[4] Between Srinivas's conception of Sanskritic Hinduism as a generalized all-India phenomenon and Marriott's description of one village as the locus of interacting Little and Great Traditions, there appeared to me to be a gap which might be filled by a synchronic and functional type of field study.

## Defining the Unit of Field Study

The unit of field study proved to be much smaller than the "intelligible unit of study" with which our methodological discussions in the Chicago seminar had dealt—namely, a total civilization in its full historical and geographical sweep. I did not, of course, expect to encompass the history of Indian civilization within a few observations and interviews carried out over a period of several months. But I must confess I entertained some hope of making contact with Indian civilization on an all-India level. The basis of this—as it turned out—naive hope was the assumption that, if Hindu traditions were still cultivated by professional specialists and if Sanskritic Hinduism, at least, had an all-India spread, a strategic selection of the main types of such specialists should offer a quick access to the structure of the civilization. I was not sufficiently familiar with India to feel confident in my selection of the "strategic" specialists, but, with the help of my reading and the advice of some who knew India better than I did, I obtained introductions to caste genealogists (Bhāṭs) in Uttar Pradesh, a subcaste of bards (Cāraṇs) in Rājasthān and Saurāṣṭra, some individual *sādhus* and pandits in Benares, a Sanskritist in Madras, a cultural historian in Bombay, and several political-cultural leaders in New Delhi. While this rather broad geographical spread was in part an accident of the location of my advisers, it seemed to assure a genuine all-India scope to my inquiry.

When I arrived in India, I quickly saw that, however strategic such a selection might appear from 10,000 miles away, it did not take sufficient account of the cultural and noncultural realities of the Indian scene. The sheer physical problem of traveling around to these various points in India would leave little time for even a preliminary study of any of these groups. But this was not the decisive obstacle; in the end, I did get to almost all these regions and to several others. A more serious obstacle to my original program arose from the fact that, even if I had been able to make studies of these various groups, I did not see how I could directly relate them to one another and to Indian culture as a whole. Perhaps one deeply learned in the history of Indian civilization and familiar with its regional and local varieties could have brought off such an integration, but to a neophyte the task appeared overwhelming. The regional variations alone were sufficient to give me pause. Indians in the north and south did not speak the same language or identify with the same tradition.

Beset by such difficulties, I decided to abandon the plan for an all-India unit of field study and to reformulate a plan that would limit the study to one region. Because I had met in Madras a very knowledgeable Sanskritist sympathetic with the study, and because Madras itself seemed to be a rich center of cultural activities. I selected the Madras area for an exploratory study. This selection, however, still left open a number of other alternatives. Should I set the bounds of the study by the boundaries of the linguistic region, that is, all of the Tamil-speaking country; should I concentrate on a village or a city, or on one group of specialists, or perhaps on one individual or on one institution, like a temple? Had I been doing an intensive field study over a longer period of time, I should probably have chosen the smallest manageable unit and concentrated on it alone. Since I was interested in charting the topography of Indian culture, its general terrain, and its different mountains, valleys, and river sources, such a procedure would have given me too narrow a perspective. For my purpose, it seemed better to begin with a rich and complex cluster of Indian culture so that I could find representatives of the major kinds of cultural institutions, cultural specialists, and cultural media. Such a cluster was offered to me by the cultural activities and institutions of the city of Madras and the adjoining towns of Conjeeveram, Mahābalipuram, and Chingleput, as well as about six villages on the immediate outskirts of

Madras. It is difficult to characterize such a cluster with any degree of precision, and perhaps it would be futile to try for great precision. It might be characterized geographically in terms of the land area covered and in terms of the different kinds of settlement units included within it. But since my criteria of selection were not geographical, this characterization would be misleading. The cluster could also be described in terms of political-administrative and cultural categories. Madras is the capital of the state, Chingleput is a district seat, Conjeeveram is an ancient temple and pilgrimage city. These characterizations, although quite apposite, were not the basis of selection. Perhaps the characterization that comes closest to describing my actual unit of field study is that which describes it in social terms as a community of people. For it was primarily the subcaste of Smārta Brahmans in the Madras area whose culture I found myself studying most persistently and intimately. It was their rites and ceremonies, their households, temples, and *maṭha,* their Sanskrit and *Āyurvedic* colleges, their storytellers, devotees, patrons, scholars, and spiritual leaders that I got to know best.

But even this description of the unit is inaccurate. For I did not set out to study a community of Smārta Brahmans, and because of the dispersed character of this community, I doubt that it would be possible to do a community study on them. Through a series of coincidences, I simply found that members of the Smārta Brahman community were also leading representatives of the Great Tradition of Sanskritic Hinduism. While most of these representatives have face-to-face interpersonal relations, the relationships among these representatives alone would be a very fragmentary segment of the social relations to be found in the community as a whole.

On the other hand, I was not prevented by a concentration on the Smārta Brahmans from studying other subcastes of Brahmans, like the Śrīvaiṣṇavas, or non-Brahmans, like the followers of Tamil Śaivism. Sometimes I was led to take notice of these "out groups" by the Smārtas themselves, e.g., of the non-Brahman performers of classical *bharatanāṭya* dancing and Carnatic music, because the Brahmans are patrons and connoisseurs of these arts; sometimes I came upon these other groups quite independently—as in the case of village folk plays, still performed by lower castes in the villages and in the cities.

## Defining the Units of Observation: Cultural Performances

When I got my program of observations and interviews in the Madras area under way, I discovered what I suppose every field worker knows, that the units of cogitation are not units of observation. There was nothing that could be easily labeled Little Tradition or Great Tradition, or "ethos" or "world view." Instead, I found myself confronted with a series of concrete experiences, the observation and recording of which seemed to discourage the mind from entertaining and applying the synthetic and interpretative concepts that I had brought with me. These experiences had an intrinsic fascination, which also tended to discourage the broad, reflective view to which I had been accustomed. As I grew more familiar with my environment, however, I gradually saw emerging the relation of the woods to the trees. There *were* units of observation; they were quite distinct from the interpretative categories, but I came to see by what mental operations one might pass from the one to the other.

I was helped to identify the units of observation not by deliberately looking for them but by noticing the centrality and recurrence of certain types of things I had observed in the experience of Indians themselves. I shall call these things "cultural performances," because they include what we in the West usually call by that name—for example, plays, concerts, and lectures. But they include also prayers, ritual readings and recitations, rites and ceremonies, festivals, and all those things we usually classify under religion and ritual rather than with the cultural and artistic. In the Madras area—and India generally, I suspect—the distinction cannot be a sharp one because the plays are more often than not based on the sacred Epics and Purāṇas, and the concerts and dances are filled with devotional songs. The religious rituals, on the other hand, may involve the use of musical instruments, songs, and dance *mudrās* similar to those used in the concerts by cultural "artists." One of the leading Madras newspapers daily lists forthcoming cultural events under three headings: "Discourses," for religious readings and discourses on the sacred books; "Entertainments," for performances of plays, dances, and concerts—mostly classical; and "Miscellaneous," for meetings of political and professional groups, public lectures on current topics, and receptions.

As I observed the range of cultural performances (and was allowed, sometimes asked, to photograph and record them) it seemed to me that my Indian friends—and perhaps all peoples—thought of their culture as encapsulated in these discrete performances, which they could exhibit to visitors and to themselves. The performances became for me the elementary constituents of the culture and the ultimate units of observation. Each one had a definitely limited time span, or at least a beginning and an end, an organized program of activity, a set of performers, an audience, and a place and occasion of performance. Whether it was a wedding, an *upanayana* (sacred thread) ceremony, a floating temple festival, a village *Poṅgal* festival, a ritual recitation of a sacred text, a *bharatanāṭya* dance, or a devotional movie, these were the kinds of things that an outsider could observe and comprehend within a single direct experience. I do not mean that I could, even with the help of interpreters, always understand everything that went on at one of these performances or appreciate their functions in the total life of the community. And sometimes even the "limited" time span was not limited enough: I was not accustomed to sitting through a four-hour movie, a play or devotional gathering that lasted all night, or a reading that took fifteen days. But it consoled me to observe that the local audiences did not sit through these stretches of time either; they would doze, talk, walk around, go home and come back, and find other resources for diverting their attention. Yet, despite such qualifications, whenever I looked for the ultimate units of direct observation, it was to these cultural performances that I turned.

## Analysis of Cultural Performances

Once the units of observation had been identified, my interest in the conceptual ordering and interpretation of the observed revived. How were the cultural performances interrelated so as to constitute "a culture"? And were there among them persistent patterns and structures of organization, perhaps diverse patterns of cultural tradition, which were related as Little Tradition and Great Tradition? Two types of ordered patterns suggested themselves almost at once as being particularly obvious and natural. One grouping included the cultural performances that marked and celebrated the successive stages of the individual life cycle from birth to death (the *rites de passage*), and the other marked nature's cycle of seasons, phases of the moon, and the like. I was somewhat surprised to find, however, that neither grouping had any special prominence in the minds of my friends and acquaintances. In fact, I do not recall a single instance when anyone identified a particular cultural performance as belonging to one or the other of these two groups. In formal discussions of the *āśrama* system and in discussions of a Brahman's duties, the individual life cycle is used as an ordering principle. But this usage is highly abstract and conventionalized and rarely takes account of the prevailing local rites and customs. When I found that the ordering of cultural performances by these distinct principles was not in the forefront of consciousness of the participants and did not in any case include all of the cultural performances I had observed, I ceased to regard these principles as compellingly "natural." It occurred to me then that the cultural performances may be susceptible to a number of different types of patterning, varying in explicitness and degree of significance for cultural analysis. I therefore re-examined my materials to see what some of these alternative patterns might be.

### *The Cultural Stage*

One type of analysis might study the place where the cultural performance occurs. The home, for example, is the center for a fixed cycle of rites, ceremonies, and festivals (including both the life-cycle and nature-cycle rites), and the temple is a center for another set of daily rites and periodic festivals. This division is consciously recognized, and there are two quite distinct sets of ritual functionaries, domestic and temple priests, who may conduct the rites in the two places. Temples and pilgrimage places are also specialized with respect to the type of deity to whom they are dedicated and the kind of motive for which they are visited: to have a specific request granted; to fulfil a vow; to expiate for sins; to gain spiritual edification, for example. Beyond the home and the temple is the *maṭha,* not so much a center for cultural performances as a seat of the highest spiritual authority of the sect, the *jagadguru,* who approves the annual religious calendar and whose blessings and advice are much sought after. The more secular performances of popular culture are put on in public halls before mixed audiences and are usually sponsored by cultural associations or *sabhās,* when they are not completely commercialized. In the villages, they may still be performed in the houses of well-to-do patrons or in the temple hall, but there, too, the institution of the community center is introducing a new kind of stage, less closely tied to individual, caste, and sect.

In all of these institutions, much goes on that is culturally significant but may not be part of an organized cultural performance. This is particularly true of the informal and casual cultural "training" that children receive from their parents. But this function, too, is probably being increasingly professionalized and institutionalized in training centers—schools, Sanskrit academies, dancing schools.

An analysis of cultural performances in terms of their institutional settings would be relatively comprehensive both as to the range of performances and the range of performers and institutions to be found in South India. It cannot deal, however, with those types of performance that have no fixed or recurrent institutional base—e.g., a folk play (*terukkūttu*), which is given in a village field or city lot, or a group of devotees who sing devotional songs along a street or country road. It also fails to include certain types of cultural specialists whose primary function is not to participate in or conduct cultural performances but to give advice about proper times (astrologers) or to supply the necessary props (imagemakers). Thus, a construction of the cultural pattern that starts from institutional settings would have to be completed with constructions that include noninstitutionalized performances and "nonperforming" cultural specialists.

### *Cultural Specialists*

One wants to know more about a cultural specialist than can be learned from watching him perform: his recruitment, training, remuneration, motivation, attitude toward his career, his relation to his audience, patron, other performers, and his community—all matters that can best be discovered by interviewing the specialist himself. While all of these things cannot be directly observed in the field, some aspects of them can be observed in favorable circumstances, for example, the training process or the performer's relation to an audience. In the main, however, the analysis of culture in terms of the careers and social roles of the professional cultural specialists is, like the institutional analysis, a construct for analyzing observable cultural performances. Redfield has suggested that such a construct is a specialization and extension of the social anthropologist's constructs of "social structure" and "social organization" to a community of cultural specialists; he therefore has called it the "social organization and the social structure of tradition." [5]

The Madras area provided representatives of five types of specialists that I had on my original list as well as a considerable number of others that I had not previously known about. The only type I did not get to hear or meet were the local bards and caste genealogists, although I was told that there were some in the area. Most of the specialists I interviewed were affiliated with special cultural institutions—temple priests with the temples, domestic priests or *purohitas* with household ceremonies, Sanskrit pandits with Sanskrit schools and colleges, a Sanskrit research scholar with the university, and a whole group of reciters, storytellers, singers, dancers, dramatic performers, and instrumental musicians with the cultural associations or *sabhās*. The press, the radio, and the movies have also developed new types of cultural specialists in the form of editors, program directors, story writers, and producers, and I interviewed several. As far as possible I tried to observe the performances of these specialists in their respective institutional settings as well as to interview them outside of these settings. There was also a group of cultural specialists, as I have already mentioned, without any fixed institutional affiliations, who nevertheless still play an active role in transmitting traditional culture. Among them were a specialist in Vedic *mantras,* an astrologer, a maker of metal images for temple and domestic shrines, leaders of devotional meetings, and an *Āyurvedic* doctor.

Whether associated with an institution or not, the cultural specialist rarely stands alone. Supporting him are usually other specialists and assistants, a teacher or guru, a patron, an organizer of performances, an institutional trustee, a public critic of the specialty. Occasionally I was lucky enough to interview the several representatives of such a functionally linked series, e.g., a dancer and her patron, a dance teacher, student dancers, the organizer of a dance school, and a publicist and critic of the classical dance. The patron, organizer, and critic are usually not themselves specialists, although they may know a good deal about a particular specialty and play an important role in setting standards of public taste and criticism. In this respect, they function as cultural policy-makers. I also found cultural policy-makers who assumed responsibility not merely for formulating the aspirations and standards governing a particular cultural specialty but for an entire cultural tradition. The head of a *maṭha* in the region, a svāmī and *sannyāsin,* highly respected and influential, showed much concern about the future of orthodox Hinduism in the area and throughout India. Another svāmī, without any institutional affiliation, was through public lectures urging a policy of democratizing the Vedas. Such matters, too, were the concern of some people who held political office and who were in a position to affect public opinion and legislative policy.

### *The Social Organization of Tradition in the Village*

In the villages, too, one can find cultural policy-makers, especially among individuals associated with the introduction of village development plans and extension services. The heads of the village development committees and youth leagues, the social recreation officers, the village-level worker, although primarily concerned with agricultural improvements, sanitation, and similar matters, are also affecting cultural aspirations and policies. The building of new village schools, community and recreation centers with their libraries, radios, and community stages, are creating in the village single centers of cultural life that formerly revolved around its several temples.

The villages lack the variety of cultural specialists to be found in the cities and towns. In the villages I visited, a temple priest, a domestic priest, and a schoolteacher seemed to be the usual minimum. Several villages had more specialists, but the social organization of tradition in the village still differed from that of the city because it involved less specialization, less full-time and professional activity, and depended more on traveling specialists from other villages and nearby towns. In one village, the temple priest is also something of a pandit, a ritual reciter of sacred texts, a singer of devotional songs, and an astrologer—functions that tend to be carried out by different people in the city. In this same village, a resident dramatics teacher trains the village boys to perform in purāṇic plays, but he is also a drummer and the village potter. There are no professional dancers, actors, doctors, or image-makers in this village, although residents know about these specialists from having seen them in neighboring villages and towns or occasionally when they pass through the village. Specialists representative of the newer mass media—the newspaper, radio, and film—are of course not to be found in the villages.

I heard about villages in South India that until recently were the homes of famous musicians, dance teachers, poets, and pandits and were active cultural centers. This situation is no longer common, however, since it depended on grants of village lands or on grants of temple privileges to families of specialists. Except for the occasional village that is the seat of a famous shrine, the village looks to the city and to the planning committee for its cultural specialists. Even the most traditional cultural specialists told me how their itineraries have shifted from the villages to the towns in the last twenty years because the most educated and "cultured" villagers have moved to the cities and towns.

Despite the declining position of the village as a center for cultural specialists, for several reasons, one nevertheless still finds a strong sense of cultural continuity between village and town. Until recently, many villages were active centers of traditional culture; even today, some of the basic cultural institutions and specialists are the same in both village and town. Moreover, in the Indian countryside, there is what Oscar Lewis[6] has called a "rural cosmopolitanism" built up in part by the network of caste and kin ties and in part by the traveling cultural specialists. Finally, in the cities and towns there is a cosmopolitan folk culture, sometimes little modified from its village counterpart and sometimes assimilated to the mass culture of the urban center. Perhaps the most striking aspect of the continuity in culture between village and city is the common stock of mythological and legendary themes shared by both villager and city man. The same stories from the *Rāmāyaṇa,* the *Bhāgavatapurāṇa,* and the *Mahābhārata* are recited, sung, and played in both village and city. Even among a colony of untouchables who were otherwise culturally impoverished I found a teacher who knew these plays teaching boys to act them out. It is because they perform and know the same stories that we can say that villager and urbanite belong to the same culture and civilization. Or, to put it more cautiously and more operationally, a contextual analysis of epic and purāṇic stories would probably disclose an underlying continuity of mental outlook and ethos between the villager and the urbanite.

## Cultural Media

To describe the cultural continuity between village and town in terms of a common stock of epic and purāṇic stories is to shift attention from the cultural specialists and their social organization to certain elements of cultural content. Before I went to India, I knew these stories as occurring in printed books called the *Rāmāyaṇa,* the *Mahābhārata* and the *Bhāgavatapurāṇa,* parts of which I had read in translation. This knowledge gave me a welcome sense of recognition when I heard some of the stories, but it did not prepare me for the rich variety of ways in which they are told and retold. Seldom did I come across an Indian who had read these stories as I did, simply in a book. This is not how they learn them and it is not how they think of them. There is a sense of intimate familiarity with the characters and incidents in the references made to Hariścandra, Rāma and Sītā, Krishna, Arjuna, and Prahlāda, as if the world of the stories were also the everyday world. Many children are told these stories from an early age by parents and grandparents, but this is by no means the only way in which they learn them. The very tissue of the culture is made from purāṇic themes. Practically every cultural performance includes one—in song, dance, play, recitation, and exposition. Characters and scenes are ever present on the colored lithographs used in homes and public halls (as well as in the brilliantly colored figures on temple towers, for example, on the modern Śrī Kapālīśvara temple in Mylapore, Madras). The cultural and physical landscapes are literally and imaginatively painted with them.

As I grew familiar with the different ways in which the stories were communicated in the Madras area, I realized that the modes of communication—the "cultural media"—were themselves worthy of study, for it was these forms and not printed books that carried the content of belief and practice expressing the living outlook of a majority of the population. Such media, too, are "cultural" in two other senses: In their differentiation of forms as song, dance, and drama, they constitute what is popularly considered "culture"; and these formal differentiations are in turn well articulated with other aspects of the culture and society. Cultural specialists, for example, are distinguished according to their mastery of the different media—in singing, dancing, acting, knowledge of Sanskrit, technique of dramatic recitation, and the like. Even when a performer is a hereditary specialist, his status is not taken for granted but is judged in terms of his proficiency in the medium.

Spoken language is the pre-eminent cultural medium; it is a constituent of culture, symbolizes elements of belief and practice, and, as an activity, articulates with other aspects of sociocultural organization. Nonlinguistic media, however, also played an important role in the cultural performances I observed. Song, dance, acting out, and graphic and plastic art combine in many ways to express and communicate the content of Indian culture.[7] A study of the different forms of cultural media in their social and cultural contexts would, I believe, reveal them to be important links in that cultural continuum which includes village and town, Brahman and non-Brahman, north and south, the modern mass-media culture and the traditional folk and classic cultures, the Little and the Great Traditions.

From my limited observation, I cite one example to illustrate the possibilities for such inquiry. The *Rāmāyaṇa* is probably one of the most popular sacred texts in the area and is communicated through a variety of cultural media. One—called *Rāmāyaṇa pārāyaṇa*—is a daily ritual reading of a canto of the Vālmīki Sanskrit text. It is done in the household by the Brahman householder or by a special Brahman reader, and at the temple by a Brahman reciter. The reading is continued until the entire text is completed, and then a new cycle of readings with the same or another text is begun. I have called it a "ritual reading" because it is a prescribed religious duty for all Brahmans; it is done before a sacred shrine by a Brahman, and the correct repetition of the holy words in Sanskrit is as important as understanding their meaning. In these respects, it resembles recitations and chanting of Vedic *mantras* and may be considered a part of the sacred culture. Another form of reading is expository. Its chief purpose is to explain the story in the regional language, Tamil, and to draw moral lessons. Depending on the erudition of the *paurāṇika* and of his audience, the text is Sanskrit or a Tamil version composed by a Tamil poet, Kamban, about 700 years ago. Expository recitations are usually given in public halls, although they may also be given in private homes and in temples. Brahmans most frequently are the expounders, but non-Brahmans do it also. A third form, *Harikathā-kālakṣepam,* resembles the second in using expository narration in Tamil as the chief medium but differs from it in adding relevant songs from Sanskrit, Telugu, Kannada, Hindi, Marathi, and Tamil with musical accompaniment. The performer in the latter case must be something of a singer, a linguist, and an "artist," as well as a dramatic storyteller. This art form is relatively recent in the Tamil country, having been developed about 250 years ago from Mahārāṣṭrian models. It is practiced by non-Brahmans as well as by Brahmans, and one of the outstanding artists is a woman. Then there is the variety of dance and dramatic forms, traditional and modern, through which themes from the *Rāmāyaṇa* are presented. Folk as well as classical forms are used, and both have been adapted to such mass media as the film.

A detailed analysis of cultural media would cast much light on the ways in which cultural themes and values are communicated as well as on processes of social and cultural change. The ritual reading in the sacred setting seems to be the oldest form and differs from the others in types of institutional setting, specialists, values expected, and amount of Sanskrit used. Yet it is possible to see strong links of continuity between this form and the less ritualized forms of popular culture. Even the most recent of the mass media, the movies, draws heavily upon the older cultural media and on the common stock of traditional devotional and mythological stories.

## From Field Study to the Study of a Total Civilization

Some anthropologists advised me before I went to India not to spend much time preparing myself by studying the history of Indian civilization or reading the Indian epics and other texts. A field study, they said, has a strict obligation to record only those realities which the field worker himself can observe within a limited area and what is within the living memory of the people he interviews. Historical and literary research would only clutter the mind with preconceptions and should be done, if at all, after the field work is finished. Although I did not take this advice, the course of the study would seem to justify it: I was compelled to limit my attention to a particular group of people within one region restricted enough to be brought under a single conspectus of interrelations; I had to set aside generic conceptual categories about total civilizations in favor of concrete units of observation like cultural performances; and even the analysis of cultural performances runs in terms of constituent factors such as cultural institutions, cultural specialists, and cultural media, which in part, at least, are amenable to the direct observation and interview of the field worker.

Yet the necessity of concrete research does not quite end the story. The purpose of the study was to test some general concepts and hypotheses about Indian civilization as a whole—particularly about the cultural continuity of its Great and Little Traditions across the barriers of village and town, caste and caste, region and region, past and present. How can the results of a limited field study be relevant to hypotheses so general in scope? How can the "cultural pattern of Indian civilization" be found in a regionally delimited cultural cluster with a very shallow historical depth? Must we then abandon the civilizational frame of reference or reconsider how a limited and functional field study is relevant to the study of a whole civilization in its full regional and temporal scope?

Methodologically, there are two different ways to relate a limited field study to a total civilization. One way is to consider the unit of field study—whether it be a village or a cluster of villages and towns—as an isolate that contains within it the culture pattern. Once the pattern is delineated for one field unit, it may be compared with the pattern found in similar units in other regions until enough cases are studied to give good measures of central tendency and of the range of variation in patterns. To give historical depth to such patterns, it would of course be necessary to supplement the field studies with historical and archaeological studies of similar isolates in the past. This procedure results in a view of the cultural pattern of a civilization as a kind of statistical aggregate of the patterns of all the cultural molecules, past and present, that have been isolated for study.

If, however, a civilization is, as Redfield writes, "a great whole in space and in time by virtue of the complexity of organization which maintains and cultivates its traditions and communicates them from the great tradition to the many and very small local societies within it," [8] then it is doubtful whether the procedure will reveal the required complexity of organization. Within a delimited unit of field study, such as I started with, it was possible to find a variety of cultural institutions, specialists, and media that link Brahman and non-Brahman, villager and townsman, one sect and another, to a common cultural tradition. But if a unit is to disclose the cultural links with the past and with other regions, it cannot be regarded as an isolate but must be considered rather as one convenient point of entry to the total civilization, as one nodule in the organized network of cultural communication to which Redfield refers. Different field studies may of course choose different points of entry—in terms of size, character, and location—but the interest in comparing their results will be not to count them as instances for statistical generalization but rather to trace the actual lines of communication with one another and with the past. The general description of this organization in its most embracing spatial and temporal reach will then be a description of the cultural pattern of the total civilization.

In closing this preliminary report, I should like to mention several lines of cultural communication that lead out from my chosen unit of field study into other regions and other times. The pilgrimage to the Ganges and to other sacred spots is undertaken by many ordinary people, but one also hears of many *sannyāsins* who have been to the Himalayas or who are planning to retire there. Thus does the sacred geography of the land extend cultural consciousness beyond one region. One *harikathā* artist I interviewed told me that she has performed all over India, as well as in Burma and Ceylon. Outside of the Tamil-speaking areas, her audiences rarely understood her Tamil narration but never failed to respond to her songs and pantomime because they were familiar with the purāṇic and epic stories she recited.

The links to the past are plentiful in a culture based until recently on the transmission of oral and written texts within families of hereditary specialists. An image-maker I interviewed still knew a separate Vedic *mantra* to help him draw each image and occasionally consulted on difficult points ancient manuals (*Śilpaśāstras*) that had been handed down to him on palm leaf manuscripts. Specialists on different types of *śāstras* as well as on the Purāṇas are still regularly consulted to settle difficult cases, and Vedic prayers and chanting still accompany many rites and ceremonies. To follow up these various strands would require competence in the different regional languages, in Sanskrit, in Indian cultural history, and other subjects, and more time than is usually given to a single field study. It is obviously a task that requires cultural historians, linguists, and Sanskritists, as well as field anthropologists.

Occasionally one finds, especially among the cultural leaders and scholars of Tamiḻnāḍu, persons whose outlook seeks to comprehend the total pattern of Indian civilization and to define its Great Tradition. A Sanskrit scholar, a Smārta Brahman, sees Sanskritic and Vedic Hinduism as the Great Tradition that has in the course of history incorporated many elements of folk and regional cultures not included in the Vedic one. He sees the formative process as a constructive Sanskritization that has conserved existing practices and customs, has reduced a bewildering mass to some cultural homogeneity, and has resulted in a refinement and "civilization" of lower practices. A Vaiṣṇavite Brahman pandit, on the other hand, spoke of two lines of tradition that he had inherited: one "familial and spiritual"—the Vedic—and the other "spiritual only"—Vaiṣṇavism. The latter has its scriptures, rituals, temples, *maṭhas,* saints, and functionaries that overlay a Vedic foundation and that he shared with non-Brahman Vaiṣṇavites. A non-Brahman Śaivite scholar made the cleavage between the Vedic and Tamil traditions sharper still. Respectful to the former, he identified with a Śaivism whose medium was Tamil and whose institutions, practices, and beliefs were, as he described them, largely non-Brahman and non-Sanskritic. And then there are individuals who speak only of a great Tamil and Dravidian tradition and who actively reject the Vedic and Sanskritic tradition as cunning impositions of a northern, Aryan, Brahman "fifth column." Representatives of this group, pursuing a program of de-Sanskritization, have rewritten the *Rāmāyaṇa* as a drama in which Rāvaṇa is the southern hero, and Rāma the northern villain.

All of these views represent in one sense "autodefinitions" of the Great Tradition, since they all begin from some special vantage point—usually inherited—of occupation, caste, sect, and region. But they can also serve, especially the more scholarly and informed among them, as valuable guides in the effort to add regional scope and historical depth to a limited field study.

## Notes

1. Robert Redfield, "The Social Organization of Tradition," *FEQ* 15, No. 1 (November, 1955): 13–21.
2. Robert Redfield and Milton Singer, "The Cultural Role of Cities," *EDCC* 3, No. 1 (October, 1954): esp. 64–73.
3. Srinivas, *Coorgs* (see note 15 to Chapter 2, above).
4. McKim Marriott, "Little Communities in an Indigenous Civilization," in Marriott, ed., *VI* (see note 6, Introduction to Part One).
5. Redfield, "Social Organization of Tradition."
6. Oscar Lewis, "Peasant Culture in India and Mexico: A Comparative Analysis," in *VI*.
7. An ancient manual on the classical dance beautifully expresses this organic interrelationship of different media: "The song should be sustained in the throat; its meaning must be shown by the hands; the mood (*bhāva*) must be shown by the glances; time (*tāla*) is marked by the feet. For wherever the hand moves, there the glances follow; where the glances go, the mind follows; where the mind goes, the mood follows; where the mood goes, there is the flavour (*rasa*)." *The Mirror of Gesture: Being the Abhinaya Darpana of Nandikesvara,* trans. by Ananda K. Coomaraswamy and Duggirala Gopalakrishnayya (New York: E. Weyhe, 1936). p. 35.
8. Redfield, "Social Organization of Tradition."

# 4 / *The Social Organization of Sanskritic Hinduism in Madras City*

## Introduction

On the first trip to India, I decided to map the "cultural topography" of Sanskritic Hinduism in Madras City—its cultural structure, social organization, and trends of change. Madras was the choice because on a preliminary visit to the city we found a rich cultural life still going on there with a convenient daily directory of events published in a local newspaper, *The Hindu,* under the heading, "Today's Engagements." Moreover I met there in Dr. V. Raghavan, Professor of Sanskrit, a guide whose profound knowledge of Sanskrit culture and Hinduism and quick and sympathetic understanding of my study made him an ideal learned informant. After the background and purpose of the study were explained to Dr. Raghavan, the problem of choosing a unit for field observation resolved itself. After consulting the daily announcements in "Today's Engagements" and weighing his suggestions, we selected each day for visiting several performances, people, and institutions that he regarded as representative of Sanskritic Hinduism. When he was free, he often accompanied me. At other times, he sent introductions and another "guide." Each day's trip was an adventure of discovery of some new aspect of a Great Tradition. Frequently I met people and learned about events, which I followed up on my own. When I had a chance to read over my notes after these trips, I usually asked Dr. Raghavan to explain items not clear to me at the time. Through this general procedure, it was possible to observe and learn about the rites, functionaries, and institutions that my learned informant considered essential to Sanskritic Hinduism, as well as many local regional rituals and institutions. Much of the action was centered in Madras City and particularly in the section of Mylapore, with its imposing Śiva temple, public hall, and concentration of Brahmans. Some of it, however, was dispersed in other neighborhoods of Madras City, villages outside the city, and several towns and shrine centers nearby. It soon became obvious to me that a Great Tradition cannot be delimited geographically by the boundaries of a small residential community but has a topography that follows the distribution of its sacred places and the movements of its specialists along the cultural and social networks that bind together the specialists and their clients.

As the evidence accumulated, it also became clear that the structure of Sanskritic Hinduism was not so simple as I had thought. All major components of a Great Tradition were indeed present, but there were several variant versions—Smārta Brahman, Śrīvaiṣṇava Brahman, Madhva, and Śaivasiddhānta non-Brahman. Dr. Raghavan, I learned, was a Smārta Brahman, a follower of Advaitavedānta, and an adherent of the Śaṅkara *maṭha* and its Śaṅkarācārya at Conjeeveram. The discovery of these sectarian or denominational differentiations within the structure of Sanskritic Hinduism created something of a crisis for my method, since I had assumed that there would be a single more or less uniform structure, at least for orthodox Hindus, and that Dr. Raghavan represented a more or less orthodox position. This methodological crisis was resolved by dropping assumptions about a uniform structure and regarding Dr. Raghavan's selections and interpretations as one learned informant's self-definition of Sanskritic Hinduism in terms of *his maṭha,* temple, domestic and temple priest, astrologer, and so forth. My task as an anthropologist then appeared to be not to say which denominational version was *the* orthodox or correct version of Sanskritic Hinduism but simply to describe the related forms, compare their similarities and differences, and try to see by what transformations one denominational structure was related to the others.

This solution to the methodological problem now seems somewhat similar to Levi-Strauss's approach to the structural study of myth and other cultural forms. At the time, however, Levi-Strauss had not fully published his theories. I found encouragement for the structural approach in D'Arcy Thompson's morphological studies of biological forms, and I borrowed his apt phrase, "the comparison of related forms." [1]

Dr. Raghavan's version of the Great Tradition—that of a Smārta Brahman and a follower of Śaṅkara and Advaitavedānta—represented only one of several interpretations, but it was nevertheless a broad and inclusive one that consolidated many elements from local and regional traditions. Although I stopped looking for *the* Great Tradition and gave up the effort to select *the* orthodox version of Sanskritic Hinduism, I continued to find the comprehensiveness and catholicity of Dr. Raghavan's position highly productive of anthropological insight. Dr. Raghavan became more than a learned informant whose personal religious beliefs, practices, and affiliations provided data for an objective interpretation of Hinduism. He became also a friend, a fellow inquirer, and a colleague with whom I could discuss and plan ongoing research. Several of the papers Dr. Raghavan wrote at this time, e.g., "Variety and Integration in the Pattern of Indian Culture" and "Methods of Popular Religious Instruction in South India," still seem to me important contributions to our understanding of the dynamic and intimate relationships between Sanskritic and popular Hinduism.[2] We have continued our friendship and intellectual association, and I continue to learn from Dr. Raghavan's many publications. On a recent visit to the United States and Europe, he drafted the following statement on Hinduism, which expresses not only the synthesis of an Advaita view of the Great Tradition but also its contemporary relevance:

> Five thousand years old, Hinduism, the most ancient among the living religions of the world, is also most modern, putting forth new forms, new interpretations and new expressions. In a religious activity or in a person today, you see not only the most ancient Vedic hymns recited, the most ancient sacraments like Initiation (*upanayana*) gone through but also the adoration of most recent saints and their devotional hymns and songs. It is this vitality that imparts to Hinduism the character of *Sanātanadharma,* perennial *religion* or *philosophy*.
>
> Hinduism combines also the most abstract and individual philosophy of the highest intellectual principle with the most simple and popular forms in which social and congregational participation expresses itself in a variety of ways. Along with the belief in the one ultimate Reality, the basis of the whole universe, enunciated in the Upaniṣads and expounded by India's greatest philosopher, Śaṅkarācārya, whose successors continue to function as active religious heads today, it has also the worship of manifold forms of divinity—incarnations of God in diverse names, forms, and ethos, such as Śiva, Viṣṇu, and Rāma and Krishna, and the Goddess Devī, each of which has its own esoteric, religious, and philosophical significance. According to one's stage of evolution and background, one can choose one's deity and continue the worship until, rising rung by rung, one reaches the highest where all forms dissolve into the one formless. Because of this free choice of approach, Hinduism has developed a philosophy of coexistence with other religions and has always been tolerant and hospitable to other faiths like Islam or Christianity. From the worship of the sacred pipal tree and Tulasī plant, and the worship of the nine planets, everything has its place, time, meaning, and eventual fruitfulness; nothing is lost. Not only do gods who are dead in ancient Greek or other civilizations live in Hinduism but also, because of this inner principle informing them as forms in a gradually ascending ladder, what would otherwise be animism or superstition forms an integral part of a continuous upward effort.
>
> As in object of worship, so in way of worship. If you are intellectual, sit and meditate on the truth in solitude; if you are emotional and given to attachment, worship the different gods, go to temples, pray, sing, and love; if you are given to activity, observe the ordained duties, sacrifice, sacraments, rites, rituals, pilgrimages, baths, and so on; or do the acts prompted by your ethical and moral impulses. The various religious activities are for purification and sublimation of man's faculties and nature. Acts help devotion, and the two are sustained by spiritual knowledge, whose complete realization they bring about in course of time. Thus, one is still a Hindu, even if one is not on one of these paths or is at the same time or various times on all these paths—which is a despair to others who swear by one book, one prophet, and one path and follow a religious foreign policy of "Come into our fold or be damned for ever."
>
> The middle path of devotion, or *bhakti,* and its manifold theistic forms constitute the most widespread and patent forms of Hinduism and also its attractive aspects. They are at the same time the basis and inspiration of the religious institutions of holy places and waters, of pilgrimages and baths, of temples and festivals, and of sculpture, painting, literature, and the arts of music, dance, and drama.
>
> All art, indeed all activity, is oriented to the religious goal, but the most efficacious discipline for the purification of the faculties and sublimation—indeed for keeping body fit, mind alert, and in poise—is Yoga.

For a full view of all these, there is nothing like a visit to the great country of India, the mother of Hinduism, Buddhism, and Jainism, which also affords a hospitable home to Zoroastrianism, Christianity, and Islam.[3]

## A First Approximation to Structure

The structure and organization of Sanskritic Hinduism in Madras City can be described in terms of its sacred geography, its sacred specialists and literati, and its sacred calendar of rites and ceremonies. The following descriptive summary of the structure and organization is based on a direct field study and is not a description of the normative structure embodied in the scriptural texts, although the texts and their interpretation appear in the field observations.

### *Sacred Centers*

Four kinds of sacred places circumscribe a Hindu's ritual life: his home, his temple, his *maṭha* and the places of pilgrimage, some far away. Of these, the home is the most important; it is the center for daily observances and for all family rites. The temple, usually near the home, probably ranks second in importance, at least as measured by frequency of attendance. For an orthodox Hindu, daily visits to the temple are not unusual. Visits on festival days and on special occasions to ask for boons or to do penance are made by the orthodox Hindu and the less orthodox as well. A pilgrimage to the Ganges and Benares is a devout Hindu's life ambition, and pilgrimages to other sacred rivers and sacred shrines, to Rameswaram and Tiruppati, for example, are made to carry out special penance, to fulfill vows, and to ask for specific favors.

The *maṭha,* although visited not more than once a year by the less faithful and about every two or three months by the devout, occupies a unique position in the structure. It is the seat of the *jagadguru,* the chief guru, the highest spiritual authority of his sect, to whom the worshiper looks for spiritual advice, penance, special blessings, and the defense and propagation of the faith. Formerly, the *jagadguru* exercised the ultimate judgment in religious disputes that could not be settled by caste pañcāyats and other local bodies and had the authority to excommunicate and to prescribe penance; this function has now fallen into disuse.

### *Sacred Specialists*

Different kinds of sacred specialists are associated with each type of sacred center: *purohitas* with the household; *gurukkaḷs* at the temples; special kinds of both at each place of pilgrimage; and authorities in *Dharmaśāstra,* Vedānta, the Epics, and Purāṇas; and *sannyāsin* and their disciples at the *maṭha.* The list includes only the leading specialists, not their assistants, the different classes of temple "servants," and so forth. Between the domestic priest and family priest,* on the one hand, and the

* "Officiant" would be a more neutral designation, but since it has become customary to use "priest" I follow this somewhat misleading usage.

head of the *maṭha,* on the other, an important difference exists: The former are mainly ritual technicians whose competence is judged by simple pragmatic tests, whereas the latter is distinguished for his holiness, his learning, and his wisdom. The domestic priests, however, are regarded with greater respect than the temple priests, because they generally have more Vedic learning. At the same time, the temple priest exercises a more essential function, since he must convey the worshiper's offering and message to the temple image, whereas the domestic priest is regarded as a dispensable assistant to the householder, to be used "in place of a book."

A group of specialists in different degrees of association with a ritual structure play important roles within it. The group includes the Sanskrit pandits learned in the rules and obligation of ritual, who are consulted on cases of pollution and marriage, for example, and the astrologer, who knows not only the ritual calendar but also the auspicious and inauspicious days for undertakings, and can cast horoscopes, and disclose what fate is revealed in the constellations, stars, and planets. Like the weather man, the astrologer can only forecast and warn. To alter events, he may recommend other specialists, such as the *mantrika* or the *Āyurvedic* doctor. The *mantrika* goes beyond diagnosis and prognosis; he has at his disposal specialized *mantras*, *yantras,* and rituals to propitiate the deities and to counteract the work of other *mantrikas.* Although the *Āyurvedic* doctor is willing to prescribe some *mantras* and Sanskrit prayers, especially for mental troubles, his instruments of preference are certain herbs and medicines prescribed in the ancient treatises. In a few cases, the value of such remedies has been verified by modern research.

The knowledge required for the construction of temples, houses, and other places was also traditionally considered a part of the sacred tradition; it extends to makers of images in stone and metal (*sthapati*), architects, and other craftsmen. Some still follow the rules of the *Śilpaśāstras.* Where major temples are being constructed, as in Orissa State at the time of this study, whole communities of them may camp on the grounds.

Humanistic specialists in some of the sciences traditionally considered auxiliary to the study of the Vedas are found in a modern Sanskrit college: pandits who specialize in Sanskrit phonetics, grammar, and poetics, in logic and Vedic exegesis, and in the most sacred science of all for its adherents, Advaita philosophy and theology.

## *Sacred Rites*

Two important differentiations apply to the sacred rites: domestic as against temple rites and Vedic as against purāṇic rites. The first differentiation is according to place of performance and kind of officiant, and the second according to the kind of scriptural sanction. The domestic rites, particularly the daily observances and the rites of passage (*saṃskāras*), are predominantly Vedic and are based on the *Gṛhyasūtras;* the temple rites and ceremonies are predominantly purāṇic and are based on the Āgamas and Purāṇas. Some domestic rites are purāṇic, and some Vedic elements also exist in temple rites. The Vedic rites are considered older than the temple rites; they are performed in presumably more ancient and sacred terms and ritual, addressed to a different set of deities, and restricted to the twice-born castes. The temple rites and festivals are considered post-Vedic, use a different terminology (although in Sanskrit) and a different ritual, are addressed to purāṇic deities and saints, and are participated in by all castes.

The link between temple and domestic rites is purāṇic—the *pūjā,* or special "attentions" and offerings to images of the purāṇic deities. These images are essentially the same in temple and household, except for size and stability. The essential contrast, then, is between the *pūjā* to an image and the imageless Vedic fire sacrifice. The two rites probably represent different cultural traditions that have grown together. In the household the purāṇic tradition overlays the Vedic, and the householder and his *purohita* conduct both types of rites. A *Gaṇapatihoma* even merges elements of a Vedic rite with a purāṇic deity. In the temple, at least in the South, the purāṇic tradition prevails and is maintained by a special class of temple priests.

There are also analogies between the temporal cycles of the domestic and temple rites. Just as domestic rites include a cycle of daily observances from morning to night and another cycle of *saṃskāras* marking the important events of an individual lifespan, so temple rites follow cycles of daily worship and seasonal festivals. The daily *pūjās* offered to the images in the temple bear some resemblance to the individual's daily cycle in the household, and the seasonal festivals set by the phases of the moon and the zodiac mark the important events—birth, marriage, and the like—in the life cycle of the gods and the festivals of the kings.

The preceding summary describes a generic structure abstracted from the particular sacred places, specialists, and rites that constitute the field data, the evidential basis, for inferring the generic structure. Instead of asking the reader to take the existence of such an evidential basis on faith, I shall describe the data from which the structure was inferred in some detail, making use of actual field notes. By retracing the order of discovery of the structure in the field, this procedure will enable the reader to check the author's inferences and will also furnish insight into the existential and functional interrelations among the different structural components of the Great Tradition in the context of daily life.

## The Domestic Sphere

### Jagadguru, *or Teacher of the World*

Within just a few days during our first visit to Madras, about a dozen acquaintances mentioned Svāmī Śaṅkarācārya, head of the *maṭha* near Conjeeveram. A museum director mentioned that the Svāmī had sent a special blessing for one of his exhibits, a businessman told of a treasured gift from the Svāmī, several people spoke of his broad knowledge and influence. Someone displayed a book that carried an eloquent appreciation of the *jagadguru.* None of these references was solicited; they came up naturally in the course of conversation. Dr. Raghavan wired the Svāmī's manager at the *maṭha* to see if an appointment could be arranged with His Holiness the following Sunday. On Saturday night, a messenger from the Svāmī informed Dr. Raghavan that the guru had taken a vow of silence for Sunday but suggested a Monday or Tuesday meeting. We agreed that Dr. Raghavan's fourteen-year-old son, Kalidas, would go with me on Monday, since he had been to Kanchi before, knew the way, and also knew the Svāmī.

I picked up young Kalidas, who carried two packed straw baskets and a camera. On the trip to Kanchi, Kalidas read in my copy of *Murray's Handbook*[4] and told me that he did not particularly want to become a Sanskrit scholar but would rather be a scientist. He was in the fourth form and was taking courses in Tamil, English, Sanskrit, mathematics, physics, chemistry, and biology. (He is now an engineer.) But he was obviously deeply moved at visiting Svāmī Śaṅkarācārya.

Within the low-walled grounds of the *maṭha* were three or four gray stucco buildings, several platforms, a small porch, and a grove of trees. Inside the gate, several young men silently reclined or sat on the near platform. They looked curiously at us but soon returned to their thoughts. Instead of going into one of the buildings, the manager led us by a large shade tree, where he greeted a seated person I had not noticed and whom I then realized must be the Svāmī, although the meeting remained notably casual and unceremonial. After placing a tray of bananas, flowers, and several other objects on the ground before the Svāmī, Kalidas backed away about five feet, prostrated himself on a small straw mat in front of the tree, and then sat up cross-legged on the mat. He had changed from his white cotton *dhotī* into a red and gold silk one. The Svāmī returned my Indian-style greeting by holding his right hand up to his chin, palm toward me, and smiling. He asked through his interpreter whether I was accustomed to sitting on the ground or whether I would prefer a chair near the mat. I chose to sit on the mat directly in front of him.*

The Svāmī had an ochre cloth wrapped loosely around his lower body and legs and draped over one shoulder and his head. He wore a wreath of small green leaves from the sacred Bilwa, with several garlands of flowers around his neck, which had been offered by his devotees. He leaned against the tree trunk in a relaxed way and touched one of his crossed feet in his lap. This guru of all the world, as orthodox South Indians saw him, was slim but not emaciated. His face was youthful, but his white beard testified that he was no longer a young man.

The guru first asked me what countries I had visited before coming to India, what languages I knew, and where I had traveled in India. My answers were not translated but were repeated slowly in English, while the Svāmī's speech was full of English words. During the meeting, he addressed several English sentences to me. He knew some English but preferred not to speak it or thought his knowledge of the language was not good enough for conversation.

We then talked about whether the influence of religion was increasing or decreasing. I told him that church membership and interest in religion had probably increased in the United States since the war, but that no

* See photographs following page 174.

one knew whether the trend would last. He said that formal and organized religion and "congregations" had weakened in India but that personal faith had increased—both in the villages and in the towns—and that pilgrimages were continuing.

As the Svāmī was speaking, a small lizard scurried around behind him. Concerned that it might be poisonous, I called the attention of the interpreter to it. "Oh, that is just a little animal," he said, "poisonous if it bites." The Svāmī glanced at it and went on talking with a smile.

The Svāmī referred to an organization known as the "Black Shirts" as one of the major antireligious forces in South India. It numbered, he said, about 200,000 members and was openly atheistic. One of the leaders lived in Conjeeveram, should I wish to meet him. The movement had originated, the Svāmī thought, in the British "divide and conquer" policy and did not represent the mentality of South Indians.[5]

We talked about the problem of poverty in India and the efforts being made to solve it. The Svāmī said that the land collected by the Bhūdān movement would have to be improved and that much government help would be needed. The community development program was working better, but it also was not enough. The real problem, the Svāmī said, is that, with the rising standard of living, people now want whatever they see, and especially things from other parts of the world. The problem of poverty cannot be solved by private or government methods or by nonviolence, for they cannot reduce the standard of living. In the past, he continued, the hereditary caste system had prescribed a simple life for laborers and Brahmans and had allowed luxuries to the other two classes only as incentives to the development of the "arts." During the last 500 years, however, the domination of India's politics and commerce by foreigners had corrupted all classes of the population and made them want luxuries. If the hereditary caste system were restored, he thought, the poverty problem would be solved. The Brahmans, as he has been trying to show them, should set an example by leading simple and austere lives.

The Svāmī expressed a belief that the caste system was related to the achievement of salvation, *mokṣa,* because all classes can get spiritual salvation only by doing their appointed tasks. The spiritual and the social problem are the same for him, and there is no conflict between them. Hinduism, he added, has sometimes been called a kind of socialism.

The Svāmī definitely does not approve of universal public education. Each group, he contends, should be taught what it needs to know to perform its functions and given some popular religious instruction but no more. Talent could be recognized and given special opportunities, but to do so was compatible with the performance of caste duties. The weaver-poet Kabīr, he said, did not give up weaving when he became a saint. A system that provides the same education for all creates many problems.

Covering his head and speaking more calmly, the Svāmī spoke of the simple life and a simple diet. Pointing to the green foliage, he said that a diet of leaves, fruit, and milk should suffice for men. This healthy diet neither destroyed life nor created many wants. The message he wished us to carry away was that the problem of poverty could be solved only by the spiritual and moral development of the individual; if it is not to be solved in this way, we would do better to leave it alone, for not all problems can be solved practically. He had no objection to community development but remarked that it deals only with temporary problems; it is also necessary to work on the eternal problems.

In another interview several months later, the Svāmī spoke in greater detail about the problems of ritual pollution, Hinduism's weakening "sociological" foundations, and the organization of the *maṭha*. The first interview, however, had conveyed to me his position as a spiritual leader and cultural policy-maker. Though he can and does participate occasionally in large organized public meetings and temple-car processions, and his authority is great, his followers and outsiders consider it a major privilege and boon to meet him quietly under his tree.

### Purohita, *or Domestic Priest, and the Ritual Calendar*

*Family.* N. V. S. Dikshitar is a domestic priest (*purohita*) who helps Dr. Raghavan with rites, ceremonies, and worship. I talked with him at Dr. Raghavan's house. The *purohita* is thirty-eight years old and is now resident in the Mylapore section of Madras City. His native village is in the Chingleput District, and his family has lived there for at least eight generations. The village was granted to them in the times of the Nawabs of the Carnatic region in honor of their devotion to Vedic learning and performance of Vedic sacrifices. The family has also produced scholars in different Sanskrit *śāstras.* The *purohita* remembers that his ancestors performed the Vedic sacrifices of *garuḍacayana, somayāga,* and *agniṣṭoma* both for themselves and for others. Even now, there are Vedic altars in his village near the Śiva temple.[6]

The *purohita*'s father died in 1935. An austere man in his habits, the father was always deep in rounds of Vedic and religious observances, on which he spent most of his property—300 acres of wet land and 200 acres of dry land. Although the father was averse to city life, the first two sons—the *purohita* and his elder brother—had to migrate to Madras in 1936 and 1941, respectively, to augment the family income. Both now officiate in the city as *purohitas.*

*Education.* Until his father's time, the *purohita* told us, the youngsters of the family usually started Vedic recitals immediately after their sacred thread (*upanayanam*) ceremony. Because family circumstances were poor, he and his brother first went to a modern school and studied Tamil, English, mathematics, and other subjects for a few years. After that, they were sent to Tiruppati, the famous hill-shrine near Madras, to complete their entire Veda in the Vedic school. As followers of the *Yajurveda,* they have mastered that one Veda. It took him six years to do so. His elder brother had started his eight-year-old son on Vedic study.

*Clients and patrons.* The senior *purohitas* in Madras are well established and have many clients. Younger ones have a smaller number of clients; the *purohita* has only ten families. Intent on conducting his own austerities, he does not have time for a large number of clients. According to an unwritten convention, a *purohita*'s fees depend on his clients' income. A well-to-do medical doctor pays him 30 rupees per month. Others pay less. He and his brother together maintain a joint family of thirteen members in Madras. They are not given to luxuries and require at least Rs. 250 per month for expenses. They live in a rent-free house that has been made available to them by the doctor; the rest has to be made up from other fees. This does not give the family much room for financial planning, and they will try to take more clients. Dr. Raghavan told me that, because of their integrity, they will not try to increase their income by extracting greater fees from their clients, as some *purohitas* do.

The *purohita* thinks a revival of interest in Hinduism has taken place in the last seven or eight years, and he finds interest and sincerity among his clients. The younger members of his family are being brought up as *purohitas,* although the Dravidian movement has created animosity among non-Brahmans toward Brahmans and especially towards *purohitas* as the critical agents. *Purohitas* have been manhandled and pelted with stones on dark streets. In his own locality, the *purohita* told us, the non-Brahmans have a certain regard for his sincerity. He is a strict vegetarian, does not take coffee, or anything in a hotel, and tries to be active in "public life" by going to readings of the *Rāmāyaṇa,* collecting money for a small *maṭha,* and performing other community functions.

### Saṃskāras *and Calendrical Rites*

*The* purohita's *duties and the ceremonial calendar.* With Dr. Raghavan's active participation, the *purohita* described the essential rites, Vedic and purāṇic, performed by South Indian Brahmans, especially Smārtas. A printed almanac called *Dṛggaṇitapañcāṅga* was frequently consulted to confirm their memories. The almanac is a new type based on the nautical almanac for greater accuracy and is sponsored by the Svāmī Śaṅkarācārya.[7]

*Vedic rites.* The *purohita* performs a group of major Vedic rites for his doctor client. The annual *śrāddha* ceremony is conducted for dead ancestors, and there are monthly libations of water and *sesamum* (*tarpaṇa*). If there are no parents living, the latter rite is performed every new moon. The *upanayana* (sacred thread initiation ceremony for boys), marriage, birth, naming, first feeding, and funeral rites are also included in this group of essential Vedic services. A group of optional and quasi-Vedic rites, performed on birthdays, when special oblations are given for longevity, may consist simply in prostration to the sun. Another group of minor Vedic rites following a marriage are the nuptials, the parting of the hair of a pregnant woman (*sīmantonnayana*), and the rite to induce the birth of a male child (*puṃsavana*). The last two are now done together and are usually announced in the same invitation. The *gāyatrī* verse is repeated at dawn, noon, and sunset and is now confined to Brahmans, except in some regions, such as Kerala, where it is also recited by Kṣatriyas. The daily cleaning of teeth and a purificatory bath are performed upon first rising.[8]

*Purāṇic rites.* During the year, most of the rites performed are purāṇic but also make use of Vedic *mantras.* The *purohita* does not necessarily have a major role, but the householder may ask him to assist. Dr. Raghavan performs his own domestic purāṇic worship (*pūjās*); some of these sacred occasions include temple worship.

The *purohita* does a daily *pūjā* at the medical doctor's house every morning about 8:00 A.M. The doctor's family, if free, watches these *pūjās* in the shrine room where the images of the deities are kept. On Tuesdays and Fridays, the *purohita* conducts special *pūjās* with the whole family in attendance.

Periodically, *pūjās* are held for the different deities. During the January solstice, the sun and cows are worshiped at the festival of *Poṅgal.* The fourteenth day of the dark half of the month of Māgha (February-March) is very sacred for Śiva worship both in the temple and at home. During this *Śivarātrī* day, everyone fasts and goes to the temple. Rāma's birth is honored on the ninth day of the light fortnight of the following month, *Rāmanavamī.* The spring solstice is *Citrāviṣṇu.* No *pūjā* occurs on this occasion, but oblations are offered to ancestors. Smārta Brahmans and Advaitins observe a special day in May in honor of Śaṅkara (*Śaṅkarajayantī*). When the sun turns south in mid-July, *tarpaṇa* is performed for ancestors, usually with the help of a *purohita.* It is called *dakṣiṇāyana.* In August comes a Vedic rite, the *upākarman,* when all the sacred writings including Pāṇini's grammar and the Purāṇas are reviewed, and a new sacred thread is put on. These recitals used to be spread over four months of the rainy season; now they are telescoped into a single day, and only the first lines and titles are recited. *Yajurvedins* and *Ṛgvedins* alone do this review in August; the *Sāmavedins* do it later, usually in September. On the day after the total review, the *gāyatrīmantra* is repeated 1,008 times (*gāyatrījapa*). The same *mantra,* repeated at least once daily by Brahmans, is considered the most efficacious of all Vedic prayers and is conducive to the destruction of the year's accumulated sins. The *purohita* just recites a few formulae, and the family themselves recite the *mantra.*

Following the *gāyatrījapa* is the *saṅkalpa*—a mental resolution to perform or to undertake specific actions.

Each religious act starts with a *saṅkalpa,* a resolve to do a particular sacred act. While this brief *saṅkalpa* figures in all religious acts, the *upākarman* described above is the occasion for a very long "resolve," a *mahāsaṅkalpa,* in which the performer identifies his space-time situation in the cosmic process by reciting according to Hindu Sanskrit texts the geography of the world up to his village or town, the time-cycles of the universe from creation to his performance, and the process of cosmic creation. He then recites all the kinds of sins likely to be committed by man in his manifold weakness in order to cleanse the evil through this act of *upākarman.* The *mahāsaṅkalpa* is repeated bit by bit by the *purohita* and the performers. Its slow and impressive pace sets the tone and spirit of the performance.

At the end of August, Krishna is worshiped late at night (*Kṛṣṇajayantī*). Gaṇeśa is worshiped in August-September on *Vināyakacaturthī.* Lakṣmī, goddess of prosperity, is also worshiped in August.

The dark fortnight of September is sacred to all the ancestors (*Mahālayapakṣa*). Special *tarpaṇas* are offered at that time to all the ancestors and to dead distant relatives, teachers, friends, and to all who had died without male issue. Their names are recited, and water is offered. Ceremonies culminate on the new moon day of the fortnight. The more devout perform the *tarpaṇas* every day, but generally one does it only on one day, the day of the fortnight when one's mother or father died.

Beginning with the new moon day in October—*Daśahrā*—Devī is worshiped for nine days in her triple aspects as Pārvatī or Durgā, Lakṣmī, and Sarasvatī. In the South, the festival is called *Navarātri* (nine nights). The worship culminates with a Sarasvatī *pūjā* on the ninth day. All books and manuscripts in the family are worshiped on that day, while artisans worship their tools and machines. The doctor puts sandal paste on his instruments and operating table.

The tenth day after *Daśahrā* is called the "victorious tenth" (*Vijayadaśamī*). On this day, Devī goes out and destroys the *asuras*. Kings in ancient times worshiped their armies, staged military tournaments, and went out on token expeditions of victory. The day is an auspicious one for starting a child in school, beginning a job, or taking some other initiative. The season is a gay one, with decorations of houses and temples, visitors, and recitations.

*Dīvālī,* which is a major festival of lights in the North, is celebrated in another form in the South. In December, however, another festival of lights, *Kārttikai dīpam,* is celebrated in homes and temples. It is connected with the legend of Śiva burning Tripura. The women take the lead in this festival, and a *purohita* is not called. The great *Kārttikai dīpam* festival in the South is that of the Śiva shrine at Tiruvaṇṇāmalai near Madras.

Between mid-December and mid-January comes a very sacred month (Mārgaśīrṣa). Early morning *pūjās* performed during this period are especially praiseworthy, and the *purohita* has been doing them for the doctor. Morning *bhajana,* public readings, and recitals are also held at this time.

*Vaikuṇṭha Ekādaśī,* which is sacred for Viṣṇu, falls during this same period. It is observed by fasting and prayer at temples and is celebrated in a grand way at the big Śrīraṅgam temple.

Another festival falling in Mārgaśīrṣa is *Ārdrādarśana*. On this day, Śiva is worshiped in homes and temples in his form as Naṭarājan. The festival is especially important at Cidambaram, the site of an important Śiva temple. The *purohita* performs *pūjās* for the doctor in the morning and evening, and the family goes to the temple. A special offering of sweet rice and vegetable soup called *kali* is prepared for Śiva on this day.

Just before the winter solstice, women perform a preliminary ceremony, *Bhogin*. They put on new clothes and have a special feast. The rite marks the end of the inauspicious winter and the beginning of the more auspicious season celebrated by the *Poṅgal* festival.

All the rites and ceremonies mentioned so far are regarded as essential, and usually no one omits them. Other ceremonies vary according to region, family, and other circumstances. The *purohita*'s doctor, for example, is a great believer in Rāma. He reads the *Rāmāyaṇa* frequently, repeating the text every month, and also has the *purohita* read it. Every Tuesday, he has a special *pūjā* for the deity Subrahmaṇya.

Actual observation of domestic rites gives a somewhat different picture of the ritual structure. The *purohita*'s description is not false, but it tends to understate the variation in importance among different rites, the number of different kinds of specialists involved, the trends of change, and the disagreements over ritual policies. For their daily observances, many Smārta Brahmans do not use a *purohita* and perform only a few obligatory rituals—perhaps a morning bath, the recitation of the *gāyatrīmantra,* and a brief reading from one of the Epics or Purāṇas. For special functions, on the other hand, many *purohitas* and other specialists may be called to perform elaborate ceremonies.

The domestic rites include a series called *saṃskāras,* which marks the phases of the individual's life cycle.[9] They are Vedic rites; their number and kind are prescribed in the *Gṛhyasūtras.* The *purohita* did not give a complete list of them, for not all are equally important or regularly observed. The most important today, in terms of family expenditure, number and distinction of guests invited, and number of Brahman priests officiating, are the sacred thread, or *upanayana,* ceremony and the wedding. For these ceremonies, a family will have a special *pandal* or foliage-canopy constructed in front of the house—or at a special hall if the house is not large enough—will make elaborate kitchen preparations, and will invite as many as 1,000 or 1,500 guests for both the ceremony and the reception that usually follows. More than one *purohita* is required at these large affairs, and the family *purohita* is usually accompanied by his relatives and other *purohitas* who assist him in the rites and perform the Vedic chanting. One Smārta wedding we attended had about twenty-five *purohitas,* and, although the regular family *purohita* took the lead in conducting the ceremony, the others helped him several times in the proper procedure. The Brahmans bring with them small bags of cloth or string to carry away the gifts they will receive: a coconut, perhaps some cloth for *dhotīs,* several small coins that must be distributed by the host for the several acts in the final part of the ceremony, and so forth.* Most leave immediately after the formal ceremony and do not stay for the reception and entertainment. They, the repositories of the Vedas, along with the kinsmen and friends of the bride and bridegroom, have witnessed the marriage sacrament.

In the conduct of the ceremonies, the fiction is maintained that the Brahman hosts themselves know both the procedure and the various Vedic and Sanskrit *mantras,* although this is rarely the case. At a wedding, the couple and their fathers are prompted by the *purohita* step by step; they repeat after him the various *mantras* word by word. During the climax of a sacred thread ceremony, when the *gāyatrīmantra* is imparted to the boy under a white cloth, the *purohita* whispers the *mantra* to the boy's father, who then whispers it to his son. The mother is also under the

* See photographs following page 174.

cloth at this time. In one ceremony I attended, the father knew many of the Sanskrit verses, but the *purohita* told him which ones to recite at particular points.*

The center of these Vedic rites is a sacrificial fire into which the *purohitas* continually throw ghee, rice, and different kinds of grain as they recite. Guests sit talking on rows of chairs under the *pandal* outside while the ceremonies are going on. The men and women are usually separated but not strictly so. There is a good deal of going in and out of the house. At one end of the *pandal,* a rapid hand-drummer and a trumpeter periodically play auspicious music and women sing the customary wedding songs.

## *A Pandit Redefines Orthodoxy*

The minor Vedic *saṃskāras* are at present performed in their proper sequence only by the most orthodox Brahman families. Others either neglect them or assimilate them into the major rites. For the boy, many of the minor rites are performed on the occasion of his sacred thread ceremony and for the girl on the occasion of her wedding. This process of consolidation and assimilation of minor rites occasionally presents the more orthodox family with the dilemma of repeating the same rites twice or being out of step with changing times. Pandits who are experts on ritual are usually called in to give advice. Their decisions not only bring into relief the sources and standards of orthodoxy as applied to particulars but also reveal how the standards are redefined in the process.

Dr. Raghavan had spoken several times of a problem involving the forthcoming sacred thread ceremonies of his two sons. According to the *Dharmaśāstra* texts, certain rites must be observed for every male Brahman before the sacred thread ceremony. These rites are a birth ceremony when the umbilical cord is cut (*jātakarman*), a naming ceremony (*nāmakaraṇa*) on the eleventh day, a first feeding ceremony by the end of the sixth month, and a first tonsure ceremony at the end of the third year. It has recently become common practice to perform most of these rites on the eve of the sacred thread ceremony at age twelve or thirteen. Dr. Raghavan had had them performed for his sons at the times prescribed in the sacred texts; now he felt embarrassed that he should have to perform them again with the sacred thread ceremony. To resolve the matter, he consulted one of the pandits from the Sanskrit College who was an expert on the *Dharmaśāstras.* I accompanied him and asked the pandit about other cases.

The pandit said he was consulted on about two cases a month and that his brother, who is a greater authority than he on the *Dharmaśāstras,* was consulted on about ten cases a month. Most consultations concerned problems of pollution caused by a death in the family—not the mere fact of pollution but special details and procedures. In one recent case, for example, a boy's grandmother had died about two months after the death of his father. The boy had already performed the funeral rites for his father but was also expected to perform a special rite—the *sapiṇḍīkaraṇa*—for

* See photographs following page 174.

his grandmother. Ordinarily, a year must elapse before it can be performed, but in this special case it would have to be performed earlier.

In a second case, the pandit found himself in disagreement with another expert, who had ruled that a boy who had not yet assumed the sacred thread could not recite the *mantras* in the funeral ceremonies for his father. The pandit thought this was a high-handed *obiter dictum,* since the texts prescribe that a son should perform funeral rites for his parents, and the question of the *upanayana* does not arise. The boy's family followed the latter advice, and the first expert conceded his error when he was shown the textual prescriptions. Usually, an elder relative performs the obsequies for a young boy.

Sometimes quick decisions have to be made in the course of a ceremony. One family, for example, had gone through the preliminaries for a sacred thread ceremony when the boy's mother began her menstrual period. The situation created a deadlock, because a woman in pollution cannot take part in any religious ceremony, but the mother's participation is required for the completion of the sacred thread ceremony. The family was prepared to postpone the ceremony for four days, since menstrual pollution lasts for three days and the woman is purified by a bath on the fourth day. It so happened, however, that there would be no early auspicious day for the ceremony after the third day. A postponement would have to be for an indefinite period, and all the invited guests and the *purohitas* would have to be sent away. The pandit decided that the mother could take her fourth-day bath on the third day and that the ceremony could be completed then.

Dr. Raghavan then described his problem. The pandit listened carefully and gave his considered judgment: The *Dharmaśāstras* prescribe a preliminary tonsure for sacred thread ceremonies, therefore the tonsure should be performed; the other preliminary ceremonies could be omitted. Dr. Raghavan seemed satisfied with this resolution, and we went on to discuss other cases.

The pandit told of a case based on the *Mīmāṃsāśāstra,* which illustrates how logic must sometimes take precedence of the prescription in the sacred text. There is a rite called *jāteṣṭi,* based on the *śruti* texts, which parents are obliged to perform for the prosperity and health of a child. Normally, this rite should precede the birth rite of cutting the umbilical cord, a ritual based on the subsidiary *smṛti* texts. Yet the order of the rites is reversed, because, until the child's umbilical cord is cut and he has taken the mother's milk, he has not yet been brought into being and cannot have health and prosperity bestowed on him.

Local customs sometimes decide cases, especially if the sacred texts do not explicitly proscribe the customs. In the South, for example, it is customary for a man to marry his maternal uncle's daughter, although this type of marriage is not sanctioned in the sacred texts. In Tamil the same word means both nephew and son-in-law; similarly, another means both uncle and father-in-law; and a third denotes niece and daughter-in-law. Marrying a paternal uncle's son, on the other hand, is considered incest. Dr. Raghavan suggested that the particular act during the marriage in which the maternal uncle takes the bride on his shoulder and the paternal uncle takes the groom on his could be understood as a symbolic renunciation of rights.

The pandit ranked the authorities he used to decide cases in the following order: first, the most sacred writings, the *śruti*—the Vedas, the Upaniṣads, and the *Brāhmaṇas;* second, the somewhat less sacred texts; the *smṛti,* which includes the *Dharmaśāstra,* the Epics, and the Purāṇas; third, the opinion of a disciplined wise man, a *śiṣṭa,* where gaps or conflicts are present in the sacred texts; and finally, local customs that are not proscribed by the sacred texts.

The pandit thought that there was much less opprobrium now than formerly toward pollution arising from postpuberty marriages. Legislation has contributed to this change, but changing circumstances also play a part. Dr. Raghavan said he was at first surprised to find years ago that girls in ritual pollution were permitted to prepare food in Poona.

Although the Indian legal system is now largely based on "modern" law, the pandit cited a number of instances in which he had been consulted on Hindu law by lawyers who wanted to find precedents based on the sacred texts. In the case of a widow suing for some state support, he was able to cite the ancient principle that a woman should not be left adrift and in the last resort should be provided for by the state Rāj.[10]

### *Another Pandit on Urbanization and Deritualization*

The pandit's testimony emphasizes the continuing importance of the problems of pollution, particularly those occasioned by the death of a relative, and indicates how the belief in pollution affects the performance of all rites. The testimony of a second pandit, an expert in the ritual requirements of marriage, reinforces this conclusion and also suggests some trends of change in ritual behavior and attitude associated with the movement of Brahmans from village to town and city.

Although S. V. comes from a family that has produced pandits for twenty-one generations, he does not consider his occupation an inherited one. One hundred years ago, he said, all Brahmans would have known enough Sanskrit to qualify as pandits; now only about 1 per cent, at a liberal estimate, would so qualify. Brahmans are too busy having to make a living, he said, as he introduced his son. His son has an M.A. in history and works in the post office; the pandit called the son worldly, a *laukika,* and himself a *vaidika,* one who follows the Vedas. His family had come from a village in South Arcot District thirty-five years before to settle in a Madras suburb. The pandit is distinguished for his knowledge of the *Dharmaśāstra* and the Purāṇas. He told us that he was one of the few people who had thoroughly studied all the eighteen major Purāṇas. A few years ago, at the suggestion of Svāmī Śaṅkarācārya of Conjeeveram, he had made an extensive tour, lecturing on the Purāṇas. His son brought out for us large streamers that had been used to announce the discourses and listed the eighteen Purāṇas as well as the names of twenty towns, cities, and villages where lectures had been given. The pandit had found great interest and enthusiasm everywhere he went, and the *jagadguru* gave him a special title in honor of his tour. Although he is an old man, he was considering another tour.

Like the pandit from the Sanskrit College, S. V. is occasionally consulted for his special knowledge of the *Dharmaśāstra* and the Purāṇas. He, too, is most frequently asked about problems involving pollution, but he also gives advice on marriage questions. If two families have the same legendary ancestors (*pravara*) in their patrilineal families (*gotras*), they cannot intermarry, and he is often asked to determine the extent of similarities in *pravara*. Each *gotra* traces its lineage to a prominent set of *ṛṣis*, or primeval sages, and if two *gotras* have at least one *ṛṣi* in common, this is considered *samānasapravara*, or similar lineage, and is an impediment to marriage.

He traced the lineage of a *gotra* through the *Dharmasindhu* by Kāśīnātha Upādhyāya,[11] a digest of ancient texts. This collection is based on the *Dharmaśāstra* and the Purāṇas, and gives the history of about 100 different *gotras* up to about a thousand years ago. He did not think many errors occurred in updating the histories, because each family knew its *gotra* and kept its history. If a family had married within its *gotra*, it would have been excommunicated. A Brahman is taught the name of his *gotra* at the sacred thread ceremony and must repeat it, together with the name of his *sūtra* and his Veda, every time he meets an elder.

Among the historic 100 *gotras* are also some non-Brahman *gotras*, but non-Brahmans do not come to consult him.

In case of doubt about *gotra* descent, Pandit S. V. would refer to the book and compare family *gotras* for overlaps. In a recent case, he had advised against the intermarriage of representatives of the *Kauṇḍinya* and *Saṅkṛti gotras*. The families took his advice, but had they disregarded it, nothing very serious would have happened, except that very orthodox people would probably not have gone to their house. Sixty years ago, he felt, such a marriage would have been regarded as incest, and the couple would have been excommunicated.

The pandit showed us a genealogical chart of his family. It covered only seven generations, because, if anyone within the seven generations died, all relatives would be polluted for ten days. Between the seventh and fourteenth generation, the pollution lasts only three days. The terms are prescribed by the *Dharmaśāstra*, at least for the paternal line.

On the maternal side, the pollution extends for three generations, and the period is much shorter. If a mother's brother dies, for instance, the pollution lasts three days; if a mother's brother's son dies, the pollution lasts one and a half days; and if the mother's brother's son's son dies, then the pollution lasts only twelve hours. There is no pollution on the maternal side in cases of birth, but on the paternal side the pollution extends to both birth and death. Many of the questions about which S. V. is consulted concern the number of days one must wait in pollution before a *śrāddha* ceremony can be performed. To decide such cases, he uses the book *Āśauca*, a compilation from the *Dharmaśāstra* and the Purāṇas by Vaidyanātha Dīkṣitar in the eighteenth century.[12]

Foreign travel is also polluting. An uncle of S. V. went to England for six months. When he returned, he came to the pandit's father to find out what he must do to be purified. The father prescribed more than forty *saṃskāras,* including the sacred thread ceremony, to remove the pollution and restore his twice-born status. Dr. Raghavan said that, on his return from his first foreign voyage to Europe, he and his wife had made a pilgrimage to Rameswaram and had undergone some purification rites there.

A girl marrying after puberty, after the age of nine or ten, is polluted and needs to be purified. Now that legislation prohibits early marriage, many girls are, strictly speaking, polluted. Years ago, marriage to such a bride would have been considered equivalent to marrying a girl of lower caste, but now it is taken casually; only about 5 per cent of the pandit's associates have special rites—*homas*—performed for the girls, and the trend is away from such rites.

Widows of all ages are not considered auspicious enough to participate in rites. They must shave their heads like a *sannyāsin's,* hear no music, use no sandalwood or flowers, eat only one meal a day, use no *tilaka* mark, and wear a white robe. These rules are strictly observed in the city by perhaps 10 per cent of the pandit's associates, and in the villages by about 50 per cent.

On his tours, the pandit had found many Brahmans leaving the villages because they had too little land or other property to support them. In the towns and cities, they met people from various regions with different customs. Their only common ground was *bhakti.* As a result, they developed an interest in religious activities, *harikathā,* and public purāṇic discourses, which allowed them "to forget themselves in public places." At home, they lacked the interest and the time to perform customary rituals. Those who remained in the villages were more observant of the orthodox routine of the *karmamārga* than were those who came to the city.

In observing the restrictions against intercaste and intersect marriages, however, the pandit estimated that about 90 per cent of his associates conformed. Vaiṣṇavite, Mādhva, and Smārta Brahmans do not intermarry, nor do the different subgroups of Smārtas. These restrictions are not in the *Dharmaśāstra* or Purāṇas but are a matter of traditional observance, *śiṣṭācāra,* and they are steadily disappearing.

The pandit did not appear to take very seriously the matching of horoscopes in marriage. Where there is some doubt about matching horoscopes, he would ask the couple to place a flower in his copy of the *Rāmāyaṇa.* If the passage where they placed it was a "happy" one he would advise marriage; if not, he would advise against it. The matching of horoscopes, he added, is not mentioned in the *Dharmaśāstras* or the Purāṇas.

On food restrictions, the pandit will allow vegetarians to eat eggs for medical reasons, but he counsels them to purify themselves afterward.

While we were talking, a young *purohita* who is a disciple of the pandit came by. He has fifty families as clients and described the main *pūjās* he performs for them: "*Sūryanamaskāra* for their health, Lakṣmī *pūjās* on Fridays for their business, *Īśvaran* or Śiva *pūjās* for their prosperity." "How do your clients decide whether you are helping them?" he was asked. "They would not keep me, if their business did not improve. Because they keep me, I know that their fortunes are improving." "What else besides health and prosperity do you help them to get?" I asked "What else is there?" "Sons," it was suggested. "Those too." "Salvation?" "No, that one does for oneself."

## *Some Optional Domestic Rites*

Sometimes the consolidation and timing of domestic rites are dictated by purely practical needs. This is apt to be true of the optional rites, both Vedic and purāṇic. At the house of a Smārta Brahman merchant, for example, I observed the practically simultaneous performance of a first birthday for his son and a *Gaṅgāpūjā* for his mother. The same *purohitas* and almost the same preparations were used. The rite for the child was performed first. It consisted of oblations in fire with the recital of *mantras* for long life and health (*Āyuṣahoma*). It ended with two young women waving a plate of red turmeric water in front of the child while singing an auspicious song in Tamil.* The ceremony, called *Ārati* (remover of distress), is conducted throughout India at the end of all auspicious functions.

After the birthday rite for the son, the *Gaṅgāpūjā* began. Several brass pots of water were brought in and placed in the center of a rice-powder diagram on the floor in preparation for the *Gaṅgāpūjā*. The pots contained sacred Ganges water brought back by the child's grandmother, who had recently completed a pilgrimage to Benares and the Ganges. The pots were then covered with flowers, gifts of cloth, and other offerings. The *purohita* and his assistant chanted *mantras* invoking the Ganges and other holy rivers, as well as some purāṇic verses that included a long prayer to the Ganges. The child's father passed out coins to the *purohitas* at different stages of the ceremony and served breakfast to Brahmans afterwards. Some of the Ganges water was distributed to relatives and several guests for ceremonial use.

At the home of another Smārta Brahman family, I witnessed two domestic rites performed about a week apart, conducted not by the regular family *purohita* but by an expert in this type of rite who was called from Malabar. The first rite was a *Gaṇapatihoma,* or oblation with eight offerings of ghee, honey, grains, coconut, and sugar cane to the elephant-headed god Gaṇeśa, or Gaṇapati. Its purpose is to remove obstacles, to bring an enterprise to fruition, or to bless a newborn child. On this occasion, it was performed to remove some obstacles in the householder's career.

The second rite, a *Durgāpūjā,* was also intended to remove obstacles and enemies and to promote health, prosperity, and long life. But the beneficiary was the householder's wife. The Malabar specialist conducted the *pūjā,* and he and his assistant performed a rather elaborate ritual, spreading white rice-powder diagrams on the floor, heating small pieces of camphor on a charcoal brazier to use in ritual lamps, plucking rose-petals with the recitation of each *mantra,* ringing bells, waving

* See photographs following page 174.

flames, and prostrating themselves. At one point, the householder placed some rupees on a plate together with a plantain and a coconut and extended them toward the expert while repeating after him the following formula: "The master of the house, his wife, children, and descendants for whom this *pūjā* is done offer this to you." While the householder and his wife prostrated themselves, the specialist held the plate toward them and recited some formulae. Then all walked around the flame and uttered prayers asking for forgiveness of sins and mistakes. The specialist, taking in each hand some of the rice powder from the diagram and a handful of the rose petals, recited the following formula: "For all in this room, men, women and children, may any defect existing in their bodies be cast out." After sprinkling some water, he handed out the holy ash (*vibhūti*) for all to put on forehead and mouth. The *pūjā* concluded with a prayer for peace and prosperity and an end to enmity.

After the ceremony, I was told that the elaborate ritual was essential because the effectiveness of the *pūjā* depends on correct performance, prayers, and the faith in it. The householder also explained that when he was planning to have the *Gaṇapatihoma* done, he decided to have the *Durgāpūjā* performed also because his wife had not been too well, and if they missed the last Friday of the month, which is auspicious for worship of the mother goddess, there would not be another time for it soon. He also said that the two rites had been recommended to him by Dr. Raghavan's astrologer, who was from Malabar.

### Jyotiṣika, *or Astrologer*

A meeting was arranged at Dr. Raghavan's house with an astrologer, and at one point we were joined by Dr. Raghavan's brother, who also knows a good deal about astrology.

The astrologer was a forty-eight-year-old Nāyar from Malabar. He had been employed for many years as a Sanskrit teacher in a Madras City high school. A private practitioner of astrology, he was widely popular among varying strata of society, rich and poor, big folk and small. For four generations, his family had been devoted to astrology, *Āyurvedic* medicine, and Sanskrit. Some members had specialized in one branch, others in another. They were also known for their skill in propitiatory *pūjās* and toxicology, especially snake bites. They knew many *mantras* and medicines for snake bite. One was an adept in snake *mantras* that drew out the venom. Even the astrologer's mother knew Sanskrit well; she had started to read it during her sixth year. His mother's mother had been a poet in Sanskrit and in Malayalam and had been able to converse in Sanskrit. His mother's brother was a professor of Sanskrit at a college in Tanjore District, where the astrologer had studied. His father was a Nāyar and an *Āyurvedic* doctor and astrologer. His wife's grandfather was a famous *Āyurvedic* doctor who had treated Dr. Raghavan, his wife, and Dr. Raghavan's uncle. The astrologer's family are not Kaṇiyars or Paṇikkars, the hereditary astrologers of Malabar; they had taken it up on their own and considered themselves just as proficient.

Before going to the Sanskrit College near Tanjore, the astrologer had attended a modern school, where he had studied English, mathematics, and science; outside of school, he had studied Sanskrit, astrology, and medicine under two Nambūdiri Brahmans and a Menon. Finishing the modern school at the age of sixteen, he had continued with tutors until the age of nineteen. From his nineteenth to twenty-sixth year, he had specialized in grammar at the Sanskrit College. There, too, he had studied astrology during his spare time and had become so good at casting horoscopes that his teachers and fellow students frequently consulted him. After the Sanskrit College, he spent one year at Annamalai University preparing to teach. Immediately thereafter, he got a post in a Madras high school teaching Sanskrit. At school, he is frequently consulted on astrological questions and for other matters and is often called on to give religious discourses. Married, he has two daughters and one son. His son was just coming up for his final examinations. The son was not being taught astrology because the father wanted to bring him up "in the modern way, on science subjects." *

There are two different methods of astrology, the astrologer explained: One is the "normal *śāstric* method" of prediction based on the position of the planets. In the second, questions are put and cowrie shells are thrown to help give the answer. The second method, *aṣṭamaṅgalapraśna,* is very elaborate. He uses only the first, which he illustrated with reference to several horoscopes. In Dr. Raghavan's horoscope, Saturn, on the day of our meeting with the astrologer, occupied the tenth house—the place of work—and was also the lord of the eighth house. The indication, therefore, is that there were always obstacles to the fruits of his labor. There are remedies suggested in *śāstric* texts. On an earlier occasion, Dr. Raghavan had consulted modern-type astrologers about a position at 1,200 rupees per month that had been offered to him by the Governor of Bihar. The astrologers told him that he would go to Bihar, but the Nāyar said that he would not go and that he would never leave Madras. (He has not done so.) The modern astrologers knew modern types of subject matter and Western methods, but our friend felt that they were not good enough at reading indications.[13]

The Nāyar astrologer knew the horoscopes of all his clients by heart. He had about 150 regular clients and "numberless" occasional ones. Frequently, clients will meet him on the street and ask questions. Without consulting any notes, he remembers their horoscopes and gives them the indications. He receives presents but takes no regular fees, valuing, he says, the friendship of his clients more than their money.

Several more successful predictions were cited. A refrigeration engineer had quit his job to start his own agency and was not doing very well when he consulted the Nāyar on Dr. Raghạvan's recommendation. The astrologer predicted that the engineer would go to England and that his prospects would improve upon his return. The man did go, and his situation did improve.

In another case, a former civil servant wanted to become a lawyer. The astrologer had advised him to perform certain propitiatory rites, which he

* The son, I have since learned, has gone into a modern technological occupation but has also blossomed into an astrological consultant.

did. The application was favorably acted on in the courts, and the man is now a highly successful lawyer.

Although the astrologer, who is a religious person and a worshiper of Devī, was willing to advise on all kinds of cases, he turns down "unsavory" questions, such as whether a man should take a second wife, or what to do about a woman's misbehavior. A prudent and ethical astrologer should not deal with such questions, he said, but there were astrologers who did so.

In selecting a wife, the important thing was to match horoscopes. One client's major worry had been to find a suitable bride for his wife's brother. The astrologer had rejected one horoscope as "not suitable for your family," and had recommended another. After seeing the girl, the friend reported that both her appearance and her horoscope were suitable for his brother-in-law.

In another case, the parents had to consider many difficulties. The horoscopes predicted longevity and happiness for the couple but indicated that a bad period for the boy would be sustained by a good period for the girl, and that bad characteristics on one side were balanced by bad on the other. A boy's family does not consider a wife's short life expectancy a defect, but her family will worry about it. In matching horoscopes, the astrologer considers some ten different points, including longevity, health, temperament, and whether there will be issue.

He felt sure that his predictions had improved as a result of his experience. He was much bolder now in making certain types of predictions, about cases of tuberculosis and other diseases affecting specific parts of the body, for instance. On the other hand, he had been unable to foresee the outcome of horse races and finds it difficult to predict the results of financial investments, about which many people inquire, and political elections. The *śāstras* provide no guidance for such predictions, since the original purpose of astrology was to fix the correct times for certain rites.

Dr. Raghavan's brother then explained some "modern applications" of astrology. In the case of horse races, the disposition of the planets when the race begins may be taken as a starting point. In picking a horse, many different systems are used. As for investments, the fact that different planets govern different metals has relevance for other commodities. For example, when the sun is 18 degrees in Gemini, in July, the indication is that cotton prices will go up.

The Nāyar astrologer recommended special rites to his clients on the basis of his predictions. The purpose of the rites, he said, is to alleviate specific evils or to nullify the effects of an unfavorable indication. If Saturn is in unfavorable position in a person's horoscope, for example, then that individual should go to the temple every Saturday (Saturn's day) to propitiate the planet and should also fast at night. Special *pūjās* can be performed either at home or in temple; they are more effective at home. In certain cases, however, they must be performed at a temple, such as *pūjās* to Saturn or to all nine planets together; or if a person is born with Mercury in combustion, that is, within 10 degrees of the sun, then he must go to a Viṣṇu temple and light ghee; if Jupiter and Venus are not favorable, then Brahmans should be fed in a temple; if Saturn is weak or unfavorable, beggars and Harijans should be fed. When Dr. Raghavan and his wife passed through a bad period of Saturn, they fed cripples on Saturdays.

The astrologer said that he also sent his clients to *mantrikas* and doctors as well as to temples. When he recommended that a *bhagvati pūjā* be performed for a friend's wife, he also recommended a *mantrika* from Malabar who knew special *mantras*. He does not recommend doctors by name but according to whether they are "English" or *Āyurvedic* doctors. English doctors, he said, are all right for injections and operations, but if Mars is unfavorable in a horoscope, he tells his client not to go near an "English" doctor, for Mars indicates weapons and instruments.

Dr. Raghavan pointed out that horoscopes are not mentioned in the sacred scriptures. In the *Rāmāyaṇa*, a reference is made to a horoscope at Rāma's birth, but there is no reference to a matching of Rāma's and Sītā's horoscopes. There are no such references in the *Mahābhārata*. Although the astrological treatises have a long history, they are not part of the sacred scriptures; they were later developments from the Vedāṅga, or appendages to the Vedas (*Jyotiṣa*, or *Astronomy*, for one). The inclusion of idols of the planets in temples is based on astrological references in the *smṛtis*. Dr. Raghavan remarked that, while some astrologers, like this Nāyar, were religious, others were generally secular, although they may suggest religious acts as remedies.

Dr. Raghavan's brother noted that, although Eastern and Western astrology are alike in some respects, the Eastern system is based on a lunar rather than a solar calendar and has more planets and different houses for them. The Western system, however, is known in India, and many astrologers use it along with the Indian.

In response to a question about the utility of predictions, the astrologer replied that it was pleasant to know of a fortunate event in advance and that it was best to be forewarned about an unfortunate one. Several stories illustrated that one cannot escape one's fate, even if one knows about a future calamity. In one tale, a man had been warned by an astrologer that his death would result from an encounter with a crocodile in the Ganges. Knowing this, he moved south to stay away from the Ganges. Death's emissary then assumed human form and was born into his family. The god, a very accomplished musician, persuaded the man to study with his teacher, a guru in Banaras, and offered to accompany him there. When they reached the Ganges, the god pushed him into the river to the crocodiles, saying: "You tried to cheat me of your fate!"

The Nāyar always tries to tell his clients whether his predictions are exact or not. Correct predictions depend on the character of the data, he believes, and sometimes mistakes creep in when the data are inexact. The fact that many people do not know their exact time of birth is a common source of uncertainty in predictions. Dr. Raghavan added that the astrologer's predictions will also depend on a knowledge of the particular society and its conditions. In the United States, for example, it is possible for anyone to move from manager of a shop to President, but in India a man with a small shop can move only to a bigger one; he cannot become Prime Minister. When an astrologer predicts prosperity for a particular individual, that good fortune will be within the limits set by his society and his condition in it.

When I drove the Nāyar home, he told me that another name for an astrologer is *daivajña*—knower of or believer in fate, destiny, and divine dispensation. A belief in God is essential, he added, if one wants to be a good astrologer. He worships the planets himself, and regularly does *pūjās* to them at a special home shrine.

Several weeks later, on the Malabar coast, we talked about astrology with two members of the "educated unemployed," one of whom was a college graduate. They complained of the widespread opinion that Malabar is full of astrologers and magicians. Astrology, they said, is used by many people as a consolation for being unemployed. "If you can read it in the stars, you can conveniently forget the political system." As a last resort, they supposed, it might be justifiable. In any case, they were sure it was now more popular in Tamiḻnāḍu than in Malabar.

## Āyurvedic *Doctor and Dispensary*

*Dispensary cases.* Men, women, and children sat on low benches in the dispensary, waiting their turn to see Doctor K. They did not have too long to wait; the doctor, seated at his desk in full view of the patients, was quick. In twenty minutes, he had examined and prescribed for twelve people. The first case was a shriveled old woman. The doctor felt her pulse. She told him she had had "some enlargement of the heart" and that her case had been declared hopeless by other doctors. He wrote out a prescription for heart disease medicines, which the patient took to a pharmacy counter on one side of the room where two assistants made up the preparations from bottles of herbs. The second case was a child with a skin eruption on her legs. The doctor diagnosed the case as eczema, felt the lymph glands, and prescribed two medicines, one for internal use and one for external use. He had seen the child twice before and said that she would be cured in about a month. The third and fourth cases also involved eczema—on a woman's hand and over the entire body of an older man. Case five was a woman of about forty-five, who complained of digestive troubles. The doctor diagnosed "a hypofunctioning of the digestive juices" and prescribed some tablets. The next case was also a digestive disorder. Case seven was an old man with diseased gums who complained of pain. The doctor gave him a powder that he prepares himself and that gives immediate relief. A child with swollen cheeks was case eight. The doctor said the boy suffered from albumen in the urine and prescribed a salt-free diet. If he did not improve soon, the doctor would send him to a hospital. For case nine, a man of sixty-five who said he could not see clearly, the doctor prescribed an eye lotion prepared from coconut water and several herbs. Cases ten and eleven were an infant and a man with "fever," and case twelve was a woman with swollen feet and ankles, for whom the doctor prescribed some bitter tablets. Her disease he called sclipadarin.

All the patients looked grateful for the brief attention they had received and usually put a small coin in a box as they passed the doctor's desk on their way to the drug counter.

*Organization of* Āyurvedic *dispensaries and medicine.* After the patients had left, the doctor explained that this was only an "outpatient dispensary" and that he referred serious cases to the general hospital. The dispensary had an endowed income of 3,000 rupees a year. Of this, the doctor received a nominal remuneration of 100 rupees a month; two assistants received 85 rupees per month; and medicines (bought from a special cooperative) came to about 120 rupees per month. The deficit was made up by contributions from patients, of whom there were about 200 a day.

The State has some 400 dispensaries using the *Āyurvedic* (Sanskrit), the Siddha (Tamil), or the Yunānī (Urdu) systems of medicine.[14] These dispensaries are run by district boards or by the municipalities. The doctor said that the state had only one good hospital of Indian medicine and one good college of indigenous medicine. *Āyurvedic* doctors who are organized into an association, may be divided into three groups in South India: (1) the hereditary physicians who learned medicine from their fathers (about 1,200), (2) those who have studied in recognized schools of indigenous and *Āyurvedic* medicine (about 800), and (3) graduates of the College of Indigenous Medicine (about 1,500). The college also teaches "modern" scientific medicine, and about 100 of its graduates practice both the indigenous and the modern systems. The hereditary doctors really do not know the workings of the human body; by their ignorance, he said, they "spoil our good name."

*Medical education.* The doctor had studied two years of science (up to the intermediate level) in the university before being admitted to the College of Indigenous Medicine, where he had spent five years. The latter curriculum included "allopathic" subjects as well as Indian medicine. He had studied anatomy, physiology, ophthalmology, surgery, and botany of Indian plants, among other subjects. At the College, "allopathic" medicine was taught by teachers from "modern" colleges, and Indian medicine by pandits who knew the Sanskrit texts. The teaching was in English and Tamil, the examinations in English. The doctor had always taken notes in English. He had learned to prepare herbs during his first year, had worked in an *Āyurvedic* dispensary in his third year, and had learned to take cases in his fourth year. For his examination, he was asked to prepare specific medicines and to examine patients in the presence of other doctors. Of the total five-year program, about 60 per cent was devoted to *Āyurvedic* and about 40 per cent to modern medicine. Recently, the proportions had been changed to 60 per cent modern and 40 per cent *Āyurvedic.*

In this mixed system, graduates may practice either system, and almost all have chosen to practice modern medicine. Although all Indian universities conduct examinations in Indian medicine and award the diploma of *Āyurveda Śiromaṇi,* few people take the diploma. Representatives of the Indian system claim to deal successfully only with "constitutional diseases," not with emergencies or operations. Indian medicine is good for functional disorders which the body can rectify of itself, the doctor said, but it cannot, according to him, cure organic diseases. It may also be useful for preventive purposes.

Traditional *Āyurvedic* training, the doctor said, was very different from the way the pandits now teach in the College of Medicine. His own pandit had been apprenticed to a teacher at the age of eight. For ten years, he had lived, slept, and eaten with the teacher's family, watching everything, learning to pound and grind the herbs and eventually working together with his master. In his spare time, he had studied Sanskrit literature—the *kāvyas,* grammar, poetics, and elementary Sanskrit. He had memorized the *ślokas* by repeating each one 100 times. Even now, he could recite the standard text of *Aṣṭāṅgahṛdayam.* The doctor said that the books on medicine were considered to have been written by the *ṛṣis* and were all perfect; some thought it would be a sin to try to improve them. In his opinion, however, the books do not always give very specific treatments; they leave room for much improvisation by the individual doctor.

Nowadays, many of the traditionally trained pandits prepare pupils for university examinations in *Āyurveda;* by serving as teachers in quasi-modern *Āyurvedic* colleges, they are helping to change the old system, although without adequate knowledge of the "modern" system.

At fourteen, the doctor had suffered from a skin disease, and his father took him to a famous "allopathic" specialist. For six months he took many different medicines, but none of them had any effect. He was then taken to another famous "modern" doctor, who told him to run up and down the beach until he perspired and he would be cured. He ran up and down the beach many times but was not cured. Still another doctor told him to smear sodium thiosulphate on his body and to stand in the sun. The medicine produced a foul smell but did not cure him.

Finally, at nineteen, the doctor had gone to the College of Indigenous Medicine and within two months was completely cured by its prescription—a daily 15-minute application of *sesamum* oil to his skin and exercise. He also gained weight. He was so impressed by the results that he decided to study Indian medicine. His decision was taken against the wishes of his family, who were Smārta Brahmans and well-to-do, educated merchants with no faith in *Āyurvedic* doctors.

After graduating from the College of Indigenous Medicine at twenty-five, he had worked for seven years as an honorary physician in this same dispensary under a senior physician. They treated about 300 people a day. The senior doctor never asked for money but ran the dispensary as a charitable institution. The older man also had a private practice from which he earned about 1,000 rupees per month.

During the war, the doctor had left Madras and had gone to work in several dispensaries run by district boards. After the war, he had come back to Madras and opened a free dispensary for a scavenger colony in Triplicane. He worked there on a part-time basis for about ten years, spending the rest of the time in his family's textile store. Ten months before our visit, the senior physician in the present dispensary had died, and the doctor had come to keep the clinic from being closed.

In 1938, the doctor had organized an association to promote good health and to educate the public about health. Through this association, he had distributed books of prayers and *ślokas* that provide "recreation" for some people and help them forget their troubles. He had gotten some of the books from Śaṅkarācārya.

*Practice, methods, and techniques.* The doctor's patients do not pay consulting fees. It is not the custom. They pay for medicines and injections. In the dispensary, the patients give what they can, usually about ½ anna. The doctor said he did not think this was a good system of remuneration, because many doctors concocted and prescribed worthless medicines in order to get some compensation. He quoted George Bernard Shaw: "If one tries to deceive another, he will be deceived in turn."

The doctor felt qualified to practice "allopathic" medicine and had done so in the district board dispensaries, but he no longer had any desire to practice it because he thought he could do better with Indian medicine. His serious cases he sends to "allopathic" doctors.

For diagnosis, he draws upon the "allopathic" side and uses all modern aids—e.g., feeling the lymph glands. He sends a patient's sputum to be examined for tuberculosis bacilli, and he uses the thermometer, the stethoscope, and the blood pressure gauge. Pandits, he said, oppose these tools and thus block progress in Indian medicine. A knowledge of modern medicine is necessary in order to make a correct diagnosis and to avoid dangerous treatments. For example, a pain in the heart may be from the stomach and not from heart disease.

The rivalry between allopathic and indigenous medicine, according to the doctor, is chiefly financial. Ten years before, the government had ordered that allopathic doctors could not also practice *Āyurvedic* medicine. The order was later revoked. The Indian Government is not favorably disposed to Indian medicine, he said, because it is a capitalistic government and has an interest, as chief producer of medicine and drugs, in modern medicine.* It is difficult to procure *Āyurvedic* drugs. The doctor and some of his friends have organized a cooperative society with revenues of 300,000 rupees a year to manufacture *Āyurvedic* medicines. The society has been successful, but it still has a problem in developing adequate preservatives.

The dispensary does not distribute birth control information. The doctor said that some believe birth control is a sin because Manu had said that it was necessary to propagate. He admitted that many of his patients have too many children, but he could not tell them so. "They do not know about such things." Birth control was necessary; the lack of abstinence is one reason for ill health. He himself had only one child, a daughter.

For patients complaining of ghosts and other mental disorders, the doctor prescribed the reading of prayers (some of them in Sanskrit), rest, baths, and "noninterference." He also had several effective medicines that will improve mental disorders in a month. Among them are *Brāhmī* and *Sūpāntana,* which are good for reducing blood pressure and for bad mem-

* The government of India has since been encouraging *Āyurveda* with funds for special centers, research, and development.

ory. The doctor gave me some books that describe the preparation of these drugs and also asked me to take a sample of *Brāhmī* with me.[15]

The usual Indian diet is not healthy, the doctor believes. He recommends bland milk diets to his patients. Spices in themselves are not bad. Tamarind, for example, is a good laxative. For hyperacidity, he prescribes lime, buttermilk, and raw vegetables. In the dispensary, he has about eighty different herbal medicines whose preparation he has supervised. Before I left the dispensary, he showed me a very special little bottle of a black powdered herb, opened it, and asked me to take some. It was, he said, a stimulant to digestion and would give me a good appetite for lunch.

### *Sanskrit College and Students*

When Dr. Raghavan and I visited the Sanskrit College in Mylapore, we were greeted by a member of the faculty, the Secretary, and the Principal. In the low-walled, tree-shaded college yard are two main buildings, a two-story building in which most of the classes are held, and a one-story building that serves as a dormitory for the students. Also in the college yard is a small building containing the library of the Kuppuswami Sastri Research Institute, which is used by members of the college.

The first faculty member we met introduced himself as an M.A. who teaches comparative philology, the history of Sanskrit literature, and "a bit of English." The Secretary told us that the college had been founded in 1906, before the University of Madras taught any Sanskrit. At first, its teachers were all old-style pandits, but some of them later took university examinations and degrees; now one member of the faculty has a master's degree but has no training as a traditional Sanskrit pandit. At present, the college has six faculty members and thirty students. The students pay no fees; they receive free board and lodging and 25 rupees per month from scholarship funds that come in part from a private endowment and in part from government funds. They are selected on the basis of the Sanskrit entrance test given by the Department of Public Instruction. Mostly from Brahman families, the students have had advanced Sanskrit training in other schools or at home. Dr. Raghavan added that in other districts and schools, many non-Brahmans also studied Sanskrit and that a strong tradition of Sanskrit learning exists among Śaivite non-Brahmans. In the village of Śrīperumbudūr, site of a famous Vaiṣṇava shrine, there is also a Sanskrit college that draws its faculty and students chiefly from Śrīvaiṣṇavas.

Sanskrit training is at present a labor of love, according to Dr. Raghavan. A Sanskrit pandit can be employed as a manuscript copyist in the orientalist libraries, a teacher of Sanskrit in secondary schools and colleges, a research scholar in a university department (a university diploma is necessary for this), or a public speaker on the *Rāmāyaṇa,* the Vedānta, and the Purāṇas, and can give religious discourses in temples and private instruction in Sanskrit and Vedānta in private homes.

Although the Purāṇas are not taught in the college, several faculty members give popular expositions of these texts and augment their small salaries in this way.

The four-year curriculum includes Sanskrit poetics and grammar, *Mīmāṃsā* or Vedic exegesis, Advaitavedānta, logic, *Sāṅkhya* and Yoga systems, comparative philology, history of Sanskrit literature, and some English. The medium of instruction is Sanskrit; most of the students can read and speak it fluently. Original treatises are used and committed in part or whole to memory.[16]

The Secretary of the college, who seemed to have a practical turn of mind, told us that modern education—especially scientific and technological education—had recently begun to compete with Sanskrit learning. The students in the college have no opportunity at present to acquire scientific education; that would be too expensive. He said that the only hope of preserving Sanskrit learning is to incorporate some modern subjects and scientific and technological study into the college's curriculum by adding a year to the present program. Then graduates of the college would at least be able to earn a living. Proposals to reorganize secondary education to include some classical education, if carried out, may also help by providing teaching posts.

The emphasis on "bread-and-butter" problems stimulated a counter-discussion of the higher values to be gained from a Sanskrit training. The consensus was that such study is a liberal education and one of the best means of training the mind and its faculties. Thorough study of Vedānta gives the student a philosophy of life, guarding him against too much faith in modern technology.

Advaitavedānta is taught as a sacred subject in the college, since it is the philosophy and theology of the college's sponsors and founders, as well as of most of its staff. It is taught only in the mornings and never after food has been taken. Other Vedic studies are not taught because of limited funds.* The college is anxious to develop both Vedic and Purāṇic studies. Pandits now teach students these subjects on a private basis. In a few other Sanskrit institutions in Madras State, the Vedas are also especially taught for *purohitas.* The present curriculum of the college would qualify a student as a Sanskrit pandit to expound the Upaniṣads. It would not give a domestic or temple priest the training he needs, nor would it qualify him to be a *paurāṇika,* a *mantrika,* an astrologer, a *sthapati* or an *Āyurvedic* doctor—all historical branches of Sanskrit learning. The ancient system in which every village has pandits specializing in these different branches of knowledge is now dying out.

After gaining some background information about the college, we observed some of the classes. The first class we entered was an advanced one in *Mīmāṃsā.* The students were discussing how the meaning of words in a Vedic context differed from their usage in an ordinary context. The teacher recited the lesson and the students listened silently, glancing occasionally at the text before them. The discussion of semantics and the

* They are now taught with a grant-in-aid from the Central Sanskrit Board of the Education University, New Delhi. A course in *Jyotiṣa* has also been added and an *Āyurvedic* college and dispensary have been started.

different ways in which the meaning of a word may be determined had a very modern ring. The second class, on Advaitavedānta, was held in a special shrine room. A garlanded picture of Śaṅkarācārya of Conjeeveram hung on the wall. The students all washed before entering and sat on the floor in front of their teacher, who put on a silk scarf. One topic for the day was from Śaṅkara's commentary on Chapter 2 of the *Vedāntasūtra*. The teacher first summarized the preceding chapter and then related it to Chapter 2. In Chapter 1, he said, Śaṅkara, using the Vedic texts as his authority, proved that all texts of the Upaniṣads refer to one supreme being, omnipotent, omniscient, who does not differ from the individual soul. In Chapter 2, Śaṅkara examines this position logically, showing that it cannot be contradicted by the findings of other systems. After analyzing these other systems, Śaṅkara refutes their contentions against Advaita. After his exposition, the teacher asked questions, and the students answered in unison in a very few words. Dr. Raghavan said that both questions and answers were in the text and that this ancient method of teaching "by discussion" goes back to the Vedas.

The third class was an elementary one in *Mīmāṃsā*. The text taught was the *Jaiminīyanyāyamālā*. The teacher expounded the text, and a student would read a few words of it. The discussion was about how the rules for interpreting texts would be helpful for understanding the *Dharmaśāstra*. A particular text—a Vedic passage referring to sacrificial acts—was used to illustrate the method of interpretation. One of the passages to be interpreted was, "The stone is the performer of the sacrifice." The use of "stone" here, the text pointed out, was metaphorical.

The last class we visited was on Sanskrit grammar and was taught by the Principal to one student. The subject was the different kinds of roots and conjugations discussed in the *Siddhāntakaumudī* of Bhaṭṭoji Dīkṣita. The Principal asked questions, and the student gave short replies. I was curious about the Sanskrit root of *"nāṭya"* as in *"Bharatanāṭya,"* and the Principal constructed a sentence to illustrate the discussion of the roots: *"Bharatanāṭya* is very pleasing to the eyes of the onlookers." He then asked the student to parse the sentence and to explain the grammatical significance of every word. The student was puzzled at first but with a little help from the Principal eventually concluded that *"Bharatanāṭya"* was a compound word, that it signified the art of dance expounded by Bharata, and that its construction was like that of "Pāṇini's grammar."

On coming out of class, I talked with a group of students who had been playing volleyball. One who knew more English than the rest translated for us. They told me that they pass five hours a day in class; they spend two years each on logic, grammar, and comparative philology, and four years each on poetics, *Mīmāṃsā* and Advaitavedānta; they get to go home twice a year; and nine out of thirty are taking final examinations this year. Two know music, and one plays the drums; one is already a graduate in mathematics; only two know English. They said that they did not feel any conflict between Sanskrit and modern education. Their faith in the value of Sanskrit persists, but they also recognize the value of modern education and of Hindi. If they had the opportunity, they would be interested in getting a modern education in addition to the Sanskrit one.

They would also favor a more general entrance examination, including mathematics, science, and social studies. Most of them do regular *pūjās* and wear Brahmanical tonsures with tufts. Conducting religious readings and discourses in their villages during their vacations interests many of these young men. Several had heard a noted Svāmī's discourses on the Upaniṣads but thought them too general and wide of the mark for specialists, although they were all right for a more popular audience. The students liked to go to modern entertainments, including the cinema. The Congress Party, they thought, had done much useful service for the country but was weak on the cultural side.

At this point, our student interpreter spoke up. Not so orthodox as some, he said, he would like to visit Europe and learn what Western scholarship had contributed to Sanskrit studies. He came from a family of Telugu Brahmans and was just finishing his first year in the Sanskrit College. He had been speaking Sanskrit from the age of six, having learned it from his father, who is very interested and active in Sanskrit learning. Our interpreter could have gone into chemical work but preferred to become a research scholar in Sanskrit. He has had no difficulties with his studies and has time to relax and read on his own. When I left, he gave me a pamphlet containing his father's Sanskrit translations of some of Tolstoy's writings.

## The Temple Sphere

### Gurukkaḷ, *or Temple Priest*

M. Swaminatha Gurukkaḷ, then a man of fifty-three, is the temple priest of a large Śiva temple in Mylapore. One afternoon I met him and his son (who acted as interpreter) in a private library near the temple, and we had an opportunity to talk for several hours.

*Family history.* The *gurukkaḷ* is very proud of his family. He said that they have been temple priests for 1,000 years. He referred to a book, *Hālāsyamahāliṅgam,* which tells how Rājādhirājā Cōḻa brought the family from the Godāvarī district. According to a work by Aghora Śiva Ācārya, his ancestors were also *ācāryas* in the Amardaka *Maṭha*—a Śaiva *maṭha.*[17] They have been priests in the Mylapore Temple for the past four generations. Previously, they had been priests in a village temple of Chingleput District for about 150 years. For the past 25 years, no family member had had any occupation other than that of a *gurukkaḷ,* except for the son, who now teaches Sanskrit at the Vivekānanda College. The family, including four sons and four daughters, all live together with M. S. Gurukkaḷ and his wife.

The imposing temple has two sets of priests; one set is in charge during the first fifteen days of the month, and the second set takes over for the second fifteen days. The *gurukkaḷ* and his four sons and six to eight relatives constitute the first set. Relatives are called in for special occasions and are paid each time. The second set also consists of four permanent members—the *gurukkal*'s sister's husband, his sister's son, a stepbrother, and another brother.

Both sets, I was assured, belong to the hereditary line of *gurukkaḷs* and are equal in status and authority. In case of a dispute, M. S. Gurukkaḷ is consulted and decides the question. This system is the same in all South Indian temples, although the periods may be differently divided.

*Trustees and Priests.* By special powers of the Hindu Religious Endowments Board, one key has been given to the *gurukkaḷs* as key guardians for the last eight years. The *gurukkaḷs* are responsible for conducting the *pūjās* and festivals and decorating the temple deities. The trustees decide how large a festival to have and plan it, but they consult the *gurukkaḷs,* who must carry it out. The *gurukkaḷ* is the only one allowed to touch the deity and therefore to do a *pūjā.*

*Education.* The *gurukkaḷ* studied under his father from the age of ten, learning all the temple requirements—the *Āgamas,** the *mantras,* the 32 *mudrās*†—by observation and practice alone. From other pandits, he learned Sanskrit and the Vedic portions required for his temple duties—the *Yajurveda* and the *Baudhāyanasūtra,* as well as something of other Sanskrit subjects. His studies lasted from his tenth to his twenty-eighth year; he was first allowed to perform *pūjās* at the age of eighteen or twenty. On festival occasions and for the establishment ceremony, he was permitted to conduct *pūjās* at other temples, even when his father was not present. He was married at sixteen.

*Duties of a temple priest.* The daily routine begins with a *pūjā* about 7:00 A.M.; another takes place at noon; and a third at 6:00 P.M. A special *pūjā* for the *liṅgam* is held at 9:30 P.M. For the main deity of the temple—Kapālīśvaran, a manifestation of Śiva—a *pūjā* is held four times daily; for the other deities—Gaṇeśa, Subrahmaṇya, and Devī—*pūjās* are held three times daily, and for the small shrines only once, in the morning. In performing the *pūjās,* the *gurukkaḷ* follows the same sequence each day; he begins with Gaṇeśa, then goes to Sūrya, *Śivaliṅga,* Devī, and Subrahmaṇya, and then to the smaller shrines. It takes him about an hour and a half to make a full round, including the *nāga* (snake) stones and the tree shrines. *Puṉṉai* is the chief sacred tree under which the goddess in the form of a peacock worships the *Śivaliṅga* Kapālīśvaran. The peacock is represented in stone, and a *liṅga* stands by its side underneath the tree.

Whether there are many worshipers present or not, the *gurukkaḷ* performs the *pūjās.* In 1942, during the wartime evacuation of Madras, he and his family stayed behind and conducted *pūjās* despite the lack of worshipers. He will not volunteer to tell the legends of the temple and its shrines unless he is asked by the inquisitive. Most of the worshipers, he thinks, do not know the true legends.

*Arcanas* are special *pūjās* performed only at the request of worshipers, who bring offerings of coconut, camphor, fruit, and the like. In a typical case, the worshiper hands the *gurukkaḷ* the offerings and requests that he do a *pūjā* to a particular deity, informing him of his name, *gotra,* star, and the particular desire, if any, for which he requests the *pūjā.*

The *gurukkaḷ* places the offerings before the specified shrine and says the *saṅkalpa* in Sanskrit: "On behalf of this devotee of such a name, *gotra,*

*** Manuals of practice and religious worship governing the temples.**

**† Hand gestures used by the priest in ritual.**

and star, and for the fulfillment of such and such a desire, I offer this *pūjā* to you." Sanskrit is the language of all *pūjās,* but recently there has been a demand for the use of Tamil.

Very few worshipers come for salvation (*mokṣa*). Most people resort to *arcanas* for the removal of sins or for the gratification of specific desires; they want position, wealth, power, health, successful marriage, success in examinations, and victory in legal cases and in elections. When a worshiper comes for the removal of sins, he does not name his sin. The worshiper thinks of it himself but does not tell the priest. In these cases, as in seeking salvation, he merely says: "It is my duty to see you."

If a worshiper's wish is fulfilled, he will usually return and ask that a bigger *pūjā* be performed in thanksgiving. In these, all the particulars are recited. "And if his wish is not granted, does he blame you for the failure?" "Oh, no. They do not blame me. I am only the postman. I don't open the letter; I merely transmit it to the deity."

As for providing spiritual advice, the *gurukkaḷ* said that he was not a moral guardian or spiritual guide; his job was to perform the *pūjās.* People with specific requests for *pūjās* may have been sent by an astrologer or *purohita.* They may also go for spiritual advice to Śaṅkarācārya or other *ācāryas.* Others go to doctors. People do not come to this temple to make or fulfill vows, although the custom exists elsewhere.

*Temple festivals, or* utsavas. One or two festivals occur every month. The *gurukkaḷ* must then decorate the deities, perform the *pūjās,* and carry out other duties. The major festival—the *Mahotsava* or *Brahmotsava* in March or April—consists of the following steps: (1) A flag is raised on the golden flagstaff and flies for ten days. A *pūjā* is performed the first day. (2) A fire is kept burning in the *yāgaśālā* for ten days. (3) A burning torch is drawn through the temple streets in all four directions to purify them. The rite is called the *vāstuśānti.* After dragging the torch through the four streets, the *gurukkaḷ* bathes. (4) The metal image of the temple deity, Kapālīśvaran, is decorated and placed on a palanquin each day, and on the seventh day it is placed in the temple car and taken along the four streets.[18]

*Temple congregation and attendance.* The *gurukkaḷ* was not familiar with the Western notion of a religious congregation. His temple is managed by a particular family, so far as *pūjās* are concerned. Regular worshipers, mostly Śaivites, come to it. Worshipers can make contributions for a deity at the temple office and a small payment to the *gurukkaḷ* when they receive the holy ash (saffron). Beyond this, there did not seem to be a fixed religious community for a particular temple. Worshipers come according to their religious urge; they are under no obligation to come or not to come. Even if a person does not come, he is not considered irreligious or bad. On festival days, the number of worshipers is larger than at other times. Many non-Brahmans come, including Harijans. Throwing up his hands, the *gurukkaḷ* said that he could no longer distinguish Harijans from other groups.

*A school for* Gurukkaḷs. About a week before our visit, the *gurukkaḷ* had started a school for the children of his family. Concerned about their ignorance and their inadequate preparation for their profession as temple priests, he organized the small school at the temple where they live. He teaches them how to enter, how to stand, the names of the different deities, and so forth. He demonstrates and then asks them to repeat. It does not matter if they do not yet understand the meaning; that will come later. Formerly all temples had such schools, he said, but they have "faded," and modern education does not appreciate the value of repetition and memorizing.

On the way home, the *gurukkaḷ* asked me to stop by his house to see the school. A group of about six youngsters aged from four to ten gathered to meet us. The *gurukkaḷ* asked the youngest child to step forward and recite. With his hands folded on his chest, the boy haltingly recited several Sanskrit *mantras*.

### *The Temple and Some Temple Festivals*

The Śiva temple in Mylapore, Śrī Kapālīśvara, which Dr. Raghavan and his family attend occasionally and whose head priest I interviewed, was originally located where the St. Thomé church now is. It originated in Pallava times. The present structure, however, is striking, intricately carved, brightly painted, and built along the general lines of the traditional South Indian temples: A square wall with carved towers encloses the shrines, and a rectangular temple tank adjoins the temple.

More than fifty different shrines are inside, grouped in clusters, including not only those of the chief deities, Śiva and Pārvatī, Gaṇeśa, and Subrahmaṇya, but also the nine planets, sixty-three Śaivite saints, many lesser deities, and several sacred trees and snake stones.[19] A Śaivite does not restrict himself to the worship of Śiva but considers it meritorious to make the rounds of all the shrines in a fixed order. Some of the shrines have a special significance and are worshiped on particular occasions, such as that of Saturn on Saturdays, or when things are not going well; the snake stones and sacred trees are invoked for fertility. Sometimes worshipers can be seen spending more time at one shrine, although generally they pause just long enough at a particular shrine, Gaṇeśa, for example, to go around it several times and to make obeisance before it by slapping their cheeks, holding the earlobes with crossed hands, and dipping at the knees. If the priest happens to be performing a *pūjā* to a particular image, a crowd will gather before that shrine to get a view of the image (*darśana*), heat from the camphor flame waved before the deity, and some of the *prasādam*, or blessing, from the priest in the form of holy ash and a flower or two. Then they recite a hymn and prostrate themselves before the deity.

The atmosphere in the temple yard is casual. Those making the rounds of the shrines seem absorbed and pay little attention to each other. There are always small groups standing or sitting and talking. Merchants who sell sweets, toys, cloth, flowers, and flower petals set up shop just outside the temple walls. Some merchants have small improvised shrines outside the temple. On the steps of the temple tank, where lotuses float on the surface of the water, people wash clothes or themselves.

A wealthy non-Brahman family is said to have recently renovated the

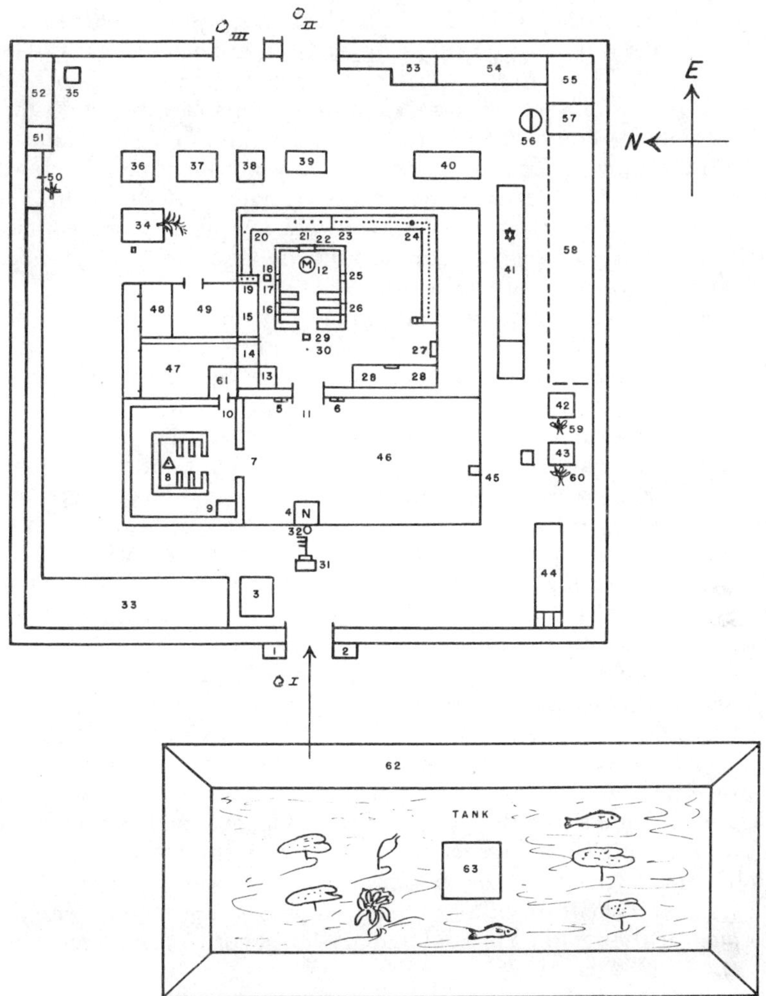


Figure 1. Plan of the Śrī Kapālīsvara Temple with a bird's-eye view of the temple tank (February 16, 1955)

temple. The trustees of the temple formerly had the power to open and close its gates, to hire and dismiss the temple "servants" (employees), to collect temple contributions, and to organize the temple festivals. Their power has now been limited by the Hindu Religious Endowment Board, which approves the hereditary temple trustees or selects new ones and supervises the expenditure of temple funds to prevent misuse and misappropriation. The Board has also announced a policy of including Harijans in the temple management and among temple servants. The office of the temple, which is in the temple yard, always appeared very active, with about six busy office workers. The temple, as an institution, is public. There is no particular owner except in rare cases, as the great Kāmākṣī shrine in Kāñcīpuram (Conjeeveram), which belongs to the Śaṅkarācārya of the Kāmakōḍi *maṭha* and the renowned Naṭarājan shrine at Cidambaram, which "belongs" to the *dīkṣitars,* the priests of that temple. The hereditary trustees of a temple are responsible for maintaining and supporting the temple. For centuries, their families have inherited lands and properties endowed for this purpose; many non-Brahman landowning aristocrats are of this class. Some of the big Śaiva non-Brahman *maṭhas* also have the duty of maintaining a whole temple, several temples, or particular services in specified temples with the resources of the properties in their custody.

In addition to the daily worship, many festivals are celebrated at the temple. Some are purely local in character, others are of all-India scope; some are based on the solar calendar, others on the lunar calendar; some are celebrated outside the temple, some only inside the temple. For the largest and most important temple festival, the annual festival (*Brahmotsava*), which comes in late spring, the deities are taken daily in procession and, toward the end of the festival, in the huge temple car (a kind of elaborately carved wooden chariot). For the lesser festivals, a palanquin or small platform is used. The movable metal images of the deities (*utsavavigraha*) are used in these processions and not the stone images (*mūlavigraha*), which are fixed. Every temple has a double set of images, one movable and one fixed.

Since it is a Śiva temple, special importance is attached to celebrations in honor of this god. One festival honors Śiva in his aspect of the cosmic dancer, Naṭarājan. Leaves, coconuts, and flowers are offered on this occasion, usually in late December or early January. Other deities are similarily worshiped on this day. During our visit at 6:30 A.M., worship was in progress to Gaṇeśa, the nine planets, Subrahmaṇya, and the temple flagstaff, among others. In the temple courtyard, a musician was leading a band of small girls and boys in a *bhajana* of devotional songs. The children carried a small drum and a harmonium. In the temple sentry box, two men of the temple choir played the long horn (*nāgasvara*) and the drum.

On the same day, Dr. Raghavan and his family held a Naṭarājan *pūjā* in his home. It took two hours to prepare special food for offerings to a garlanded painting of Naṭarājan. The *pūjā* included all *upacāras* ("attentions" offered to deities), and the entire family participated. One relative sang some Śiva songs in honor of the occasion.

*Mahāśivarātrī,* the great night of Śiva at the end of February, impressed us as the most solemn and widely celebrated Sanskritic festival of our stay in Madras. Worship starts early in the morning, lasts through the day, and continues all night. Dr. Raghavan's entire family visited the temple during the early evening. The Śiva temple precincts were full of people from about 5:00 P.M. on, and many individuals wore costumes rarely seen in the city. The Raghavans brought flowers and fruits for offerings. In the early evening, a procession with music wove through the narrow residential streets around the temple. Later in the evening, we entered the temple precincts. Crowds were at every shrine—files including young men marched around the planets' shrine. Many worshipers, especially older women, seemed to have set themselves up for the night in the temple grounds or near a favored shrine. The largest crowds were entering and leaving the major Śiva shrine, which, at least on this evening, was plainly marked with neon letters in Tamil, ŚIVA.

*A floating festival.* A less solemn occasion is the floating festival,* when the temple deities are brought out for a ride on the float in the temple tank, a block-long pond. Before the evening procession, one of the priests drags a burning stick around the temple streets to purify them. Then a band of musicians, playing instruments including a *nāgasvara,* a drum, several clarinets, and bagpipes, led a procession of the images of Śiva and Pārvatī down one of the temple streets. Two large umbrellas and gas torches were carried alongside the deities. Behind them, a group of about six Brahmans chanted the Vedas, followed by some non-Brahmans of the temple choir singing Tamil hymns. Occasionally, auto traffic on the street temporarily separated the chanters from the rest of the procession.

When the procession reached the corner of the tank farthest from the temple, the whole group moved to a float strung with electric bulbs, the images were placed in the center, and a *pūjā* was performed. A group of men on the steps of the tank began to pull the float around the tank. On the first night of the festival, the float is pulled around three times, on the second, six times, and on the third, twelve times. Ropes on pulleys connected the float to the fixed platform in the center of the tank. To keep the float from getting too close to the tank steps, a man in a small boat adjusted the pulleys.

Throughout the festival, street merchants, tattoo artists, and sideshows competed with the float. To attract attention, vendors rubbed their balloons to produce a squeak and waved pinwheels in the wind. A bright moon over the temple towers and tall palms furnished a "transcendental" backdrop for the noisy, crowded scene.

Our friends explained the purpose of the festival: All the attentions shown to an earthly ruler are shown to the divinity. Just as a king would enjoy a ride on a float, so does a god. This is a "pastime" festival like the "swing" and "hunt" festivals. There are "boat songs" with special melodies. Their explanation placed the crowd, the fireworks, and the noise in perspective. "It is a cool moonlight night; the people have come out after a warm day; it would be pleasant for anyone to take a ride on the temple float around the tank."

Māsimākam, *or* Mākam *Festival.* Not all festivals are held in the temple grounds. The *Māsi Māgha,* or *Māsimakam,* which comes in the Tamil month of Māsi (February-March), is particularly auspicious for bathing away sins and receiving boons. On this occasion, temple images are brought to the seashore.

On *Māsimakam* day, although friends had not mentioned that it was an important occasion, in fact a major festival (particularly at Kumbakōṇam in Tanjore District), an ardent *bhakta* non-Brahman acquaintance told us he wanted to take us to a big festival. We drove north-

* See photographs following page 174.

ward with him along the seashore to an area accessible to some of the poorer districts of the midcity and walked the quarter-mile or so toward the sea.

The approaches were rough and weed-grown, and fluttering advertisements told of circuses and carnivals. Thousands of people, most of them poor, were walking toward the sands. Along the paths were mendicant holy men, "holy freaks," such as a saffron-robed boy with a distorted tiny head, and sellers of balloons, flowers, plaster figures, and food. The crowd grew steadily larger. Police cars were parked at the approaches, and police were directing the foot traffic with electrified megaphones.

Large temporary pavilions spread out close to the sea. They had been erected by some of the principal temples of the city and contained portable, ornately dressed deities. Sounds of music on the beach came from the bands of itinerant families and from the musicians of various temporary temple pavilions. Other temporary sheds held sideshows, waters from the sacred rivers, and relics.

Whenever a deity was moved or became visible, the crowd pressed forward. Because the festival, propitiating Jupiter, among other planets, is held on a full-moon night, the crowds became even greater after nightfall.

### Sthapati, *or Image-maker, and the Consecration of a Temple Image*

Before a temple or domestic image can have any sacred powers, it must be consecrated in a special ceremony. I observed one such ceremony in a small temple in a Madras suburb at the invitation of an image-maker (*sthapati*).

The street on which the *sthapati* lived is called Kallukkāran Street or Stonemason Street, after the numerous families of stonemasons and image-makers who once lived there. Now only one such family was left on the street, the *sthapati*'s. He lived there with his wife, his daughter, his son, and a younger brother. His place of work was on the ground in front just off the street, and the living quarters were behind a partition. The *sthapati*'s family had lived in Mylapore for eight generations, having come from a village in South Arcot District. A framed picture of his father, who had recently died at the age of fifty-six, was reverently brought out. The father was holding a palm-leaf manuscript. The *sthapati* explained that his father had been something of a scholar and had left six manuscripts to the family.*

The *sthapati* himself is thirty-four. He is the only one of seven brothers now practicing his father's profession in Mylapore. A younger brother, aged twenty-eight, makes images for a temple in the north near Aijmer. All the other brothers, except for one aged twenty-two, who is assisting him, are employed in related crafts in Madras. The oldest, who is thirty-six, works as a metal-caster in the Madras School of Arts. The youngest, aged eighteen, is an engraving assistant in the same school, and another, a man of twenty-five, is an artist in a Tamil journal's office.

The family belongs to the Kammāḷan caste—a generic name. They are also called Viśvakarman Brahmans, one of the five *gotras* of artisans. The

* See photographs following page 174.

other four were founded by Manu, Maya, Tvaṣṭṛ, and Śilpin, although the *gotras* themselves have different names. The name Bhāṣyam Sthapati means that the image-maker belongs to the Pratinisi *gotra,* whose founder is Viśvajñāna (or Viśvakarman). His family worships Subrahmaṇya, and the community as a whole, including the family, worships the goddess Kāmākṣīyammaṉ.[20]

The *sthapati* was modest about his technique. It is very ancient, he said, and the lore had been handed down by tradition. He melts the metal in small containers over a fire in the ground. The fire is fanned by a small hand-bellows, not directly but through a connecting hole in the ground. Both the container and the bellows he used were modern products. The molten metal is poured into a kind of plaster-of-paris mold made of a fine grade of sand that the *sthapati* gets from the river bed. He told me that the mold was an innovation that he had introduced. His father did not know about the fine sand and used only clay. The mold is built up around a model of the image. The model is made of wax (*kuṅkiliyam*) and castor oil. When the mold is fired, the wax runs out and the metal can be poured in through holes left for the purpose. In other words, he uses a variant of the *cire perdu* (lost-wax) method.

An order for an image is usually placed only by the deity's name, with no picture or detailed description. The *sthapati* knows the different images well and makes a sketch from which to model the wax. In drawing the sketch, he preserves the image's traditional proportions. Taking a thin strip of palm leaf, the *sthapati* showed me how by folding and refolding it he could mark the proportions without using any rigid straight edge. He then quickly sketched one of the deities in the *tribhaṅgi* pose. He noted that the chest was double the length of the head, the waist was just the length of the head, the left hand was one and a half times the length of the face, and the right hand three-quarters as long as the face.[21] (See Figure 2.)

Alongside the *sthapati,* an old man was hammering a silver piece of metal. He was a metalworker from Kumbakōṇam in Tanjore district and a specialist in the making of breastplates. The present piece had been ordered by a local temple for a stone image of Saturn that was to be consecrated the next morning, and the *sthapati* invited me to go to the ceremony. He gave me a circular with a drawing of the Saturn image that announced the ceremony.

On the way to the temple the next morning, we talked about the clients for images. The Āñjaneya temple—named after Hanumān—had ordered the metal cover for a fixed price of 200 rupees. The *sthapati*'s father had made a bronze image of Hanumān for the temple and several other images. Recently, the demand for temple images had increased. Formerly, the clients, the temple patrons, were mainly kings and Zamindars. Now people get together and contribute toward the purchase of a temple image. Individuals also order images for domestic shrines and other religious purposes; these are similar to the temple images but smaller. He also sells some images, especially the bronze Naṭarājan, to the Handicraft Emporium and to the Victoria Technical Institute, which cater to tourists.

The most common images the temples order from him are those of

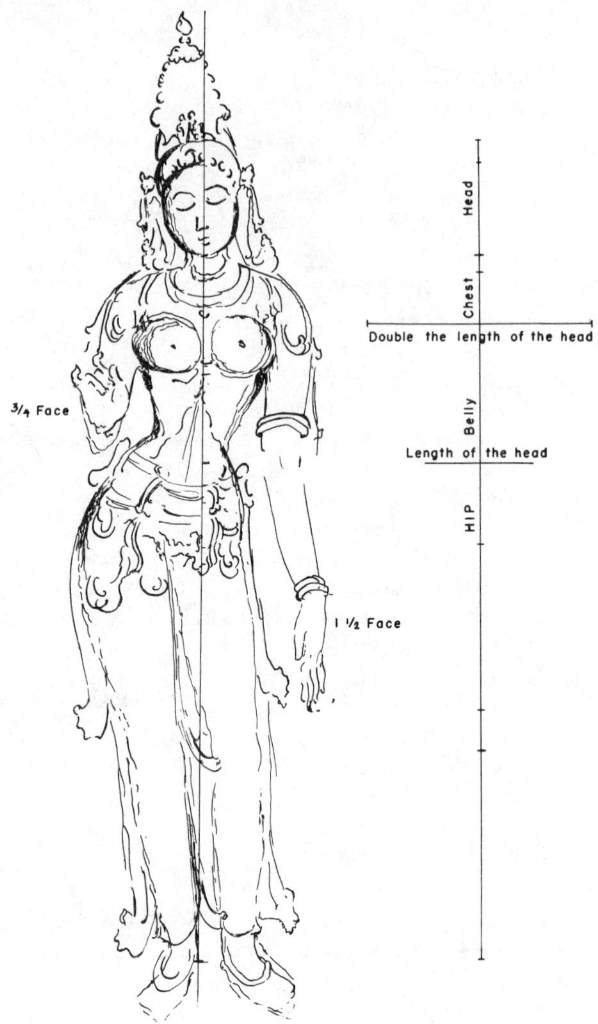


Figure 2. Tribhaṅgi pose

Subrahmaṇya, Gaṇeśa, Rāma, Krishna, Somaskanda, and the goddesses Piḍāri and Māriyamman.

Abhiṣekam *ceremony.* Almost all of these and several other deities were represented in the small temple where the *abhiṣekam* was about to be performed. It was a small temple among huts and houses in an old suburb of Madras. When we arrived it was raining, and a small crowd was already waiting under umbrellas for the ceremony to begin. The front enclosure of the temple housed separate shrines for the nine planets; also shrines for Gaṇeśa and Śiva; Rāma, Sītā, Lakṣmaṇa, Bharata, and Hanumān; Subrahmaṇyam and his two wives, Vaḷḷi and Devasenā; a large shrine for Āñjaneya (Hanumān), after whom the temple is named.

The shrine, like the others, was guarded by two stone temple guardians, or *dvārapālakas.* Three different images of Hanumān stood in the shrine: a large permanent stone one, a small one of green crystal, and the movable bronze image made by the *sthapati*'s father. A shrine for Śrīnivāsa Perumāḷ, a form of Viṣṇu, completed the shrines on the front side of the temple. All the shrines contained, in addition to the main deity, the deity's animal "vehicle," and other objects. The Gaṇeśa shrine contained a *liṅgam* in a round base, the *avaidya,* and, as we paused before it, one man explained that the two symbols represented the cosmos. Another agreed: "Yes, the male and female principles are the origin of the cosmos, the container and the contained."

Among the shrines at the rear of the temple was a standing stone image of Gandhi, a pair of wire eyeglass frames on his nose and his crooked wooden walking stick leaning against the wall. The priest said that the same *pūjā* is performed for the Gandhi figure as for the temple deities, with Vedic *mantras.* On January 30, the day of Gandhi's death, a special service is performed, and food is distributed to poor people. To the right of the Gandhi statue were some *nāga,* or snake, stones at the foot of a pipal tree and a mango tree. These trees represent a married pair, and women without children come to propitiate the deities. A table altar with five brass pots of water on it stood a little to the right in front of the trees. The water pots were being sanctified for the ceremony by the Vedic chanting of four priests, who poured ghee into a fire. One of the priests referred to a notebook handwritten in the *grantha* script;* another had a printed book, with parallel passages in Sanskrit and Tamil. To the right of the priests was a *pāmbu puṟṟa,* or snake pit, and in front of this the sacred *tulasī* plant. To the extreme right of these stood the main Saturn shrine, the object of the day's *abhiṣekam* ceremony.

This temple is only about eighteen years old, and about 500 people come to it regularly. They are mostly Brahmans of all sects living in the suburb, but the founder of the temple, a *mantrika* who says he can cure insanity and snake bites, has made a special point of getting non-Brahmans as well to come to the temple. The *mantrika,* a middle-aged man with intense eyes, smiled as all this was explained to me. He nodded approvingly as a bystander told the visitor, "Yes, it is a well-known fact that *mantras* can draw out the venom of a poisonous snake bite."

One of the functionaries then informed us that people had gathered and the ceremony could now be completed. The chanting stopped. A small procession, led by a horn, drums, and cymbals, was formed around the brass pots of water. A priest lit a sacrificial lamp from a fire, put a peeled banana on a spit, and, to the accompaniment of a bell, poured ghee from a small cup over the banana into the fire. The *mantrika* cut a lemon and squeezed it over the brass pots. Three men came forward, lifted one of the small brass pots, and placed it on the head of an old man. Just as the pot touched the old man's head, he shook and trembled and would have collapsed if the three carriers had not caught and supported him. A bystander remarked, "God himself has entered into the pot and that is why he couldn't carry it."

* The *grantha* script was developed in Tamil country for writing Sanskrit.

The whole procession, with men carrying the four brass vessels, walked around the temple once, stopping finally in front of the Saturn shrine. With horns blowing and bells ringing, the metal plate was placed on the image, water from the vessels was sprinkled over it, and lamps were waved in front of it. The crowd surged forward to touch the flames and to be sprinkled with some of the sanctified water, which they caught in the palms of their hands and sipped.

The *sthapati* said that the idol-maker plays an important role in these ceremonies. It is he who "opens the eyes of the image." He explained that he does not finish the eyes of the image in his shop but comes with his tools to the temple when the image is installed and draws a circle around the eyes to open them. He had done this for the Saturn image the day before. The *sthapati* told me he performs a *pūjā* for Ganeśa before he casts an image. He and his father shared the same regard for the images they made for others as they have for their own. His family, he added, is quite religious. He does not go to the meetings of the antireligious people, because that would hurt his profession.

The *sthapati* likes best to work on the Naṭarājan image because he can improve it. I bought two different Naṭarājans from him and saw that he does get an individual variation into his work.

The *sthapati* told me that he had watched his father work a long time before he was taught the proportions. Depending on his interest, his father would teach him on an auspicious day. He started with wax models. Some mistakes were made at first, but not many. No special ceremony was held when he made his first image, but he was very happy about his success. Even taking into account his improvement of the clay medium, he thinks that his father's wax models were cruder than his own. Each worker has a somewhat different way of working, and the *sthapati* thinks that he can recognize different workers' products.

Only one other family of *sthapatis* lives in Madras, but a state association of *sthapatis* had recently been formed. It is called the Tamiḻnāḍu Śilpin Art Association, has the purpose of fixing image prices, and now numbers ten members. The association has asked the central government for a grant of 30,000 rupees to develop their art in Tamiḻnāḍu. The *sthapati* thinks there is every chance that they will get it. The money would be used in part for a school and teachers.*

His father, the *sthapati* said, had some books on the art. They had been taken to the family's village during the war and would be brought back to the city eventually. His father's books included five important manuscripts on *Śilpaśāstra—Mānasāram, Mayamatam, Kāśyapam, Karmakoṣṭham,* and *Mūlastambham*. The last, he said, goes back more than 100 years. Dr. Raghavan later told me that he knew of the first three, which had been printed, but that he had not heard of the last two.

The *grantha* script is used in these family books. The *sthapati* knows the script but does not need to use the books. He said that he had learned

* A government school for *sthapatis* at Mahābalipuram and a government manufacturing center for bronze images and artware have since been established. The Śaṅkarācārya of Kāñcī has also sponsored annual Āgama Śilpin conferences attended by large numbers of traditional *sthapatis,* archaeologists, and other scholars.

the important things by heart from his father. When he has some special problem, he refers to the books. He has consulted them on such questions as the origin of his caste, the exact name of an image, or how to finish an image. For each image, he knows a Sanskrit *śloka* that describes its form. The *ślokas* must be recited before examiners to prove that one is a *sthapati.* We asked him to recite a *śloka,* and the young Sanskritist with us thought that the one he then intoned was a very corrupt rendering. He asked the *sthapati* for the Tamil version and translated that into English:

> The chest should be like the face of a young cow,
> thighs like the plantain, nose like the *sesamum* flower,
> feet like the tortoise: This is the form of Rāma.

The *sthapati* sketched a picture of Rāma to illustrate the *śloka.* He began with the chest, which did look like the face of a cow. Then, at one side, he drew a *sesamum* flower, a plantain, and a tortoise to show their resemblance to the nose, thighs, and feet.

### Mantrika *and Mental Healer*

The *mantrika* came to see me the next day, at my invitation, accompanied by the temple priest. The priest was a Śrīvaiṣṇava, and the *mantrika* was a Smārta Brahman. The *mantrika* said that he was sixty-five years old and that he had inherited his profession from his father. He was very proud of his father, especially of his name, Jata-Vallabha Ramaswamy Aiyer.* His father had come from a village in Chingleput District and was a Sanskrit scholar. The *mantrika* had come to Madras thirty-five years ago and lives with his wife, daughter, daughter-in-law, and grandchildren in West Mambalam, Madras City.

The *mantrika* is not learned in Sanskrit, but he says that he learned all the *mantras* from his father, the short ones first, the longer ones later. Until the age of twelve, he was like other children, but at that age he assumed the sacred thread, was married, and began performing *pūjās.*

The *mantrika* tried to explain the theory of *śakti,* the female divine principle, which he said was at the basis of his practice. Since he knew little English, and his interpreter, the temple priest, was not familiar with the theory, the exposition was not very coherent. There are four kinds of *śakti,* he said; *jñānaśakti* for expanding the brain and concentration, *bodhaśakti* for diagnosing ailments, *kriyāśakti* for treatment and for building houses and temples, and *icchāśakti* for obtaining specific objects of desire.[22] The *mantrika* regarded himself as especially qualified in diagnosing possession by evil spirits. He can also prescribe treatment for different ailments, especially for ghosts, of which he has from fifty to a hundred cases daily. Ghosts, he said, are mental troubles for which he has some special herbs as well as amulets, or *yantras.* Different kinds of ghosts, or *ātmās,* can "catch" a person and make him hang himself, fall from a building, and do other strange things.[23] The *jaṭāmuni* is a giant ghost;

* "Aiyer" is a Smārta honorific, a Tamil form of the Sanskrit word, *ārya.* Ramaswamy a famous deity name. Jata-Vallabha is a title gained for proficiency in Veda and recitation.

the *ladamuni* a dancing ghost; the *kāmamuni* a ghost that looks like a dark shadow; and the *śūramuni* resembles a fire and feels hot to the touch. To determine what kind of ghost is troubling a patient and how serious it is, the *mantrika* takes a lime and gives it to his client, asking him to smell it. Then the *mantrika* looks at the lime under a magnifying glass. If it turns red, the case is hopeless; a yellow color is a good sign. He then places the lime in a small box and concentrates on it. If the lime shakes in the box, a ghost troubles the patient. The *mantrika* can see the body of the patient in the lime and can tell which part of his body is affected. If an intermediary has touched the lime, he will see that body. Because a lime has been handled many times at the market, one must wash it well before using it. He was emphatic that he never puts questions to the patient or permits him to talk before the lime is examined. Just by looking at the lime, he said, he could also tell what I was thinking. Europeans, too, come to see him. They do not have the same diseases as Indians because they are not afraid of ghosts. They do not have "mind troubles," only body sickness; and they want to know how to invest their money.

The best time for the *mantrika* to see clients is just before sunrise, after he has performed his morning *pūjās*. He can also diagnose after sunset, but he does it mostly in the mornings. He learned the lime *pūjā* from his father, who let him watch and then gave him small cases to try. It is important, the *mantrika* said, not to become frightened while performing *pūjās*, for they are highly dangerous and may even be fatal to the performer. One of his sons had become frightened during a *pūjā* and had died at the age of 18, only three months after his marriage.

Such *pūjās* may also be harmful to others. The *mantrika* knew two brothers, one of whom, a doctor, had gone to the United States while the other stayed in India and lost the family wealth. The one that stayed home called in a *mantrika* to work mischief against the doctor. When the doctor returned, he called in another *mantrika* to counteract the first. Now the first *mantrika* cannot eat and loses money, and his clothes inexplicably catch fire. Since a kind of professional code prescribes that *mantrikas* will not harm one another, the first *mantrika* found himself in trouble because the god to whom he performed his *pūjās* turned against him.

The *mantrika* told more stories to demonstrate the power of *mantrikas* in general and his own powers in particular. Once he had gone to a meeting called by Svāmī Śaṅkarācārya. At the gate the constable stopped him, because he mistook him for a non-Brahman. The *mantrika* scratched one of his own arms to let the blood flow. The constable fainted, and the Svāmī himself came out to usher the *mantrika* into the *pūjā* room.

The *mantrika* claims he was the first to take Harijans into temples and into Kāñcīpuram. He said he had done so because he believed that "God wants everybody." He then drew the *Oṃ* symbol on a piece of paper and, taking a key, traced it on my face. The first man, he said, was descended from a frog or a monkey. Did I know why man was called a monkey? Because when he combs his hair before a mirror he looks like one. There is no caste or creed.

He does not charge his patients fees. They give what they like in presents or money. If he is called out of Madras, he asks for train fare and hotel costs. When a new temple is built, and he is asked to write a *mantra* for the foundation stone, he gets a fee. He wrote a special *mantra* for the *abhiṣekam* ceremony the day before.

Although he prescribes herbs for others, the *mantrika* has never taken any medicine himself, because he follows a proper diet and believes in God.

The *mantrika* has never gone to a "modern" doctor. He would be willing to accept physical therapy and surgical operations from modern doctors but not their medicines. They can be trusted when they feel the pulse, but not when they use the stethoscope. Because many modern doctors just talk to the patient and do not feel the pulse before prescribing medicines, he cannot have faith in them. He had once seen a doctor examine a patient with a stethoscope when the earpieces were not even in his ears, but around his neck. Turning to me, he said: "If you get a fever, don't go to a modern doctor; just do not eat for a day and it will go away."

The *mantrika*'s patients are roughly 75 per cent non-Brahmans and 25 per cent Brahmans; they include about as many men as women and include both rich and poor. When a rich patient offers to give him anything he wants if he will cure him, the *mantrika* jokingly replies by asking for half of Madras. Both villagers and townspeople come to him for treatment.

The *mantrika* invited me to watch him practice his art. The next day, I went to the same suburb where I had gone with the *sthapati*. The *mantrika*'s house was very near the temple. It was modest, with two main rooms and a closet-sized room, which he called his *pūjā* room. He introduced me to an elderly man I had not seen before and to several members of his own family. Some children and neighbors who had gathered in the doorway were sent away. I was handed a slip of paper, one side of which listed sixteen different "kinds of *śakti* that exist in mankind." He said this list would explain what he had talked about the previous day.[24]

On the reverse side of the paper was a diagram and list of eight directions (*tikku*) with a god (*devatā*) and planet (*navagraha*) for each.[25] The *mantrika* said he also had some knowledge of astrology and practiced it occasionally as a sideline. He brought out a large white card, measuring about 1 foot by 2 feet, in the center of which was a human figure with a planet marked for each part of the body: the sun for the head, the moon for the neck, Mercury for the arms, Jupiter for the waist, Venus for the stomach, and *Ketu* for the feet. Distributed about the figure were the "twelve zodiacal houses," arranged in the following manner:

| | | | |
|---|---|---|---|
| *Mīna* | *Meṣa* | *Ṛṣabha* | *Mithuna* |
| *Kumbha* | | | *Kaḍakam* |
| *Makara* | | | *Siṃha* |
| *Dhanus* | *Vṛścika* | *Tulā* | *Kanni* |

This system of correspondences, the *mantrika* explained, was helpful in diagnosing bodily diseases. Only recently, a lady had come to him thinking that she was the victim of another *mantrika,* but he had found that she was suffering from a disease in a particular part of her body and had told her that a doctor could cure her.

*A case of ghosts.* In order to give a demonstration of how he diagnoses and cures "ghosts," the *mantrika* put away the card and asked the elderly interpreter to describe his own case. The interpreter said that about two years before, ghosts had come and troubled him every night for two or three minutes. They were black "appearances" like shadows and would stand before his bed or walk in the air without speaking or touching anything. His wife and daughter occasionally saw them, too, and the whole family would shout together sometimes. The interpreter assured me that he believed in God and was a devotee of Viṣṇu. His prayers had brought no relief. He had also consulted other *mantrikas,* who had been unable to help him. A friend had recommended that he come to the *mantrika* for help.

Using the procedure of diagnosis with a lime described above, the *mantrika* had told our interpreter the name of his enemy and where he lived and had further assured the man that he would have no relief from ghosts until an amulet (*yantra*) that had been buried under a certain tree in his enemy's village had been dug up. At the interpreter's request, the *mantrika* and a friend had gone to the village, where they found the *yantra* in that exact spot and brought it back to Madras. The *mantrika,* by performing further *pūjās* with his box, found which spirit (*devatā*) was responsible and, by applying counter-*japa,* stopped the ghost's effects. The interpreter had had no more trouble with ghosts, nor had his wife or daughter. He then showed us a small silver *yantra,* which the *mantrika* had given him for future protection.

On further questioning, I learned that the enemy was the father-in-law of the interpreter's son. The son had married about five years before and had lived happily with his wife in Madras. The daughter often visited her father's village, but the interpreter had been to her father's village only once after the marriage and never before. The father-in-law visited his daughter about once a year. The interpreter had never openly quarreled with him and had never mentioned the ghosts to him. "What good would it do? He would only go back to his village and get his *mantrika* to do worse things." He preferred to avoid trouble in the family and so kept silent. He thought that the father-in-law's motive was to separate the family.

The interpreter's son is a clerk in the railway office. The interpreter is a retired high school teacher who had taught English, science, and mathematics. He now lives about six or seven miles from the *mantrika* and regards him as a good friend. He had seen him cure many other cases of ghosts and could testify to his skill. Not long before, a sick man had been brought to him. The *mantrika,* after making the lime diagnosis, said the patient would die in two days and refused to take the case. "It happened so."

After this introduction, the *mantrika* suggested that I might want to test his skill. I was given a notebook with a list of questions in English, such as: Should I lend any money? Will I continue to have friends? Will I pass the examinations? Should I invest in stocks? I was asked to pick one of the questions by number, then to choose another number up to 7, and finally to look on another page of the notebook for the answer to my question. I had picked the question about friends, but the answer did not correspond, since it said it was safe to lend money. The *mantrika* said that he had compiled these notebooks in English especially for Europeans. He showed me another notebook, a very old one, which had come to him from his father and contained special *mantras* for different ailments, arrays of numbers, and much else. He also showed me some newspaper clippings about his role in the fight to open temples to Harijans.

Not at all discouraged by the failure of the first test, he told me he would now demonstrate the lime diagnosis. Handing me a clean scrap of paper, he asked me to write on it a question that I wanted him to answer, then to fold the paper, and place it in an envelope. Not knowing then how we would return to the United States I wrote, "Will we return home by plane or boat?" The *mantrika,* without looking at the paper, went into his *pūjā* room to concentrate. I was permitted to watch at a distance through the open door. On the walls of the room were *śakti* images, masks, and effigies. On a small table before which the *mantrika* sat were two monkey skulls painted a rose color, several silver and bronze images, and the box with a silver cover. Inside the box was a black stone carving of Hanumān, covered with a black ointment. The *mantrika* placed a lime inside the box; taking a wooden stick with a cloth wrapped around one end, he gently tapped the monkey skulls and the lime. After each tapping, he would look intently into the box and write with chalk on a small slate. He said later he saw "moving pictures" on the black interior of the box. After ten minutes, he emerged with the slate and asked me to open the envelope and read my question. After hearing it, he excitedly pointed to a small drawing in one corner of the slate, which he said represented an airplane. We all examined it; to me, it could also have represented a boat. Then he told us that there was more on the slate. He had written in Tamil that I had no children, that like a missionary I was more interested in traveling to foreign lands than in staying home, and that I was not much interested in women.

On leaving the *mantrika*'s house, I suddenly remembered that I had never been asked to touch or smell the lime; I still wonder whether this was an oversight or whether it was because he was not diagnosing a disease or a case of ghosts. In any case, we returned to the United States by plane, although we tried several times to get passage on a ship.

## Competing Self-Definitions of Sanskritic Hinduism: Orthodoxy and the Sects

The encounter with non-Vedic scriptures and with some non-Brahman specialists came as something of a surprise, since I had assumed that all the representatives of Sanskritic Hinduism were Brahmans and that the Vedas were the ultimate scriptural authority for the Great Tradition. But

Dr. Raghavan assured me that there were many non-Brahman representatives of the Great Tradition and arranged for me to interview two of them, as well as a Śrīvaiṣṇava Brahman who was a Vedic scholar and also an expert on non-Vedic rituals. My discussions with these people obliged me to revise my conception of the structure of Sanskritic Hinduism in order to take account of variations in caste, sect, and linguistic region. I shall first describe the interviews and then analyze their implications for a revised definition of the structure of Sanskritic Hinduism.

### *Śrīvaiṣṇavite* Ācārya, *or Domestic Priest*

*Family.* The *ācārya* comes from a Brahman family who have been Śrīvaiṣṇava domestic priests (*ācāryas*) and pandits for about fifteen generations. He was born in Kumbakōṇam in Tanjore District and still lives there with his father, mother, wife, and two young sons. Occasionally he comes to Madras to lecture on Vedic topics, see disciples, and participate at cultural functions. On one of these visits, Dr. Raghavan arranged an interview with him.

*Education.* Between the ages of five and twelve, the *ācārya* had attended an "English" school, but when he was twelve his father had started him on serious Sanskrit studies. He had studied the *kāvya* and *nāṭakas, Mīmāṃsā,* Vedānta, and the *śāstras.* He also learned his family Veda, the *Yajurveda,* by reciting it after his father many times. He had gone on to learn some of the other Vedas, three *maṇḍala* of the *Ṛgveda,* six *khaṇḍas* of the *Atharvaveda,* and portions of the *Sāmaveda.* He explained that every Brahman gives his *gotra, sūtra,* and Veda as a greeting. His family belongs to the *Sotamarṣaṇa gotra,* the *Āpastambasūtra,* and the *Yajurveda.*

He had learned the Purāṇas and the Epics by himself; by the age of three or four, he already knew the stories, having heard them from his mother and at public recitations.

The pandit continued his Sanskrit studies until the age of twenty-four. He had been married at fifteen. Since turning twenty-four, he has spent most of his time in "propagating the Hindu religion" and in Vedic studies. An outstanding Vedic scholar, he considers himself a specialist in *Mīmāṃsā.*

On his father's death, the pandit will, as the oldest son, "automatically succeed" the father as *ācārya* to about 300 Vaiṣṇava families in Kumbakōṇam and scattered parts of India. Until then, his father must "do it all"; it would be "the greatest sin" to replace him. Even if the son moved to Delhi, he would not be permitted to serve his father's clients there; they would have to send for the father or go back to Kumbakōṇam.* He is allowed to teach disciples and to lecture on Hinduism, but not to perform any of the rituals. Even when he accompanies his father to ceremonies, he sits and watches without taking part.[26]

*Vedic and Śrīvaiṣṇava heritages.* In the *ācārya*'s family, Śrīvaiṣṇava doctrine and Vedic culture mix. They have inherited two lines: the

* Dr. Raghavan later told me that this is not a uniform practice, that younger members of the family, if apprenticed, are allowed to officiate.

Vedic, which is both a family line and a spiritual one, and the Vaiṣṇava, which is only a religious line going back to Nāthamuni, a Śrīvaiṣṇava saint of the tenth century.

Both Vedic sacrifices and Vaiṣṇava rituals are performed by the family, but there is an important difference between them. The Vedic sacrifices must be supported by the *śruti* or *smṛti* texts; the Śrīvaiṣṇava rituals are sanctioned only by tradition. Moreover, the Vedic rituals are common for all Brahmans; the Śrīvaiṣṇava ones are not and are also performed by some non-Brahman followers of Śrīvaiṣṇavism. In the Vedic rituals, a priest is not strictly necessary, although the householder may use a *purohita* as an assistant "in place of a book," to pass along the appropriate *mantras.* No intermediary is necessary between God and the worshiper. The *purohita* performs the rituals on behalf of the householder. There are two major kinds of Vedic ritual: *ekāgni* (one fire), an individual rite, and *tretāgni* (three fires), one that requires assistants. Similarly, some Śrīvaiṣṇava domestic rituals are performed by the householder, such as the daily *pūjās,* and some, e.g., the *Puruṣasūktahoma,* require the assistance of others.

Temples are not Vedic institutions but are post-Vedic. Temple rituals are governed by the laws of the Āgamas. These Āgamic scriptures are of two kinds: Śaiva *śakta* and Vaiṣṇava.* Āgamas are not Vedic in the details of the ritual; they only employ Vedic *mantras.* The Vaiṣṇava and other Āgamas that govern temples require a temple priest through whom alone the worshiper can approach the shrine. In each of the sects, the temple priest has a different name. Vaiṣṇava temple priests are called *bhaktācāryas;* Śaiva ones are called *śivācāryas* or *gurukkaḷs.* There are also non-Brahman temple priests, especially in village temples, who are called *pūjāris.* "Temples and priests always go together."

Rituals are usually classified into three categories: *nitya* are performed without expectation of return and only to please the gods; *naimittika* are occasional sacrifices; and *kāmya* make specific requests, often for worldly pleasures. Anything that aims at something other than God's unity is *kāmya.*

Women are not included in Śrīvaiṣṇava rituals but are included in Vedic ones.

*Functions of a Śrīvaiṣṇava* ācārya. The *ācārya* is called upon to perform such ceremonies as birthdays, deaths, marriages, and daily *pūjās,* as well as two special Śrīvaiṣṇava rituals: the *samāśrayaṇam* and the *śaraṇāgati.* The former is the initiation ceremony for Brahmans and, after a child's eighth year, for non-Brahmans. It consists of five parts: the bestowal of a baptismal name, branding and wearing of caste marks, special *mantras,* and authority to perform idol worship. The *śaraṇāgati* ritual is kept secret and must be administered only by *ācāryas.*

The *ācārya* is also expected to teach Śrīvaiṣṇava doctrine to his clients, in his own house or theirs, though not in temples. Payment is for the specific services he performs, according to the inclination of the client. He also receives some support from the special disciples whom he teaches. In Kumbakōṇam, ten families of Vaiṣṇava *ācāryas* serve about 1,000 families

* There are also Āgamic texts on the worship of Sūrya, Gaṇapati, and Kumāra.

of the sect. Some families of Smārtas also call upon the *ācārya*'s father to conduct Vedic rituals for them. According to his rough estimate, some 1,000 practicing Śrīvaiṣṇava families and 2,000 such Smārta families live in Madras City.

*Personal views and interests.* The *ācārya* plans to bring up his oldest boy as an *ācārya*. The boy will not be allowed to do nonreligious work, since he must continue the family tradition. The younger son will probably go into some other line of work to help support the family. The *ācārya*'s own younger brother is working in a bank.

The *ācārya* has a strong interest in religious studies and in reconciling religion and science. He made many references to "P.C.," which was his abbreviation of the title of Edward Tylor's *Primitive Culture.* He had also read other works of Tylor's, John Lubbock's *Prehistoric Times,* and James Frazer's *Golden Bough.* He usually reads in the library after preaching. Tylor gives much information, he finds, about Sūrya and sun worship. He says he believes anthropology should be begun during the early years of one's life, like mathematics; he teaches his disciples that the world needs to know more about comparative religion, the science of religion, the philosophy of religion, the psychology of religion, and the history of religion. The present clash between Dravidians and Aryans arises because of ignorance; if more people studied anthropology, they would not make such mistakes, he says.

In his talks on the radio and in public lectures, the *ācārya* tries to approach religion in a scientific manner by explaining the mystic devotion to Krishna and why it is necessary to worship God. His mission in life is to revive the Vedic ideals, he said; he has written for a leading English-language newspaper articles on Vedic polity, Vedic morality, and the position of women in the Vedas. His viewpoint is that the development of democracy, from Aristotle to the French and Russian revolutions, can be better understood with the help of the Vedas.

The *ācārya* asked me to send him some modern books about the relation between science and religion. So that I would not send books already known to him, he mentioned that he had read David Hume's *Treasure House of Living Religions,* works by Sir Arthur Eddington, Sir James Jeans, Max Planck, Alfred North Whitehead, General Jan Smuts, and J. T. Sunderland's *The Existence of God Proved.*

### *Śaivasiddhānta Scholar*

To acquaint me with a non-Brahman scholarly representative of Sanskritic Hinduism, Dr. Raghavan arranged a talk with a Śaivasiddhānta scholar, who held a bachelor of arts degree and a teaching license. The scholar spoke English well. Born in Madras sixty-eight years before, he was a retired district education officer who had worked in the Madras State Department of Education from 1915 to 1943. After his retirement, a Southern university asked him to serve as registrar for three years. Although he was the first in his family to get an "English" education, the scholar has continued his family's active devotion to Hindu religion and, especially, to Śaivasiddhānta.* His father had studied with two famous teachers who were also Sanskrit scholars, and he himself had been initiated by a famous guru, Śrī Pambam Swamigal. He has written and lectured on Śaivasiddhānta,[27] has been active in a Śaivasiddhānta association, and has helped to organize weekly group-prayer meetings.

Religious instruction in the schools was very much on the scholar's mind; he deplored recent trends in the "modern" schools. As a district education officer, he had supervised elementary and secondary schools in towns and villages and had tried to provide a greater role for moral and religious instruction. The schools, with the exception of the Christian ones, did not show much enthusiasm for religious instruction, however. Some use was made in schools of selections from Tamil literature—the *Tirukkuṟaḷ* and Auvaiyār's alphabet song, but little more. One of the obstacles to introducing more religion, he had found, was the "English" method of teaching, which distrusted abstractions and taught the child "only what is in the region of the five senses." This method does not make use of the child's powers of memory and overlooks the possibility that he can memorize many things that will be of value when he grows up. The scholar still remembered much of what he had learned sixty years before. According to the older method, after the children had learned to read and write, the teacher would read and give the meaning of the passage, then the children would recite the same passage from memory the next day. In addition, they heard purāṇic reciters in the temples and other places.

*Religious revival.* As the years went by, the older method deteriorated, and interest in religion slackened. During the 1930's, a revival set in as a reaction to the attacks made by the Dravidian movement. The attacks had political and economic bases and were aimed at the Brahman community's alleged dominant position. Since Hindu religion was also attacked in the process, non-Brahmans such as himself had also felt threatened and had taken steps to counteract the "Drāviḍas." In 1929 and 1930, he had sent a questionnaire to the Śaiva associations proposing a conference to discuss the anti-Hindu situation, as well as such questions as what a Śaiva should believe about Śaivism, God, and the purpose of life. The subsequent meeting was attended by about 100 representatives of the associations, and a statement was issued. A second and larger meeting, sponsored by the non-Brahman svāmīs of two major Śaivite *maṭhas* followed. At the second meeting, which was attended by about 2,500 people, the statement of the previous meeting was discussed and amplified to include a section on the importance of wearing sect marks. Brahmans also attended the meeting in large numbers.

*Saints and sacred scriptures of Śaivism.* The Śaivas look upon four Tamil poet-saints as their chief *ācāryas:* Appar, Sambandar, Sundarar, and Māṇikkavācagar. Between the second and eighth centuries A.D., these saints defended Hinduism against Buddhism and Jainism. A collection of sacred hymns in Tamil, called *Tēvāram,* was written by the first three men, and another collection, written by the fourth, is called *Tiruvācakam.*

Śaivas accept as their authoritative scripture the Śaiva Āgamas in San-

* *Śaivasiddhānta* refers to the scriptural texts, theology, and sect of Tamil Śaivism.

skrit and the Vedas, as well as the Purāṇas and Epics. But a portion of their scriptures is also in Tamil; besides the *Tēvāram* and *Tiruvācakam* it includes a larger collection of hymns, the Tamil *Tirumuṟais;* a collection of 3,000 stanzas, the *Tirumantiram,* which were composed between the third and sixth centuries; and fourteen philosophical treatises, the *Siddhāntaśāstras,* which expound the philosophy of Śaivasiddhānta. One of the most important treatises is the *Śivajñānabodham,* which contains the essence of Śaivism and was written about the thirteenth century. Although all these works are in Tamil, they derive their authority from the Vedas and the Śaiva *Āgamas.*

*The basic elements of Śiva worship.* Śiva worship, the scholar said, is found all over India and in some respects is pre-Aryan. Its basic elements include worship of the *Śivaliṅga,* in which the Lord without form is seen in one's own soul; the wearing of the sacred ashes; utterance of the five sacred syllables, *na-maś-śi-vā-ya;* and the wearing of the sacred beads (*rudrākṣa*). Specific aspects of worship and belief will depend on the individual's stage of spiritual development. Subsidiary deities and other *mantras* may also be added. Although the *Śivaliṅga* is worshiped in temples by every Śaivite, each individual has his own deity and will change deities according to his stage of development. There are four stages of development, or paths, for Śaivites; *caryā, kriyā, yoga,* and *jñāna.** The last is the highest, and it leads to loving communion with the Lord. Both householders and *sannyāsins* (wandering holy men) may follow these paths, but now there is a dearth of *sannyāsins.*

The original Śaivites, he said, were Brahmans, but all grades of non-Brahmans—Bāṇiyas, Vēḷāḷars, Harijans—are also Śaivites. In fact, the majority of non-Brahmans in Tamiḻnāḍu are Śaivites. Most of the temples are Śaiva also; according to tradition, there are 1,008 Śaiva temples and 108 Viṣṇu temples. There are also Śaiva *maṭhas* and a provincial Śaiva association—the Śaivasiddhānta Mahāsaṅgam—founded by two svāmīs, which sponsors meetings and lectures, issues a journal, and was then celebrating its fiftieth anniversary.

The scholar said that he liked to look on India as the abode of the gods, from Mount Kailās in the north, whose lord is Śiva Mahādeva, to Cape Comorin in the south, over which the Lord's consort Pārvatī rules. His own life aim, he said, is *tapas* (asceticism). Before parting, he gave me a pamphlet containing some of his lectures on Śaivasiddhānta.

### *For the Great Tradition, a Non-Brahman Village Patron*

I first met R.J.P. at a sixtieth anniversary celebration in honor of his son-in-law's parents. We were told he was a well-to-do non-Brahman landlord from a village near Tiruccirāppaḷḷi and was helping to pay for the celebration. He was president of his village *pañcāyat* board and of the horticulture society, a director of the school, and very active in philanthropic and cultural activities. The Brahman who introduced him had great respect for R.J.P. as a patron of Sanskrit learning and traditions. The patron was tall and handsome, with a small pointed mustache that

* These are the four parts of all Āgamas, Śaivite or Vaiṣṇavite.

set off his angular features and a courtly, considerate manner. Although he was himself a visitor in the house and to the city, he took the lead in seeing to everyone's comfort, offering chairs, food, and other courtesies. At a second meeting in the same house, for a *Śaktipūjā* conducted by an aged specialist in Tantric *mantras* whom the patron had invited, the impression of aristocratic dignity and politeness increased.

On our third meeting, I was taken to the upper story of a two-story house where I found R.J.P. just fresh from a nap. He had brought his daughter by car to Madras for confinement in one of the city hospitals, where she had given birth to a son, and both mother and child were doing well. The family was now waiting for an auspicious day to return to his village: According to their reckoning one would not occur for about six days, and they would wait. I proceeded—a bit too single-mindedly, as I appreciated afterward—to put to him a series of questions about the extent to which the traditions of Sanskritic Hinduism were still alive in his village.

R.J.P. said his family had been principal landholders in the village for about 300 years. Some of them had been Diwans to the Nāyaka kings. They owned 600 to 700 acres of paddy land, which in their region is now worth about 5,000 rupees per acre. The population of the village is 3,000, with 15 to 20 castes represented. The village includes about 70 Brahman houses, comprising about 500 individuals, and there are also Kaḷḷas and Ādi Drāviḍas. It has a *trimūrti* temple, for all castes and sects, which is older than the temple in nearby Śrīraṅgam. The main festivals come on March 16 and in the spring and summer. The festivals begin with that of the village goddess, Piḍāri Amman, at which a goat is sacrificed and its blood tasted as a blessing by non-Brahmans. Festivals in April and May honor Śiva and Viṣṇu. Six *purohitas* live in the village. The *vaidikas* read the Purāṇas every day; public readings are held in the temples during specially sacred periods, such as the month of December. *Harikathā* recitations of the *Rāmāyaṇa* usually take sixteen days, and *bhajanas* are also held. A few dance teachers and some musicians also live in the village. A group of professional actors—*vinodins*—is invited to sing ballads and to dance. These performances are most frequent during festivals and are held near the temple, but some are also held during marriages and similar private ceremonies. Local radio programs originating at the regional station in Tiruccirāppaḷḷi include devotional themes. There are no *sabhās* for concerts and cultural performances outside of the city. *Terukkūttu* folk dances take place in the fields.

Some of the *purohitas* in the area know the rudiments of astrology and use it to determine the times for sowing and harvesting and to cast horoscopes. *Mantrikas* from other villages are consulted, as are *Āyurvedic* doctors from the nearby town of Tiruccirāppaḷḷi. A village stonemason knows Sanskrit, and R.J.P. had sent him to Śrīraṅgam for further study.

The village area has a Śaivasiddhānta *maṭha*—probably the first Śaivite *maṭha*—and one or two *sannyāsins* in one family.

The village school goes up to the third form, with nineteen teachers and 500 pupils of all castes and both sexes. As the village landlord, R.J.P. had started this school in 1932. Although it has since received government aid, it still costs him about 2,000 rupees per year, while the government contributes 3,000 rupees. After the third form, those students who can continue their schooling go to the next village, a pakka municipality, or to Śrīraṅgam, a temple city. The village has no library. About six radios are in operation, including one in the community center, but no films or newspapers reach the village. However, because the village is close to Tiruccirāppaḷḷi, the people have some access to films and journals.

Most Brahmans in the village own land, about five to ten acres per family. Congress and the Dravidian movement are the main political parties.

After responding to my questions, R.J.P. began to speak freely about what was preoccupying and troubling him. As he talked, he became more expressive and, although his voice never rose or showed tension, his sincerity and simplicity increased. His was certainly the most lucid, disarming, and modest statement of the "Indian faith" I had heard in India, and I was sorry not to have been able to record it verbatim. The following is an attempt at reconstruction.

R.J.P. does not think India has been making much progress along the right path. "We are trying to out-Herod Herod." Indiscipline runs loose in the social, moral, and educational spheres, he said. Everyone thinks he can talk about everything, without decency, because now he is free. Before, people had at least been afraid of sin; now the political trend makes materialists of everyone. The change had come, R.J.P. thought, in the last twenty years. Ten years before, there had been much discussion about moral and religious instruction, but the result was more attention to physical and mental, not moral, education. The younger generation was being brought up in a very different atmosphere from the one in which R.J.P. had been brought up, and the change had come about because of the political situation. Under the sanction of freedom of speech, all things are permitted. Students lack respect for their teachers and engage in strikes; the young no longer respect their elders and lack faith in God or in religion. This is true to some extent of his own sons.

The public problem is how to give the young the proper attitude through education. R.J.P. did not know how to do the job. He was still thinking about the problem as parent, teacher, and organizer of a school. Teachers had organized guilds with thousands of members. Their groups represented many years of experience with young minds, and he respected that experience and their resolutions for educational reform. But nobody does anything, he stressed, everybody just talks about education. "What is the right education for our children and our village? I am unable to understand."

India's Basic Education Program, he thought, proposes reforms to fit public prejudices. He did not believe that such reforms would solve the problem. They are a product of the "political mind" not the "practical mind." "What tomorrow will be, they do not care. The trend of public opinion in the last five years has not been progressive. That is my humble opinion. Public opinion doesn't pay respect to education but wants education to pay. It asks 'how much' from fees, from government, from people. The teachers are not content, so they pass resolutions and have strikes."

Education, he continued, is a matter of molding young minds to the proper path. Now they are spoiled by stories in the cheap magazines and novels. Everyone has become ambitious to become a minister of government or a wealthy man. In the past, many more had contentment and respect for good things. Now no one is satisfied, and every satisfaction leads to more greed. If people were willing to work for a better position, it would be all right, but they want to strike for it or they use "We want it" as a political slogan.

"Which way the wind now blows," R.J.P. could not say. Politically, he had always been neutral. Since he had always been independent, he cannot even call himself an "independent."

He believed in God's grace for all who have faith. God is always great; He knows what to say and how to say it. All three *Śaktis—icchā, kriyā,* and *guṇa*—are needed. What is needed now is the right direction, not more wants. R.J.P. therefore believed that an *avatāra* was coming, perhaps from the West, "like yourself." Millions of insects are born and die every day, for God's purpose and for the world's purpose. God is great; He knows what is; He knows how to save. We are always saved. When there is no faith, people worry and political leaders make use of these worries. Some good things lie in our future, he thought—world unity, for example, whether as preached by Christ or by Vivekānanda. It must come. "This is my humble opinion, the opinion of an obscure man in one little corner of the world."

He regarded people as more and more materialistic, however. They think they can get everything for themselves. They think of their worth in rupees and of their belongings, not peace of mind. How to give them peace, in America or in India, was the problem for R.J.P.

Everybody becomes an *avatāra,* he told me. Nehru is an *avatāra;* he has handled a difficult situation well. Someone must now come and see that everyone *works* for the peace of the whole world, a real peace, not a political peace. The unity of India is not enough. "We want peace for the whole world, not only for India. We want a real *avatāra*—an x—a great soul. That's what is wanting now, in my humble opinion. People now sign letters only with a signature, no 'faithfully' or 'sincerely yours.' What we need is more sincerity and truth, not Americanism, Chineseism, Germanism, or any kind of -ism.

"May God grant us good faith in Him so that we can be more happy and really happy. *Karmamārga* and *bhaktimārga* are not enough; we are consciously losing our faith.

"New winds are blowing. Where is the other strength? When there was danger of a Japanese invasion, I had only a picture of *Him* and thought only of my faith in *Him* and of his grace. Then my *pūjāri* came with a *prasādam,* precisely at that hour to satisfy my faith, my want. That is why, as an Indian, I repeat the name Śaṅkara, the commander of God's wishes. I put my faith in him and in no other—not in friends or relatives. I am only a poor soul of 120 pounds' weight, who may collapse at any moment or be blown away. With my faith, I feel safe everywhere, even from the H-bomb, a master of myself, not harmful to others, but useful to others. Nobody can be an enemy to us. We are His children, and how can a father be cruel to his son? The light is within; the lights in the village, the town, the house do not matter. Getting goodwill is all that matters. We came into the world bare and alone and we go out of it the same way. Let us therefore be friends with everybody. That is what religion teaches—the Vedas, the Āgamas, and the rest—love to all, and then there will be no war."

I felt the poignancy of R.J.P.'s discourse. The voices of his family downstairs receded, the bare electric bulb hanging from the ceiling looked dim, Madras itself seemed far away. I felt that I was beginning to understand the "Indian point of view" and how its faith gave comfort and warmth to its adherents, much like other faiths. I was reminded of the twenty-third psalm and mentioned it to R.J.P. He apparently did not know it.

Because it was getting late, and I did not want to impose on R.J.P.'s hospitality, I stood up and started to say goodbye. Standing up also, he turned toward a window sill on which were placed a small cup of ashes, a lithograph of one of the deities, and the head of a cut flower. He explained that this was his improvised home-shrine. Lifting the flower and holding it at arm's length, he pointed out that it had the shape of a *nāgaliṅgam,* with the petals hanging over the stamen like cobra heads. It was, he thought, remarkable for a flower to resemble so closely one of God's manifestations. God, he added, is everywhere and in every form. All flowers have some fragrance. If we believe that God is in every form, where is the quarrel between householders, castes, or nations? If we believe that He is everywhere, we shall not be afraid of anything. "This is my Indian faith. We worship God in some specific form and make offerings to Him, but since He is in everything, we do not need to make offerings to Him. The same holds true about the picture and the ashes. They are only symbols to remind us of our faith and of the inner light. So this *namaskāra,* which I now make to you, is only a folding of the hands, a gesture, but it is meant to convey to you my feeling and goodwill. This is my humble opinion, the opinion of one self in this little corner of the world."

## *Definition Versus Comparison of Related Forms*

> In a very large part of morphology, our essential task lies in the comparison of related forms rather than in the precise definition of each.—D'Arcy Wentworth Thompson, *On Growth and Form* (Cambridge and New York, 1942), p. 1032.

There are obvious similarities in sacred centers, sacred specialists, and sacred rites between the Śaiva and Śrīvaiṣṇava forms of Hinduism and the structure of Sanskritic Hinduism previously described. Household, *maṭha,* and temple, domestic and temple priests, Vedic and purāṇic rites, and scriptures are to be found in all three. Structurally, their similarities might be described as isomorphs or at least homomorphs of the same Great Tradition. This description would not be completely accurate, however, for there are significant differences among the different versions. The Śrīvaiṣṇava *ācārya* had pointed out some of these differences: Special Vaiṣṇava rituals are not sanctioned by the Vedas or the *smṛtis* but are post-Vedic and are governed by the special manuals of worship—the Vaiṣnava Āgamas. These Āgamas require a special kind of temple priest to mediate between the worshiper and the image; they are considered to be on a par with the Vedas and *smṛtis* in the canon of Śrīvaiṣṇava or Śaiva scripture, which also includes a set of Tamil hymns and texts composed by Vaiṣṇava and Śaiva saints. The Śrīvaiṣṇava must also undergo a special initiation ceremony under a guru, whether or not he is of a "twice-born" caste and has been through the sacred thread ceremony. Finally, while the Vedic rituals are obligatory for all Brahmans, the Śrīvaiṣṇava rituals are performed only by Śrīvaiṣṇava Brahmans and non-Brahmans of this sect.

A similar set of differences distinguishes Śaivism from the orthodox versions of Sanskritic Hinduism: the inclusion of special Āgamas and Tamil hymns of Śaivite saints in the scripture, initiation by gurus, who are accessible to non-Brahmans as well as to Brahmans, and so on.

Other differences in structure between the sects and the orthodox position include the content of scripture, language, rankings of scriptural authorities, the relative emphasis placed on domestic and temple rites, the kinds and roles of specialists, recruitment of members and specialists, and transmission of traditions. Sect marks, philosophy, and theology also differ. Historically, the sects have stressed the devotional side (the *bhaktimārga*), whereas the orthodox position has stressed ritual observance (*karmamārga*) and knowledge (*jñānamārga*). The non-Brahman patron's confession of faith indicates that this is still true and that a highly personalized universalistic faith transcending family, caste, sect, and nation is inherent in Hinduism.[28]

How far do these differences call for a redefinition of the structure of Sanskritic Hinduism, and how should a revised definition deal with the variations in language, sect, caste, and philosophies of salvation? Westerners are apt to press for a single uniform definition; Indians are more willing to tolerate the diversified and amorphous structure; they refer to each sect as having its own "tradition" (*sampradāya*). Their attitude has a scientific justification, as the quotation from D'Arcy Thompson suggests. Where variation in form occurs, it is best to study the variations and compare the related forms, rather than to attempt a precise definition of the "orthodox" form. What I have described as "The Structure of Sanskritic Hinduism" on the basis of the observations in Madras City has validity as a first approximation and as comprehending the Hinduism of one group of Smārta Brahmans. The Hinduism of other groups and of the sects must be compared with it, not for the sake of arriving at a single and uniform definition, but to discover their similarities and differences, interactions, and interrelations. Much of the comparison starts from variations in contemporary structure and form, but we shall quickly encounter problems of history and change as we probe the reasons for the similarities and differences *among* the variations. Is temple worship, for instance, a late development and a superimposition on Vedic domestic ritual, adapting some of its forms to a nondomestic setting; or is the temple rite an absorption into the Great Tradition of modes of worship that may have prevailed in pre-Vedic times? Here, a historical question confronts us, the answer to which would clarify the structural affiliations of domestic and temple ritual.

The morphologist's problem in biology, "whether two different but more or less obviously related forms can be so analyzed that each may be shown to be a transformed representation of the other," has its analogue in the morphology of cultural forms. The question leads here as elsewhere to a study of the dynamic processes capable of effecting the required transformation in cultural forms. Since related cultural forms, however, are not wholly independent of each other, a deductive construction of cultural dynamics must be liberally tempered with historical and regional studies of cultural variations in time and space. As these studies are pursued, we shall become more interested in the continuing processes of cultural integration and cultural differentiation and less in the precise definition of a single cultural pattern. For greater understanding of the dynamics of Indian culture, I believe that a comparative and historical study of sect formation would be fruitful, since the sects and, recently, the religious and secular reform movements have been the chief agents and vehicles for cultural and social change.

If we abandon the search for a single definition of *the* structure of Sanskritic Hinduism, we should abandon with it any exclusive identification between this structure and *the* Great Tradition. There are different structures composed of different proportions of Sanskritic and non-Sanskritic elements. The less Sanskritic sectarian versions are not necessarily closer to the Little Tradition because they include vernacular scriptures, non-Brahmans, and devotional and image-centered worship. In fact, sectarian distinctions are often not too important today in the villages or even among large numbers of people in towns and cities. Moreover, many would regard some elements of sectarianism—temple architecture and sculpture and universalistic themes, for example—as part of the Great Tradition.[29] Smārta orthodoxy, on the other hand, not only includes the learned Sanskritic tradition but has also incorporated many local customs and "lower" practices and beliefs, including the *Atharvaveda,* the Epics and Purāṇas, and along with them much of what the heterodox sects have stressed from Buddhist and Jain times to the present. Dr. Raghavan's graphic characterization of his many practices and beliefs—"I am a museum"—conveys the catholicity of the Smārta position.[30]

## Transformations of Sanskritic Hinduism: Preliminary Indications

### *The Cultural Drift of Orthodoxy*

There are many indications of change within the structure (or structures) of Sanskritic Hinduism and some signs that the entire structure may be undergoing a radical transformation. In the process of what I have called "redefining orthodoxy," we find evidence of an inherent flexibility, which permits a variety of changes that do not destroy the structure. The application of scriptural rules to particular circumstances inevitably requires the establishment of some order of precedence among the rules, the resolution of conflicts among them, and an adaptation to local and exceptional conditions. The Sanskrit pandit's description of how he ranks sacred authority and decides difficult cases clearly shows that Sanskritic Hinduism possesses a flexible structure. Logical reasoning, local customs, and the convenience of the parties concerned all have weight in the application of rules to particular circumstances, and if such nontextual considerations do not override revealed and traditional scripture, at least they go beyond its explicit prescriptions and proscriptions. Cognizance is taken in this manner of changing practices and fashions, and elements of local and Little Tradition are assimilated to the Great Tradition. We see here a process that officially sanctions the cultural drift to which any standards of orthodoxy are subject.[31]

The cultural drift of orthodoxy, which is inherent in the structure of Hinduism, raises serious questions about how recent many changes really are. Upon first observing the way in which minor life-cycle rites were being assimilated into the major rites of the sacred thread ceremony and the marriage ceremony, I assumed that the change had begun in the city within the last twenty-five years. Later I discovered that Thurston had mentioned the same trend at the turn of the century and that the Abbé Dubois had already noted it in the eary 1800's.[32] Becoming interested in the historical question, I checked several authorities on *saṃskāras,* with even more surprising results. P. V. Kane, taking note of modern practices in India as a whole, has written that most of the *saṃskāras,* except for the *upanayana* and marriage, have fallen into oblivion. He also noted that the naming and first-feeding ceremonies were now performed "in a popular way" without Vedic *mantras* or priests, that the hair-cutting was done on the same day as the *upanayana,* and that the birth ceremony, or *jātakarman,* is conducted on the same day as the first feeding. His account corresponds in a general way to the contemporary Madras picture. More surprisingly, however, Professor Kane goes on to say that "this state of things has continued for centuries," because the penances for nonperformance of the minor rites have never been very great—at most the forfeit of a cow or some money—and because the authors of the later *smṛtis* and digests were of an accommodating spirit, prescribing easier and easier substitutes for the minor rites, concentrating on the major ones.[33] In modern times, the penances for nonperformance of the minor rites continue to be light: four annas for each rite up to the tonsure, and eight annas for the tonsure.

Another authority on the *saṃskāras,* K. V. Pandey, essentially agrees with Professor Kane. He stresses the many changes and developments in the history of the minor rites and suggests additional reasons for their decline: Buddhism and Jainism had emphasized a religion of devotional practices rather than of ritual observance; the *mantras,* being in archaic Sanskrit, produced indifference in the masses, who could not understand them; and the bifurcation of society into religious and secular spheres turned the rites into mere ceremonies. In more recent times, Professor Pandey contends, the fear of criticism by foreign rulers, particularly the Moghuls, led to secrecy or to nonperformance of the rites, while Western rationalism and skepticism further undermined their appeal among the educated. He appears to believe that the efforts of the Ārya Samāj to revive the rites have not had much success and to be equally doubtful about the attempts at reform by the Brāhmo Samāj, first by removing idolatry and other "unprogressive" features and then, under Keshub Chunder Sen's influence, by trying to create a new set of rites combining old and new elements.* The new rites consisted of a *homa* sacrifice; *ārati* (waving of flame before an image); a *Durgāpūjā;* a Sanskrit hymn with 108 names of God; Caitanya's religious dances; prayers to the Ganges, the moon, and fire; and a form of Christian baptism and communion.[34]

My Indian friends certainly had no notion that they might be misleading me when they spoke of a change as being "recent" or distinguished present from former practices. The chief sources of my misinterpretation were probably, first, an Indian sense of time that differed from mine (I learned later that 500 or even 1,000 years was often spoken of as "a short time"); and, second, my assumption that a change that had occurred in their lifetime had not happened to others many times in the past.

### *Technical Modernization of the Sacred Culture*

Evidence of technical modernization within the structure of Sanskritic Hinduism is abundant: We see the neon lights in temples; the use of a microphone for Vedic chanting; mechanical cookers to prepare food for pilgrims; and pilgrims traveling by automobile, train, airplane, and shrine-owned diesel buses. Special pilgrim trains regularly take two-month tours of sacred places. Changes of this order do not greatly alter the ritual culture; in fact, they tend to enlarge the culture's scope by including more people, over a larger territory, and within a shorter time span than was possible with the older means of transportation and communication. Driving up the hills of the Tiruppati shrines may not involve as much physical penance as walking, but then modern means of transportation have their own rigors.

An improved nautical-type almanac for fixing festival dates, finding auspicious days, reading horoscopes, and forecasting is another example of technical modernization. Another possible example is the adaptation of astrology—Eastern and Western—to forecasting the stock market, political elections, and the kind of doctor a client should consult. The development of astronomy without reference to astrology, on the other hand, begins to look like a technical modernization that goes beyond the traditional structure in which the two branches of learning had been closely linked. The case of medicine seems similar: An *Āyurvedic* doctor's incorporation of thermometers, stethoscopes, bacteriological tests, and

* The Ārya Samāj and the Brāhmo Samāj were two religious reform movements founded in the nineteenth century by, respectively, Svāmī Dayānanda Sarasvatī and Rājā Rāmmohan Roy.

other modern diagnostic devices into his practice represents a modernization of the traditional system of Indian medicine that does not transform it radically. If, to be sure, these changes should bring with them acceptance of the entire theory and practice of modern medicine and its associated system of training, then the transformation would be far-reaching indeed. We would then see a change both in the traditional learning and in the *Āyurvedic* educational system.

### *Transformations in the Transmissive System*

The case of *Āyurvedic* medicine is especially instructive, because it shows very clearly both the continuities and the discontinuities of cultural change. The three kinds of *Āyurvedic* doctors—the hereditary ones who have learned from their fathers and pandits by the apprentice system, those who have studied in schools of indigenous medicine, and those who are products of the mixed system taught in the College of Indigenous Medicine—represent three stages on a scale of modernization. It seems clear from the increasing emphasis on modern medicine in the mixed curriculum, as well as from the preponderantly greater number of those who choose to practice "allopathic" medicine, that the modern system is winning out. It will not be any the less Indian for being "modern." The Yunānī and Siddha systems, once considered to be outside the Sanskritic *Āyurvedic* system, are now regarded as part of "indigenous Indian medicine," in contrast to what is now called "Western," "English," or "allopathic" medicine. Yunānī, a Hindu name for Arab medicine, comes from the Sanskrit word Yavana, meaning Greek and "people from the West." [35]

The degree of modernization represented by the College of Indigenous Medicine has not yet affected the Sanskrit College. Nevertheless, the college secretary believes that the incorporation of some elements from modern scientific and technical education is necessary to preserve the college and enable its graduates to earn a living. The students feel no conflict between traditional and modern learning; they would like to have more science, mathematics, and social studies. Apart from these impending changes, the Sanskrit College already has a mixed educational system. The curriculum consists chiefly of some traditional branches of Sanskritic learning, such as grammar, logic, Vedic exegesis, and Advaita philosophy; it has, however, added several modern subjects, among them comparative philology, the history of Sanskrit literature, and the English language. Vedic and purāṇic studies are not included in the curriculum, although they may be in the future if funds become available.* The Vedas are taught at several special schools and are also still transmitted in a few families by the *gurukula,* or apprentice, system;† the Purāṇas are learned informally from storytellers, reciters, and dramatizations. Several other branches of Sanskrit learning have been detached from the traditional corpus and been "modernized" as independent fields of study. This group includes not only medicine but also law, mathematics, astronomy (with

* Vedic has since been added.

† An apprentice system in which the pupil lived at his guru's house and performed services for his master.

astrology), music, dance, drama, the graphic and plastic arts, and architecture. All are taught either as university subjects or in special professional schools. They are no longer considered sciences auxiliary to the Vedas, as in the curriculum of the Sanskrit College.

Although the teachers at the college are predominantly Sanskrit pandits trained in the traditional way, many now study to pass university examinations and obtain university degrees, which in their eyes possess both greater prestige and more practical value than the old system. The teacher's classroom methods retain something of the old system: emphasis on oral transmission of sacred texts (printed books being used as aids to memory only) and a concern for ritual purity, at least in the teaching of Advaita. The organization of the teaching into hour-long classes on different subjects taught by different teachers, with recreation periods, is strikingly different, however, from the *gurukula* system, where the student lived in his teacher's house for twelve years or more. The Sanskrit College is a recent and transitional educational institution, which must compete with the teaching of Sanskrit subjects in the high schools, arts colleges, and universities.

Practically all the specialists interviewed had attended an "English" or modern elementary school between the ages of six and twelve; there they learned Tamil, English, mathematics, and some science. Their Sanskritic education usually followed, being acquired either from their fathers, from another guru, or at a special Sanskrit school. The two major complaints of the former district education officer and the Śaivasiddhānta scholar against the "modern" schools are representative of this group's opinions: (1) Modern education deprecates the need for memorizing sacred texts as a means of transmitting a tradition and insists instead on appeals to the pupil's direct experience; and (2) modern education neglects moral and religious instruction in favor of a secular approach that weakens respect for parents, teachers, gurus, and God.

Despite such complaints, which are of course heard elsewhere, most of the traditional specialists accept "modern" education and are bringing their children up in this way. The astrologer does not want his son to be an astrologer; the sons of Sanskritists are adopting scientific and technical careers. The only significant exceptions to this trend seem to be the hereditary sacred specialists—the temple priest and the two domestic priests, and the Telugu Brahman in the Sanskrit College, who had rejected a chemistry career. All these trends are mutually dependent and interactive. As an occupation becomes less closely tied to family and caste, so the task of keeping sons in the careers of their fathers, or of operating a domestic apprentice system, becomes increasingly hard. The introduction of competitive examinations, government-supported schools, and government licensing of professions makes it difficult to stop short of a system of "modern" education. Mechanical developments, such as printing and industrial manufacture, bring with them new products, new skills, and new demands, making many old products and methods obsolete. Programs of economic development even call for a system of "basic" education that is closer to direct experience of contemporary life than is the modern "English" school.

Under these conditions, the question arises whether the structure of the Sanskritic tradition can be maintained at all—whether the coming of the secular welfare state introduces a kind of structural change that cannot be redefined within the traditional framework. Have we here, in short, not only a series of transformations within the structure of the Great Tradition, but a transformation of that tradition?

### *The Prospect of Structural Change*

This question troubles many of those whom I interviewed; in their references to the weakening of the caste system, antireligious movements, the neglect of *śāstric* learning, and materialism, they reveal some anxiety about the future of Sanskritic Hinduism. They see many changes as expressions of large-scale political, economic, and cultural movements affecting India as a whole; others they see, however, as the familiar process of deritualization within the Brahman community itself. Concern was most explicitly phrased by the Sanskrit College pandit, the expert in the Purāṇas, who said that only a small proportion of Brahmans are now followers of the Vedas (*vaidikas*) and that the majority, including his son, are worldly-minded (*laukikas*). The situation, in his view as well as that of Svāmī Śaṅkarācārya and others, implies a Brahman abdication of their traditional role, or *dharma,* which was to cultivate Sanskrit learning and ritual and to serve as spiritual exemplars and guides to others. The process of "de-Sanskritization" is manifest in different ways: the small number of Brahmans sufficiently well versed in the Vedas and *śāstras* to qualify as pandits; the laxity in ritual observances, not only in the daily domestic observances, but in the general attitude toward post-puberty marriage, marriage within the same *gotra,* preparation of food by menstruating women, foreign travel, nonvegetarian diets, alcohol drinking, the behavior of widows, the departure from traditional occupations, the desire for luxuries, and the changing attitude toward untouchables. Continuing strictness is reported about intercaste marriage and the observance of pollution in cases of the death of relatives, but the general trend of diminishing Brahman observance of ritual obligations is particularly visible in the towns and cities.

As if to compensate for their ritual lapses, some Brahmans have been turning to devotional and revivalistic forms of religion. The pandit called this a turning away from the path of ritual observance, *karmamārga,* and from the path of meditation, *jñānamārga,* and a shift toward the path of devotion, *bhaktimārga.* Many do not even stop here, he said, but have become outright atheists and materialists (*nāstikas*).

The picture that orthodox people paint may be a dark one, depicting a moral "fall," but it is perfectly intelligible and familiar to my informants, who expect confusion and the violation of *dharma* in this wicked age of *Kaliyuga* (one that goes back several millennia).

The effect of the de-Sanskritizing trend has been to stimulate efforts at a Vedic and Sanskritic revival. The *purohitas* who have returned to their family occupation and the temple priest who has opened a school for his own and his relatives' children are examples. Others come to mind: an association, the Dharma Śiva Saṅgam, to arrange free sacred thread ceremonies for "destitute boys," funeral ceremonies for "the poor who die helpless," and Sanskrit classes and lectures on religion and *dharma;* and another association, the Āstika Sabhā, to propagate Hindu religion by holding religious discourses and Vedic classes. Young men learn Vedic chanting in these classes and are invited to perform at weddings and other functions.

Such efforts at revival do not and cannot limit themselves to a restoration of Vedic orthodoxy. A total restoration would be impossible, considering that the very standards of orthodoxy have been changing and that technical, educational, and general social changes require new approaches. Changes of this order prompted orthodox Brahman groups to go beyond a Vedic revival and to cooperate with sectarian and non-Brahman groups in a common defense against antireligious movements. The association of Śaivism referred to by the Śaivasiddhānta scholar, an association of the heads of all *maṭhas* to contest legislation against *maṭhas,* and the sponsoring of *Tiruppāvai-Tiruvembāvai* conferences are clear-cut examples of these "interfaith" efforts.

Reactions of this kind indicate that not all contemporary changes are a product of cultural drift; many are the results of deliberate changes in cultural policy, cultural leadership, and organization. In both types of changes—directed and undirected—new values and standards are emerging that transform the previous judgments as to what constitutes proper and improper behavior. To cite one example, many no longer consider later marriages sinful; they are becoming part of a new pattern. Behavior and beliefs formerly considered a "fall" from virtue by orthodox standards are now justified in terms of "scientific progress" and "democracy." In order to determine how far these transformations are continuous with the older structure of Sanskritic Hinduism, it is necessary to trace them in detail.

We shall first examine the hypothesis of a change from ritual and learned orthodoxy to devotional and popular religion, and then look at certain changes in cultural policy and leadership.

## Notes

1. Claude Levi-Strauss, *Tristes Tropiques* (New York: Atheneum, 1964); *idem, Structural Anthropology* (New York: Basic Books, 1963); and D. W. Thompson, *On Growth and Form* (Cambridge: Cambridge University Press, 1942).

2. V. Raghavan, "Variety and Integration in the Pattern of Indian Culture," *FEQ* 15, No. 4 (August, 1956): 497–505; *idem,* "Methods of Popular Religious Instruction in South India," in Singer, ed., *TI* (see note 6, Introduction to Part One, above); and *idem,* "The Relevance of Hinduism in the Modern World," in *Kamakoti Vani* 1, Nos. 1 and 2 (Michilipatnam, Andhra Pradesh, January-February, 1969): 15–21, 33–40.

3. V. Raghavan, February 25, 1967.

4. *Murray's Handbook: India, Pakistan, Burma and Ceylon* (London: John Murray, 1949).

5. The leader was the late C. N. Annadurai, who organized the Dravidian Progressive Federation (DMK) as an offshoot of the Dravidian Federation (DK). See R. Hardgrave, *The Dravidian Movement* (Bombay: Popular Prakashan, 1965), for a brief history of the movement. Collections of the Svāmī's sayings are published in P. Sankaranarayan, comp., *The Call of the Jagadguru* (Madras: Ganesh & Co., 1958).

6. Professor H. Daniel Smith, Department of Religion, Syracuse University, has produced a series of films of domestic and temple rites in Madras. These are distributed by the Syracuse University Film Library. A useful introduction to the domestic and temple rituals of South India, including both a discussion of ritual handbooks and some direct observation, is Diehl, *Instrument and Purpose.* See also Louis Dumont, "Definition structurale d'un dieu populaire tamoul," *Journal Asiatique* 241, No. 2 (1953): 255–70.

7. My colleague David Pingree has kindly supplied the following information about the *dṛgganita* system: "Basically, the *dṛgganita* system is simply a revision of the parameters for the mean motions of the planets which appear in the *parahita* system, which Haridatta proposed in A.D. 683; the *parahita* parameters are those of the *Āryabhaṭīya* of Āryabhaṭa (A.D. 499)." See also Pingree's review of the basic text of *dṛgganita* edited by K. V. Sarma, *JAOS* 87, No. 3 (1967): 337–39.

8. The *gāyatrī* verse, *Ṛgveda* III: 62.10, in English translation: "We meditate upon that adorable effulgence of the resplendent vivifier, Savitar; may he stimulate our intellects." Translated by Raghavan in V. Raghavan, *Prayers, Praises and Psalms* (Madras: G. A. Natesan & Co., n.d.). An alternative translation by J. A. B. van Buitenen: "We wish for that most desirable gift of the God Impeller (the sun), who must set our thoughts in motion."

9. For a mainly "textual" description and analysis of the *saṃskāra,* see Raj Bali Panday, *Hindu Saṃskāras: A Socio-religious Study of the Hindu Sacraments* (Benares: Vikrama Panchang Press, 1949).

10. For the relationship of modern Indian law to traditional Hindu law, and customs, see J. D. M. Derrett, *Introduction to Modern Hindu Law* (London: Oxford University Press, 1963); *idem, Religion, Law and State in India;* and Marc Galanter, "The Displacement of Traditional Law in Modern India," *Journal of Social Issues* 24 (October, 1968): 65–91.

11. Kāśīnātha Upādhyāya, *Dharmasindhu* (*-sāra*) (1790), "now the leading work in matters of religious observances in the Deccan," according to P. V. Kane, *History of the Dharma Śāstras* (Poona: Bhandarkar Oriental Research Institute, 1932–62), 1:463.

12. Vaidyanātha Dīkṣitar, *Aśaucha* (n.p., n.d.).

13. B. V. Raman, *Manual of Indian Astrology* (Bangalore: n.p., 1953), is currently consulted by local astrologers.

14. Charles Leslie has applied anthropological methods to the study of Indian systems of medicine. See Charles Leslie, "Professional and Popular Health Cultures in South Asia," in Morehouse, ed., *Understanding Science and Technology. Aṣṭāṅgahrdaya,* a medical treatise by Vāgbhaṭa.

15. See Ramalingayya, *Vaidya Yoga Ratnāvali* (Madras: Madras State Indian Medical Practitioners' Cooperative Pharmacy and Stores, 1953), and *idem, Unani Pharmacopeia* (Madras: n.p., n.d.).

16. Daniel Ingalls discusses the traditional Sanskrit training of Brahmans in "The Brahman Tradition" in Singer, ed., *TI.* Staal, *Nambūdiri Vedic Recitations,* describes the traditional techniques of Vedic transmission; *Jaiminīya Nyāyamalā* is a mīmāṃsā text. The *Siddhāntakaumudī* of Bhaṭṭoji Dīkṣita is the most widely used grammatical text for Sanskrit in India. It is basically a rearrangement of the *sūtras* of Pāṇini.

17. The *Hālāsyamahāliṅgam* of Rājādhirājā Cōḻa.

18. The traditional manuals of temple ritual compare these ceremonies to preparing the ground by plowing, leveling, measuring, and making a square. See Diehl, *Instrument and Purpose,* and Kramrisch, *The Hindu Temple.*

19. The following list of the Śrī Kapālīśvara Temple shrines is reproduced as written down by the son of the temple priest, with Sanskritized forms added in brackets:

i. Small Gate Entrance
ii. Big Gate Entrance
iii. Third Entrance (open)
1. Sri Kalpaka Ganesh [Śrī / Gaṇeśa]
2. Sri Murugar
3. Sri "Angampoombāvai"
4. Sri Nandikeswarar (Bull) [Nandikeśvara]
5. Sri Ganesar [Gaṇeśa]
6. Sri Murugar
7. Entrance to Sri Karpakambal Temple
8. Sri Karpakambal [Kaṟpakāmbāḷ]
9. "Palli-arai" (Nuptial Room) [Paḷḷiyaṟai]
10. Entrance to Safe Room (Twillery)
11. Entrance to Sri Kapaleswaran Temple [Kapālīśvara]

12. Om, Sri Kapaleeswar [Kapālīśvara]
13. Bronze Sham Mukar [Ṣaṇmukha]
14. Sri Nataraja [Naṭarājan]
15. Sri Arumkar and 63 Nayanars [Aṟumukar / Nāyaṉārs]
16. Sri Durgambal
17. Sri Brahma
18. Sri Chandikeswaran [Caṇḍikeśvara]
19. 3 Goddesses: Sri Saraswati, Sri Durga, and Sri Laksmi, in the order from South to North [Sarasvatī, Durgā, Lakṣmī]
20. Sri Bhairavar [Bhairava]
21. Nalvar (Appar, Sundaran, Manikkavācakar, Jnanasambandar)
22. Unnamahenvar
23. Sri Linga, Rishaba, and Sri Ganesh [Liṅga, Ṛṣabha / Gaṇeśa]
24. Sri Surya among 63 Nayanars [Sūrya]
25. Sri Dakshina Moorthī [Dakṣiṇāmūrti]
26. Sri Ganesh
27. Mirror in front of Sri Nataraja
28. Sri Kapaleeswar and Sri Karpakāmbāḷ (Utsawar) (Bronze idol) [Utsava]
29. Bronze Nandi
30. Bali Peetha [Balipīṭha]
31. Flag staff
32. Big Bali Peetha
33. Vahana Godown (Godown of Vahnas or vehicles)
34. Peacock Temple
35. Sri Sanisvaran (Saturn) [Śanīśvara]
36. Sri Sundarasvar [Sundareśvara]
37. Sri Navagraha (Nine planets)
38. Sri Jagadeeswan [Jagadīśa]
39. Sri Ganesar
40. Sri Annamalai [Aṇṇāmalai]
41. Sri Murugar
42. Sri Palani Andavan [Paḻani Āṇḍavan]
43. Sri Vaīllā Nayanar (Saiva saint of special importance to this temple)
44. Navaratri Mandapam [Navarātrimaṇḍapa]
45. Sri Hanuman in the pillar [Hanumān]
46. Mandapam [Maṇḍapa]
47. Silver Vahanas Godown
48. " " "
49. Ordinary Godown
50. Temple office
51. Yāga Śalai [Yāgaśālā]
52. Kalyāna Mandapam [Kalyāṇamaṇḍapa]
53. Cow-herd
54. Godowns
55. Madapalli (kitchen) [Maḍappaḷḷi]
56. Temple well
57. Sandal paste–preparing room
58. Garden
59. Bilva tree
60. Maha-Bilva tree [Mahābilva]
61. Iron Safe room
62. Tank steps, 32 in number
63. Neerāli Mandapa [Nērāḷimaṇḍapam]

20. On the artisan claims to be Viśvakarma Brahmans, see E. Thurston, *Castes and Tribes of South India* (Madras: Government Press, 1909), 3:113, and Stella Kramrisch, "Traditions of the Indian Craftsman," in Singer, ed., *TI*, pp. 18–24.

21. See Kramrisch, "Traditions of Indian Craftsman"; A. Coomaraswamy, *The Arts and Crafts of India and Ceylon* (London: T. N. Foulis, 1913); *idem, The Indian Craftsman* (London: Brobsthain & Co., 1909); and Milton Singer, "Changing Craft Traditions in India," in Wilbert E. Moore and Arnold S. Feldman, eds., *Labor Commitment and Social Change in Developing Areas* (New York: Social Science Rescarch Council, 1960), pp. 258–76, for further discussion of traditional techniques and values of the craftsman.

22. See also Diehl, *Instrument and Purpose,* for the theory of *śakti* in South India.

23. *Ibid.,* p. 274 n., translates *jaṭāmuṇi* as a "kind of demon" and identifies it as a god. The translation "ghost" was used by the interpreter.

24. The *mantrika* listed sixteen kinds of *śakti* that exist in mankind:

1. Iccha Śakti
2. Akaraṇa Śakti
3. Vishesa Śakti
4. Kriya Śakti
5. Maya Śakti
6. Tatwa Śakti
7. Sankalpa Śakti
8. Chalana Śakti
9. Bhoga Śakti
10. Bodha Śakti
11. Bada Śakti
12. Vimiti Śakti
13. Kalpana Śakti
14. Thorta Śakti
15. Kripa Śakti
16. Laya Śakti

25. Here are the *mantrika*'s diagram and list of the eight directions, together with the corresponding deities and planets (words in parentheses and brackets have been added):

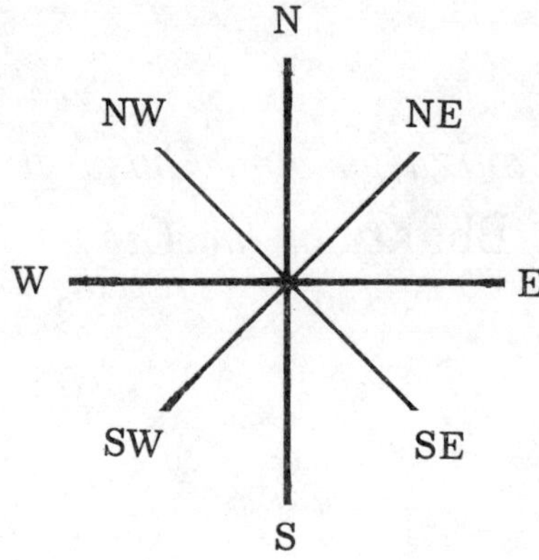


| Name of *tikku* (*diś*) [direction] | Name of *devatā* [deity] | | Name of *navagraha* [planet] |
|---|---|---|---|
| 1. East | Inoran | [Indra] | Sukran (Venus) |
| 2. S. East | Agoni | [Agni] | Chandram (Moon) |
| 3. South | Eman | [Yama] | Angarakan (Mars) |
| 4. S.W. | Niruthi | [Nirṛti] | Rahu |
| 5. West | Varman | [Varuṇa] | Sani (Saturn) |
| 6. N.W. | Vayu | [Vāyu] | Kethu |
| 7. North | Kuberan | [Kubera] | Guru (Jupiter) |
| 8. N.E. | Isanam | [Īśana] | Putan (Mercury) |

26. Śrīvaiṣṇava rituals and philosophy are described in Rangachari, *Sri Vaisnava Brahmans.*

27. See Sri S. S. Pillai, *Talks on Saiva Siddhanta* (Sivananda Nagar, Himalayas: Vedanta Forest University, 1954).

28. For parallels among the South Indian sects, see Farquhar, *Primer of Hinduism.*

29. See introduction to E. A. Burtt, ed., *The Compassionate Buddha* (New York: New American Library, 1955).

30. Raghavan, "Variety and Integration" (note 2, *supra*).

31. The concept of "cultural drift" is derived from Sapir's "linguistic drift": "The drift of a language is constituted by the unconscious selection on the part of its speakers of those individual variations that are cumulative in some special direction." Edward Sapir, *Language: An Introduction to the Study of Speech* (New York: Harcourt Brace & Co., 1921), p. 155. See also F. Eggan, "Cultural Drift and Social Change," *Current Anthropology* 4 (1963): 347–55. In the present application, the "cultural drift of orthodoxy" refers to the cumulative drift of standards of orthodoxy in a particular direction under the influence of changing practices and interpretations of those practices.

32. Thurston, *Castes and Tribes,* and Abbé Dubois, *Hindu Manners and Customs* (Oxford: Clarendon Press, 1899), p. 277.

33. Kane, *History of Dharma Śāstras* II, 1:199–200, and Panday, *Hindu Saṃskāras* (note 9, *supra*). See also Farquhar, *Outline of Religious Literature* (note 3, Chapter 2, above).

34. Panday, *Hindu Saṃskāras,* pp. xxviii and 546.

35. See Leslie, "Health Cultures," (note 14, *supra*).

# 5 / *Urbanization and Cultural Change:* Bhakti *in the City*

## Introduction

Chapter 3 on the cultural pattern of Indian civilization stressed the problems of method presented by a field study of a Great Tradition and proposed the concept of a cultural performance as a useful unit for field observation. I had found that the social organization of Sanskritic Hinduism extends beyond the specialists, rites, and institutions described in Chapter 4 and includes another group of specialists and performances, to be described in this chapter. I learned about the latter group while exploring the former, but the relationship between them at first appeared puzzling and presented some problems of interpretation. Because many informants talked about the cultural performances in such terms as concerts, artists, art music, classical Indian dance, dramatic recitals, and social play, I assumed that they represented a secular, aesthetic culture distinct from the ritual and religious culture. My interpretation was, of course, based on the familiar Western dichotomy between religion and culture. I also assumed that the aesthetic culture was modern—the effect of urbanization and secularization—while the religious culture was traditional and ancient.

These assumptions and interpretations were mistaken. In India, religion includes culture, and culture includes religion, even in a metropolitan center. Classical art, too, is a yoga.

I began to interpret the relationship between religion and culture more perceptively when I noticed that my Indian friends tended to identify *pūjās,* weddings, sacred thread ceremonies, musical concerts, or dances as performances of their culture. This observation led to the formulation of the concept of a "cultural performance" as a minimum observable unit of both religious and secular culture. Analysis and comparison of cultural performances provided a fruitful method for dealing with the problems of the relations between religion and culture and of the effects of urbanization on both. In applying the method in Madras, I perceived that religious and cultural forms shaded into each other on a single continuum of religio-cultural experience. Songs, words, and gestures of a ritual observance, for instance, reappeared in a classical dance program. That a professional dancing girl (*devadāsī*) should begin her classical program with an invocation and *pūjā* to a deity struck no one as incongruous. The dancer told me afterward that she dedicated her work to God and that foreign students could not really master classical Indian dancing because they did not really "believe."

The close relationship between religion and culture extends into all fields of urban culture, including the film, radio, theater, and music concerts. Through analysis of cultural performances, it was easy to see how the folk play and folk ballad were adapted to the city vacant lot or the film, and how the stories from the Epics and Purāṇas were endlessly told and retold in recitation, song, drama, and dance. Aspects of the Great Tradition, Little Tradition, and modernity were all caught up in this popular purāṇic urban culture.

"Secularization," however, did not seem to describe the cultural effects of urbanization, although there was certainly a good deal of "technical modernization" of traditional cultural media. One general difference between urban cultural events and the more narrowly religious performances in the home or temple was the greater freedom from caste or sect identification. Neither performer, performance, nor place of performance was identified with any particular caste, sect, or religious community. Frequently, all that was required for admission to public performances was a contribution or entry fee. The lack of other restrictions suggested that the religious culture was being democratized rather than secularized in the city. I saw, too, that the people who came to these various manifestations of religious culture had regular occupations in the economic and cultural life of the city, that they were businessmen, engineers, film producers and technicians, bankers, teachers, laborers, porters.

The best clue for understanding the effect of urbanization on Sanskritic Hinduism came in my interview with a *paurāṇika.* He had attributed the shift from ritual observance to devotional observance among urban Brahmans to their migration to the towns and their need to "think of God" and relax.

This same formula of a shift from ritual to devotion had also been mentioned by Pandit S. V. at his explanation for the decline in ritual observance in the city but I had not given it much thought until the time came to analyze the wide range of cultural performances and to understand their relation to urbanization. Then it became clear that the shift from ritual to devotion did indeed extend to much of urban culture. I termed "deritualization" the decline in ritual observance represented by the abbreviation, consolidation, or omission of many domestic rites. The spread of *bhakti,* or devotion, into many modern cultural performances and cultural media had no special designation but was easily confirmed by comparing the internal themes and messages of the performances and the explicit attitudes of the performers and their audiences.

Many regular followers of such events remarked spontaneously that *bhaktimārga,* the path of devotion, was "an easier path to salvation" in an urban setting and in "this modern age" than *karmamārga,* the path of strict ritual observances, or *jñānamarga,* the path of meditation and *śāstric* study.

Between the decline in ritual observance and the increase in devotional religion a complementary, functional relationship exists, since the loss in religious merit that results from the former is to some extent made up by the latter. Although I found some evidence for this complementarity in the observations and interviews of my first two visits to Madras, it was on the third visit that, in a study of some leading industrialists, the importance of this complementary relationship as a mode of adaptation to modern changes became clear.

I shall now present some examples of the method of comparative analysis of cultural performances. The following generalizations concern the changes in religious orientation adopted by Madras Brahmans under the influence of the urban environment. These changes are verbalized by some of the Brahmans as involving a change in preference among the ancient paths to religious salvation within Hinduism.

## The Widening Path of Devotion in Urban Culture

### Paurāṇika, *or Storyteller*

The storyteller, or *paurāṇika,* sat on a raised platform, his feet crossed under him, reciting the coronation of Rāma. On the floor of the large hall in the high school sat some 500 listeners, men on one side and women on the other—smiling, attentive. The hall was full, and there were people on the balconies and in the alcoves. The *paurāṇika* recited in short, rhythmic phrases, both in Sanskrit and in Tamil. Periodically, several people in the audience would shout "Rām, Rām" and "Jai Rām." This shouting was usually started by a very busy man who walked about the room greeting newcomers and giving messages. On either side of the platform stood a large ceremonial lamp. Directly behind the *paurāṇika* was a small garlanded altar, the main part of which was a lithograph of Rāma and Sītā. As the *paurāṇika* reached the end of the story of Rāma's coronation, someone waved a flame in front of the picture and rang a bell.

When the cries of "Rām, Rām" died down, the active man stood up to make a speech. Like most of the other men in the audience, he wore a white *dhotī,* and his chest was bare except for a sacred thread across it. From the folds around his waist a thick packet of documents protruded. This packet and his active manner made him stand out. I later learned that he worked in a bank and was one of the organizers of this series of discourses on the epic *Rāmāyaṇa.* Speaking in Tamil, he said that the series had been very successful and that 1,000 rupees had been contributed to the *paurāṇika,* as well as many additional individual gifts. He then introduced a friend of his, a member of the Indian civil service who had recently been transferred to Madras from the north. The civil servant wore a *dhotī* and no shirt. He was tall and well built, wore glasses and a stylish Western haircut. He spoke in English, using many Sanskrit phrases and *ślokas.* An elderly pandit with a top knot translated almost simultaneously into Tamil.

The civil servant grew more and more impassioned and eloquent. His theme was that there is not and could not be any real happiness in this life. The audience responded to his message and his Sanskrit quotations with sighs of assent. The *paurāṇika* continued to sit on the platform with a benign smile on his face.

After the meeting, the organizer arranged for me to interview the *paurāṇika* at the railroad station the next morning.* The *paurāṇika* would then be free from other people who wanted to see him and would have at least an hour before his train left.

When I arrived at the station, the organizer of the program was already on the platform. He greeted me with a vigorous "Rām, Rām" and led me to a small car parked near the station. The *paurāṇika* was in the back seat, and the owner of the car sat behind the wheel. The latter man, who operated an auto parts store, had driven them to the station. We all squeezed into the little car, with the organizer and the store-owner acting as interpreters for the *paurāṇika* and offering opinions of their own.

The profession of *paurāṇika* was not hereditary in his Brahman family; he was the first to turn to it. From the age of nine to thirteen, he had studied under a village pandit. Between the ages of thirteen and twenty-two, he was employed in agriculture in the village. As a child, he had listened to many *paurāṇikas* among relatives and friends in his village but did not decide to make it his career until he was about twenty. At that time, he occasionally read discourses, and finding an interested and appreciative audience, was seized with the desire to "give out." From his twenty-second to his twenty-fifth year, he lived in town and studied the Vedānta under a famous svāmī and *śāstrin*.

The *paurāṇika* said that he had no special technique of recitation. He simply follows the ancient, traditional way, "the way of dedicated souls." As he recites he gathers momentum, and the words "just come." He follows the Vālmīki text of the *Rāmāyaṇa,* giving important passages in Sanskrit with an occasional Tamil paraphrase. His seniors had taught him the main background for his discourses. He never uses written notes. He listens for "fresh and sweet things" from the ancients and takes care to remember them. When he started, he used to recite with the text in hand, rendering the meaning of each stanza in "an interesting manner." After fifteen years of repetitions, he found that the important portions "stuck to his mind" and that he could dispense with the text. He has specialized in reciting the *Bhāgavatapurāṇa* as well as the *Rāmāyaṇa*.

The *paurāṇika* now travels primarily to towns, visiting villages much less often than in the past. He attributes the change to the migration of the "cultured" people—that is, Brahmans—to the towns, and their need for more "relaxation" and opportunities "to think of God." Formerly, the "cultured" people had lived in the villages and learned philosophy from the *śāstras*. Now they live in the towns and are not educated in the *śāstras,* so they need to listen to recitations of the Purāṇas and the Epics. They have changed from *karmamārga* to *bhaktimārga,* from ritual observance to devotion.

The auto parts dealer suggested another reason for the change: In the villages, people live a quiet life, but in the towns they are upset by antireligious movements and look for a defense against them. The antireligious

* See photographs following page 174.

threat had probably begun about fifteen or twenty years before. The *paurāṇika* agreed.

The *paurāṇika* had observed another change, a shortening of the period of recitation. He used to spend six months to a year in a complete reading of the *Rāmāyaṇa*. Now he usually does it in fifteen days and the *Bhāgavatapurāṇa* in eighteen days. Among the considerations behind this change were his need to attend to family problems—a prolonged absence from home was impractical—the need to complete other ceremonies and religious functions, and the fact that as he grows older he must make shorter-range plans. He had been giving readings for more than thirty years and must soon think of his retirement. The auto parts dealer added that, as many Southerners moved north, the *paurāṇika* was asked to travel over a wider area and thus had less time for any single engagement. The *paurāṇika* agreed that more extensive travel might also be a factor in the shortening of his readings. He and other reciters make frequent visits to the North Indian areas of Bombay, Calcutta, and Delhi. Nevertheless, he felt that he could still give the essence of the *Rāmāyaṇa* or the *Bhāgavatapurāṇa*. He pointed out that the old days had also had a tradition of short readings.

During a fifteen-day reading, the *paurāṇika* will read the *Rāmāyaṇa* from beginning to end. He does not break the story up into separate episodes, such as the marriage of Sītā or the coronation of Rāma, or announce each episode in advance as some reciters do. He admits, however, that certain parts of the story do stand out, and he gives them the importance they have in the original text. He does not try to dramatize or "vulgarize" these incidents.

The continuing popularity of the familiar stories, the *paurāṇika* explained, was a "divine dispensation." The Epics and Purāṇas are great works with an inner vitality, quality, and discipline of which the listener never tires. They are called in Sanskrit "the eternally new." Moreover, there is religious merit in hearing the recitations. Faith in the *śāstras* destroys past sins, the "bad accumulations in the mind." Even hearing the sound vibrations will clear up bad tendencies. Then, too, as people hear and understand the moral teachings, they will carry out the precepts and overcome their evil tendencies. They will, for instance, show more respect for elders and parents and for chastity and will do more to achieve harmony in the family. The moral ideals, rather than the details of the stories, were important.

The *Rāmāyaṇa* used to be more popular than the *Bhāgavata,* the *paurāṇika* said, but now people are becoming more interested in other truths and are equally willing to listen to the *Bhāgavata*.

The *paurāṇika*'s opinion of *harikathā* recitations and of *bhajanas* reflected his concern for maintaining the austere, disciplined reading of the Vālmīki text which he does so well. He saw nothing wrong with the *harikathā* method itself; its value depends on the particular artist. He felt that many artists are now overly inclined to cater to the lowest tastes of the audience and to introduce extraneous elements. *Bhajanas* were useful and could fascinate the learned as well as the unlearned. His own readings had more appeal for Brahmans than non-Brahmans, because he used more of the Sanskrit original and tried to maintain the pure, traditional way of recitation.*

When the *paurāṇika*'s train came into the station, I asked if I might make a contribution to his work, but he refused, saying that he accepts gifts only in the presence of the deity, as the night before.

The organizer invited me to his house to meet his family. He spoke ecstatically about the purāṇic readings and discourses:

"It is a tonic, a sweetmeat for us, a food for us. We live on it. It gives us a memory for life. It charges the air with the divine presence and calls up vivid scenery before our eyes. When I listen to the story of Rāma, I become exhilarated, I forget the day's events, all my troubles in business or in my family. I become completely absorbed, relaxed, and refreshed."

He had recently been in England on a business trip and had taken every opportunity to visit English church services. He said he found little difference between the preaching of a sermon and a purāṇic recitation. In both cases, the speaker expounds and expatiates on a particular text. He had found the English church audience more disciplined and better behaved than an Indian audience, however.

The meeting organizer had no Sanskrit education, but he had heard many of the stories as a child in his village. He had attended college for three years and had then gone to work in a bank, where he remained for twenty years. He was forty-three years old and had four children.

The organizer has arranged daily lectures at his home and two on Sundays. He also holds *bhajanas* there. Because not many people had come to his home recently, he now helps organize the meetings in a public hall. He had made all the arrangements for this last series of readings and had collected 1,000 rupees and numerous other gifts for the *paurāṇika*. He was disappointed that more of his friends had not come.

He had sent out more than 1,000 invitations, but only about 100 of those invited had appeared.

What he appreciates most about the *paurāṇika,* he said, is fidelity to the Vālmīki text and the avoidance of the anecdotes and jokes told by other reciters. He had first heard the *paurāṇika* about four years before and had since brought him to Madras four times. He would not listen to anyone else now.

His personal guru is the headmaster of the high school, "a very learned and wise man," who was also the translator for the North Indians at the meeting. The headmaster gave discourses on the Upaniṣads every Thursday evening at the organizer's home.

The owner of the auto parts store was also a good friend of his. This businessman considered it a great privilege to drive the *paurāṇika* each day from the organizer's house where he was staying to the high school hall for his discourses. He had felt especially privileged to bring him to the railroad station.

The organizer thought that listening to *Rāmāyaṇa* readings was an ideal form of religious discipline for people like himself and his friends, Brahmans without much Sanskrit training. It involves much less effort

* There are also some gifted Brahman and non-Brahman expounders of the Tamil *Rāmāyaṇa* of Kamban.

and work than Yoga. "You don't have to do anything; it just comes and your mind is inspired by the recitation."

## *Cultural Change and Cultural Process*

The *paurāṇika* had related the increasing dominance of towns, rather than villages, in his itinerary and the associated cultural change, the shift from the path of ritual observance (*karmamārga*) to the path of devotion (*bhaktimārga*). His explanation may be interpreted at three levels of generality. At the most general level, it implies the possibility of choice among the major paths to salvation. This interpretation fits in with the often-stated doctrine that Hinduism offers three alternative paths to salvation, the above two and *jñānamārga,* the path of knowledge, and that different individuals or groups may choose whichever one is most suitable. A second interpretation would associate "ritual observance" with orthodox Brahmanism and "the path of devotion" with the less orthodox sects of Vaiṣṇavism and Śaivism or with non-Brahman Hindus. At this level, the shift appears as a departure from orthodoxy in the direction of sectarianism. Finally, at a third level, the *paurāṇika* seems to be saying that a group of urban Brahmans, who have neglected the ritual observances and scriptural studies they used to follow in the villages, now feel the need for the easier path of devotion.

These three interpretations are not mutually incompatible, since they occur at different levels of generality. But the third and most particular interpretation implies that a group of Brahmans is exchanging the path of orthodox religious discipline for a painless religiosity of devotion because of urbanization, increased mobility, and the need to defend themselves against antireligious and anti-Brahman movements. The last factor is somewhat paradoxical, since it suggests that, were it not for the challenge of antireligious movements, these Brahmans would become completely secularized. In the past the shift from ritual orthodoxy to devotion and the growth of heterodox sects may also have been associated with increasing urbanization, travel, and skepticism. Buddhism and Jainism seem to have sprung up in such an environment.[1] Perhaps what we are encountering today is one of those recurrent patterns within Indian civilization. And, if one accepts this cyclical view, one might venture to predict that today's urbanization will not result in secularization, since Buddhism did not, after all, prevail in India and the materialistic and atheistic sects have been almost completely forgotten. Like Buddhism, the antireligious and anti-Brahman movements are likely to be absorbed.

Yet it seems unwise to equate present events to cyclical processes, even in India, where the disposition to do so is very strong. The present does not merely repeat the past; former heterodoxies have been incorporated into later orthodoxies, just as Buddhism influenced the Advaita philosophy of its most effective opponent, Śaṅkarācārya. Novel elements of today may eventually find their way into some future orthodoxy. To identify these novelties, it is necessary to record the particularities of the present before subsuming them as instances of more general, repeating processes. Cultural change in India is characterized by striking continuities, but there is change.

## *Urbanization and Cultural Change*

It was not only the *paurāṇika* who testified to the recent shift from village to town and city. Similar testimony came from specialists in the other cultural media. Storytellers, as well as dance teachers, dancers of the traditional type, producers of plays, pandits, and cultural critics also reported more scope for their activities in urban centers than in the villages. Census data indicate a general movement of the population to urban centers. The proportion of urban population in Madras State has increased from 11 per cent in 1901 to 19 per cent in 1951, with the greatest increase in the largest cities. The population of Madras City, for instance, grew from 500,000 in 1901 to 645,000 in 1931 to 1.5 million in 1951. Between 1941 and 1951, the rate of population growth for Madras City (60 per cent) was greater than that for Madras State (40 per cent).[2]

Tamil Brahmans have participated in the general movement to the cities. In Madras City, their numbers increased from 14,450 in 1901 to 41,700 in 1931, while their population in the state as a whole grew from 416,000 to 495,000 during the same period. The census does not enumerate Brahmans separately after 1931, but there is no reason to suppose that the earlier trend has been reversed. In any case, during the first thirty years of the twentieth century the Brahmans took the lead in coming to an urban center like Madras for education and for jobs in teaching, government, law, cultural activities, and, to a lesser extent, in production, commerce, and transport.

Probably the most important single factor in facilitating the urban movement of the Tamil Brahmans has been their literacy both in English and in Tamil. In 1931, for example, the literacy rate of Brahmans in Madras State was 62 per cent in Tamil and 23 per cent in English. Their nearest competitor, the Komaṭṭi (a banking and trading caste), registered 33 per cent and 2 per cent, respectively. Twenty years later, in 1951, the literacy figure for Madras State as a whole was only 28 per cent, and for Madras City 61.4 per cent. In view of the fact that between 1901 and 1931 the literacy of the Tamil Brahmans had almost doubled, while their literacy in English had almost tripled, we may safely assume that the trend for 1931–51, for which we have no separate census figures, has been in the same direction if not of the same magnitude.

In view of the pronounced migration of Brahmans to the largest cities and their superior literacy in both traditional and modern media, it is not surprising to find storytellers and other cultural specialists converging upon the urban centers. What remains more difficult to determine are the precise effects of these urbanizing trends on the traditional culture.

What, in particular, happens to the Great Tradition as its chief repositories, the Brahmans, move from their ancestral villages and sacred centers into a modern metropolitan center like Madras? The *paurāṇika* gave us a general clue to the nature of the cultural transformation involved: Ritual orthodoxy gives way to a devotional, revivalistic type of religion. But whether this development leads to a secularization of the Great Tradition, a complete deritualization of the orthodox culture, or the creation of a new mass urban culture cannot be inferred from a change in the path of observance. Some of the orthodox will obviously continue ritual observances in the urban environment in various degrees. What happens to the structure of ritual orthodoxy under these conditions? Again, not all the cultural media that have developed in the city have originated there. The press, radio, and movies, it is true, are recent urban creations. But most of the urban cultural media are known in the villages, too, and are frequently associated with *bhakti* movements there. What happens to these media and their specialists as they come to the city and interact with the mass media and their specialists?

### *An Easier Path to Salvation:* Bhakti

The path of ritual observance (*karmamārga* or *karmayoga*) and the path of devotion (*bhaktimārga* or *bhaktiyoga*) are two of the three standard paths within Hinduism that lead to eternal bliss and salvation. The third path is that of knowledge (*jñānamārga* or *jñānayoga*). The three paths have been interpreted as providing a variety of roads open to an individual depending on his degree of spiritual evolution and type of personality:

> To those intent on work, there is *karma-yoga,* the path of fulfilling the ordained duties and performing such meritorious acts as have been prescribed by scriptures. To those who are of an emotional nature, whose heart is not satisfied with impersonal acts or principles of ethical conduct and in whom there is an inner cry for hugging a supreme personality to whom it could pour forth its love and homage, there is the path of devotion, *bhakti-yoga.* And to those of the highest class who can revel only in the Abstract, there is the path of knowledge, *jñāna-yoga,* and the goal of realizing the one impersonal Absolute Brahman, which is of the essence of Being, Light, and Bliss, *Sat, Cit,* and *Ānanda.* Truly cultivated, these are not mutually conflicting, but different paths to the one ultimate goal.[3]

What is particularly significant about these paths in Madras City today is that orthodox Brahmans traditionally committed to the paths of ritual observance and of knowledge are turning to the path of devotion, that they seem to be doing this as a result of moving to the city, and, finally, that the paths themselves are acquiring some new content and form in an urban setting.

There is a very general consensus among the Brahmans of Madras City that they have neglected the path of knowledge (*jñānamārga*) and the path of ritual observance (*karmamārga*). The path of devotion (*bhaktimārga*) is now the most popular and considered to be a last defense against atheism. As one public speaker put it: "We modern men and women who have learned, or are being taught, that we need not follow the *śāstras* but can follow our own inclinations are sure to derive very great spiritual profit and mental comfort by studying the hymns of the popular saints." This is a constant refrain in the speeches of cultural leaders, who never tire of extolling devotional purāṇic recitations, plays, films, and music and dance concerts as an accessible path to salvation open to "modern" man. Even Svāmī Śaṅkarācārya, the spiritual leader of Advaitins in Madras State, who does not regard *bhakti* as a very deep or lasting form of Hinduism, has sponsored conferences of Tamil hymn-singing for "inculcating the spirit of *bhakti* among the people at a time when atheists were doing their best to poison the minds of youngsters through propaganda."

The turning to devotional religion is, in part, a response to antireligious movements and trends and, in part, represents a distinctive development of religious and popular culture in an urban environment. To some extent, this development is a continuation or revival of traditional devotional movements in which Brahmans have always played a leading role, but it has also entered into modern cultural and mass media and serves new needs.

*Bhakti* movements are very old in India and have been traced all the way back to the Vedas.[4] Most generally, however, they have been associated with the post-Vedic and post-Buddhist sectarian movements: Vaiṣṇavite primarily in North India, Śaivite and Vaiṣṇavite in South India. In Tamil tradition, there are sixty-three Śaivite singing poet-saints (called Nāyaṉārs), whose canon of hymns (*Tēvāram*) was collected in the tenth century A.D., and twelve Vaiṣṇavite singing poet-saints (called Āḻvārs), whose canon of hymns (*Divyaprabandham*) was collected in the eleventh century. These hymns, together with the *Bhāgavatapurāṇa,* particularly the story of Krishna's life, are part of the scriptures of Tamil Śaivism and Vaiṣṇavism, and have been placed on a par with the Vedic and Āgamic scriptures.

Traditionally, the doctrine of *bhakti* taught that religious merit and even salvation could be acquired by those deficient in *śāstric* learning, ritual observance, and ascetic penances if they would but love the Lord and sing His name and praises in the presence of other devotees (called *bhāgavatas*). This doctrine gave the movement a mildly anticaste and anti-intellectual tone. The following verses illustrate the mood of many Tamil hymns:

> Though they give me the jewels from Indra's abode,
> Though they grant me dominion o'er earth, yea o'er heaven,
> If they be not the friends of our lord Mahādeva,
> What care I for wealth by such ruined hands giv'n?
>
> But if they love Śiva, who hides in His hair
> The river of Gaṅgā, then whoe'er they be,
> Foul lepers, or outcastes, yea slayers of kine,
> To them is my homage, gods are they to me.
>
> Why bathe in Gaṅgā's stream, or Kāverī?
> Why go to Comorin in Koṅgu's land?
> Why seek the waters of the sounding sea?
> Release is theirs, and theirs alone, who call
> In every place upon the Lord of all.

Why chant the Vedas, hear the *śāstras'* lore?
  Why daily teach the books of righteousness?
Why the Vedāṅgas six say o'er and o'er?
  Release is theirs, and theirs alone, whose heart
  From thinking of its Lord shall ne'er depart.

Why roam the jungle, wander cities through?
  Why plague life with unstinting penance hard?
Why eat no flesh, and gaze into the blue?
  Release is theirs, and theirs alone, who cry
  Unceasing to the Lord of wisdom high.

Why fast and starve, why suffer pains austere?
  Why climb the mountains, doing penance harsh?
Why go to bathe in waters far and near?
  Release is theirs, and theirs alone, who call
  At every time upon the Lord of all.[5]

The sentiments of an easier path to salvation have naturally been popular among non-Brahmans and lower castes. They have given devotional groups the distinctive emotional tone of a brotherhood of mystical devotees of Krishna or of Śiva. Among some devotional groups in contemporary Madras, the emotional tone persists, but the brotherhood is now conceived in terms of modern democratic and equalitarian ideology. And Brahmans from orthodox families have become active participants and leaders of the devotional movement. The devotional movement in Madras City has become ecumenical, an expression of democratic aspirations within Hinduism. It links village and town, traditional and modern, the folk and classical, and sacred and secular spheres of culture. It brings together, at least within the religious and cultural sphere, different castes and sects, linguistic and religious communities. Historically, devotional movements have had similar tendencies but have usually resulted in the formation of exclusive sects. The contemporary movement inspires not so much sectarian and denominational formations as a diffuse emotion of brotherhood, which softens the rough edges of group differences.

### *Urban Pastoral:* Bhajanas

The kind of cultural performance that is closest in form and spirit to the older *bhakti* movements is a form of group hymn singing called *bhajanas.* The gatherings are very informally organized as part of temple processions around the streets of the city or in private homes and halls.* Older men distinguished for their devotion and knowledge of the songs (and known as *bhāgavatas*) act as *bhajana* leaders, but many *bhajana* groups meet without special leaders. Some of the leading singers, of whom there are about 100 in Madras City, come from families who have been devotees for four or five generations. Every Saturday evening, it is usual for these groups to hold a *bhajana* at home with friends. The sessions usually last three or four hours and consist chiefly in chanting the Lord's name and singing devotional songs. A larger all-night *bhajana* is held

* See photographs following page 174.

about once a month. For these, it is usual to have a leader who knows the technique and also some musicians. The more elaborate of the long *bhajanas* include not only chanting of the Lord's name but also a greater variety of songs and an acting out by the devotees of the story of Krishna and his beloved milkmaids, or *gopīs,* as well as of the wedding of Rādhā and Krishna.

A full *bhajana* program, several of which I attended, includes a complete *pūjā* to Krishna, who is invoked with songs, in lithographs on the walls, and in a lamp placed on the floor in the center of a circle of devotees. All of the "attentions" (*upacāras*) offered to a temple image by a priest are offered to the lamp by the singing devotees. The offerings are chiefly in the songs, although some articles, like fans, garlands, and sandal paste, are also used.

One leading devotee, a well-educated *bhāgavata* who very kindly gave me running comments on the *bhajana* in which he was participating, explained that these "attentions" represented "services of all kinds." My devotee friend declared: "We let the Lord enjoy all kinds of happiness, comforts, conveniences, and so forth. We offer them to Him as servants or devotees who always think in this way, 'What shall I do to the Lord next? What service shall I offer? Shall I hold an umbrella for Him? Shall I fan Him? Shall I do this thing for Him? Shall I do that thing for Him?' and so forth. We do all imaginable kinds of service to Him."

As they sit singing in a circle around the lamp, the devotees imagine themselves to be milkmaids or *gopīs* playing with Krishna. "The philosophy here," the *bhāgavata* explained, "is that all men and women in the world are spiritually women, and the Lord alone is male, because the woman's love for her lord or husband is the greatest possible love, and we can acquire such great love only by imagining ourselves as women—as the *gopīs*—and love the Lord, calling after him."

The marriage of Rādhā and Krishna in a complete *bhajana* is an imitation of an orthodox Hindu marriage. Its form, according to the *bhāgavata,* was supposed to have originated in Sītā's marriage to Rāma. In *bhajanas,* the Vedic part is usually left out, but all the rest is included. The pictures of Rādhā and Krishṇa are carried by the devotees as they enact the roles of bride and bridegroom. A marriage string (*tāli*) is put on Rādhā's neck in the picture; the devotees' feet and those on the pictures are painted with sandal paste or turmeric powder; the pictures are taken in procession, flowers are thrown, *pān supārī* is offered, a miniature swing is used, and so on. Some of the Rādhā-Krishna love songs for this part of the *bhajana* are taken from Jayadeva's *Gītagovinda* and are sung in Sanskrit.

The songs and dances of the *bhajana* follow a definite sequence that is known to experienced devotees and can also be learned from printed books. The songs come from various traditional sources—the *Bhāgavatapurāṇa*—and from the regional devotional songs. Some are in Sanskrit, others in Tamil, Telugu, Hindi, and Marathi. There are many songs in praise of the ten incarnations of Viṣṇu and also some in praise of Śiva, "to show that we do not dislike Śiva, though we have been praising Krishna all along."

The dances include the *rāsakrīḍā,* a Krishna dance, and the *kummi* and *kōlāṭṭam,* both folk dances, the former usually performed by women at work. The dances were called "sports" by my *bhāgavata* informant, a translation of *līlā.* They represent the *gopīs'* expression of joy at being with Krishna. "There may be several other sports as well—all imagined to be those the *gopīs* resort to as they are now most happy, having got Krishna back and being able to enjoy His company once again. Happy people will sport in a variety of ways."

In the eyes of the devotees, the climax of the *bhajana* comes when they embrace one another and roll on the floor to take the dust from each other's feet. A young devotee, a college instructor and the *bhāgavata*'s son, explained that this part of the *bhajana* expresses "the spirit of equality without respect to young or old, caste or creed. Each devotee shows that he considers the others his equals and is willing to worship them as the Lord." One of the verses that they sing at this point says: "Let us purify ourselves with the dust that has fallen from the feet of the devotees. Let us praise the two glorious feet of our guru. Let us enjoy the bliss by mutual embraces and attain ecstasy."

Local interest in *bhajanas* has greatly increased in the last twenty years. Non-Brahmans as well as Brahmans hold *bhajanas,* although Brahmans predominated at the ones I attended. There are *bhajanas* of the "sitting" type, where only Tamil songs—usually from the *Tēvāram*[6]—are sung and where Brahmans do not take the lead. Non-Brahman Vaiṣṇaiva *bhajana* halls and *bhajana* parties are also common.

The fifteen to twenty devotees I had seen at two *bhajanas* were mostly Brahmans and had been doing these *bhajanas* together for about six or seven years. They were all personal friends and had generally developed their friendship from meeting at the *bhajanas.* "That is why the *bhajanas* are so good; they make us friends. We accept all, we accept even foreigners."

Women who attend the *bhajanas* may also join the singing, although they usually sit silently on the side. In the last ten years, there have been efforts to organize all-female *bhajanas,* where women do the singing and the men are silent. In fact, there are now probably as many *bhajanas* of women as there are *bhajanas* of men.

### Bhakti *in the Storytelling Media*

A less dramatic kind of devotional performance consists of readings and recitations from the Epics and Purāṇas. India is a storytelling civilization. Stories from the *Rāmāyaṇa,* the *Mahābhārata,* and the *Bhāgavatapurāṇa* are a staple upon which the Indian imagination feeds in all parts of the country. While I was in Madras, I saw hundreds of people daily sitting in public halls avidly listening to the recitation of familiar stories. The reciters were usually professionals (called *paurāṇikas*); some were Brahmans, some non-Brahmans, some were Śaivite, some Vaiṣṇavite, and there were women as well as men among them. One woman I heard usually had an audience chiefly of women, while the male reciters drew mixed audiences but with the men sitting on one side of the hall and the women and children on the other. The style of recitation varied from the austere, erudite manner of the pandit, who would not depart from the Sanskrit texts he knew well, to the folksy, humorous, and anecdotal manner of the reciter who traded on his histrionic and comic talents rather than on his learning. An individual recitation lasts two or three hours, although it is customary to arrange a sequence lasting seven or fifteen days.

Not all the reciters were professionals. In the home, parents and grandparents will tell the stories to the children. And if the householder is orthodox, he will also read, or have read, a canto from the *Rāmāyaṇa* (or *Mahābhārata,* or a Purāṇa) every day as part of his morning prayers. Because the section on the discovery of Sītā (*Sundarakāṇḍa*) has greater merit, it will be read at the rate of seven cantos a day. This ritual type of reading is usually done in the Sanskrit text and is carried on over a period of about a year and a half until the entire Epic is completed. Then a new cycle of reading is begun either in the same text or in another, such as the *Mahābhārata.*

Recitation of stories from the Epics and Purāṇas, whether done by amateurs or by professionals, in ritual Sanskrit or in the vernacular, is only one of the media through which these themes are presented. The same stories may also be sung in ballads, danced, dramatized, painted in pictures, carved on temple towers, and written in books. Each medium has its own special development and combines in many ways with several of the others. The variety of storytelling media is reflected in the numerous Sanskrit words for "story"—*kathā, harikathā, kālakṣepam, pravacana.*

Historically, all of these media have been used to communicate and transmit the traditional religious culture. Professional specialists in the media are known from remote times, performing in the temples of village and town and in palace courts on the occasion of religious festivals, weddings, and royal celebrations. These media came to have a special "popular" function because the masses of the people were not ritually excluded from them as they were from Vedic ceremonies and recitations. For the orthodox, this distinction persists today, the Vedic culture being reserved to the Brahmans and "twice-born," the epic and purāṇic literature being the vehicle of dissemination for the "masses." [7] Yet many changes have occurred and are occurring to blur and shift the distinction. Non-Brahmans, śūdras, and untouchables are being given direct access not only to temples but also to Vedic rites, artificially revived, and to discourses on the Upaniṣads. Brahmans not only participate as performers, patrons, and organizers of the popular cultural media but also have become an eager audience for them. The development of the newer mass media of print, radio, and movies has not eliminated the older cultural media or the traditional themes but has transformed and incorporated them. The increasing concentration of population in urban centers has also brought with it changes in cultural media, specialists, and places and occasions of performance. How far all these changes have produced a mass, secular culture different in values and in organization from the traditional religious culture is a question that I shall now consider.

## *Cultural Effects of Mass Media*

Mass media such as the movies, the radio, the daily newspaper, and the printed book tend to reinforce the trend toward greater popularization. Whether privately or governmentally controlled, they cannot afford to cater to a limited caste, sect, or linguistic group but must seek to maximize the audiences for continuous performances of their media. Popular entertainment is for them a more important value than religious merit and salvation. The technology and organization of the mass media make these shifts possible and introduce, as well, new characteristics in the cultural transmission that are quite different from the traditional cultural media.

The most important of these characteristics is that the mass medium produces an impersonal record—on paper, wax, wire, tape, or film—that exists separately from both performer and audience and can be mechanically reproduced. As a result, the program can be transmitted to mass audiences quickly and in practically any location.

There is a further difference in quality as well as in quantity. The mass media develop their own times, places, and occasions of performance on a principle of continuous daily "showings." This fact cuts them off from the ceremonial calendar geared to the important events of the life cycle and the agricultural cycle, which were the major occasions for the cultural media. On these new occasions and cultural stages, it becomes possible to bypass the distinctions of caste, sect, language, and sponsorship that were important in the traditional performances. Another difference is that the cultural media were equally at home in village and in town, and traveling performers used to spread a living cultural network over the countryside. The mass media, on the other hand, are centered in the large city and require elaborate mechanical equipment and personnel to operate. Although their programs are sent to towns and villages, the impersonal record, rather than the performers, travels. The performers remain in the urban centers.

These distinctions tend to place the mass media in a relation to the traditional culture, its social structure, and its religious values that is very different from the relation of the cultural media to those traditional elements. A constant repetition of themes in the mass media is no longer regarded, at least by the producers, as "eternally new" but is merely a source of dependable income or an obstacle to novelty. The cultural tradition, which in India is thought of as being transmitted from what has been revealed to the seers (*śruti*) and through that which is remembered (*smṛti*) by pandits and storytellers, undergoes a transformation when it is transmitted impersonally over the mass media without the benefit of seers, gurus, or reciters.

## Bhakti *in the Films*

But even the changes introduced by the mass media have not yet resulted in a secularization of religious culture. Print, radio, and film are used to disseminate purāṇic stories and devotional music, and *bhakti*-inspired audiences have their own ways of personalizing the impersonal mass media. In Tiruppati, in some of the bigger temples of the Tamil country, and in Annamalai University, the loudspeaker and phonograph record are used to broadcast devotional music, hymns, and prayers. Recently, the availability of tape recorders at about 1,000 rupees has permitted a number of people to keep recordings of such devotional recitals at home and to listen to them regularly. The hymns recited at the Tiruppati shrine in the small hours of the morning to wake up the Lord have been tape-recorded and kept by some devotees.

The example of the "mythological" and "devotional" films is instructive. During our stay in Madras, a non-Brahman and practically illiterate chauffeur kept urging us to see the film *Auvaiyār,* which was then very popular and which he characterized only in an enthusiastic murmur as *"bhakti, bhakti."* We did eventually see the film and also interviewed its producers. The story is about the female saint and poet, Auvaiyār, of the Tamil country who goes about performing miracles with her devotional songs. Usually, each song is connected with an incident teaching a moral lesson, and, as it is sung, the incident is dramatized on the screen. A giant image of Gaṇeśa was kept in the theater lobby.

The technique of narrative song sequence in the *Auvaiyār* film has also been used in other devotional and historical films, as well as in radio dramas and in epic-like narratives about Gandhi and the Congress Party struggle for independence. It is an adaptation of a village ballad form called "bow song" (*viḷḷuppāṭṭu*) to urban mass media.[8] One person responsible for these adaptations was the producer and director of the film *Auvaiyār*. A folk poet by avocation, he is known as "the Bobby Burns of Tamil" and has a nickname that means "soaked in the soil." He has composed more than 1,000 folksongs in village meter on harvest festivals, weddings, war, and modern themes. The village background of folk plays, folksongs, ballads, and purāṇic recitations to which he was exposed as a child have provided him, he believes, with great literary wealth. His was the only Brahman family in the village, and their relation to the non-Brahmans was very good. He came to Madras in 1935 at the age of twenty-five, but mentally he still lives, he says, in the village. He goes back at least once each year. And in town, he tries to live as in the village with some thirty-five to forty relatives under one roof—including four different generations.

*Auvaiyār* is expected by its producers to run for five years and make a large profit for the company. Its great success has encouraged Indian film producers to turn once more to "devotionals" and "mythologicals" as dependable investments. One film producer stated that about 80 per cent of the stories in Indian movies are now traditional, reflecting the desire of the movie companies to play it safe by relying on the familiar. Many of these traditional stories are drawn from the Epics and Purāṇas or from stories about the lives of regional saints like Auvaiyār or Caitanya.

This trend, which represents a return to the mythological themes of the early Indian films, is considered regressive by some modern producers. They do not feel that traditional subject matter is as "educational" as "social" or "landscape" films. The educational value of the "mythological," according to one producer, is restricted to "what has already happened." This comment sounds paradoxical to a Westerner but probably reflects the Indian's realistic acceptance of his mythology. The same producer also worries a good deal about whether a medium like the films is not too powerful in a country like India, "where people are so ready to believe." He seemed particularly impressed by the case of an actor who had played the role of a saint in one devotional film and was for several years afterward followed around and worshiped by large crowds, as if he were really a saint.

On the other hand, the producer was convinced that the filmmaker must think of the Indian "man in the street," the rickshaw puller in the city and the villager, as his audience and suit the film to their taste and understanding. Film music and dancing cannot be classical or even authentically Indian. Film music is a mixture of Spanish, Hawaiian, and Indian, and the dancing is a mixture of streamlined classical Indian dances and European styles like the waltz.

Not all Indian films have traditional or devotional themes. As in the United States, comedy and variety films are also quite popular. There is an Indian "Costello" who is in such great demand at the studios in Calcutta, Bombay, and Madras that he spends much of his time flying from one studio to another. This emphasis, too, needs no special justification in the filmmakers' minds: "The cinema is often all the rickshaw puller or the villager has. It has to combine everything in an evening's entertainment—dancing, comedy, fighting, romance, and lots of songs." The villagers see the films in the nearest towns or in the village at the mobile theaters sent out by the film companies or the government. The government films are documentaries, shorts, and information films and must also be shown in urban theaters.

### *The Folk-Urban Continuum in Dramatic Cultural Media*

Comedy, variety, social, and educational films belong to an international urban culture and are not especially associated with the devotional outlook, as the mythological, devotional, and historical films are. Yet even these more purely "international" films retain many distinctive Indian features—traditional song and dance forms, the combining of many different media in one program, long and rambling sequences, the use of regional languages. The mass media have brought in new urban forms of devotional and nondevotional storytelling, but they are also still linked in themes and techniques to the folk and traditional storytelling media.

A similar continuum can be traced in popular urban drama. The village folk play (*terukkūttu*) has migrated with the low-caste communities and thrives on city lots as vigorously as it once did around village temples. As in the village, these are all-night performances, given about four times a year during festivals and important occasions. The actors are all amateurs, young men of the community who are rehearsed for several months by an older man who happens to know the plays. The most popular ones are based on incidents from the *Mahābhārata* and *Rāmāyaṇa* and from

Tamil epics and legends, all familiar to the audience. Comic interludes and farce, usually having no relation to the play, help to sustain interest through the night. There are also presentations of garlands and gifts to the leading actors on first appearance, because they are the important people who organize the plays and raise the money for city license fees. This little ceremony and the colorful costumes of the leads give a touch of glamour to the kerosene-lighted, roped-off lot on which Arjuna and Draupadī, Rāma and Sītā, Kōvalan and Kaṇṇaki act and sing their roles.

While the folk play persists unchanged in the city, there has also developed within the last fifty years a form of popular devotional drama that corresponds to the devotional films and the urbanized forms of Purāṇic recitation. Specializing as the other media do in mythological, devotional, and historical themes, the devotional play incorporates some elements—bright costumes, professional lighting, and stage effects—of the court theater and of the modern stage. To a Western observer, the action in these devotional plays seems predominantly of a tableau form, with occasional songs and dances and numerous sound effects and trick stage effects. Their form serves to highlight the mythological incidents and personages and to present each in as luminous a manner as might be desired from a chromolithograph.

Devotional plays are probably the most popular dramatic performances in Madras, with all classes of the population paying to see them at a commercial theater. They have been developed by a professional actor and producer, Nawab Raja-Manickam, who has a reputation for *bhakti*. Before the curtain goes up on one of his plays, puffs of smoke roll out under it and from the sides, indicating that he is performing a *pūjā* to Gaṇeśa. He has produced plays based on Rāmdās and on the life of Christ, as well as on South Indian deities like Murugan, to teach the message of devotion and national unity. The first scene in the Murugan play *Kumāravijayam* opens with a singing tableau representing Indian unity. Various figures, all young boys, appear with papier-maché heads of Gandhi, Nehru, and other Indian leaders, as well as regional types, against a backdrop showing a temple, a mosque, and a Christian church.

This devotional drama is a more colorful and urbanized form of the folk play. It is performed by professionals on a commercial stage for mixed audiences and uses modern stage techniques. Its themes remain devotional and its tableaus are more akin to the painted scenes on temple towers than to the modern theater.

Within the last fifty years, however, there has been rapidly developing in the city a modern theater that cuts across caste and sect and has some resemblances to Western theater. Sponsored at first by amateur dramatic societies, particularly of male college students, the movement is now in the hands of professional companies, performing in permanent theater halls. The amateurs, particularly the Suguṇa Vilāsa Sabhā, undertook to stage a great variety of plays in a variety of languages, Kālidāsa in Sanskrit, Shakespeare in English, and plays in Tamil, Telugu, Canarese, and Hindi. They also occasionally took them to the country and to Ceylon. The professionals are more limited in scope. As in the cinema, which is the chief medium now for popular drama, the aim is to reach a wide audience, so Tamil is the major language. Types of plays are categorized, again as in the film, into devotionals, mythologicals, and historicals, on the one hand, and socials and comedies, on the other. The first group is regarded as representing the indigenous Indian theater and the latter as being largely Western-influenced. The Sanskrit drama is virtually neglected by the professionals, although a recent Sanskrit revival may bring it back into popular esteem. In the National Drama Festival organized in 1955 in New Delhi by the newly formed National Academy of Drama, a performance of Kālidāsa's *Śakuntalā* started the program. In the regional competition for this festival in Madras, of the six plays presented, all were in Tamil and one had the English title, *Oh What a Girl.* The play finally selected for presentation in New Delhi, after some controversy among several local drama groups, was a Tamil historical play.

The social play replaces the traditional purāṇic stories and the traditional media of presentation with modern problems and prose dialogues. It corresponds to the novel, the short story, and modern poetry and tends in the main to be cultivated by a similar group of people, those with modern education and in the middle and upper classes. The urban theater prefers to use Tamil and the other Indian vernaculars or even English. It is also more secular than the traditional drama in being less determined by caste and sect. Performances are in public halls open to all who can pay the price of admission. The times and occasions of performance are not geared to temple festivals or other religious occasions; they are brief and are set in accordance with the commercial and cultural exigencies as perceived by the owners of the theaters, the performers, and their organizers and sponsors. In these respects, dramatic media resemble the cinema and the radio and tend to develop their own "festival" calendar.

The involvement of drama in the political arena is reminiscent of the storytelling media. Both the state government and the national government have shown active interest in dramatic activities. In addition to the officially sponsored academies and drama festivals, there has also been use of dramatic media to tell villagers the story of independence, of the five-year plans, and of specific projects for village improvement. Both the traditional and the modern dramatic forms have been employed for this purpose. And not only the government has made political use of drama. Private voluntary groups and opposition political parties and movements have made similar use of this medium.

## The Classicists

Pervading almost all cultural media and mass media and appealing to all classes of the population, the path of devotion has become a main highway. It is not surprising that Brahmans, too, should find themselves on it as performers, patrons, and audience. Those belonging to *bhāgavata* sects of course find this situation congenial to their traditions, despite the novel elements that have appeared in it. Many Smārtas have also been drawn into it, although their tradition has stressed the paths of knowledge and ritual more than that of devotion.

Not everyone, however, has taken the path of *bhakti*. Beside it and overlapping it, another path, far smaller, is clearly discernible. This is the path of classical art cultivated by a very distinctive class of patrons, critics, and connoisseurs, among whom Brahmans predominate.

The classicists are not regular or frequent participants in *bhajanas,* which they regard as too emotional and uncontrolled a form of religious expression, suitable perhaps for less cultivated people. If they go to purāṇic recitations, they prefer the austere *paurāṇika* who knows the Sanskrit texts well and adheres faithfully to them, rather than the reciter who caters to popular tastes and humor. They may not always have sufficient command of Sanskrit to follow the texts, but they nevertheless insist on purity of standards.

They regard the musical form of purāṇic recitation known as *harikathā* as an art form superior both to *bhajanas* and to traditional recitation without music. In the field of the drama, they fail to see how the modern social play has improved on the classical play, and they prefer the devotional and folk play to the "social." Highest in their esteem are the classical South Indian dance, the *bharatanāṭya,* and the classical South Indian or Carnatic music, vocal and instrumental, which they consider the very peak of aesthetic achievement.

For the classical critics there is, in other words, a definite hierarchy of cultural media and performances. This hierarchy depends not only on the general character of the media but also on the degree of sophistication, knowledge of the art tradition, and taste with which they are rendered. As one ascends the hierarchy, the values of popular entertainment as well as of *bhakti* diminish, and the values of "pure art" become more important. The "pure art" at the top is to some extent "art for art's sake," but it is not completely secularized. It represents a fourth and distinctive path to release and the absolute, and a kind of sublimation of the paths of ritual observance and knowledge.

### *Story and Song:* Harikathā

The distinctive technique of reciting called *harikathākālakṣepam* uses songs in several languages—Sanskrit, Tamil, Telugu, Kannada, Marathi, and Hindi—dramatic exposition in Tamil, and musical accompaniment; it is considered an art form, since it demands a knowledge of music, languages, and dramatic technique. This form of *harikathā* was developed in the Tanjore Court about 100 years ago through adaptation of a Mahārāṣṭrian form. During the 1950's the senior Madras performer in this technique was Saraswati Bai, a lady Brahman noted for her knowledge of both North Indian and South Indian music, her gifted voice, her excellent pronunciation of a wide range of Indian languages, and her erudition and good taste in the selection of song and story material. Her style of *harikathā* is regarded as a unique combination of the best styles of her predecessors.

Krishna Bhāgavatar of Tanjore is credited with the creation of the distinctive Tamil *harikathā* from the Mahārāṣṭrian model. Saraswati Bai, who claims descent from him through her guru or teacher, believes that this form began in the South in the nineteenth century. In a personal interview, she gave the following account:

> Before that, there were just long recitations of stories from the *Rāmāyaṇa* and other Purāṇas. During the reign of the Marāṭhā Court, a *harikathā* artist from the North, Ramachandra Morgar Bhava, came on a pilgrimage to Tanjore. He came during the four sacred months—July-October—when he was not supposed to travel. So he stayed at the court and gave *harikathā* performances. The princess heard him and was very much impressed because this was very different from the *paurāṇika's* way of telling stories. She had a protegé, Krishna Bhāgavatar, at the court who was then fourteen years old and was learning the violin. She and the minister wanted him to learn *harikathā,* and, simply from watching R. M. Bhava, he learned the art in one year.
>
> The princess then arranged for performances on successive days, the old man performing the first day, and the boy the second. Afterward, she said that Bhava's performance must be heard but the boy's performance must be heard *and seen.* She meant that the boy's acting and dancing were improvements over the singing of Bhava. Krishna Bhāgavatar also introduced Tamil as the language of the narration. Bhava had used Marathi. He was a Mahārāṣṭrian Brahman. My guru knew and admired Krishna Bhāgavatar.

Saraswati Bai's guru, Pandit K. Krishnachar, was a Sanskrit pandit in the Christian College of Madras and, although himself not a *bhāgavata,* was a thorough student of the art and of South Indian music. He gave up his teaching duties at the college when he decided to train her as a *harikathā* performer. He taught her Sanskrit as well as *harikathā* and was always present at his pupil's performances, even when she toured.

Saraswati Bai has been awarded several titles, including those of "expert musician" (*Gāyan Paṭu*) and "expert in *harikathā* performance" (*Kīrtan Paṭu*). She considers herself equally a storyteller, a singer, and a religious teacher. "All three must be present in equal proportion; no one is primary." She does not restrict her moral teaching to one special lesson or sect but teaches about Hinduism. She performs before both Vaiṣṇavite and Śaivite sects. She comes from a Mādhva Brahman family. Her repertoire of stories about Śiva, Viṣṇu, Subrahmaṇya, and many other gods is usually taken from the *Rāmāyaṇa, Mahābhārata,* minor Purāṇas, and the hagiology of the saints. She recounts the same story many times but insists that there is no such thing as "repetition." People love to hear the same story over and over and will call for it in advance. A popular favorite is the story of Nandaṉar, the Tamil Śaivite Harijan saint, which she thinks she has told at least 10,000 times.

She is willing "to tell any kind of story everywhere, provided it is about God. But the essence must be devotion (*bhakti*) and I would not sacrifice this anywhere." In her view, *harikathā* is the most appropriate medium for the expression of *bhakti.* In a public speech she said: "Music is not only a medium of entertainment in this world but also the means of realizing the Godhead."

She performs for festivals and festivities, usually of special castes; marriages; temple festivals; before institute and *sabhā* associations; and before maharajas. She has performed before the maharajas of Mysore,

Travancore, Cochin, and others. "Three generations have heard me; I have been doing it for forty-eight years." Marriages are the most frequent occasions, festivities next, temple festivals third, performances for *sabhās* and maharajas least. She attributes a decline in the number of temple festivals to the spread of atheism. To some extent, too, musical associations and concerts are taking the place of temple festivals. She has given *harikathā* performances all over India, in Calcutta, Bombay, and Benares, as well as abroad, in Rangoon and Ceylon. Before foreign audiences who do not understand her Tamil narration, she always selects songs in the language of the region, and with these and her "mono-acting" she can hold them. Indian audiences are, of course, already familiar with the stories and have shown great enthusiasm wherever she has gone.

She has also traveled to the villages. "I have not spared a single village and not a single village has spared me." Whenever she has traveled by cart, crowds of villagers would come out to greet her and would follow her from one village to another. The arrangements for village performances are usually made by a landlord, who invites her for a marriage or a temple festival. The landlord gives a fee for her, her musicians, and her guru; the villagers will give her shawls and other presents. The musicians include a drummer who has been with her for nearly forty years, a harmonium player who has been with her almost as long, and a supporting singer who also plays cymbals. The harmonium is used instead of the *tambūrā* for a drone because the *tambūrā* is big and difficult to transport. The traveling party also includes her cook and servants.

Each trip used to last two or three months, but now she goes only for a week or ten days. A manager makes the arrangements for the distant trips; for the near ones she makes them herself. Local arrangements are usually made by the inviter, who pays all the expenses of the party and, in addition, pays her a fee. When she was in Bombay she received a fee of about 2,000 rupees. For performances close to Madras, she usually receives about 600 rupees. No written contracts are drawn, but "it is all written in letters, so it is like a legal contract."

Village audiences and town audiences are not too different, she said, but she has found village audiences more appreciative of both her stories and her music—not because they are more religious, but because "they just respond better." Thousands of villagers will come to hear her from neighboring villages. Southerners show more interest in art and music than Northerners, and when they settle outside of South India they always organize music and art activities. In Rangoon, Burma, where there are many "overseas Tamils," 10,000 people came to hear her at one performance.

The epic and purāṇic stories are also still recited in the villages in the old style by *paurāṇikas* but now not as much as in the cities, where the *paurāṇikas* receive more recognition and are paid more. In her opinion, the *harikathā* performances are probably more popular than the regular readings, which go on for periods of six months to a year, because they are for special occasions and distill the essence of the teaching in a short time—about four hours.

There are many *harikathā* performers now, both women and men, and she knows them all. When they are in town, they come to her for advice. She has helped many of them to get started.

The most difficult thing in *harikathā,* she says, is to take the many different parts in a single story. She has been highly praised on this score. One admirer has written: "I have seen her, in her *kālakṣepams,* put great actors in the histrionic field to shame by her masterly impersonation of the characters of a Rāvaṇa, a Hanumān, or a Garuḍa, a giant or a cooing bird, a *bhakta* or a scoffer, a lover or a libertine, a god or a goddess, a saint or a sinner, a man or woman, king or peasant, with equal ease and yet remain in her decorous sari—'rich but not gaudy'—the sweet, simple, generous and loving Lady Bhāgavata she has been and is today." [9]

These varied roles acquire knowledge, too, of the appropriate dialects, of some Urdu for the story of Rāmdās, and of Tamil slang for that of Nandaṉar. *Harikathā* is a kind of concentrated drama, a monodrama, in which one gifted actor enters swiftly a whole series of characters, moods, and manners.

The day before my interview, a local newspaper announced that the Indian Government was going to use *harikathā* to publicize the five-year plans. Saraswaṭi Bai said she hoped that the government would set up a national academy for *harikathā,* as it has set up an academy for letters and the dance; otherwise the art would be lost. I asked her whether *harikathā* could be used to get people to dig pits and clean wells, whether devotional songs were not inappropriate for this purpose. This question evoked much laughter from her and the members of her family who were present. But then she said, seriously: "No, the devotional songs would not be appropriate. But I would be willing to compose new songs if I were asked. This is a matter of patriotism, and I would be willing to sing about pits and wells, too."

Several *harikathās* about Gandhi's life have been written and performed. One was recorded by another lady *bhāgavata* who comes from a Brahman Vaiṣṇava family in Mysore. In her version, the story of Ghandi's life is told after the fashion of the lives of the saints. In fact, Gandhi is treated as an incarnation (*avatāra*) of God who has come to deliver India from foreign domination. Gandhi's death is also effectively told as the death of a martyr. Gandhi Bhāgavatar (Rājarām), a Tamil Smārta Brahman and a Tamil poet, was a pioneer in this line.

To tell Gandhi's story, the reciter uses all the songs and Sanskrit verses that are used in the traditional *harikathā.* She begins with the famous song of the Gujarati saint Narasimha Mehta, which starts with the words "*Vaiṣṇava janato*" and declares that "he is true devotee of Lord Viṣṇu who knows the suffering of others." It was Gandhi's favorite song. The reciter emphasizes the great faith that Gandhi had in devotion and in the recital of Rāma's name. Gandhi's doctrine of help and uplift for the poor and his belief in equality are also stressed.[10]

### *Classical South Indian Dance and Music*

In *harikathā, bhakti* is still an important element, although considerations of artistic and dramatic technique and learning also loom large. In the classical South Indian dance called *bharatanāṭya* and in classical South Indian or "Carnatic" music, aesthetic standards and the rules of art predominate. In fact, these two media are the most frequently associated with the ideas of classical art. They are almost never referred to without the prefix "classical." Their more active revival is dated from two political events, the Madras meeting of the Indian National Congress in 1927, and the All-India Khādī and Swadeshi Exhibition organized by the Tamiḻnāḍu Provincial Congress Committee in Madras in 1935.

On the occasion of these meetings, local cultural leaders organized an All-India Music Conference in 1927 and a Music Festival in 1935. Until then, voluntary organizations called *sabhās* had arranged periodic public performances of music and *harikathā*. Apart from the publicity given at these times to dancing and music, one of the most important results was the organization of the Music Academy of Madras. Proceeds remaining after the expenses of the All-India Music Conference of 1927 had been met were donated by the Reception Committee of the Congress for the founding of a Music Academy. The Academy soon became an important center for the promotion of Indian dance and music. It has sponsored regular performances of leading artists, holds annual conferences at which both scholars and artists exchange knowledge, encourages new talent, sponsors music and dance schools, and tries to set high standards of public taste. The *Journal of the Music Academy* has become an all-India forum for learned discussions of the technicalities of Indian music and dance and enjoys an international circulation as well. The success of the Music Academy stimulated the organization of other voluntary associations, and now there are about twenty "cultural *sabhās*" in Madras carrying on similar programs. During the Christmas season, which usually falls in the Hindu holy month of Mārgaśīrṣa, the different cultural associations vie with one another to bring the best artists to Madras and to put on the most interesting programs. The most elaborately planned program is that of the Music Academy, which usually consists of expert demonstrations and discussions in the morning, popular auditions and programs in the afternoons, and classical concerts in the evening. Two of the halls most frequently used for these programs are the Museum Theater in Egmore and the Rāsika Rañjanī Sabhā (Association Which Pleases Connoisseurs) of Mylapore.

Cultural associations, or their leaders, also organize special local programs for visiting dignitaries and foreign cultural delegations, and for the national drama, music, and dance festivals that are now held in New Delhi on Republic Day. The programs are not always the same, although there is usually a common core of classical South Indian dance and music in them. In 1955, on the occasion of the Congress meetings at Āvaḍi near Madras, free cultural programs for the delegates and visitors included, in addition to classical music and dance, several varieties of folk dances, a puppet show, a dummy horse dance, a folk play, a devotional drama, a social drama, and devotional singing, or *bhajanas*.

The Music Academy and the other local cultural associations, while tolerant of "folk" and "popular" culture, regard the promotion of classical music and dance as their own primary responsibility. Their influence has secured a hearing for the "classics" on the radio and, to a lesser extent, in films and has prompted the organization of state and national academies of music, dance, drama, and letters. They are the institutional representatives of the classic revival. Although Brahmans have played an active part in their formation, they are not restricted with respect to caste or sect.

### *The Revival of Classical Dancing:* Bharatanāṭya

The "revival," strictly speaking, was not only a revival but brought in major innovations—particularly in the dance. Before it was revived, it was known as the *nāc* or *sādir nāc* and was performed by hereditary families of dancing girls. They were called *devadāsīs,* servants of God, because they were usually "dedicated" or given to particular temples, where they sang and danced at the temple processions. Their "dedication" involved a "marriage" to one of the deities in the temple so that they could not become widows. Any children they had would take the mother's father's name and could inherit his property as well as the mother's. The dancing girls were trained to sing and dance by professional teachers known as *naṭṭuvaṉārs,* men who came from hereditary families of teachers and musicians and were also attached to the temples. Some of them were the male members of the *devadāsī* community, while others came from a different community. The dancing girls, their teachers, and musicians performed not only on the occasion of temple festivals and ceremonies but also for private parties, particularly weddings, and at palace parties. Special troupes of dancing girls and musicians were sometimes permanently attached to the courts.

Because of the association of some of the dancing girls with prostitution, an "anti-*nāc*" campaign was waged at the turn of the century by British and Indian reformers to stop temple dancing and "dedication" of girls to temples. In 1905, the Executive Committee of the Prince and Princess of Wales' Reception Fund unanimously decided that there should be no performance by *nāc* girls at the entertainment to be given for their Royal Highnesses at Madras. In 1947, Madras State forbade "dedication" and temple dancing.

After the revival, the dance came to be called *bharatanāṭya;** daughters of respectable families, including Brahmans, now take it up; it is taught in high schools, and in diluted form has become one of the most popular items in cultural programs in the films, on the stage, and at private gatherings. Although in the recent past it was developed in South India, especially around Tanjore, it is now popular all over India and has also been performed abroad by Uday Shankar, Ram Gopal, Shanta Rao, and other dancers.

The major agents of the change are, as usually happens, transitional

* *Bharatanāṭya* means dance based on the technique originally laid down by the sage Bharata, author of the oldest surviving text in the art, the *Nāṭyaśāstra.* The name was introduced and used by Dr. V. Raghavan, who played a significant scholarly and academic role in the renaissance of the art. Previously, the dance had been called the art of *bharatam, sādir,* or *nautchnāc.* The terms *bharatam, bharataśāstra,* and *nāṭya* are still in use.

figures. Three kinds of transitional figures have played an important part in transforming the *sādir nāc* into *bharatanāṭya:* dance critics, the traditional dancing teachers, and some dancing girls.

*Dance Critic*

One influential critic highly respected by friends of the art and by professionals was K. V. Ramachandran. His perspective was gained from a wide academic background, since he was a keen student of ancient Indian sculpture and painting and of all aspects of traditional culture. He was a technically well-informed critic of classical dance and music and a sharp-tongued enemy of mass culture and everything he considered counterfeit.[11]

K. V. Ramachandran wrote one of the first technical appreciations of *bharatanāṭya* in a series of articles published in 1935 in the magazine *Triveni, Journal of Indian Renaissance.* This journal, founded in Madras in 1928, became a major organ of the cultural revival in the South, in form and format like the old *Dial.* The articles are highly detailed analyses of the dance movements of the *nāc,* still so called at this time, and of its affiliations with the Brahman dance drama, the Tamil folk play, and Bharata's *Nāṭyaśāstra.* The article is illustrated with photographs of many of the movements posed by Ramachandran and his wife.

After 1942, K. V. Ramachandran lived in Coimbatore, where he did a flourishing business making and selling a popular hair tonic. He discovered the formula about 1929 when his wife began to lose her hair after the birth of their first child. They were then living in Madras, where he ran a small druggist shop. The success of the tonic enabled him to devote more of his time to the study of classical Indian dance and music. He has also studied Western music, because he regards himself as a "citizen of the world whose antennae spread all over the world." He knows Mozart, Beethoven, Wagner, and Handel and is especially fond of Debussy, in whose music he finds Javanese influences.

K. V. Ramachandran comes from a Smārta Brahman family learned in music and Sanskrit. Four of his uncles were musicians, and some of his cousins were pandits. He had studied music and Sanskritic tradition. He first became seriously interested in the classical dance when he was in college in Madras from 1915 to 1919. The stimulus was his reading of Coomaraswamy, Otto Rothfeld, and E. B. Havell. But even as a boy he had been attracted by the aesthetic charm of the dance and used to watch the *devadāsīs* and their dancing teachers at marriages and temples as often as he could, both in the city and when he went to the villages during vacations. At that time, there were at least 500 professional dancing teachers in Madras and many *devadāsīs.* The anti-*nāc* movement had not yet come to a head, and public concerts were not yet popular. He thinks that the first public dance concert was held in Madras in 1933 and that Chokkalingam Pillai was the teacher.

His reading of secondary works on the dance stimulated him to go to some of the original sources, like Bharata's *Nāṭyaśāstra,* and to the temple dance sculptures at Cidambaram and Tanjore to reconstruct the original forms of the classical art. The dance poses on the temple sculptures, while valuable, have to be reconstructed with caution, since they represent only a single "frozen section" within a moving sequence. However, he believes that through a careful study of these literary and temple sources and of the "authentic living traditions of the art" in Java and Bali as well as in India, it is possible to recover the true classical dance.

After his marriage in 1925, he encouraged his wife to learn dancing from a professional temple dancer in Mylapore and from a Brahman dancing teacher who taught her the art of interpretation (*abhinaya*). He often corrected his wife's poses as well as those of professional dancers who came to him for advice. He also encouraged his daughters to take up dancing and singing.

K. V. Ramachandran believes that Brahmans have always played an important role in transmitting the classical dance. Because of their knowledge of Sanskrit and rhetoric, they were especially qualified to teach *abhinaya*. This tradition has almost died out, although remnants of it can still be found in the dance dramas (*bhāgavatamelānāṭaka*) performed by male Brahmans in a few Tamil and Telugu villages. At some point, the Brahmans taught the art to the guilds of non-Brahman teachers or, *naṭṭuvaṉārs,* who have jealously guarded it since.

The *devadāsīs,* too, have played an important part in keeping the dance traditions alive, Ramachandran believes. The dancing girls rarely married but were kept as concubines by well-to-do patrons. The children were raised by the mother and her relatives without any stigma. The male members of the community were usually dancing teachers and musicians and married within the community. Whatever faults moral reformers may have found with their social life, Ramachandran thinks their mode of life did not prevent these professional dancers from achieving very high standards of proficiency, taste, and judgment in the art and general culture as well.

K. V. Ramachandran's sympathies have always been with the Congress movement, although he did not belong to the party. He ran classes for Harijans when Gandhi was in jail and has always been a nationalist at heart. As a child he used to have his hands caned for singing the patriotic anthem "Vande Mātaram." * His elder brother was active in the movement, for which he went to jail, and later became a leading journalist. Ramachandran does not, however, believe that the Congress Party has been very sympathetic to cultural pursuits. He cannot regard seriously its claims to extend the Swaraj to Indian culture. He regards the founding of the Music Academy in 1927 on the occasion of the Congress Party meeting in Madras that year as merely a coincidence, and the Madras 1935 Music Festival sponsored by the Tamiḻnāḍu Congress Committee, in which he himself participated, was of the same character. "The political movement just makes a show of patronage but has really very little influence and

* Originally a poem by the Bengali novelist Bankim Chandra Chatterji in the late-nineteenth-century novel *The Abbey of Bliss.* Later turned into a proto-national anthem by pre–World War II terrorists.

never picks the right people. The politicians are like flies on the wheel of culture."

His attitude toward present trends is highly critical. Dance performances have been commercialized, "the mob calls the tune, the art has lost refinement, and the artists are interested only in revenue." The emphasis on translating all songs into Tamil so that everyone can understand them has not increased the number of people who really understand the music. And "acoustical cranks," who are quite unmusical, have become music critics.

But he is not without hope for the future: "We will die before these things die." With a long-range view and a "better class of people," the classical arts can be kept alive. The proper approach would be first to understand what you have, then to clear up misconceptions, and only then to develop new forms within the old framework. He thinks even temple dancing could be restored if political conditions were favorable, since people at large are not bothered by "morality."

In Indian villages today, little survives of the classic forms. They have more of the folk arts, which, he supposes, may be "the soul of the classics, like a child lisping" but do not become important until they have been influenced by classical forms.

In his view, the renaissance of Indian culture that started with great hopes in the 1920's proved a failure. The "cinema people" have taken it over, and now "the monkey has got it." Indian culture has become more and more attenuated in every generation and, "like a child with an enlarged liver, lives on in an enfeebled way." The development of modern dance and music schools has "merely increased the scope for fraud."

It had been possible for a classical culture to flourish in the past because performances were regularly held in temples and palaces; patrons were musicians and connoisseurs; audiences were highly critical; and artists were responsive to this atmosphere. Now audiences are very uncritical, and the "artists play down, not up, to the audience." In the past, artists had considered it a privilege to perform before the deity, and there was no stress on personality and the ego; compositions were impersonal and anonymous. The cultivation of the art through family tradition also enhanced cultural values.

A student of Tamil before he studied Sanskrit, K. V. Ramachandran believes the present "left-wing" effort to Tamilize the arts is culturally suicidal. Although *bharatanāṭya* developed in Tamil country, its life source has been its connection with Sanskrit. Without this connection, it will dry up or have a lopsided development.

K. V. Ramachandran regards the classical dance as an expression of a spiritual reality. In his presidential address in 1956 to the Indian Institute of Fine Arts in Madras, he referred to some of the religious elements in the dance, especially to its connections with temple worship. He speaks of the first item on a *bharatanāṭya* program, the *alarippū,* as "a divine adoration." "While the main root connects *nāṭya* with the Vedas, others connect it with the Āgamas, which govern and regulate temple worship and tantric rituals."

Secularizing trends in the dance he regards as unfortunate: "By secularizing it, we have converted it into an affair of the drawing room; and imported the spirit of the market place into the tabernacle. . . . all our arts were auxiliary to our religion; a restoration of faith in that religion might help to restore the arts." [12]

*Traditional Dance Teacher*

The image of the classical dance constructed by the dance critics needs to be supplemented by the reports of surviving traditional teachers and dancers. One dancing teacher is now conducting a *bharatanāṭya* dancing school in Madras. I had an opportunity to visit his school and to interview him twice and also to learn from him something of the traditional ways of teaching and dancing as practiced in the villages.

The city dance class was held in a small school hall during hours when classes were not in session, about two hours early in the morning and another two hours in the late afternoon. I visited it one afternoon and watched teacher and students communicate perfectly without the use of language. The teacher sat cross-legged at one end of the room. He vigorously tapped the time with a small round stick and chanted it in nonsense syllables. With his free left hand, he described hand and foot positions for the different steps. Occasionally, he put down the stick and used both hands to describe these positions. His hand movements were intermittent and highly abbreviated, but the pupils followed them intently and were guided by them and by the beats of the stick through the complex intracacies of *bharatanāṭya*.

There were eight students in the class, a young girl from Orissa, an older Pārsī girl from Bombay on a government scholarship, an American woman from New York, and five little girls from eight to ten, most of whom came from Brahman families in the city. They were all learning *bharatanāṭya*. Only the small girls knew the teacher's language, Tamil; the others communicated with him through the dance's gestures and rhythms.

The class and teacher were sponsored by the Indian Institute of Fine Arts, a cultural association devoted to the promotion of classical Indian dance and music. "We teach only the purest classical type of dancing," said the wife of the Institute's secretary, who had received me at the class. She and another official of the Institute were proud that Chokkalingam Pillai, the dancing teacher, attracted students from all over India and from abroad. The Institute had given diplomas, representing usually the completion of three years' training, to at least twenty dancers. Some of them had become professional dancers, but many were interested in the art only for its own sake; the families of the younger students were interested not in having their daughters become professional dancers but in having them learn a social accomplishment.

Chokkalingam Pillai is a traditional dancing teacher, a *naṭṭuvaṉār,* who once taught *devadāsīs*. He is the son-in-law of Meenakshisundaram Pillai of Pandanallūr Village, a famous *naṭṭuvaṉār* who, before he died, had attracted some of India's best dancers to study with him in his village.

There are three different families of dancing teachers in Pandanallūr Village: Chokkalingam's family, Meenakshisundaram's family, and a third family. All three are related and directly descended from a famous "Tanjore quartet" of *naṭṭuvaṉārs.* They have been historically attached to the two temples in the village, one Śiva temple and one Viṣṇu, to some temples in surrounding villages, and to the big temple in Tanjore, about 50 miles away. Chokkalingam Pillai believes that the families of dancing teachers in the village can trace their affiliation to the Tanjore temple back to the Cōḻa kings who founded it in A.D. 900.

Chokkalingam insisted that the community of dancing teachers was in no way related to the community of dancing girls (*devadāsīs*) whom they taught, contrary to the opinion that the women of the *naṭṭuvaṉār* community were sometimes dancing girls and that the men of the *devadāsī* community were dancing teachers and musicians. The two communities do not intermarry or interdine. No dancing girl would be allowed to sit in front of a *naṭṭuvaṉār;* she only came to the house to learn.

Meenakshisundaram Pillai, who had taught the art to Chokkalingam, came from a distinguished family of musicians and dancing teachers; his mother was the daughter of Ponniah, one of the famous Tanjore quartet. Meenakshisundaram first studied in the village and was then sent to Tanjore City for further study. He learned Tamil, Telugu, and Sanskrit well enough to compose songs in these languages. Some of his songs were in praise of the deities in his village temple. He also learned singing, violin, dancing, and dance theory from digests of Bharata's *Nāṭyaśāstra.* In Tanjore, he had married the daughter of his guru, the son of another of the four Tanjore brothers, Sivananda. When he returned to the village, he taught music, dancing, and singing. Among the famous dancers who had studied with him were Shanta Rao, Mrinalini Sarabai, and Ram Gopal. He died in 1954 at the age of eighty-six. One son and several sons-in-law carry on his tradition.

Chokkalingam's early memories are of young girls from *devadāsī* families and boys from the whole community coming to learn dancing and music from his father-in-law. The children would begin their training in their fifth year. Some came to live with his father-in-law, others returned home daily. The routine of the house was very strict. It began at 5:00 A.M. with music lessons for all. The first meal of the day, cold rice and curry, was served at 7:30. From 8:30 to noon, the girls practiced dance steps under his father-in-law's supervision, and the boys sat on the side following with sticks of their own. Mistakes, whether made by the girls or by the boys, were punished by slaps or rappings with the stick. Shaming insults with the help of the other children were also used.

After the noon meal, and between 1:00 and 4:00 P.M., the children went to a modern school to learn languages. Tamil was the medium of instruction, but Telugu songs were also learned. On their return, there was dance practice again from 4:00 to 6:00, music lessons from 6:00 to 8:30, lessons in *abhinaya* (interpreting songs through dance gestures) from 8:30 to 10:00, another rice and curry meal at 10:30, and to bed at 11:00. They did not find this routine exhausting, Chokkalingam Pillai said, because "the food was right." [13]

Serious lessons began when a child was about ten and continued until about the thirteenth year. Thus the total training period usually lasted seven to eight years. The completion of the training was marked by the pupil's first performance—*aranġēṟṟam.* It was usually given in a temple and only by the girls; there was no special ceremony for the boys, who always assisted their teacher and never performed independently.

At the *aranġēṟṟam* ceremony, the teacher usually received presents from the mother of the pupil as well as from others. Thereafter, if the pupil performed in public and received any compensation, she would give half to the teacher, who assisted at such performances by keeping time with small cymbals.

The system had continued until seven or eight years before, when temple dancing girls were abolished by law. Chokkalingam and his father-in-law were brought to Madras by Rukmini Devi who, although herself a Brahman, learned to dance and organized a dancing school at Kalākṣetra. He does not think, however, that the old methods of instruction can be followed now or that the same type of dancers can be produced. The pupils have less time for training, and the traditions are not in their families.

Chokkalingam's family was attached to a temple in a village several miles from their home village of Pandanallūr. To this village, some members of the family went every day to participate in the *pūjās* held at the temple. Dancing by the dancing girls was involved in these *pūjās* in the form of *mudrās* (hand gestures) to the nine deities of the nine directions. In these *pūjās,* the *naṭṭuvaṉār* kept the time with cymbals and drums, and the *pūjāri,* or temple priest, gave the orders. Sometimes there was singing and pipes.

The biggest performances came at the *Brahmotsava,* the chief annual temple festival, which comes in April and lasts for ten days. The festival begins with the hoisting of the temple flag and a propitiation of the nine gods of the directions. Once the flag has been hoisted, no villager can leave the village until it has been lowered at the end of the festival. During the festival, the *devadāsīs* would dance for about an hour and a half each day, accompanying the processions of the gods and dancing at the street corners. The *naṭṭuvaṉārs* assisted at these dances and also helped with the morning and evening *pūjās.*

The ninety-minute festival dance program was quite similar, Chokkalingam Pillai said, to the present *bharatanāṭya* programs, both in arrangement and in types of songs used. The songs were mostly devotional about Krishna and the *gopīs* and other gods. In a dance program that one of his pupils had performed in 1954 in Madras, we found only one song out of ten that could not have been used at the temple festival. It was written by Ponniah Pillai, one of the famous *naṭṭuvaṉārs* of Tanjore and a relative of Chokkalingam. This song praised a human being, the only type of song that was prohibited at the temple.

> Oh my friend! I am deeply in love with Him
> Take Him quickly and secretly
> He Rāmaliṅga endowed with all good qualities and a generous mind.

I feel the cool moonlight very hot.
Manmatha [God of Love] is tormenting me with his arrows.
Do take him here at once.

Even to this prohibition there is an exception. At the Tanjore temple, e.g., on the eighth day of the festival, a dance-drama called *Kuṟavañji* is performed by the dancing girls in honor of King Sarbhoji. There was no *Kuṟavañji* at his village, but it is performed at other temples in honor of the elephant-headed deity, Gaṇeśa.

Another song addressed to Śiva on the same program would have been allowed in temple dances. The dancer does not sing these songs but acts them out with a standardized gesture language (*abhinaya*) as they are sung in Tamil or Telugu by specialized singers. The second song was written by Marimuttu Pillai, a devotional singer.

Will He not come down the street
Oh! if only He could favor me with a fleeting glance
That Lord Naṭarājan, who burnt Manmatha and Tripura
Oh! if only He would tarry in front of my door and have a word with me
That I may conquer the God of Love whose arrows are tormenting me?
Time does not move
I have none to carry my message of love.
I am blameless:
He whose dancing feet are worshipped by Lord Brahmā and Viṣṇu, the three thousand holy Brahmans of Cidambaram and all the celestials
Will he not come down the street and favor me with a fleeting glance?

For their participation in these festivals and the performance of their other temple duties, the *naṭṭuvaṉār* family usually received two or three rupees a month and a portion of the cooked rice offerings from the temple. The *devadāsīs* received less than this. The *naṭṭuvaṉār* family could also augment their income by taking pupils and by performing at marriages, private parties for a "big man," and other festivities. The structure of the dance programs was the same on all of these occasions, although the songs were usually "lighter." But the "lighter" songs were also devotional. Even maharajas at their parties insisted on hearing the songs in honor of their deities. Some of the temple songs were in honor of local temple deities and could not be used outside, but in general all the songs were similar.

In the old days, village audiences knew as much as town audiences. They knew who the best dancers and teachers were and would go for miles to other villages to see them and to appreciate the science of the art. Now the audiences in the city *sabhās* and in the villages do not know very much about the art, but the audiences in the towns are beginning to learn.

Chokkalingam compared some of the local dance forms to *bharatanāṭya:* the Brahman dance-drama (*bhāgavatamelānāṭaka*) is found in just a few villages. In technique, it uses similar pure dance steps (*nṛtta*) and the same interpretative gestures (*abhinaya*), but, because it is performed by males, it does not have the "soft" movements of the *bharatanāṭya*. So far as he knows, the *naṭṭuvaṉārs* did not teach the Brahman *bhāgavatas,* although each group may have learned from the other.

The folk play—*terukkūttu*—has very little of the dance in it—no *nṛtta* and a bit of *abhinaya*. It is all devotional, based on purāṇic themes, and depends on narration.

Some folk dances have steps corresponding to those of *bharatanāṭya,* although they do not use much *abhinaya*. Villagers have performed the *kōlāṭṭam,* or stick dance, in temples during October and November, in praise of Lord Krishna. Pillai, who knew it from his village, has introduced a form of it, the *piṉṉal kōlāṭṭam,* in the institute school.

Before we left, I asked the *naṭṭuvaṉār* whether Americans could learn *bharatanāṭya*. He said he had had some good students and went out of his way to praise the American woman then studying with him. But he doubted whether they really learn it if they do not begin young and "believe." He had similar doubts about the younger generation of Indian students, for they, too, lacked dedication.

### *Dancing Girls*

The *devadāsīs* and their dancing teachers were not attached to temples exclusively. Royal courts also made claims on their time. There is a record of a troupe of Tanjore dancing girls, dancing teachers, and musicians who were in the service of the Maharaja Sayajirao III of Baroda until Baroda was merged with Bombay.[14] Two of the dancing girls, who were retired with pensions in 1941, came from *devadāsī* families attached to the Kāmākṣi Temple at Tanjore, and two of the dancing teachers were grandsons of the Tanjore dancing teacher whose granddaughter had married Chokkalingam's father-in-law. The entire group had come to Baroda from Tanjore as the dowry of the Tanjore princess who had married the maharaja in 1879.

At the Baroda palace, the troupe was subject to the supervision of the State Department of Artists, which fixed the regulations and printed them. The two dancing girls together earned 433 rupees per month, and their musicians received a total of 272 rupees per month. A dearness allowance was later added. The dancers had to provide their own costumes.

Strict rules governed leaves and discipline. The women were given a regular monthly leave of four consecutive days and three months' maternity leave with pay. All the artists had to register in a special book every Saturday at the State Department. If Saturday was a holiday, they had to go the following working day. The dance team had to perform for the maharaja every Wednesday and Saturday after dinner. Dance performances also had to be given in Durbar for ceremonies and for distinguished visitors. No performances were required when the maharaja was away. The superintendent was required to give the dance team at least two hours' notice before a performance. Gifts in cash and presents from the audience had to be surrendered to the superintendent, who divided some of it among the artists and put the rest into the state treasury.

The dance repertoire included the standard *bharatanāṭya* program (it was called the "Tanjore *nāc*" at this time) and some "light" dances at the end. The five "light" dances, which were performed by the two dancing girls as a team, were called the Rādhā-Krishna dance, the kite dance, the scorpion dance, the drunkard's dance, and the snake charmer's dance. Although the dances included some *bharatanāṭya* movements and gestures, they were, in general, freer and more frivolous than the regular *nāc* and very popular with the court audience. As was the custom, the ruler's name was included in some of the dance songs. A Tanjore song in honor of Śivājī, coming in the *varṇa* part of the program, was slightly changed to honor the Maharaja of Baroda.

When the original dancing girl, Gowri, retired fifty-two years after she was brought to the Baroda court at the age of ten, the maharaja had a metal statue made of her in one of her dance poses at a cost of 50,000 rupees. It is still in the Lakṣmīvilāsa Palace in Baroda.

In 1949, when Baroda merged with Bombay, the State Department of Artists was abolished. A dance department was, however, organized in the M. S. University of Baroda, with the son of one of the Tanjore dancing girls as a dancing teacher. *Bharatanāṭya* and *kathak* dancing are taught, and both the B.A. and M.A. degrees are awarded.

The National Academy of Song, Dance, and Drama (Sangeet Natak Akademi) selected for the first time in 1955 outstanding Indian artists in music, dance, and drama for "Akademi awards." The award for the outstanding *bharatanāṭya* dancer was presented by the President, Rajendra Prasad, to Balasaraswati of Madras.* Balasaraswati's great-great grandmother was a famous *vīṇā* player, and her mother is a famous singer. Yet she is a transitional figure belonging neither wholly to the family tradition of *devadāsīs* nor to the modern trends that she is helping to bring in. She is the only one of four daughters who took up dancing and did so against her family's wishes. Because of the anti-*nāc* movement, she had few opportunities to see the old-style dancing during her childhood. And she was not "dedicated" to a temple. She had been trained by a *devadāsī* who was once attached to the Mylapore temple and by a *naṭṭuvaṉār* from Tanjore. Her dancing, usually to be seen at public concerts, is distinguished for its expressive *abhinaya*. Because of her artistic proficiency and because she is now considered a representative of the authentic classical tradition, the Music Academy of Madras sponsors her dancing school where, with the help of her teacher's son, she teaches *bharatanāṭya* to young girls of different classes and families of Madras.

When we interviewed her at the Music Academy, her mother, brother, and young daughter were present, as well as several other visitors, including some friends and supporters of her school. Her family is one of twenty-five *devadāsī* families who have preserved the traditions of the community in Madras. Among them are singers, instrumentalists, dancers, and dance teachers. There is no settled division of labor, but taste determines the choice of occupation, except that the men of the community are usually the dance teachers.

She had heard of Brahman dancers and thought that they had contributed to the development of *abhinaya*. She had known one, Ganapathi

* See photographs following page 174.

Sastri. However, she did not show much interest in the theory of the dance, in temple dance sculptures, or in Bharata's *Nāṭyaśāstra.*

She had performed *Kuṟavañjis,* the *devadāsī* dance dramas, and told us the story of the play about King Sarbhoji as well as the occasions on which it used to be performed in the villages.

She regarded her training as the secret of her success and of her ability to act the different roles of the dance songs. The methods of dance training are now changing and, in her opinion, for the worse. She did not think a restoration possible and felt that the present products were "too inferior to offer to God." She did not consider future prospects for the dance very encouraging, although "it depends on providence." She found it embarrassing to say which was her favorite role.

In her school, she made no distinction between amateurs and professionals and would take anyone. The usual course in other schools lasts six months, but she considered five years a minimum for talented youngsters who begin at the age of six. She adapted her methods of instruction to the age of her pupils in order to take account of growth in stature, body control, and the like. Foreign students, she thought, could learn the pure dance steps (*nṛtta*) but did not easily master the proper gestures and expressions for the interpretive parts or *abhinaya.*

She did not go to movies of dancing because she did "not want to spoil the art." However, she would consider making a movie on her own conditions.

She has danced before leading members of the Indian Government but did not enjoy it because it was obvious from their faces that they did not understand the art or follow the songs. A far more knowing and appreciative spectator was the Sardar-i-Rasat of Kashmir (son and heir of the deposed maharajah) who had recently come to see her dance, and had followed every step and song.

### *Carnatic Music*

The classic revival in music has had a smoother, if less spectacular, course than in dance. Music has not been so closely associated with the controversial dancing girls. Although many famous musicians have come from the *devadāsī* community, Brahmans and other castes have also cultivated the art for a long time. Technical development in music has a long continuous history in the South and has reached greater specialization and refinement than the dance. Technical virtuosity with instruments like the *vīṇā,* the *flute,* the *mṛdaṅgam* (South Indian drum), and the *nāgasvara* (or long pipe) has been so highly developed that it is not at all uncommon to hear concerts devoted exclusively to performances on these instruments. Vocal music is similarly highly developed, and the large number of "modes" (*rāgas*) gives the individual singer, who is as often a female as a male, great opportunity for virtuosity. While some of these instruments still have a ritual use, particularly the long pipe and the drum, which are played at weddings and other functions to frighten away evil spirits, their purely musical development began very early. The ancient Tamil epic of the second century A.D., "The Lay of the Anklet," mentions four kinds of *vīṇā,* five kinds of flute, and thirty-one kinds of percussion instruments and lays down the technical qualifications for singers, both male and female, drummers, flutists, and *vīṇā* players. It includes other discussions of music. The system was based then, as it is today, on melody and rhythm and a basic scale of seven notes.[15]

Many features of the southern musical system are also described in Sanskrit treatises, such as the *Nāṭyaśāstra* of Bharata, where it is directly derived from Vedic chanting, and later treatises like the thirteenth-century *Saṅgītaratnākara* of Śārṅgadeva. From the sixteenth century, when the Carnatic composer saint Purandara Dāsa flourished, Southern or "Carnatic" music developed in distinction from Northern or "Hindustani" music. The present classical form of the Carnatic system is usually attributed to three Tanjore composers, all Brahmans, of the early nineteenth century: Tyāgarāja, a Telugu living near Tanjore, and Muttusvāmī Dīkṣitar and Śyāma Śāstrī, both Tamils. They are often accorded a position in the recent history of classical Southern music equal to that of the Tanjore quartet of dancing teachers in the nineteenth century. After them, critics see a decline in musical development because of an overemphasis on rhythm, a failure to coordinate theory and practice, loss of princely and patrician patronage, and weakening of the *gurukula* system of training. The revival aims at restoring the Carnatic classical tradition to its historic path.

### *Definitions of Folk, Popular, and Classical*

Music critics frequently refer to the distinction between "classical" and "folk" music as equivalent to the ancient Sanskrit contrast between *mārga* and *deśī.* In a paper on "Popular Music and Classical Music," V. Raghavan of Madras University systematically defines the folk-classical distinction in music and traces some of the historical interaction of the two types. He includes in "popular music" folk music as well as popularized classical and "light" music. He finds the main difference between "popular" and "classical" in the rendering: "when the rendering is sophisticated, it is art or classical music; when it is plain and simple, it is the popular or folk variety." Sophistication depends on rules and principles into which an art has been codified and systematized. Just as "to evolve a principle and to conduct oneself in conformity to it is the mark of culture," so it is in art where the standard of judgment has evolved from "artistic criteria." Connoisseurs care for and enjoy high aesthetic standards, whereas the layman likes other things. "That is art-music in which artistic considerations alone prevail; the moment one sings down to the populace, one relaxes the high austerity of his art."

Folk or popular music then, Raghavan finds, is not bound by strict rules and principles and is characterized by features likely to appeal to popular tastes: simple rendering; accentuated and obvious rhythm; group singing; stereotyped, monotonous form; emphasis on words; basis in a festival, a season, or an event; emotional and dramatic tone. These elements are present in art-music but must be "duly proportioned" and made subservient to "expression." Melody (*rāga*), rhythm (*tāla*), and idea and feeling (*bhāva*) must be "evenly integrated" into a "fine synthesis."

Even the classical pieces of the great musicians, who have been mostly saints and teachers, are often overloaded with thought and words, and, "when they are rendered as vehicles of teaching or as means of devotional transport, they depart from the concert and take the turn toward *harikathā* and *bhajana*."

Art-music should evoke its *rasa* (mood) by the actual music and not by importing extraneous elements.

> To evoke *rasa* with the words alone is to surrender music to poetry; to evoke it through overloading one's rendering with pure feeling is to surrender it to drama; to evoke it by pure music is really pure music, and the *rasa* which this pure music evokes leaves far behind that realm in which the mundane sentiments of *śṛṅgāra* (love), *vīra* (heroism), etc., have their meaning; it is that ineffable bliss in which one gets absorbed as in *samādhi* (Yogic concentration). Thus does *nāda* (sound) become the nearest portal to the *Brahman* (world spirit).

Raghavan concludes that in "art-music" "the canons and requirements of art, the rules of balance, harmony, proportion, propriety, concentration on pure artistic resources to the exclusion of adventitious circumstances are to hold sway or absolute sway." To dilute these strict standards and to make concessions in any direction to please a lay audience is to make the music popular "or if it is purposely done for subserving another art or other purpose, it is applied music." [16]

## *Influence of Folk and Popular Music on Classical Music*

In the same paper, Raghavan describes how "folk" and "classical" music have interacted with each other. He further develops the view, which he has stated more comprehensively elsewhere, that the historic formation of the major Indian cultural tradition has involved an interaction with local and regional traditions. "Almost always, the major cultural tradition spreads out and consolidates itself over new regions by absorbing, incorporating within itself, and adjusting to its own scheme such of the local elements as are valuable and attractive. So do all major traditions become national cultures, of significance to every region and group of people." [17]

This give-and-take cultural process is particularly clear in music and dance, although it may also be traced in language, social organization, and in other areas of human activity. Many of the musical scales (*rāgas*) have regional and tribal names and probably represent sophistications of tribal melodies. The association of the *Rājamātaṅgī rāga* with the *vīṇā* as the goddess of music may be connected, he suggests, with a tribe called Mātaṅgas who were once numerous and artistically endowed but later were degraded socially as Cāṇḍālas and untouchables. Numerous musical technical terms, names of instruments, and varieties of voice are still in the local language of Western India and reflect the movements of the cultural tradition across India. Not only does *deśī* terminology occur in classical music, but the treatises stipulate that a musician is not entitled to the foremost status of *Gandharva* unless he is proficient in both the *mārga* and the *deśī* styles.

In the classical dance, too, there are *deśī* strands. The treatises on music and dance describe local and folk dances. Jayasenāpati's *Nṛttaratnāvalī* devotes its last three chapters to the varieties of folk dances. According to V. Raghavan, Someśvara, the author of another treatise, "was captivated by the dance of the hunters, the *goṇḍali,* and systematized it in a set scheme and described it in his work from which it passed into the regular repertoire of dancers elsewhere also." [18] Raghavan finds these folk influences beneficial; they contribute "a frequent invigoration and enrichment of the main tradition by local forms which are fitted into the basic technique and higher ideology of the classical tradition. The *deśī* supplied the material, the *mārga* refined it and assigned it to a place and wove it into the larger and richer scheme. The popular and the classical were the two currents, so as to say, of the energy of our culture. Our art and culture thus soared forth like the image of Pārvatī and Śiva in one, the Ardhanārīśvara, a synthesis of the two into an inseparable unity." [19]

## Summary and Implications for a Theory of Cultural Change

### *Little and Great Traditions in Village and City*

In India, Little and Great Traditions are not neatly differentiated along a village-urban axis. Both kinds of tradition are found in villages and in the city in different forms. Folk and ritual performances survive in fragments in the city, but they are very old forms and are common in villages and towns. The popular devotional and classical forms are essentially urban developments of the last 100 years, although they have more ancient precedents. The modern urban forms are the most recent of all and are essentially urban in origin. These five different kinds of performances are but points on a single continuum when we compare their media, performers, language, place and occasion of performance, and themes.

In such folk forms as the folk play and ballads, the performers are generally non-Brahman men; in the case of dances and songs, they are usually women. There is some hereditary cultivation of skill within certain families, particularly in ballad-making, but in general the performers are amateurs who "pick it up" or are trained by some teacher. The language of the folk forms is usually a regional dialect of Tamil or Telugu and is rarely written or printed. Non-Brahman village temples have been the sites for the performance of the folk plays on the occasion of seasonal festivals, while the songs, dances, and ballads may be performed at almost any place and time. The audiences are generally members of the non-Brahman community. Purāṇic themes are mixed with themes from local legend and history and from the commonplaces of daily life. Folk performances are close to the Little Tradition pole of cultural performances but are not completely cut off from Great Tradition influences.

At the opposite pole, but still found in villages as well as in towns, are the ritual performances, the life-cycle rites and ceremonies, temple festivals, chanting and recitation of scriptures, and, until about 1947, temple dances and religious dance dramas. These belong to the sacred sphere of the culture and are closely associated with Brahman priests and pandits as performers, teachers, and patrons. The performers are men, except for the community of temple dancers, and belong to families who have cultivated the special media for many generations. The verbal texts used are generally Vedic and classical Sanskrit and have been transmitted through an oral tradition, although books are used as aids to memory. In some Vaiṣṇavite and Śaivite rites, Tamil hymns and scriptures have been incorporated into the ceremonies. The themes are mainly Vedic and purāṇic. Some ritual performances differ in one other respect from other kinds of cultural performance: The daily rites performed by householder or temple priest do not require an audience; they are addressed only to a deity.

The popular devotional and classical types of cultural performances that have developed in an urban environment differ from the village forms in a number of important respects. The duration of the performance is much shorter in the city: A purāṇic recitation usually lasted from six months to a year in the village; in the city, it has been condensed into seven- or fifteen-day sequences. The devotional films and plays, as well as the *harikathā* performance, do not exceed three or four hours, whereas a village folk play or temple festival play went on through the night and, at the major festivals, for ten days. The performers at urban performances are nonhereditary professionals who have usually been trained in modern schools. They come from all communities, Brahman and non-Brahman, and include women as well as men. Since the place of performance is a public hall or theater and the occasion is the performance itself, there are no caste or sectarian restrictions on the audience. The language of the popular devotional performances is predominantly the urban colloquial vernacular of the region, with some verbal texts in Sanskrit and other Indian languages. Sanskrit is used by the more erudite performers in *harikathā,* in classical concerts, and of course in Sanskrit plays. Stories from the Epics and Purāṇas and from the lives of the regional saints continue to provide the major thematic material for the urban forms, but secular and political themes play an increasing role.

The greatest transcendence of local folk and ritual forms occurs in the strictly modern urban forms—the social play, the social film, the short story, and the novel. Here, the language is predominantly a regional vernacular or English, and the themes are the social, economic, and political problems of the day. The language and the distinctive cultural content of some of these problems—intermarriage of castes, the plight of the villager, a foreign-trained graduate's qualms about an arranged marriage—add a distinctive flavor to this younger branch of a worldwide urban culture.

## *Two Rhythms in Culture Change*

The differentiation of folk, ritual, popular, devotional, classical, and modern urban cultural performances in relation to urbanization suggests that more general processes of change are operating in different spheres of culture. The differentiation between classical (*mārga*) and folk (*deśī*) in art styles is paralleled, as Raghavan has pointed out, in the field of language by the differentiation between *saṃskṛta* (perfected, refined, civilized) and *prākṛta* (unrefined, vernacular), and in the field of social customs by the distinction between customs sanctioned either by *śruti* (revealed scripture) and *smṛti* (remembered scripture), or by local usage (*deśācāra*) and family usage (*kuladharma*).[20]

Each sphere of culture seems to be subject to opposing directions of change, one type of change tending to push a given cultural sphere in the direction of greater refinement and strict codification, the other in the direction of maximum popularity and practicality. At any given time, the content of a given cultural sphere is something of a compromise between the two extremes, a range of intergrading cultural forms. The prevalence of the refining tendencies sustained in several departments of culture over a long period will result in a level of aesthetic and intellectual achievement deservedly called a Great Tradition.

The question now arises as to whether the operation of opposing rhythms of change within different spheres of culture is merely formal and structural or whether there is some direct and organic relationship among changes in the different spheres. Is there, in particular, a distinctive pattern of change that a Great Tradition undergoes in a metropolitan environment? Perhaps a process of secularization?

Culturally, the effect of urbanization, so far as the Madras case is concerned, has been to shift attention and activity away from ritual observances and sacred learning and to fields of popular culture and the arts. This change carries with it a shift in values from those predominantly connected with religious merit to those of mass entertainment and aesthetics. There are also associated changes from cultural media to mass media and from sacred centers and occasions of performance to cultural centers and secular occasions. Movie actors and concert artists compete with priests and pandits as performers. First nights succeed "first fruit" ceremonies.

It would be inaccurate, however, to apply the Western concepts of secular urban mass culture and of "art for art's sake" in interpreting these changes. There are, indeed, secularizing tendencies, but they have not yet cut off urban culture from the traditional matrix of sacred culture. There is no sharp dividing line between religion and culture, and the traditional cultural media not only continue to survive in the city but have also been incorporated in novel ways into an emerging popular and classical culture. Much of the urban popular culture is an extension of the path of devotion (*bhaktimārga*), more easily accessible to modern man than the paths of strict ritual observance (*karmamārga*) or the path of sacred knowledge (*jñānamārga*). The classical arts, as well, offer a special path or discipline for those able to cultivate it that is akin to yogic concentration.

Nor are the religious interpretations of popular and classical culture limited to the verbalizations of religious leaders. The interpretations are borne out by the many continuities in themes, media, and audience reaction that link the urban culture to the traditional sacred culture. The films and other mass media, although disposed by technical and economic organization to cater to a mass market without respect to caste, creed, or language, have nevertheless found it profitable to draw on the old mythological and devotional themes and to adapt freely the media of folk and classical culture. The newer political themes introduced with the struggle for independence, and now with economic development, are also effectively communicated when joined to the traditional themes and media. The effect of the mass media, in other words, has not so much secularized the sacred traditional culture as it has democratized it.

In the revival of classical South Indian dancing and music, the strands connecting these arts with the sacred culture are evident. The revival, to be sure, has its creative aspects, particularly in having introduced new classes of people as teachers, performers, and audience. It also tends to make the concert stage and the social recital, rather than the wedding or the temple procession, the normative cultural forum for the performance of these arts. The hereditary teachers and performers, however, or those directly trained under them, remain in the greatest demand and have the highest prestige. And a program of authentic classical dancing or music is still pretty much what it was when it formed part of a ritual calendar. The *pūjās* of invocation, the devotional songs, the hand gestures (or *mudrās*), many of the dance movements, and the musical instruments used for village festivals 50 to 100 years ago are now used by modern artists in city concerts. In judging their performances, the critics and connoisseurs will apply standards of technical virtuosity and aesthetic refinement, but they take for granted the purāṇic themes and also judge whether the performance is a "worthy offering to the deity."

Many of the media, or elements of them, enter into the performances of more popular culture—purāṇic recitations, devotional plays, *bhajanas*—since the difference between popular and classical culture rests not on a sharp difference in kind of media or theme but depends rather on the degree of sophistication and technical refinement and the balance among aesthetic, devotional, and entertainment values that characterize the performance.

The continuum of media and themes extends right into the sphere of ritual observance. The *pūjās* and *mudrās* of the temple and domestic priests are clearly similar to the *pūjās* performed in *bhajanas,* devotional plays and films, and classical dancing. And there are analogies between the modern classicists' doctrine of pure music, with its insistence on preserving fixed rules of art and its de-emphasis of the meaning of the words, and the ritual necessities of Vedic chanting. In the *Sāmaveda* chanting, for example, there is a highly developed technique of vocal and instrumental music with specialized singers and musicians. The singing was part of mystic sacrifices and highly esoteric. The *sāman* singers are still reluctant to disclose their special techniques. The verses of the *Ṛgveda* furnish the libretto for this singing, but there are also many syllables without particular meaning (*stobhas*) that are used as aids. The mystic efficacy of the singing depends on the correct enunciation of the sounds, and it thus became all-important to repeat the sounds each time without any change.[21]

Classicism in art may be a sublimation, if not an actual derivation, of ritual singing and dancing. And popular mass culture, to which it is opposed, is itself an extension of the devotional reaction to ritualism. The dialectic of the two rhythms of cultural change continues on a new plane, with some new, some old, media and themes.

The new plane on which this dialectic of cultural rhythms is operating is an urban one. Although several of the older ritual and village folk forms survive in the urban environment of Madras, the distinctive cultural developments in the city have been the revival and modernization of classical forms and the creation of popular devotional forms in each of the major media—literature, purāṇic recitation, drama, music, and dance.

These classical and devotional forms are not without ancient precedents, but their immediate and contemporary sources are urbanized ritual forms and urbanized folk forms. Urbanization has adapted the traditional forms to create modern versions of class and mass culture. It is also beginning to produce a form of urban culture that derives neither from the sacred culture nor from the local folk culture, a cultural form from another urbanized culture—as in the novel, the social play, the symphony—or a creative synthesis of indigenous and foreign sources.

### *A Profile of Urbanized Literati*

To this point, the discussion has been primarily cultural, based on a comparative analysis of cultural performances. Can such a method throw any light on the sociological question raised at the outset: Are the Brahman literati turning into intelligentsia in the urban environment? The results of the cultural analysis suggest that urbanization differentiates the literati into social types corresponding to the cultural types of performances. They imply the existence of ritualists who follow the path of ritual observances (e.g., domestic and temple priests and strictly orthodox householders); sages who follow the path of sacred knowledge (e.g., pandits, yogins, svāmīs); popularizers who follow the path of popular devotionalism (e.g., the purāṇic reciters, *bhajana* leaders, dramatists); and classicists who follow the disciplines of the classical arts. All of these groups are literati in the sense that they seek through their activities to continue the Great Tradition. But the last two types, the popularizers and the classicists, represent new urban types who seek to restore, revive, or adapt elements of traditional culture under modern urban conditions. The ritualists and the sages are old literati types who are found in a metropolitan center but do not feel at home there.

In this scheme of classification, only the modernists, who seek to introduce modern and Western cultural forms even where they conflict with the traditional culture, would be classed as intelligentsia. Among them are writers of novels, short stories, and modern plays; producers of films; performers and composers of Western music; and scientists.

The folk performer (bard, reciter, actor) is a proto-*literatus* who cultivates the cultural forms of the Little Tradition. In India, however, where Little, Great, and urban traditions interact so freely, he also performs some of the functions of the literati and of the intelligentsia, bringing the local traditions into the culture of the city and taking the city's cultural products back to the countryside.

This typology of social roles, suggested by a typology of cultural performances, deserves to be checked against direct sociological studies of the groups concerned. Such studies, I think, will find a good deal of overlap, because there is a continuity of social types, as there is of cultural forms. The modernist film producer who attends *bhajanas* regularly is not an unusual person, and the new literati are also responsible for introducing some novel forms within the frame of traditionalizing change.

Rather than scan the cultural data for additional indications of social typology, I should prefer, in these closing pages, to sketch a composite profile of the urbanized Brahman literati in Madras City and then attempt some explicit generalizations about types of cultural change.

Madras City would not appear to be a very good place to study the Great Tradition of Indian culture. It is a large metropolitan center and a major cultural, political, and commercial center of South India. Nevertheless, it presents an unusually good situation in which to trace the heterogenetic transformation of a Great Tradition that results from secondary urbanization, because the leading professional representatives of that tradition, the Brahmans, and the non-Brahman merchant patrons, have been closely associated with the city from its very beginnings in 1640. They have come to the city from adjoining villages and towns to help build up its educational, cultural, administrative, and economic services and to take advantage of these services. For these tasks, they were particularly well qualified by their relatively high literacy, linguistic abilities, and long association with learning and literary activities. As they exercised their abilities within an expanding urban center and passed through the modern educational system into modern professions, they came to perform in increasing numbers the role of intelligentsia, or agents of cultural change, and less and less that of traditional literati. They found in their new preoccupations less time for the cultivation of Sanskrit learning and the performance of the scripturally prescribed ritual observances, the two activities for which Brahmans have had an ancient and professional responsibility. They have not, however, completely abandoned these activities, and, to some extent, they have developed compensatory activities that have kept them from becoming completely de-Sanskritized and cut off from traditional culture.

They continue, for example, to make pilgrimages to Benares and the Ganges as well as to many of the shrine centers in South India, albeit with modern means of transportation and new motives of patriotic and cultural sightseeing added to the old religious ones. They employ family priests (*purohitas*) to help them conduct domestic rites, and those who can afford it are very lavish in observance and expenditure on the occasion of a sacred thread or wedding ceremony. They go to the temple several times a year for the big festivals and visit their *jagadguru* and their *maṭha* at least once a year. They have actively resisted legislative restrictions on these sacred institutions and have formed organizations to finance ritual activities and to promote Vedic learning. While they deplore the passing of the old *gurukula* system of education and the decline in the number of *śāstric* pandits, they are interested in keeping Sanskrit learning alive and support moves to incorporate more of it into high schools, colleges and universities. Their ritual status as Brahmans may have declined somewhat through increasing violations of some of the pollution taboos and a generally more careless attitude toward them, but the taboos against intercaste marriages are still very strong, and pollution from death or birth in the family and from many other sources is still carefully expiated.

Above all, urban Brahmans have taken an increasing interest in popular religious culture, traditionally designed for the lower castes, women, and children. They form *bhajana* groups; listen to recitations of the hymns of Tamil saints; and organize and attend purāṇic recitations, devotional plays, and movies, and discourses in English or Tamil on the Upaniṣads delivered by non-Brahmans, contrary to *śāstric* sanction. These cultural performances are increasingly held at public halls and theaters rather than in temples or at domestic ceremonies and are open to all without respect to caste or sect. They are considered an extension of the devotional form of religion of the older *bhakti* cults and sects to a democratic mass culture. Brahmans not only make up part of the audience but are also among the leading performers, directors, and writers of these programs.

A relatively small group of more educated and sophisticated Brahmans (and non-Brahmans too) have kept aloof from mass religious-cultural activities. To their taste, these activities are too emotional, unrefined, and unauthentic. They are classicists and insist on greater fidelity to the ancient Sanskrit texts in readings and recitations and on the superiority of purely artistic values (as articulated in the ancient *śāstras* and exemplified in temple sculpture and cultivated by hereditary performers) to the values of popular entertainment or even religious devotion. This group is responsible, both as leading critics and as an audience of connoisseurs, for the revival of classical South Indian dancing and music. The revival, as some of the more percipient classicists have observed, is not entirely backward-looking. It contains such creative innovations—linking it to the modern urban scene and to its popular culture—as a change in the methods of instruction from the apprentice system to the modern school; a change from hereditary families of teachers and of performers to nonhereditary teachers and pupils drawn from all quarters, including the most respectable families; and the substitution of the social accomplishment or a commercial career for a ritually defined role. Some classicists deplore these innovations and call for a total restoration of the traditional system —temple dancing, the apprentice method of teaching, and a practically hereditary professionalization of performers and teachers. Others are content to seek a wider hearing for classical culture in the mass media and to raise the levels of popular taste. Most classicists look upon their classicism not as a secular doctrine of "art for art's sake" but as a distinctive path of release and religious salvation, akin to yogic concentration.

### *Cultural Structure and Social Organization of Cultural Traditions*

The above summary combines social and cultural description and makes no attempt to set out the special concepts and hypothetical processes implicit in this chapter but only occasionally discussed in direct fashion. In concluding, it may be useful to make the theoretical implications of the case study explicit.

A cultural tradition needs to be conceived both culturally as a cultural structure and societally as a social organization. As a structure, it is made up of sequences of cultural performances combining various cultural media, verbal and nonverbal, performed at cultural centers by professional and semiprofessional performers. Performances, media, centers, and performers have a complex and differentiated structure of their own. It is possible to place each structure along a continuum between two poles—an uncultivated Little Tradition of folk culture at one end and a cultivated and learned Great Tradition at the other. There seems to be constant interaction between the two extremes, whether one looks at performances, texts and media, cultural centers, or cultural performers. In India, the Great Tradition is still closely tied to a sacred culture, so that the performances are frequently religious rites and ceremonies; the centers are temples and shrines; performers are priests and spiritual teachers; and the media are linked to a canon of sacred scripture and myth. Urbanization has secularized this sacred culture in some degree, but the line between the sacred and the secular spheres is never very sharp or constant.

It is natural to look beyond the concept of a Great Tradition as an aspect of several differentiated cultural structures and to regard it as something of a governing pattern and principle of an integrated culture. Or at least we are tempted to look for the total culture pattern of a civilization in its Great Tradition, which is usually highly articulated, sophisticated, and comprehensive. Can we, however, identify this integrating pattern of the Great Tradition through a comparison of the similarities and differences among the cultural forms to be found in each of the parts of the cultural structure?

This procedure may with unusual virtuosity and good luck uncover such an over-all pattern, but more frequently it seems to result in a highly fictive construct. I do not mean to say that civilizations (or simpler cultures for that matter) do not have over-all integrating patterns, only that it is necessary to supplement the cultural analysis by a societal one to discover the patterns that are actually operating in a concrete situation. There are a great many different ways in which the elements and partial structures of a cultural tradition could be organized into unifying patterns. The problem is to discover those ways in which they have actually been organized. And to do that requires a knowledge of the social organization of tradition, of how particular communities of people are related to particular cultural performances, centers, media, and performers.

In India, communities of tribes, castes, and subcastes; villages and towns; and religious and linguistic groups overlap. And each kind of community has its distinctive organization of common cultural traditions. The social organization of Indian traditions may, of course, be studied in any of these kinds of communities, although it would take a great many different studies of the different groups in different parts of the country to establish a solid basis for generalization about India as a whole. In South India, one particularly useful kind of group to study is the sect-like denominational groups within Hinduism. Each has a comprehensive version of the tradition, and by comparing in detail the social organization, personnel, and institutions, particularly the *maṭhas,* of the major sects, Vaiṣṇavite and Śaivite, it is possible to arrive at a general picture of the over-all structure of Hinduism within the region where the sects' constituencies are to be found. This procedure will not, to be sure, yield a single authoritative version of the Hindu Great Tradition, but rather a structure of related and overlapping versions. An outside observer cannot say which version is most authoritative without assuming the vantage point of a particular sect or group.

## *Types of Cultural Change and Cultural Process*

Neither the cultural structure nor the social organization of a tradition remains fixed and unchanging over time. One of the main interests of the Madras study has been to determine what kinds of change in Hindu traditions are related to urbanization. Some processes are primarily cultural, and some are societal as well as cultural. Let us now attempt a more explicit and precise analysis of these processes in terms of their dimensions and agencies.

Cultural change, like any other kind of change, has a temporal dimension which it is useful to distinguish into linear and cyclical varieties. Linear types of cultural change imply a specification of a date or approximate date that allows us to fix a "before" and "after" division. Modernization of a cultural tradition is a linear type of change in this sense. It implies that the tradition has been transformed into a form that did not exist before a certain date. For purposes of the Madras study, we have taken the early seventeenth century as a dividing line between modern and traditional. Pre-British India is taken as traditional India. Not all changes in the modern period, however, constitute modernization. Pilgrimage, for example, although it has incorporated modern means of transportation, still seems to conform to its traditional pattern. It is useful, in other words, to consider whether any particular change in tradition is continuous with the structure prevailing before a certain date, or whether the structure has been replaced by a new one. In the former case, we might speak of the change as a traditionalizing type, in the latter as a modernizing type. The changes in the pilgrimage pattern have been traditionalizing, but the changes in the educational system have been modernizing. If the change results in a structure that is neither quite like the traditional one nor a predominantly new one, we might speak of a compromise formation.

The establishment of the Madras College of Indigenous Medicine, for example, was a deliberate attempt to construct a compromise formation between traditional Indian medicine and modern medicine, but the college seems to be going in the direction of modernization. A more stable case of compromise formation is in the field of popular culture where the traditional cultural media and purāṇic themes have been adapted to the mass media of print, radio, and film and linked to a democratic interpretation of the traditional devotional (*bhakti*) movements and ideologies.

Cyclical cultural processes do not require reference to a "before" and "after" dividing line. They are recurrent processes which, of course, take time, but the temporal duration of the process is a cycle that may recur within the traditional or the modern period. Sanskritization and de-Sanskritization are cyclical processes in this sense. And while, in general, modernizing changes are likely to be de-Sanskritizing and traditionalizing changes to be Sanskritizing, exceptions may occur. The Sanskritization of the Camārs described by Bernard Cohn[22] is for them a modernizing process, since it has changed their traditions into novel forms. The Westernization of some Brahmans, on the other hand, who approve of alcoholic drinks, nonvegetarian diets, and widow remarriage, may be both a de-Sanskritizing and a modernizing process if considered in relation to their previous traditions, but may be traditionalizing if considered in relation to the traditions of lower castes who drink alcohol and eat meat, or even if considered in relation to the earliest Vedic traditions, when such customs seem to have been sanctioned for Brahmans.

The processes of Sanskritization and de-Sanskritization involve, in other words, an essential reference to a particular set of cultural norms or values, which takes us beyond the temporal dimension, linear or cyclical. Since these norms will vary for different groups and change over time for the same group, it is necessary in analyzing such processes to specify both the group and the time during which the norms in question prevail. The time reference is not necessarily introduced here as a baseline for judging linear change, but as a way of locating the cultural content which is being transformed. The transformation may be either cyclical or linear. Whether or not the changes in cultural norms will change the total structure of the tradition will depend on many things—the balance between traditionalizing and modernizing changes, the speed of the change, the degree of looseness or flexibility built into the tradition, and, ultimately, the judgment and actions of those considered the "authorities" among the literati. They regard many changes as continuous with their Great Tradition and are incorporating them within a redefined orthodoxy. They regard a few changes as fundamental threats to the tradition and have actively organized resistance and defense against them.

There is a kind of built-in flexibility within the orthodox Vedānta position that permits an easy incorporation of a wide variety of changes. The pandits who are called upon to decide difficult cases say they follow a fixed hierarchy of authorities and standards in their deliberations and decisions. At the top of the hierarchy are the revealed scriptures (the *śruti,* including the Vedas and Upaniṣads). Next come the remembered scriptures (the *smṛti*), including the treatises on religious law, the Epics and Purāṇas, and the auxiliary sciences. In case of a conflict among scriptures, the opinion of a wise man should be consulted. Local customs and usages and, finally, individual conscience may be followed if the scriptures are not relevant.

This hierarchy gives the wise man—the pandit, the guru, the head of the *maṭha*—a comfortable scope for interpretation and reconciliation of scriptural sanctions. He quite freely invokes considerations of logic, experience, the convenience or inconvenience of a particular circumstance, and local usages in reaching his decision. In this process, the wise men and particularly the learned literati are an institutionalized agency for changing tradition, so long as they regard change as primarily preservative of the tradition's essentials.

The long-run result of the process has been consolidative and selective. Some elements of language, learning, and the arts, as well as of ritual custom, disappear (e.g., Vedic sacrifice); new ones are added (e.g., temples and monastic organizations). Aspects of heterodox sectarian movements and of tribal and regional custom are assimilated to orthodoxy. Fragments of Little Traditions have been absorbed into the Great Tradition, and the culture of the villages and tribes has, in the long run, also been responsive to the authoritative teachings of literati. And just as a large and famous temple will contain numerous shrines to stones, snakes, trees, and the planets, as well as to the pantheon of major deities, so a learned and sophisticated Brahman will make offerings to these shrines and follow many local and family usages, as well as adhere to a very abstract Advaita philosophy. As one of them said, describing just this kind of situation, "I suppose I am a museum."

Some limits are recognized, however, to what can be assimilated by the orthodox tradition. The anti-Brahman, anti-Sanskrit, anti-Hindu movement now popular with some Tamil groups is certainly looked upon as an attack upon the essentials of Hinduism. And the weakening of the caste system, particularly as a ritual structure, is viewed in the same light by the more orthodox. Svāmī Śaṅkarācārya, the most authoritative spokesman for Madras Smārtas, thinks that what is distinctive and essential in the nature of Hinduism is the caste system considered as a set of hereditary family disciplines. If they decline, he thinks Hinduism will not be very different from other religions, many of which have similar systems of ethics, theology, and philosophy but lack the hereditary sociological foundation for them. The Brahman community, he believes, has become lax, for one reason and another, in the observance of the disciplines of diet, marriage, social intercourse, ritual observance, and sacred learning. He is inclined to appeal to devout non-Brahmans to preserve the essentials of Hinduism in these difficult times, since the *śāstras* make less severe demands on them and they are able to conform.[23]

Even in the face of this uncertain future, the Svāmī and his Brahman followers remain detached and resilient. Their long-run cosmic perspective gives them a hopeful serenity in the face of disturbing changes. Discussing the restrictive legislation against temples and *maṭhas,* one Brahman said cheerfully: "Well, many of the temples and *maṭhas* are only 700 or 800 years old. They have been destroyed before and revived. New values must be admitted. Life will grow, if old values are not destroyed. Life is one huge, infinite ocean in movement."

## NOTES

1. This argument has been made by Paul Masson-Oursel. See Paul Masson-Oursel, Helena Wilman Grabowska, and Philippe Stern, *Ancient India and Indian Civilization* (New York: Barnes & Noble, 1967), p. 143.

2. Figures are based on the 1951 census. By 1961, the rate of growth had decreased. In 1951–61, the population of Madras City increased by 22.11 per cent to approximately 1.75 million, while the population of Madras State grew by 11.9 per cent to 33,686,953. The proportion of urban population in the state increased from 24 per cent in 1951 to 27 per cent in 1961.

3. Raghavan, "Some Leading Ideas" (see note 14, Chapter 2, above).

4. V. Raghavan, "The Vedas and Bhakti," *The Vedanta Kesari* 42, No. 8 (Madras: December, 1955): 330–36.

5. Tirunāvukkarasu Svāmī (more commonly referred to as Apparsvāmī), in F. Kingsbury and G. E. Phillips, *Hymns of the Tamil Śaivite Saints* (Calcutta: Associated Press, 1921), pp. 51 and 57.

6. The hymns of Tiru Jñāna Sambamdamūrti Svāmī, seventh century A.D.; Sundaramūrti Svāmī, ninth century A.D.; and Tirunāvukkarasu Svāmī (Apparsvāmī), seventh century A.D.

7. Raghavan, "Methods of Popular Religious Instruction" (see note 36, Chapter 2, above).

8. For an account of the "Bow Song" outside of Madras, see K. P. S. Hameed, "Bow Song: A Folk Art from South Travancore," *Tamil Culture* 5, No. 3 (July, 1956): 274–84.

9. *Commemoration Volume* in honor of Srimati C. Saraswati Bai (Madras, 1939). See also Y. B. Damle, "A Note on Harikatha," *Bulletin of the Deccan College Research Institute* 17, No. 1 (Poona, October, 1955): 15–19.

10. I am indebted to V. Raghavan for information about this Gandhi Kathā.

11. I have recently learned that K. V. Ramachandran has unfortunately passed away. Since the account here of his views and activities is based largely on personal conversations with him, I have left it in the historical present.

12. Interviews in Madras with K. V. Ramachandran, 1954–55.

13. Cf. the dancer Shanta Rao's account of her training in B. Zoete, *The Other Mind* (London: Victor Gollancz, 1953).

14. Moban Khobar, "Bharata Natya in Baroda," *India Institute of Fine Arts: Proceedings* (Madras, 1954). The author was head of the Department of Dance at the Maharaja Sayajirao University of Baroda.

15. *The Śilappadikāram,* trans. with notes by V. R. Ramachandra Dikshitar (London: Oxford University Press, 1939), pp. 57–62.

16. V. Raghavan, "Popular and Classical Music," *Journal of the Music Academy* 28, i–iv (Madras, 1958): 100–106.

17. Raghavan, "Variety and Integration" (see note 19, Chapter 2, above).

18. Raghavan, "Popular and Classical Music."

19. *Ibid.*

20. *Ibid.*

21. V. Raghavan, "An Outline Literary History of Indian Music," *Journal of the Music Academy* 23, i–iv (Madras, 1952): 64–74. For a musical analysis of the *Sāmaveda* in relation to classical Indian music, see A. H. Fox Strangways, *The Music of Hindostan* (Oxford, 1914).

22. Bernard S. Cohn, "Changing Traditions of a Low Caste," in Singer, ed., *TI,* pp. 207–16.

23. Personal interviews. See also Sankaranarayanan, comp., *Call of the Jagadguru* (note 5, Chapter 4, above), a discourse delivered by Śrī Śaṅkarācārya during his stay in Madras in the autumn of 1957.

# PART THREE / *MYTH, RITUAL, AND SOCIAL CHANGE*

# 6 / *The Rādhā-Krishna* Bhajanas *of Madras City*

## Introduction

During my first visit to Madras, Dr. Raghavan and other friends had reservations about the hypothesis that the decline in ritual observance and the increase in devotional religion were consequences of recent urbanization and modern life. Such changes have occurred many times in the past, they pointed out. *Bhakti* movements were very old, and the *Bhagavadgītā* does sanction the path of devotion, especially for the salvation of women, children, and Śūdras, alongside the more demanding paths of strict ritual observance and yogic meditation. Their arguments were unsettling and persuasive, especially when Dr. Raghavan documented them in historical studies that related *bhakti* to the Vedas and described the methods of popular religious instruction.[1] Yet I could not abandon my strong impression of something new about these religious developments in twentieth-century Madras and of an intriguing relationship between the traditional movements and modern urban life. To explore them further during my second visit to Madras City, I decided to make an intensive and detailed study of the Rādhā-Krishna *bhajanas,* a form of group devotional singing and praying. For several reasons, the *bhajanas* offered a good opportunity to explore the impact of the city on religious change. In form, at least, they resembled the older *bhakti* movements; their "urban pastoral" content and imagery focused on the story of Krishna as cowherd and his relation to the milkmaid *gopīs*—with songs, dances, and dramatizations portraying a village landscape. The fact that many *bhajana* participants were Smārta Brahmans who pursued weekday professional and middle-class urban occupations made the ceremonies especially relevant for a study of the effects of urban life on cultural traditions.

During my first trip to Madras, I had attended several Rādhā-Krishna *bhajanas* and had noted that some Smārta Brahmans actively participated in them. It looked then as if the *bhajanas* were among many diverse expressions of devotional (*bhakti*) religion that had become popular in an urban center. I did not understand at that time why Smārta Brahmans, generally Śaivite, should be so closely associated with a Krishna cult, nor did I know very much about the historical and textual sources of the *bhajanas,* their different types, social organization, social functions, and meanings. The intensive study of the Rādhā-Krishna *bhajanas* turned up some interesting answers to these questions and also an unexpected psychological relation between some ancient myths and rituals, contemporary social changes, and the individual's quest for salvation.

The *bhajanas* did not originate in Madras City; their history and tradition go back in Tanjore District to the seventeenth century. The founders and codifiers of the tradition were Smārta Brahmans, whose collections of songs and commentaries were brought about 1900 to Madras City, where they have become popular with professional and middle-class people. The leading devotees who have developed the *bhajanas* in the twentieth century were also influenced by the devotional traditions of Bengal, Mahārāṣṭra, Uttar Pradesh, Gujarat, and Rājasthān and have incorporated songs from saints from these regions and languages into the Madras *bhajanas.*

A textual analysis of the songs and commentaries associated with the Rādhā-Krishna *bhajanas* of Madras City, such as T. K. Venkateswaran has done, shows that they can be related to the medieval and early modern *bhakti* movements.[2] A contextual analysis, on the other hand, shows that they also have features whose significance and function lie in recent urban and political developments. For example, the multilingual, intersect, and intercaste tendencies of the *bhajanas* and *bhajana* songs surely represent a defensive reaction and a positive culturally integrative alternative to the separatist regionalism of the pro-Tamil, anti-Hindu, anti-Sanskrit, anti-Brahman Dravidian movement. The organization of neighborhood, occupational, and citywide *bhajana* groups on a wide variety of occasions represents an attempt to institutionalize a form of religious association and activity that will bridge the gap between the caste- and lineage-restricted domestic cults, the sect-linked temples and *maṭhas,* and the purely secular forms of urban association. Such forms of religious expression and association as the *bhajanas* also inspire participants, perhaps only intermittently, with the desire to become "true devotees" throughout their lives and offer them a path to spiritual salvation requiring no very great renunciation of their urban occupations and way of life.

The Rādhā-Krishna *bhajanas* are not limited to these three meanings and functions, nor do these three have the same importance for all participants. They do seem to represent a cluster of current functions and meanings that go far to explain the special attraction of the *bhajanas* for some urban Brahmans and non-Brahmans.

The aspirations and ideals expressed in the *bhajanas* are not always realized in daily life. Many friendships are formed in *bhajana* groups, and some become lasting, cutting across caste and sect lines. By and large, however, the *bhajana* associations follow the lines of caste and sect. Among the *bhajana* groups I studied—those chiefly organized by Smārta Brahmans—55 per cent of the members were Smārtas, 10 per cent were Śrīvaiṣṇava Brahmans, 10 per cent were Mādhva Brahmans, 20 per cent were non-Brahmans, and 5 per cent were unclassified. These figures are based on an analysis of donations for major *bhajanas* during 1959–60, and they correspond to observations of actual attendance at *bhajanas* during

1954–55 and 1961. Those *bhajana* participants who report that they forget caste differences in the *bhajanas* also indicate that these feelings do not last long afterward. Some who are brought close to a vision of Krishna by *bhajana* songs and dances confess that a direct vision is a rarely attained consummation of a *bhajana.*

Because *bhajana* aspirations are rarely fully realized, one might dismiss them as ineffective. To do so, however, would be to misinterpret the role of the *bhajanas* in everyday life and to overlook an important practical function of the *bhajanas*—namely, to dramatize and act out in the *bhajana* program aspirations and ideals that are rarely realized in daily life and may even lack general acceptance. Some of the more thoughtful *bhajana* participants claim, with apparent reason, that the acting out of such aspirations in the *bhajanas* turns men's minds and sentiments in the "right direction" and eventually influences their daily conduct as well.

An analysis of the mutual salutations and prostrations of devotees in the *bhajanas* and of their "sports" with the milkmaids (enacted by male fellow participants) as cultural performances shows that the *bhajanas* dramatize *both* the modern ideal of social equality and the ancient yearning for salvation through supreme devotion to a deity. The analysis reveals a close relationship between the "ritual" and "mythological" aspects of a *bhajana* performance, on the one hand, and its influence on daily life, on the other. This relationship accounts for the *bhajanas'* influence on the participants' thought, feeling, and behavior. The basis for this relationship is the "identification" of a *bhajana* performer with his role in the story of Krishna and the *gopīs* from the *Bhāgavatapurāṇa.* He tries to talk, walk, act, feel, and think as they did in the purāṇic stories. An underlying aim of such identification is to generate and sustain in the devotee a particular mood or feeling (*bhāva*) of love, anger, sadness, fear, and so forth. The constancy and intensity of the mood, rather than the specific quality of emotion, is, for the devotee, the prime consideration. To the extent that he succeeds in the identification he will be not only acting out a mythological story in a ritual drama but also attuning his personality to new roles. Through the process of identification, the aspects of his cultural traditions that a participant chooses to affirm become vehicles for innovation.

Evidence for the thesis that the mechanism of psychological identification, or role-playing, is the dynamic link between the myth and ritual of the *bhajanas,* on the one hand, and the attitudes and behavior of the *bhajana* participants, on the other, came from the testimony and life histories of some participants. The thesis, as a matter of fact, was originally suggested to me by one participant's vivid and dramatic account of his personal search for salvation through the *bhajanas.*

Once the principle became clear, additional evidence for it appeared in other kinds of cultural performances in Madras, such as the mythological, historical, and devotional films, plays, recitations, songs, and dances. For example, a popular Madras dramatic reciter of stories from the Epics and Purāṇas told me that the most difficult and satisfying aspect of her art was to take many different roles in a single story. Her audiences praised her "masterly impersonation of the characters of a Rāvaṇa, a Hanumān or a

Garuḍa, a giant or a cooing bird, a *bhakta* or a scoffer, a lover or a libertine, a god or a goddess, a saint or a sinner, a man or a woman, king or peasant." Knowledge of the appropriate regional languages and dialects, songs, and gestures and a strong dramatic and narrative sense were required in this art form, *harikathā,* or "monodrama"—a kind of concentrated drama in which the performer enters swiftly into a whole series of characters, moods, and manners.[3]

A famous Madras film idol similarly told me that he had identified with his roles in mythological and historical films and considered himself well cast in the more martial roles—Kaṭṭabbomman and Karṇa—because of a legend that his community had descended from Cōḻa warriors. The audiences (largely non-Brahman) who flock to his films share his identification, expect him to conform to it in his private and public life, and have organized fan clubs all over the state to keep the image alive and do good works in his name. He in turn has tried to live up to the part—as a great hunter (he has his own game preserve and many mounted trophies), a benefactor and protector of the poor and unfortunate, and a fighter for South Indian Tamil identity.

These identifications also explain how traditional mythological and legendary stories, rites, and ceremonies can serve contemporary moral and social purposes by providing support for social equality, national and regional identity, or community development. The *harikathā* reciter, for example, would be willing to use her songs to encourage people to dig wells and pits for the development effort, since "it is a matter of patriotism." Several recordings of *harikathās* about Gandhi's life recited in the traditional manner emphasize Gandhi's great faith in devotion and his doctrine of service on behalf of the poor. One record opens with Gandhi's favorite song, written by the Gujarati saint Narasimha Mehta, which declares that "he is a true devotee of Lord Viṣṇu who knows the suffering of others."[4]

To arrive at an adequate understanding of the meaning and functions of the Rādhā-Krishna *bhajanas* in Madras City, it was not enough to observe the *bhajanas,* discuss them with participants and others, or collect life histories from the participants. The philosophy and theology of the *bhajanas* turned out to be an indispensable key for their interpretation. Their philosophy of devotion is intimately associated with the history of *bhakti* and sectarian movements. The songs sung at the *bhajanas* and the casual comments of some *bhajana* participants suggested the existence of such a philosophy, but its significance did not begin to become clear until one *bhajana* participant, S. Krishnaswami, expounded his personal view in a series of letters he wrote me after my return to the United States. I later encouraged his son, T. K. Venkateswaran, then a Fellow of the Center for the Study of World Religions at Harvard University, to expand on his father's work by writing a study of the philosophy and theology of the South Indian *bhajanas* as represented in the *bhajana* songs, the scriptural texts, and the lives of the early *bhajana* leaders. T. K. Venkateswaran gladly agreed to do so, since the project would fit in with his plans for a study of the *jīvanmukta* in the Advaita tradition, that is, the saint who puts off his own spiritual salvation in order to help others.

The value of T. K. Venkateswaran's textual study immediately suggested the feasibility of a broader collaboration between anthropological and literary-historical approaches to the study of Krishna worship. Because the Madras *bhajanas* incorporated elements of several other regional traditions, especially those of Bengal, Mahārāṣṭra, and Uttar Pradesh, it seemed promising to compare the Krishna cult in these different regions on the basis of textual and contextual studies. A personal meeting with Caitanya and Rāmakrishna devotees in Calcutta* had already suggested strong similarities between the South Indian and the Bengali traditions. My colleague at Chicago, Edward C. Dimock, Jr., who was studying Bengali Vaiṣṇavism, confirmed the point. Together with other colleagues, we held a Krishna seminar in Chicago during the summer of 1962 and invited T. K. Venkateswaran and Thomas Hopkins to participate. The results of the seminar were so encouraging that we presented a preliminary report in a symposium on "The Krishna Legend: Variations on a Theme" at the 1963 meeting of the Association of Asian Studies. Dimock's paper and mine were first published in the journal, *History of Religions.* The joint studies on Krishna were later published by the East-West Center Press. In a foreword to the volume, Daniel Ingalls noted the significance of such explorations for the Indological study of Krishna. The significance of the *Krishna* volume for the anthropological study of myth, ritual, and society has recently been noted by Victor Turner.[5]

Anthropological studies have successfully demonstrated the functional relations among myth, ritual, and social structure in preliterate religion, but they have been far less successful in analyzing world religions. One major difficulty is that, in the latter case, myth and ritual are embodied in an elaborate corpus of scriptural texts, cultivated by literate specialists and functionaries and embedded in highly specialized institutions. The anthropologist also finds that historians of religion, philosophers and theologians, orientalists, and philologists have preceded him. These scholars have in the main concentrated their attention on literary and historical studies of the textual corpus and generally have not dealt with the relationship of the texts to living people and institutions—precisely the relationship that interests the anthropologist. Until quite recently, however, the anthropologist has either lacked the necessary linguistic and historical knowledge of the textual corpus or has deliberately cut himself off from such knowledge, adopting a rather narrow interpretation of functionalism, in which he seeks to show that a body of myth and ritual exactly reflects an existing social structure and also legitimizes it.[6]

The significance of the Krishna study is that it shows how the methodological constraints imposed by the cleavage between the textual and contextual approaches can be overcome through a collaboration between textual scholars and anthropologists. The study limits such collaboration to

* Caitanya (A.D. 1486–1533) was a religious leader in Bengal who inspired a revival of Vaiṣṇavism. See Edward C. Dimock, Jr., *The Place of the Hidden Moon: Erotic Mysticism in the Vaiṣṇava-Sahajiyā Cult of Bengal* (Chicago: University of Chicago Press, 1966). Śrī Rāmakrishna (1836–86) was a modern Bengali saint whose teachings of religious synthesis were brought to the West by Svāmī Vivekānanda. See *Sri Ramakrishna: The Great Master* (Mylapore, Madras: Sri Ramakrishna Math, n.d.).

a single cultural theme—the worship of Krishna as child and lover in India—but the results seem to warrant its extension to other themes and problems, such as the worship of Rāma and Sītā, of Kālī, the cow, and others. The Krishna study shows how a great traditional text about Krishna, such as the *Bhāgavatapurāṇa,* is related to regional texts and literary traditions and the local forms of Krishna worship in which these texts appear. The specific variations in the forms of worship and in the interpretations of the texts according to historical period, linguistic region, sect, caste, and tribal-peasant-urban cultural levels are identified for at least three different regions of India: Tamiḻnāḍu, Bengal, and Uttar Pradesh. A basis for an all-India "unity in cultural diversity" is demonstrated in this study both by the recurrence of similar episodes from the *Bhāgavatapurāṇa* in the different regional developments and by the interregional cultural "networks" created by traveling gurus, missionary sects, itinerant reciters and performers, the religious pilgrimage, and related institutions and specialists.

One unanticipated result of the Krishna study was that it presented overwhelming and convergent evidence against a narrow structural and functional theory in which myth and ritual reflect and legitimize an unchanging social order. The authors of every contribution to the study found that the social and psychological functions of the Krishna stories and ceremonies seemed to express aspirations that were in some respects diametrically opposed to the existing status quo. This point is most dramatically shown in McKim Marriott's account of "role reversals" during a North Indian village *Holī* festival, but it is also a persistent and unequivocal theme in all the other essays, including the historical studies of the *Bhāgavatapurāṇa* by Thomas Hopkins and J. A. B. van Buitenen. In a broad sense, it may be "functional" for a set of myths and rituals to express opposition to an existing social order or to some aspect of it; if so, however, this "functionalism" differs sharply from the "classical" functionalism that seeks to demonstrate, by tracing isomorphisms among myths, rituals, and social structure, that myths are "charters" for existing social institutions. The "functionalism" of the Krishna study is a more adequate approach to a social anthropology of civilizations and may be more adequate for the study of primitive cultures as well.[7]

## History of the Madras *Bhajanas*

In Madras City a form of congregational devotional worship—called *bhajana*—is becoming popular and seems to be developing into a Hindu cult that links the cults of temple and domestic worship. Superficially, the *bhajanas* resemble the older devotional cults (*bhakti*) within Hinduism, emphasizing recitation of divine names and worship of personal deities. But the contemporary *bhajanas* show many features that are distinctive of the region within which they have developed, of the social groups that support the development, and of the problems confronting contemporary Hinduism as it tries to adapt itself to modern urban conditions. The *bhajana* programs followed in Madras today probably derive from a codification and a philosophy attributed to three teachers who lived in Tanjore District near Kumbakōṇam in the seventeenth century. The names of these three gurus are invoked in some *bhajana* songs at the very beginning of a *bhajana* program. They are: Bodhendra, Śrīdhara Veṅkaṭeśa (or Ayyarvāḷ), and Sadgurusvāmī. It is quite likely that the use in the *bhajanas* of devotional songs by saints from different regions, the centrality of the Rādhā-Krishna story, and the general selection and sequence of songs go back to these founders. Influences from other individuals and regions, however, particularly from Bengal and Mahārāṣṭra, are also evident. In Madras City, the movement is only about fifty years old and may have been brought in by leaders who came from Kumbakōṇam in Tanjore District. Since the end of World War II, *bhajana* groups have multiplied rapidly in the city and have also become fashionable in smaller towns and villages. The meeting of a *bhajana* group usually takes place at a private home and is attended by a mixture of castes and sects, with middle-class professionals and Smārta Brahmans predominating. The relation of *bhajanas* to the full range of religious-cultural performances that may be found in Madras City has been discussed in Chapter 5 above.[8] In this chapter, I shall discuss the different types of *bhajanas,* their social organization, transmission and leadership, and their meaning and function as cultural performances.[9]

## Types of *Bhajanas*

While the word *"bhajana"* is in common use in South India, it does not have a very precise meaning. The usual translation is "prayer" or "devotional song." In North India, *kīrtan* and *saṅkīrtan* are used as rough synonyms. The meaning of the word can best be clarified by reference to the types of performances that are called *bhajanas* in Madras City. At least five different types are called *bhajanas* and may be observed in contemporary Madras: weekly, monthly, annual, morning, and occasional. A sixth type, daily *bhajanas,* is no longer a common occurrence.

### *Weekly* Bhajanas

The weekly type is an evening gathering of relatives, friends, and neighbors in a private home for about three hours from 7:30 to 10:30 P.M.; Saturday night is the most popular choice, although some groups meet on Thursday or other nights of the week. The men of the group, usually about a dozen, sit in a circle or in rows on the floor and lead the singing, while the women and children sit to one side and join in the refrains. The standard pattern is for the leader to recite or sing a phrase, like "Let us sing the name of Govinda," and for the audience to respond by repeating the name, or by shouting "Jai, Jai" ("be victorious") or a similar phrase. In the kind of refrain called *nāmāvali* (necklace of names), it is customary to begin slowly and then to speed up the recitation, and with each repetition to raise the pitch gradually to correspond to the seven pitches, or *svaras,* of the Carnatic system of music and then to lower it in the reverse order. These *nāmāvalis* are the emotional thermometers of a *bhajana.* When accompanied by cymbals and *chiplas* (a kind of castanet), a drum, and sometimes a harmonium, the *nāmāvalis* can become very intoxicating. However, if an audience tends to be carried away by too much repetition of *nāmāvalis,* the leader has a diplomatic way of returning to a slower pace of recitation or singing, by interrupting the *nāmāvali* with a set phrase, such as "Let us remember the Lord who is the life of the *gopīs.*"

The opening refrains and *nāmāvalis,* starting with the chanting of "Hari Nārāyaṇa! Hari Nārāyaṇa!," invoke the names of various deities—Rāma, Govinda, Mahādeva, Viṭṭhala, Gaṇeśa—and famous devotees. These are usually followed by a recitation of fourteen or more Sanskrit stanzas that sum up a kind of "unformulated creed" of the *bhajana.*[3] Some stanzas honor the three gurus and other great devotees, such as Prahlāda, Nārada, and Arjuna. In other stanzas, the underlying philosophy of the *bhajanas* is stated: namely, that singing about Krishna will bring salvation, that such singing is obligatory for Brahmans, and that people who have "fallen" or committed "sinful" acts can be saved in this way. This is followed by *tōḍayamaṅgalam, nāmāvali,* and *gurustuti.* At least one song each is sung from *Gītagovinda, Kṛṣṇalīlātaraṅgiṇī,* Bhadrācala Rāma Dāsa, Purandara Dāsa, Tyāgarāja, Sadāśiva Brahmendra, Kabīr Dāsa, Mīrābāī, Caitanya, and other devotees. Then comes the major ritual part of the weekly *bhajana:* a *pūjā* (religious offering) to Krishna and Rādhā. There are also *pūjās* at the very start and toward the end of the *bhajana,* but these are very brief—with offerings of flowers and food to the lithographs of Krishna and Rādhā on the wall, a recitation of 108 names, and the waving of a camphor or wick light (*ārati*). The *pūjā* that follows the stanzas is far more elaborate. It is performed by a leading devotee; other devotees participate to varying degrees, but all participate even if their favorite deities are not Krishna and Rādhā.

The major *pūjā* takes from about forty-five minutes to an hour and follows more or less the steps of domestic and temple *pūjās.* It differs from them in performing some of the steps mentally or symbolically—for example, the image of the deity is not actually bathed; the *bhajana pūjā* uses lithographs rather than metal or stone images; it changes the sequence of steps and introduces songs that are not part of domestic or temple *pūjās.* The sixteen "attentions" (*upacāras*) offered to a deity in the other *pūjās* are offered in songs in the *bhajana pūjā.* Miniature metal images, garlands, fans, and so forth may be used if they are available. Some of the songs are addressed not to Krishna but to Rāma; because of their appropriateness, they are sung anyway. Vedic *mantras* and Sanskrit stanzas used in domestic *pūjās* are also chanted with flower offerings. The first *mantra* of each Veda and the first *sūtra* of each *śāstra* are recited as offerings. And there are stanzas to glorify sacred texts, sacred places, sacred trees, and sacred days. Tamil and Sanskrit songs of the Āḻvārs are sung, and the *pūjā* concludes with invocations of auspiciousness (*śobhanam* and *maṅgalam*) to Rāma and Krishna, and with some *nāmāvalis.*

In the next part of the *bhajana,* the three gurus—Bodhendra, Śrīdhara Veṅkaṭeśa, and Sadgurusvāmī—are praised in Sanskrit songs and stanzas. Most detail is given about Bodhendra, who is described as "the author of one hundred works on the efficacy of the Divine Name," as enjoying and sporting "in the sea of Rāma's name," and as having heroically repudiated the differentiation between Hari (a title of Viṣṇu) and Śiva. Śrīdhara Veṅkaṭeśa is said to be concerned with Śiva's name; only Sadgurusvāmī is said to be concerned with Krishna. "In his mind, the Lord of the Yadus, the lotus-faced Lord Krishna, plays with Rādhā in an uninterrupted manner." These devotees and others, such as Tukarām and Nāmdev, are said to be "good men" who are "full of peace" and who "work for the welfare of the people like the spring. / Having themselves crossed the fearful ocean of *saṃsāra,* / They help others to wade through with ease and spontaneity."

Following the praise of the gurus is a series of songs in many different languages about or by different regional saints, each followed by a *nāmāvali.* Jayadeva's *Gītagovinda,* a passionate medieval Sanskrit poem on the love of Rādhā and Krishna, heads this list. One *aṣṭāpadī,* or canto, is sung during each weekly *bhajana* until the entire work of twenty-four *aṣṭāpadīs* is finished; then the first *aṣṭāpadī* is repeated, and so on. The others songs include some from Nārāyaṇa Tīrtha's *Kṛṣṇalīlātaraṅgiṇī,* a Sanskrit work about Krishna's pranks and "sports"; another Sanskrit song also about Krishna by Sadāśiva Brahmendra; a Telugu song about Rāma by Rāmdās; some of Purandara Dāsa's Kannada songs to Krishna; Gopāla Krishna Bharati's Tamil song to Śiva; and one of Tyāgarāja's Telugu songs on Rāma. Except for Jayadeva, all the composers were South Indian, but some songs from North Indian saints are also included: a Hindi song by Kabīr on Rāma, a Hindi song by Mīrābāī on Krishna, and a Marathi song by Tukarām on Viṭṭhala. Most of these saints' songs deal with the personal discovery of refuge in a particular deity. Mīrābāī's, which is perhaps the most personal, will serve as one illustration:

> When the decorative stub on the *pādukā* [wooden sandal] of my great teacher touched me, I forgot the world. I obtained an inner peace and bliss.
>
> Wherever I looked, I beheld only the feet of my teacher.
> Everything else was *māyā* to me, like things seen in a dream.
> Birth and death—this ocean of *saṃsāra* has dried up.
> I have no anxiety about the seeking of a plan to cross it.
> Govinda protected Gokula village by holding aloft a mountain.
> When I sought refuge in him, he turned my vision inward.

After a short *pūjā* to Krishna and other deities come the concluding songs and stanzas of the *bhajana.* These consist of a verse and *nāmāvali* saluting and asking for the special protection of Gaṇeśa, Sarasvatī, Subrahmaṇya, Śiva, Pārvatī, Rāma, Sītā, Āñjaneya, Krishna, and Garuḍa or Vainateya. In these supplications, the supplicants' needs are rarely mentioned—only the qualities and deeds of the deity. Lines from a Sanskrit song by Bhadrādrivāsa will illustrate this peculiarity:

> O joy-giver of the *gopīs,* of the festival of Gokula village,
> O Govinda, glory to you. Do protect me.
> O Son of Nanda, moon-faced one, your face is charming. Do protect me . . .

The closing invocations of the *bhajana* (another *maṅgalam*) ask for auspiciousness for Krishna and his devotees, and also for all people:

> All welfare and auspiciousness to the people. Let the rulers of the earth rule in the righteous way.
> Let there be ever auspiciousness for the cows and the Brahmans.
> Let all the people in different countries [*lokas*] be blessed with happiness.
>
> Let there be rain in the proper season,
> Let the earth be full of crops,
> Let this *deśa* [country, nation] be free from poverty and misery,
> Let the Brahmans be free from fear.[10]

Of the last two invocations, one asks that Hari (Viṣṇu, or Krishna) be remembered in all places where devotees assemble, and the other asserts that "Brahman alone is [ultimately] real," to which the audience replies, "*Oṃ.*"

At the end of the *bhajana,* the special food of the day, already offered to the deity in the *pūjā,* is distributed to all as a "favor" (*prasāda*) of the Lord. The sharing of the *prasāda* in a symbolic communion is as essential to the *bhajana* as is the singing together.

### *Monthly* Bhajanas

The second type of *bhajana,* called a *divyanāmabhajana,* or *dīpabhajana,* is generally a monthly affair. Once a month, usually on a Saturday night, a group of twenty to forty people meet from about 7:30 in the evening until about 6:00 the next morning to conduct this type of *bhajana.* Not everyone comes at the same time or stays throughout the night. Some of the children are taken home to sleep; others try to stay awake as long as they can until they fall asleep on their mothers' laps. Adults, too, come and go according to personal convenience. Many songs and stanzas from the weekly *bhajana* are also used in the monthly *bhajana,* but many others are added, particularly about Krishna's activities and "sports" (*līlās*) with the *gopīs,* or milkmaids. The heart of the monthly *bhajana* is the singing, dancing, and dramatizing of these songs by the devotees as they sit or dance around a small lighted ritual lamp symbolizing Krishna's presence, imagining themselves to be *gopīs.*

The invocation of Krishna's presence into the lamp takes place in two steps. First the lamp is decorated with a garland of flowers and lighted by a leading devotee of the group, as it stands under lithographs of Krishna and Rādhā on the wall. A light-offering is then made to the deity in the lithograph, accompanied by a Vedic *mantra.* This symbolizes a transfer of power from the lithograph to the lamp. After the host has distributed flowers and scented sandalwood paste to the active male devotees, the leader takes the lighted lamp in his hand; while he holds the lamp and dances clockwise around the floor with it, four songs, two in Sanskrit and two in Kannada, are sung. The lamp is then placed on a small wooden pedestal in the center of the floor, decorated at that spot with geometric drawings of rice powder. As long as the lamp is in the center of the floor, it is regarded as a spot made sacred by Krishna's presence. The action of the *bhajana* takes place as the devotees sit or dance in a circle around the lamp.

The themes of the *bhajana* are based mainly on incidents in Krishna's life as described in the *Bhāgavatapurāṇa,* but they are expressed and elaborated in songs from various regional saints: Vijayagopāla, Bhadrādri, Nārāyaṇa Tīrtha, Rāmdās, Mīrā, Āṇḍāḷ, and others. In one of the most dramatic parts of the *bhajana,* the devotees, after they have been dancing and singing the *gopīs'* play with Krishna, suddenly sit down and sing the *Gopīkāgītā,* lamenting Krishna's disappearance from their (the *gopīs'*) midst and begging him to return. To re-enact and celebrate Krishna's reappearance, the devotees stand, sing, and do a number of dances considered appropriate expressions of joy by the *gopīs* as they "sport" with Krishna again. These dances are based on South Indian folk dances usually performed by women. They include the circular dance (*rāsakrīḍā*), in which there is imagined a Krishna, who has multiplied himself so that there is a Krishna between every two *gopīs;* a churning dance, in which the devotees pair off, cross hands, and embrace; a stick dance (*kōlāṭṭam*); and a *kummi* dance (the last two being country folk dances).

The songs sung during and after these dances include folk songs and songs in Sanskrit and other regional languages. They also sing a group of philosophical songs in Tamil, called *Siddha,* composed by Tamil sages known as Siddhars; *abhaṅgs* in Marathi by Turkarām and Ekanātha; songs on the ten manifestations of Viṣṇu, and songs on Śiva and other deities.

After these dances and songs, each devotee prostrates himself before the others and then rolls full-length clockwise around the lamp to take the dust from the feet of the other devotees. When he gets up he is embraced by the other devotees.*

In a final circumambulation, the devotees go around the lamp singing a Sanskrit song about Krishna. A song is then sung in praise of Śiva, another in praise of Jagannātha, followed by a *nāmāvali* on Govinda and a stanza in praise of Āñjaneya. Women and children join in these songs for the religious benefit of the entire *bhajana.* A light-offering is made to the lamp and then to the lithograph. The leading devotee now picks up the lamp and, singing the third *aṣṭāpadī* from the *Gītagovinda,* dances with it, then returns it to its original place under the lithograph. The other devotees prostrate themselves toward the lithograph, indicating that Krishna's power has been transferred back to the picture. Another light-offering is made to the lithograph, and the *bhajana* closes with the same invocation of auspiciousness (*maṅgalam*) used at the end of weekly *bhajanas.*

This type of *bhajana* is also performed on the occasion of a festival, on Rāma's and Krishna's birthdays, and on days commemorating the birth and death days of the gurus Bodhendra, Ayyarvāḷ, and Sadgurusvāmī. It may also be performed on the birthday of some member of the family or when a noted Bhāgavatār comes to visit. Shorter forms of the *bhajana* may last four or five hours.

* See photographs following page 174.

*Annual* Bhajanas

The third type of *bhajana,* the marriage of Rādhā and Krishna (*Rādhā kalyāṇam*), which is performed annually, has a special and pre-eminent status among *bhajanas,* because, in the story of Krishna, his marriage to a favorite *gopī,* Rādhā, represents a consummation of Krishna's romance with the *gopīs,* and because on the allegorical plane the marriage symbolizes the human soul's union with the Absolute. The preparations and arrangements for this type of *bhajana* are far more elaborate than for the others. Hundreds of people come to it, requiring a very large house, a small hall, or, as is customary, a street pavilion (*pandal*) like those used in actual marriages. Professional musicians are frequently employed and also Vedic priests (*purohitas*), who know the ritual of an orthodox Hindu wedding, to chant Vedic *mantras.* The number of devotees who come to one of these *bhajanas* may be so large that it is necessary for them to form several concentric circles when they start to sing and dance, or for many to drop out from active participation. At one *Rādhā kalyāṇam* I attended, the host thinned out the circle of devotees by arbitrarily tapping individuals on the back at random and asking them to withdraw.

The marriage part of the *Rādhā kalyāṇam bhajana* usually takes about six hours and is performed on a Sunday morning following a lamp-type *bhajana* the preceding night. However, it is now customary to have the marriage *bhajana* culminate a ten-day program of *bhajanas* that is becoming the great festival (*Mahotsava*) of *bhajanas* for the year, echoing, perhaps, the traditional ten-day temple festival. During these ten days, *bhajanas* are performed, usually in the evenings, grouped according to special regions and composers. In 1961, one Madras festival included special *bhajanas* based on the *Gītagovinda* and the *Kṛṣṇalīlātaraṅgiṇī,* on songs of the Tamil Śaivite saints (*Tēvāram*) and Vaiṣṇavite saints (*Tiruppāvai*), and on songs by Mīrābāī, Kabīr, and Purandara Dāsa. Individual singers and *bhajana* parties from different regions were featured during the festival. Recitations with songs (*harikathā*) on Krishna and other purāṇic themes were also given, and comic relief was provided by mimicry and imitations.

On the Saturday night preceding the marriage *bhajana,* there is a discourse (*jāṉavāsam*) to welcome the bridegroom (Krishna) to the bride's (Rādhā's) house for the marriage. It is followed by an all-night *bhajana* combining features of the weekly and the monthly *bhajana* types but using more objects (fans, metal images, garlands) than are usually used when the ceremonies are performed separately. Some 200 to 300 people may come to this all-night bhajana and remain until it ends about 4:00 the next morning. After the devotees and other guests have had a chance to get a few hours' sleep, either at the place where the *bhajana* is held or in their own homes, they gather again early in the morning. A small party is formed under the leadership of a distinguished devotee to go beg for rice and other presents for the wedding. The leader wears the traditional costume of devotees on this occasion and carries a *tambūrā* and begging bowl. Housewives come out to put their gifts in the bowl or are visited at their doors by members of the party. This custom is called *uñchavṛtti.*

While the party is out, the *bhajana* proper begins with a brief *pūjā* and with invocations, stanzas, and *nāmāvalis* similar to those used at the beginning of the weekly *bhajana.* Songs from the monthly *bhajana* are also used. It is usual for each *bhajana* leader to sing songs from his own tradition. The marriage ceremony is obviously the most popular part of the *bhajana,* and by the time it is ready to begin as many as 500 people may have gathered in and around the pavilion. The ritual of the marriage ceremony follows that of an orthodox Hindu marriage of the South Indian type, with variations, especially in the use of songs that are peculiar to the Rādhā-Krishna *bhajana.* The most important song is the twenty-second *aṣṭāpadī* of the *Gītagovinda,* which expounds the union of Rādhā and Krishna. Telugu songs on the same theme are also used.

Much of the ritual is acted out by the male devotees. Rice mixed with turmeric powder and water is pounded in a mortar with a pestle, and groups of devotees take turns dancing with the pestle toward and away from images of Krishna and Rādhā while singing a song of auspiciousness to Krishna. The dance is said to be a village dance common during the South Indian harvest festival (*Poṅgal*) and is interpreted by some devotees as a dance of the *gopīs.* A similar combination of rice and turmeric powder is used for marriages and domestic *pūjās,* but the pounding is omitted. The bride and bridegroom, represented by lithographs and metal images, are anointed and adorned. Turmeric powder and limewater, and a red substance (red is an auspicious color) are applied to their feet to beautify them and as a good augury for them. Gifts of cloth are placed under the images, and Vedic *mantras* for marriage are recited by the Vedic priest. A thread moistened with turmeric and carrying a gold pendant at one end is hung around the neck of the bride. This is an emblem of marriage when tied by a bridegroom around the bride's neck and is called the *tāli.* As at a regular marriage, the lineage of the couple is recited for three generations on each side, giving the names of the father, the father's father, and the father's grandfather.

Some of the ritual resembles that of a Western marriage—for example, the throwing of rice and flowers at the couple—and seems to express the blessings and joy of the audience. Among the songs sung to convey this joyous mood is one by Nārāyaṇa Tīrtha saying: "I see Krishna here with His eight other wives—all in resplendent glory." Many of the Rādhā-Krishna songs are also used in Hindu marriages. At this point in the ceremony, the day's priest is given a present of money and perhaps some other gift (*sambhāvana*). Further attentions are then bestowed on the couple: Their feet are painted again, flower balls are exchanged, they are given a ride in a boat and a swing. Much of this is done only in song and symbolically, but some of it is acted out. If a small swing and metal images are available, the leader will swing them to and fro while singing two or three Sanskrit and Tamil songs about Rādhā and Krishna. The bride and bridegroom are also supposed to address satirical Telugu verses (*padyas*) to one another.

One of the most moving parts of the ceremony is that of putting Rādhā and Krishna to sleep. Sanskrit and Kannada lullabies are sung, a light-offering is made, and a curtain is drawn to give the bridal couple privacy and to symbolize their union. One of Jayadeva's songs is sung, asking Rādhā to go to Krishna (*Aṣṭāpadī* 21). A slightly humorous conversation between Rādhā and Krishna is sung in Sanskrit by one devotee. Their sleep is indicated by the singing of a lullaby and by a period of silence while the devotees close their eyes and meditate. Distinguished devotees are selected to act as guards at each of the four gates of the palace. Their leader sings a song for each direction, asking the guards to see that all is well, and the devotees respond. After another brief silence, Sanskrit, Tamil, and Telugu songs are sung to Krishna in a *rāga* for waking.

With offerings of flame-light and milk, the *bhajana* closes after a final *maṅgalam*. The presents are then distributed to the devotees, and food is also given to them, as well as to all the participants and to the poor. These large wedding *bhajanas* always include a feeding of the poor. Sometimes a leading devotee will make a speech to close the ceremonies, although the festival may go on for another day, with additional discourses, street processions of Rādhā and Krishna around a temple and tank, and a special celebration in honor of Hanumān. On the last day of the festival, *Aṣṭāpadīs* 23 and 24 are sung.

In the last few years, a Sītā-Rāma marriage (*Sītā kalyāṇam*) and a Vaḷḷi-Subrahmaṇya marriage (*Vaḷḷi kalyāṇam*) have been added as annual *bhajanas,* but they have not yet become as popular as the Rādhā-Krishna marriage *bhajana.* One section of the city that celebrates all these marriages has changed its name to Kalyāṇam Nāgar—town of marriages.

The swing festival (*Dolotsava*) is sometimes included at the end of a monthly *bhajana,* in which case it comes in the early hours of the morning. At the marriage *bhajana,* it usually comes, in abbreviated form, about noon. The swing festival is also part of a Hindu wedding and was probably held in the past as a garden festival in spring and summer.

### *Morning* Bhajanas

The fourth type of *bhajana* is a street *bhajana* conducted very early in the morning, and occasionally at night, around the temple tank.* This observance is especially popular in the holy month of Mārgaśīrṣa. Among Krishna devotees, the explanation of these *bhajanas* is that the *gopīs* waked at 3:00 A.M. during this month and sang and prayed to the goddess Kātyāyanī (Pārvatī) for Krishna's hand. A leading devotee will sometimes organize and train a band of children to sing early morning *bhajanas.*

The devotees believe that the human year is a day for the gods. The twelve months of the human year represent the twenty-four hours of the divine day. The month of Mārgaśīrṣa is holy and auspicious for gods, since it represents the two-hour "interval" from 4:00 to 6:00 A.M. for them, the time when they wake from sleep and begin to be active. Each subsequent month represents another two hours. That is why the *gopīs*

* See photographs following page 174.

are said to have chosen this month for Kātyāyanī *pūjā*, or *kratan*,* and why *bhāgavatars* hold *bhajanas* in the morning.

The songs at morning *bhajanas* are similar to those sung at other types of *bhajanas*, with *nāmāvalis* and Tamil songs, Śaivite as well as Vaiṣṇavite, more common than at other *bhajanas*.

The pattern of the morning *bhajanas* is also followed during festivals on full-moon nights and when the temple deities are taken in procession. On these occasions, *bhajana* parties follow the deities, along with Vedic chanters and singers of *Tēvāram*.

### *Special* Bhajanas

The fifth *bhajana* type is not an independent kind of *bhajana* but a selection or combination of the preceding four types, for performance on some special occasion. The most common occasions are the visit of a dignitary, a wedding, Republic Day, and other holidays. *Bhajana* groups are invited to an individual's house to conduct these *bhajanas*, or some active group may organize a number of them on its own premises. Many of the *bhajanas* given during the *bhajana* festival are occasional *bhajanas* of this type.

### *Daily* Bhajanas

A sixth type of *bhajana*, the daily *bhajana* or *nityabhajana*, is no longer commonly observed, although it is reported to have been more common, at least among very sincere devotees, a generation ago. This type of *bhajana* is performed daily in one's house for an hour or two in the evening, with members of the family and perhaps a few neighbors and friends attending. About fifteen songs on different deities, gurus, and saints, in Sanskrit, Telugu, Tamil, Marathi, and Hindi are sung each day, a different set each day for the first twenty-four days, and then the cycle begins to repeat. It has been reported that the Divine Life Society at Rishikesh conducts evening *bhajanas* the year around. In Madras, only the well-known devotee Gopālakrishna Bhāgavatār is said to conduct daily *bhajanas*.

## Social Organization of the *Bhajanas*

The basic unit of *bhajana* social organization is the social group that meets weekly to conduct an evening *bhajana*. It is usually a small neighborhood group comprising the members of one or two households. The organizers and active participants are generally male adults, although in the last four or five years a few *bhajanas* have been organized by women. A weekly *bhajana* group will include father and sons, women and children of the household, several other relatives who may live in the same household or nearby, and friends and acquaintances from one or two other households in the immediate vicinity. These friends are not family relations, although they may belong to the same subcaste; the friendship

* A *pūjā* or rite according to the white *Yajurveda Śrautasūtra* of Kātyāyana.

is usually based on neighborhood acquaintance or on professional or occupational association. If some members of the *bhajana* group move away, the weekly *bhajana* meetings rotate from one household to another, unless the distances are too great, in which case a new *bhajana* group is formed in the new neighborhood. The formation of local *bhajana* groups is quite informal and spontaneous. New ones are organized constantly in various parts of the city, but not all survive with equal vigor and seriousness. Some of the groups are closely tied to a father, grandfather, or great-grandfather who was a distinguished devotee and who himself conducted *bhajanas*. Most local groups do not have a very long and continuous history.

The more successful a local *bhajana* group becomes, the more quickly its membership expands beyond the small neighborhood group. New members are attracted from outside, or the local group expands its membership by its own organizational activities. This is especially apt to be the case for the monthly and annual *bhajanas,* when large numbers of people participate. Several local groups may combine on these occasions, but it is also likely that one of the more active groups may organize the larger *bhajanas* in its name.

This process can be illustrated by an example from Mylapore, one of the Madras suburbs, where one of the local *bhajana* groups, first formed in 1945, has sponsored annual as well as occasional *bhajanas.* The group elects officers, solicits donations, prints announcements and invitations, and issues an annual report with an audited account of its revenues and expenditures. During 1959 and 1960, in addition to conducting its usual Saturday night *bhajanas,* it organized daily morning *bhajanas* around the temple streets for about two weeks at the end of December (during Mārgaśīrṣa); was invited to conduct *bhajanas* in private homes and public institutions on fifteen occasions in various parts of the city; held special *bhajanas* five times on its own premises—the home of one of its members—to honor distinguished visitors and to celebrate holidays; and organized marriage *bhajanas* for Rādhā and Krishna for ten days in January and for Rāma and Sītā one day in April and again for a day in November, when it also held a one-day marriage *bhajana* for Vaḷḷi and Subrahmaṇya. Each of the marriage *bhajanas* included feeding of the poor. The group also organized *bhajana* pilgrimages to places of religious interest.

The organization of so many activities sometimes puts a strain on the resources and cooperativeness of the group. On one occasion, when it was invited out of town to conduct a *bhajana* at someone's home, the host expected the *bhajana* to go on through the night. One of the officers, however, decided that a three-hour *bhajana* was sufficient for the occasion. The decision so offended another officer that he resigned his post in protest.

The major activity of the group is the organization of the annual marriage *bhajana* for Rādhā and Krishna and the associated *bhajana* festival, which goes on for ten days. Donations are solicited for this purpose by members all over the city in offices and homes. In 1959 and 1960, about 2,000 rupees were donated by more than 800 people. About 700 of these donations were of 2 rupees (about 50 cents) or less. The donors represent many different classes and occupations. Of the 322 that could be identified, about 55 per cent were Smārta Brahmans; 10 per cent Śrīvaiṣṇava Brahmans, 10 per cent Mādhva Brahmans, 20 per cent non-Brahmans, and 5 per cent of the donations were made in the names of women. The occupational representation is definitely middle class and professional and includes government, education, business and industry, law, medicine, religion, journalism, and the arts. The government group includes a retired high-court judge, a retired deputy collector, and a member of the state legislative assembly; the education group includes the principals of two colleges, a university professor, and several teachers; the business group includes a bank officer, the director of a steel factory, chartered accountants, shopkeepers, and merchants; the arts group includes actors, employees of a film studio, and musicians. Probably the most numerous groups are office assistants, Vedic *purohitas,* and medical people. Not all donors are necessarily active participants in the *bhajanas,* and not all participants make donations, but there is considerable overlap between the two groups.

The money collected for the 1959–60 festival was spent approximately in the following manner: the pavilion, 119 rupees; orchestra, 261 rupees; *pūjā* 78 rupees; food for the poor, 518 rupees; flowers, 62 rupees; procession, 35 rupees; camphor, 119 rupees; printing, 366 rupees; transportation, 154 rupees; carpet, 50 rupees; cloth for gifts, 225 rupees. A balance of about 255 rupees was used for the expenses of weekly and occasional *bhajanas.* The group is also hoping to collect enough money to construct its own permanent building.

The organizational drive and leadership of this Mylapore *bhajana* group probably come from two of its officers, one an outstanding and highly respected Tamil writer and journalist, a Smārta Brahman; and the other a successful chartered accountant, a Śrīvaiṣṇava Brahman. They live next door to each other in one of the newer sections of Mylapore. The accountant's house is now used for weekly and special *bhajanas,* and the street in front for the marriage *bhajanas.* The accountant is also a leading worker in the Congress Party of Madras, and he has organized the distribution of free CARE milk to poor children, using his house as a distribution center. The milk distribution cards carry the name of the *bhajana* group as well as his own name.

In 1958, through the initiative of officers of the Mylapore *bhajana* group, a conference was called of all leading devotees in the city. As a result of the meeting, an association of Madras devotees was organized under the title Madras Bhāgavata-Mahā-Sammelanam Samāj. Officers and a governing body of about fifty members were selected. The association is a federation of *bhajana* groups in the city and hopes eventually to include all *bhajana* groups in the state. About forty-five local Madras *bhajana* groups were affiliated with it in 1961 and paid dues of one or two rupees a year. The association now holds a conference once a year, when it elects officers, discusses its plans, and conducts special *bhajanas.*

The activities of the association are similar to those of the Mylapore local group but are more extensive. It undertakes to furnish *bhajana* leaders to any group in or out of the city that requests them. One of the secretaries estimated that there are now about 500 requests a year and said that he goes out about three times a month to lead *bhajanas*. When the association sends out a *bhajana* leader, he is usually given the cost of his transportation and a gift by his host. Other association services include regular notice of *bhajana* meetings all over the city and the organization of special *bhajanas* when there are visitors and on other occasions.

Not all the local *bhajana* groups in the city are affiliated with the association, nor are they all as highly organized as the Mylapore group. Some of them regard so much organization as uncongenial to the spirit of the *bhajana*. One group, led by the son of the famous Madras devotee S. V. Aiyer, claims not to have any fixed program of performances or even a regular meeting time. It sends out no invitations, requires no special arrangements, and makes no collections, because the leader believes such organization leads to quarrels and to expectations of privileged treatment that are contrary to the spontaneous feelings of love and equality that should prevail among devotees. The group does seem to follow a regular program in its weekly meetings, as established by the leader's father. The program begins with a recitation of the divine name (*nāmasaṅkīrtana*), songs in praise of the guru and father, of Rādhā and Krishna, and of the saints. It concludes with an *aṣṭāpadī* from the *Gītagovinda*, a song from the *Kṛṣṇalīlātaraṅgiṇī*, and one of Mīrābāī's songs. A special feature of the group's *bhajanas* is the more active participation of the women, although they sit separate from the men. We find an influence here both of the Caitanya type of *bhajana* and of Mīrābāī.

The type of *bhajana* performance and the kind of social organization are clearly interrelated. Each type of *bhajana* calls for a somewhat different kind of social group and social organization. On the other hand, the composition of the social group and its organizational propensities definitely affect the type of *bhajana* performance. Each local group introduces some variations of its own into the program, and, as the groups get larger, the sources of these variations become more diversified. The variations are in turn codified into a fixed program that soon becomes traditional. Whatever the long-run outcome of this interaction may be, there is no doubt that the trend of the last fifty years in Madras *bhajanas* has been toward larger-scale organization and greater formality and fixity in the program. There is continuity with the earlier seventeenth-century codifications of the traditional program, but there are also many innovations of regional and national significance. An urban, centralized organization, the Madras Bhāgavata-Mahā-Sammelanam Samāj, has developed to take official charge of the movement, with practically all media of modern communication at its disposal and with good prospects for a permanent institutional center of its own. This organization sponsors a regular festival calendar that parallels and intersects the traditional calendars of temple and domestic worship. Professional musicians, Vedic priests, semiprofessional devotees, and expensive ceremonial arrangements are employed for the larger *bhajana* performances. Printed *bhajana* books have made it easier for a large number of people to follow a uniform program.[11] Affiliated groups have been formed by Tamils in Calcutta, Delhi, and other large cities in and out of India, and there is a plan to extend the movement into villages and towns of Tamil̲nāḍu.

It is arguable whether these developments can be characterized as the formation of a new "cult" or of a "Great Tradition." Perhaps "modernization and urbanization" of an old cult and tradition is an apter characterization. They are in any case a significant growth in one cultural tradition of contemporary Hinduism. The nature of this tradition and the processes involved in its growth can be further clarified by a discussion of the leadership, transmission, support, and meaning of the *bhajanas.*

## Leadership and Transmission of the Rādhā-Krishna Cult

Leaders of *bhajanas* are those who know the songs best or have a reputation for devotion. Sometimes the two criteria do not coincide: Those with musical skill do not always have a reputation for devotion, nor are the devotees necessarily musically gifted. Special roles in the performance of *bhajanas* are usually reserved for elderly and distinguished devotees—the conduct of a *pūjā* and the carrying of the lamp in the lamp *bhajana.* These devotees may or may not be musical and familiar with the ritual. On the other hand, the role of priest in the Rādhā-Krishna marriage *bhajanas* is usually assigned to a professional Vedic priest, who is paid for his services. Some priests, who may come with no interest in *bhajanas,* eventually cultivate an interest and become members of regular Saturday night *bhajanas.* They do not, however, forgo their fees for performing the marriage service.

The role that a devotee plays in a *bhajana* does not itself determine his leadership status. On the contrary, if a devotee has a reputation for devotion he is invited to conduct *bhajanas.* What testifies to such a reputation? One answer to this question was framed by a leading Madras devotee in a speech he gave in 1960 to close the celebration of a Rādhā-Krishna marriage *bhajana.* His answer set severe standards for a true devotee; he who looks like a devotee only during *bhajanas* is not a true devotee. He is like a workman who does not think about his work after hours; he is only a "*Bhajana* workman" who knows the sequence of songs and has the musical skill to sing them. To become a true devotee, he must be a devotee throughout his life: pure in speech, thought, and action. He must be sincere and firm in his belief that all beings in the world are children of God and that everything—whether calamity or good fortune—happens by His grace. He must be rid of egoism, be humble to all, and speak in a sweet manner. Although this speaker did not seem to think that singing *bhajana* songs would quickly transform the singers into true devotees, he nevertheless urged cultivation of friendship with groups of devotees and singing as the best means available in this age for meditating on God and asking His forgiveness and help.

This austere ethical interpretation of the requirements for a true devotee is not, I think, shared by average participants in *bhajanas.* They are more apt to agree with the same speaker's admission that the devotional path (*bhaktiyoga*), being available to all and not requiring any external aids, is a more accessible path to salvation in this age than the path of knowledge or of works. They may not disagree with the qualities stipulated for a true devotee, and they would certainly greatly respect anyone who possessed those qualities, but in choosing *bhajana* leaders they will settle for less: Anyone who manifests sincerity and constancy in his devotion qualifies as a leader.

*Bhajana* leadership is formalized in two different ways—through the organization of *bhajana* societies and through the guru-disciple relation. When *bhajana* societies have adopted a formal organization, the election or appointment of officers is a way of designating leaders. Among the officers now serving in some *bhajana* societies, some are obviously distinguished for the quality of their devotion, and others rather for their organizing abilities, acquaintance with a wide range of people, and interest in seeing the Rādhā-Krishna movement become an organized movement. It is perhaps paradoxical that a cult that emphasizes spontaneous, personal devotion should become an organized social movement, but the transformation could not take place without the help of the organizing type of leader. It may even happen that the same individual provides both the spiritual and the organizational leadership (the devotee who made the speech on the qualities of a true devotee is an example). There is an institutional precedent for this in the heads of the South Indian monasteries, whose spiritual authority has been recognized by the Indian Supreme Court to depend on their secular property rights.[12] The most common situation in *bhajana* organizations, however, is more akin to the separation of secular and religious leadership, as in the temples.

### *Gurus and Disciples*

The guru-disciple relationship is not generally considered a formalized relationship, since anyone is in principle free to choose his guru, and a guru is in principle free to accept or reject a disciple. What makes the relationship formal is the requirement of a formal initiation ceremony in which the guru imparts a secret *mantra* and a set of instructions to the disciple. When a guru or group of gurus is recognized by a series of disciples, a particular cultural tradition (*sampradāya*) is established, and its authentic transmission is traced through a chain of disciples, who in turn become gurus to the next generation. In this sense, every Indian sect or philosophical school forms a cultural tradition. Each traces its evolution through a historical or putative chain of disciples to a founding guru or gurus. The Vedas are traced through certain families to the original revelations of *Ṛṣis* or Seers; Buddhists look to Buddha as the founding guru; Jains to Mahāvīra; Smārta Brahmans to Śaṅkara; Mādhvas to Madhva, Śrīvaiṣṇavas to Rāmānuja; Liṅgāyats to Bāsava; Sikhs to Guru Nānak; and the Rāmakrishna followers to Rāmakrishna and Vivekānanda. In the South Indian Rādhā-Krishna cult, three gurus are recognized as having given the Rādhā-Krishna *bhajana* its canonical form. The three are praised in stanzas recited at the very beginning of each *bhajana*. Other saints from other regions and periods whose songs are sung in the *bhajanas*—for example, Caitanya, Tukarām, Mīrābāī, Kabīr, and Purandara Dāsa—have also been assimilated to the South Indian *bhajana* tradition, but they do not have the pre-eminent status of the three gurus.

There does not yet exist a generally recognized chain of disciples of the three gurus, although one occasionally hears attempts to trace such a chain. By reciting stanzas in praise of the three gurus, contemporary devotees make themselves disciples in unilateral fashion, so to speak. There are, however, devotees who have been initiated by an older generation of devotees, who in turn claim spiritual descent from the three gurus. One who has been thus initiated, a retired film actor, is also an officer in one of the *bhajana* societies and is frequently called upon to lead *bhajanas* in different parts of the city. He is usually asked to lead the *bhajanas* of his society during the Rādhā-Krishna marriage ceremony. On this occasion, he comes dressed in the traditional costume of a devotee, with a turban around his head and a *tambūrā* under his arm. This is the costume that the guru who initiated him wears when he visits the city. In his domestic shrine, the retired film actor has pictures of the three gurus, of two Mahārāṣṭrian saints, of a family guru who is said to have reached the age of 161, of Gopālakrishna Bhāgavatar, who initiated him into the *bhajana* field, and of the initiation ceremony. He also keeps on display near the shrine a string of beads, called *sūtram,* that he received when he was initiated, with which he counts the names of the deities. This devotee's family comes from a town in South Arcot District. His grandfather, father, brother, he, and two of his sons have Śrī Veṅkaṭeśvara as their chosen deity. Two of his other sons, however, have chosen Durgā and Murugan as their respective favorite deities.

In addition to Gopālakrishna Bhāgavatar, who is a master among living *bhāgavatars* and who has published a standard collection of *bhajana* songs in Tamil, other gurus are frequently mentioned who are within living memory of the present generation. All are said to have conducted *bhajanas* according to the program laid down by the three founding gurus, but each is also credited with some individual innovations.

One of them is Tillistana Narasiṃha Bhāgavatar, who is said to have been the first to print in *grantha* script, at Kumbakōṇam in the early 1900's, a collection of *bhajana* songs based on Sadgurusvāmī's codification. Narasiṃha Bhāgavatar, a Telugu Smārta Brahman, was invited to Madras City for *harikathā* recitals and for *bhajana* parties. The parties are remembered by T. V. Seetharama Aiyer, who came to Madras from Kumbakōṇam in 1904 to become the librarian of the Hindu High School in Triplicane. He describes the *bhajanas* of this period as emphasizing classical music and being restricted to Brahmans. Sūlamaṅgalam Svāminātha Bhāgavatar also recalls Narasiṃha Bhāgavatar and other early *bhajana* leaders.

Three of the leaders were contemporaries and are frequently singled out for special mention: Rāmacandra Aiyer, S. V. Aiyer, and Kōthamarāma Aiyer. All three came to Madras from Tanjore District and were familiar with the *bhajana* tradition deriving from the three gurus. Through their personal experience and travels, each of them added to this tradition something from Bengal, Mahārāṣṭra, and North India.

Rāmacandra Aiyer, popularly known as "Hari," a retired elementary school teacher, came to Madras about 1913 from Tanjore District to live with his younger brother, who had a government job in the city.

"Hari" conducted *bhajanas* in his brother's house and wherever asked. He is said to have started the *Rādhā kalyāṇam* and *Sītā kalyāṇam bhajanas* and also to have added Sunday *bhajanas.* He died in 1953 at the age of seventy-three.

Veṅkaṭaramana Aiyer (or S. V. Aiyer) called himself "Mīrādāsī" because he believed Mīrābāī had possessed him. The incident is described in the following words by a contemporary:

> As this blessed devotee lay on his back one starlit night, on the top floor of his residence in Madras, a voice beckoned to him and bade him look at a meteor in the sky. There actually was a meteor then in the sky, and this *premi* [lover] saw a blue figure descend therefrom and reach his side. As it approached him, he recognized it to be Mīrā enveloped in a dazzling cool blue light. From that time onwards, Mīrā possessed him and he felt he was a tool in the hands of Mīrā who was herself living in the blue boy of blessed Vṛndāvan.[13]

The incident changed S. V. Aiyer's life and behavior. From then on, he imagined that he was a *gopī,* at least in his own house, and he lived in an ecstatic condition. His gait, smile, and talk became "naturally attractive and bewitching." He dressed daily in a cape, put on anklet bells, and went out with a begging bowl to beg for rice. On his deathbed, when he could not move his limbs or speak much, he asked his disciples to write "Rādhā-Krishna" on his tongue, and when this was done, he felt ecstatic.

S. V. Aiyer came from Tanjore District to Madras for his education. He studied Sanskrit, German, and Latin, among other subjects. In 1900, he was employed as a superintendent in the Accountant General's Office. This was probably the time of the Mīrābāī incident. In 1914, he was transferred to Calcutta for about two years, and after that to Delhi. While in Calcutta, he learned at first hand about the Caitanya movement and drew inspiration from Caitanya's life. Although S. V. Aiyer, too, followed the *bhajana* program of the three Tanjore gurus, he was probably responsible for innovations giving greater prominence to Mīrābāī songs and to Caitanya-type *bhajanas.* His son, who is one of his devoted disciples, believes his father took the *bhajana* out of the hands of the professional devotees who conducted it for fees in the homes of the well-to-do. He mixed with the poor, he stayed up late at night, and, above all, he taught that all formalities could be dispensed with in *bhajanas* if the devotees loved Krishna and believed that he was merciful. The son reports that when the father would say to the family, "Let us do some *bhajanas,*" the children would ask, "With what?" The father would then tell them not to depend on externals but to sing the Lord's praises. He would even permit them to keep their shoes on, since he believed that the Lord was so merciful that he would forgive any mistakes the devotees might make.

S. V. Aiyer probably also introduced the type of *bhajana* where men, women, and children all sit together, singing and developing the same ideas.

A third Madras guru, Kōthamarāma Aiyer, was a contemporary and close friend of S. V. Aiyer. He, too, came from Tanjore District. He studied at Madras Christian College, where he received his B.A., and later studied law and took a B.L. degree. He was a lecturer in English at the Arts College of Madurai and served as headmaster in several high schools before he was appointed to the post of manager in the Administrator General's Office in Madras City.[14]

Kōthamarāma Aiyer annually visited the Pandharpur shrine for Lord Viṭṭhala in Mahārāṣṭra. Once, when his superior officer refused to give him leave, he resigned his job and made the pilgrimage anyway. He learned Marathi in order to study the works of the Mahārāṣṭrian saints and their songs. He sang these songs in the *bhajanas* that he conducted weekly and on special occasions. In 1921, he built a temple for Lord Viṭṭhala in Triplicane, a Madras suburb, with a *Bhajana Mandira* (*bhajana* hall), and established a permanent endowment for daily worship in order to fulfill a vow he took when he resigned his position. Before he died in 1934 at the age of seventy-three, this pioneer in the *bhajana* cult had published, in Telugu script, a number of books for the use of devotees.[15]

Another complete collection of *bhajana* songs, also in Telugu script, was published by M. S. Subrahmaṇya Aiyer, a superintendent of the Madras Postal Audit Office, under the title *Nitya Bhajanāvali.* This collection, intended for daily *bhajanas,* contains fifteen sections of twenty-four songs each; one song may be taken from each section, so that there will be no repetition until the twenty-fifth day. M. S. Subrahmaṇya Aiyer knew all the songs by heart, and it was said that if all *bhajana* books were to become extinct, they could be brought out again with his help. He conducted daily *bhajanas* at his house, as well as other types of *bhajanas* wherever he was invited to conduct them. His wife and three daughters would join the chorus of the daily *bhajanas* at home, and they also conducted *bhajanas* when invited to other women's homes. He had two sons, both of whom died in youth.[16]

The guru-disciple relationship, according to some students of Hinduism, offers a pure personal and religious relationship that transcends Hindu society and culture. This interpretation seems to be an overstatement, in view of the many formalities, social and cultural, that surround the relationship in India. There is a definite etiquette governing the behavior of guru and disciple toward each other, and, in the older *gurukula* system of education, this etiquette defined a kind of apprenticeship not only in religious matters but in secular and technical crafts as well. It may be true, however, that the characteristically Indian guru-disciple relationship, as a mutual, voluntary relationship between individuals, provides a channel for transmitting and changing cultural traditions that is independent of the channels defined by the hereditary social groupings of family, caste, sect, language, and region. This is in any case an interesting hypothesis to explore in connection with the transmission of the Rādhā-Krishna cult in South India.

The facts we have already adduced concerning this cult give great weight to transmission through chains of gurus and disciples. The same facts, however, also show that transmission is not wholly independent of the social structure but sometimes follows the grain of that structure and sometimes cuts across the grain. Predominating among the leaders and followers of the cult is a subcaste of Brahmans, the Smārta Brahmans. On the basis of a preliminary estimate, about 55 per cent of *bhajana* participants in Madras City are Smārta Brahmans. Among *bhajana* leaders, the percentage is much higher. In South India, then, the Rādhā-Krishna cult is cultivated by particular social groups. But not all Smārtas are Krishna worshipers, and there are also other Brahman subcastes, the Mādhvas and Śrīvaiṣṇavas, as well as some non-Brahmans, who belong to the cult. The figures suggest that in about 45 per cent of the cases the guru-disciple relationship may cross subcaste, caste, and sect lines.

If we look at family histories, we find that some families have cultivated the Rādhā-Krishna cult for four to five generations, while in others only one generation has practiced it. Since the father is normally the first guru for his children, it is not surprising that the sons should follow the traditions of their fathers. But continuity is a result more of childhood upbringing and paternal example than it is of creed. Since every individual is free to choose his favorite personal deity (*iṣṭadevatā*), the sons may, and sometimes do, choose deities different from their fathers', as in the case of two sons of the retired actor who took Durgā and Murugan as their favorites. In such cases, the pictures or images of the sons' deities are simply added to the family shrine.

## *A Crisis of Choice*

We do not know enough details of the family histories of the three Tanjore gurus or of the Madras gurus to say in each case how far there was a departure from family traditions. It is likely that each individual introduced innovations that are now publicly recognized. In the family history of one highly respected Krishna devotee in Madras, there is evidence of profound personal choice and, in theological language, of a "call," although there does not appear to be any innovation in the family tradition. This devotee, now about sixty-nine, feels that he inherited his love for Krishna from his father, his grandfather, and his great-grandfather, all of whom were great devotees of Krishna, although he received his formal initiation and *sūtram* from an ardent devotee named Rādhākrishna Bhāgavatar of Ammaṅguḍi, who had retired from the railway service. He has passed this love on to his sons. As a child, he was brought up by his father—his mother had died when he was four days old—in an atmosphere completely permeated by love of Krishna.[17]

> My father was the first person on whom my eyes were set. He is my spiritual *guru,* and he has left me and my sons his legacy of extreme and inimitable love for Śrī Krishna.
>
> It is said in *Bhāgavata* that *bhakti,* or devotion to God, should be taught to men and women while they are young—when their minds are most receptive, impressionable, retentive, and fresh. My father believed in this and used it to great advantage while teaching his pupils.

The reality of Krishna was conveyed to the impressionable boy not so much by didactic instruction as by his father's whole-hearted devotion:

When my father initiated me in my early devotion to Śrī Krishna, there were no formal rites or ceremonies whatever. My *bhakti* just grew as informally as my early secular education did. My mere constant movement with my father (who was a veritable embodiment of *bhakti*) and his very company at all times inspired in me, without my knowledge, ardent *bhakti* even at my early age, or rather because of my early age. The very air of the house was saturated with love for Śrī Krishna. His divine name was ever in the mouth of my father. When he began to do some work or other, he said that Śrī Krishna would help him to do it. When he was confronted with some trouble or difficulty, he said that Śrī Krishna would help him out of it. Before he took his food, he would offer it to Śrī Krishna. If he was in need of something, he said that Śrī Krishna would enable him to get it. If he planned to do something, he would invoke Śrī Krishna's aid to do it successfully. "Śrī Krishna" was his father's and his grandfather's chosen god, and he got Him for himself by heredity or inheritance. I got Śrī Krishna as patrimony from my father. I inherited Him from my father as I inherited his landed property. When he was tired, he would say, "Śrī Krishna." He gave the name Krishnasvāmī to me so that as often as he called me by name he could remember Śrī Krishna, and he did call me very frequently.

This natural growth of Krishna love was challenged and recovered during a "religious upheaval" experienced in college:

While I was in Madras Christian College for the B.A. Honors course, a professor taught us Christianity. He eulogized Hinduism for the first six months of the term, and during the remaining three months he undid his work practically and eulogized Christianity. He made it appear that Hinduism was only a bundle of superstitions. As I was always very earnest about religion, I could not reconcile what he had taught us of Hinduism with what he taught us of Christianity. He had gained my heart and my ears in the first six months by saying things that my heart was after and endeared himself to me. He had gained my trust or confidence, and I considered his words as Gospel Truth. He had worked upon my mind very successfully. I could not decide easily what attitude I should take toward the two religions presented to me. I was a youngster and a student. He was an elderly person and my professor. A mental conflict appeared in me. I was comparing the two religions for several days in the light of what the professor had said of them in his very beautiful English, fluent and impressive, gripping like that of a wizard. A great religious upheaval took possession of me now, which lasted for days. One day, however, I came across a book of Śrī Rāmakrishna's sayings compiled by Svāmī Abhedānanda that led me to read all the sayings of the saint available and all the literature concerning Him. This was the first time that I knew of Śrī Rāmakrishna. I had not heard of him before. I read Svāmī Vivekānanda's *My Master* and his other works. I discussed questions with Svāmī Śarvānanda, then the head of Śrī Rāmakrishna *maṭha* in Madras. He was a man of [spiritual] realization, who was very useful to me at that time. In the Rāmakrishna literature, I came across references to and accounts of Lord Gaurāṅga or Saint Śrī Krishna Caitanya of Bengal. I read two or three books on this saint. Śrī Rāmakrishna hailed from Bengal, too. I was told Śrī Rāmakrishna was an *avatār* of Śrī Krishna Caitanya, who was himself an *avatār* of Śrī Krishna. I picked up the Bengali script with a view to reading the original literature on and of these saints. I read two or three Sanskrit books of this category in the Bengali script. Many were

> the books that I read at this time. I used the Library of the Theosophical Society, Madras, as well. The result of all this was that I caught hold of Hinduism again and found myself completely deluged by the sweeping flood of Krishna Love that I had once had and that I had lost sight of and grip of for a time. I do not know how this was effected, I mean this revival of Krishna Love in me. It is enough to say that I experienced it in some mysterious way without my knowledge. I was thereafter for some days alive with a new vigor or force of spirituality of the Devotion Type centering round Śrī Krishna and I was absolutely unconscious of everything around me. I muttered the word Śrī Krishna in season and out of season, spoke of Him and sang of Him likewise. I was not aware of sunset and sunrise for a few days and the time of the day. . . . A strong foundation was laid in the spiritual structure of my being, and all doubts departed, never more to return in my lifetime. I found solutions now for all the problems of life, of human society in all the countries, of the whole universe, to be brief. I lead an easy life now, and my heart and my mind are now carefree. I say to myself and with Śrī Rāmakrishṇa that the end and aim of life is to see God, and I am praying when I can to Śrī Krishṇa for this. My hairs used to stand on end at the mere mention of the name "Śrī Krishna," and tears of joy would trickle down freely from my eyes. It was indeed the most happy period in my life. It is true that I did not care for the family at that time, and I sometimes thought of adopting more severe measures for attaining God-realization forthwith. My father was naturally alarmed. But my fervor abated, and I could again attend to the normal duties of life. My father always thought that I was safe in Śrī Krishna's protection, and I thought and think so, too. I feel He is lending His helping hand to me at all times. He has helped me in life on several occasions, remaining invisible, of course, and if He becomes visible to me at any time, I shall then have reached the goal. I find that *bhajanas* help me a lot in my spiritual aspirations, and I attend them whenever I can.

It is to be regretted that this kind of detail is not available for the life-histories of other devotees, particularly those recognized as leaders of the Rādhā-Krishna cult. When it becomes available, we shall have a great deal more insight into the relative parts played by the guru-disciple relationship and by family, caste, and sect membership in the transmission of Krishna worship, and into the scope for individual choice. Several tentative conclusions, however, may be drawn from the fragmentary evidence presented. The evidence suggests that, far from being an independent mode of transmission that transcends the social structure and the culture the guru-disciple relationship operates as the very lifeline of the culture and the social structure. In theory, it is a voluntary relationship between two individuals, but these relationships are not found in a vacuum. Each person brings to the relationship a background of group affiliations and culturally defined outlooks. When these are shared between guru and disciple, there is likely to be continuity in the transmission with the disciple's inherited traditions of family, caste, sect, and so on. When these are not shared, there is likely to be some discontinuity, at least from the individual disciple's point of view. This generalization cannot be made in an unqualified way, since there are different levels of the social structure and of the culture that may or may not be shared. A guru with no family relation to the disciple may help bring him back to his family tradition, as Svāmī Śarvānanda seems to have done with Krishnasvāmī. A father, on the other hand, acting as a guru, may not succeed in rearing all his children to follow the family cult, as in the case of the retired actor. Whenever discontinuities in the transmission emerge, there is the possibility of innovation and new cult formation. And in this sense, the Rādhā-Krishna cult may be an innovation among Smārta Brahmans in South India—a possibility I shall discuss later.

The discontinuities and innovations need not create serious problems, since, in principle, every Hindu is free to choose a favored personal deity of his own. The freedom exists even for Advaitins, who do not find the quality-less monistic absolute as emotionally satisfying as a loving personal God with concrete attributes. The degree of deliberate choice exercised by an individual, however, will necessarily vary with his age and the accidents of his personal history. Children brought up in a family of Krishna worshipers are likely to imbibe the cult without being conscious that they have made a choice, unless their beliefs and practices are later challenged. Adults, on the other hand, may, for reasons not always clear to themselves, suddenly decide to worship a deity outside the usual choice of their family, caste, or region. One of the interesting features of the Rādhā-Krishna cult, perhaps characteristic of Hinduism, is the latitude that it allows for both kinds of choices—the innovative choice as well as the choice of affirmation. In the *bhajanas,* one frequently finds active participants whose personal deities are not only not Krishna but no aspect of Viṣṇu. The *bhajanas* are in this respect like the family shrines—capable of incorporating the diverse personal choices of their participants.

## *The Role of Smārta Brahmans*

The Rādhā-Krishna cult in Madras draws its leadership and massive support from Smārta Brahmans. We have estimated on the basis of the Mylapore figures that about 55 per cent of the contributors and participants in the *bhajanas* are Smārtas. The Smārta Brahmans' predominance among the leadership of the movement is even more striking. All three Tanjore gurus were Smārtas, as were the Madras pioneers, and most of the contemporary leaders.[18] The emergence of a Rādhā-Krishna cult among Smārta Brahmans is perplexing, in view of their reputation and status in South India. As followers of Śaṅkara and Advaitavedanta, Smārtas have traditionally accepted a monistic, monotheistic theology in which worship of personal deities is considered a sign of spiritual immaturity. Insofar as worship of a particular deity has been associated with Śaṅkara's name, it has been Śiva, and not Viṣṇu and his manifestations. In theory, Smārtas say they worship five (or six) deities impartially—Śiva, Viṣṇu, Devī, Gaṇeśa, Sūrya (and Subrahmaṇya). Smārtas also have a reputation for being orthodox in following the traditional (*smṛti*) rules of ritual observance and in cultivating Sanskrit learning in all its branches. Their approach to religion has been intellectual and scholastic, rather than the popular, emotional approach of Krishna *bhakti,* which some of them feel to be intended for Śūdras, women, poor people, and other groups excluded from the "high-church" approach. In Madras today, there are Smārtas who look upon the Rādhā-Krishna movement as "too emotional" and who may even refer to it as an "aberration," but there is no doubt that the movement is popular among a large segment of the Smārta Brahman group and draws its main support and leadership from them. In other parts of India the Rādhā-Krishna cult is supported mainly by Vaiṣṇavas and by non-Brahmans.

When I asked people in Madras why a Rādhā-Krishna cult had emerged among Smārta Brahmans, I received a variety of replies. Two of the most frequent were that Smārta Brahmans take the lead in organizing religious and cultural functions generally and that they worship the five deities. The former is a restatement of the fact needing explanation, and the latter states a permissive condition; it does not explain why they should cultivate a Vaiṣṇavite tradition. One Śrīvaiṣṇava Brahman, a leading Rādhā-Krishna devotee, suggested that Smārtas have taken the active lead in Rādhā-Krishna *bhajanas* because these are new to them, but an old tradition among Śrīvaiṣṇavas. The suggestion is an interesting one; it does not, however, take account of the fact that Vaiṣṇava *bhajanas,* in Madras at least, are part of the temple service; they are not held in private houses, nor are they generally multilingual and attended by diverse sects. They are confined to the singing of songs, some about Rādhā and Krishna, from the canon of Tamil Vaiṣṇavite saints.

The special role of Smārta Brahmans in the development of a Rādhā-Krishna cult is probably to be explained by a number of other considerations. One might argue that, because Smārtas have been so closely identified with orthodox ritual observances and with Sanskrit learning, they have felt the need to develop Krishna *bhakti* as an "easier path to salvation," since their middle-class and professional occupations, their Westernized education, and their increasing secularism have made the older and more difficult paths less accessible to them.* Advaitavedānta would not stand in their way if they wished to embrace Krishna worship, since for an Advaitin such worship may be as good a stepping stone to self-realization in the Absolute as any other mode of worship. And there is also in Advaita a kind of built-in dialectic to transcend sectarianism of any kind, which disposes Advaitins to favor inter-sect, if not antisect, movements. The head of the Śaṅkara *maṭha* at Kāñcī, who is one of the leading spiritual authorities for Advaitins in South India and who personally does not regard Krishna worship as a very orthodox form of Hinduism, nevertheless supports the *bhajanas* and urges joint public performances of Śaivite and Vaiṣṇavite prayers and songs. He has also lent his support to the organization of an association of the heads of *maṭhas* of all sects in the South to represent the interests of the *maṭhas* against legislative restriction.

No doubt some of these interfaith activities are a common defensive measure against the trend of increasingly secular legislation and, particularly in Tamilnāḍu, against the outspoken and sometimes violent anti-Brahman, anti-Hindu attacks sponsored by two regional political parties, the Dravidian Federation and the Dravidian Progressive Federation. The Smārta Brahmans, however, have been the first to see these trends as a

* Chapters 4 and 5 above give supporting contemporary evidence for such an explanation.

danger to Hinduism and to respond by joining and organizing movements that cross sect, and even caste, lines. Although the predominance of Smārta Brahmans in the Rādhā-Krishna cult associates that cult with one particular subcaste, the ideology and traditional theology of that subcaste predispose it to play an ecumenical and even cosmopolitan role in guiding the responses of contemporary Hinduism to the challenges of modernization and secularization, and to the divisiveness stemming from caste, sect, and regional differentiation.

This kind of role is not one that the Smārta Brahmans have assumed only in the last generation or so. In South India, the role is a historic one for them. When their leader and codifier, Śaṅkara, led a Hindu restoration against the Buddhists in the eighth and ninth centuries, he tried to build an all-India Hinduism that could rise above the doctrines and practices of any particular group or region. This founding pattern has been confirmed through the vicissitudes of later South Indian history. Although the Vijayanagar emperors, the Nāyakas of Tanjore, and the Marāṭhā rājās of Tanjore were by personal religious persuasion Vaiṣṇavites, they generally adopted religious policies that extended toleration (and sometimes temples and village grants) to Śaivites, Smārtas, Jains, Muslims, and Christians. Histories of these dynasties suggest that outstanding Smārtas and Advaitin scholars influenced these policies: Madhvācārya under the Vijayanagar, Appayya Dīkṣitar and Govinda Dīkṣitar under the Tanjore Nāyakas, and a large number of Advaita *ācāryas* under the Marāṭhā rājās of Tanjore.[19] One of the three Tanjore gurus who codified the Rādhā-Krishna *bhajanas,* Śrīdhara Veṅkaṭeśa, came from a village in Tanjore that had been given to forty-six pandits of his court by Śāhjī. The village became a seat for scholarly study of language, literature, philosophy, and medicine as well as religion.

Since the three dynasties that ruled over the Tamil country were all foreign to that region, they brought into the culture of the area languages and literature and religious, musical, and other forms that combined with the local forms to produce a cosmopolitan Tanjore culture, of which the multilingual Rādhā-Krishna *bhajanas* are one striking development. Smārta Brahmans, by virtue of their special traditions, were qualified to make a unique contribution to this culture. The uniqueness of the contribution consists not only in the many excellent literary, linguistic, philosophical, musical, and other works produced by Smārta Brahmans, but especially in the capacity to build ever new syntheses from the cultural currents flowing into the South. Some of these syntheses—the Rādhā-Krishna cult is undoubtedly one—have resulted in transformations of Smārta traditions, changing a preference for Śiva to devotion to Krishna, and perhaps, too, upgrading devotional Hinduism generally in relation to intellectual and ritualistic Hinduism.

The critical role of the Smārta Brahmans in the transmission of the Rādhā-Krishna cult has thus involved them both as a group and as individuals in the making of innovative choices that have changed their own traditions in some respects. That they are also involved in making choices reaffirming other aspects of their tradition makes it easier for them to accept the changes.

### Meaning and Function of the Rādhā-Krishna *Bhajanas*

The preceding discussion of the historical role of the Smārta Brahmans in the leadership of the Rādhā-Krishna cult suggests that the *bhajanas* may be performing three kinds of functions: (1) providing an easier path to salvation in an age when the paths of strict ritual observances, religious knowledge, and ascetic withdrawal have become difficult or inaccessible, (2) reducing the consciousness of caste, sect, and regional differences and the tensions generated by this consciousness, and (3) providing a philosophy of devotion for believers. I should now like to examine the evidence for these interpretations of the *bhajanas.*

The range of relevant evidence is very broad and the varieties of it rather complex: There is the observed behavior at the *bhajanas,* programed and unprogramed; the explanation of this behavior by participants; the speeches of leaders on the meaning and functions of *bhajanas;* observed behavior of participants outside the *bhajanas;* the life histories of participants; the *bhajana* songs; the history of the *bhajana* tradition and its relation to *bhakti* movements; the social organization and transmission of these movements; and the philosophy and theology of the *bhajanas* expounded by the texts and leaders recognized by the participants. In interpreting the function and meaning of the Rādhā-Krishna *bhajanas,* I shall try to take account of the full range of evidence.

From the point of view of the Smārta Brahmans, accentuation of differences between castes, sects, and linguistic regions is disruptive and generative of harmful tensions. Whatever reduces consciousness of these differences will therefore, in their opinion, have a socially intergrative effect. The Rādhā-Krishna *bhajanas* are viewed by some of their leaders as moderating the tension-producing differences. Many features of the *bhajanas* contribute to this function. Linguistic regionalism, for example, is bypassed by the use of songs in various languages composed by saints from different regions of India or sung in praise of such saints. On special occasions, *bhajana* groups from Mahārāṣṭra and other parts of India are invited to Madras to participate in the local *bhajana* programs. Caste differences are minimized by inviting non-Brahmans to *bhajanas,* by feeding the poor and even untouchables on the occasion of the marriage *bhajanas,* and by the salutations and prostrations of the devotees to one another irrespective of caste. Many participants say that "there is no caste in the world of devotion" and that they "forget their caste differences in the *bhajana.*" By holding the *bhajanas* in private homes or public halls rather than in temples, sectarian differences are also muted.

To those who know the history of the religious devotional (*bhakti*) movements of medieval India, the antiparochial, anticaste, and antisect features of the *bhajanas* will sound familiar. It would be an incomplete interpretation, however, to say that the Rādhā-Krishna *bhajanas* of Madras City are merely survivals of an old tradition. In contemporary Madras, specific trends are at work that give the *bhajana* movement a special significance. There is, for example, an intense pro-Tamil, pro-Dravidian agitation that is aggressively opposed to the use of Sanskrit and Telugu, two languages associated with Brahman cultural hegemony in Tamilnāḍu. The agitation is also directed against the Brahmans as an alien Aryan priesthood from the North, which was supposed to have foisted "superstitious" religious practices and beliefs on the South for its own private gain. In this particular context, the multilingual, multicaste, and multisect *bhajana* may be seen as a defensive effort to unify the very groups that the pro-Dravidian movement tends to divide: Tamil and non-Tamil; Brahman and non-Brahman; Śaivite, Vaiṣṇavite, and all "believers" in Hinduism. In this respect, the integrative functions of the *bhajanas* are related to developments in Madras City and the state that are only about fifty years old.

Consistent with the integrative function, but perhaps independent of it, the *bhajanas* may also be seen as providing forms of sociability and intimacy in an urban setting that transcend kin, caste, sect, and region. Although each local *bhajana* group usually begins with a family household, it quickly expands to include neighbors and friends from office and shop who are not kin and who may even come from a different caste, sect, or linguistic region. Newcomers to *bhajana* groups are usually brought by neighbors or by professional colleagues. The weekly *bhajana* remains essentially a neighborhood group; the monthly *bhajana* overflows neighborhood lines; and the annual *bhajana* festival draws crowds from all parts of the city. Thus, *bhajanas* in a large city may perform functions quite different from those they have performed in villages and small towns. For an urban population that is still village-conscious and many of whose members return to their native villages for family ceremonies about once a year, the pastoral themes and activities of the Rādhā-Krishna stories must add a village flavor to city life. This flavor is not, of course, otherwise missing from the city, for many city people keep cows and buffaloes, and there are streets of houses in parts of the city that might have been directly transplanted from nearby villages.

An American observer of the Rāḍhā-Krishna *bhajana* is apt to interpret the informal sociability and friendly atmosphere, the mixing of castes and sects, the mutual embracing and prostrations, as expressing a democratic spirit of equality. He may even find some *bhajana* participants, especially among the younger members, who will so interpret these features of the *bhajana* to foreigners. As he talks with more participants and learns more about the *bhajanas* and their history and philosophy, however, he will soon discover that to interpret the *bhajana* in terms of democratic ideology can be very misleading. One *bhajana* leader and respected devotee, for example, emphatically disclaims any political implications of the *bhajana*. He is opposed to the Congress government and particularly to its democratic egalitarian tendencies. The best form of government, in his opinion, is a benevolent monarchy based on an aristocracy of talent and wisdom, as were the monarchies of Aśoka and the British Rāj. Another leader of the same *bhajana* group is an active Congress worker, and he sees democratizing effects in the *bhajana*. These effects consist, for him, in the improvements of non-Brahman speech, attitudes, and behavior that come from association with Brahmans. The sociability of *bhajanas* may appear to be more "democratic" than meetings segregated by caste or sect;

yet a full analysis of this sociability points to sources that have little to do with democratic ideology and more to do with *noblesse oblige,* the need for friends in a big city, the need to find a substitute for strict ritual observances, the prestige of opening one's house for religious meetings, and so on. Similar observations apply to other apparently "democratic" features of the *bhajanas,* such as feeding the poor, mutual prostration, the use of songs from different regions, and so forth. When one looks at them closely, they turn out not to be very "democratic," or at least they are not so interpreted by the participants. The feeding of the devotees and of the poor is regarded by many participants as a ritual requirement of a *bhajana,* without which it would be incomplete and inefficacious. The mutual prostrations are commonly interpreted by participants as expresions of humility and of respect to the element of divinity present in other devotees. "They do not prostrate to one another but to the Lord Krishna who is between them."

The problem of conflicting interpretations of the *bhajanas*—which include conflicting opinions among participants, as well as differences of interpretation between participants and nonparticipants—can be resolved, I believe, by widening the range of evidence and the frame of interpretation. The problem will not be solved so long as we restrict ourselves to individual items of observed behavior at the *bhajanas* and to participants' explanations of these items. We must in addition view the *bhajanas* as cultural performances designed to bring religious merit to participants. From this point of view, the activities of the *bhajana* are rites that find their sanctions in scriptural texts and their interpretations in a theology and philosophy based on these texts. To interpret the meaning of the observed behavior at the *bhajanas* and to assess the opinions of participants about this behavior, it becomes necessary to relate behavior and opinion to rite and text and to the philosophy expressed there. Some of the philosophy is contained in the *bhajana* songs—those, for example, that tell the devotee not to be ashamed to sing the names of the Lord with other devotees as a means of acquiring merit. Such songs are taken as scriptural texts sanctioning *bhajana* recitation and singing. Most of the songs, however, are ritual texts, which happen also to express invocations, supplications, and many other forms of devotion to Krishna, Rāma, and other deities. The more comprehensive philosophy and theology of the Rādhā-Krishna *bhajana* is formulated in other scriptural texts, in commentaries on them, and in the writings and sayings of leading devotees. T. K. Venkateswaraṇ has made a preliminary study of the texts from the point of view of nondualist theology (Advaitavedānta) and Krishna devotion (*bhakti*).[20] It is clear from his study that such observed features of the *bhajana* as informal sociability, mutual prostration, singing, dancing, eating together, and the use of songs in different languages all have specific scriptural sources and sanctions and may be interpreted in terms of theological doctrines of "calling," "surrender," the presence of divinity in all things, and so on.

According to his account, the behavior of the devotees in embracing each other, taking the dust from one another's feet, and making mutual prostrations is sanctioned by references to instances of similar behavior in the *Bhāgavatapurāṇa* and in other Purāṇas cited in a treatise on *bhajanas* by the devotee Sadgurusvāmī. A stanza from the *Bhāgavata* is quoted in this treatise: "By ignoring those who belong to oneself, those that mock at oneself, by giving up the sense of bodily conceit and shame, one [the devotee] should offer prostrations [even] to the horse, the outcaste, the cow, and the donkey."

The theological implication here is that the devotee should recognize and see God in all things, although "the presence of God in men has a clearer [and] more significant dimension."

Following Sadgurusvāmī, Venkateswaran also points out that the salutations are a reversal of the Vedic observance, at least for Brahmans, in which salutations are offered only to an older person by a younger person with an appropriate formalized recitation of one's *pravara, gotra, sūtra,* and Veda.

This reversal in salutation has not led, however, to a reversal in other behavior. The new salutation has become formalized and restricted to the appropriate phase of a *bhajana* performance. One elderly and distinguished devotee explained that, although it would not be becoming for him to prostrate himself before a younger devotee, he does prostrate himself before the devotees as a group. On one occasion, he had met a *bhajana* group coming toward him and prostrated himself before it. The group turned out to include his son.

While the behavior at the *bhajana* tends to become formalized and ritualized, it is not without significance for behavior and social relations outside the *bhajana* context. A lucid and penetrating explanation of what this significance may be was given by one devotee:

> The relation between devotees as one of complete equality is only their *ideal.* They wish to make it a matter of fact and a reality. But, at the same time, it does not replace the traditional respect of sons for fathers, of young for old, of the less devout for the more devout, of the lower castes for the higher castes, and so forth. Devotees fall at each other's feet and take the dust of the feet of each other and place it on their heads, embrace each other, and do other such things. It needs *constant* practice of these things so that they may become perfect equals. In actual life, the equality has not yet been achieved or realized. It is only the *ideal,* and devotees wish to reach this ideal sooner or later. It has not yet come, as I have said before. Fathers do think that they are superior to their sons, the elders do think that they are superior to youngsters, the more devout do think that they are superior to the less devout, the high-caste devotee thinks that he is superior to the low-caste devotee, and so forth. Thus they *think* one way and *do* another way when they exhibit equality or express democratic sentiments. There is no correlation between their *mind* and *body.* They do not act alike. They think one thing and do another thing. When by constant practice, their minds imbibe equality as their bodies express it, the ideal is reached by the harmony between the mind and the body. The two then act alike, and there is correlation between them. Until then there is no talk of complete equality as the body expresses equality and the mind does not. What the body expresses is thus only a gesture of the ideal to be attained, and *constant* gesture of this kind

will bring about the ideal in its own good time. The body expressing equality and the mind expressing inequality produce insincerity in a person, a great sin in a devotee.

This explanation is particularly valuable for its suggestion that the *bhajana* is a kind of acting out in dramatic form and bodily gestures of an ideal, for the purpose of evoking in men's minds the sentiments and attitudes that may eventually bring their behavior closer to the ideal.

There are indeed *bhajana* participants who report that the *bhajana* evokes such sentiments in them. Some non-Brahman participants testified that at the moment of the *bhajana* they felt that "all are equal in the midst of God." They also added, a little sadly, that the feeling did not last. A few reported more continuity in their states of mind and seemed to have acquired reputations for being "true devotees throughout life." Such reputations do not require complete withdrawal from the world, for most devotees are householders who carry on their mundane responsibilities. Even the most withdrawn and mystical of the Krishna devotees carry on their daily tasks. One of them said he was aware of the power of *bhajanas* to reduce caste differences and bring about other social effects, just as he was aware of the power of a candle flame to burn one's finger, but he was "not enamored of this power." Yet the same devotee insisted that Rādhā-Krishna devotees were especially conscientious and efficient in their daily work, since they did not want to give critics any grounds for saying that *bhajanas* distracted people from work. There is also evidence of direct carryover of behavior and attitude from *bhajanas* in the reports of devotees who appeal to, and are helped by, other devotees in matters of jobs, loans, and other needs.

The salutations and prostrations at *bhajanas* are thus related to an ideal of equality but not in a direct and obvious way. The relationship has been discovered by tracing the links between the behavior and the scriptural texts whose sanctions convert the behavior into symbolic and ritual acts. The meaning of these acts in the ritual context is explained by the theological and philosophical doctrines associated with the particular cult. The meaning of the acts for the nonritual everyday context will be found through analysis of the testimony of observant and thoughtful participants who are also familiar with the theological meaning. This method of determining the "meaning" of *bhajanas* can be applied to other items of observed *bhajana* behavior. I propose now to apply it to determine the meaning of the behavior that is so central to the monthly type of *bhajana,* namely, the singing and dancing of the devotees about the lamp. This behavior is more complex than the salutations and prostrations, since it consists not of discrete single acts but of a connected sequence of acts that tell a story, the story of the milkmaids' (*gopīs'*) infatuation with Krishna, of Krishna's "sporting" with them in the woods, of his separation from them, and of their final reunion.* The story provides a kind of "script" and "choreography" for the singing, dancing, and dramatization of this type of *bhajana.* The general principle of interpretation, nevertheless, remains valid.

* See photographs following page 174.

Just as the Western observer is apt to interpret equalitarian features of a *bhajana* directly in terms of democratic ideology, so he tends to interpret the singing and dancing in terms of the emotional and orgiastic tendencies of Western religious cults. The devotional *bhakti* movements in Hinduism are in a sense more "emotional" than the paths of ritual and knowledge and occasionally lead to ecstatic behavior. But they are not governed by uncontrolled and irrational emotions. The path of devotion is also a discipline, a yoga, subject to well-understood rules and based on a "rational" philosophy. This philosophy assumes that the emotions expressive of certain human relations—for example, servant to master, child to parent, friend to friend, lover to beloved—are appropriate ways to express a devotee's attitude of devotion to a deity. A devotee is free to choose the kind of relationship he will assume toward a deity, being guided by the example of famous devotees who have gone before him. Once he has chosen a particular relationship, the devotee will discipline his emotions and actions to accord with the requirements of the relationship. He will act out the role as sincerely and as well as he can in the hope of evoking a reciprocal response from the deity.

An additional aspect of this philosophy prescribes the singing of divine names and devotional songs, the reciting of scriptures, and the joining with other devotees in song and dance as the best means of expressing devotion and gaining salvation.

Much of what happens at the Rādhā-Krishna *bhajana* can be explained by reference to this philosophy of devotion.

The story of Krishna and the *gopīs,* or at least major episodes from it, is well known to the participants from the *Bhāgavatapurāṇa* and other scriptural texts. Many of the songs they sing are based on these texts and provide the built-in scriptural sanction for the action at the *bhajanas.* Some of these songs, as well as the Purāṇic texts, also attribute a theological meaning to the story, that is, the *gopīs* represent the human soul in search of salvation; because their love for Krishna is so constant and intense, it is transformed into a spiritual and blissful devotion to a transcendent deity; the circular dance in which Krishna has multiplied himself to dance between every two *gopīs* symbolizes how devotees are related to one another through their relation to God, and so on.[21]

If some of the *bhajana* actions are a ritual dramatizing of episodes from the Krishna story that have a transcendental theological meaning, it remains to be explained why groups of male devotees in Madras City should choose this medium to express their devotion. The answer to this question requires testimony from individual devotees and information about their individual and family histories, as well as reference to the philosophy of devotion. Since the *gopīs* represent any human soul, any devotee is free to identify with them. In Vaiṣṇavite doctrine, at least, there is also the belief that all souls are female and that Viṣṇu is the only male. Then there is the psychological tendency of devotees to look for concrete and successful models of devotion to imitate. In Vaiṣṇavite theology, such models may even be necessary as intermediaries.[22]

Beyond these general considerations, the *gopīs'* love for Krishna occupies a unique position as a model of devotion because of its extraordinary intensity and constancy. Through this intensity and constancy, what begins as carnal love becomes transmuted into a "holy" and "spotless" love, because it is bestowed on a god. Indeed, according to the philosophy of devotion, any emotion—hate, anger, fear—if directed *constantly* toward a god will lead to salvation, although love is the most "fruitful" emotion. This would not be true if love or the other emotions were directed to mortals, because these relations are not permanent and because unpleasant emotions would provoke unpleasant reactions. But God, being eternal, is quite indifferent to the kind of emotion shown. The *gopīs'* love for Krishna is so intense, the most intense possible kind of love and devotion, because it is a kind of lawless love, the love of married women for their lovers. It is not subject to the discipline, respect, and obedience of wifely love. The conclusion of this line of reasoning is logical enough: If the devotees persist in their imitation of the *gopīs'* love for Krishna and that of his favorite, Rādhā, their own devotion too will become as intense and effective as that of the milkmaids, and they will be rewarded by the physical presence of Krishna and by the blessedness that the *gopīs* achieved. This is not an easy attainment, especially for male devotees, but it can, with constant practice and discipline, be achieved—at least so the devotees believe.

This explanation for identifying with the *gopīs* applies to devotees whose personal deity is already Krishna as well as to those who have chosen other deities. The following statement from a devotee already devoted to Krishna restates the general theory and makes the application to *bhajana* behavior:

> The love of a woman for her husband or for her lover is very much more intense than any other sort of love in the world, and I mentioned the *gopīs,* Rādhā, Rukmiṇī, Satyabhāmā, and so forth, as instances in point. Their love was indeed transcendent. Even when the husband or the lover is a man, the woman's love for him is of a very high order, and when the Lord Supreme is the husband or the lover of a woman, you can find no other love excelling or surpassing this love. The ladies mentioned above can therefore be said to be the most blessed in the world. If we concede this, we can ourselves aspire for this kind of supreme love for God. We can imagine ourselves to be these women or at any rate ordinary women, imagine that the Lord is our husband or lover and bestow the maximum love on Him. *Whatever we think intensely, we become that soon.* Mind makes the man. Think constantly that you are a sinner, and you are that. Think that you are virtuous, and you are virtuous. Think constantly that you are a woman and that God is your husband or lover, then you will be a woman and God will be your husband or lover. It is for this purpose that in *bhajanas* a lamp is lit up and placed in a central place and that spiritual aspirants go round and round it singing the Lord's glories. The Lord is invoked to be present in the lamp, and the spiritual aspirants imagine themselves to be *gopīs* playing with Śrī Krishna. You know the philosophy here that all men and women in the world are spiritually women, and the Lord alone is male—the Puruṣa. The love of the *gopīs,* Rādhā, Rukmiṇī and Satyabhāmā, explains the principle of the human soul being drawn to the Supreme Soul and getting merged in It. Likewise, Sītā represents the human soul, and Rāma the Supreme Soul; Pārvatī the human soul and Śiva the Supreme Soul; Vaḷḷi or Devasenā the human soul and Subrahmaṇya the Supreme Soul.

In the opinion of this devotee, an awareness of the theological meaning of the *gopī* story or an imitation of the *gopīs'* external behavior will not automatically lead to attainment of the blessed state. What are required are a love for Krishna as deep and constant as theirs, a renunciation as great as theirs, and, perhaps, Krishna's grace. *Bhajanas* may stimulate a sense of these qualities, but they do not assure them; they dramatize the ideal to be attained in gesture and behavior. According to this devotee, because the *gopīs'* love for Krishna is a love among equals, it is

> bound to be more intense and more sweeping than love between a superior and an inferior. Fear, respect, a sense of inequality, an absence of liberty . . . are all distracting factors in the intensity of love.
>
> The *gopīs* had their own husbands, but they chose to transfer their love to Śrī Krishna, who they thought was their lover. They were captivated and charmed by His entrancing and fascinating beauty of form and by His bewitching personality. Their love was infinitely more intense than the love of Rukmiṇī, Satyabhāmā, and the other wives of Śrī Krishna for Him. The love of the *gopīs* for Śrī Krishna was wild and dashing like the storm or the gale, and it swept everything before it. It was like the "wild west wind" described by poets, and it knew no check or restraint. The *gopīs* forgot themselves absolutely. They forgot their own bodies, their dress, their homes, their people (husbands, sons and daughters, parents-in-law, and so forth), and forgot the time when they met Śrī Krishna. They were not aware how the time was gliding and were quite unconscious of their surroundings and of what happened to them. They had given up everything for Him. In this respect, they were like the holy *sannyāsins,* or ascetics; like Buddha, for example, who had given up his kingdom, wife, son, father, mother, friends, and so forth, for the sake of Truth. They were like the great, ancient Ṛṣis of India who had sacrificed all their earthly pleasures and possessions for seeing God and remaining with Him for all time. The love of the *gopīs* for Śrī Krishna was carnal. It was lust. But Śrī Krishna transmuted it completely into holy and spotless love for God, for He was God and they were mortals, and His grace enabled them to rise to immortality in the least possible time or interval. The *gopīs* thus cast off their mortal nature and became Divine in nature by mixing with the Divine Śrī Krishna.

For men to identify themselves with the *gopīs* and their "wild love" is "rather difficult." But

> if a man can do it, by dint of constant practice of his thoughts, infinite gain is the result, in his spiritual aspiration and practice. Persistence is the most vital thing needed—constancy of emotion or attitude toward God. If it is present, the quality and content of the emotional feeling do not matter if you want slow realization of God and do matter if you want quick realization, easy, pleasant, and so forth.

Although the quality of emotions expressed by a devotee may not matter, the object does matter: "A male devotee should on no account pose as a lover or husband of a female manifestation of the Lord, for example, Durgā or Lakṣmī or Sarasvatī or Rādhā. Such love is completely ruled out. It is prohibited and is considered the worst sin in life." A male devotee imagining the Goddess to be his Consort and loving and worshiping Her as such is certainly ruled out. He may worship Her and love Her in any other relationship and praise Her. This is not ruled out. A devotee must never imagine a Goddess to be his Consort, spouse, wife, or lady-love. He may imagine Her to be anything else for him. . . . So, it follows that the praise of Pārvatī, Durgā, Lakṣmī, Rādhā, and so forth is *not at all* ruled out in a *bhajana*. . . . A goddess can be imagined to be his mother, sister, child, or friend but should never be imagined to be his wife or consort. . . . A devotee may also imagine himself to be a servant of a goddess.

Female devotees find it easier to identify with the *gopīs,* although in contemporary Madras women are not generally active in Rādhā-Krishna *bhajanas.* There are, however, famous women devotees who imagined themselves lovers of Krishna. Two are Mīrābāī, from the province of Rājasthān, and Āṇḍāḷ, from Tamiḻnāḍu. Each literally believed she was Rādhā and the consort of Krishna and wrote many moving hymns expressing her devotion. Some of them are sung in the Rādhā-Krishna *bhajanas.* There is a Tamil collection of Āṇḍāḷ's hymns known as *Tiruppāvai.*

There were also a man and wife, Harnāth and Kusuma Kumārī, both of whom imagined themselves to be Rādhā and worshiped Krishna. They are now worshiped as saints.

Famous male saints who imagined themselves female lovers of Krishna are also numerous. In addition to Caitanya and Rāmakrishna, there is the great Vaiṣṇava teacher in the South, Vedānta Deśika, who described his experiences in a drama, *Acyutaśataka.* In the South, there is a festival every year for this saint. On the fifth day of the festival, his image is dressed as a woman (*mohinī*) and taken in procession facing the idol of Krishna, and both are worshiped that day by devotees who are husband and wife. In the Tamil Śaivite tradition, the saint Māṇikkavācagar imagined himself and other devotees as women, with Śiva as their lover. His devotional songs are still well known—in a collection called *Tiruvembāvai.*

The most detailed description we have of the use of *gopī* love as a means of reaching Krishna is that given in the biography of the modern Bengali saint Śrī Rāmakrishna, compiled by one of his disciples.[23] Even as a child, Rāmakrishna liked to act the parts of women characters—such as Rādhā and her companions. Putting on a woman's dress and ornaments, he would take on the gestures, voice, and movements of a woman. "The village women would say that nobody could recognize him then. . . . With his love of fun, he would often pass in that disguise in front of men, with a pitcher under his arm, to fetch water from the Haldārpukur; and no one would ever suspect that he was not a woman!" [24]

In his adolescence, "knowing that the *gopīs* of Vraja had Krishna, the embodiment of pure Existence-Knowledge-Bliss, as their spiritual husband through love, because they were born as women, he used to think that he too would have been blessed to love and have Krishna as husband, had he been born in a female form." On these occasions, he imagined he had become a child-widow with long hair, living simply on coarse food, spinning yarn, singing songs about Krishna, and weeping for him to come.[25]

As an adult, Rāmakrishna undertook a systematic discipline of devotion as a woman to Krishna. In Bengali Vaiṣṇavism, this devotion is classified as "the Sweet Mood" (*madhurabhāva*), one of the several devotional moods that a devotee may assume toward a deity. For about six months, Rāmakrishna wore women's clothes and ornaments (sari, gauze scarf, bodice, artificial hair) and mimicked the movements, speech, smile, glance, and gestures of women. Some of the women he knew "were so much charmed by his womanly deportment and by his genuine care and affection for them that they regarded him as one of them and could not at all maintain their bearing of bashfulness, hesitation, etc., in his presence." He prayed, longed, and wept for Krishna, and under the sense of separation from Krishna "drops of blood oozed out then . . . from every pore of his body. . . . All the joints of the body seemed slackened or almost dislocated, the senses completely desisted from functioning, and the body lay motionless and unconscious sometimes, like that of a dead man—all because of the extreme anguish of the heart." Believing that he could not attain the vision of Krishna without Rādhā's grace, Rāmakrishna identified with her. "He was very soon blessed with the vision of the holy form of Rādhā, devoid of the slightest tinge of lust. He now saw that this form also disappeared into his own body like the forms of other deities when he had had their visions." Through his constant feeling of identification with Rādhā, he believed his love for Krishna became as profound as hers. "He became so much absorbed in the constant thought of himself as a woman that he could not look upon himself as one of the other sex even in a dream." In this way, he attained a vision of Krishna, and the form of the vision united with his own person. "We have heard from the Master himself that at that time he lost himself completely in the thought of Krishna and sometimes regarded himself as Krishna and all beings, from Brahmā down to a blade of grass, as forms of Krishna. When we were frequenting Dakṣiṇeśvara and were in his company, one day he plucked a flower of grass, came to us with his face beaming with delight, and said, 'The complexion of Śrī Krishna I used to see then (at the time of practicing the *madhurabhāva*) was like this.' "[26]

None of the devotees participating in the Madras Rādhā-Krishna *bhajanas* has reported attaining similar visions of Rādhā or of Krishna as a result of *bhajana* participation, although many have been influenced by Rāmakrishna and his movement. One devotee, however, reports that as a youth he did see Krishna once, but has since lost sight of him. He hopes to recover this vision as the *gopīs* did after Krishna disappeared from their midst. In the meantime, his participation in *bhajanas* gives him a sense of "infinite joy" and a "seeming" presence of Krishna. What he aims at is an ascetic's life, but he will probably remain a householder and be content with its small gains.

Commenting on his desire to see Krishna in the concrete form in which he stood before the *gopīs,* as described in the *Bhāgavatapurāṇa,* this devotee says he does not see Krishna now, although he has "a very vivid sense of His presence." He "longs to see Him again as the *gopīs* did." And he compares his loss with that of the *gopīs:*

> Even the *gopīs* lost sight of Him for a *short* while, but He appeared before them again very soon and they felt blessed. It occurred on a bright new moon night in autumn in the most pleasant groves of Vṛndāvana on the banks of the holy Yamunā, near the town of Mathurā and the village of Gokula, at some distance from Delhi.

There is no doubt that, at least for this devotee, the enactment of the *gopī* episode in the *bhajana* has a deep personal meaning:

> It is a long, *long* while, a very long while indeed since I lost sight of Him in 1918. It is now 1960. He has not yet appeared before me again, because I am not able to think of Him and of His sweet attributes constantly, even without a moment's break. The *gopīs* actually shed tears of grief at His separation and cried out aloud with extreme love for Him. This pleased Him to give them again His company. I am not able to do so. They had renounced everything in the world for Him. I am not able to do so. One can see Him if one loves Him in the extreme, i.e., if one loves Him only and none other and nothing else. I am not able to do so. The renunciation of the *gopīs* is greater than that of any other person in the past, present, and future. It is an *ideal* to be reached by men and women.
>
> I long to reach this ideal, and I long to have their deep love for Śrī Krishna. I should love Him as *well* as they did. I am not able to do so. Until I do so actually, therefore, I cannot *see* Him, and the moment I do so I can *see* Him.

During the *bhajanas,* this devotee says, his mind is "deeply engrossed with the attributes of Krishna" and that he "seems to see Him . . . and to enjoy His company." But when the *bhajana* is over, his mind is centered on other things "like money straits at home, duties to the family members, things that I should do for them and which I have not yet done, and so on, which may cast a gloom over my mind. . . . I feel infinite joy while attending a *bhajana,* and there is this joy in me all the time that I sense continuously a great happiness." This kind of vision, he admits, is not the same as that of the *gopīs* or Rāmakrishna. Their vision lasts forever, "without a second's break," for the devotee sees the deity "as vividly and as actually or truly as I see you or as you see me or as you and I see others in the world today." However, Krishna appears to him in dreams sometimes, "but it is not often enough." He also believes that Krishna sometimes shows His favor to one unasked, and that He may do so in his case, "but one cannot count on it for a certainty in one's life." Meanwhile, he feels that he has to make himself fit to receive His grace. "This is my life at present. There is the desire in me now for God realization. It should grow from strength to strength. My love for Him must increase to a very, very great extent for me to attain the goal in life, and I feel His hand in it."

The ideal toward which he aims is the life of an ascetic and not of a householder, he believes, but he wishes to practice as much of that life as he can as a householder.

> Whatever is gained is a gain, however small it may be. I am now sixty-six years old, and it is time for me to achieve the maximum spiritual attainment. One must accomplish something at least in one's life, and death may overtake one at any moment. I think of Dr. Johnson's bewailing in the church on his birthday. He said, "One more year of my life is gone today, O Lord! and I have not done anything worth my while in learning to love You." I feel like him and wish to do something worthwhile spiritually, at least as much as is possible.

It is clear from this Krishna devotee's life history that the story of Krishna and the *gopīs* is taken as a parable of the individual's spiritual odyssey. What happens to the *gopīs* happens to any individual in search of salvation. The *gopīs'* love explains "the principle of the human soul being drawn to the Supreme soul." So deeply ingrained is this identification with the *gopīs* in the minds of some devotees that when I asked this devotee in a private conversation how the devotees' love for Krishna leads to mutual love among the participants in the *bhajana,* he replied by spontaneously describing three different incidents from the *Bhāgavata-purāṇa* in which the *gopīs* discover each other's love for Krishna, come to share that love with one another, and so develop a mutual love. He did not think it necessary to mention explicitly that something similar takes place as contemporary devotees imitate the *gopīs.* But the identification with the *gopīs* and Krishna worship is not fanatical or exclusive. In the *bhajanas,* participants sing the praises of, and identify with, other devotees of Krishna as well as with those of Rāma, Śiva, Subrahmaṇya, Gaṇeśa, and other deities. Outside the *bhajanas,* too, many devotees are explicit about this flexibility and, if they are Advaitins, relegate Krishna devotion to the sphere of individual choice and personal preference, a choice, however, that may be the ladder to the impersonal absolute without qualities. As this same devotee explained:

> The one God appears in many forms or manifestations—as Viṣṇu or Nārāyaṇa, Śiva, Rāma, Krishna, Vināyaka, Subrahmaṇya, Durgā and so forth—to please the different kinds of devotees in the world, of different temperaments and inclinations and of different outfits of intellect and heart. It is like the same person appearing in cinemas or picture shows as different persons at one and the same time. It is thus silly or stupid for Vaiṣṇavas to hate Śiva, for Śaivites to hate Viṣṇu, and so forth. To me, the Lord is Śrī Krishna, to you He is God the Father, to the Muslim He is Allah, to one He is Rāma, to another Śiva, and so on. There should therefore be the most perfect catholicity in the world in the matter of religion. If it exists, equality will establish itself among different individuals and different groups of men and women, and legislation for social evils, which is no remedy at all, is quite unnecessary. So, *bhakti* brings all the hearts in the world together in their common vibrations of yearning for God and is attained in the easiest way possible. If sugar and sugar candy are given, it is possible that one person prefers to have the candy and another the sugar. A person may have greater relish for a particular victual than for another. He may not hate the latter. Thus, preferences will always exist in the world, and it is good that they exist.

The interpretation of the Rādhā-Krishna *bhajanas* as ritual dramatizations of the ideals of social equality and of supreme devotion to God seems to me to accord with observed behavior, with the statements of participants, and with the religious texts. This interpretation does not imply that all participants share these ideals to the same degree or with the same self-consciousness. It implies only that the *bhajanas* are dramatic cultural performances in which the ideals are symbolically acted out. In this respect, the *bhajanas* belong with a large class of other cultural performances that have become media for the expression of devotion (*bhakti*)—devotional plays and films, dramatic recitations of stories from the Epics and Purāṇas, dances based on epic and purāṇic themes, devotional songs, and the like. Many different kinds of people participate in these performances for many different kinds of individual reasons. The meaning and function of the performances will of course vary with different individuals and their psychological needs. We have tried to pick out several clusterings of meanings and functions for the Rādhā-Krishna *bhajanas* that are linked to the changing role and status of the Smārta Brahmans in Madras, to contemporary conditions and ideologies, and to the perennial Indian quest for individual salvation.

The clusterings of meanings and functions have different psychological and historical sources and motives and, perhaps, different destinies. But in the Rādhā-Krishna *bhajana* movement of Madras City, there seems to be a temporary convergence and interpenetration of the different meanings and functions. Confronted by the increasingly secular and impersonal social life of a large urban center, orthodox Hindus find it increasingly difficult to cultivate their highly intellectualized, scholastic traditions or to follow the numerous rituals prescribed for their caste, sect, or family. At the same time, the Dravidian movement for linguistic regionalism, with its championing of Tamil against Sanskrit, Telugu, Hindi, and other Indian languages; of non-Brahmans against Brahmans; and of "rationalism" against "superstition" drives the orthodox Hindu, and particularly the Smārta Brahman, to a defense of his religion, his culture, and his caste. Under these circumstances, many find appealing such a devotional cult as the Rādhā-Krishna *bhajana,* which permits them to pursue an easier path to individual salvation while simultaneously countering the political trends of the times. For the love that leads Krishna devotees to yearn for Krishna also brings them into intimate social contact with their urban neighbors of different caste, sect, or language, and to a sharing as devotees in the mutual affection that inspires their faith. Whether the Rādhā-Krishna *bhajanas* will develop into a casteless, sectless, ecumenical form of Hinduism is difficult to say. Already tendencies have appeared toward new forms of ritualization, intellectualization, and sectarianism that make such an outcome unlikely. There is no doubt in the minds of devotees, however, that the Rādhā-Krishna *bhajanas* of Madras City have, like Krishna's descent to rectify specific evils on earth, become the timely instrument of an integrative and unifying religious movement.

## Notes

1. Raghavan, "Vedas and Bhakti" (see note 4, Chapter 5, above), and *idem,* "Methods of Popular Religious Instruction," (see note 2, Chapter 4, above). See also V. Rag-

havan's work on the poet saints, "The Great Integrators," *Akashvani* (*Indian Listener*) 31, No. 39 (September 25, 1966): 1–2 and 10.

2. T. K. Venkateswaran, "Rādhā-Krishna *Bhajanas* of South India," in Singer, ed., *Krishna,* pp. 139–72.

3. See Chapter 5, above.

4. *Ibid.* Recordings of Gandhi *Harikathās* include Śrī K. P. Yadugiri Kumari, "Gandhi Mahatmyam Bala Bharathi," and *idem,* "His Master's Voice" (28010 to 28013); see also Damle, "Harikathā" (note 36, Chapter 2, above). The use of traditional themes in songs, plays, recitations, and other media in community development programs is described in Mayer, Marriott, and Park, eds., *Pilot Project: India.* James Peacock, *Rites of Modernization* (Chicago: University of Chicago Press, 1968), describes a somewhat analogous use of traditional cultural media in East Java.

5. See Singer, ed., *Krishna;* Turner, *Ritual Process*; and Dimock, *Place of Hidden Moon.*

6. For further discussion of this problem, see Chapter 2 above and references in note 2, Introduction to Part One.

7. For discussion of this newer functionalism, see the following entries in the *International Encyclopedia of the Social Sciences* (New York: The Free Press, Macmillan, 1968): Clifford Geertz, "Religion," pp. 520–26; Edmund Leach, "Ritual," pp. 576–82; and Victor Turner, "Myth and Symbol," pp. 398–406.

8. Originally published in Singer, "Great Tradition in Madras," *TI,* pp. 141–82 (note 2, Chapter 2, above).

9. The present account is based on observations and interviews in and around Madras City in 1954–55 and 1960–61, as well as on continuing correspondence and conversations with friends from Madras.

10. These stanzas are translated and discussed in Venkateswaran, "Rādhā-Krishna *Bhajanas*" (note 2, *supra*). Translations of other stanzas and songs that follow, unless otherwise identified, are by T. K. Venkateswaran.

11. A *bhajana* book edited by Gopālakrishna Bhāgavatar is highly popular. Its program is widely followed.

12. *Supreme Court Journal* 16 (Madras, 1954): 335–61.

13. This biographical material has been made available to me through the kindness of S. V. Aiyer's son.

14. Biographical material made available through the kindness of T. S. Vasudevan.

15. Kōthamarāma Aiyer edited the following volumes: *Bhajana-Paddhati;* Śrī Jayadeva's *Gītagovinda;* Śrī Nārāyaṇa Tīrtha's *Kṛṣṇalīlātaraṅgiṇī; Hindustān Kīrtana Mālā,* comprising the songs of Mīrābāi, Kabīr, Tulsī Dās, and others; *Bhajana-Utsava paddhati* (Rādhā, Rukmiṇī, and Sītā *Kalyāṇams*); and *Divyanāma Saṃkīrtana* (singing and dancing devotees around a lamp). He also published a Tamil translation of Śrī Gñānadeva's Marathi commentary on the *Bhagavadgītā* (known popularly as *Gñāneśwari*).

16. This biographical information came to me through the kindness of T. S. Krishnaswami.

17. These biographical data are based on personal interviews and correspondence.

18. The earlier historical role of Smārtas in Krishna worship is discussed by Venkateswaran in "Rādhā-Krishna *Bhajanas.*"

19. T. Venkata Ramanayya, *Studies in the History of the Third Dynasty of Vijayanagara* (Madras: University of Madras, 1935); K. R. Subramanian, *The Maratha Rajas of Tanjore* (Madras: K. R. Subramanian, 1928); and V. Vriddhagirisan, *The Nayaks of Tanjore* (Annamalainagar: Annamalai University, 1942).

20. Venkateswaran, "Rādhā-Krishna *Bhajanas,*" pp. 141–44 and 161–65.

21. The philosophy and theology of Krishna devotion are discussed in Singer, ed., *Krishna,* by Thomas J. Hopkins (pp. 3–22), Edward C. Dimock, Jr. (pp. 41–63), and Venkateswaran. See also Archer, *Loves of Krishna,* and Mukerjee, *Lord of Autumn Moons.*

22. Cf. Singer, ed., *Krishna,* p. 51 (Dimock).

23. Saradananda, *Sri Rama Krishna.*

24. *Ibid.,* p. 63.

25. *Ibid.,* p. 239.

26. *Ibid.,* pp. 234–35 and 237–39.

# PART FOUR / *MODERNIZATION AND TRADITIONALIZATION*

# *Introduction*

The first two Madras studies found the Great Tradition of Sanskritic Hinduism very much alive in an urban setting. As I pursued a contextual study of that tradition's specialists, centers, rites, and cultural performances, its social organization and cultural topography began to emerge. The approach also identified some processes and trends of change in the Great Tradition under urban influence—among others, technical modernization and cultural drift, deritualization, increase in devotional *bhakti,* and classic revivals in music and dance. The studies, however, raised but did not answer an important question—namely, whether continuing modernization in the form of urbanism, industry, science, and modern education would totally transform the structure and organization of Sanskritic Hinduism. Two diametrically opposed answers had previously been given to this question. One asserted that continuing modernization would inevitably bring about a total structural transformation of Sanskritic Hinduism and would replace the joint family with the nuclear family, caste with class, and religious beliefs and rituals with secular and scientific ideologies. The second answer, on the contrary, asserted that such a transformation of tradition could not occur in India because the traditional beliefs and institutions were incompatible with modernity and would necessarily obstruct the further progress of modernization. Max Weber's name is closely associated with the second position, but it was also widely known in the classical nineteenth-century dichotomy between "traditional" and "progressive" societies. A third, compromise position attempted to reconcile the first and second positions by asserting that "traditional" societies such as India would not modernize until they had eliminated their traditional institutions, beliefs, and values. Gunnar Myrdal's *Asian Drama* argues essentially this third position.

My third Madras study presents evidence for a fourth position—one that recognizes the continuing coexistence and mutual adaptations of India's cultural traditions—Great and Little—and modernity. This position asserts none of the possibilities envisaged in the first three positions—the inevitable and linear transformation of a traditional culture and society into a modern one, the unchanging and obstructive persistence of a traditional society and culture, or the hypothetical modernization of a traditional society if it were to abandon its traditional institutions.

If one accepts the dichotomy between traditional and modern societies, the fourth position of a coexistence and mutual adaptation between tradition and modernity sounds paradoxical and anomalous. To make such a position plausible and persuasive, it is necessary to frame a conceptual model of Indian civilization that combines the long-run telescopic perspective of culture history with the short-run microscopic perspective of social anthropology. Chapter 7, "The Social Organization of Indian Civilization," attempts to formulate such a theoretical framework for a social anthropology of Indian civilization by combining some aspects of Alfred Kroeber's thinking with aspects of Robert Redfield's. The chapter also demonstrates the plausibility of the model for India through a review of recent research.

The Kroeber-Redfield model of Indian civilization allows us to envision the possibility that Indians may be modernizing without necessarily abandoning their traditional institutions, beliefs, and values. The study of the Madras industrial leaders in Chapter 8 describes how such a possibility has in fact been realized by a small group of families in the short-run perspective of the present three or four generations. Part Five, entitled "Beyond Tradition and Modernity," extrapolates from the results of the short-run studies to the cultural-historical perspective of Indian civilization as it modernizes by traditionalizing innovations.

A summary of Chapter 7, "The Social Organization of Indian Civilization," was presented at the New Delhi meeting of the International Congress of Orientalists in January, 1964. The chapter reviews the progress of recent anthropological thought and research toward a social anthropology of Indian civilization from the point of view of the problem of specifying the unity and continuity of Indian civilization. W. Norman Brown had recently discussed this problem from an Indological point of view in his presidential address to the Association of Asian Studies. His rejection of the cataloguing of discrete cultural traits and his suggestion that cultural unity and continuity be looked for in organizing principles and in the field of values and attitudes was a congenial starting point. A similar approach was being pursued by M. N. Srinivas, Louis Dumont, David Mandelbaum, McKim Marriott, Bernard S. Cohn, Surajit Sinha, and other anthropologists.[1] The time seemed ripe for a systematic review of these trends for an international and Indian audience of scholars. Using Redfield's latest thoughts on the structure and organization of civilizations as a model, the chapter compares this model with that of A. L. Kroeber and then discusses the results of mainly anthropological research in the light of these models. The comparison of Redfield and Kroeber had been suggested to me by an exchange between them in 1958.[2]

For my work on India, the 1964 paper played an important role. In trying to put together an explicit and systematic statement of the Redfield approach to the study of civilization and in assessing the approach in terms of recent research, I believe I came to have a better understanding of the relationship between the cultural and the social in the "structure" of Indian civilization, as well as of the processes that modify the structure. Social relations and social networks are important not only as aspects of a social structure but equally as media for the transmission of cultural traditions. The networks of social relations, in other words, are cultural as well as societal.[3]

The social organization of Indian civilization, however, includes more than a network of social relations communicating cultural traditions. It also includes processes that change both the social networks and the cultural traditions. In "The Cultural Role of Cities," Redfield and I had suggested that the processes of cultural and social change might be usefully related to the primary and secondary patterns of urbanization, and I tried to follow up these suggestions in my Madras studies.

The "Social Organization" chapter raises the question whether, in view of the existence in India of variant models for "Sanskritic Hinduism," as well as of non- or anti-Sanskritic models, a more general conception of the Indian Great Tradition should be defined, perhaps in terms of S. K. Chatterjee's "Indianism." [4] The paper does not answer this question except by implication in the conclusion. There it is suggested that the Indian concept of cultural identity is a changing one and is highly selective. Elements from different Great Traditions, Little Traditions, and modern cultures are variously included. These elements, as expressed in myth and legend, history and ceremony, not only represent a sense of a shared past and a common culture but also suggest that Indian civilization is becoming more "modern" without becoming less "Indian." [5]

After the Orientalist Congress in New Delhi, I went to Madras to continue my research there. By this time, I was convinced that the dichotomy between "traditional" and "modern," whether in the popular form of Western "materialism" versus Eastern "spirituality," or in the more sophisticated social science form of "traditional" versus "modern" societies, was not a useful theoretical guide for understanding India. There were just too many cases of coexistence and interaction between the "traditional" and the "modern." The more important and interesting task was to find out more about the processes and mechanisms of cultural change involved in these coexistences and interactions and about how Indians were becoming more "modern" without becoming less Indian.

For my third visit to Madras, I had prepared two tentative research plans, both designed to explore the ways in which cultural traditions are modernized. The first was designed to study how successful industrialists related their economic activities to their religious beliefs and practices, family life, and caste affiliations. The topic had been suggested by my 1961 meeting with Anantharamakrishna, Madras's leading industrialist, and I was counting on his help. The second would study how modern cultural media, especially the films, were becoming vehicles for the cultivation of new regional and national cultural identities.

When I got to Madras, I learned of Anantharamakrishna's recent death. With the help of R. K. Venkataraman, at that time Madras State Minister of Industries, and Mr. Chitty-Baboo of the commercial office in the local American consulate, I was soon able to compile a list of leading industrialists in Madras City and collect current information about their companies and recent industrial development in Madras State. I deliberately set out to find the most successful industrialists in the city, irrespective of caste or religion. Most of the rest of my stay in Madras was spent in interviewing and learning about industrial leaders.

The first report of the industrialist study was presented to a meeting of the American Society for the Study of Religion in April, 1964, and was expanded during the winter of 1965 at the Center for Advanced Study in the Behavioral Sciences at Stanford. A portion of it was presented at a Wenner-Gren Foundation conference on "Structure and Change in Indian Society" organized by Bernard Cohn and William Rowe at the University of Chicago in June, 1965. This paper was published in revised form in the conference volume as "The Indian Joint Family in Modern Industry." It emphasizes the structural compatibility of traditional joint family organization with industrial entrepreneurship and documents some of the specific ways in which Madras industrial leaders have adapted the traditional joint family in an urban and industrial environment. The paper proposes a modification of the usual anthropological use of "the genealogical method" to make that method suitable for a study of industrialization and cultural change. In earlier studies, I had already found the compilation of individual and family life histories a simple and fruitful field method for the study of ritual specialists and devotees. The extension of the method to industrialists and their families was an obvious next step, one that was encouraged by my colleagues Fred Eggan and David Schneider.[6]

The distinctive approach of the industrialist study, Chapter 8 here, to an understanding of modernization is the analysis of family "adaptive strategies." The analysis shows, I believe, the ways in which the industrial leaders innovate while maintaining certain aspects of their cultural traditions and social institutions. Max Weber and others who have emphasized the ritualism and traditionalism of the caste system have also occasionally noted its adaptability and flexibility. They have not recognized, however, that the system persists and changes precisely through the specific adaptations of the old and the new that individuals and groups are willing and able to make. The particular kinds of adaptations, such as compartmentalization, ritual neutralization of the work sphere, vicarious ritualization, and the others used by the industrialists may not be the only kinds involved. And the nature and interrelations of these adaptive strategies need a good deal more study and analysis. No doubt remains in my mind, however, that these are some of the important mechanisms and processes underlying the modernization of Indian cultural traditions and social institutions. Adaptive strategies have probably been operative in Indian civilization for a very long time, but the arena, material, and results of their operation at any given time may be novel.

In the case of the Madras industrialists, we do not yet see the total transformation of traditional social structures and values predicted by some social science theories of modernization or demanded by some ideologists. The joint family has not been replaced by the nuclear family, caste by class, ritual and religious belief by science and secular ideologies. Instead, the adaptations are "compromise formations," which with varying degrees of stability combine novel and traditional elements. The industrialists' adaptations are like the interactions between religion and economic activity that Weber found among the early Puritan industrial capitalists, and they bring about in the Indian case, as in the Western one, not so much a revolutionary transformation of society and culture as the formation of an industrial cultural tradition alongside the existing agricultural and commercial traditions. The European "compromise formation" differs from the Indian as seventeenth-century European religion, culture, social structure, and political and economic organization differ from those of twentieth-century India, but the adaptive processes in the two cases are similar. The Madras industrialists believe, as did their Puritan counterparts, that they are "fated to succeed" in industry according to their own doctrines of predestination. In twentieth-century Madras, however, the Indian version of the "Protestant Ethic," that is, the Hindu ethic, is more likely to produce a spirit of socialism than a spirit of capitalism, as the theodicy of the caste system is transformed into a theodicy of the industrial system. Not only are the industrial leaders prepared to continue as managers of a nationalized industry, although most would rather not see the private sector nationalized, but a leading spiritual authority of South India also refers to Hinduism as a "kind of socialism."

## Notes

1. W. Norman Brown, "The Content of Cultural Continuity in India," *JAS* 20, No. 4 (August, 1961): 427–34; Brown, *Man in Universe;* M. N. Srinivas, "The Nature of the Problem of Indian Unity," in Srinivas, *Caste in Modern India;* Louis Dumont, "For a Sociology of India," in Dumont and Pocock, eds., *Contributions to Indian Sociology* 1, No. 1 (April, 1957): 7–22; Mandelbaum, "Study of Complex Civilizations" (see note 6, Introduction to Part One, above); Marriott, "Little Communities" (see note 33, Chapter 2, above); Bernard S. Cohn and McKim Marriott, "Networks and Centers in the Integration of Indian Civilization," *Journal of Social Research* 1, No. 1 (Ranchi, September, 1958): 1–9; Cohn, *India;* and Sinha, "Tribal Cultures," in Singer, ed., *TI,* pp. 298–312 (see note 29, Chapter 2, above).

2. See Kroeber, *Anthropologist Looks at History,* Foreword.

3. Earlier formulations of the relationship between social networks and cultural transmissions were made by McKim Marriott, Robert Redfield, Bernard S. Cohn, Surajit Sinha, and myself. A first attempt to synthesize the formulations was made in the preface to Singer, ed., *TI.*

4. M. N. Srinivas accepts most of these revisions and indeed has contributed to some of them. See Srinivas, *Social Change in Modern India.*

5. The changing character of India's cultural self-image is also discussed in the preface to Singer, ed., *TI,* and in Chapter 1, above. Marriott discusses changes in cultural self-image as an aspect of national policy in McKim Marriott, "Cultural Policy in the New States," in Geertz, ed., *Old Societies and New States.* See also David Mandelbaum, "The World and View of the Kota," in Marriott, ed., *VI;* Orans, *The Santal;* and Bernard S. Cohn, "The Pasts of an Indian Village," *Comparative Studies in Society and History* (*CSSH*) 3, No. 3 (April, 1961): 241–49.

6. The contribution of W. H. R. Rivers's "genealogical method" to the development of social anthropology is discussed by David Schneider and Raymond Firth in their introduction to the new edition of Rivers's *Kinship and Social Organizations* (London: Athalone Press, 1968). See also two articles in the *International Encyclopedia of the Social Sciences* (see note 7, Chapter 6, above): F. Eggan's "Kinship Systems" (4: 390–99), and M. Singer's "Culture" (3: 527–41). Raymond Firth, "Family and Kinship in Industrial Society," *Sociological Review* Monograph No. 8 (1964), and Milton Singer, "The Indian Joint Family in Modern Industry," in Singer and Cohn, eds., *Structure and Change,* discuss applications to industrial society.

# 7 / *The Social Organization of Indian Civilization*

## The Unity and Continuity of Indian Civilization as Postulate and Problem

The concept of the unity and continuity of Indian civilization is both a commonplace and a problem. Its validity is usually regarded as self-evident. Yet, when scholars begin to inquire into the exact nature of this unity and continuity and into the ways in which they are attained, they quickly encounter many unanswered questions. In his paper "The Content of Cultural Continuity in India," the American Indologist W. Norman Brown concludes that, while there has been a highly developed civilization on the Indian subcontinent since the third millennium B.C., with many elements of cultural continuity, it remains a problem to say what has given Indian civilization its distinctive character and vitality.[1] He says he does not believe the question will be answered by making a catalogue of the hundreds of cultural traits (such as the use of the swastika, the sacredness of the pipal tree and of the cow, the joint family and the caste system, asceticism, the doctrines of *karman* and rebirth and of *ahiṃsā*) that persist across large spans of Indian civilization. Even if the historical and ethnic origins of these traits could be traced, this knowledge would not be sufficient, he contends, to discover the vitalizing principle of Indian civilization. That principle, he suggests, lies in the field of values and attitudes and not in the material production of arts, literature, and the sciences or in particular skills, customs, institutions, or forms of thought. He analyzes, as one example of such a basic value, the notion of duty and the stress on correct action.

Professor Brown's approach to the problem of cultural continuity in Indian civilization seems to me most fruitful. Unfortunately, not being a Sanskritist, I cannot personally emulate it as much as I should like to. It is an approach, however, that appeals to the social and cultural anthropologist, because it poses the problem of cultural continuity in terms of the discovery of a distinctive organizing principle (or principles), rather than in terms of a catalogue of recurring cultural traits, and it directs us to look for these principles in the field of values and attitudes.

In another paper, "The Nature of the Problem of Indian Unity," the

Indian anthropologist M. N. Srinivas sees Indian unity threatened by the tensions created by differences in locality and region, language, caste, and religion.[2] These differences are not necessarily incompatible with loyalty to the Indian nation, if there is a hierarchy of loyalties and if there is no overriding drive to homogenize the differences into a monolithic uniformity of language and culture. "Tensions and conflicts at a particular level maintain the identity and separateness of groups of the same order, but these groups can and do unite at a higher level." The fact that a person stands for his village in relation to other villages, or for his caste against other castes, does not prevent him from being an Indian in relation to non-Indians. Moreover, each of the subnational groupings performs some integrating function, since it may cut across other differences; for example, regional loyalties may cut across differences in caste, religion, village, and town. Given a balanced regional development, continued economic growth, and a tolerance for linguistic and cultural differences, Professor Srinivas sees India emerging as a strong and united country.

It is not my concern here to argue whether Srinivas's optimism or his implied commitment to a secular and democratic state is justified by current trends. What is more to the point of the present discussion is that he conceives the problem of Indian unity not as a problem of attaining an all-India cultural uniformity and homogeneity, but rather as a problem in managing the complexities of a multilingual, multicaste, multireligious, and multilayered civilization. That the recent political unification of the country by a national movement dedicated to democratic political institutions and processes may indeed offer the best prospect of converting the "primordial ties" of traditional group associations into the "civil ties" of citizenship is an opinion I personally happen to share with Professor Srinivas. His conception of India as a unity in diversity need not stand or fall, however, with any particular political form of organization, since it is possible to apply this concept of unity in Indian civilization to the pre-British and premodern periods.

## How to Think About a Civilization: The Kroeber-Redfield Models

If the continuity of Indian civilization is to be looked for in some distinctive organizing values and its unity in an organized coherence of social and cultural differences, do we have any general forms of thought that will help us to sketch in imagination the profile and organization of a civilization so persistent and so unified? I believe such thought forms can be found in ethnology, culture history, and social anthropology. Although the main field of development for these disciplines has been the simpler primitive societies and cultures, the more complex cultures and civilizations have become subjects of study in recent years. The transfer of methods and concepts from the field of the "primitive" to that of civilization is not without its difficulties, and many changes in the disciplines are required to bring it off. Nevertheless, it seems to me that the progress so far made by anthropological studies in India, Southeast Asia, China, Japan, the Middle East, Europe, and North and South America justifies us in speaking of an "anthropology of civilizations." I should like in particular to draw upon the ideas of two of the foremost contributors to this recent development—A. L. Kroeber from the side of culture history and ethnology, and Robert Redfield from the side of social anthropology—for the kind of imaginative construct of Indian civilization we are seeking. I shall then examine some recent anthropological studies of Indian civilization to see how far they support such a construct. I shall also indicate possibilities of cooperation between the social-anthropological students of contemporary Indian civilizations and the historical and Indological students of Indian civilization.

For Kroeber, every human culture is a composite historical growth out of elements most of which have been borrowed from other cultures. This observation holds for those grand complex cultures called "civilizations" as well as for the simpler primitive cultures. In spite of the foreign origins of the bulk of their cultural inventories, however, most cultures succeed in reworking and organizing these elements into a distinctive over-all pattern or style. Such total culture patterns or styles are not arbitrary and sudden impositions; rather, they represent gradual drifts toward consistency and coherence of the subpatterns and substyles in the different spheres of culture—literature, music, painting, sculpture, religion, philosophy, science, social organization, and so forth. The total pattern or style of a culture thus represents an assemblage or organization of lesser styles and patterns.

> A civilization, as the assemblage of the styles followed by the inhabitants of a certain area through a certain duration of time, could then consist of a style or manner of government, added to a style of law, and another of social relations; further, a characteristic manner of production and economy, of religious belief and organization; plus what we ordinarily call its styles of literature, art, music, and building.[3]

Once crystallized, a total pattern or style gives a culture its distinctive character, and its changes a particular shape and direction. In this way, it represents an element of continuity and constancy in a culture. In the case of self-conscious cultures, total culture pattern and style may receive articulation in the form of a self-image and world view formulated by the more articulate members of the culture.

But total patterns and styles may themselves undergo change even in the simplest and most stable of cultures (although the absence of documentary historical records makes this difficult to demonstrate). In the complex civilizations, changes in total culture patterns and styles are the rule, and these changes can be used to trace the profile for the rise and decline of a civilization. In his work *The Configurations of Culture Growth,* Kroeber has collected data showing that the greatest intellectual and aesthetic achievements of the major civilizations tend to cluster together in limited periods of time. In the case of Indian civilization, he finds two such periods of cultural florescence, the first around 500 B.C. and the second between A.D. 400 and 600. The Indus phase he sets aside as insufficiently documented.

Kroeber calls these peaks of culture growth "culminations" or "climaxes" and interprets them as the realization of the potentialities implicit in a particular *total* pattern or style. He also finds that the growth peaks tend to coincide with periods of successful organization of ideas, standards, and substyles. As a culture adds new elements, it also tends to become more highly organized, and this in turn increases its capacity to assimilate still more new elements. Successful incorporation of new elements can thus lead to greater productiveness. This kind of cultural creativity and assimilation of new elements Kroeber finds running ahead of cultural organization before a period of culmination is reached, but he finds it lagging behind after culmination, when organization leads to repetition, rigidity, and sterility. The civilization may then decline altogether or may, after a period of dormancy, enter upon a fresh period of cultural creativity by "reconstituting" its basic patterns and styles.

Kroeber believes there is evidence for such reconstitutions in the case of China in the period between A.D. 200 and 600 and, in the case of the West, in the periods between 500 and 900 and between 1300 and 1550. The present strains and unsettlement in the West probably reflect the throes of a second stage of reconstitution of Western civilization, analogous to that of 1300–1550, with population, wealth, curiosity, knowledge, enterprise, and invention still in an expanding phase.

In one of his very last essays, "Periodization," Kroeber refers to growth tendencies, at least in the fields of art and science, which show an acceleration and internationalization of stylistic change. Because of rapid means of communication, modern man is no longer under the dominance of one style at a time but has within reach "an international pool of styles." A gifted artist or scientist may, under these conditions, originate a number of different styles in a single lifetime. Kroeber cites Picasso as an example of this possibility, which he regards as "an indubitably new phenomenon and perhaps a precursor of more to come." This phenomenon has also been noted in the recent growth of science, but in this field the acceleration and spread of different styles of scientific thought and research is kept from turning into fad and fashion by the general cumulative and irreversible direction of growth.[4]

Kroeber's observations may be extended to changes in *total* cultural styles and patterns where the "new kind of phenomenon" also seems to be appearing. In the past, the interflow between cultures and civilizations was generally a flow and fusion of culture elements or element complexes, not of total ways of life. To be sure, total style patterns or particular cultures did change, but they did so very slowly and under conditions of "protective isolation" from other cultures, not often as a result of direct borrowing. Now, with the increasing intensity of culture contacts, there is an acceleration not only in the interflow of culture elements or even of styles in specific arts or sciences, but of total life-styles as well. The "international pool of styles" is now beginning to wash away the regional differentials of the world's cultures, although the pool may still contain a rich enough variety of styles to make possible differentiation on some basis other than the regional.

Redfield began thinking about civilizations from the perspective of a study of small communities as they functioned in the present. In contrast to Kroeber's cultural historical approach, which is telescopic, diachronic, and cultural, Redfield's starting point was microscopic, synchronic, and sociocultural. In his later work, particularly after 1951, when he enlisted Sinologists, Islamists, Indologists, historians, and philosophers to cooperate with anthropologists in a project for the comparison and characterization of civilizations, Redfield began to develop ideas for a social anthropological study of civilizations that is macroscopic and historical. These ideas, however, grew naturally out of his first major study, *The Folk Culture of Yucatan.*[5]

In the Yucatan study, Redfield and his co-workers compared four different communities (a tribal village, a peasant village, a town, and a city) in order to analyze and explain the cultural contrast between the Spanish and modern "urban civilization" of the northwest area of the peninsula and the more indigenous and "primitive" southeast. The general conclusion of this study was that the relative order of the four different communities on the map of Yucatan, from tribal village to city, corresponds to an order of decreasing isolation and homogeneity and of increasing secularization, individualism, and cultural disorganization. Redfield called this order a "folk-urban continuum," with a folk type of society and culture at one end and an "urban civilization" at the other. He also suggested the following general hypotheses: (1) that the primitive and peasant societies (as isolated, homogeneous local communities) tend to have the general character of a "folk" type of society; (2) that as they come into contact with urbanized society they change in the direction of an "urban" type; and (3) that the different changes are interdependent, as changes in some of the characteristics of a society tend to bring about, or at least "go with," other changes.

The "folk-urban continuum" is a one-dimensional, linear continuum connecting different points on a map. The four communities selected for study are four separate "points," treated as if they all exist at the same time without essential interrelation; "civilization," meaning chiefly Spanish and modern Western, is associated with one of the "points," the capital city of Merida. The Mayan civilization, having been "decapitated" by the Spanish conquest, does not enter the picture. Redfield was quite aware that the model had historical implications, chiefly along the lines of the age-area principle. He wrote, for example, that it could be used to reconstruct "a sort of generalized hypothetical account of the history of the culture" of Yucatan as a whole. "In a similar way, it might be validly asserted that a comparative description of communities encountered as one goes from Paris southward through Marseilles, Algiers, the Sahara, and then the Sudan [now Mali] would provide the vague outlines of the culture history of Western Europe." But he believed that this would be "a crude way to derive even the most tentative historical conclusions." While he used the available history of Yucatan, the study of the whole "follows a comparison of present conditions in one community with present conditions in the others." The historical dimension is left to historians and archeologists.[6]

In his later thinking, when he had become interested in the study of historic civilizations, it occurred to Redfield to adapt the "folk-urban continuum" to the study of the "human career" and to the development of particular civilizations. He first began to do this in his *The Primitive World and Its Transformations*[7] and was actively preoccupied with the task at the time of his death in 1958. While he regarded his thinking along these lines as very tentative and exploratory, there is no question that the extension of the "folk-urban continuum" provides a most fruitful form of thought for research on civilizations.

By thinking of early civilizations as historical developments from the small, isolated precivilized "folk" societies and cultures, Redfield added *time* as a second dimension to the "folk-urban continuum." He added more than this, for civilization is reached not just with the appearance of a single urban center but with a transformation of the folk societies (by the food-producing and urban revolutions) into a variety of new societal and cultural types interrelated in a variety of ways. Among these new types Redfield noted especially the "peasant," for whom living off the land is a way of life but who is at the same time dependent on towns and urban centers for many essential goods and services. In these urban centers appear new specialists of all sorts, including reflective intellectuals and reformers, with new world views and ways of life.

Given historical depth, the "folk-urban continuum" is no longer a line on a map but a great volume, perhaps a sphere, in which any point may be connected to other points by networks of lines. A civilization is now to be represented by such a great sphere in its totality, and not just by one point on a line. For Redfield, a civilization had both a "societal structure" and a "cultural structure." The "societal structure" consists of the total network of social relations that connect the communities of different kinds to one another over long periods of time. This structure is formed by networks of marriage and kin, trade and work, religious pilgrimage, and political administration and organization, which join together different villages with one another and with urban centers. It is a structure of networks and centers of many different kinds, in which communities, little and great, are the unit "points" and the social relations between them the connecting lines.

The "cultural structure" of a civilization is the structure of its ideas and the products of ideas, that is, of its cultural traditions. This structure, too, is compound and complex, as is the societal structure, for there are in every civilization the "high" cultural traditions of the reflective few (the Great Tradition) and the "low" folk traditions of the unreflective many (the Little Tradition). These different levels or dimensions of a civilization's cultural structure interact constantly with each other. The rates and results of the interaction depend on the kinds of social organization that exist in a civilization for the transmission of the different levels of tradition. In this respect, the cultural structure depends on the societal structure of the civilization. For the Great Tradition tends to be cultivated and transmitted by intellectual specialists ("literati"), teaching in schools and temples located in special kinds of centers; the Little Tradition, on the other hand, tends to develop and to be transmitted among the unlettered without benefit of specialized teachers and institutions. Between the learned specialists of the Great Tradition and the unlearned masses, however, there generally exist in most civilizations many kinds of intermediary specialists and institutions, which act as channels of transmission between the "higher" and "lower" levels of tradition. In fact, the entire "societal structure" of social networks of a civilization may function as transmissive channels for the communication of the different levels of tradition among the different communities connected by the networks. Redfield's notion of "a social organization of tradition" invites us to study the societal structure of a civilization not only for its own sake but also as an organized means for communicating the different levels and components of a civilization's traditions from one generation to the next and from one community to another.

The precise rates and results of interaction between Great and Little Traditions will of course vary from civilization to civilization, depending on the kind of societal structure and the cultural content of the cultural structure. It will also depend on whether the civilization in question is in a "primary" phase of development or in a "secondary" phase. In the "primary" phase, the Great Tradition has developed indigenously from precivilized local cultures and, although carried to a reflective level and systematized, remains essentially homogeneous with the Little Tradition. In this phase, Great and Little Traditions are dimensions of each other, and there tends to be a consensus about the order of "highness" and "lowness" among the different communities in the civilization. In its "secondary" phase, a civilization tries to incorporate cultural elements from other cultures and civilizations. This process will tend to weaken consensus about the order of levels in tradition and to weaken the cultural integration between city and country.

In our joint paper, "The Cultural Role of Cities," Redfield and I distinguished the primary and secondary phases of a civilization as "orthogenetic" and "heterogenetic" types of cultural change.[8] We also tried to relate the two types of change to the cultural roles of different kinds of cities, specialists, and institutions, that is, to the cultural roles of different kinds of societal structures. Although our analysis was illustrated with many references to particular civilizations, including India, it was intended as a mental construct, not as a history of one or many civilizations. Such a construct cannot be used to classify civilizations into "orthogenetic" and "heterogenetic" types, for every known civilization is a mixture of indigenous and nonindigenous elements. In the study of any particular civilization from this point of view, the main problem is not to disentangle the indigenous from the nonindigenous elements but rather to identify the net results of the operation of both "orthogenetic" and "heterogenetic" change and to describe the processes and organized institutional arrangements that bring these results about. It may well be that a civilization can absorb many foreign elements over a long period of time without losing its essential character. Most major civilizations seem to have had this capacity in some phases of their careers. This capacity depends not only on the societal and cultural structure of a civilization but also on the character and rate of encounters with other cultures. The two peaks of achievement in Indic high culture that Kroeber has identified were undoubtedly influenced in some degree by foreign stimuli. Yet the continuity of form and content was so great that these developments now appear as different phases in the development of a single Great Tradition. Whether Indian civilization's encounter with Islam or with European civilization has resulted in a similar net balance of "orthogenetic" over "heterogenetic" change is a more controversial question. The encounters in these cases were far more massive, prolonged, and coercive, and the results are not yet stabilized.

I should now like to consider recent anthropological research on Indian civilization in the light of the Redfield and Kroeber models. Their models were, of course, developed in relation to ongoing research, including that in India, not in a vacuum. We should also note the differences between the two models, as well as the similarities, when we try to apply them jointly to India. It is obvious, I think, that Redfield's later concept of "civilization" is broader than the earlier, not only in going beyond the notion of Western urban civilization, but also in envisaging a civilization as a complex assemblage of communities and cultures of different levels and kinds, coexisting in mutual dependencies, of different kinds and degree, over vast stretches of time and space. This concept begins to approach Kroeber's notion of a civilization as an assemblage of culture patterns and styles, but it also differs from it in several important respects. Kroeber systematically abstracts the cultural aspects of a civilization from its social aspects. He is certainly aware of the social aspects and occasionally takes them into direct account. But he sees the task of culture history as essentially a history of culture, with social structure and social organization subordinated.

Redfield, on the other hand, tries to maintain parity between culture and society. A civilization has both a social structure and a cultural structure. Redfield would, I feel sure, have accepted Kroeber's analysis of the cultural structure into component patterns, styles, and growth profiles. But he wanted also to associate each cultural structure with an organized structure of communities and to trace how each community, and groups within it, may develop subassemblages of life-styles. These "subcultures" are for Redfield not only substyles of different spheres of culture—law, religion, literature, art, music, and so forth—as they are for Kroeber; they are also the organized ways of life of a series of connected concrete communities.

## From Village to Civilization

When social anthropologists began to do field studies in India after it had achieved independence, they generally selected a village community as the unit of field observation. Some of the reasons for the selection were practical: Most Indians lived or had lived in villages and regarded them as the basic units of social life; also, the villages were becoming the concern of uplift movements and of community development programs. There was, however, another reason: The village seemed to represent a small, relatively isolated and self-contained community, in which the social anthropologist might study how the different parts of village social structure were related to one another and to village culture. The Indian village seemed to fit the social anthropologists' image of a "primitive isolate," which had been made the hallmark of social anthropology—as distinct from the fields of ethnology and ethnography—by Malinowski, Radcliffe-Brown, and their students.[9]

As they learned more about India, however, some social anthropologists recognized that their choice of the village community as a unit of field study reflected more the prevailing preconceptions of their discipline and of general opinion than it did the realities of Indian social life and culture. In 1953–54, Robert Redfield, McKim Marriott, and I organized a seminar on Indian village studies at the University of Chicago, to which we invited eight outstanding social anthropologists to discuss their respective field studies in eight different regions of India, in the light of two questions: (1) To what extent is the Indian village an isolated and self-sufficient "little community"? (2) What can be learned from village studies about Indian civilization as a whole? The social anthropologists unanimously found that their villages no longer fitted the image of a "primitive isolate," and some were skeptical about the isolation and self-sufficiency of the Indian village in the past. They reported, on the contrary, that each village was linked to other villages in its region and to towns and cities by complex networks of social relations based on caste, kinship, and marriage, trade and occupation, religious pilgrimage, and admistrative and political organization. In some respects and under certain conditions, the village was an organized unity with which a villager identified, but the numerous "extensions" of a village embedded it inextricably in a wider society and culture.[10]

About the same time as the Chicago seminar, five of the social anthropologists, together with eight others, were contributing brief progress reports of their field studies to the *Economic Weekly*. With the exception of one isolated village in Kulu studied by Colin Rosser, none of the villages reported upon in the *Economic Weekly* series suited the classical "isolate" image. M. N. Srinivas, who contributed to both series, concluded in his introduction to the volume of the *Economic Weekly* reports that "the villager's social field is . . . much wider than his village. Kin, economic, religious and other social ties enlarge the field to include a circle of neighboring villages. . . . The completely self-sufficient village republic is a myth; it is always part of a wider entity." [11]

If the discovery that the village is an integral part of Indian society and culture has made the social anthropologists' image of the "primitive isolate" obsolete in Indian anthropology, it has also created new opportunities and new problems for the anthropological study of Indian civilization. The small community of the village with its extensions now offers the scholar an opportunity to study many features of Indian civilization in microcosm—to learn how, e.g., parliamentary institutions operate at the village level. Many social anthropologists have responded to these opportunities by making specific studies of the networks of marriage, caste, trade, politics, and religion that link particular villages to the wider world of Indian civilization. Their researches are gradually disclosing in what ways the societal structure of India varies in nucleated and dispersed villages, in different regions, and particularly as between the loosely meshed networks of the North and the closely meshed networks of the South. Underlying this variety, there also seem to be many interregional networks and similarities lending considerable plausibility to the hypothesis that India is characterized by a distinctive societal structure of networks and centers, a structure that has enabled it to integrate communities of many different degrees of complexity and types of culture.

Once we postulate an intricate structure of networks and centers as comprehending the societal structure of Indian civilization, we are free to select a great variety of social units for a field study. In addition to the village, we may choose as units castes, tribes, sects, *sādhus,* temples and *maṭhas,* sacred cities, specialists, and markets and towns, as well as regional segments of particular kinds of networks. Each of these represents a special kind of microcosm of the macrocosm that is Indian civilization and will therefore contribute to our knowledge of the total societal structure. The choice of a unit should not, however, be too much influenced by apparently "natural" territorial divisions, for, as L. Dumont has emphasized, it is the structure of social relations associated with a territory that makes the territory culturally significant and not conversely.[12] In his study of the social organization and religion among the Puṟamalai Kaḷḷar of South India, Dumont found that the smallest independent social unit among these Kaḷḷar was not the village but the province (*nāḍu* in Tamil), which comprises a collection of patrilineal, patrilocal lineages with a common religious cult. In this case the chief of the province is also the chief of the lower lineage chiefs as well as of the lineage cults.[13]

The significance of the networks and centers of Indian civilization is not exhausted when their structure of social relations has been traced and described. Equally significant is the function of networks and center as media of cultural communication and cultural exchange between village and village, village and urban center, region and region, region and center, caste and tribe, educated and uneducated. The networks that extend the villager's social relations beyond the village also extend his cultural horizons. Oscar Lewis, noting the widespread intervillage networks of intermarriage and caste in North India, contrasts this "rural cosmopolitanism" with the more formal networks of trade, administration, and pilgrimage that characterize relations among the more "inward-looking" Mexican villages.[14] It is not only the cultural consciousness of the villager that is affected by networks and centers; everyone's is. The societal structure circulates culture (material, intellectual, and spiritual) through the sphere of Indian civilization, and it needs to be studied in this role as organizer and transmitter of cultural traditions. Only with the help of such studies shall we be able to understand the gradual and emerging synthesis of different language groups and cultures that seems so characteristic of Indian civilization.

A study of the social organization of Indian civilization is not likely to result in the demonstration of the existence of a single homogeneous culture or of a single set of values and beliefs. But it does seem likely to demonstrate how certain commonalities of the culture spread, and why the spread may have been wayward and uneven in some places.

Since this is a new field of study for social anthropologists, there are not yet many new researches to report. A pioneer study is M. N. Srinivas's book *Religion and Society Among the Coorgs,* in which he analyzes the manner in which the domestic and local cults of the Coorgs are linked to regional and all-India cults.[15] McKim Marriott, in "Little Communities in an Indigenous Civilization," has also shown that the festivals and pantheon of an Uttar Pradesh village are related by processes of "universalization" and "parochialization" to the wider cultural traditions of "Sanskritic Hinduism." [16] In 1958, I edited a symposium on *Traditional India: Structure and Change* for the *Journal of American Folklore,* including papers by eleven social anthropologists, as well as several Sanskritists and cultural historians, on the social organization of the transmission of cultural traditions in Indian civilization. This volume also includes a report of my own study of "cultural performances" in Madras City as channels for the transmission of both folk and classic culture, both traditional and modern values.[17]

There is also some interesting material on the social organization of cultural traditions in Louis Dumont's study of the Kaḷḷars and in L. P. Vidyarthi's study of Gayā as a sacred center and of the Gayāwāls as sacred specialists.[18] G. S. Ghurye's book *Indian Sādhus* also belongs in this field.[19] Beyond this, there are a number of journal articles and undoubtedly some new monographs in preparation.

The amount of work already published does enable the social anthropologist to say something about how the transmission of cultural traditions has been socially organized in India and by what processes different levels of tradition have been brought into contact and a position of mutual influence in villages and in urban centers. I shall begin with the process of spread that Srinivas calls "Sanskritization."

## Sanskritization and Cultural Mobility

The most fruitful and influential anthropological study of the interrelations between little and great communities and between Little and Great Traditions in Indian civilization is that of M. N. Srinivas, *Religion and Society Among the Coorgs of South India.* The study is notable not only as a monograph on Coorg society and religion but even more for its analysis of "Sanskritization" as the process whereby the Coorgs, and many other groups, have been integrated into Indian society and culture. Srinivas's use of this concept has stimulated much discussion and research. As a result, the concept has undergone some revision and generalization, in the course of which some scholars have questioned the appropriateness of the term "Sanskritization" for the various processes now connoted by it. I shall retain the term in Srinivas's original usage and indicate in what ways later discussion and research call for the recognition of different processes and perhaps new terms.

As used in the Coorg study, "Sanskritization" refers essentially to a specific kind of cultural mobility—a mobility that brings groups outside of Hinduism into the fold and raises the cultural status of groups already in it. This cultural mobility takes place within the caste system. Non-Hindu groups are Hinduized by becoming castes, and lower castes rise to the cultural status of higher castes as they adopt vegetarianism, teetotal rules, and the deities, rites, and myths of "Sanskritic Hinduism" as defined in Sanskrit literature and philosophy and as practiced by Brahmans. Many groups have thus Hinduized themselves in a generation or two, Srinivas believes, by taking over the customs, rites, and beliefs of the Brahman and other higher castes. He expresses the belief, moreover, that this process has been going on for more than 2,500 years and has been responsible for the spread of Sanskritic ideals and beliefs throughout the subcontinent and to the remotest hill tribes.

"Sanskritic Hinduism" is, in Srinivas's conception, a model style of life, embodying a complex of practices and values associated with Brahmans and with the Sanskrit scriptures—a model style that has spread throughout India and even abroad through the process of "Sanskritization." It includes vegetarianism and teetotalism, wearing of the sacred thread, performance of life-cycle rites by Brahman priests, with the use of Vedic *mantras* and vegetarian offerings, prohibition of widow remarriage, acceptance of the *varṇāśrama* system, a pantheistic bias in theology, and belief in the doctrines of *karmaṇ, dharma,* rebirth, and release. This lifestyle thus would seem to provide such a standard and measure for the unity and continuity of Indian civilization as we are seeking. It specifies a stable complex of values and attitudes that may contain Professor Brown's vitalizing principle of Indian civilization. It approximates, as well, the great traditional dimension of Indian civilization. And since "Sanskritization" is a two-way process in which elements of local culture are absorbed into "Sanskritic Hinduism," we have here a mode of interaction between Little and Great Traditions.

Further research by Srinivas and other anthropologists has resulted in some revisions of his original formulations. The revisions have not in the main invalidated the existence and importance of "Sanskritization" but have rather made more precise the conditions and scope of its operation. I shall indicate how they have led to a more general theory of cultural mobility.

Although a particular group may profess to adopt the values and lifestyle of "Sanskritic Hinduism," they may fall far short of it in their daily practice. The eating of meat and the drinking of alcoholic beverages, for example, have been frequently observed among such groups. Some of them acknowledge the discrepancy and simply take the position that "Sanskritic Hinduism" is an ideal way of life to which they aspire. They may not succeed in realizing it in full detail; they are content to achieve some of its diacritical marks: the wearing of a sacred thread, using one of the *varṇa* labels, employing a Brahman *purohita,* and the like. Other groups, however, will not admit that their behavior is discrepant; they insist that they are indeed comforming to a model of "Sanskritic Hinduism" that sanctions meat-eating, drinking, aggressive behavior, gambling, and so forth.

This anomalous situation may be clarified by distinguishing local versions of "Sanskritic Hinduism" from all-India versions. The local version may use the four *varṇa* labels—Brahman, Kṣatriya, Vaiśya, and Śūdra—but the defining content of these labels varies with locality and needs to be empirically determined for any particular locality. It has also been discovered that the relative prestige and rank of the different *varṇas* tend to vary with locality, time, and group. In many areas, for example, the kingly or martial life-style has a rank equal with, or sometimes higher than, that of the Brahman. Groups in these areas who wish to improve their status do so by adopting some of the stigmata of the Rājpūt life-style, i.e., by "Rājpūtizing" their way of life.[20] Even the life-style of the merchant and peasant have been taken as models in localities where these groups are dominant.

In view of these findings, we must say that "Sanskritic Hinduism" does not set up one single life-style—that of the Brahman—as an ideal model but allows for a number of different model life-styles, each with a distinctive complex of values, and that the precise content and the relative rank of these models vary with time and locality. The Indologist will probably not find this conclusion very surprising; it seems to agree with the way in which the *varṇāśrama* doctrine is interpreted in the sacred texts. Yet it remains to be seen whether the results of textual studies will coincide with those of the contextual studies of the anthropologist. One textual scholar, J. F. Staal, criticizes M. N. Srinivas and other anthropologists for underestimating the geographical and historical variability of the Great Tradition of "Sanskritic Hinduism." [21] So far as the past is concerned, this is a research problem for historians and Indologists, not for social anthropologists. V. Raghavan's preliminary survey of the variety and integration of Indian civilization indicates the kind of studies that need to be done to determine the formation of "Sanskritic Hinduism" as a Great Tradition and its later transformation by contact with regional and local tradiions.[22] In his paper "On the Archaism of the *Bhāgavatapurāṇa*," J. A. B. van Buitenen has, with considerable success, applied and extended the concept of "Sanskritization" to the authors of the *Bhāgavata* who were probably trying to transcend the *varṇa* scheme through a *bhakti* movement.[23]

## Attributes Versus Interactions in Caste Mobility

In the meantime, the social anthropologist who studies the very recent past needs to learn a great deal more about how the local versions of the Great Tradition are related to local behavior and to all-India models and behavior. McKim Marriott has brought some new light to this problem by distinguishing between attributional and interactional criteria for the ranking of castes in a locality.[24] He maintains that the relative ranking of different castes in a locality depends not on the attributes of their way of life, actual or professed, but on the kinds of interactions they have with other castes, particularly in the taking and giving of food and water and in their participation in ritual services. In his view, a caste may Sanskritize its way of life without rise in status, if it does not change its interactions with other castes. On the other hand, a caste may raise its status without changing its attributes in dress, diet, pantheon, rites, and beliefs, if it changes its interaction with other castes.

Marriott's interactional analysis offers a promising objective technique for determining caste ranking, which, in preliminary studies, coincides with the subjective collective opinions of the villagers. Studying collective opinions, he and four other anthropologists have compared caste ranking in villages of West Bengal, Bihar, Mahārāṣṭra, and Uttar Pradesh.[25] Out of 176 castes in these villages occurring in regional lists of 36 each, only nine types of castes were common to the four regions: Brahman, Rājpūt, Merchant, Barber, Potter, Weaver, Washerman, Oilman, and Leatherworker. The nine castes form a similar hierarchy of just five ranks in the different regions, with Leatherworker at the bottom; Weaver, Washerman, and Oilman always above Leatherworker; Barber and Potter always above them; Rājpūt and Merchants always above Barber and Potter; and Brahman and Rājpūt always ranked at the top. Within each of the five ranks, the ranks of particular castes vary by region and locality. The technique of studying local opinion can thus use the data of local studies to build regional and interregional comparisons and can eventually lead to an objective all-India rank hierarchy.

It remains to be discovered whether this five-rank hierarchy of castes is the same in other regions and does represent an all-India hierarchy. It is already evident that this kind of analysis has important implications for any definition of "Sanskritic Hinduism" as an all-India Great Tradition, especially if the all-India classifications and rank hierarchy of castes determined by opinion and interactional analysis do not coincide with the classifications and rank hierarchy in "Sanskritic Hinduism." In that case, there would be two all-India versions of the caste system, one, called "the *varṇa* theory," based on the opinions of the educated and the doctrines of the texts, the other based on the behavior and opinions of the uneducated villagers. M. N. Srinivas and David Mandelbaum seem to take this duality as the real state of affairs.[26] A second possibility, no less interesting, is that the two versions may coincide. In that case, one would have to say either that the villagers know the *varṇāśrama* doctrines of "Sanskritic Hinduism" and conform in their actions accordingly or that "Sanskritic Hinduism" has incorporated village behavior and opinion into its doctrines.

Marriott seems to incline to a third possibility, different from both the hypothesis of duality and that of non-duality. He envisages a kind of parallelism between interactional and attributional ranking based on a division of jurisdiction between them. Interactional ranking is "more to be expected as the logic of untutored, untraveled villagers" and rests on detailed objective knowledge of daily interaction in a particular locality. Attributional ranking, on the other hand, is more likely to be found in situations of cultural heterogeneity where educated people, lacking an intimate acquaintance with the day-to-day interactions in a village community, fall back on "the generalities derived from Brahmanical texts." He predicts, therefore, that it is more likely to be used by Brahmans, the educated, the urban, the more Westernized Indian, the Western social scientist, and, generally, by the stranger to the village community. He says that each mode of analysis "has peculiar reference to social relations of a distinctive type—interactional to social relations in the little community, attributional to those in the great community."[27]

Attributional analysis thus seems to express a cultural or mythological generalization about the social structure, whereas interactional analysis is based on "highly particularized intensive studies" from which "an accurate and intelligible picture" can be "constructed only by laborious comparison." Until these intensive studies and comparisons are made, attributional theory, "inaccurate as it may be and untrue to the nature of village thought . . . offers an approximation to general truth that is at least more accessible than knowledge of the details of ritual interaction in hundreds of thousands of villages." Marriott also expects that "interactional ranking will become increasingly difficult to find and study" because "interactional ranking may be expected to give way increasingly to an actual spread of attributional ranking" with the increase in urbanization, education, geographic mobility, and the influence of Brahmanical and Western social ideologies.[28]

There is a fourth possibility, a kind of modified duality, which I should like to propose. This possibility arises from the fact that even uneducated villagers all over India show familiarity with some version of the *varṇāśrama* system and apply its categories and philosophy to themselves as well as to others. Many of these villagers also seem to believe that rank does depend on cultural attributes and that they can improve their rank by adopting some of the attributes of "Sanskritic Hinduism." Marriott is probably correct when he suggests that villagers think this way more in reference to the remote supravillage context than in reference to their own village, in which context their thinking is more interactional. Yet it is difficult to believe that the villager compartmentalizes his thought and action into two distinct and parallel systems, one for use in the little community, the other for the great community. It seems to me more plausible to assume that there is a constant and mutual interpenetration between the two systems, even at the village level. The villager's experience with his local village social structure is bound to influence his conceptions and understanding of the wider structure of Indian civilization. Conversely, what he has learned of the wider structure from teachers and sacred texts must have some influence on the way he conceptualizes the local structure. If this assumption is valid, then there are likely to be some connections between the system of rank and classification he uses locally and the system he uses for supralocal reference. Changes in local realities that affect rank and mobility will probably be reflected, however loosely and indirectly, in the villager's thinking about the supralocal system, just as national political, legislative, and economic changes are beginning to change some villagers' thinking (and action, too) about the local rank hierarchy.

It is not possible, given the present state of our knowledge, to determine which of these four possibilities represents the closest approximation to the truth. Each certainly deserves to be taken as a working hypothesis for further research using both interactional and attributional analysis.

## Westernization and Sanskritization

In his Coorg study, Srinivas made several references to Western influence and noted briefly that improvements in communication—newspapers, radio, films, and books—have contributed to greater Sanskritization. Several years later, he published an essay, "A Note on Sanskritization and Westernization," in which he analyzed how Westernization and Sanskritization reinforce one another and in what respects there is a conflict between the two processes.[29] Although the analysis refers chiefly to Srinivas's studies in Mysore, it also takes account of observations by other anthropologists in Madras, Orissa, Uttar Pradesh, and Madhya Pradesh, as well as of several conference discussions at which Srinivas presented his views.[30] The paper represents, therefore, a generalized analysis of the relations between Westernization and Sanskritization in the light of recent field research and critical discussion.

Under "Westernization" are included technical improvements in communication and transportation, urbanization, industrialization, the new occupational opportunities that come with them, and Western-style education, as well as the civil and military institutions of parliamentary democracy and the new occupations associated therewith. Most of us would probably prefer to call this collection of changes "modernization," although many of them were introduced into India under British auspices. In any case, these changes do seem to have contributed to an increase in "Sanskritization." Many castes have successfully Sanskritized their way of life and improved their ritual status as they have improved their economic, educational, and political positions. Cultural mobility has been closely tied to economic and political mobility, in the present as in the past. The only major exceptions to this rule are the Harijans, who are sometimes prevented from improving their cultural status by the dominant castes of their localities. Harijans now have available to them the alternatives of withdrawing from the local system completely, by migration to other areas or by conversion, or of taking advantage of administrative, judicial, legislative, and political means for the improvement of depressed and scheduled castes. Studies by F. G. Bailey show that both alternatives are being adopted.[31]

The alternative of "Sanskritization" also continues to remain popular with lower castes, in spite of its social ineffectiveness. Bernard Cohn has reported that in the Uttar Pradesh village he studied, while a depressed caste was trying to raise its status by "Sanskritizing" its customs and beliefs, the locally dominant caste was modernizing.[32] The same observation has been made in other areas and has led Srinivas to formulate the generalization that, while the lower and middle castes are Sanskritizing, the upper castes are modernizing. However, this generalization should be examined in conjunction with another in which Srinivas asserts that the upper castes are both more Westernized and more Sanskritized than the lower and middle castes, implying that Sanskritization generally tends to precede Westernization.[33]

The tendency for Westernization (or modernization) to supersede

"Sanskritization" has suggested to some that traditional Indian culture, and the caste system as well are about to disappear. Srinivas is skeptical of this opinion, and I must say I share his skepticism. There are several different kinds of changes going on with modernization; one is the introduction of a new life-style model—the Western and European—that does not replace the old models but is simply a new addition to the traditional repertoire of ways to live. There is some indication that the new model is being accepted by educated Indians all over the country. With some it may be chiefly a matter of dress, diet, speech, and manners; with others it goes deeper into modern science and political ideologies. Yet this group is far from having alienated itself from the traditional culture and social structure of family, caste, region, or nation.

Those who have not accepted the new Western life-style as an ideal model are nevertheless subject to many modern influences as regards education, occupation, political activity, and performance of ritual obligation. There are many orthodox Brahmans, especially in the urban centers, who have received modern education in India or abroad and who have gone into the modern professions of law, medicine, engineering, scientific research and teaching, industrial management, parliamentary politics, and the civil service. These people continue to regard themselves as good Hindus, even if they do not have time for all the traditional ritual observances and Sanskrit learning. They are also often among the chief contributors to Hindu *maṭhas* and temples and the leaders of movements for cultural revival.

In the eighteenth and nineteenth centuries, as Srinivas points out, these people may have experienced some cultural shock and conflict when they first encountered the British and European style of life, which sanctioned cow slaughter and beef-eating, alcohol, remarriage of widows, and divorce.[34] They must also have been stung by the European criticisms of many Indian customs and beliefs. Today, however, these groups are accommodating themselves to modern ways with little psychological or cultural conflict. The explanation for the smooth accommodation lies not so much in the individual traits and qualifications of the group—although it is quite intelligent, well trained, and enterprising—but in the richness of Indian culture and the flexibility of its social structure, which enables them to modernize without losing their cultural or social identities. Brahmans, and other castes, too, have always been allowed to take up new occupations if their traditional occupations could not support them. The distinction between sacerdotal Brahmans (*vaidikas, yogins*) and worldly Brahmans (*laukikas, niyogins*) is of old standing. And the values of wealth, power, and pleasure, while perhaps subordinated to those of doing one's duty and of attaining release, have always been accepted as essential to the complete scheme of life. If today castes of all kinds participate in politics, in business, or in science and the professions, they can apparently do so without renouncing their cultural heritage or even all of their caste rules. Modernization is not for them or for the Westernized and educated sector incompatible with "Sanskritization" or with the preservation of the traditional social and cultural structure. In some studies of shifts away from traditional occupations in Bengal, Nirmal

Kumar Bose has found that while the upper castes have shifted to modern professions requiring higher education, the lower castes have shifted to modern jobs requiring little literacy.[35] Similar results have been reported by Richard Lambert for Poona factories and by Martin Orans about Santāls working in Jamshedpur.[36] The Santāls who work in Jamshedpur have accepted industrial employment as an alternative to living on the land without giving up all their traditional culture. "Having a job at Tata is like having land," they say. "You can pass it on to your son."

## Summary and Conclusion

The unity and continuity of Indian civilization is for the scholar both a necessary postulate and a problem; a postulate because the impression of unity and continuity is overwhelming, a problem because objective and precise verification of the impression, in the face of a long and changing history and a great diversity of languages, castes, tribes, religions, regions, villages, towns, and cities, is often difficult to provide. For a clarification of the problem, this chapter draws upon recent trends of thought and research in anthropology, particularly ethnology, culture history, and social anthropology. The models of a civilization developed by Kroeber and Redfield offer in combination a fruitful way to think about the continuity and unity of Indian civilization. From Kroeber we take the conception of a civilization as a coherent and historically derived assemblage of culture styles and patterns. Civilizations in his view have distinctive growth profiles, which show culmination of their patterns, reconstitutions in new styles, or decline. The growth is in part influenced by the absorption of new culture elements and styles from other cultures and in part by indigenous innovation. Under modernization, civilizational styles have shown a tendency to accelerate and to internationalize.

The application of Redfield's theory of a "folk-urban continuum" to historic and living civilizations gives us a conception of a civilization as a structure of communities of different scales of complexity and of different cultural levels. In his view, the earliest civilizations probably developed indigenously from local precivilized folk societies through the agricultural and the urban revolutions. These transformations created many new social and cultural types within the societal structure of "primary civilizations," including the peasantry. The early developments probably differentiated as well the cultural traditions into the "higher" levels cultivated in special centers by the educated and sophisticated (Great Traditions), and the "lower" levels (Little Traditions) familiar to the uneducated in the villages and towns. Encounters of primary civilizations with alien precivilized or civilized cultures were in some cases traumatic and disastrous, in others a stimulus to a "secondary" phase of growth and development. The outcome in each case depends both on the character of the encounter and on the character of the civilization. The study of such encounters is advanced through detailed study of the institutions, specialists, and media of which a civilization makes use for the transmission of cultural traditions, internally and externally (that is, the social organization of tradition).

Viewed in the light of this model, Indian civilization has a long growth profile in which several culminations are visible (probably about 2500 B.C., 500 B.C., and between A.D. 400 and 600) and during which its style patterns have been reconstituted several times without loss of continuity in total culture pattern. It probably entered its "secondary" phase of development quite early without essential impairment of cultural creativity or of its Great Traditions of high culture. It is debatable whether a cultural decline set in after A.D. 1000, in the middle period. But it seems likely that another phase of cultural "renaissance," reconstitution, and creativity emerges in the modern period, stimulated by the encounter with Europe.

This telescopic view of Indian civilization, while congenial to the culture historian, does not find favor with the social anthropologist who wishes to understand the social structure and workings of contemporary villages and other small communities. Recent village studies in India reveal, however, that the social anthropologist has discovered that the Indian village is not an isolated, self-sufficient social unity; rather, it is tied to the wider society and culture by many ties of marriage, caste, trade, religion, and politics. This discovery is producing a kind of research that gives considerable support to the conception of Indian civilization as a coherent structure of rural networks and urban centers, which at the same time acts as a medium for the mutual communication of Great and Little Traditions and of other cultural differences between and among tribes and castes, linguistic regions, regions and center, town and country.

One of the most widespread ways in which the cultural exchange takes place is through the process that M. N. Srinivas first studied and called "Sanskritization." The process is essentially one of cultural mobility through which groups have been incorporated into Indian civilization by adopting a set of practices, beliefs, and values that Srinivas calls "Sanskritic Hinduism" and identifies primarily with the Brahman way of life. The process of "Sanskritization" has enabled lower castes within the civilization to raise their status in a generation or two.

Further research and critical discussion has contributed to a more general conception of "Sanskritization." In the first place, the Brahman way of life is not the only model for Sanskritization. The life-styles of the warrior, even of the merchant and peasant and the saints, are also sometimes adopted as models for cultural mobility. In the second place the process incorporates into the system not only Hindus but also Jains, Buddhists, Pārsīs, Muslims, Christians, and other groups that do not consider themselves Hindu. In view of these considerations, it would be more appropriate to think of "Sanskritic Hinduism" not as a single set of beliefs and practices defining one life-style, that of the Brahmans, but rather as a complex pattern of beliefs and practices associated with several different life-styles. For this normative pattern, S. K. Chatterjee's word, "Indianism," is perhaps a more acceptable designation than "Sanskritic Hinduism." [37] If we accept this change, then we might also refer to the process of "Sanskritizing" as "Indianizing."

Whether the process of cultural mobility is called "Sanskritization" or "Indianization," it is compatible with Westernization and modernization, a conclusion that Srinivas and some other social anthropologists accept, although others have challenged their view. The weight of present evidence seems to me to show that, while modernizing influences are undoubtedly changing many aspects of Indian society and culture, they have not destroyed its basic structure and pattern. They have given Indians new alternatives and some new choices of life-style, but the structure is so flexible and rich that many Indians have accepted many modern innovations without loss of their Indianness. They have, in other words, been able to combine choices that affirm some aspects of their cultural tradition with innovative choices.

In a civilization as old and developed as that of India, the sense of cultural identity is highly self-conscious, variable, and many-layered. One begins to understand something of it from reading the late Prime Minister Jawaharlal Nehru's *Discovery of India* or former President S. Radhakrishnan's *Hindu View of Life*.[38] Some of it is expressed, as well, in the myths and histories of local tribes, castes, families, and regions. At the village level, as at the national, there are many images of the past, not one. Bernard Cohn, in an interesting account of the different "pasts" he found in one village, speculates "that a society is modern when it does have a past, when this past is shared by the vast majority of the society, and when it can be used on a national basis to determine and validate behavior." [39] Because of regional, communal, and class differences in their views of the past, Indians do not as yet share such a past, he contends. This is, of course, a highly subjective question, not very much studied as yet by objective methods. If the thesis that there are socially organized patterns of cultural continuity and unity in Indian civilization is valid, then there should also be, as the subjective expression of this, some widely shared sense of a multilayered common culture with a common past. My impression is that there is and there has been such a self-image of Indian civilization, which expresses itself in mythology, traditional history, and the cultural performances of the festival calendar. Such a self-image varies in degree of sophistication and accurate knowledge among different groups and may also include different local histories for different local groups, each of which may look at the past from its own point of view. But each local history and mythology tends to be linked to all-India history and mythology by the very social networks, institutions, and specialists that extend the villagers' social field. In his article on "The Historical Value of Indian Bardic Literature," Christoph von Fürer-Haimendorf writes that a class of traditional bards in West India "not only recount the history and mythology of their clients, but being literate, are also familiar with Hindu mythology, and have in their repertoire a number of episodes from the *Rāmāyaṇa* and other Hindu Epics." [40] How another group of living bards and genealogists, the Bāroṭs of Gujarat, actually go about converting local into national myth and history has recently been described by A. M. Shah and R. G. Shroff.[41] The process of building a single collective memory is, moreover, not restricted to bardic genealogists. All the literary, graphic, and performing arts have contributed to it—through recitation and dramatization of purāṇic and epic materials, dance forms, songs, sculpture and painting—as V. Raghavan in particular has emphasized. The modern media of film, radio, newspapers, magazines, and books have reinforced the traditional cultural media in this function. Through historical and devotional films, recordings, temple ceremonies, articles, and books on Indian history and archaeology, as well as through Republic Day celebrations, the sense of a shared culture and past seems to grow every day more vivid, making Indian society more "modern" without making it any less "Indian."

## Notes

1. Brown, "Content of Cultural Continuity" (see note 1, Introduction to Part Four, above).
2. Srinivas, "Problem of Indian Unity" (see note 1, Introduction to Part Four, above).
3. Kroeber, *Anthropologist Looks at History,* p. 40.
4. *Ibid.*
5. Redfield, *Folk Culture of Yucatan.*
6. *Ibid.,* pp. 340–42.
7. Redfield, *Primitive World and Its Transformations.*
8. Redfield and Singer, "Cultural Role of Cities" (see note 3, Introduction to Part One).
9. Bronislaw Malinowski, *Argonauts of the Western Pacific* (New York: E. P. Dutton, 1922), and A. R. Radcliffe-Brown, *The Andaman Islanders* (Glencoe, Ill.: The Free Press, 1948; first published in 1922).
10. Participants in the 1953 University of Chicago Seminar on Indian Village Studies are listed in note 7, Introduction to Part One. Papers presented at the seminar were published in Marriott, ed., *VI.*
11. Srinivas, *India's Villages.*
12. Dumont, *Une sous-caste.*
13. *Ibid.*
14. Lewis, "Peasant Culture" (see note 33, Chapter 2, above).
15. Srinivas, *Coorgs.*
16. Marriott, "Little Communities" (see note 33, Chapter 2, above).
17. Singer, ed., *TI.* See also introductions to Part One and Part Two, above.
18. Dumont, *Une sous-caste,* and Vidyarthi, *Sacred Gayāwāl.*
19. Ghurye, *Indian Sādhus.*
20. Surajit Sinha, "State Formation and Rajput Myth in Tribal Central India," *Man in India* 42, No. 1 (January-March, 1962): 35–80.
21. J. F. Staal, "Sanskrit and Sanskritization," *JAS* 22, No. 3 (May, 1963): 261–75.
22. Raghavan, "Variety and Integration" (see note 19, Chapter 2, above).
23. J. A. B. Van Buitenen, "On the Archaism of the Bhāgavata Purāṇa," in Singer, ed., *Krishna.*
24. McKim Marriott, "Interactional and Attributional Theories of Caste Ranking," *Man in India* 39, No. 2 (June, 1959): 92–107.
25. McKim Marriott, "Caste Ranking and Food Transactions: A Matrix Analysis," in Singer and Cohn, eds., *Structure and Change.*
26. David Mandelbaum, "Social Perception and Scriptural Theory in Indian Caste," in Stanley Diamond, ed., *Culture in History: Essays in Honor of Paul Radin* (New York: Columbia University Press, 1960). See also Srinivas, "Varna and Caste" (see note 26, Chapter 2, above).
27. Marriott, "Interactional and Attributional Theories."
28. *Ibid.* See also Marriott in Silverberg, *Social Mobility.*
29. Srinivas, "Sanskritization and Westernization" (see note 21, Chapter 2, above). See also other references in note 5 to Chapter 9, below.
30. See the references in notes 6 through 9, Chapter 9, below.
31. Bailey, *Caste and Economic Frontier.*
32. Bernard S. Cohn, "The Changing Status of a Depressed Caste," in Marriott, ed., *VI,* and *idem,* "Changing Traditions of Low Caste" (see note 22, Chapter 5, above).
33. Srinivas, "Sanskritization and Westernization."

34. Srinivas, *Social Change in Modern India.*
35. N. K. Bose, "Some Aspects of Caste in Bengal," in Singer, ed., *TI.*
36. Lambert, *Workers, Factories and Social Change;* Martin Orans, "A Tribal People in an Industrial Setting," in *TI;* and Orans, *The Santal.*
37. S. K. Chatterjee, "The Indian Synthesis—and Racial and Cultural Intermixture in India," presidential address, All-India Oriental Conference, Poona, 1953.
38. Nehru, *Discovery of India.*
39. Cohn, "Pasts of Indian Village" (note 5, *supra*).
40. C. von Fürer-Haimendorf, "The Historical Value of Indian Bardic Literature," in Philips, ed., *Historians of India, Pakistan and Ceylon.*
41. Shah and Shroff, "Vahīvañcā Bāroṭs of Gujarat" (see note 23, Chapter 2, above).

# 8 / *Industrial Leadership, the Hindu Ethic, and the Spirit of Socialism*

## Max Weber on the Roles of the Protestant and Hindu Ethics in Industrial Development

The most frequently alleged obstacles to modernization in India are perhaps the ritualism of the caste system and the doctrines of fate (*karman*), rebirth (*saṃsāra*), duty (*dharma*), and salvation (*mokṣa*), which are supposed to constitute a theodicy for the social system's moral and metaphysical justification. Max Weber's classic statement of this position in his work on the sociology of Hinduism and Buddhism is well known. Recent restatements by K. W. Kapp, Gunnar Myrdal, and others do not go beyond Weber's formulation, although they are not so much concerned as Weber was with the historical question of why industrial capitalism did not originate in India, and they have the benefit of about fifty years of further research and discussion since Weber wrote. In the perspective of later research and discussion, what is surprising about Weber's statement, and *a fortiori* about the later restatements, is the way in which dogmatic, sweeping generalizations about the effects of Hinduism and the caste system on the economy are juxtaposed with highly differentiated and realistic qualifications. In the current discussions, such juxtapositions often take on a bizarre, paradoxical tone: After much evidence is given to show how flexible and adaptive Hinduism and the caste system have been in the face of economic and social change, the conclusion is illogically drawn that a major precondition for economic development and modernization is the elimination of most traditional institutions, practices, and beliefs. A closer look at the *locus classicus* of this paradox, Weber's work, in the light of some recent research, will, I believe, yield a more logical and positive conclusion about the compatibility of traditional Indian society with modernization.[1]

> Every new technical process which an Indian employs signifies for him first of all that he leaves his caste and falls into another, necessarily lower. Since he believes in the transmigration of souls, the immediate significance of this is that his chance of purification is put off until another rebirth. He will hardly consent to such a change. An additional fact is that every caste makes every

> other impure. In consequence, workmen who do not accept a vessel filled with water from each other's hands cannot be employed together in the same factory room. Not until the present time, after the possession of the country by the English for almost a century, could this obstacle be overcome. Obviously, capitalism could not develop in an economic group thus bound hand and foot by magical beliefs.[2]

In the chapter "Caste Forms and Schisms," in which Weber most explicitly discusses the effects of the caste system on the economy, we find similar assertions such as these:

> It was impossible to shatter traditionalism, based on caste ritualism anchored in *karma* doctrine, by rationalizing the economy [page 123].

> The effects of the caste system on the economy . . . were essentially negative . . . this order by its nature is completely traditionalistic and anti-rational in its effects [page 111].

> Hinduism is characterized by a dread of the magical evil of innovation [page 122].

In the very same chapter from which these statements are taken, Weber has analyzed with considerable perspicuity and some reference to empirical data the different kinds of mobility in the caste system occasioned by residential and occupational mobility of caste members, as well as by property differentiation and technological change. He also takes note of changes in ritual practices and traditions that are associated with these economic and technical changes, in words that adumbrate M. N. Srinivas's later theory of "Sanskritization." When Weber wrote, there was already sufficient evidence of industrial capitalism to attract his attention. And he had some interesting observations on the dispositions of different castes and communities to become entrepreneurs, commercial and administrative employees, and factory workers. He was impressed by the increase in commercial investment and the accumulation of wealth, especially among the lower castes that had gone into business and industry, and he praised their "superior adaptability to the rational pursuit of profit."

Why, in view of all this, should he, and others who followed him, have insisted so dogmatically that Hinduism and the caste system are essentially negative and antirational in their effects on economic activity? One reason, I think, why Weber drew such negative conclusions was that at the time he was writing, before World War I, industrialization was just beginning in India under a British administration reluctant to encourage competition with Manchester and Birmingham. The growing pains in recruiting factory labor, absenteeism, factory discipline, finding venture capital, markets, and the like, were clearly evident and recalled to Weber the problems of European industrialization in its early period. His generalizations, however, go beyond these specific difficulties of transition. It is "extremely unlikely," he wrote, that "the organization of modern capitalism could have originated on the basis of the caste system" or be facilitated by it after being imported from Europe. The "core of the obstruction," he found, is not in any particular difficulties; it is "embedded in the 'spirit' of the whole system: A ritual law in which every change of occupation, every change in work technique, may result in ritual degradation is certainly not capable of giving birth to economic and technical revolutions from within itself or even of facilitating the first germination of capitalism in its midst" (page 112).

Beside this "ritual law," the mobility and adaptability of different castes, the industriousness of Indian artisans, and the resourcefulness of entrepreneurs shrink in Weber's view to insignificant and almost imperceptible proportions. The overwhelming potency of "the ritual law" derives, according to Weber, not only from the organization of occupations and economic activity in terms of a caste system and a hierarchy of ritual purity and pollution. It derives from the combination of such a system with a "theodicy" that justifies the system in terms of an ethic and theology based on the belief that one's status in the present life is determined by actions in a previous existence and that one's status in a future life will be determined by the net balance of merits and demerits accumulated in the present and past lives. The two doctrines of personal fate (*karman*) and rebirth (*saṃsāra*), which according to Weber constitute "the dogmatic foundation" of Hinduism, when linked to the caste system through a rational and deterministic moral order, gave that order "irresistible power" (page 131). Since this order, in Weber's interpretation, places "the supreme premium on ritual correctness and the performance of caste duties, the only way in which members of impure castes can improve their future social opportunities is to lead an exemplary life according to caste ritual. In this life there is no escape from the caste, at least no way to move up in the caste order" (page 121).

Weber sums up his analysis of the theodicy with an eloquent flourish at once echoing and disagreeing with Marx's *Manifesto:*

> *Karma* doctrine transformed the world into a strictly rational ethically-determined cosmos; it represents the most consistent theodicy ever produced in history. The devout Hindu was accursed to remain in a structure which made sense only in this intellectual context; its consequences burdened his conduct. The *Communist Manifesto* concludes with the phrase "they [the proletariat] have nothing to lose but their chains, they have a world to win." The same holds for the pious Hindu of low castes. He too can "win the world," even the heavenly world; he can become a Kṣatriya, a Brahman, he can gain Heaven and become a god—only not in this life, but in the life of the future after rebirth into the same world pattern [pages 121–22].

Weber's conclusion from this analysis is not only that it is "impossible to shatter traditionalism, based on caste ritualism anchored in *karman* doctrine, by rationalizing the economy," but, conversely, that it is impossible to rationalize the economy in such a traditional and ritualistic social order.

> It could not have occurred to a Hindu to see the economic success he had attained through devotion to his calling as a sign of his salvation. And what is more important, it could not have occurred to a Hindu to prize the rational transformation of the world in accordance with matter-of-fact considerations

and to undertake such a transformation as an act of obedience to a Divine Will [page 326].[3]

From this alleged incapacity of the Hindu, Weber deduced another: namely, that India could not have many economic successes of a kind and quantity sufficient to originate or to take over and develop industrial capitalism.

When I tell orthodox Hindus about Weber's theory, they are astonished. "If that were true," they usually reply, "how could we have lived and done so many things—built temples, ships, and empires, fought wars and organized agriculture, crafts, and trade?" There must be some misunderstanding, they feel, of the relations of religious belief and ritual to daily life. Even the sacred scriptures, they point out, recognize the need for rulers, administrators, traders, and artisans, as well as priests, scholars, and saints. Not everyone can be or needs to be an ascetic who renounces the world for a simple life of austerity and meditation. Most people must act in the world and meet their obligations to family, caste, and society. As they approach retirement, they will transfer their responsibilities to the next generation and turn more to meditation and prayer.

Weber was, of course, familiar with the scriptural doctrines of the four orders (*varṇas*) of society, the four stages (*āśramas*) of life, and the accomplishments of Indian civilization. He even tends to exaggerate Indian dynamism in his references to "unbridled lust for wealth," "ferocious warfare," and "unbridled lust of relentless conquest." Why then are his conclusions so negative?

To understand and evaluate Weber's conclusions about the negative and irrational effects of caste and Hinduism on the economy, it is necessary, I believe, to compare his analysis of the Indian case with his study of the role of the "Protestant ethic" in the rise of European industrial capitalism. From his European studies, Weber was led to believe that the origins and development of industrial capitalism required a class of entrepreneurs dominated by a set of values and motivations which he designated as a "capitalistic spirit." These values included a willingness to work hard, to save and reinvest, to order one's economic activity in a methodical and rational manner, to anticipate the future, to take risks, to keep accurate accounts of profits and losses, to stick by one's word, and to give fair measure. Those who manifested such a "spirit" most strongly, he further contended, were a group of enterprisers who belonged to the Puritan Calvinistic branch of the Protestant Reformation. From the association between groups of early merchant capitalists and groups of Calvinists, he concluded that there must be an "affinity" between particular forms of religious beliefs and particular motivations for economic activity. He then proceeded to infer the psychological links that could transform a Calvinist's anxiety about his ultimate salvation into a "capitalistic spirit" of enterprise.

In his studies of India, China, and Asia generally, where he did not see anything resembling the development of European industrial capitalism, Weber reasoned that the religions of those countries must lack the counterparts of a "Protestant ethic" that would provide the characterological foundation for the economic motivation required, as one among several factors, to spark and foster a development of industrial capitalism. With this initial hypothesis, he then undertook a detailed and highly informed analysis of Hinduism and Buddhism. He located the alleged irrational "spirit" of Hinduism in the caste system and the theodicy of fate (*karman*), rebirth, and duty (*dharma*); in an excessive ritualism and reliance on magical helpers; and in the use of orgiastic, other-worldly paths to salvation.

"No community," Weber wrote, "dominated by inner powers of this sort could out of its substance arrive at the spirit of capitalism"—or, for that matter, could take over capitalism as an imported artifact. "Instead of a drive toward the rational accumulation of property and the evaluation of capital, Hinduism created irrational accumulation chances for magicians and soul-shepherds, prebends for mystagogues and ritualistically or soteriologically oriented intellectual strata" (pages 325 and 328).

In support of this far-reaching conclusion, Weber tried to show by detailed analysis that, in relation to everyday conduct, Hinduism obstructs occupational change and technical innovation through the ritualism and traditionalism of caste, and that its belief system, unlike that of the Calvinists, provided no rationale whereby a striving for other-worldly salvation could be transformed into a this-worldly discipline and a positive social ethic.

Weber's thesis on the rise of European industrial development has stimulated a considerable polemical literature. His negative counterpart of that thesis in Asian economic development has aroused much less interest, until quite recently. The reason for the renewed interest would probably have astonished Weber, for, in current discussions, Weber's studies are drawn upon and extended not as a plausible historical explanation of India's failure to develop an early form of industrial capitalism but rather as a recipe for current policies that will achieve rapid industrial development. This recipe recommends the abolition or abandonment of the caste system, the joint family, most ritual observances and practices, the beliefs in *karman*, rebirth, *dharma*, cyclical *yugas*, *māyā*, renunciation—in fact, practically all the institutions, practices, and beliefs characteristic of Hinduism—as the best way for India to achieve economic development, social reform, and a modern democratic state.

This prescription is naturally offered more often by non-Indians than by Indians, considering its highly unrealistic, "off-with-their-heads" nature. Yet there are Indians, too, who take Weber's diagnosis seriously and who have proposed such "revolutionary" measures for economic development as the elimination of many traditional values and practices on the grounds that these traits are incompatible with a modern society.

Not all recent discussions of these problems can be blamed on Weber, of course, although most authors of such efforts have directly or indirectly been influenced by him and have tried to convert his historical analysis into a contemporary policy and program for economic development. The resulting stereotypes of India (and of Asia) as a "backward," medieval society are so apt to flatter the ethnocentric conceits of Europeans and

Americans that the policy prescriptions flowing from these diagnoses seem to be very sensible ways of "Westernizing" and "modernizing" Asian nations. We can, in fact, find most of the elements of this approach in the ideology of "the white man's burden," which was in its heyday before Weber wrote.

The appeal of this ideology to Europeans as a source of diagnosis and prognosis is irresistible. As late as 1914, the British director of a new Department of Industries in Madras, which had been belatedly created to encourage commercial enterprise, expressed the following opinion of the obstacles to industrialization in that Presidency: "None of these entrepreneurs had the haziest notion as to what industry really meant. . . . The root of the trouble lies in the Indian social system—the caste system."

Because of its water-tight division of labor, he argued, the caste system precludes cooperation, stifles progress, discourages independent thought, leads to the acceptance of authority rather than reason, and diverts the intellect to empty philosophical speculations. His conclusion sounds familiar: "Manufacturing as at present carried on in Europe is out of the question," unless the Indians accept the fact "that modern industry is an essentially Western conception and one therefore that must be approached from the Western, or practical point of view." [4]

Certain analogies between Weber's analysis of the European case and the Indian case exhibit the underlying structure of his argument.

1. He assumes in both cases that the decisive factors in accounting for economic motivation are not biological and racial differences or universal instincts and impulses for gain and power but the ways in which education, environment, and culture have organized the biological impulses.

2. He assumes in both cases that the respective social systems are dominated by "inner spirits," which express that system's character and determine its future directions of change. For the European case, he locates this "spirit" in a "Protestant ethic" and a "spirit of capitalism," and for the Indian case he finds it in a "Hindu ethic" and a "Hindu character."

Weber's use of the nineteenth-century "spirit" or *"geist"* seems to me close to the more current and acceptable anthropological concepts of "cultural configuration," "basic personality structure," and "cultural character."

3. In both cases, he tries to derive the "spirit" of the total social system from a specific religious and ideological "theodicy" which "explains" and "justifies" the social system. In the European case, however, the social system "explained" and "justified" by the Calvinistic theodicy is not the existing traditional social system but the system as it will be when reformed, whereas, in the Indian case, the social system "explained" and "justified" by the theodicy is the existing and ancient traditional caste system.

4. In both cases, the effects of the "theodicy" on individual motivation and behavior are deduced by a hypothetical and introspective method in which Weber asks how he would feel and act if he were a "believer" in each of the respective theodicies. In the European case, however, he had firsthand experience and knowledge of the Protestant "believers" and

their social backgrounds to guide his "psychocultural" derivation of an ideal-typical Puritan personality type. In the Indian case, he seems to have relied chiefly on the scriptural texts and on European Indologists' interpretations of them for his construction of the ideal-typical Hindu. Although familiar with some empirical data in census and administrative reports, Weber did not give such information much weight in his derivation of Hindu character. This is perhaps the main reason why his psychological portraits of the Puritan and the Hindu are so different in spite of the many parallels between Calvinistic and Hindu predestination theologies.

5. In both cases, Weber assumes that there is a two-way causal relation between the social system and the religious ideology. The social structure, economy, and political and legal systems all influence the religious system and are in turn influenced by it. Because Weber was, however, interested in demonstrating the independent influence of religious ideology on the economy, especially in the case of Calvinism, he tended to take for granted the reverse influence of the social system in his *Protestant Ethic and the Spirit of Capitalism* and concentrated instead on the dynamic role of religious ideology in bringing about change in the social system by way of its psychological effect on believers. His analysis of the Indian case, on the other hand, tends to emphasize the conservative effects of the religious ideology on the traditional social system.

Given the great similarity of underlying assumptions and approach, which seems to me generally valid, why should the conclusions in the two cases be so diametrically opposed? Weber and his supporters would probably answer that Hindu society, religion, and personality are diametrically opposed to European society, religion, and personality. I believe there is more to the argument than that and have already indicated that some of the differences in conclusions depend on differences in Weber's methods and assumptions. Let us see how such differences may have influenced his conclusions and whether these conclusions can be tested by empirical research.

On the basis of his analysis of scriptural texts, Weber identifies the "dogmatic foundation" of Hinduism in two doctrines, fate (*karman*) and rebirth (*saṃsāra*). What is problematic about his argument is not his assumption that belief in fate and rebirth are widespread but the notion that there is in Hinduism a kind of official, orthodox core of religious and metaphysical doctrine with a uniform and unchanging interpretation, in spite of the diversity of heterodox schools and sects. Weber was probably encouraged to make such an assumption by reading the Indological scholars of his day. These scholars have tended, as Kalidas Bhattacharya has recently observed, to bestow on one school of Indian philosophy, Advaitavedānta, the seal of orthodoxy. They have further singled out the other-worldly and ascetic aspects of this philosophy as the dominant interpretation of its doctrines. Weber's conclusion that there can be no escape from the "iron law" of caste and ritual, except through renunciation of this world for an other-worldly ascetism, is directly influenced by this special interpretation of Advaita. Although his work includes a well-informed discussion of the *Bhagavadgītā* and the *bhakti* sects, he does not really follow through the implications for his general thesis of alternative paths salvation. Nor does he give much attention to the man who seeks his salvation through action (the *karmayogin*) or to the enlightened one who chooses to remain in this world to help save his fellow men (*jīvanmukta*). These paths are both compatible with Advaita.[5]

A second assumption leading Weber astray is that there must be a specific and uniform psychology for all Hindus resulting from adherence to an orthodox Hindu creed. He posits a psychology that includes a "dread" of rebirth and redeath, a "dread" of innovation and change, as well as passivity and fatalism, irrationality, mysticism, and other-worldliness.

To a large extent, this psychology of the Hindu believer is a hypothetical construction—what Weber supposes that he or Everyman would feel if he believed in the doctrines of *karman* and rebirth. But Weber insists that the negative consequence of these beliefs for behavior follow ineluctably, whether or not the believer is aware of the connection. ("The fact that the devout individual Hindu usually did not realize the grandiose presuppositions of *karma* doctrine as a whole is irrelevant for their practical effect, which is our concern" [page 121].)

How can Weber be so sure of these psychological consequences? His certitude derives directly, I believe, from his assumption that the entire traditional social and cultural order is governed by a single inner "spirit" or "principle," which he thinks he has identified in "the law of ritual." Given this principle and the associated theodicy of *karman* and rebirth, the individual Hindu's social and moral order must become, according to Weber, completely determined not only as a logical construction of thought but also as psychological feelings and dispositions to act.

If the results of Weber's analysis were only hypothetical and ideal-typical constructions, they would not do much harm. However unrealistic the constructions of the "spirit" of the social system and of the psychology of Hindus have been, they can still be useful stimuli for empirical research. Certainly his earlier and parallel constructions of an ideal-typical Puritan capitalist in European society were fruitful hypotheses for research and have stimulated much useful discussion.

The problematic aspect of Weber's assumptions emerges when the ideal-types are confused with empirical realities. In an ideal-typical "traditional" order governed by an "iron law" of ritual, there may well be ideal-typical Hindus living in magical dread of change and innovation and seeking to escape from the wheel of rebirth and redeath through other-worldly ascetic austerities or orgiastic mystical rites. At this level of imaginative construction, perhaps the only way to change the "traditional" order is to construct an ideal-typical "modern" order in which ideal-typical secular Indians, completely liberated from traditional institutions and beliefs, can proceed to modernize their economy and society.

What has all this to do with empirical realities? "Traditional" Indian society has been a changing society, and the Hindus who have been agents of these changes have not been prevented by caste, ritual, or religious beliefs from making innovations. Even Weber pays tribute to their flexibility and resourcefulness when he writes,

> The law of caste has proved just as elastic in the face of the necessities of the concentration of labor in workshops as it did in the face of a need for concentration of labor and service in the noble household. All domestic servants required by the upper castes were ritually clean. . . . The principle, "the artisan's hand is always clean in his occupation," is a similar concession to the necessity of being allowed to have fixtures made or repair work done, personal services, or other work accomplished by wage workers or by itinerants not belonging to the household. Likewise, the workshop was recognized as "clean." Hence, no ritual factor would have stood in the way of jointly using different castes in the same large workroom, just as the ban upon interest during the Middle Ages, as such, hindered little the development of industrial capital, which did not even emerge in the form of investment for fixed interest [pages 111–112].

Weber's psychological analysis of the effects of the Calvinistic doctrine of predestination or election on individual Puritan believers postulates a "salvation anxiety," which is allayed by a rational, methodical dedication to success in one's "calling." Evidence of success in the form of wealth or expansion of enterprise symbolizes that the believer may be on the right path to salvation and thus reinforces his devotion to his "calling" and the pursuit of success; this in turn reduces his "salvation anxiety" still further. Such essentially is Weber's theory of how a Protestant ethic is related to a capitalistic spirit in individuals. The relation is not logical but psychological and appears plausible in the light of what we now know about defenses and reaction formations against anxiety. It is, however, puzzling to find that, for Weber, the psychological effects of the Hindu ethic are wholly negative and antirational, producing a passive, mystical, and otherworldly ascetic Hindu bent on escaping from this world, in contrast to the active, this-worldly ascetic Puritan who seeks his salvation through mastery and transformation of this world.[6]

This is an especially puzzling contrast because there are several striking parallels between Calvinistic and Hindu eschatology, and it is not clear why the psychological effects of the one belief system should be so diametrically opposed to those of the other. Through their emphasis on personal destiny and fate, both systems should arouse "salvation anxiety" in believers. In both, a vocational ethic enjoins industriousness and dedication to one's "calling" as a moral duty. Competence and success in one's calling are also linked in both to a transcendent goal of spiritual salvation. In Hinduism, the link has been described in the lofty philosophical doctrine of the *Bhagavadgītā,* which assures to householders, women, and Śūdras a path to salvation in the performance of their daily work, provided their performance is not motivated by a desire for the selfish enjoyment of the fruits thereof. Tilak, Gandhi, and other modern Hindu leaders applied this analogue of the "Protestant ethic" to justify programs of political and economic activism.[7]

Weber's contrast between the active Puritan and the passive Hindu is all the more puzzling in view of the moral activism of the *karman* doctrine. If a man's present condition is determined by his past actions, and his future will be determined by his present and past actions, then he is the master of his fate, as Weber recognizes. Why, then, should he become passive, pessimistic, fatalistic, and an incompetent failure? For Weber, the decisive difference between the Protestant and Hindu cases seems to be the Hindu belief in rebirth and "redeath." He interprets this belief as implying that one's actions cannot improve one's condition in this life; they can affect future lives only. Therefore, Weber deduces, no matter how active and enterprising a man may be, he can do nothing about his condition in this life, and the prospect of an infinite sequence of future lives and deaths can only be disheartening and enervating: "To any thoughtful and reflective person, life destined to eternal repetition could readily appear completely senseless and magical" (page 133).

Weber's analysis proceeds on at least three different levels: the *textual*, the *contextual*, and the *ideal-typical*. At the textual level, he expounds and interprets the philosophical doctrines contained in particular scriptural texts very much as an Indologist would. Weber has selected a restricted range of texts and has identified the two doctrines of *karman* and rebirth as the dogmatic core of Hinduism. At the textual level, the two doctrines are sometimes associated with fatalism, pessimism, and passivity. These attitudes, however, are not direct logical consequences of the belief in *karman* and rebirth, but they derive from an additional assumption made in some of the texts, especially the Buddhist, that all life is suffering and that the cause of suffering is desire. Without this additional doctrine, the great chain of life linked in cycles of rebirth presents as grand and awesome a vision as that of biological evolution. Even with the doctrine of suffering, some of the texts, such as the *Bhagavadgītā*, offer paths of escape through ritual observance, disinterested action in this world, and devotion to a deity (*bhakti*), as well as through meditation and knowledge.

At the ideal-typical level of analysis, Weber asks what a devout Hindu would feel and do if he believed in *karman* and rebirth. His answer that such a Hindu would be fatalistic, pessimistic, and passive and would seek escape and consolation from his despair through other-worldly ascetism or mystic transports suggests that he has constructed his ideal-typical Hindu from a particular selection of textual doctrines and has interpreted the psychological consequences of these doctrines for believers in a way that agrees with the interpretations of some Western Indologists:

> Most people were left numb before the problem [of salvation] and gave it up. They took the attitude that success was beyond them. They might just as well do so and leave the effort to persons of greater intellectual capacity and strength of will. They greatly admired such persons, but for themselves they would be content with a modest effort, living by a simplified ethical code that would reduce evil *karma* and increase good, and so palliate the misery of future existences, though not cure it. They would placate the minor godlings of disease, child-bearing, prosperity; worship the great gods who were confessedly not the Absolute; deal only with what they had the intelligence to grasp or the imagination to conceive. They would merely make the best of a situation that for all their practical purposes was hopeless.[8]

At the contextual level, Weber asks what individual Hindus of specific occupations, castes, and sects believe and how these beliefs influence their behavior. There is some reference in Weber's essay on Hinduism and Buddhism to the different beliefs and attitudes of different status and interest groups—intellectuals, middle class, masses; Jains, Muslims, and Hindus. This sociologically differentiated picture is nowhere reconciled with the ideal-typical construction derived from interpretations of scriptural doctrine.

The articulation between the textual and contextual levels is closer in *The Protestant Ethic,* where Weber uses sources that are closer to a contextual level of analysis than his construction of the ideal-typical Hindu: popular religious literature, sermons, histories of particular groups, biographies of individuals and families. In Weber's studies of Hinduism and Buddhism, although he discusses the evolution of particular sects and religious movements, this history is largely doctrinal. The argument of some that Indian history is essentially doctrinal and mythological overlooks the wealth of contextual clues scattered in tales, plays, folklore, and family histories. Perhaps such material was not available to Weber.

It is just this contextual problem of how ordinary people interpret and apply religious and philosophic beliefs in everyday life that interests the social anthropologist. It is from social anthropological studies that we may hope to learn whether the conclusions of Weber's ideal-typical analysis (that the effects of Hinduism on everyday life are essentially negative and antirational) are valid. The contextual level of analysis does not exclude the textual level but presupposes and complements it. It does so not only because knowledge of the textual tradition furnishes a useful background for the study of the folk traditions but even more because the study of the folk traditions frequently encounters the texts and textual specialists as integral components of folklore. Whether or not ordinary folk are familiar with the doctrines of the scriptural texts, how they apply them in everyday life depends very much on their contact with textual specialists—and cultural centers—which mediate such knowledge to them. A contextual study of the ordinary Hindu's religious beliefs and ritual practices must therefore include as an essential part the role of the textual specialist and his texts.[9]

If we look only at the mutually exclusive "traditional" and "modern" orders at the ideal-typical level, "modernization" may appear as a revolutionary change in type of social structure and culture. When we look at specific individuals and groups, however, it is difficult to find much evidence for such exclusive orders of society or total structural transformations. "Modernization" at the contextual level becomes a rather more complicated and interesting process whereby individuals and social groups adapt the new to the old and the old to the new. This, at any rate, is what I found in a study of how a small group of successful industrial leaders in Madras City adapt their social institutions, ritual structure, and belief system to their economic activities, and how they adapt their economic activities to their cultural traditions. In the remainder of this chapter, I should like to analyze the adaptations of these industrialists and consider the implications for a theory of modernization and cultural change.

## Industrial Leaders in Madras City

The following pages report an application of a contextual approach to a study of the relationship of industrial leadership to Hinduism in Madras City. The report emphasizes the roles in industrialization of the joint family, the caste system, and Hindu rituals and beliefs, since these are the three aspects of Hinduism most frequently singled out as major obstacles to industrialization and economic development in India.

The study is preliminary and incomplete in several respects. It deals primarily with the families of industrial leaders (owners and managers) and not with those of workers and other industrial employees. The analysis and conclusions are not, therefore, intended to apply to all industrial occupations. A more serious limitation arises from the fact that I had no opportunity to collect the "traditional" kinship systems of the families studied. The absence of such data makes it very difficult to generalize about trends of change in their kinship systems brought about by industrialization. To some extent, this defect can be mitigated by reference to some of the excellent kinship studies now available on some of the South Indian groups,[10] and I have used them where relevant. But in view of the numerous variations among different families, castes, communities, and regions, the use of such studies does not solve the problem. In a complete study, the "traditional" kinship systems of just those families who have moved into industry and urban living would have to be reconstructed as they existed in their native villages and towns. The point of departure for such a reconstruction would be the genealogies provided by living members, which would need to be supplemented with local historical studies of these families.

Most of the data were collected from January through March, 1964, when I was in India; some of the background information was collected on the two earlier trips in 1954–55 and in 1960–61. The industrialists were selected by asking knowledgeable people, including other industrialists around Madras City and in other places, to name the leading Indian industrialists of the city, and by identifying the owners or managing directors of companies in the city with a capitalization that would fall into the census definition of "large" or "very large" industry. In the end, the two lists coincided fairly closely. Seventeen were in the city at the time and available for interviews. To the list I added the State Minister of Industries, who played a decisive role in encouraging private-sector industry, and, for purposes of comparison, the general manager of a very successful public-sector industry. The nineteen industrialists were not, then, all "entrepreneurs" in the classical economic sense of the term and will therefore be referred to as "industrial leaders."

Statistical and historical information about industrial development and particular industries in Madras City and Tamiḻnāḍu was obtained from the State Ministry of Industries, the Superintendent of the Census in Madras City, the Madras Record Office, the records of the Commercial Office of the American Consulate in Madras, and literature published by some of the companies.

The nineteen industrial leaders are not necessarily a "representative sample" of industrial leaders in the State or in India. They are a group of identified individuals and families known to be playing a significant role in industrial development. The Minister of Industries referred to them as "the cream of the industrial class." For purposes of an inquiry into the social character and motivations of a newly emerging class of successful industrial entrepreneurs, it is precisely "the cream," the pace-setters and creators of new standards, that needs at this point, I believe, to be studied.

The industrialists are also the most relevant group for a test of Weber's thesis, for they represent the closest parallel to the successful Puritan capitalists who were the empirical basis for Weber's analysis of the Protestant ethic and the spirit of capitalism in Europe and the United States.

The essential facts about the industrialists can be quickly summarized. Five are managing directors of their companies, five are directors, four are chairmen, three are partners in their firms, and one is a general manager. All were born in villages or small towns, and all now live with their families in a metropolitan center. Their move into industry is relatively recent. Ten entered between 1931 and 1940; five entered between 1941 and 1950; three entered between 1951 and 1960; and one entered in 1962. Seven were the founders of their companies; in six other cases, the leader's father was the founder; in one case a father-in-law, in one a mother's brother, and in one a grandfather. Their occupations before going into industry were self-employment in banking and trade (nine), government service (four), and employment by private business firms (four). Two entered business directly after completing college or professional training. Five of the nineteen have never been to any kind of college or professional school. Of the fourteen who had attended college, eight had specialized: two in accounting, three in science, two in economics, and one in automotive engineering.

Nine of the industrial leaders are Brahmans from Tamiḻnāḍu (seven Smārta Brahmans and two Śrīvaiṣṇava Brahmans); four are Ceṭṭiyars, a traditional Tamil trading caste; one is a Mudaliyār, a Tamil peasant caste; one is a Kammar, a peasant caste in Andhra; two are from Muslim families, one of which has lived in Tamiḻnāḍu for several hundred years and the other recently came from Hyderabad and Bombay; one is from a Gujarati Hindu merchant family which migrated to Madras City in 1919; and one is from a Syrian Christian family that came to Madras from Kerala.

The significance and explanation of these facts is not so easily summarized. A deeper analysis is required that goes beyond the social-survey type of data. Each of the industrial leaders, for example, is affiliated with several different kinds of social groupings—family, caste, religious sect, linguistic region, class, political party, and others. Which of these affiliations explains the individual industrialist's behavior? The usual answers to this question, including Weber's, are based on inferences from the kinds of kinship system, or caste system, or system of ritual and religious belief, to putative individual psychology and behavior. This procedure tends to explain individual behavior by reference to social and cultural systems of which the individual is a member, on the assumption that (1) all the social and cultural systems of which an individual is a member, and all aspects of each system, are equally relevant for a particular individual, and (2) the specific behavior of individual members of a "system" replicates the generic characteristics of the system without significant variations or nonsystemic traits. To avoid these assumptions, I propose first to describe the concrete involvements of the individual leaders in industry and then to relate them to as much of the postulated "systems" of kinship, caste, ritual, and religious belief as seems directly relevant. Generalizations about the role of these respective "systems" in inhibiting or facilitating industrial leadership will then be considered at a higher level of abstraction.

By proceeding from the observed concrete adaptive behavior and belief of particular individuals and groups to the more abstract levels of conceptualized "systems" and "structures," I hope to bypass a number of dilemmas that have confronted Indian anthropology and social anthropology in general. These dilemmas include such questions as whether the joint family, the caste system, and the system of Hindu ritual and belief persist in a "modern" urban and industrial setting or whether they "break down" and are replaced respectively by the nuclear family, a class system, and secular ideologies. Discussion of these questions is often inconclusive and confused, it seems to me, not at the level of empirical facts, although data are not as plentiful as could be desired, but because of failures to recognize the different levels and kinds of abstractions within which the questions are posed.

At the level of "structural" analysis, these questions are answered by definition and methodological assumptions, since the time perspective is synchronic and the relevant "structural types" have by definition been abstracted from significant change. It is no surprise, then, to find "structural" analyses insisting that the joint family, the caste system, and Hinduism persist as structural types and adducing some selected empirical evidence to support that position.

When "structural" analysis, on the other hand, assumes a diachronic perspective, it insists equally that the significant changes are all "structural," in that they involve total transformations of "structural types," for example, from joint to nuclear family, from caste to class, and from Hinduism to secularism. Selected empirical evidence is also usually mustered to give plausibility to this set of conclusions.

Apart from the contradiction in conclusions, these forms of structural analysis are unable to deal with the commonplace empirical facts of the coexistences of joint and nuclear families, of caste and class, and of religion and secularism—coexistences, moreover, of long duration that may, in some cases, antedate Westernization. From the point of view of "structural" analysis, the coexistence of "types" can only appear anomalous or as indications of a "transition" from the "traditional" to the "modern" types.

Efforts to resolve these dilemmas by introducing more rigorous definitions of the "structural types" and subtypes or by statistical surveys of their relative frequency of distribution have not been any more successful.

At the level of statistical frequencies, the question of "persistence" and "breakdown" does not arise unless the normative structures of the culture are invoked, and if they are, the dilemmas reappear so long as one remains at the level of "structural" analysis.

A more fruitful approach to these problems may be to reverse the procedure and direction of inference. Instead of trying to draw conclusions about individual behavior and belief, and empirical persistence and change, from "structural" definitions and *a priori* assumptions, why not begin with the ways in which particular individuals and groups make use of their family, caste, religious affiliations, and networks in particular fields of activity, such as the city and industry, and then consider what these facts imply about the congruence or incompatibility of "structural types"? This is, in any case, the procedure I shall follow in trying to assess the reciprocal effects of urban industry on such characteristic Indian institutions as the joint family, the caste system, and Hinduism. Perhaps we shall find by following this procedure that there are forms of change and persistence in these "structures" and "systems" that transcend the structuralist's dilemma: either synchronic equilibrium or diachronic total transformation.

## The Role of the Joint Family in Modern Industry

The relationship of industrialization to family organization in Europe and the United States has long been a subject for discussion and theorizing. The earlier views of the economic historians and social critics, which blamed "the industrial revolution" or "private property" for destroying the family by putting men, women, and children into factories for long hours, have been replaced by the less apocalyptic views of the sociologists, who have restated the relationship as a transformation in family type. According to this theory, the extended preindustrial family system has been transformed under the influence of industrialization into a nuclear or elementary family system. Support for this theory has been marshaled in statistics that purport to show an increasing trend toward nuclear families in industrial countries, as well as in the argument that the structure of the extended family system is functionally adapted to an agricultural society but dysfunctional in an industrial society, while the nuclear family is functionally adaptive in an industrial society but dysfunctional in an agricultural society.

Although treated as axiomatic in many sociology textbooks, this theory has been challenged during the last fifteen years from three different directions: the documentation by social anthropologists of the variety of family systems in different parts of the world; the discovery by social historians that the nuclear family may have been prevalent and a cultural norm in Europe and the United States even before industrialization; and the finding by sociologists and social anthropologists that many families in American and European cities maintain widespread kin ties.[11]

These findings have reopened many of the questions previously considered to be settled about the relations of family organization to industrialization. Some sociologists have tried to take account of the comparative study of family systems in reformulating the general theory. Goode, Nimkoff, Levy, and Moore and Feldman, among others, show familiarity with cross-cultural studies and a strong interest in them.[12] Levy's recent formulation is perhaps characteristic of this group of sociological writers:

> One of the special characteristics of relatively modernized societies is their quite unusual type of family unit. Whatever the previous ideal family structure was, during the transition toward relative modernization, the ideals always change toward what anthropologists and sociologists call a multilineal conjugal family, unless they already took that form.[13]

Social and cultural anthropologists would be more likely to stress the variety of adaptations to industrialization, as well as the initial variety of kinship structures. There are some anthropologists, however, whose interest in universal generalizations is almost as strong as that of the sociologists and who are tentatively reformulating the relationship of industry to family organization in terms as general as those of the sociologists. Among the products of these approaches, Raymond Firth's paper "Family and Kinship in Industrial Society" illustrates a characteristic familiarity with recent sociological and historical studies and a lucid trial reformulation of a general theory. His reformulation, based on recent studies of kinship in London, is more circumspect and differentiated than the sociologists'.

> What the development toward an industrial society probably does is to break down the formal structure of kin groups, except perhaps that of the elementary family, which is most resistant. The lineage, the extended family, the large cooperative cognatic kin unit is likely not to survive as its members disperse into industrial employment and their traditional resources and authority structures lose meaning. But personal kin ties tend to be retained on a selective basis. Indeed, they may be even strengthened if the physical isolation of the elementary family is promoted by industrial, urban, conditions. There is no reason then to think that extra-familial kin ties are likely to decrease in our modern Western society. They fulfill a function which, though not strikingly obvious, is almost certainly important for the social life of individuals and family units.[14]

I will attempt to trace the implications of some recent studies of the relationship of the Indian joint family to urbanization and industrialization, including a preliminary study of my own in Madras City. I shall be interested not only in the extent to which the Indian case fits the kind of generalization formulated by Levy and Firth but even more in the new approaches that the Indian case suggests for a study of the problem within the framework of social anthropology.

### *Is the Joint Family Breaking Down?*

Recent discussions of what is happening to the Indian joint family under the influence of urbanization, industrialization, and modernization parallel in many respects the general trends just summarized. The tendency of these discussions is to question earlier conclusions that the joint family is breaking down and is being replaced by the nuclear family. Census data previously used to support such conclusions are now being reinterpreted or disqualified on the grounds that the data gave only information about household size, an unreliable index of family type. The entire question of rural-urban distributions of joint and nuclear families is being reconsidered in the census, other statistical surveys, and case studies.

These reconsiderations and the new studies based on them offer a substantial challenge to the thesis of a linear transformation of the joint family into a nuclear family under the influence of urbanization and industrialization. They show, for example, that large joint families are more prevalent in urban than in rural areas and vary in prevalence with region and caste, that nuclear households are as prevalent in villages as in cities, and that such rural-urban distributions may have been common in the past. They also show that nuclear households, in both villages and cities, may, with the changing domestic cycle of marriages and births, grow into joint households and decline with separations and deaths into nuclear households again. "Jointness" in these studies has become a complex, multidimensional thing including common residence and meals, common worship, common property, and the maintenance of kin ties even among separated households that may no longer have any joint property.

With this growing sophistication, it is no longer possible to support conclusions about the breakdown of the joint family by citing statistics on the frequency of nuclear households. The burden of proof has shifted: One must distinguish the cultural ideal of the joint family from its actual occurrence, and attitudes and sentiments from behavior. Different types of joint families (lineal, collateral, and others) must be distinguished, as must different types of nuclear families. I. P. Desai has, in fact, proposed a classification of joint-family types based on different aspects of jointness as well as on the number of generations within a household.[15]

In view of the increasing complexity, questions of how we are to define "joint family" or "nuclear family" are now frequently raised. Is a household composed of parents and their married sons and daughters-in-law who have not yet had children to be classified as nuclear or as joint? Some writers would classify such a household as nuclear because it does not consist of at least three generations. Others classify it as joint because it represents a phase in a domestic cycle that will soon grow into a proper joint household as grandchildren are born. Others carry the domestic cycle analysis one step further and see a joint family growing out of every nuclear family.

The authors of these studies and discussions have reacted so strongly against the "breakdown" and linear transformation theories that they sometimes give the impression that the joint family never changes except by eternal recurrence of the nuclear-to-joint-to-nuclear domestic cycle of growth and decline.[16]

Yet, despite all the new evidence and argument, one continues to suspect that the joint family has been changing. Even if one accepts the validity of the domestic cycle analysis, we still do not know whether the rate of reformation of joint families out of their nuclear "seeds" is greater or less than it was in the past, and similarly for the rate of fission of joint families into nuclear. And how can the argument of the functional incompatibility of the joint family with urban life and industrial organization have any cogency if the joint family never changes but only recurs? The critics have, I believe, introduced greater sophistication into the discussion but have yet to come to grips with the problem of change.

By arguing that a joint family is more than a matter of household size or composition, of common residence or common property, or of the ratio of nuclear to joint households, critics have introduced, albeit implicitly, the more abstract concept of the joint family as a social structure embedded within the framework of a specific kind of social system. As a social structure, a joint family is a network of social relations among persons related in specified ways. Their social relations are crystallized in a set of mutual obligations within a framework of law or customary usages which defines appropriate norms of behavior for each category of relative. Whether a particular group constitutes a joint family depends on whether it is held together by the kind of social network in question, that is, whether or not the individuals within it are disposed to discharge toward one another the set of rights and duties specified in their religious scriptures, legal code, and customary usages. The presence or absence of joint residence, joint property, a particular set of kin, and so forth is relevant only insofar as it is a part of the total structure of obligations. The presence of any particular feature does not necessarily make a group of people a joint family, nor does its absence deprive the group of that status.

The concept of social structure, as is well known, derives from Radcliffe-Brown. Its application to the Indian joint family may be carried one step further by noting that the joint family, as a social system, may be analyzed into several distinct components: the kinship terminology; the categories of relatives designated by the terminology; and the rules of marriage, residence, descent, inheritance, and authority. The Indian joint family is usually characterized in terms of these components as follows: It is patrilineal in descent, patrilocal in residence, patriarchical in authority, and has an inheritance rule that divides family property equally among adult males lineally related within at least four generations. Since there are significant variations in each of these components in different regions, castes, tribes, and religious groups, such a characterization cannot be taken for *the* Indian joint family. It may, however, be taken as a characterization of a dominant structural type of Indian joint family. And I shall so take it in this chapter, setting aside for the time being the matrilineal systems and the other "deviations" from the dominant type.

It is this dominant type of joint family that some social anthropologists and sociologists have in mind when they assert that the Indian joint family is breaking down because its "structure" is incompatible with industry and modern urban living.

Generalizations about the functional incompatibility of industry and the structure of the joint family, insofar as they are empirically based, usually cite three kinds of supporting evidence: (1) the prevalence of the nuclear family in industrialized countries, such as England and the United States;

(2) examples of how well adapted the joint family was in an agricultural condition of society; and (3) examples of industrial backwardness in countries where an extended or joint family is prevalent. I have already referred to recent re-examinations of the first kind of evidence in which historians and sociologists have suggested that a nuclear-type family may have preceded industrialization in these countries and that industrialization may actually broaden the network of some kinds of kin ties. There is also a special kind of fallacy to be noted in the use of the second and third kind of evidence. Cases of successful adaptation of the joint family to agricultural conditions are not really comparable to cases of unsuccessful adaptation under industrial conditions. And since the duration and geographical scope of agricultural conditions are so much more extensive than those of industrial ones, the selection is doubly biased: The end product of a prolonged and widespread process of trial-and-error adjustments is compared with the early, sporadic efforts at adapting to industrialization.

A biased selection of the evidence can be avoided and a more adequate understanding achieved of the functional relations between industrialization and the joint family by studying successful industrial families in the context of a society with a strong tradition of joint-family organization. Such a study would trace the histories of successful industrial families in terms of basic social components: residence, household size and composition, maintenance of kin ties, occupational succession, class and subcaste affiliation, education, control and inheritance of joint property, authority structure and household management, religious beliefs and practices, and the like. The patterns of intergenerational persistence or change in these components can then be interpreted in relation to one another and to the associated processes of urbanization, industrialization, and modernization in which the families are involved. The interpretations would not be linear, causal statements about the effects of urbanism or industry on the joint family but would rather analyze the variety of forms that the joint family structure assumes in specific urban and industrial conditions and their adaptive, functional significance under these conditions, and would identify the major variables that might account for the observed variety of adaptations. Generalizations drawn from this kind of study would, of course, be restricted in scope, being limited by the nature of the sample and the stage of industrialization of the society from which it is drawn. They would nevertheless suggest hypotheses about basic processes of adaptive change that could be tested with other family histories in more advanced stages of industrialization.

*Joint family management in Madras industry.* While all of the industrial leaders whom I interviewed were born in villages or small towns, all of them now live in a metropolitan center. The majority, about twelve out of nineteen, live in small nuclear households with their unmarried children. When their daughters marry, they go to live with or near the husband's family. When the sons marry, they are "kicked out" of the parents' home, as one leader who likes American slang described it. The trend to a smaller number of children is unmistakable: In only one case out of eighteen has a leader had significantly more children than his father. He was an only child but has eight children himself. In the other cases, the reverse trend is dominant, usually going from a range of five to eight children for the father to a range of one to three for the son. Belief in, and practice of, birth control are widespread among the leaders. One of them had himself sterilized about twenty-four years ago and persuaded all the male members of his family and about 3,000 of his male employees to do the same. But the move to the city has not destroyed large family households. At least four of the leaders maintain very large joint households, and three others have moderately large ones. When the married sons are "kicked out," they may not be kicked very far. They may be given a bungalow in a family compound or a house nearby. Contact is also maintained with relatives in village and town through visits to them on the occasion of weddings, births, deaths, and other important events, and through donations to a local school, college, clinic, hospital, or temple. Relatives also come to the city for life-cycle rites or to ask for help, and they send children to be raised and educated in the city.

The move into industry has also brought changes in joint-family organization, but it has been accompanied by a carryover and adaptation of traditional joint family principles into the sphere of industrial organization. Except for the public sector industry and one private company, all the companies are family firms, including even the very largest public limited companies in which the controlling family owns only a small fraction of the stock. Effective family control has been maintained through a number of organizational devices, the most important of which are to have the company's affairs managed by a "managing agency" that is owned and controlled by the family, to organize the company as a subsidiary of a "parent" company that is family-controlled, and to appoint members of the family to the managing directorship and to the board of directors of the company. These devices of indirect control are familiar in the United States and Europe, where they have also developed with the separation of ownership from control in the modern corporation. And it is probable that they were introduced into Indian business under British and Western auspices. I should like to suggest, however, that the separation of ownership from control has parallels in the structure of the joint family, which make it relatively easy for Indian joint families to adapt the principles and practices of household management to industrial organization.

Controlling authority in the Indian joint family resides in the family head or manager, usually the father or eldest male. He makes the major decisions on all important questions, including the disposition of joint family property. Generally, he is expected to consult other members of the family, but his decisions are supposed to be binding on all once made. If the manager of the family is the father, he "owns" a portion of the joint family property. His portion may be but a fraction of the whole, since, in the South Indian patrilineal system, he shares the joint family property with his sons, grandsons, and great-grandsons. Each of them has a right to a portion of the joint property when it is divided; a right to ask for a division, if of age, or through his guardian if not; and a right to be consulted on important decisions concerning the management of joint family affairs. Members of the joint family who are not coparceners are entitled to maintenance but do not have a say in the management or in the questions of partition.

The relationship of the manager of a joint family to the coparceners and other family members is thus analogous to the relationship of the managing director of a company to its board of directors and stockholders. In each case, there is a separation of ownership from control. The controlling authority does not necessarily own a major portion of the shares but has the major responsibility for making key policy decisions on the affairs of the group with due consultation. And in each case the maintenance of an undivided, expanding organization depends on the decision-making abilities of the manager and the acceptance of his authority by the "owners."

The structural and organizational parallelism between joint-family management and business management is not merely formal. It is appreciated by the industrial leaders and sometimes made the basis of a direct extension of the same principles from the rural joint-family household into modern industry. In fact, the tables of organization of some of the industrial firms resemble a genealogical chart of the coparceners of joint family property.

The process of extension usually begins with the way in which the father trains his sons. There are seven families among my group who have clearly extended the traditional pattern of joint-family organization in their industries. In three, the father, who was the founder of the family industries, was quite aware of the advantages of joint-family organization in industry and deliberately set about to train his sons from an early age to this pattern. The description of one of these three families is quite characteristic of all of them.

The father, who died in 1955 and was described by one of his sons as a very severe "disciplinarian," had inculcated mutual respect and tolerance in his five sons from an early age. Each son was encouraged to pursue an educational career suited to his interests and abilities in engineering, finance, arts, or business administration. The eldest son lives in the family village and manages the family lands; each of the other four sons has a specialized industrial responsibility, managing a separate operation in the family business. In addition, two grandsons have also been trained and brought into the business, and several others are being trained to come in.

The "founding father" laid down the following rules for the conduct of all family enterprises:

1. No member of the family should have property of his own or outside investments.
2. No member should maintain a separate bank account outside the joint-family account; all of a member's financial transactions should be known to the others.
3. All profits should be reinvested in the family business.
4. Shares in the business should be held only by the descendants in the male line.

5. All the houses and automobiles used by the family should be owned by the company and be made available to family members when they work for the company. In addition, each son's wife could draw a fixed allowance for the expenses of her separate household and for entertainment and travel.

These rules, which are simply an adaptation of traditional joint-family practices to industrial life, were in practice modified in some respects. When the father retired, he sold his holdings in the business, which were equal with those of each son, to his five sons at par value, in equal shares, for about fifteen lakhs of rupees. He then gave the cash to his three daughters. Each son is supposed to provide for a similar division in his will. The procedure is intended to keep the holdings in the family and also to avoid "son-in-law problems." Recently, however, some granddaughters and grandsons have received shares in the business. And, after the father died, the brothers agreed to leave their estate to a family trust, which will then run the business. Such a trust is required under present laws to spend 75 per cent of its holdings for the purposes for which it was created but may retain 25 per cent subject to municipal and business taxes. At present, the family makes a variety of charitable contributions, religious and secular, totaling about two lakhs of rupees per year.

All major company decisions are discussed at informal meetings of the brothers, which take place at least once a month. Decisions require complete consensus, on the assumption that if anyone has a reasonable proposal he should be able to persuade the others. Two members of the third generation, sons of the oldest brother, are already on the board of directors of the company, and several others are being groomed for such posts.

*Cycles of authority*. There are indications that some younger sons, and grandsons, of the present generation of founders are not generally content to follow in their fathers' or grandfathers' footsteps and need to be given scope and opportunity for making their own decisions, if the industrial enterprises are to be kept within the family. In several cases, fathers and grandfathers are aware of the restlessness of the younger generation and have given the young men special projects to manage and develop. One hears of more cases of restlessness among the third generation than among the second generation: Grandsons of founders are more likely to break away from their fathers and the family business than are sons of founders. There is probably an alternating generational cycle at work here that is a function of the structure of authority and affection in the joint family, as modified by the personality of the father and by changing opportunities.

A strong father who has broken with *his* father may succeed in raising his sons as a loyal "band of brothers" who will not break away from him or insist on a division of the family property, even after his death. But the more successful he is in this, the more submissive his sons will have become, and the less authoritarian they will be as fathers. Other things being equal, this is probably the "psychodynamic" explanation of the relatively greater rebelliousness of the third generation over the second.

Other things are rarely equal, however. A man may not have enough sons, or opportunities for industrial leadership may change from generation to generation and in relation to opportunities for political and other kinds of leadership. The recent emergence of industry as a field for leadership in Madras is underlined by the fact that, of the nineteen leaders interviewed, eight were of the first generation of their family in industry, ten were of the second generation, and only one was of the third generation.

In starting industrial enterprises, the present generation of seven founders departed from traditional family occupations and started on new paths. It is therefore relevant to ask whether the founders also "broke" psychologically with their fathers. The information on this point is quite interesting. In one case, the father strongly disapproved the son's occupational choice; in three cases, the sons quarreled with the fathers and left home between the ages of seventeen and twenty-one to make their own way in Madras City. Two quarrels concerned the father's alienation of the mother's affections by taking a concubine or a second wife. In the third quarrel, the son set up a new household at the age of eighteen with his mother and his mother's brother just one year after arriving in Madras City. The mother's brother was also his partner in the firm he eventually founded.

In two other cases, the fathers had died when the sons were still young, aged six months and thirteen years, respectively. One of the fatherless boys was raised in Colombo, Ceylon, by his mother's brother, who also became his father-in-law and initiated him into trade and money-lending. When he started his own industrial enterprise, he took as a partner his mother's sister's husband. The second fatherless boy was raised by an elder brother, whom he eventually took as a partner in his first industrial venture.

Six of the seven leaders who were founders, then, did experience some kind of psychological break with their fathers. Of the twelve "nonfounders," two mentioned having lost their fathers while still young and none mentioned quarrels with the fathers. One leader who lost his father was raised and adopted by one of his father's brothers, was taken into the family business, and is now a managing director of one of the family's industrial subsidiaries. In the second case, the father died when the son was seven; the boy was sent to Madras City to be raised and educated by his mother's brother, who had already founded a successful family business in trade. He has since succeeded his uncle as leader of the family business. None of the other ten nonfounding leaders seemed to have experienced a psychological break with his father, or at least none revealed any special feeling about the problem. All but one are continuing in the family business.

The role of substitute father in cases where a leader lost or quarreled with his father and left home was taken by a mother's brother in three cases, by an elder brother in one case, by a father's brother in one case, by employers in two cases, and by an unspecified person in the last case. The substitute father generally also initiated the boy into business and became closely associated with him in an industrial career. What kind of person became the substitute father depended in part on the reasons for the break with the father and in part on the availability of brothers, uncles, sympathetic employers, and others.

Before we conclude, however, as some American studies have done, that a psychological break with the father is a necessary or sufficient condition for industrial leadership, we should remember that most of the ten nonfounders who presumably suffered no psychological break with the father have already demonstrated effective and successful industrial leadership. We also need more information than we have about whether the founding fathers of nonfounders experienced a break with *their* fathers, as well as information about the relations of the present founders with their sons and about the sons who broke with their fathers and did not become industrial leaders.

### *Conclusion on the Joint Family in Industry*

Until quite recently, a prevailing sociological theory asserted that the joint and extended family structure was everywhere and inevitably transformed into nuclear family structures under the influence of urbanization and industrialization. The theory was based on the alleged history of such transformations in Europe and the United States and on the alleged functional incompatibilities of joint and extended family structures with such requirements of urban and industrial life as residential and occupational mobility, a highly complex and specialized division of labor, a monetized economy, advanced scientific and technical training, large capital requirements, and corporate organization. The comparative studies by social anthropologists of diverse family systems did not at first seriously challenge this theory, because they dealt chiefly with the simpler societies and because they tended to concentrate on synchronic analysis of presumably stable social systems. The situation generated a series of false dilemmas between generalization and comparison, between worldwide uniformities and regional and cultural diversities, and between structural transformation and structural stability. Only as sociologists have become interested in the comparative studies of social systems, and social anthropologists in structural change within complex societies, have these false dilemmas ceased to dominate discussion and has a more productive convergence of sociological and anthropological approaches begun to develop.

The method of analyzing family histories has been used by sociologists and social historians to study social and occupational mobility. It has also been used in genetics and medicine to trace pedigree patterns in the inheritance of selected traits. In social anthropology, however, the approach, known after W. H. R. Rivers as the "genealogical method," has been somewhat arbitrarily restricted to oral genealogies and the synchronic study of social systems. Rivers himself did not so restrict the method but looked upon it as a promising way to get data for recent social history.[17] I should like to suggest that Rivers's genealogical method, if freed from the synchronic restriction, does indeed offer a powerful means of collecting social data for the study of both structural change and structural continuity of family systems and of other kinds of social structure. It seems to be an especially appropriate method for the study of what happens to the Indian joint family in an urban and industrial setting.

In a preliminary application of the method to study a group of outstandingly successful industrial leaders in Madras City, I found that, while there have been striking changes within three generations in residential, occupational, educational, and social mobility, as well as in patterns of ritual observances, the changes have not transformed the traditional joint-family structure into isolated nuclear families. On the contrary, the urban and industrial members of a family maintain numerous ties and obligations with the members of the family who have remained in the ancestral village or town or have moved elsewhere. And within the urban and industrial setting, a modified joint-family organization is emerging. The metropolitan industrial center has simply become a new arena for the working of the joint-family system.

The natural history of the process is similar to the changing relations of the "stem" and "branch" families in Japan, although primogeniture is not a regular feature of the Indian joint family. When a member of the Indian joint family first moves to the city and goes into industry, he may become a "deviant" and peripheral outpost in relation to his family's ancestral seat and traditional occupation. As he succeeds and prospers, however, when he marries, begets children, and builds an urban house and an industrial empire, he soon establishes a "branch" center in relation to the ancestral estate. Eventually, as ties with the natal village or town become attenuated and as more relatives move into the city and into industrial occupations, the urban "branch" may become a new "stem" sending out new shoots into other cities and towns with every new branch office or plant of the family company.

This natural history is characterized by the operation of adaptive processes, some of which change the structure of the traditional joint-family system and some of which minimize the conflicts with the new conditions. Among the adaptive processes identified in Madras are *compartmentalization* of the domestic and social sphere as "traditional and religious" and of the industrial sphere as "modern and secular"; *vicarious ritualization;* the separation of ownership and control both in the organization of the family and in the organization of the industrial corporation; and the extension of the practices and principles of household management of the rural joint family to business management.*

The possibility and effectiveness of these adaptations depend on the existence of structural congruities between the joint family system and the requirements of modern industry and urban life; upon the intelligence, motivation, and ability of the actors; and upon a favorable legal structure and climate of opinion.

It is perfectly true that modern industry in India is characterized generally by such features as urban location, the separation of place of work from the place of residence, a widely extended market for products and services, a monetized economy with an institutionalized credit system, a

* See p. 315 ff. below.

complex division of labor and an occupational structure based on highly specialized technology requiring scientific research and technical training, a separation of legal ownership from management, and a hierarchical structure of management interested in the intergenerational continuity of the enterprise. But it is not at all true that the joint-family system is structurally and functionally incompatible with these features of modern industry and therefore either is a major obstacle to the development of industry or is inevitably destroyed by the progress of industry. On the contrary, the foregoing evidence drawn from the family histories of successful Madras industrial leaders suggests that the traditional joint-family system and many of the practices associated with it offer some distinct advantages for organizing an industrial enterprise.

The joint family provides a nucleus of capital that can be used for the technical and specialized education of its members, for starting new ventures, and for operating or expanding existing industries. In the living four generations of a common ancestor, his sons, grandsons, and great-grandsons who constitute the coparceners of joint-family property at a given time, the family provides a well-structured pattern of authority, succession, and inheritance based on the relationships of father and sons, brother and brother, uncle and nephew. This structure, as it turns out, also meets many of the requirements of industrial organization for direction, management, diversification, and continuity. Decisions can be taken by mutual consultation and consensus. The varied talents of family members can be trained and utilized for a variety of industrial operations—fiscal, administrative, or engineering, as the case may be—within the parent company and in the establishment of subsidiaries. As older members retire and withdraw from active life, the continuity of capital and management is replenished from the pool of joint-family friends and personnel. With a living horizon of three or four generations visible at any given time and its extensibility into the future limited only by the family's fertility, the scope for industrial foresight and planning seems practically unlimited.

The structural congruence between joint-family organization and the organization of industrial firms seems at first sight to be so great that one wonders how the opinion of their inherent incompatibility ever got started. The harmonies I have sketched are to be found in the hypothetical "ideal" circumstances only. In practice, there may be many disturbing factors: an insufficiency of mutual trust and cooperation among the coparceners, an insufficiency of sons and grandsons, or inadequacies of ability and motivation. In addition to the internal failures, there are the external disturbances emanating from discouraging laws and taxes, public criticism, unfavorable economic conditions, industrial problems including the growing capital requirements, and threats of nationalization. In view of many sources of possible disturbance of the "ideal" pattern of adjustment, it is surprising to find, among the cases of our industrial leaders, several approximations of the "ideal."

The relative frequency of occurrence of joint families versus nuclear families in industry, however, has not been a major interest here. This study has not been a statistical survey but an analysis of a few identified families that have produced successful industrial leaders. The main interest of the analysis has been in the ways in which these families have functionally adapted their preindustrial social structures to industry, in the varied range of their adaptations, and in the major variable factors that account for this range. Among the factors, we have identified the following as perhaps the most important: the demographic patterns of births and deaths in particular family lines; the patterns of child-rearing, especially of sons by fathers; the occurrence of "pioneer" types of personalities; the availability of economic opportunities; the tax structure and the legal framework generally; national industrial policy; and the attitudes of public opinion toward family dynasties in industry. Secular and religious ideologies play their part, too, but chiefly through their influence on the other factors. Hinduism, as such, is not a major factor, although the way in which specific Hindu rites and doctrines have been adapted by these industrial families shows analogies with Max Weber's analysis of the relation of the Protestant ethic to the rise of European capitalism.

The internal and external limitations on the joint family in industry are not absolute or decisive. They must be taken into account in assessing the future of the family firm, but they may also be modified by counterefforts. The Hindu Code's admission of daughters to equal inheritance with sons, for example, would seem to undermine the patrilineal, patrilocal kind of joint-family organization of industry by bringing in daughters and their husbands and children. Yet there is no intrinsic reason why the patrilineal, patrilocal family pattern should not eventually adapt itself to the broader pattern if it proves functional for industrial organization. In fact, I have noted several cases where sons-in-law have been brought into the business because there were not enough sons available. It is likely that urban residence patterns will minimize the distance married daughters move away from the parental household. The psychological tension between father-in-law and son-in-law is not in any case any greater than that between father and sons, and the tension among brothers-in-law is probably no greater than that among brothers.

The reluctance of sons to follow their fathers' occupational careers can also be neutralized, as some of the industrialists have found, by giving the sons responsibilities that will satisfy their desires for challenge, initiative, and independence.

In any case, the future of the Indian joint family in industry does not depend on the conversion of Hindus to a Protestant ethic or on the increasing spread of nuclear-type families. Such changes may only change the specific forms of family organization without destroying the family principle. What is more likely to destroy the family basis of industrial organization is a tax policy that makes it impossible for families to accumulate sufficient capital for starting or expanding a business, or a policy of nationalizing the private-sector industries. Although many of the industrial leaders said that they would be willing to continue as managers of public-sector industries in the event of nationalization, one wonders whether their motivations would not undergo profound changes if their industrial activity were completely divorced from family organization.

## The Roles of Caste, Class, and Traditional Occupation

A surprising feature of the caste affiliations among the Madras industrial leaders is the disproportionate number of Brahmans, nine out of nineteen. The number is unexpected in terms of both the scriptural theory of traditional caste occupations and the alleged conflicts between the strict ritual requirements of a Brahman's daily routine and a career in industry.

In Madras, and in India generally, industrial organization is perhaps too recent a development to be considered the traditional occupation of any caste. Yet it seems plausible that the castes whose traditional occupation has been trade and money-lending would be the most qualified and most likely to take to industrial enterprise and that the traditional artisan castes would become the skilled labor force for industry, leaving the unskilled jobs for the untouchables.

Quite apart from the fact that this *varṇa* theory of industrial organization makes no place for Brahmans or Kṣatriyas in industry, it does not account for the actual caste distribution among the Madras industrial leaders. Another theory is needed to explain these facts. One explanation usually given in South India for the presence of Brahmans in business and industry is the discrimination against them in government service, political office, and the universities, which was introduced by special legislation and anti-Brahman political movements. With these opportunities closed, so the argument goes, ambitious and able Brahmans have turned to commerce and industry for new opportunities.

That argument is certainly plausible and probably applies statistically to a general trend. It is not, however, well confirmed by the specific cases in hand. Not one of the Brahman industrial leaders gave this reason for his or his family's entry into commerce or industry. The reasons they did give seemed to have little to do with such an explanation. One Brahman family, for example, had gone into trade two generations before because the grandfather was so orthodox that he could not perform his regular ritual observances under the restrictions of any kind of government office routine. Another Brahman had come into industry only after retiring from government service, and a third had turned his attention to industrial development because he became convinced that it was the best way for India to solve its many economic problems.

Four of the Brahman families had come from such localities of Tirunelvēli District as Kalliḍaikkuṟicci and Āḻvārkkuṟicci, where Brahmans have been noted as traders and bankers for more than 300 years. It does not require any reference to anti-Brahman movements to explain why a Brahman from this area goes into business and industry. In the eighth case, there was no background of government or professional service in the family, and, because of the father's early death, the son had had no opportunity for professional education.

Out of nine, then, there is only one Brahman family in which the shift from government service and the higher professions into business and industry may have been influenced by recent anti-Brahman discrimination, although even in this case such pressure is not acknowledged.

It is quite likely that the effects of anti-Brahman discrimination will become more noticeable in the future when the generation of children now in school grows up.

Present political agitation in Madras State against Brahmans by the Dravidian political parties extends to Brahmans in business as well as to those in the professions and in government service, and Brahman industrialists will occasionally lose government contracts as a result. Since large-scale industry is regulated by all-India laws, however, the Brahman industrialists in Madras at the time of my study were not yet greatly alarmed by the agitation, especially if their factory was outside the limits of the city, then under DMK control. Some of them make financial contributions to the DMK, even if they personally prefer the Congress Party or the Swatantra Party. They are in any case willing to deal realistically with some of the DMK-controlled trade unions in their plants. One of the Brahman industrialists boasted that he was on very friendly terms with the leaders of the DMK union in his factories and that they found no reasons to oppose him, since he treated them in a sincere and friendly manner and even invited them to dine with him at his house.

The variety of castes and communities among the industrial leaders, as well as the relatively large number of Brahmans among them, may be peculiar to Madras City and its history. The second largest industrial center in Madras State, Kōyamputtūr, is said to be dominated by Nāyaḍus, with practically no Brahmans and only a few Ceṭṭiyars in industrial leadership. Among entrepreneurs in medium and small-scale industry in the State as a whole, however, a recent study reports that after Nāyaḍus, Brahmans had established the largest number of firms. The frequencies of firms for different communities is given in Table 1.[18]

Table 1
Distribution of Entrepreneurs According to Social Community

| Community | Frequency[a] |
|---|---|
| Nāyaḍu | 21 |
| Brahman | 12 [b] |
| Ceṭṭiyar | 8 |
| Nāyakkar | 3 |
| Punjabi | 2 [c] |
| Christian | 2 [d] |
| Gujarātī | 1 |
| Kaundan | 1 |
| Ācāri | 1 |
| Muslim | 1 |
| Total | 52 |

[a] Refers to number of firms established by entrepreneurs in each category.
[b] Includes one partnership between two Brahmans and a Christian.
[c] Established by the same individual.
[d] One of these entrepreneurs is a European permanently settled in India.

The "overrepresentation" of Brahmans among the industrial leaders cannot be explained by the *varna* theory of traditional caste occupations or by the recent anti-Brahman movements in the State. Nor can such explanations account for the presence among the industrial leaders of members of two South Indian peasant castes, two Muslims, and a Syrian Christian. In fact they explain only the presence of the Ceṭṭiyars and the Gujarātī, who claim trade and banking as the traditional occupation of their castes. If, therefore, there is some common factor that predisposes a man toward entry into industry and success, it is not trade as a traditional caste occupation but something else. On the basis of an analysis of the social backgrounds of the Madras industrial leaders, I believe that the common factor is to be found in the previous occupation, and the experience, training, and education of the individual leaders and of their families.

### *The Roles of Previous Occupation, Experience, and Education*

The Madras data offer substantial support for the argument above. Thirteen of the industrial leaders I studied had come into industry from banking or trade as a previous occupation. The group includes six of the Brahmans, three of the Ceṭṭiyars, the Mudaliyār, the Gujarātī, the Syrian Christian, and one of the Muslims. Four came in from government service; two of them were Brahmans, one was the Andhra Kamma, and the other was the second Muslim. With one possible exception, their work in government service had given them specialized training and experience and knowledge that was directly relevant for their later careers in industry.

The banking and trade group includes four in deposit and commercial banking, one in stock brokerage and investment banking, one in shipping, and two with car and bicycle agencies. Those from government service include two former Indian Civil Service (ICS) men, one Member of Parliament, and one railroad engineer. Two of the four who had been employees worked as chartered accountants, one worked for an electrical firm, and one for a textile firm. Two of the leaders had entered industry directly after their professional training.

The leaders' identification of their father's and grandfather's occupations tends to support the same pattern. Eleven of the fathers were classified in trade and banking, four in government service, and three as landlords. The fathers' fathers' occupations were given as commerce for seven, government service for two, and law for two; one was identified as a "Sanskrit pandit," another as a "Tamil poet," the rest as landlords.

Education is almost as relevant for a successful industrial career as previous occupation and experience, although specialized scientific and technical education is a recent development. Early training and socialization is also important. The founding fathers who had "escaped" their own fathers' domination seemed to have been in a majority. On the other hand, as fathers they had been the most successful in socializing their own sons into the methods and ways of business. Among this group were Brahmans, the Syrian Christian, and members of other castes, although early inculcation of methodical business disciplines is a long-standing custom only among the Cețțiyar trading castes.

A college education is not—or, in the present leadership generation, was not—an essential prerequisite for industrial leadership, judging from the educational background of the Madras industrialists. Five of the nineteen had never been to any kind of college, and three of the five are "founders." Of the fourteen who had had some college education, eight had specialized (two as chartered accountants, three as Bachelors of Science, two as Masters of Arts in economics, and one in automotive engineering). Of the four "founders" in the college-educated group, three had had some specialized education and one had not. Within this group, there seems to have been no specialized education that particularly qualified a man for industrial leadership. One chartered accountant is a "founder" and another is not. Of the three Bachelors of Science, one was a "founder," but none seemed to think that his specialized scientific education had prepared him for his industrial role, and two of them, in fact, had shifted to advanced work in economics and politics. The third said that, if he were reborn, about the only change he would make would be to take a degree in economics instead of in geology. Those who had taken advanced degrees in economics seemed to make good use of their training in the analysis of industrial problems for specific industries as well as the problems of industrial development in India generally. Three of the leaders had taught themselves engineering; one had done so despite the lack of previous college training, one on the basis of an arts degree, and one on the basis of a Bachelor of Science in geology and an M.A. in arts. Some experience in related occupations and in the technical training programs sponsored by the British in India during World War II had given them the opportunity for this specialized learning. Only the automotive engineer had passed directly from his specialized training into a line of work in his father's enterprise that made full use of his training.

Over a four-generation perspective, there is a definite upgrading of educational qualifications, as well as a tendency for the families to specialize in engineering and scientific fields. None of the fathers or grandfathers of the industrial leaders without college education had any college education themselves. On the other hand, all the sons of these leaders are college-trained or are now in college, and in at least three of the families, the sons have received technical engineering training in England.

Of the fathers of the fourteen industrial leaders who had had some college education, five had had some college, four had had none, and in five cases the information was not definite. Of the paternal grandfathers, seven had not been to college, four had received legal training, and the information was not available in the other cases. Two of the grandfathers without college training—the "Sanskrit pandit" and the "Tamil poet"—had attained a high level of learning within the traditional culture.

The sons of the college-educated leaders have, for the most part, exceeded their fathers in level of education completed, in degree of specialization in science and engineering, and in specialized study abroad. For example, nine of the fourteen leaders have sons who have been trained in engineering or in industrial chemistry; in six of these cases, the specialized education was received in England or the United States. In several cases where the sons are now in school, the fathers are planning to send them abroad for scientific or technical training. One thirteen-year-old, the son of a leader with about two years in a commercial college, is being prepared to enter Harvard.

The opportunities for specialized scientific and technical training abroad have been increased by technical collaboration agreements between the Indian firms and American, English, Japanese, French, Swiss, and German counterparts. Seventeen of the nineteen Madras leaders' companies have such collaboration agreements with foreign industrial firms. These agreements, usually drawn for a ten-year period, provide that two or three Indian specialists per year will be sent abroad for training and that foreign consultants will be sent to train and advise Indian specialists in India. The technical collaboration agreements have become the main channels for the transfer of foreign technical skills and probably rival the formal educational channels, although the Indians who receive highly specialized training under these agreements have usually already completed their advanced technical training, either in India or abroad.

While the industrial leaders are generally too busy to take time off for extended periods of training, their frequent trips abroad to negotiate agreements, as well as to look for markets or products, have given them opportunities to learn about new technical processes and products and the organization of industry. One leader, who has played an active role in Madras's industrial spurt between 1957 and 1965, testified that his observation of European and American factories during a U.N.-sponsored tour had convinced him of the importance of industrial development for India's future.

The tendency for particular families to upgrade their educational level over several generations and for their members to follow closely related lines of specialization is, of course, nothing new. What is new is the kind of education and specialization followed. The influence of modern education is being channeled through particular family lines. In the father's or grandfather's generation, "modern education" meant education in the arts and sciences for positions in the civil service or in law, teaching, medicine, or chartered accounting. In the present generation, it has come to mean specialized, usually postgraduate, education in economics, science, engineering, or business administration. The son who wants to study comparative literature, say, is considered a deviant and has to be brought back into the family line of specialization.

How this transition from the "older modern" to the "newer modern" education has been made is illustrated by one family. Law and government figure in the careers of the older generation—the father and grandfather and the father's five brothers had all been in government service, primarily in railway offices. Five brothers-in-law in the industrialist's generation were also in government service; one brother was a teacher, another a lawyer. The brothers' and sisters' sons and the leader's own children reflect the newer trend toward a specialized technical profession. The industrialist's son has a Ph.D. in chemistry, as does his elder brother's son; a younger brother's son is an electrical engineer. Among his four sisters' sons, four are engineers; one holds a Ph.D. in chemistry and works for the Indian Atomic Energy Commission; and one is a medical officer in the Air Force. A university professor, a government administrator, and an army officer are also among them. The occupations of the younger generation also illustrate the diversification of government services, which are coming to include many different kinds of highly trained technical professions.

Where the industrial leader's own family does not provide enough scientific and technical personnel for a company, and usually it does not, specialized members of other families are employed. The personnel manager in one of the firms had a grandfather who was a teacher; his father was a civil engineer, and his father's two brothers are engineers. Of his own brothers, one is an engineer, one a mathematician, one a geographer, and one an eye, ear, nose and throat specialist. All of his mother's sisters had married university teachers, and all of their children had married doctors. His wife's brother is a world-famous scientist living abroad, and his wife's uncle is a famous Indian scientist. His own sons are being given modern technical education.

The family of an eye surgeon in the medical center maintained by one of the companies for its employees shows an equally remarkable degree of specialization. The surgeon's grandfather was a village officer, and his father was an engineer. His father had four brothers; the eldest was the village officer, the second a photographer, the third an automotive engineer, and the fourth operated a fleet of buses. Two of his own brothers and his sister's husband are also engineers, and another brother is a cotton specialist. Among his and his brothers' and sisters' children, eleven are engineers (civil, mining, marine, radio, mechanical, and chemical). The photographer uncle's two sons are also engineers.

These family specializations in engineering and scientific fields are providing a pool of the specialized skills needed in modern industry. As industry becomes more and more dependent on science and technical research, its rapidly changing character may render any particular scientific specialty obsolete. At present, however, the tendency for industrial families in India to concentrate on scientific and technical education for their children is functional for industrial development.

### *Growth Patterns of Industrial Enterprises*

Individual industrialists and their families have put together the components of previous occupation, experience, and education in different ways to build their respective enterprises. Their different adaptations to changing opportunities have resulted in different industrial growth patterns. Those who were in trade or banking, for example, had frequently had opportunities to learn something about manufacturing processes, costs, market conditions, new ventures, and sources of capital. A striking example is the small bus operation begun by the father of one of the industrialists in 1912. By 1916 the father had also become a dealer in tires and automobile parts imported from the United States, and by 1922 a dealer in cars and trucks. With a General Motors franchise, he organized his firm as a private limited company in 1929 and added auto insurance and financing to the trucking and bus service and the auto and truck dealership. In 1930, he started to manufacture automobile bodies, and in 1936, auto parts. Service and gasoline stations were added in 1939, retreading of tires in 1943. Thus, by 1946, when he launched a full-fledged automobile plant in Madras City, he had already accumulated a great deal of practical knowledge about the financing, operation, servicing, and manufacture of motor vehicles and their components. Although he had some college education, it was not until two of his sons in the 1930's and, later, two of his grandsons studied for several years at an institute of technology in the United States that there was an injection of specialized scientific and technical knowledge into the operations of the company. Three other sons who have had some college education without specialization are also in the business. One of the three, who had not finished college but who had made himself into a "finance pandit" by voracious reading, is most ambitious to expand the family enterprises into a great industrial empire.

A somewhat different growth pattern from trade and banking is illustrated by the father and grandfather of one of the Ceṭṭiyar leaders. With a little schooling, the grandfather had entered business at the age of fourteen and had accumulated before he died about a crore of rupees through overseas banking and the purchase of 30,000 acres of paddy land in Burma, Ceylon, and Indochina. He brought his three sons into the business during World War I while they were still in their teens. Before the outbreak of World War II, anticipating the instability and turbulence that came to Southeast Asia, they transferred their banking operations to Madras City and started a small manufacturing industry there in 1938. By 1949, they were able to negotiate collaboration agreements with British and American firms for the manufacture of bicycle tire tubes, cycle saddles, diamond chains, dynamo sets, lamps, and other useful parts. Three of the grandsons were sent to England for technical training in the collaborating British plants and are now in the family business; one grandson, the leader in question, entered the business at nineteen when he graduated from Presidency College in Madras with a Bachelor of Science in geology. Each of the grandsons had served a practical apprenticeship in the business for about five years before being given managerial responsibility for one of the company's subsidiaries. There is probably a good deal of plausibility to the argument that the family's experience in commercial banking has given its males practical knowledge in handling money and taking risks, as well as insight into a wide variety of industries.

A third example illustrates growth arising from government service. In this case, the leader had served in the ICS for twenty-five years before entering industry. During his ICS career he had become an adviser on industrial development in Madras State, and during World War II he was in charge of technical manpower training. His practical experience, coupled with a B.S. and an M.A. from British universities, enabled him after the war to develop a group of industries that manufacture sugar, cement, industrial machinery, and other products. His father and grandfather were landlords holding about 200 acres in a village not far from

Madras City. He was the first in his family to receive a higher education and go into the ICS. All his brothers and sisters still live in or near the native village. His two sons were both trained at the Massachusetts Institute of Technology, one in chemical engineering and the other in business administration, and were brought into his business; they live in Madras City near their father. His daughter married an MIT graduate whose father is an industrialist in another part of the state, where she now lives. Her three sons are in a local technical institute and will be sent to MIT, where they will be trained to go into her husband's and father-in-law's business.

These three growth patterns, as well as those of the other companies, show how entrepreneurial families make the transition from a predominantly agricultural society to industry. Capital, special knowledge, and experience are accumulated from land, money-lending, trade, or government service. These resources are used to start a small industrial firm. Then, as the firm expands and sons and grandsons, or other relatives, are educated and brought in, the firm is usually converted into a private limited company, and after that into a public limited company with diversified interests in a number of related enterprises controlled by a family managing agency or in other ways. Fourteen of the seventeen private-sector family companies followed this growth pattern. The three exceptions followed similar growth pattern but had been established by British entrepreneurs in 1786, 1889, and 1925, respectively.

### *Emergence of an Entrepreneurial Class in Madras City*

The different backgrounds of the industrial leaders and the different paths by which they came into industry strongly suggest that factors such as individual and family experience, previous occupation, education, and capital in relation to available opportunities have been more decisive than caste affiliation and traditional caste occupation in the recruiting of the industrial leadership of Madras City and in favoring successful careers. In some cases, traditional caste occupation may have predisposed a family to the acquisition of such a background, but in most cases there has been a departure from traditional caste occupation. Industrial entrepreneurship is not, therefore, the preserve of any particular caste or traditional "business community" but has attracted able individuals from several castes, including Brahmans and cultivating castes whose traditional occupations would at first glance seem to be quite remote from industry. The association of members of these castes with industry cannot be explained by invoking a general theory of caste and caste occupation but can be explained by detailed individual and family life histories and the social, economic, and political history of Madras City. The ways in which family histories are related to the growth patterns of individual industries has already been suggested. A brief sketch of the commercial and industrial history of Madras will indicate how an indigenous class of entrepreneurs drawn from several different castes arose and how the qualifications, orientations, and organization of this class have been changing.[19]

The East India Company came to India for trade, as did the other

European companies, although Vasco da Gama said he came to find Christians as well as spices. Francis Day picked the site of Madras City in 1639 for the English company, because it was a region noted for superior weavers and dyers and one where printed chintz and blue cloth could be bought for less than the Dutch had to pay at Masūlippaṭṭaṇam. The officers of the East India Company were primarily traders until the end of the eighteenth century. They used Indian merchants as brokers who made cash advances to weavers for the production of cloth to be exported and also sold imports from Europe. For the official company trade, "chief merchants" were appointed; they in turn sent junior merchants through the countryside. For their private trade, the company officers employed Indian "Dubashes," as well as "free merchants" licensed by the Company. The free merchants included British, Portuguese, Jewish, Armenian, and other traders.

The chief Dubash for Dupleix, the French Governor of Pondicherry, was Ānanda Raṅga Piḷḷai, who recorded in his diary that "the merchants are all Chettis, Komutti, Brahmans, and Guzaratis; those in the company's service are mostly Brahmans and Vellalas." [20] He contrasted the Hindus, who were the company's merchants, held all the "big appointments," and were wealthy, with the Christians, who "form only a sixteenth of all the people here, and all are poor" save the family of one Christian Dubash. Brahmans thus seem to have been active in Madras trade from the early days of the company, along with Ceṭṭiyars, Vēḷāḷars, and other South Indian castes.

By 1710, there were twenty-nine free merchants among the residents of Fort Saint George, and some of them were in silent partnership with East India Company officers. Several of the famous British firms, such as Parry and Company and Binny and Company, originated in this way.

The free merchants, chief merchants, and Dubashes started meeting together very early. In 1673 they met twice a week in Blacktown, the ancestor of the present Georgetown. In the 1670's chief merchant Kasi Verona formed a joint stock company with seventy-five other merchants. They raised capital to the extent of 20,000 pagodas (gold coins), which was divided into 200 shares. The affairs of the company were managed by twelve representatives of the shareholders, who sent out twenty junior merchants to purchase cloth and sell European imports. These early merchants came from various castes and communities—Ceṭṭiyars, Nāyakkars, Mudaliyārs, and Piḷḷais, as well as Brahmans.

The office of chief merchant was abolished by the East India Company in 1775, and special company servants were appointed to deal with the weavers directly and to sell the company's goods. In 1800, all company servants were forbidden to trade privately, and by 1813 the East India trade was opened to all free merchants. In 1833 another charter took the company out of trade and turned it into an administrative body.

The decline of the company's trade monopoly and trading activities left the field open to the free merchants and former chief merchants and their assistants. Private merchants, primarily European, organized the Madras Chamber of Commerce in 1836 to express and protect their common interests. The Indian merchants did not organize a chamber of commerce until 1909, when the failure of a leading British bank in Madras shook Indian confidence in British integrity and competence and gave Indians the courage and the opportunity to organize an Indian bank in Madras City. This bank, the Indian Bank, was organized by a Smārta Brahman in collaboration with Ceṭṭiyars, Mudaliyārs, and other castes.

The distribution of castes in Madras business before World War I showed a pattern similar to the current one. A directory of leading Madras business houses published in 1914 lists, as one gathers from the names, sixteen Ceṭṭiyars, eight Tamil Brahmans, four other South Indian Brahmans, eight Muslims, seven Mudaliyārs, four Nāyaḍus, four "Dosses," two Paṭēls, and a scattering of individual Christians, Pārsīs, Siṅghs, and other castes and communities. Apart from the concentration of seven of the Ceṭṭiyars in commerce and banking and five of the Muslims in hides and skins, there is no other pattern of caste or community concentration. The majority of the businesses were selling operations, but several included manufacturing as well: wood, printing, carriages, textile mills, motor cars, and bicycles. The earliest printer in this group started business in 1863, and the earliest textile mill was begun in 1883.[21]

With the coming of Swạdeshi and the growth of the national movement, a new class of Indians was also attracted to commerce and industry. It entered the field for patriotic reasons—to help make India economically independent and able to compete with European manufacturers. "The older type of Indian businessman is often very astute, but his methods are not of the best. The new type is usually not a man of affairs at all but rather an academic person who happens to be an enthusiast for the development of indigenous enterprise and the defeat of what he considers 'the exploitation of India.' "[22]

The creation of imperial and provincial departments of industry after World War I, the winning of independence, and the several five-year plans have brought this type to the fore, not so much in the private sector as in the public sector and in various state and central government agencies. The academic type of industrial leader is no more drawn from particular castes and communities than is the practical type, although, being educated for and connected with government service, he may now often come from those castes and communities that have sent most members to the universities and into government service.

In the private sector as well as in the public, another type of industrial entrepreneur is now emerging: the engineer and technician. This type has been rising since independence, especially in small light industries such as die casting, electroplating, enameling, woodworking, foundry forges, and tool and die making. It has been greatly helped by the government-financed "industrial estates," which provide factory space, capital, training, experience, and research and marketing information. Industrial estates have been successful in Madras State in attracting entrepreneurs and productive capital. By the end of the Second Five-Year Plan, there were nine estates with 237 factory units in the state and an investment in production of 8.61 crores of rupees. One hundred twenty-eight of the units are in the Guindy estate just outside of Madras City; 283 more factory units in thirteen new estates have been sanctioned under the Third Plan. Ninety-one of them will be located in Madras City District.

In the field of small- and medium-scale industry, the entrepreneur with engineering or scientific training is appearing with greater frequency. Among the fifty-two firms, small and medium, in Berna's study, the largest number were established by graduate engineers (see Table 2).

Table 2
Distribution of Entrepreneurs According to Immediate Economic and Technical Background [23]

| Entrepreneurial Background | Frequency |
|---|---|
| Rural artisans | 5 |
| Domestic merchants | 10 |
| Factory workmen | 6 |
| Graduate engineers | 12 |
| Importers | 5 |
| Manufacturers | 4 |
| Cultivators | 4 |
| Miscellaneous | 6 |

NOTE: Frequency refers to number of firms established by entrepreneurs in each category.

Among the leaders of the large industrial firms I studied in Madras City, the graduate engineer is in the minority. Only one of the leaders had been trained in engineering (automotive), although three others had taught themselves engineering. Among their sons, nephews, and grandsons, however, the trend toward engineering and scientific training runs very strong.

The foregoing historical sketch is not intended to be a commercial and industrial history of Madras City. Instead, I wanted to suggest that detailed historical studies of commercial and industrial developments are needed to trace the association of the members of particular castes and communities with particular economic activities. Such histories should take their point of departure from specific economic developments and the specific ways in which particular families have become associated with them, rather than begin with general histories of castes and communities, valuable as these may be for other purposes. A history of the textile industry in Kōyamputtūr or in Madurai and of the specific Nāyaḍu or Ceṭṭiyar families that have been most active in it, for example, would be more relevant than a general history of the Nāyaḍus or Ceṭṭiyars as a "business community." Similarly, a history of specific industrial developments in Madras City and of the particular individuals and families most active in them would be more illuminating than a history of Brahmans, Ceṭṭiyars, or Mudaliyārs as "business communities." It is not an entire community that develops specific lines of economic activity, but only a small number of families and individuals from within that community. And even where traditional occupations may predispose members of a particular community to go into one line of economic activity rather than another, as in the case of Ceṭṭiyar money-lending and trade, it is still only a small and highly localized fraction of the community that may be so "predisposed" by special experience, abilities, opportunities, and other circumstances as to take the lead (for example, those Ceṭṭiyars who developed banking and commerce in Southeast Asia before World War II, or the Kalliḍaikkuṟicci Brahmans who developed manufacturing industries in Madras City). We need localized occupational histories of these families and individuals rather than "community" histories that prejudge the role of caste in economic activity.

### *Does the Caste System Persist in Industry?*

The question of the caste system in industry has two facets: (1) To what extent do the industrial leaders tend to give preference to members of their own caste or religious community in recruitment and promotion of employees? (2) To what extent does the distribution of employees in a factory accord with traditional caste occupations?

It is generally assumed around Madras City that industrial leaders give preference in recruiting and promotion to members of their own subcastes and religious communities. A "Brahman firm" is said to hire Brahmans; a "non-Brahman firm," non-Brahmans; and a "Christian firm," Christians. The leaders deny this. Most of them claim to follow enlightened personnel policies based on professional job classifications, and specialized skill, knowledge, and training requirements. Some of them observe that, because their firms have branches in several different states and sell their products all over India to different castes and communities, they are obliged to select their employees on a national basis as well. One Brahman estimated, however, that from 60 to 70 per cent of his office staff and about 4 per cent of the factory workers were Brahmans. A Ceṭṭiyar leader estimated that about 150 of his 3,000 employees were Ceṭṭiyars.

To reconcile these divergent views is not easy, since the problem is essentially a statistical one, and accurate statistics are not easy to come by. It is especially difficult to compile statistics that accurately measure the role of such relevant factors as education, training, skill, and experience. If a member of a particular caste or community has been given preference over a member of another, is it because of his caste or because of his superior education and skill? We know that in the past some of the higher castes, especially the Brahmans, were able to become much better qualified educationally than the lower castes. With the rapidly increasing educational opportunities since independence, however, this situation no longer holds. The educational level is rising for all castes and communities, although the highly skilled and specialized managerial types of training are still genuinely in short supply.

Another set of complications in interpreting the available statistics arises from the fact that industrial personnel policy is subject to an all-India labor code, to state laws, to the demands of trade unions, and to the awards of arbitration boards, as well as to the decisions of industrial leaders. Employees in most factories, for example, insist on seniority as a primary criterion for wage rates and promotions, and they demand preferences for their children in recruitment. These demands are generally supported by the unions and sometimes acknowledged in the labor code. Their effect is to structure the distribution of castes and communities in favor of some employees.

Bearing in mind these difficulties, I shall now examine some data on personnel practices and policies affecting recruitment and promotion in the industrial enterprises operated by three of the leaders, two Brahman and one non-Brahman; I shall then compare these personnel operations with the practices of the one public-sector enterprise.

The data for one of the Brahman firms were collected by a welfare department worker within it, a non-Brahman, who made a house-to-house survey of about 250 employee-families, using also some of the personnel office records (Table 3). Castes included Brahman, Mudaliyār, Reḍḍi, Piḷḷai, Ācāri, Tēvar, Ceṭṭiyar, Nāyaḍu, Yādavar, Nāyakkar, and the "scheduled castes" (former untouchables), such as Harijans and Ādi Drāviḍas.[24]

In terms of occupational spread, the Brahmans have the smallest range, being concentrated in the supervisory and clerical posts, with a lesser representation as machinists and mechanics. All other castes are widely distributed in all trades. Surprisingly, the Harijans and other scheduled

Table 3
Classification of Old Castes Engaged in New Trades[25]

| Trade | Brahmans | Mudaliyār Reḍḍi | Piḷḷai Ācāri Tēvar Ceṭṭiyar | Nāyaḍu Yādavar | Nāyakkar | Harijan or Ādi Drāviḍa or Scheduled Caste | Total |
|---|---|---|---|---|---|---|---|
| Supervisory staff | 1 | | | | 2 | 1 | 4 |
| Clerk, compounder | 5 | 2 | | 1 | | 4 | 12 |
| Machinist & apprentice | 2 | 4 | 6 | | 5 | 10 | 27 |
| Mechanic, tool-setter | 1 | 1 | 1 | 3 | 1 | 6 | 13 |
| Welder | | 2 | | 2 | 1 | 1 | 6 |
| Fitter | | 8 | 3 | 6 | 3 | 4 | 24 |
| Turner | | 1 | 5 | 2 | 3 | | 11 |
| Electrician | | | 2 | 1 | | | 3 |
| Blacksmith, hammerman, coremaker | | 1 | 1 | 2 | 2 | 4 | 10 |
| Carpenter | | 1 | 5 | | 7 | | 13 |
| Tinker | | 3 | 3 | 3 | 3 | 4 | 16 |
| Painter, liner | | 3 | 2 | 1 | 1 | | 7 |
| Binder, compositor | | 1 | 1 | | | 1 | 3 |
| Nursing orderly | | | 1 | 1 | | 1 | 3 |
| Driver | | | | | | 2 | 2 |
| Watchman | | | | 4 | | 5 | 9 |
| Attender | | | 1 | | 1 | 4 | 6 |
| Laborer, unskilled | | 2 | | 3 | 10 | 16 | 31 |
| | 9 | 29 | 31 | 29 | 39 | 63 | 200 |

castes have the widest spread, with some representation in supervisory and clerical posts and a concentration as machinists and mechanics, as well as representation in all other categories, such as welders, fitters, turners, blacksmiths, carpenters, tinkers, painters, binders, nursing orderlies, drivers, watchmen, and unskilled laborers.

An analysis of the backgrounds of 783 applicants for employment in the same company in 1963 shows a comparably wide range of trades in relation to caste, community, and other social and cultural characteristics (Table 4 in Appendix B).[26]

In the other two firms, one Brahman and one non-Brahman, the respective personnel managers cited comparable statistics, but with a proportionately smaller representation of Brahmans at the managerial and supervisory levels.

Hiring of unskilled workers usually takes place at the factory gates, and the semiskilled are recruited from the ranks of the unskilled. Interviews and tests administered by a committee are used to select skilled workers. Technical and supervisory staffs are recruited by the personnel office, and candidates are sent to the respective departments for interviews. Personnel selection in the public-sector industry is administered by a selection board, members of which are appointed by the general manager. Decisions of the board can be appealed to the general manager. He reports that he has reduced caste and community as factors in personnel selection by holding employee interviews on complaints one evening a week. Within the last two years, the number of appeals has dropped from fifty a week to one or two.

Far more significant than the occupational distribution of different castes and communities within a particular factory at a given time is the question of opportunities for upward mobility. One of the most thoughtful of the industrialists said that a new kind of caste system is likely to form in industry unless a broader base of scientific and technical education is provided. He concluded that, at present, there are four major barriers to upward mobility within the industrial system. They are, in ascending order of educational complexity: (1) ability to read and understand scientific measurements of time, pressure, heat, and the like; (2) knowledge of underlying technical principles; (3) ability to design tools and machines; (4) knowledge of pure science. He did not believe a B.A. degree was sufficient to take one over all these hurdles, but the addition of some specialized training and practical experience might make it adequate. His views were echoed by several other leaders in less explicit and systematic forms. The testimony of personnel managers and my own observations support their views.

The dividing line between the lower and the higher positions in the industrial status hierarchy is the position of foreman. It is the highest position in the hierarchy of the skilled, the semiskilled, and the unskilled workman. He may rise from the ranks, but if he does he usually cannot rise beyond this position into management or even into the office or engineering departments. The main thing a foreman needs that represents a hurdle for the factory worker is a college degree and some specialized scientific and technical training. Since blueprints are all in English, and machine markings and gauges are in English or other European languages, as are all conversation and correspondence with foreign consultants, collaborators, customers, and even top management, it would be most unlikely that a skilled workman who did not know English well could ever be selected as a foreman. In addition, if he did not have specialized scientific training and knowledge, certified by a diploma or a college degree, he could not hope to go on into the engineering department. The foreman symbolizes the wide gulf between the manual workers, on the one hand, and the technical, supervisory, and managerial staffs, on the other.

Since foremen and highly skilled workers may now receive higher wages than some office workers and assistant engineers, why do we not find more of the educated at the skilled workers' level? The explanation is the fear of status loss associated with manual work, no matter how skilled. Bachelors of Arts and even high school graduates are reluctant to work with their hands. Their reluctance is shared by the engineers and scientists who may be employed in a manufacturing plant.

The chief barrier, then, to upward mobility within the factory system is a lack of educational qualification; and to downward mobility, the fear of loss of status by taking a job involving manual work. Is this a caste system or a class system? The answer depends on the degree to which the different jobs are actually allocated to specific castes and the extent to which the rank hierarchy of jobs reflects the rank hierarchies of the caste system. On the first point, we have already noted that, while there is some clustering of particular castes in particular job areas, a considerable spread of castes over different job areas also occurs. Very few jobs in the factory are considered the exclusive monopoly of any particular caste. The traditional forms of occupational specialization are, in any case, difficult to maintain in a situation where many new kinds of jobs have to be learned.

On the other hand, there is a status hierarchy *within* modern industry, with top management at the top; skilled and unskilled workers at the bottom; and office staff and technical engineering departments in the middle. Salaries and wage rates are roughly calibrated to match this hierarchy, although some junior engineers' salaries may be lower than the wages of some highly skilled workmen.

Educational qualifications follow this status hierarchy as well. No formal education is required for the lowest ranks; a diploma is required for the post of a junior engineer; a college degree for assistant and full engineer; at least a high school pass (diploma) for ordinary clerical and supervisory posts; and a B.A. or its equivalent for the more technical and administrative posts. No formal educational requirement exists for the top management.

Whether this is a caste system or a class system is arguable. The crucial question is, What are the paths to top management and how easily can they be traveled? From my observations, I would say that it is much easier to move into top management from engineering and other technical professions than from skilled and unskilled jobs. I met only two managers who had risen from the ranks of the skilled workers; one of them was a plant manager who was British, and the other was a general manager in the public-sector industry. All others whom I met, or heard about had risen from the ranks, came out of the office, technical, engineering, or professional staffs.

Since independence, Indianization of many British firms has created opportunities for Indians to move into top management posts; in fact, there were more openings than qualified personnel to fill them. A shortage still exists at the top management level and for some kinds of technical skills. The emphasis that the five-year plans have placed on industrial development has further increased these opportunities. That shortages in managerial and entrepreneurial personnel still exist is due not to the caste system or to religious beliefs but to the discrepancy between, on the one hand, the growing opportunities for industrial leadership and management and, on the other, the low levels of literacy, lack of scientific and technical education, and absence of experience with industry that prevailed in the pre-independence period. A few examples of recent trends in Madras will support this interpretation and also suggest that both private industry and government are trying to attack the problem through broader educational and training programs.

The artisan class is itself changing. While carpenters, blacksmiths, tinkers, and other representatives of the traditional crafts are found in modern industry, modern machinery is also creating new skilled jobs for machinists, drillers, turners, tool and die designers, and the like. Sometimes the older craftsmen can make the change, but more frequently it is their children, better educated and trained than they, who perform the newer tasks. Modern artisans often consider themselves as good as clerks and engineers, marry much later than their fathers did, and walk beside their wives on the street. With sufficient experience and capital, some of them leave the factories in which they are employed to start small industrial firms of their own.[27]

This trend has been encouraged by central and state government industrial estates and by training programs at the factories outside regular work hours. Many firms are also providing apprentice training opportunities for workers and their children. Many of them will now give priority to children of employees in recruiting only if the children are properly trained.

None of the firms studied, to my knowledge, had yet introduced instruction in English into its training programs. The current linguistic controversies in Madras made this an imprudent measure. At least one of the industrial leaders, however, a member of the State Legislative Assembly, was working with the State Minister of Industries in an attempt to make education free up to the secondary level and to provide lunches and clothing for the children. Various schemes for technical and vocational training were also being put into effect.

It is not only the artisans who are being trained and retrained. Many of the industrial leaders expressed dissatisfaction with the educational qualifications and attitudes of the college graduates and engineers who come to work for them. Such graduates, they find, usually lack adequate technical training and practical experience and are much too reluctant to work directly at machines. The heads of firms have accordingly introduced apprentice programs for graduates as well, and if a B.A. or B.S. is unwilling to work at a machine he is not hired. For management and technical staff, there are also National Productivity Council seminars supported by the government. At least two of the personnel managers said that in their firms, tests of performance, as well as interviews by the different departments, were becoming increasingly important as criteria for recruitment and promotion. These companies' growing national and international contacts have also made them more responsive to the importance of broad and scientific personnel policies.

With a continuation of new opportunities in industry, the associated broadening of the educational and training programs, and the adoption of progressive personnel policies, the status system of Indian industry will come to look more and more like the management, white-collar, blue-collar "class" system of Western industry. The clustering of castes and communities in different occupations will more and more be determined by educational and skill qualifications and generic status factors rather than by caste and community.

## Conflicts and Adaptations in Ritual and Belief

Caste and the joint family are sometimes included in definitions of Hinduism. Since non-Hindu Indians may also have these institutions, we cannot regard Hinduism as coextensive with caste and the joint family. Instead, I shall take a somewhat narrower view of Hinduism as consisting of a distinctive set of rituals and beliefs. The rituals and beliefs have something to say about caste and the joint family but are not exhausted by those social institutions. In the present section, we are interested in the relationship to industry of Hinduism as a set of rituals and beliefs. The problem is one of exploring how the industrialist's ritual observances and religious beliefs affect his industrial activities and, conversely, how his life in industry affects his ritual observances and beliefs. Since there are two Muslims and one Syrian Christian among the industrial leaders I interviewed, I shall include some references to their religious observances and beliefs for comparison with the Hindus.

Max Weber's analysis of Hinduism implies that a good Hindu cannot also become a good industrialist, because the inner "spirit of Hinduism" is incompatible with industrial capitalism. One aspect of Hinduism especially singled out by Weber and others as incompatible with modern industrial life is its ritualism and magic. In this aspect, Weber includes domestic ritual observances, public festivals and ceremonies, and the "enchanted" world view, as well as the fear of pollution from intercaste contact or from contact with polluting objects and activities.

The fact that sixteen of our nineteen industrial leaders in Madras City are Hindus constitutes something of an anomaly in Weber's terms. There are several possible rationalizations for this anomaly: One is to argue that the Hindu industrialists are not good Hindus but are deviants from Hinduism; another is to say that they may be good Hindus but that they engage in industrial activities at the price of soul-shattering conflicts with their religious and cultural traditions. My evidence throws doubt on both explanations and consequently on the assumption that it is an anomaly for a Hindu to go into industry.

None of the Hindus (or non-Hindus) among the Madras industrial leaders considers himself especially orthodox. On the other hand, all consider themselves good Hindus (or Muslims or Christians) and, in some cases, even devout. All of them are well aware that they do not spend as much time as their fathers or grandfathers did on ritual observances. They are nevertheless convinced that they still adhere to the "essentials" of their religion, and they do not experience any strong sense of conflict between the demands of their religion and their mode of life as industrial leaders. The self-description offered by one fits most of the others: He described himself as "a fellow who is not an orthodox Hindu but who believes in the essential tenets of Hinduism."

Only two of them spontaneously expressed any sense of conflict; four said there could not be any conflict because business and social-religious life were in separate spheres and did not mix, while these six and the remaining thirteen had worked out mutual adaptations of the two spheres that avoid traumatic conflicts. The adaptations involve some interesting reinterpretations and restructuring of both ritual observances and religious beliefs, as well as a definite effort to formulate a positive ethical code for industry within a religious framework.

One leader who expressed some sense of conflict had experienced personal doubts about whether he was a good Brahman. He had consulted his guru, to whom he said: "Guruji, how can I call myself a good Brahman? I eat meat, drink alcohol, smoke and even dine with Harijans." His guru replied that it was unfortunate that the industrialist did such things, but that while one can never be certain about the identity of the father, there could be no doubt about the mother. Since the man's mother was a Brahman, so was he. The answer seems to have satisfied the industrialist and allayed his doubts.

Actually, at home this gentleman's family maintains many ritual observances. They are strictly vegetarian, drink no alcohol, do not smoke, and do not permit widow remarriage. They perform *pūjās* occasionally, listen to Sanskrit chants on tape, have Brahman *purohitas* who come in for special ceremonial occasions, and a pandit to tutor the children in Sanskrit. An astrologer is regularly consulted for domestic affairs, and traditional doctors are called when modern doctors fail. The astrologer is not consulted on business decisions, since that "would be tempting God too much." The family regularly visits temples and the head of their *maṭha* at Śṛṅgēri and attends *harikathā* and other devotional performances. They also help to maintain temples at the father's native town and at other shrines.

Every morning, this industrial leader prays or "pretends to pray" while washing and shaving. On the way to his office, he always asks his driver to slow down in front of a Hanumān temple so that he can salute the deity from the car with a *namaste* (joined hands) and request the god's help. He prays not for personal enrichment, he said, but to train and sharpen his mind for decisions.

His faith in God, he says, is absolute, but "God helps those who help themselves." To accomplish anything, it is necessary to exert "untiring, bone-breaking effort." If you don't succeed, there is no point in being bitter about the results. Try to do better next time by "restudying your methods, regrouping your forces, and reattacking. If you do get results, don't be elated, for what you will have achieved is due to God's will."

When he first went into business, this leader had colleagues who, in his opinion, were better qualified than he in education, experience, and ambition. He succeeded where they failed. Since he cannot see that he is superior to them in muscle or brains, he believes that "something else" has used him as an "instrument" to succeed. He says he does not know enough to say whether his actions in a previous existence, that is, his *karman,* may have favored his success, but there must be "something else."

It had not occurred to this Brahman to renounce an active life and withdraw from the world. He quoted a Tamil proverb to express his attitude toward his career and activities in industry: "If you put on the garb of a dog, then you must bark like one." In this industrial age, he thinks, many people cannot live without some expensive things: refrigerators, washing machines, clothes, and much else. It is therefore necessary for industrialists to go on making more and more of these things and to employ more and more people to do so. He once asked the head of his *maṭha,* who was staying in his home: "Most Revered Holiness, you are my guest. Do you expect me to see you every morning before I go to work?" His Holiness replied: "No, you follow your profession, for God has ordained that as long as you do that well, you are doing your duty [*dharma*]." He believes he works much harder than his employees and says he feels a strong sense of responsibility for keeping them employed and paying their wages.

Although industry is bringing many changes, this industrial leader does not see these changes as destructive to cultural and religious traditions. Perhaps 5 per cent of the changes, he estimates, are destructive of traditions. If "rich merchants in some Northern cities" start deviating from tradition by adopting easy divorce, promiscuity, and modern hairdos for the women, they will be replaced in one or two generations by others from the lower rungs who are more devoted and who will think and act along more traditional lines. The stress and strain of modern life is, if anything, returning people to tradition for guidance. The trend is manifest, he believes, in the large numbers of people attending devotional performances, visiting the temple in Mylapore, and going by the thousands to visit the heads of their *maṭhas,* in such places as Śṛṅgēri.

His code of ethics in industry is to play fair and deal honestly with others, not to covet their property, to be friendly and sincere with all without respect to caste or community, to treat wealth as a trust for supporting the largest number of people and not just for one's children and relatives, and to do one's job as well as possible. The code is a traditional one and, in his opinion, has always been followed in the domestic sphere. He thinks it should be followed in industry as well, not only as a moral duty but out of enlightened self-interest. Otherwise communal tensions will heighten and the "have-nots" will be tempted to destroy everything. His policy is to "keep your head and follow tradition."

The pattern of ritual practices and religious beliefs to which this Brahman and his family adhere is very similar to that of many of the other Hindu industrialists. There are some individual variations reflecting differences in age, education, caste, and community. One of the non-Brahman leaders, for example, does not have a sacred thread ceremony for boys in his family and is supporting a school to train non-Brahman pandits. Another leader, a Brahman, rises at 5:30 every morning to do Yoga *āsanas* for an hour in order to still "the chatterbox of the mind." He says that this routine, which he has been following for the last fifteen years, makes him fit for the whole day and helps rid him of worries. Another Brahman, a man in his forties who comes from a very orthodox family, does not engage in any kind of prayer or meditations. He said that when he is a little older he might consider it. Some families make frequent pilgrimages to Tiruppati and other shrines; others rarely go to them or to local temples. Some consult astrologers only for domestic affairs; others use them for business and stock predictions as well. One said that when he has no statistics, he consults an astrologer.

It is obvious from these examples, I believe, that while there are some conflicts between Hindu ritual and belief and modern industry, the conflicts are not so intense as to have discouraged Hindus from going into industry or to have prevented long-lasting adjustments between the requirements of Hinduism and the requirements of industry. What are the adaptive processes and strategies by which these adjustments have been brought about and maintained?

### *Sanskritization and Westernization*

When I first became acquainted with some of the Madras industrial leaders and their families, it seemed to me that the adaptations they made were very similar to those described by M. N. Srinivas as "Sanskritization" and "Westernization." Later, I found that there were other adaptive strategies involved as well. It will be easier to understand the other strategies if Srinivas's conceptions are kept in mind.[28]

Srinivas has shown that relatively low castes frequently try to raise their ritual status by emulating practices and beliefs generally associated with a Brahman life-style and that such an effort at upward ritual mobility, which he calls "Sanskritization," is apt to be accompanied by upward political and economic mobility. In his later writing, Srinivas has broadened his conception of "Sanskritization" to take into account cases of upward ritual mobility in which non-Brahmanic but Sanskritic life-styles are taken as models. He has also related the process of "Sanskritization" to "Westernization." He sees "Sanskritization" not only as a process whereby lower castes have raised their ritual status in the caste hierarchy but also as perhaps the major way in which tribal and other non-Hindu groups have been incorporated into the caste system and the Hindu fold.

In my Madras research, I used Srinivas's conception of "Sanskritic Hinduism" as a basis for interviews and observations, although the cultural inventory of the Sanskritic life-style varies with region, caste, and community and changes under the pressures of debate and controversy. As an ideal-type, the "Sanskritic" model includes abstinence from meat and alcohol; subcaste endogamy and a proscription against widow remarriage; commensality only with members of the same subcaste; wearing of the sacred thread and worship of the major deities of the Hindu pantheon; use of a Brahman *purohita,* Vedic *mantras,* and vegetarian offerings in worship; daily prayers, readings from scriptures, listening to recitations from scriptures; alms-giving and visits to temples and *maṭhas;* belief in the four orders and four stages of life (*varṇāśramas*); and belief in the doctrines that one's personal destiny is determined by one's past actions (*karman*), that one will be reborn many times in different forms according to one's deserts (*saṃsāra*); that one must meet moral obligations to kin, caste, and society (*dharma*); and that one will find release and salvation from the cycles of rebirth (*mokṣa*) by following a personal discipline of ritual observance (*karmayoga*), devotion to a deity (*bhaktiyoga*), or meditation and knowledge (*jñānayoga*).

The model of the "modern" life-style includes literacy in English and a modern education; the use of European dress, diet, and manners; a modern occupation; acceptance and use of modern technology and its products; preference for modern political institutions and political ideologies; and respect for a world view based on modern science and scholarship.

The "modern" life-style is followed by the industrial leaders, particularly in their plants and offices, and in their homes to a lesser extent. They all speak English and use it in business conversation and correspondence and on the telephone. European and American education, clothes, films, automobiles, cameras, books, journals, industrial techniques, and organization are greatly admired and sought after. In the home can be found refrigerators, washing machines, transistor radios, and, occasionally, air conditioning and the cocktail party. The idiom of modern science, technology, politics, and economics is often heard in the conversation of the leaders and their children, who also show some resistance to arranged marriages, meticulous ritual observance, and traditional social forms. Modern doctors and medicine are all held in high esteem and are consulted as a matter of course when there is any illness in the family. The leaders travel abroad once or twice a year to find new industrial methods and products as well as new markets.

One of my first departures from Srinivas's definition of "Sanskritization" occurred when I noticed that insofar as the industrial leaders did conform to a Sanskritic model it was more likely to be in their domestic and social life than in their occupational activities, where the "Western" or "modern" model was more apt to be followed. Nor were they especially bothered by the apparent discrepancy between domestic and occupational practice. The same individual or family, I observed, usually followed both models simultaneously. It was not simply a matter of changing one's behavior in different situations; there also seemed to be important functional articulations between the two spheres, articulations that were meaningful and strategic in the life histories of the particular individuals and families. In their cases, the adaptive processes seemed to have different aims and to use different means from the Sanskritizing castes analyzed by Srinivas. If the Madras industrialists were trying to conform to a Sanskritic model—and most of the Hindu ones were—it was not so much in order to raise their ritual or secular status as a caste as to restore their family's previous status or maintain their present one. Since most of the industrialists came from ritually clean castes, their family status was relatively high and in some cases declined when they entered industry. "Sanskritization" could not, therefore, have the same significance for them that it might have for low and "unclean" castes that happened to be economically successful.

In view of the differences between the life-styles of the industrialists and Srinivas's model, it becomes problematic whether the Madras industrialists are "Sanskritizing." I have continued to use Srinivas's term in cases where there is acceptance of, and some conformity to, a model of Sanskritic Hinduism but have not adopted the rest of Srinivas's theory of "Sanskritization" and "Westernization." Instead, I have tried to identify other strategies and processes of change, some of which are consistent with "Sanskritization" or "Westernization," and some of which are quite distinct. The distinctiveness of these strategies does not arise simply from the fact that some of the industrialists fail to live up to the Sanskritic model or accept an alternative non-Sanskritic model; it arises from the fact that both those who conform to the Sanskritic model and those who accept alternative models will use such adaptive strategies. The operation of these adaptive strategies changes the cultural content of both the Sanskritic and non-Sanskritic models as well as the social units to which they are applied.

### *Compartmentalization of Modern Industry and Tradition*

One leader spoke of conflicts in his immediate entourage. He cited the behavior of his wife, who after giving a cocktail party for foreign and other guests would do a *pūjā* in her *pūjā* room; his children, who wanted to arrange their own marriages; and his industrialist colleagues, who mix freely with all castes and communities at work but consult an astrologer to fix an auspicious time for a board meeting. He sees such occurrences as conflicts because they juxtapose "traditional" and "modern" practices in a way that seemed incongruous to him. Yet he, too, accepts the fact of rapid change, while wondering which changes are for the good.

Since changes have been numerous and rapid, why do not more of the industrial leaders, who are agents of some of these changes, experience a stronger sense of conflict between their religious and cultural traditions and the demands of industry? It may be that some had experienced conflicts while they were younger, or that their fathers and grandfathers had, but they had since made adaptations and grown used to the incongruities.

A clue to one important adaptive process was given by the leader who said that there can be no conflict because business and religion are different and separate spheres. Three others expressed a similar opinion. They meant "separate" both in the sense of a physical separation of the two spheres and in the sense that different norms of behavior and belief were appropriate to the two spheres. Their view obviously is a *compartmentalization* of two spheres of conduct and belief that would otherwise collide. As such, it is an adaptive process working to reduce the conflict between tradition and modernity.

While most of the leaders did not explicitly verbalize the strategy of compartmentalization, most did adopt it in their daily behavior. The physical setting for the traditional religious sphere is the home, where many of the traditional ritual observances of Sanskritic Hinduism are performed. The physical setting for modern practices is the office and factory; there English is used, Western dress is worn, contacts with different castes and communities are frequent, and the instruments and concepts of modern science and technology engage the attention.

Each of the leaders passes daily from one context to the other and symbolizes the passage by changing from Indian *dhotī* to Western shirt and trousers and from his Indian language to English. Employees at all levels change their clothes; most of the workers wear shorts and shirts to work even if in other respects (e.g., English literacy) they may not be as modernized as their employers.

The differences in behavior indicate a culturally recognized difference in the two physical settings: The home is categorized as the domain of one's family, caste, religion, and language community; the norms appropriate to these groups are in operation there. The office and factory, on the other hand, are categorized as a domain that includes nonrelatives, other castes and communities, and even foreigners; the norms of behavior there will accordingly be very different from those prevailing in the home.

Because in Madras City and in India generally modern offices and factories were historically introduced by the British, and because the top management was British or European until quite recently, the norms of conduct there were set by the British. One of the Indian managing directors of a Madras firm founded by the British defended the practice of wearing white shirts with ties and white ducks on the ground that a certain amount of formality in dress is conducive to discipline and efficiency. He deplored, by contrast, the practice of some U.S. Government officials in India, who appear publicly in shorts and brightly colored sport shirts. At the same time, this manager was diplomatically supervising the complete Indianization of the firm's personnel.

While compartmentalization is a pervasive process, it is by no means complete. There are exceptions and overlappings, although the predominant trends of behavior and the cultural norms are clear. Some exceptions "prove the rule," some require other explanations. Celebrating the *āyudhapūjā* in office and factory and closing down for festival holidays are exceptions.* These practices probably have more traditional cultural symbolism for the employees than they do for the employers and top management, just as one sees more lithographs and images of deities in the shops and work departments than in the front office. But the employers and managers do come to the *pūjās* and are willing to put up with the many festival holidays, though some would like to see the number reduced. Some of the most devout Hindus among the leaders find that the

* See p. 325.

celebrations have practical value in enhancing cleanliness and productive efficiency.

Compartmentalization is not complete in the home sphere either. Work is brought home from the office, and important decisions are discussed at home. Modern appliances and furnishings are found in many of the leaders' homes; the home may be as technically modern as the office. There are many variations; much depends on the characteristics and general background of the family. As everywhere else, the newer homes and the newer offices are the more modern. Even within the more modern types of homes, however, the older customs continue. The wives, who may not speak English, and other females of the household tend to remain in the background; they usually do not eat until the males and guests have been served, and they participate more faithfully in ritual observances and cultural performances than do the industrial leaders and other males of the household.

The home-*versus*-office-and-factory compartmentalization also holds for the employees, with some modifications depending on their level of education, income, and family background. In the previously cited household survey of workers, it was found that although only about 12 out of 200 families maintain their village connections, 96 of the houses have *pūjā* corners for the higher Hindu deities, and 91 families go on annual religious pilgrimages. In 85 cases, the males drink or smoke. Houses are clustered in compounds by caste and community. Because of the lower standards of living, the contrast between the "traditional" home and the "modern" factory is more striking for employees than it is for the employers: "The employee lives in two worlds. He works in a spacious, well-ventilated, electrically lit modern factory that houses expensive machines. He operates electrically driven machinery requiring technical skill but returns home to primitive living conditions where wives work with their hands to pound, grind, lift water, cook, and serve his meal in a smoky, ill-lit, ill-ventilated, overcrowded room." [29]

Compartmentalization is an adaptive process that permits Indians to combine the modes of thought and behavior of modern industry with traditional modes of thought and behavior without too direct a collision. So long as the home and the rest of the family maintain the traditional observances, the industrial leader and his employees feel free to depart from the traditional patterns in the office and factory, on trips abroad, and elsewhere outside the home.

Although the Madras industrialists' "compartmentalizing" has been facilitated by the physical separation of home and factory and by the British introduction of factories, compartmentalization may occur without much physical separation or foreign influence. There is no doubt, however, that participation in European-sponsored and -dominated activities must have induced in many Indians a defensiveness about their own culture, which they tried to preserve in the separate sphere of home life. The early Dubashes, for example, who served as translators, interpreters, and brokers for the Europeans, jealously worked to keep Sanskrit a sacred, secret language. Nineteenth-century reform movements were generally efforts to rediscover and purify indigenous Indian culture, instigated by Indians who were most "acculturated" to European culture.[30]

Compartmentalization of cultural differences nevertheless predates the European intrusion into India. It is an old, well-known feature of Indian life. Indians in fact show such great sensitivity to cultural differentiation based on caste, language, geographical region, religion, and life-style and have so often categorized these differences with verbal and nonverbal markers that they sound like anthropologists when talking about each other. Evidence for this observation can be found in the elaborate classifications of subcastes, occupations, neighborhoods and regions, religious communities and sects, and legal and philosophical systems. Not only was membership in classes and subclasses marked by distinctive life-styles, but each individual was usually designated by a string of names encoding all this information: family, region of origin, occupation, name of family's or individual's deity, subcaste, and sect.

Cultural forms are precisely distinguished also and classified according to different "systems"; this is true of music, dance, drama, literature, and other arts. Films, for example, are commonly distinguished and classified as "mythologicals, historicals, devotionals, socials, and comedies." Systems of music are classified into "folk" or country (*deśī*) and "classical" (*mārga*); "classical" systems are distinguished as "Southern" and "Northern" and further classified according to particular schools. Analogous classifications are made for kinds of dancing.[31]

The Indian penchant for noting and classifying social and cultural differences, as has been suggested by M. B. Emeneau,[32] represents an unusual capacity to bring the unconscious and subliminal processes of speech, thought, bodily movement and gesture, and autonomic functions into conscious awareness and to subject them to systematic analysis and control. In any case, there is no doubt that the Madras industrialists' compartmentalizing of their work and domestic spheres into "modern" and "traditional" represents a similar process of cultural differentiation and classification. It differs from the older classifications of caste, sect, and region in that it is not a mutually exclusive classification—the same individual, family, or caste can be both "modern" and "traditional." The distinction also suggests a difference between "foreign" and "indigenous" and between the old and new. These differences are not absolute, for some of the other cultural classifications are not mutually exclusive with respect to individuals and families, and not all imply cultural homogeneity or simultaneity. Members of the same family, for example, may be classified as worldly (*laukika*) or orthodox (*vaidika*) Brahmans and thus have different occupations and life-styles. Individuals and families, moreover, have been known to change caste, sect, and region.

In its adaptive function, compartmentalization resembles a process that has long been operating in the history of Indian civilization—that is, the incorporation of new groups and values into the civilization as subcastes with their distinctive ways of life and thought. This aspect of India as a plural society has been noted often and has been interpreted as the source of an ethical and cultural relativity. Each caste and religious community group has its own set of moral duties (*dharmas*) and subcultures, and, it has been alleged, there can be no common standards of ethics or of citizenship applying to all.

This relativity is, however, only relative. There is, in scriptural theory at least, an interdependence among the different groups and their respective *dharmas* that creates an organically unified and functioning society among the "federation of cultures." Each group is not free to choose any "subculture" whatsoever; it must conform to a functionally necessary *dharma,* such as that of the ruler, priest, merchant, farmer, and so forth. Beyond these functionally differentiated and interdependent *dharmas,* there is also a set of standards that applies to all members of the society irrespective of the subgroup to which they belong. Finally, there is a rank hierarchy of statuses by which some are considered "higher" than others. In traditional Hindu society, higher ranks—usually but not invariably associated with the way of life of an ideal Brahman (or of an ascetic)—became a model life-style that all groups sought to imitate in order to achieve the highest form of Hinduism and thereby raise their status in the hierarchy.

The process of incorporation and mobility of groups within Hindu society, which M. N. Srinivas has called "Sanskritization," is not the same process as compartmentalization. "Sanskritization" is a kind of assimilation of new groups and their cultures into a pre-established scriptural pattern and a submission to the norms of that pattern, while compartmentalization seems to be a way of permitting new patterns and groups to be formed outside the old by setting them aside and labeling them as "new" or "foreign."

Sanskritization represents an *orthogenetic* cultural change that evolves out of past cultural traditions, while compartmentalization represents a *heterogenetic* cultural change that seeks a mutual adaptation between the indigenous and the foreign. If compartmentalization remains stable, new and old patterns may coexist without generating intense conflicts. If it is unstable, then either the new pattern will be reshaped to conform to the old, or the old will be reshaped in the image of the new or even be displaced by the new, or perhaps some new synthesis of the old and the new will emerge.

How stable is compartmentalization, or rather, how stable are the results of the process? In some domains, the results seem at first to be quite lasting. Among medical theories and practices, for example, now classified as *Āyurvedic,* "Siddha," "Yunānī," allopathic, and modern, each is recognized as a distinctive type of medicine, and a patient is free to choose among the various alternatives. The listing of doctors in telephone directories follows this classification. Yet in recent times there have been drives, inspired by political-cultural ideologies, to compel the central and state governments to support "indigenous Indian medicine" against "modern medicine." Where students have been given free choice in medical schools, on the other hand, they have generally opted for modern medicine or have combined indigenous and modern.[33]

This example shows that compartmentalization of innovations can turn out to be unstable, either because of ideological polarization of the "traditional-indigenous" and the "modern-foreign," or because there may be a trend to choose one or the other pole, the traditional or the modern, in the gradual process of selective incorporation.

In the case of industry, the outcome of compartmentalization depends on several other adaptive strategies and processes as well. The Madras industrialists are aware that manufacturing industry represents an innovative pattern in India. One of them said, "We have no industrial tradition in India; we have a bit of a commercial tradition and a long tradition of agriculture." Their cultural categorization of industry as different and new has not kept them away from it. On the contrary, the newness has stimulated their curiosity and enterprise and a sequence of adaptations to harmonize industrial development with religious traditions and social institutions. Compartmentalization by setting aside potential conflicts between the new and the old buys the time and freedom to learn about the new and to assimilate it to the old.

### *Ritual Neutralization of the Work Sphere*

In Madras factories and offices, the workmen of different castes and religious communities join at least once a year to clean and make offerings to their machines and tools in the *āyudhapūjā*. The ceremony comes at the end of a nine-day festival when *pūjās* are offered at homes and in temples to Sarasvatī, goddess of learning; to Lakṣmī, goddess of wealth; and to Durgā or Pārvatī for general welfare. On the tenth day the factories are usually closed, and the employees clean their machines and tools and invite a priest (*pūjāri*) to come and officiate at the evening *pūjā*. Company officers may also be invited to attend. In some factories, brief *pūjās* may be held every Friday in all departments. This practice, however, depends on the individuals concerned and does not involve a closing down of the whole factory, the attendance of a *pūjāri,* or an elaborate ceremony. Some Madras industrial leaders grumble that India has too many religious festivals and holidays. Brahman leaders are apt to share this opinion with non-Brahmans, although most industrialists are willing to live with the present system. One, a Smārta Brahman, said, apropos of the cleaning done at *āyudhapūjā,* that British industrialists would have been delighted to have their machinery cleaned so economically.

The number of religious festivals and holidays allowed workers is not simply a religious matter; it is regulated by the state and central governments, forming a part of the rules for leaves. About five years ago, the Madras State Government passed a National Festival and Holiday Law, which requires that companies grant at least seven holidays a year, including two national holidays and five festivals. The unions generally negotiate for several more, which may bring the total to ten or twelve.[34]

In addition, each employee is entitled by statute to fourteen days of earned leave per year. Firms that come under the Employee State Insurance plan must also grant either twenty-six full days of paid leave or fifty-two half-days and an additional number of days of leave with full pay depending on length of service.

Ritual ceremonies are held on other occasions—on the inauguration of a new factory branch, the starting of a new venture, or the visit of distinguished guests. Some of the industrial leaders consult astrologers to determine auspicious times for such events, for board meetings, and for making business decisions.

Employees are permitted to keep images and lithographs of deities near their work and to hold *pūjās*. Occasionally, one sees images and lithographs in a manager's office, though not very often.

Because of the overlap between the festival calendar and labor laws in India, it is difficult to assess the role of ritual in industrial organization. Workers would like to increase their paid holidays, whatever their religious significance, and employers would like to reduce them. Some of the employers, however, did look upon the holidays, "if not too many," as contributing to industrial efficiency and productivity. At least one plant manager, who was British, saw in the workers' worship of their machines an attitude of technological value. Comparing the factory workers of Calcutta to those of Madras, he said that, while the Southern workers were very conscientious and were rapidly learning industrial skills, they were not so industrially "sophisticated" as the Calcutta workers. As evidence, he cited the greater number of *pūjās* the Calcutta workers hold for their machines and tools. This, he thought, showed a greater respect for the machines.

Fears of ritual pollution from close intercaste contact and interaction and from "unclean" objects and kinds of work are definitely declining in the factory context. Almost every factory maintains a canteen for its employees, serving breakfast, lunch, and tea. Except for the distinction between vegetarian and nonvegetarian and the use of Brahman cooks for the vegetarian meals, employees from different castes eat freely together in the canteens, using the same set of cups and plates and sitting at the same tables. Work teams are also usually mixed in caste and will use the same tools, aprons, goggles, washrooms, and other facilities. Outside the workshop, different castes join in union meetings, religious processions, and political activity and are in daily close contact on the buses and trains.

These practices and policies have not resulted in a general elimination of caste consciousness or in the disappearance of caste-based association. Brahmans tend to associate with Brahmans and non-Brahmans with non-Brahmans; higher castes tend to use harsh words and the singular form of address to lower castes, even in the factory setting. Factory sweeping and scavenging are still largely done by untouchables. When anti-Brahman political parties control the union, caste consciousness is deliberately intensified. Nevertheless, the mixture and interaction of castes in the industrial context is far greater than it is in the domestic setting, where different castes cluster their dwellings in separate compounds and still maintain distance among themselves.[35]

One of the most striking instances of the decline of the fear of ritual pollution in industry has occurred in leather manufacturing. Since such work may involve the handling of dead cows and other animals, and since leather itself is considered polluting, untouchables and non-Hindus have traditionally tanned hides and skins and have produced and sold leather goods. Before partition and independence, most of the tanneries and leather factories in Madras State were owned by Muslims and Europeans, and they employed low-caste and non-Hindu workers. When the British and many Muslims left, some of the tanneries and leather factories were bought by caste Hindus.

One of the industrial leaders was the first member of the Ceṭṭiyar community in Madras to go into the leather business. As a young man, he had read about Gandhi's efforts to start a tannery at Sevāgrām. Inspired by this example, he said to himself that if Gandhi, a "Ceṭṭiyar of Gujarat" (that is, a trader) could do it, so could he, a Ceṭṭiyar, or trader, of Madras. He started trading in hides and skins with his uncle, who had brought him up in Colombo, Ceylon, and had initiated him into trade. Later he rented a tannery and finally constructed his own series of tanneries. The Ceṭṭiyar community at first regarded this leader as an untouchable; as the business grew and prospered, however, the prejudice against him disappeared. He now has about 150 Ceṭṭiyars and many other caste Hindus, including Brahmans, as well as traditional leather-working castes (Cakkiliyars and Paṟaiyans), working together in the tanneries he and his relatives have established. In one, a Brahman is the chief technician. About 75 per cent of the workers live in a company hostel, where they receive board and lodging at subsidized rates and get some fringe benefits. This Ceṭṭiyar tanner is now a respected businessman in Madras City. President of the Indian Leather Technological Association and a member of the Cosmopolitan Club, he has recently helped organize a very successful leather fair in Madras. Once or twice a year, he travels to Japan and Europe to find markets for treated hides. He has, by his own example, improved the quality of treated hides by refusing to adulterate and by taking lower profit margins. Although the main market for hides and leather is abroad, he is now considering ways to develop the domestic market.

He works about fourteen hours a day and speaks of business as his relaxation. When he feels tired, he visits his tanneries over the state or travels abroad.

In most other respects, the Ceṭṭiyar and his family are devout Hindus. He is a vegetarian but will occasionally eat mutton, and he does not smoke or drink even when traveling abroad. There are no cases in his family of widow remarriage or of marrying out of his subcaste. Every morning before breakfast, he prays in Tamil in his *pūjā* room to Gaṇeśa to remove obstacles, to Subrahmaṇya for success in trade, to Lakṣmī for wealth, to Sarasvatī for learning, and to Śiva. He and his family attend both a Śiva and a Viṣṇu temple but are not affiliated with any *maṭha*. Brahman *purohitas* are called to the house for weddings and sacred thread ceremonies, and on other occasions. An astrologer is consulted for casting horoscopes and determining auspicious days on which to start new enterprises and seek new customers. Although he does not consider himself an expert, he frequently consults an astrological almanac in order "to avoid the major bad things." Both *Āyurvedic* and modern doctors are used. The wife and daughter attend devotional *bhajanas* and discourses daily, as well as classical Indian dance and music concerts and plays by the Tamil actor-producer Śivājī Gaṇeśan. Occasionally he joins them.

The industrialist believes in the basic tenets of Hinduism—*karman,* rebirth, and *dharma.* He attributes his successful career to a combination of his *karman,* divine grace, hard work, and his "never having done anything against his conscience." If reborn, he would choose the same career, and he considers it his moral duty as a human being and as a citizen to follow that career in order to contribute to others. He quotes Gandhi in support of the belief that to provide more industry and more jobs for his countrymen is better than a life of renunciation.

The traditional ritual hierarchy of castes and occupations is transformed in the industrial setting. Forms of address and informal associations may still follow caste lines, but in the large companies, at least, personnel policies are increasingly responsive to qualifications of skill, education, and performance. Although there is clustering by caste in some kinds of jobs (for example, Brahmans in clerical and supervisory posts, artisan castes in skilled jobs, untouchable castes in unskilled ones), such clustering is explicable in terms of the backgrounds of related experience and education and does not necessarily express adherence to traditional principles of caste occupation.

A status hierarchy exists, in other words, within industry as one moves from unskilled labor to semiskilled and skilled, or from clerical to supervisory, technical, and managerial levels. This hierarchy is not, however, in one-to-one correspondence with the hierarchy of ritual pollution and purity among castes, caste occupations, or products and processes. It is a hierarchy defined rather by differences in salary and cost-of-living allowances, educational qualifications, and degree of authority and responsibility. The hierarchy coincides with the ritual hierarchy where some traditional caste occupations still persist in industry, e.g., sweepers, scavengers, construction workers, carpenters, potters, and the like. As industrial plants modernize their plumbing, construction, and equipment, the scope for these traditional occupations narrows, and their visible ritual stigmata disappear. Most jobs in a modern industrial plant are simply too new in materials, techniques, and organization to fit the traditional ritual hierarchy. While some castes may try to claim a hereditary right to certain jobs on the basis of a resemblance to their traditional occupations, the jobs are in the main open to the competition of education, skill, seniority, and influence. Jobs that involve working with and dirtying one's hands are avoided by the college-educated, who prefer "clean" jobs. Even they, however, are increasingly accepting work with their hands in the face of salary differentials and apprenticeship requirements.

From the point of view of the industrial leaders and their personnel managers, the status hierarchy within a particular industrial company is not a replication of the caste hierarchy but is more like the "blue-collar," "white-collar," "management" hierarchy of European and American companies. So far as purity and pollution are concerned, they see this hierarchy as ritually neutral. Whether their employees view the hierarchy in the same light is another question and one on which I do not have much evidence. It is quite possible that employees would tend to see more of the jobs as caste-linked and with ritual significance. What we need are studies of the folk classifications and rankings of industrial occupations as seen by members of different castes who are located at different positions in the industrial structure. It would not be surprising if such studies showed that industrial jobs tend to be more caste-defined in the folk taxonomies than they are in the factory's personnel classifications or in the actual statistical distributions of castes in different jobs. The reason for this expectation is that the folk taxonomies are closer to the "at-home culture" than they are to the "at-work culture." In the domestic setting caste and ritual distinctions are still important and are accepted as a matter of course, while in the work setting caste distinctions are less important and have to compete with other modes of classification and other kinds of hierarchy.[36]

### *Ritual Neutralization and Secularization*

The tendency of jobs, products, and social relations in the industrial plant and office to become increasingly free from ritual and religious restriction is commonly referred to as a process of "secularization," "Westernization," and "rationalization." The outcome of this process, according to sociological theory, is the complete elimination of ritual, religion, and ethics from the sphere of industry. It would be better to describe the process as a "deritualization" or "ritual neutralization" of the work sphere without implying a linear trend toward "secularization" and "rationalization." In the Madras factories and offices, at any rate, what seems to be happening is not a complete elimination of ritual and religion but, on the one hand, a contraction of the sphere that is subject to ritual restrictions and, on the other, a reinterpretation and restructuring of religious and ethical principles so that they become applicable to industrial life. Traditional rites, norms, and sanctions are abbreviated and specialized or become inoperative, while new norms and sanctions also emerge. "Deritualization," therefore, does not necessarily imply "secularization" but only an enlargement of the "ritually neutral" area. I have therefore called it a "ritual neutralization of the work sphere" without, however, intending to imply that the work sphere is completely freed from ritual restrictions or that the enlarged "neutral" area is without religious or cultural significance.

While "ritual neutralization" contracts the area subject to ritual restrictions and permits new techniques, products, and social relations to develop in a "ritually neutral" context, this area is not "pure" or completely free of "pollution." It is an ambiguous borderline area, neither very pure nor very polluted. The conception of it among the Hindu industrialists, especially the older ones, is that it is a slightly polluted area. In this respect, it resembles M. N. Srinivas's description of the "ordinary ritual status" characteristic of everyday life as a condition of "mild impurity." This resemblance is not at all surprising, since it would be difficult to imagine how Indians could go about their daily affairs if they were everywhere confronted by the dilemma of having to choose between absolute pollution and absolute purity.[37]

When a particular individual or group is considering entry into industry, it is not in any case absolute ritual pollution that will enter their calculations but the *relative difference* between their previous ritual status and their anticipated ritual status in industry. Logically, there are three kinds of possible relative difference to consider:

1. If members of a caste take up a new occupation of the same degree of purity-pollution as their previous occupation or have contact with castes and products that are of a similar degree of purity, there will be no particular ritual barrier to their mobility and no change in their ritual status.
2. If members of a caste try to take up new occupations of a degree of purity higher than that of their previous occupations or try to have contact with products and castes of relatively higher degree of purity, there will be a ritual barrier to their mobility originating primarily not with themselves but with opposition from other castes and community agents.
3. If members of a caste try to take up new occupations of a degree of purity lower than that of their previous occupations or try to have contact with "impure" products and castes, they will encounter a ritual barrier maintained primarily by their own caste organizations.

Most of the Madras Hindu industrial leaders fall into the third category, coming as they do from "clean" castes whose ritual status is relatively high. They should therefore have been deterred by a fear of ritual pollution in industry, according to Weber's "ritual law." Yet, except for the leather manufacturer and the Brahman who invited untouchables to dine with him, they seemed little worried about pollution. The reasons, I suggest, why mobility into industrial employment is not greatly affected by such worries are that "ritual neutralization" leaves large areas of industry free from traditional ritual and caste restrictions and that "vicarious ritualization" and reinterpretation justify those industrial activities that may be considered polluting—and threats to one's ritual status.

"Ritual neutralization" was not first introduced with industry, as is shown by Srinivas's discussion of "ordinary ritual status" and Weber's reference to the artisan's hands and workshop being clean. The ritual neutralization of the work sphere is intensified by urbanization and industrialization for two major reasons: (1) the increase in population, along with the increase in residential and occupational mobility, makes the monitoring and enforcement of traditional codes more difficult in the urban-industrial setting, and (2) the variety of new jobs, products and social relations is not quickly assimilated into the traditional ritual structure.

Some of the traditional jobs, products, and relations (e.g., scavenging, carpentering, hierarchical authority relations, and the like) do carry over into industry. Another group of industrial products, jobs, and relations, while seen to be different from those of a traditional agricultural society, are nevertheless similar enough to traditional jobs and relations, at least on superficial inspection, to be assimilated into the traditional structure. A small iron foundry, for example, is not greatly different from a smithy, a wood-lathe operator from a carpenter, or a small textile manufacturer from the head of a group of weavers. These common-sense analogies are much harder to draw for an electric steel furnace, automatic lathes and drills, chemical engineering, and the managing directorships of industrial complexes, just as the social relations in a modern office, a plant assembly, a canteen, or a clinic are not easily analogized to the traditional social and ritual structure.

In the light of the difficulty of quickly assimilating all new industrial products, processes, and social relations into the traditional ritual and caste structures and of the competition among different castes and communities for jobs and status within industry, there is a tendency to neutralize the ritual and caste significance of new industrial jobs, products, and relations. Industry becomes a ritually ambiguous sphere in which a status hierarchy emerges defined by "secular" criteria rather than by the criteria of the traditional ritual and caste structures. The stability of compartmentalization depends on this ritual ambiguity. To the extent that the "at-home culture" and the "at-work" culture are increasingly differentiated on the basis of the amount of "ritually neutral space," compartmentalization is reinforced and stabilized.

### *Vicarious Ritualization*

If we regard industry as a set of innovative patterns, there are sources of internal tension that tend to make the compartmentalizing type of adaptation unstable if not reinforced by other strategies. Among these are the demands on time. If a person spends twelve to fourteen hours a day in his office or working on business affairs, he cannot devote as many hours as his father or grandfather did to ritual and ceremonial observances at home or to religious studies. The two contexts may be physically and culturally distinct, and time may mean different things in them and be measured differently. Yet "there are only so many hours in a day," as the leaders say, and some activities will have to give way to others. The response of the industrial leaders to this temporal conflict is, with one or two exceptions, to try to have the best of both worlds. They give a great deal of their time and energies to their industrial affairs, yet they also manage to discharge their religious and ritual obligations in such a way as to remain convinced that they are still good and even devout Hindus (or Muslims and Christians). How do they manage to do so? Not necessarily by merging the spheres of religion and business, but by a series of adaptive responses which, taken together, may be called "vicarious ritualization," since these responses involve the substitution of an abbreviated rite and ceremony for several longer rites, or the substitution of a proxy performer of the rites for the original performer.

Instead of taking four to six hours for daily ablutions and prayers, as their fathers and grandfathers did, most of the Hindu industrial leaders now take about fifteen minutes to a half-hour, if they perform these duties at all. Two or three leaders rise very early in order to give more time to these acts; some pray while shaving and washing; and some say that they will give more time to such things when they are older. Many of the life-cycle and calendrical rites and festivals are abbreviated, and some of the minor ones are consolidated and performed together with a major one. On the occasion of a boy's sacred thread ceremony, many of the minor rites that should have been performed for him earlier are performed in abbreviated form. It is also becoming usual to perform different rites for different members of the family on the same day, to save time and for the convenience of all concerned, e.g., a sacred thread ceremony, a sixtieth birthday, and a return from a pilgrimage may all be celebrated at home in quick succession with the help of a single domestic priest who has come for the occasions.

Commenting on the trend toward the abbreviation and consolidation of rites and ceremonies, several of the industrial leaders insisted that the trend did not represent secularization, since the abbreviated performances still symbolized the same attitudes and beliefs. "Although we abbreviate our rituals," said one, "the worship is no less." Several were aware of the scriptural classifications of rites into obligatory and optional, and regular and occasional, and of the doctrine that an individual's spiritual evolution may enable him to dispense with many outward rites, ceremonies, and images in favor of symbolic "mental" worship. They have learned these sophisticated doctrines from their gurus, the scholarly pandits, and their own reading. Some of their children, however, are more impatient with ritual demands and are less inclined to look for substitutions. The sons of one industrialist, in whose house an important religious leader was visiting, told their father that if they had to remove their shirts and prostrate themselves before the religious functionary every time they passed him, they would simply stay out of his path until he left. The father agreed that perhaps these salutations were no longer important, although, in other respects, he ran a "traditional" household and had ostracized a daughter who had married for love.

The abbreviation of the ritual calendar has not always meant a reduction of expenditures. On the contrary, several life-cycle rites and calendrical festivals tend to be singled out for especially lavish preparations, even if the actual performance is greatly abbreviated. Some examples are the sacred thread ceremony for Brahman boys, weddings, and the major temple festivals of one's caste and sect. Although they have been contracted from a week or more to a single day, weddings have become occasions for expensive outlays of money and elaborate arrangements. It is now fashionable to hold both the religious ceremony and the wedding reception in a Madras mansion called Abbotsbury, which is rented for the purpose, rather than in one's own house. The bride's family usually bears the cost of the religious ceremony, which is held at some auspicious morning hour, whereas the evening reception is paid for by the groom's family. Famous musicians and dance artists are hired to perform at the reception.

While the industrial leader takes an active part in the planning and financing of these major life-cycle and calendrical rites and also participates in them in order to discharge his obligations as son, father, uncle, brother, or family head, he also delegates an increasing portion of his responsibilities to professionals, friends, and relatives who serve for him. Domestic and temple priests and the women and children in his family do many of the rituals. "They have the time, so they can do it" was a frequent remark. This delegation of ritual performance is especially frequent in the case of minor rites and ceremonies. Even among Brahman industrial leaders who come from orthodox families wherein the male head was traditionally responsible for performing the domestic rites and the study and teaching of the scriptures, vicarious ritualization is a common practice. Such leaders employ domestic priests (*purohitas*) on a regular basis to come in and perform daily *pūjās* as well as to carry out the more elaborate rituals on special occasions. Pandits are hired to tutor the children in Sanskrit and the scriptures. Wives, children, and other relatives go to the temple and to pilgrimage shrines and also attend a wide range of cultural-religious performances—classical Indian music and dance, plays and movies based on mythological and devotional themes, *bhajanas,* and recitations and discourses from the Vedas, Upaniṣads, Purāṇas, and Epics. At first glance, some of the performances may resemble secular cultural events; many of them nonetheless represent expressions of devotional and even ritual religious forms with an ecumenical tendency.[38]

The industrial leaders and their families are also the patrons and benefactors of cultural religious organizations, specialists, and institutions. They make generous contributions for the repair and improvement of temples, *maṭhas,* Sanskrit colleges, shrine centers, and special celebrations and festivals. In some cases, the industrial leader's family owned and managed a temple. Such private temples have, through recent legislation in the State, been brought under the jurisdiction of a Commissioner of Religious Endowments, who appoints the temple trustees. Trustees may continue to be members of the family who previously "owned" the temple and who, in any case, may continue to consider contributions to its maintenance a family obligation. The *maṭha* with which a family is affiliated also receives financial and other support from the industrialists. When the head of a *maṭha* is on tour, transportation and other arrangements for him and his retinue are directly provided by some of the industrialists in the form of automobiles, trucks, sound equipment, lodging, board, and related amenities.[39]

The leaders' charities are not restricted to narrowly "religious" institutions, functions, and functionaries. They or their fathers have also founded or contributed to colleges, universities, student hostels, hospitals, medical clinics, employees' housing, cultural associations (*sabhās*) to provide music, dance, and the theater, along with other "modern" philanthropies. In a few cases, benefactions are provided for members of the leader's caste, sect, or linguistic region only, but in most instances no such restrictions apply, even if the facility is located in a natal village or town. Many leaders also regard as religious and charitable acts their contributions to the festivals celebrated by their employees in their factories and to the paid holidays. In one case, a leader and his brothers contribute a substantial sum annually to a Gandhian social work program run by their sister and her husband.

The family trust is becoming the most popular legal device used by industrial leaders to provide for their philanthropies. Under present Indian law, such a trust is required to spend 75 per cent of its holdings for educational and charitable purposes but may retain the remaining 25 per cent, subject to municipal and business taxes, and use the money in the family business.

By supporting temples, *maṭhas,* and religious functions and functionaries; hiring domestic priests to perform rites in his home; and having his wife, children, and relatives participate in these and other religious and cultural performances, the industrial leader is able to overcome the temporal obstacles to a strict adherence to the ritual calendar. This "vicarious ritualization" justifies him in his feeling that, despite the abbreviation and even elimination of many rites and ceremonies, he is still a good Hindu and his acts of charity are "good deeds" that help restore any spiritual merit he may have lost from personal neglect of ritual observances. He has this feeling whether he happens to have been influenced by the Gandhian and modern philosophy that wealth is a "public trust" or by the more traditional philosophy of the religious leaders, who say that "kings and rich men" must be generous in their charities.

In fact, one can find ancient precedents for both vicarious ritualization and its justifications. Contraction and consolidation of rites with changing circumstances are mentioned in the *Dharmaśāstra* literature.[40] Kings and rich merchants have from earliest times been the patrons of temples and *maṭhas,* religious sacrifices and celebrations, schools, pandits, poets, musicians, and dancers. The industrialist patron may be entering new kinds of occupation and may also be assisting with the technical modernization of temples, *maṭhas,* and shrines, as well as with schools, hospitals, roads, and irrigation, but the meaning and function of his "vicarious ritualization" is quite traditional—to transform wealth and power into religious merit and social prestige.[41] Hindu philosophy makes this interpretation relatively easy by teaching that he who pays for a religious performance gets the "merit" from it.

Precedents for "vicarious ritualization" among businessmen associated with foreigners in the history of Madras can be readily cited. Ānanda Raṅga Piḷḷai, the chief Dubash for Dupleix,* records in his diary the complaints of some Christians against him that, as soon as he was appointed chief Dubash, he began patronizing Hindu temples and honoring Brahmans; he neglected Christians, they said. He criticizes another Dubash, a Christian convert, who celebrated the construction of a church by giving a lavish feast where Hindus were invited and "all arrangements were made in strict conformity with the religious scruples of each caste." His objection was not to the lavishness of the feast but to the fact that a Christian was following Hindu customs!

> However magnificent be the style of any social act in which one indulges, if it be at variance with the established practice of the community concerned, it cannot redound to one's credit. If a man who has forsaken his religion, and joined another, reverts to the manners and customs of his former belief, he must inevitably draw upon himself contempt.[42]

* Marquis Dupleix, French Governor of Pondicherry in 1742.

When a Christian missionary regretted that Piḷḷai had not become a Christian convert, because many others would have followed him, Piḷḷai replied that such conversions were most unlikely, since Hindus, who are the company's merchants, hold many and varied appointments and considerable wealth. "Each is his own master and does not trouble about the others. If one turns to another religion, the rest would not follow him." [43]

In the eighteenth-century literature, we also find Sanskrit notices of merchants and other notables of Madras City who patronized pandits, poets, musicians, dancers, and other artists.

The Tamil trading community, the Ceṭṭiyars, have a reputation for being devout Śaivites and spending very large sums on the famous shrines and temples at Cidambaram, Madurai, Tiruvaṇṇāmalai, Tiruvāṉaikkāval, and elsewhere. Many of them have customarily set aside one pie* in every rupee of profit for charitable and religious expenditure.[44]

These historical examples show that Hindu traders and merchants were able to collaborate with Europeans without being converted to Christianity, the religion of their employers and rulers. On the contrary, those Hindu merchants who prospered from this collaboration generally increased their support of Hindu temples, priests, pandits, rites, and ceremonies.†

Vicarious ritualization is an old and well-known adaptive strategy in Hinduism and other religions as well. The need for it has been intensified by the growing ritual neutralization of the work sphere, which has contracted the area of ritual purity and pollution and has taken away time from the performance of traditional rites and ceremonies. To compensate for these changes and to restructure their religious obligations, the industrial leaders have turned to vicarious ritualization and to the reinterpretation of basic religious doctrines.

## *Reinterpreting the Essential Tenets: From a Theodicy of the Caste System to a Theodicy of the Industrial System*

Vicarious ritualization is not the only response to the temporal conflicts created by modernization, nor is the limitation of time the only source of conflict. An indivisibility of the personality—or at least a limit to one's divisibility into "industrialist," "father," "Hindu," "philanthropist," and other social roles—plays its part. As the industrialist passes back and forth between the world of industry and his domestic world, he is bound to carry with him, consciously or unconsciously, some standards and practices from one sphere into the other. He is, after all, only one individual, however many "social personalities" he may develop. While his relations with untouchables are more free in the office and factory context than in the home context, because they are two "separate spheres" with different norms, he cannot completely leave his domestic attitudes and standards at home when he goes to the office or file away his industrial standards at the office when he goes home. Leakages occur between the spheres and become

* There were 192 pie in a rupee before recent currency reforms.

† The effects on the modernizing process of this kind of encapsulation of religious behavior away from business and politics are discussed in Part Five.

sources of tension and of changes in both spheres. In one leader's home library, an engineering manual stood next to a copy of the *Bhagavadgītā*. Another leader, a Brahman, boasted that he invites union leaders who are untouchables to dine with him at home. A third leader insisted that he was more "religious" by being charitable to his employees than were those who were strict vegetarians and "observers" at home but "cheated" their employees. A fourth thought he could be an "ascetic" in his office, because he put in more than he took out. These leakages between the domestic and the industrial spheres indicate that another adaptive process is at work to accommodate conflicts. The process is one of redefining the essentials of Hinduism in order to meet the requirements of an industrial age, and changing industrial policies and practices to conform to a positive ethical code.

Vicarious ritualization enables the industrial leaders to "stretch time" to cover both their ritual calendar and their business schedules, but it does not blind them to their many lapses in ritual observances as compared to their recollection of their fathers' and grandfathers' practice.

They do not, however, see these lapses as a threat to their Hinduism, as some of their gurus do. Instead, they are redefining what the essentials of Hinduism may be in an industrial age "when everything has to be speeded up." They regard a broad simplification and streamlining of the ritual calendar as one inevitable step in religious modernization. A downgrading of ritual observance generally with a concurrent upgrading of devotional faith (*bhakti*) and a reformulation of philosophical and ethical principles is another aspect of the process of restructuring the essentials.

Their ritual orientation is not always Sanskritic; one leader, for example, organized and supports a school to train non-Brahman domestic priests. The Syrian Christian and the two Muslim families follow the rituals of their respective religions. None of the leaders is antireligious, even if he has lapsed in personal observance. In addition to the indirect support they give to ritual and devotional religion, they are for the most part convinced that they still believe in their faith's essential tenets. The conviction is based on an effort to apply and interpret such basic doctrines of their religion as personal destiny (*karman,* kismet), moral duty (*dharma*), rebirth (*saṃsāra*), God's will and God's grace, salvation (*mokṣa*), and noninjury (*ahiṃsā*) to industrial life and their own careers. Sometimes the effort is purely personal; sometimes it is based on the advice of their gurus and the spiritual heads of the sects to which they belong. Whatever the source, most leaders show a sincere and reflective preoccupation with the relevance of these religious and ethical principles for modern industry and seem to have reconciled any apparent conflicts to their own satisfaction.

At least four of the industrialists are not sure they know enough to believe in the *karman* doctrine, which holds that their present condition is a result of their past actions, although these four, as well as the others who do believe in it without qualifications, are sure there must be something, usually referred to as "God's grace" or "God's will," to explain why they have succeeded where others have failed. Increasingly this kind of explanation is invoked to explain inequalities of all kinds and not only the inequalities of caste. One industrialist remarked that after the caste system disappears he will still believe in the doctrines of *karman* and rebirth as the best explanation and justification for other remaining gross inequalities.

A belief in *karman,* or in God's grace, does not preclude for these men the importance of human effort and intelligence. As one of them put it: "Without God's will nothing can move, but if you think God is going to give you everything on a platter, you are a fool." His thought was echoed by the other leaders; effort, hard work, time spent on thinking about a project, knowledge, and genius are considered essential ingredients in success—and so is luck. Sometimes luck is interpreted as opportunity, and sometimes as just a fortuitous breeze that "blows the falling leaf in one direction rather than in another." It was not always clear how many of these ingredients were also included in one's personal fate as determined by past actions, that is, in one's *karman.* Some were inclined to include everything in *karman;* most left the issue open, beyond suggesting that ability, intelligence, and will power were inherited from one's parents and grandparents. Acutely conscious that "one's ego is always there, always claiming that it has done this, it has done that," they nevertheless believe that "*I* am not doing anything; somebody or something is directing me."

In an industrial context, the doctrine of doing one's moral duty (*dharma*) is also being reinterpreted. Practically every one of these men looked on his work in industry as a moral duty and as a necessary contribution to the good of India and the world, as well as to himself and his family. This view is similar to Gandhi's reinterpretation of the *Bhagavadgītā* as calling for a different kind of sacrifice in each age; in ours, the needed sacrifice is "body labor." Some of the industrialists were familiar with the Gandhian interpretation; others simply had a strong sense of the urgency and appropriateness of industrial production at this stage of India's development in order to provide jobs and a higher standard of living. "It is a job you've got to do and to do well. It would be a sin not to act. In a country like ours, very few can do things."

Several others had been confirmed in their industrial interpretations of their *dharma* by the heads of their *maṭhas* and by their gurus who assimilate the industrial vocation to the Vaiśya's role in the traditional *varṇa* scheme.

None of these industrialists looked upon his work or industrial life as the veil of *māyā* or wished to renounce it for the life of an ascetic or even a hermit. One industrialist interpreted the notion of *māyā* as "the irrelevant and the distracting." Industrial life is for this philosophically minded man a significant reality that will do more for future generations than agriculture was able to do. On the eve of retirement, he was putting his affairs in order. To train his successors, he was gradually delegating more and more of his daily responsibilities to them, while continuing to make the general policy decisions.

With about three exceptions, all the leaders are "this-worldly ascetics," working hard, with complete absorption in and dedication to their jobs.

One of them even reported solving industrial problems in his dreams. This kind of commitment to work was well expressed by the leader who said he could be an ascetic while working in his office, since "asceticism is putting more in than you take out."

Industrial progress is no illusion for them, despite the doctrine of endless *yuga* cycles of degradation and reconstruction.* Most of them were familiar with the *yuga* doctrine and did not let it affect their emphatic belief that progress has been made in many fields. Even if this age is a morally degraded *Kaliyuga,* they did not doubt that "tremendous progress" has been made in their country, at least since 1947, and that it would not be reversed.

Commenting on the *yuga* doctrine, another said that "the past is always golden." He added that this life may be a "corridor," but "we have to live in it." For himself, he found the transitory and the eternal reconciled in the Advaitic philosophy of the Upaniṣads. He recited an Upaniṣadic passage to me in his office with great zest and feeling, first in Sanskrit and then in English: "I am that truth. You are that truth. The entire universe is that truth. Everything is that truth. That truth, that energy which is in the sun is in you. *That* is one universal brotherhood."

The Syrian Christian and the two Muslim Indian industrial leaders said they followed practices and beliefs prescribed by their respective religions. Their faiths are not, however, as different from those of the Hindu leaders as one might expect. Kismet replaces *karman* for the Muslims. No rebirth awaits the Muslims, because after death "you black out." Kismet and God's will determine who succeeds and fails, but kismet works only if you work, too. Not all who make the effort succeed. Anything that is begun with good intentions, however, is bound to turn out well.

The Muslim family that has lived in the South for several hundred years is more observant in its religious practices than the other Muslim family, which has recently come from Bombay and Hyderabad. Members of the former family go to the mosque every night for prayer; they do not drink alcohol or smoke; and a *munśī* is giving religious instruction to their children. The leader of the more urbanized, formerly Northern family considers his family "far from orthodox Muslims." He remembers his father, once a finance minister of Hyderabad, as very religious but not orthodox. The father read from the Koran, the *Bhagavadgītā,* and the Bible daily. This religious tolerance is reflected in the family's marriages. Although the executive is married to a Muslim, three of his four brothers had married English, Swedish, and French girls, respectively; a brother's child had married a Hindu, and his own daughter is married to a Roman Catholic.

The Christian leader described his family as "Syrian Christian with a Hindu tendency." His father and brothers are graduates of Madras Christian College. The family members do not believe in *karman* or rebirth;

* An aeon in Hindu cosmology is divided into four ages, or *yugas,* called *Kṛta, Tretā, Dvāpara,* and *Kali.* Each yuga represents a progressive decline in morality and religion, and the *Kaliyuga* complete confusion and disorder, after which the world is destroyed by fire and flood. The world is then re-created and passes through another cycle of *yugas.* The present age is said to be the *Kaliyuga.*

they attribute their success to an "almighty and loving God." God should not, on the other hand, be blamed for one's mistakes. The father, who was a pioneer advocate of scientific agriculture and industrialization, had taught them to regard work as a moral duty and everything they owned as a public trust. As Christians, the family has encountered no discrimination in Madras City, where they belong to a small minority. In Kerala, where the different communities—Christian, Muslim and Hindu—are more evenly balanced, they find the inter-sect situation more serious.

The idea that behavior in industry should be governed by a code of ethical principles was mentioned by most of the leaders, Hindu and non-Hindu alike. It is very much on their minds, because they constantly hear Indian businessmen and industrialists criticized at home and abroad. They are eager to correct the popular stereotype of the Indian businessman as one motivated by a "trading mentality" to seek quick and exorbitant profits from goods that seldom meet quality standards. They concede that there are some merchants, "especially in North India," who fit this stereotype and say that it will take another ten or fifteen years to educate such traders to more enlightened and sound business practices.

Positively, most of the leaders have formulated precepts of a practical code of conduct that they hope will be enforced by the manufacturers' association, or even the government. Some of the rules they have formulated are quite traditional: Be truthful and keep your promises; do your job well; don't be lazy and waste time; use your wealth for the good of others, not just for yourself; and depend on yourself and not on others' charity. Quality control may be a modern innovation, but the obligation to give accurate weights and measures is an old one.

Some of the ethical rules the industrialists have formulated have a more modern ring: Provide equal opportunities for all to develop and grow through technical education and jobs; do not discriminate or give preference because of caste or religious community; respect the dignity of labor; promote democracy and economic welfare by raising standards of living; and work for human rights and universal brotherhood.

The rules are not a mere collection of pious platitudes; they represent a sincere effort to establish an operating code in Madras industry. The leather manufacturer's campaign against adulterated hides is only one of many examples of efforts to establish quality control. Many of the other industrialists belong to the Indian Standards Institute, which certifies quality. Others use Lloyd's to certify quality. One of the problems in effective quality control arises in the manufacture of precision parts by a large number of small suppliers who do not have the requisite experience and technical knowledge.

Although some industrialists complain that India's labor and social security laws and its tax structure are too "advanced" and burdensome for a country just beginning to industrialize, several have adopted progressive employee welfare programs of their own. Some have endowed schools, hospitals, and colleges in the city, as well as in their native towns and villages. They are also beginning to adopt personnel policies and practices that tend to emphasize skill and performance as criteria for hiring and promotion, rather than caste and community preference. Most, too, plow a percentage of their profits back into further expansion and improvement of their plants. Their charitable contributions to temples, *maṭhas,* churches, and mosques and their feeding of the poor vary from family to family; most of them have a good reputation on this score. None spoke more eloquently than the one who said that "poverty anywhere is a danger everywhere," because it causes the "evil eye" of resentment. Not all are as traditionally compassionate as another, who says he "cannot tolerate suffering" and is generous in giving 25 per cent of his income per year to charities, his staff, and the poor. This man's *ahiṃsā* precept, however, that "if you can't do your fellow men good, don't do them harm" is widely shared, with the added provision that by building industry, these leaders are convinced, they are "doing good."

While not all the industrial leaders are equally philosophical in their interpretations of "the essential tenets" of Hinduism, the range of their beliefs and the general trend of their reinterpretation of these beliefs for their industrial activities is remarkably similar: They see industrial leadership as a moral duty (*dharma*) that needs to be urgently discharged in the present age, even if it means sacrificing some traditional obligations. They see their own success in such a career as a combined outcome of their past actions or *karman,* God's grace or God's will, and their own effort, intelligence, and luck. Not all see this success as an essential road to their final liberation (*mokṣa*) from the cycles of rebirth (*saṃsāra*), but most do see it as one of the roads they must take, and they enjoy traveling it. Although industry may be only a tiny "corridor" in the cycles of the ages (*yugas*) and may be illusory (*māyā*) compared to ultimate reality, industrial life is nonetheless an unavoidably present, progressively changing reality, with a greater potential for improving human welfare than agriculture had by itself. These men have no strong disposition to renounce industrial life for the career of an other-worldly ascetic.

For these industrial leaders, the "essential tenets" of their religion have a durability and generality that will survive industry's many changes. Even if the doctrines of *karman* and *saṃsāra* have been used in the past to explain and justify the inequalities of the caste system, these doctrines will not lose their relevance with the passing of the caste system, for other inequalities to explain and justify will exist.

The scriptural and intellectual sources upon which the industrial leaders have drawn for their formulations and reinterpretations of the "essential tenets" vary with their community, education, individual talents, and spiritual advisers. Some quoted the *Bhagavadgītā,* others the Upaniṣads or the Tamil *Tirukkuṟaḷ.* It is interesting, however, that apart from some differences in detail the Syrian Christians, the Muslims, and the Hindus have come out with a similar industrial code and set of beliefs. The main difference among the Hindus is between those who have been influenced by Gandhi's reinterpretation of the *Bhagavadgītā* and other scriptures and those who are influenced by the more traditional gurus and teachers. A note of irony lingers in the fact that industrialists should find moral and religious support in Gandhi, who was so strongly opposed to industrialization. But his teachings of the dignity of labor as an appropriate form of sacrifice in this modern age and of self-reliance, truth, nonviolence, and compassion for the poor and lowly have their obvious application to modern industry.

Among the more traditional interpreters of Hinduism, two heads of Śaṅkara (Advaitavedānta) *maṭhas,* one at Kāñcī (Conjeeveram) and one at Śṛṅgēri, are influential with the industrial leaders, particularly the Brahmans. Both Śaṅkarācāryas have supported the industrial leaders in the belief that they are performing their moral duty (*dharma*) when they create industrial products and jobs or make money. The idea that one can be a good industrialist and at the same time a good Hindu, even a good Brahman, has the Svāmīs' endorsement. The Śaṅkarācāryas are less indulgent, however, about lapses from ritual observances than the leaders themselves; the Svāmīs hold a somewhat different view of the "essentials of Hinduism." One of them said that what is distinctive and essential to Hinduism is its "sociological foundation," not its superstructure of beliefs. By "sociological foundation," he said he meant the set of family disciplines regarding birth, food, marriage, death, and the like, which avoid pollution and transmit from generation to generation the proper way of life. Traditionally, Brahman families were duty bound to cultivate these disciplines to the highest degree. In recent times, however, under the pressure of economic changes and necessities, he finds that many Brahman families have relaxed these disciplines and exposed themselves and him to dangers of pollution. Under the circumstances, the Svāmī thought it would be necessary to rely more on devout non-Brahmans to maintain the family disciplines. Without such a "sociological foundation," he felt, Hinduism will disappear as a distinctive religion, since its theological and philosophical tenets are not so different from those of other world religions.

That some are born to make money, others to rule and protect, and still others to be scholars and workers is the way both these spiritual leaders interpret for this age the ancient *varṇa* doctrine. The money must be made in ethical ways, and "kings and rich men" are expected to perform works of charity.

For the other two classes, the intellectuals (especially Brahmans) and the workers, the Svāmīs prescribe a simple life without luxuries. These classes do not have much property and cannot give much to charity. If each class performed its appointed function, each would find its spiritual salvation, they say, and social problems would also be solved.

The Śaṅkarācāryas believe that present trends run counter to the śāstric prescriptions. Because people now want whatever they see, especially what is found in other parts of the world, the standard of living is rising and there is a problem of poverty. This desire for luxuries, they feel, has been created by more than 500 years of foreign domination in Indian politics and commerce. While Vinoba Bhave's land-gift movement, the community development projects, and industrialization all make some contribution to the decrease of poverty, these measures cannot solve social problems. Such problems can be solved only by the spiritual and moral development of the individual, by a return to the simple life.

This does not mean that everyone should withdraw from the world and become an other-worldly ascetic. Hindus, as they read history and the ancient treatises on war and politics, say they have always been a practical, active people. The doctrine of the unreality of the world has nothing to do with practical life; it refers to a higher level of experience. The world is a myth only in the sense that it is created by man's reactions to it and is therefore a product of human consciousness. "We do not stop eating just because we believe in the atomic theory." The world may be unreal from a certain point of view, but men must nevertheless act in this life. Spiritual leaders, however, believe that they should not develop too much attachment to things of this life. For them, a diet of leaves, fruit, and milk suffices. This diet does not destroy life and does not create many wants. It is also healthy. Among rulers and the business class, however, luxuries are needed, say the spiritual leaders, as an incentive to develop the "arts."

Although the Śaṅkarācāryas seem far more orthodox than the industrial leaders in their insistence on strict ritual observances, they do encourage the leaders, and support many intercaste and inter-sect movements. The industrial leaders, in turn, support the Śaṅkarācāryas, trying to meet their demands through a vicarious ritualization that leaves them free to follow their industrial careers. In this manner, and by redefining the "essentials" of Hinduism and extending its tenets to industry, they have been able to "modernize" Hinduism without secularizing it, or at least without losing their cultural identity as Hindus. For them, the "essentials of Hinduism" consist more in a set of beliefs and a code of ethical conduct than in a set of ritual observances. In this sense, the effect of industry is to change the traditional conception of the essentials of Hinduism from an emphasis on correct ritual observances and family disciplines to an emphasis on philosophical principles, devotional faith, and right conduct.

## Industry and Indian Traditions: A Summary

Max Weber's thesis that the "spirit" of Hinduism and Hindu society constitutes a "core obstruction" to occupational and technical change is derived from an ideal-typical construct based more on a narrow interpretation of selected scriptural texts than on observed facts of individual behavior in specific social and cultural contexts. Weber did recognize some of these facts in his analysis of the different kinds of caste schisms and mobility generated by residential and occupational mobility, property differentiation, technical change, and the growth and decline of new sects. His analysis also took some account of how Hindus adapt their ritual structure and theodicy in daily practice by ignoring, circumventing, and rationalizing ritual restrictions. The fact that there is some pollution, for example, in getting pots from a potter, a shave from a barber, and clean clothes from a launderer has not prevented these daily transactions. Transgressions of ritual restrictions result, as Weber recognizes, not only in such *ritual sanctions* as rites of purification; they frequently lead to *practical sanctions* organized by members of one's own or of other castes—ostracism, fines and penalties, and even beatings. Such secular sanctions and the relative power relations reflected in them may be more decisive constraints on action than the fear of ritual pollution *per se*.

In spite of his awareness of such realities, Weber seems not to have seriously considered their significance in counteracting what he regards as the essentially negative effects of Hindu ritual and belief on the economy. Weber's chief concern was historical: He sought to explain why industrial capitalism originated in Europe and not in India or elsewhere in Asia. He thought he had discovered one decisive factor in one particular set of religious ideas and attitudes—a "Protestant ethic"—that acted as a catalyst in the European case, and another set of religious ideas and attitudes—a Hindu and Buddhist ethic—that acted as an inhibitor in the Asian case. Today, there is less interest in Weber's "origins of capitalism" problem and more concern with the conditions of economic development. Unfortunately, Weber's ideal-typical Hindus living in "magical dread" of innovation and "redeath" still haunt current discussions. Many contend that a major precondition for economic development and modernization is the extirpation of "traditional" religious beliefs and practices and social institutions.

In a preliminary study of nineteen industrialist leaders in Madras City, my problem was to find out how a group of successful entrepreneurs relate their religious beliefs and ritual practices and their family and caste affiliations to their economic activities and policies. The results of this study indicate, I believe, that the industrial leaders not only did not experience soul-shattering conflicts between their religious and social traditions and their industrial careers, but in fact adapted the two spheres in ways reminiscent of Weber's Puritan capitalists.

Within two or three generations, these industrial families have moved from small villages and towns into a metropolitan center, modern higher and technical education, and the leadership of industrial empires. While the size of the household and the nuclear family has generally decreased, the norms of joint-family organization are still alive in the urban households and in their relations to relatives and lands in natal villages. Education and training of the young in the new technical specializations of engineering, science, and business administration and the ownership and management of industrial empires are also linked to joint-family principles. The moves into industry and the city have brought some changes in living styles and some departures from caste and religious traditions. I should like to summarize these changes and the different kinds of adaptations with respect to the roles of the joint family, the caste system, and the system of Hindu ritual and belief.

Although twelve of the companies with which the industrialists are identified are public limited companies whose stock can be bought and sold on the open market, and only three are private limited companies and three are partnerships, the industrial leaders and their families in fact control all the companies studied except the one in the public sector.* The devices through which this control is exercised are chiefly the managing agency system, the holding company, and the top offices of a

* The list of companies is given in Appendix A below.

company. By using these devices, an industrial leader and his family can control a number of public limited companies without owning a controlling interest in them, provided he and his family control the managing agency that manages the affairs of the company or a holding company of which the company is a subsidiary, or else hold the positions of managing director, director, and chairman of the board in the company. Several of these devices may be used in combination.

This phenomenon is a familiar one in European and American corporate industrial organization and has been discussed in terms of the separation of ownership and management. It has not, however, been much studied in relation to the differences in social structure and culture patterns to be found in different societies. While the managing agency system, the joint stock and holding company, the corporate table of organization, and the family trust fund were all introduced into India under British and Western auspices, the ways in which Indians have used and developed these organizational forms of modern business and industry reflect Indian social structure and culture as well as economic and political conditions. The fact that the legal separation of ownership from management in the modern corporation has not prevented Madras industrialists and their families from retaining control over these corporations says a good deal about the structure and adaptability of the Indian joint family as well as the entrepreneurial ingenuity of the Indian businessman. It suggests, at the very least, that the study of economic organization and economic history should not be separated from the study of domestic organization and family history.

The move to the city and into industry has not destroyed the joint family and its extended kinship ties. Although the data on the Madras industrial leaders' families show a trend over three generations toward smaller and separate households and toward smaller nuclear families, there is also an active cultivation of joint-family contacts with relatives in villages and small towns as well as in the cities, and with the maintenance by at least seven of the leaders of large joint households in the city. Many of the rules of the traditional joint family, moreover, have been adapted to industrial organization and management. These include the use of joint-family funds to finance the education of members and to make capital investments in industrial undertakings and a deliberate specialization and division of labor in the training and placement of sons and nephews, grandsons and grandnephews in industrial careers. The restriction of such training, placement, and shares in the business to those members of the family who are eligible coparceners to joint-family property in a patrilineal virilocal family system is also a traditional feature of the joint family. The authority of the eldest male of the family, usually the father or eldest son, to make the important business decisions with the consensus of the other coparceners, the use of joint facilities and joint bank accounts, and occasional joint households or compounds represent further extensions of the traditional rules.

These rules are not rigid; their operation depends on many contingencies—the number of males born into a family, the willingness and ability of the father and his brothers to inculcate business skills and strong family loyalties in the boys, the availability of opportunities, the legal structure, national industrial policy, and public opinion, among others. One industrial leader had married the boss's daughter, although this runs against the grain of a family system in which married daughters are expected to move away and inheritance is in the male line. With the Hindu Code's admission of daughters to equal inheritance with sons, it is probable that resistance to taking sons-in-law into the family business will diminish. Usually, married daughters have been provided for through dowries and cash payments from their fathers or brothers.

The adaptability of the traditional joint-family rules in an urban and industrial context implies an underlying congruence of the structure of the traditional Indian joint family with the requirements of modern industry—a congruence that has enabled it to survive geographical and occupational mobility, monetization of the economy, production for national and international markets, and the application of science and advanced technology to industry. Whether it can also survive complete nationalization of the economy is more problematic.[44]

No claim is made that the close articulation between family structure and industrial organization is peculiar to India or that the form such articulation takes among the Madras industrial leaders is unique. It may well be that, as more social anthropological studies of modern industrialization are made, the Madras pattern will turn out to be a variant of a common pattern. The evidence contained in a few recent studies suggests that this is indeed the case.

The caste system also does not constitute the rigid, monolithic barrier that it is usually alleged to be. Even during the preindustrial period, the complexity and mobility of castes was far greater than the doctrine of the four *varnas* suggests. Departures of some caste members from traditional occupations and the formation of new subcaste clusters around new occupations are historical commonplaces. Agriculture and commerce have historically been considered open to all castes. With industrial development came many new jobs, some of which do not fit into the traditional caste occupations and are therefore also "open" to all castes. The fact that some castes cluster around some occupations in industry is to be explained primarily not by the operation of caste principles in industry but as the effect of previous experience, education, access to capital and opportunities, job protection through seniority, and preference given to children of job-holders. These factors, rather than caste as such, explain the predominance of Brahmans (nine) and Ceṭṭiyars (four) among the Madras industrial leaders, as well as the clustering of castes in different jobs. In the case of the Ceṭṭiyar leaders, predisposing factors are to be found in their traditional occupations of trade and money-lending; in the case of the Brahman leaders, similar predisposing factors are found to occur with a departure from their traditional caste occupations. In the case of the other castes and communities represented among the industrial leaders, there is also a departure from previous caste occupation, which is usually peasant agriculture.

The degree of continuity or discontinuity of industrial employments with preindustrial ones must therefore find its explanation not in traditional caste occupations or in the caste system generally but in the specific histories of individuals, families, and caste or religious groups, histories that show how these individuals and groups first acquired special access to the experience, knowledge, capital, or opportunities needed for industrial development. Industry is too new in India and in Madras to be the traditional occupation of any particular caste. It therefore provides opportunities to all castes for entrepreneurship, management, engineering, skilled labor, and other employments. To the extent that industry still uses traditional methods and crafts in construction—carpentry, forge work, and cleaning—it also provides opportunities for the castes traditionally associated with these crafts and trades.

Some traditional occupations may be more closely related to certain modern occupations than other traditional occupations. Trade and banking, for example, are closely related to industrial enterprise, and blacksmithing is closely related to some kinds of skilled labor in a foundry. Hence, it would not be at all surprising to find that some castes are better qualified than others by experience, skill, and knowledge of special conditions to move into related industrial occupations. Experience in trade and banking or in a skilled craft, however, is not in India confined to just one caste. Members of several castes have managed to acquire some of the experience and knowledge relevant to modern industry and have been able to move into industrial occupations when opportunities came their way. Some Brahmans, having high literacy and educational qualifications, were able to fill clerical and supervisory posts; others, experienced in trade and banking, built up industrial enterprises.

Some observers are disposed to see industry as tradition-bound in India, since they find some features of the traditional caste and ritual system within it. Traditional merchant castes (such as the Ceṭṭiyars in Tamiḻnāḍu) *are* prominent in industry, and most firms are locally known as caste or community firms and are presumed to favor their particular community in recruitment, training, promotion, and contracts. Traditional artisan castes, such as those of blacksmiths, carpenters, tinkers, and construction workers, are still found in modern industry, as are the untouchable sweepers, scavengers, and others who specialize in polluting kinds of work. At first glance, at least, the status hierarchy in industry resembles the traditional caste hierarchy, both in its general outlines as a *varṇa* system and in its detailed job classifications. The observance of *pūjās* and religious festivals in offices and factories is a further reminder of the traditional ritual and festival calendar.

These traditional features within Indian industry are not, it seems to me, sufficient to prove the case for the persistence of the caste system in industry. Departures from traditional caste and *varṇa* occupations are far more numerous and significant. In Madras City, Brahmans outnumber Ceṭṭiyars and other castes and communities as industrial leaders. Former untouchables are found throughout the spectrum of industrial employments as machinists and mechanics and in highly skilled types of jobs. Some kinds of work, such as tanning and leather manufacture, previously done only by untouchables, foreigners, or non-Hindus, are now the province of caste Hindus. While there is some clustering of other caste groups in particular kinds of related jobs, the range is neither narrow nor exclusive. Many new kinds of jobs in a modern factory or office are not easily done by traditional artisans but may be by their children, who have better education and technical training. Job classification is increasingly based on technical and performance criteria and administered by professional personnel managers. In office and shop, in canteen and washroom, in union and political activities, and at religious festivals or on the journey to and from work, different castes come in constant contact and communication. As companies grow in size, they are obliged to add directors and managers from more than one caste or community in order to assure access to capital, contracts, technical agreements with foreign firms, and a national market for their products.

These modern features of industry are not likely to displace the traditional features overnight, nor are the two sets of features necessarily incompatible. A definite status hierarchy emerges in industry, and upward mobility within the hierarchy follows well-marked paths. Education, especially in English, technical skills, authority, and salary define the criteria for achievement in the hierarchy; "dirty" work with one's hands defines the negative criterion. Consequently, there can be upward mobility to management posts from white-collar office work and from "clean" engineering and technical staff but rarely from the plant staff, no matter how skilled, if the appropriate education is lacking. The shop foreman represents the highest position open to the skilled workman. The more progressive industrialists are trying to broaden the channels of upward mobility through technical training programs and are requiring "graduates" to work with their hands.

The industrial hierarchy is not, however, isomorphic with the traditional caste hierarchy. In broad outline this industrial hierarchy seems similar to that found in the United States or Europe, where, as in India, college graduates are not disposed to become factory workers, and factory workers do not easily rise into top management. I would, in fact, suggest that the source of the Indian industrial hierarchy is to be found not only in the demands of industrial organization and traditional Indian attitudes but in European models and influences as well. In Madras City, a very definite British legacy is to be reckoned with; until India became independent, managers and heads of departments in most Madras firms were British. Respect for their authority meant a respect for English language and literature, for clean hands, white ducks, shirts, and neckties. The English education sponsored by the British in India was designed generally for training clerks and office workers; it did not aim to train industrial managers, engineers, or scientists. Within the British status system also, clerks and office workers outranked skilled workers; a literary education was considered superior to a technical or practical one. A British observer at the turn of the century wrote that "the nineteenth-century education produced a philosophically-minded class, with a fine contempt for all kinds of manual labor and completely dissociated from intelligent working men. This is not a promising basis upon which to build up industries." [45]

With the growth of the national movement and the eventual departure of the British, industrial enterprise and management attracted Indians trained in science, engineering, business administration, finance, and marketing. The new types have continued some of the older British models in industry, as they have also joined with the older practical types, in some cases their own fathers, uncles, or grandfathers, to form an entrepreneurial class. Since World War II, Indian industrialists have also extended their contacts with American, Japanese, Russian, German, Swiss, and other industrial concerns. Through these contacts they have acquired new markets, capital and equipment, training, and skills. Whether the Indian industrialist follows the older British models, or the newer models from the United States, the Soviet Union, and other countries, or some combination of these, he is rapidly building a distinctive form, an Indian industrial tradition.

The conflicts the industrialist encounters with traditional institutions, beliefs, and values he contains and mitigates by *compartmentalizing* his life in industry from his domestic and social life. He categorizes the latter as his "traditional culture," although it also contains many modern features, and the former as his "modern culture," although it contains some traditional features. Both these "cultures" are Indian for him, and his daily passage between them depends on a set of adaptive strategies that not only reduce the conflicts but also provide a basis for their eventual reconciliation and integration.

Compartmentalization is especially important in understanding the role of Hindu ritual and beliefs in industrialization. To judge from the situation in Madras factories and offices and the behavior of its industrial leaders, ritual and belief are not the major obstacles they are frequently alleged to be by Max Weber and others. While fear of ritual pollution from intercaste contact and from polluting products and processes is still to be found, that fear is not a major problem in industry. Intercaste work teams, intercaste dining in factory canteens, and the use of common washing and medical facilities are all now standard practices. The manufacture of leather and other polluting products is increasingly in the hands of "clean" and upper castes, whereas before independence this was a monopoly of non-Hindus and untouchables.

The weakening and contraction of pollution is more evident in the office and factory than it is at home and in social relations. In the home, intercaste dining is rare, and many traditional restrictions still prevail. In fact, the industrial leaders seem to make a kind of compensatory effort to maintain a traditional home life and a traditional role as religious patrons (through Sanskritization and *vicarious ritualization*) while they are acting as the vanguard of modernization in the industrial sphere. By compartmentalizing their lives in this way, they are able to function both as good Hindus and as good industrialists. Their compartmentalizing is not complete and rigid, however, for they also tolerate and sometimes encourage a certain amount of ritual and religious behavior in the office and factory by allowing employees to have *pūjās* and to keep images and lithographs of deities near their machines, while giving them paid holidays during the major festivals. Some of this is, to be sure, done under the constraint of labor laws and union pressure, but many leaders also see in these rites an expression of respect both for Hinduism and for machines.

The industrial leaders follow a modern life-style in industry; they use English, Western dress, the latest machines and industrial management and design, and mix freely with all castes. At home, they continue to follow the traditional life-style, using their "native" language, dress, and diet; following many ritual observances; and adhering to the tenets and practices of their caste and religious sect. Where conflicts arise, because they do not have enough time for all the rites and festivals and a full day at the office, or because industrial activities seem to violate ritual restrictions and religious scruples, accommodations are made on both sides. The life-cycle and calendrical rites are abbreviated and consolidated without losing their symbolic significance; through "vicarious ritualization," the devout householder delegates much of his responsibility for ritual observances to a domestic priest and to those members of his family who have the time. Generous charitable endowments to temples and *maṭhas,* religious schools, functions, and functionaries help to restore the religious merit thought to have been lost through lapses in ritual observance.

In this compartmentalization, the work sphere is "ritually neutralized," that is, relatively freed from customary norms and ritual restrictions. This makes it easier to experiment with and learn about new products, processes, and social relations. Through "ritual neutralization," many traditional restrictions governing intercaste relations and contacts with "pollutants" are either suspended in office and factory or are replaced by new norms. Although some of the leaders' more orthodox fathers and grandfathers thought that going into industrial activity risked pollution from the association with foreigners, low castes, and polluting products and from the encroachments on the ritual calendar, they nevertheless went into business and did what was necessary to protect their ritual status. Their sons and grandsons, however, show much less fear of loss of ritual status from going into industry; they tend to think of industry as ritually neutral, neither very pure nor impure. Only a few occupations and products in industry, such as sweeping, scavenging, and leather manufacture, are still thought of in terms of the traditional ritual pollution and the caste structure; even some of these are being taken up by "clean castes" as modern technology removes the old stigmata. Through the operation of this adaptive strategy of "ritual neutralization," the traditional ritual hierarchy of purity and pollution is gradually replaced in the work sphere by a status hierarchy defined in terms of differences in authority, salary, and education.

Those industrial leaders who adopt "vicarious ritualization" as their strategy in domestic and social life do not cling passively to "tradition" but participate in a creative process of adaptation and development that includes many cultural revivals and innovations. In this sphere, too, traditional norms are modified and redefined. The leader's own direct participation in ritual and cultural performances is progressively reduced to a minimum, while his relations to these observances becomes increasingly symbolic and fiscal. Under these circumstances, he can remain a good Hindu, in his own eyes as well as in those of his spiritual preceptors and his community, because he continues to make generous contributions to religious and charitable endowments and because his family conforms to many observances.

The industrial leader's relation to his religion, however, is not wholly vicarious, symbolic, and financial, nor is it restricted to the domestic sphere. He also participates directly and personally in reinterpreting and restructuring the "essential tenets" of his religion for an industrial age. In his reinterpretation he not only comes to see his industrial career as a source of necessities and luxuries for his family but also may see in it his personal destiny (*karman,* kismet), an opportunity to fulfill his moral obligations to society (*dharma*), and a path to his ultimate spiritual salvation (*mokṣa*). These reinterpretations, supported in part by authoritative spiritual leaders, include the formulation of an ethical code for industry and a greater emphasis on the devotional and intellectual side over the ritual and social side of religion. At the level of philosophical and ethical beliefs, then, if not at the level of ritual observance, the industrial leaders are trying to integrate their compartmentalized traditional and modern cultures into a coherent and meaningful whole by converting Weber's "theodicy of the caste system" into a theodicy for an industrial system.

## Religious and Secular Motivations for Industry

Evidence of the kind we have presented of the adaptability of Hindu social structure and Hindu beliefs to industrialization is beginning to be recognized by some adherents of Max Weber's thesis. Yet they interpret such evidence only as showing a passive and permissive role for Hinduism in industrialization, not as showing any positive, dynamic role of the kind presumably played by the Protestant ethic in the development of European industrial capitalism. They sometimes add that the changes occurring in Hinduism under the influence of industrialization indeed prove that there is severe conflict between the two, for to become a good industrialist a Hindu entrepreneur must slough off his Hinduism and secularize his life. S. N. Eisenstadt, for example, acknowledges that Hindu society has adapted to new circumstances and developed new institutions and new secular activities because it has a high level of rationality and an openness to reinterpretation of its sacred traditions. He argues, however, that Hinduism's relatively weak "transcendental elements" and its tendency to get "embedded" in a particular social setting have prevented it from generating the motivations and commitments needed for the undertaking and performance of new secular roles and from producing the new common symbols of a national identity to support the innovative forces needed for institution-building.[46]

Before evaluating this argument, I should like to note that it represents a major shift in the emphasis of Weber's thesis. It stresses the *rational adaptability* rather than the *irrational resistance* of Hinduism to change. In so doing, Eisenstadt also shifts the discussion of obstacles to modernization from emphasis on religious belief and ritual and traditional social structure to the more cogent problems of shortages in capital, skills, industrial management, and the like. To this extent, his position represents a major concession to those who have questioned the adequacy of Weber's analysis of the sociology of Hinduism and Buddhism. In the end, however, there is an effort to save Weber's thesis by arguing that Hinduism cannot provide *positive motivations and commitment to industrial life* because it is not "transcendental" enough, as presumably Calvinism was. We may now consider this argument.

The psychological motivations that Weber found in Calvinism to support a "spirit of capitalism" were not explicit in the texts of theological doctrine. He made indirect and hypothetical inferences about the "psychology" of believers from the way industrialists interpreted Calvinist doctrines and tried to apply them in the changing circumstances of everyday life. Through such a chain of inferences, Weber arrived at his conclusion that the Calvinistic doctrine of predestination would arouse an intolerable anxiety in individual believers about their prospects for salvation, an anxiety that would lead, with the elimination of traditional institutions for allaying it, such as confession and penances, to a desperate search for "signs" of salvation in business enterprise and the accumulation of profits. The alleged transformation of a "transcendental" theological doctrine into a sanction and motive for capitalism is not, therefore, a direct logical inference from doctrinal cause to economic effect. As Tawney and others have pointed out, the change rests on a complex historical development in which religious and economic changes were mutually interactive. Whether one accepts Tawney's verdict that the Protestant ethic was a "tonic" for, rather than a "cause" of, capitalism or Weber's occasionally cautious postulation of an "affinity" between the two, we cannot simply deduce the economic relevance of Calvinistic theology from doctrinal texts but must study how these doctrines were used and interpreted by particular individuals and groups in changing social and cultural contexts.

Much the same methodological procedure must be followed when we try to assess the economic effects of Hinduism. It is not enough to speculate about the shackling inhibitions on an active life that are supposed to follow from the doctrines of Hindu philosophy and theology as expounded in the scriptural texts. One must ask how these doctrines have been interpreted, by whom, for whom, and in what kinds of circumstances. In his study of the sociology of Hinduism and Buddhism, Weber tried to use the best empirical and textual sources available to him. Since these sources were extremely limited and he did not himself have first-hand experience of India, his interpretation of the psychological consequences of "the Hindu ethic" tended to be overinfluenced, as were some of his sources, by the stereotypes prevailing in his day of Hindus as inactive, other-worldly traditionalists who alternated in their quest for salvation between a rigid caste ritualism and ecstatic orgies of other-worldly mysticism. He could not find in these sources any psychological support for a rational, methodical organization of everyday economic activities.

In my study of the Madras industrialists, as well as from my observations of other Hindus, I found that Hinduism also generates in its believers a "salvation anxiety" about how to escape from the effects of one's own past actions and the endless cycle of rebirths. The anxiety is not an intolerable one, however, that leads to an overwhelming pessimism and defeatism or to a despairing burden of sin and guilt. That one becomes good by good deeds and bad by bad deeds is taken as an inexorable law of fate (*karman*) but not necessarily as a denial of freedom of choice and action in the present or as a reason for not exercising effort, intelligence, foresight, and resourcefulness in taking advantage of opportunities to improve one's condition in this life and the next. Many paths to salvation are recognized, and only a very few individuals are qualified to follow the path of complete ascetic renunciation and mystic meditation. The vast majority must follow the life of the householder, raising and providing for families, engaging in useful work, and retiring only when too old to carry on domestic and public responsibilities. This mode of life, too, has scriptural sanction as a path to salvation, provided it is led without attachment and is guided by the prescribed moral duties (*dharma*) of ritual observances, devotion, and meditation and an ethical code that enjoins a man to tell the truth, keep his word, and help others or at least not do them harm (*ahiṃsā*). There is sanction, too, in the householder's life for the acquisition of power and wealth (*artha*) and for enjoyment (*kāma*).

Can such a world view make a positive place for the industrial entrepreneur, and will the place it makes for him give him the motivation and commitment to undertake the innovative tasks of industrialization and modernization? The answer to these questions, so far as the evidence of the Madras industrial leaders goes, must be an unequivocal "yes." Although not all the leaders are Hindus, most of the Hindus among them are strongly motivated and committed to their work, and in their own minds they link this commitment and their success to their religious beliefs and social obligations. To develop industry is, they say, "something we must do," either because they feel that happens to be the way they must work out the consequences of their past actions or because they feel that it is their moral duty (*dharma*) as individual citizens to help provide the jobs and products so urgently needed in India today. If they can carry on such activity without appropriating all its fruits for themselves, but rather increase those fruits for future generations and dedicate them to God, their work will become, they say, a "service" and a kind of "sacrifice" in the sense of the *Bhagavadgītā*, especially as interpreted by Gandhi. Such "this-worldly asceticism" does not mean for these industrialists a renunciation and withdrawal from this world and a denial of the reality of their own and India's social and economic progress. In spite of the prospect of endless cycles of rebirth and of world creation and destruction, they feel they must do what they can to overcome present obstacles and to improve the condition of this world as they pass through the "corridor of time." They are not so egoistic as to claim all the credit for whatever success they may have achieved, although they recognize the importance of personal effort, intelligence, and foresight. Beyond the ego, however, "there must be something greater," that is, God's will or God's grace, which along with luck and opportunity explains to them why they succeeded when so many others failed.

Madras industrialists see the economic success they have attained as a product of devotion to their calling and duty. They also see their careers as one path to their salvation. They believe that their individual prosperity and the material transformations wrought by their companies are expressions of a divine will, not simply the private conceits of a few individuals. These views are endorsed by their highest spiritual advisers and by the pandits who specialize in traditional Hindu law and theology. The endorsement may not extend to approval of every detail of the industrialists' behavior, but it does give the industrialist the reassurance that as a good industrialist he is also an instrument of a divine will and of a cosmic process. His Hinduism, therefore, is both a source and sanction for his commitment to an industrial career that represents his personal fate, his moral duty, and a path to his ultimate spiritual salvation.

The linking of economic activity and wealth accumulation to devout Hinduism is commonplace in India. It is recognized not only in the acceptance of wealth and power within the religious scheme of basic values or in the daily prayers addressed to Gaṇeśa and Lakṣmī for success and good fortune but also in the more general Weberian formulation that a dedication to an orthodox life will lead to economic prosperity.

Religion, however, is not the only source of the Hindu industrialist's motivation. There are for him, as there were for the Puritan industrialists, some mundane pleasures of industry.

With about three exceptions, most of the industrial leaders work hard at their jobs, keep long hours, and give their talents and undivided attention to industry. Only one, a second-generation leader, said that after he leaves the office he forgets about business and relaxes with his family by playing tennis or reading. Why do most work so hard? The satisfaction of performing their moral duty (*dharma*) through industry and working out their own and their country's salvation in this way is not the only satisfaction they derive or anticipate from their work. Even the traditional Hindu scheme of the ends of life is a quadrivium (*caturvarga*) providing for the inclusion of wealth and power (*artha*) and enjoyment (*kāma*), as well as moral duty (*dharma*) and salvation (*mokṣa*). It is quite evident from their direct statements and indirect indications that the industrial leaders are motivated by an interest in wealth, power, status, industrial production, and workmanship, as well as by moral duty and prospects of salvation. Their motives for industrial leadership are mixed, as are everyone's. In the mixture of motives, nonetheless, it is sometimes possible to discern one motive that dominates the others as a kind of overriding "passion." Considering only the "secular" motivations, the desire to amass wealth seems not to be a dominant passion for any of the leaders, and social status seems to be so for only two. For most of the others, the dominant motivation seems to be a combination of workmanship and power. These judgments are based on direct expressions of interests and attitudes taken together with answers to specific questions—"Why do you work so hard?" "If you were reborn, would you choose the same career?" "Do you ever feel like withdrawing from your work and becoming an ascetic?"—and the observed evidences of life-style, civic and philanthropic activities, and personal and family histories.

Most leaders, of course, show interest in the monetary returns from their industry, but not as an overriding passion to accumulate great wealth. They want the money, they say, to provide a comfortable life for themselves and their families, for reinvestment in their companies, and for ceremonial expenses, charities, and other good works. Beyond this, they deprecate a lust for wealth with familiar sayings such as "money can't buy everything," or "we are all buried only in muslin." The industrialists find it increasingly difficult to make the traditional distinction between necessities and luxuries in their expenditures, when so many "luxuries" are becoming "essential" for their comfort. The standard of living of these industrial millionaires is actually rather like that of a well-to-do middle-class family in the United States, although by present Indian standards a large comfortable house, a radio and refrigerator, a car, and professional college education for children are still considered expensive luxuries. With two exceptions, most of the families live unostentatiously in relatively small households. Of the exceptions, one inherited a grand palace built by his father. Its splendor is now faded, and the atmosphere resembles that of a quietly elegant museum. The other exceptional industrialist maintains a household of about twenty relatives, entertains lavishly, and owns race horses. A wedding is the one ceremonial occasion on which all the families are willing to make a big splurge.

Most of the leaders' money is tied up in their companies, and new profits are reinvested for industrial expansion. Although cognizant of financial rewards, as a group they seemed more interested in creating and building industry than in profits. The level of profit expectation ranged from 10 per cent to 20 per cent of working capital. Some claimed their present profits were well below this level. Only one seemed more interested in the profit and loss sheets of his companies than in their products and processes.

Industrial leadership, especially in the private sector, is still not the easiest path to high social status in Madras City or India generally. A state or central government minister, a high civil servant, an engineer, or a doctor commands higher status and larger wedding dowries. While in recent years several of the leading industrialists have received some social recognition and public honor, it has been chiefly for their support of temples, *maṭhas,* high schools, hospitals, and related philanthropic activities, rather than for their industrial achievements.

The relatively lower social status of the industrialist derives historically from the merchant's position in the traditional *varṇa* scheme, where he was always outranked by kings, warriors, government ministers, scholars, and scribes. The status system was reinforced by the social hierarchy the British brought to India.

Commenting in an early nineteenth-century directory of Madras Indian businessmen, a British observer praises a Smārta Brahman for going into business:[47]

> It has frequently been observed that persons who have received higher university education are apt to look upon business careers with disfavor. They generally prefer to enter government service or to join the overstocked professions of law and medicine with very doubtful prospects of success. . . . Fortunately, the pressure against business careers shown by educated people is being

> overcome; still it was courageous on the part of Mr. G. Venkataramana Aiyer, a graduate of about fifty years' standing, to have sought a future outside of government service, especially as he comes from a family connected for longer than a generation with the higher ranks of government service.

The avoidance of business careers by the well-educated and the well-connected is hardly surprising in view of the low status to which such careers were relegated in the British Indian social hierarchy, a status even lower than that in the traditional *varṇa* scheme.

The burning question in nineteenth-century Madras society, one learns, was not whether a businessman should associate with intelligent workingmen but whether a businessman, British or Indian, would ever be invited to Government House along with "respectable" people. Leaders of trade did not receive invitations to dinner at Government House as civil servants, generals, the clergy, and service-connected professionals did. At most, they might be invited for tea.

Since independence, the status and prestige of Indian industrialists has improved, though recent ideological movements such as socialism and communism have further reinforced the low social prestige of the merchant capitalist and industrial entrepreneur by pillorying the industrialist as a "capitalist exploiter" in the service of "colonialism" and "imperialism." These stereotypes are generally so crude and unrealistic that by contrast Marx's discussion of the necessary and creative role of capitalist enterprise in the evolution of industry sounds like Chamber of Commerce propaganda.

In such a climate of opinion, it is not likely that many will choose industrial leadership in the private sector as a path to high social status and public honor. The two leaders who are status-dominated have satisfied their status aspirations through such means as living in a palace, collecting titles, founding a university, buying racing stables, and cultivating the company of important persons.

Considering the problematic social status of industrialists, it is surprising to find so many able and dedicated leaders in the field who are satisfied to stay. To the question, "If you were reborn, would you choose the same career?" the most successful industrialist in Madras City answered: "I have no choice, I must have done something bad in a past life." He had no doubts about the moral or secular values of his work, but he did not consider its status as important as the government service of his father or the Sanskrit learning of his grandfather. Most industrialists said that if reborn they would again choose the same career, not only because they believed it was their *karman* or kismet or duty (four were not sure it was) but also because they derived deep pleasure from such a life. One said he would change his academic preparation from geology to economics, and another joked that he would prefer to be reborn as an industrialist in some place where taxes were lower, but only two wanted a different career, one as an architect or artist and the other in scientific research.

To Indian industrial leaders a sense of mastery and independence and a pride of achievement probably means more than it does to their American or European counterparts. As one of them put it with feeling, he was tired of being patronized, of being told by foreigners that he couldn't do this and couldn't do that. He and his brothers and father set out to prove that Indians are equal to anyone in industrial enterprise and efficiency; now the family boasts about a dozen "firsts" in their field. Their eminence has been achieved, he added, without the use of foreign experts, although he and several brothers were trained abroad and started out handling foreign sales agencies.

It is sometimes said, by Indian as well as non-Indian observers, that the Indian industrialist has an easy time of it, with a market protected by government licensing of output capacity, import restrictions, and other controls. Actually, the Indian industrialist is so beset with obstacles that an American industrialist, and probably a European one, would find his position intolerable. The system of industrial licensing carries with it many burdens: prescriptive production quotas, price controls, restrictions on foreign exchange, advanced labor laws, almost prohibitive income and estate taxes, competition from public-sector industries, and the constant threat of nationalization. In addition, shortages—of capital, raw materials, machinery and components, organized distribution facilities, and top management and highly skilled personnel—while not necessarily a consequence of government policy, are nevertheless real problems, especially for new enterprises.

In the face of such obstacles, the Madras industrial leaders show a degree of enterprise, persistence, and resourcefulness difficult to reconcile with prevailing stereotypes about them. Even allowing for their adjustment to fifteen years in a controlled economy, their spirit and outlook is dynamic and optimistic. They are not particularly alarmed by threats of nationalization; most regard these threats as irresponsible talk by people unaware of the consequences. Should their industries be nationalized, however, they say they are prepared to work directly for the government as managers of public-sector industries. One of them summed up the general attitude: "Obstacles are always there. If everything is made easy, what is the pleasure in life? You must do something." To illustrate his attitude, he told how he had persuaded a reluctant and skeptical foreign collaborator to undertake a technical collaboration agreement by sending within fifteen days a photostatic copy of an industrial license, which usually takes two years to obtain, or one year "if you know how."

The personality traits expressed in the Madras industrial leaders' beliefs, attitudes, and behavior are surprisingly similar to those Weber attributes to his "ideal type" of European capitalist entrepreneur. The Madras industrial entrepreneur, like his European counterpart, is calculating and daring, temperate and prudent, shrewd and completely devoted to his business; he avoids ostentation and unnecessary expenditure, is concerned about the confidence of his customers, shareholders, and workers, is embarrassed by the outward forms of social recognition, and sure that he gets nothing out of his wealth himself "except the irrational sense of having done his job well." [48]

On the basis of the evidence presented, it would be difficult to prove that these personality traits were "caused" by Hindu beliefs and values; but the evidence does at least suggest an "affinity" between the personality traits of the industrial leaders and their Hinduism. That their activist outlook and personality is not simply a Western import along with Protestant Christianity and industrial capitalism is, I believe, strikingly shown by their resemblance to one kind of Indian hero who is celebrated in the ancient Sanskrit tales. Such a hero shows

> a cool-headed drive to make good in the world against heavy odds, a constant cagy awareness of what is going on, concentration of attention, a readiness to act immediately on what comes into view, a presence of mind able to match wits with anyone, and a self-centered ruthlessness in taking advantage of an adversary's loss of control; on the other hand the hero shows a compassionate readiness to give up his attachments (not so much out of a sentimental regard for the needs of others as from an enlightened self-interest), fidelity to his word at all costs, and a poise and mental equilibrium that issues in dependable and wise actions.[49]

Whatever may have been the value of such character traits in the heroic age, they are at least as valuable and as functional in this industrial age as they were then. I do not call attention to these parallels between the ancient Indian hero and the modern industrial leader of Madras City on the one hand, and Max Weber's ideal European capitalist entrepreneur on the other, in order to prove that the Madras industrial leaders' personality traits and entrepreneurial spirit have been generated either by a Hindu ethic or a Protestant ethic. The conclusion we can draw from these parallels, rather, is that such traits and such a "spirit" have an affinity with more than one religious tradition—Christian, Hindu, Muslim, and others. If we accept this conclusion, then we must also explain why, if the entrepreneurial personality type was not discouraged among Indians by Hindu beliefs and rituals, Indians did not develop industrial capitalism much earlier. One answer is that much more than a personality type or a social ethic is needed to develop industrial capitalism, as Weber recognized. The important problem is not the fruitless search for the missing links in Indian history that would have produced an industrial revolution exactly like England's, but rather the question whether Indian social institutions, religious beliefs, and rituals are inherently obstructive to modernization and whether modernization will inevitably destroy Indian cultural traditions. The present study suggests that traditional Hindu institutions and beliefs are compatible with modern industrial organization and that they are being adapted by the successful industrial leaders in Madras City to supply the motivations and a positive social ethic for continuing industrialization.

## How New and Unique Are the Madras Industrial Leaders?

Because deviations from traditional caste and ritual restrictions are more evident in office and factory than in domestic and social contexts, the inference is usually drawn that industrialization is first destroying the traditional system in the work sphere and will then destroy it in the domestic and social sphere. This is the much-discussed trend toward "secularization" that is alleged to express the linear transformation of traditional societies into modern societies. The theory posits that the upper castes in urban and industrial centers are first abandoning the characteristic features of traditional Indian society and culture—the joint family, caste, ritual purity and pollution, the theodicy and "enchanted" world view—for a "modern" life-style, and then the middle and lower castes will follow them at a respectable distance through a process of "lagging emulation." The Madras study does not confirm this theory but suggests an alternative interpretation of the relation of modernization to tradition. The upper castes who have moved into the city and into industrial life tend indeed to adopt a "modern" life-style. But the tendency is more evident in their work sphere than in their domestic sphere, where they actively maintain and even strengthen their "traditional" life-styles, albeit with many modifications.

Where no major intrinsic conflicts occur between traditional Indian society and culture, on the one hand, and modern innovations, on the other, a wide variety of structural and cultural adaptations takes place in the caste system, the joint family, and the ritual and belief system, hardly noticed but playing an important part in enabling the changes associated with industrialization to go on peacefully and without destruction of traditional institutions. The ways in which some industrial leaders have adapted joint-family organization to the management of the modern industrial corporation forms an important example of this process. Abbreviation and consolidation of ritual observances make up another, perhaps less important example. Where intrinsic conflicts exist between the innovations and social and cultural traditions, adaptations are made that contain, mitigate, and often resolve the conflicts. I have tried to analyze these adaptations into several basic kinds of "adaptive strategies" followed by individual leaders and their families. Each family uses different combinations and sequences of these strategies, depending upon its particular social status, its size, talents and ambitions, the changing circumstances or available opportunities, and the reactions of others. But there are significant relations among these strategies and characteristics of the results of their operation that indicate that generic and persistent processes are at work.

The functional complementarity of these adaptive strategies and of the more casual adaptations suggests that the industrial leaders are trying to maintain an "inner" and essential core of cultural identity while experimenting with innovations. The "core" is not itself hard and unchanging, since some of the innovations are eventually absorbed into it through reinterpretation and restructuring, while some traditional elements are dropped and others are technically modernized. The operation of these adaptations has not resulted either in a complete "modernization" of the "core" or in a complete "traditionalization" of the innovations. Nor do the industrial leaders envisage such outcomes. The precepts articulated by two of them not only epitomize Indian practical wisdom and common sense for coping with technical and social change, but sound Western as well:

"Use your head and follow your traditions."

"If you are not prepared to change your traditions, you will become extinct like the dinosaur."

The adaptations made by the Madras industrial leaders to industry and urban life may now be summarized.

1. They are definitely modernizing, in the sense of taking on and developing the innovations of modern industry and urban living.
2. At the same time, they are not abandoning their traditional institutions, values, and beliefs but rather adapting and restructuring them where necessary to maintain and strengthen what they consider the "essential core" of tradition.
3. Their ritual observances are restructured to the greatest extent and their joint-family organization least. The restructuring of caste and of the "theodicy" of the caste system is intermediate between that of ritual and that of the joint family.
4. In all cases, the restructuring is greater in the industrial and work sphere than it is in the domestic and social sphere, where a compensatory effort is made to maintain, revive, and develop traditional institutions, arts, beliefs, and values.
5. The over-all outcome of the adaptations is not a linear transformation of joint family into nuclear family, of caste into class, of ritual and theodicy into secularism and science.
6. The general trend of modernization among the industrial leaders is better described as experimentation with and a gradual incorporation of innovative changes (whether of foreign or indigenous origin) into an indigenous culture that is already both "traditional" and "modern."
7. The indigenous culture is also restructured in order to accommodate the accepted innovations. The joint family is adapted to the occupational diversity and geographical mobility of urban and industrial life; ritual observance becomes more vicarious and symbolic and is supplemented by devotional (*bhakti*) and cultural performances; caste loosens its hold on occupation, residence, status rank, interpersonal relations, interdining, and intermarriage. The beliefs in personal fate, rebirth, duty, and salvation are generalized and applied to modern industrial life, thus converting the theodicy of the caste system into a theodicy of the industrial system.

The foregoing summary applies to a group of industrial leaders and their immediate families studied in Madras City in 1964. Whether similar adaptive strategies are used by the industrial leaders in other Indian cities or by other occupational groups, I do not know. It may be that the then predominance of Brahmans and Ceṭṭiyars in the industrial leadership of Madras City had resulted in a distinctive pattern of modernization that will not be found in other cities, such as Kōyamputtūr, where industry is dominated by Nāyaḍus, or in Madurai, where it is dominated by Ceṭṭiyars. Moreover, what about the many industrialists in North India—Bombay, Kānpur, New Delhi, Calcutta? It seems likely that where industry developed early under indigenous auspices, as in Ahmadabad, the strategy of compartmentalization would not have taken the same form. It is not likely, either, that skilled artisans and mechanics who become industrial entrepreneurs would confront the same kind of ritual and status obstacles as Brahmans and upper castes do, and be led to use Sanskritizing strategies for the same purpose as upper-caste industrialists. While these are plausible hypotheses, a sufficient number of studies of the adaptive strategies used by industrial leaders and their families is not at hand to establish valid generalizations. From the few studies available and an occasional autobiography or biography, one receives the impression that the adaptive strategies of the Madras industrialists are quite widespread, although they may take different forms.[50]

This is not the place to review the variations in adaptations to industry and modern life recorded in other studies. Several recent studies, however, report findings on compartmentalization and cultural reinterpretation that suggest areas where further research would be useful.

These studies indicate that the compartmentalization of the "modern" and the "traditional" is not a simple function of the physical separation of residence and work; it depends also on cultural definitions of "home" and "office." The definitions in turn depend on the specific kinds of cultural models that are socially recognized and accepted.

The physical boundaries of the "at-home culture" for example, may include an entire village or village district, an urban neighborhood, a single household, or a particular part of the house, as the kitchen. Conversely, the boundaries of the "at-work culture" may embrace an entire city, an industrial area, a single office or factory, or a work area in the house. Compartmentalization is essentially a *cognitive* separation of activities whose physical separation is symbolic of a cultural difference between "traditional" and "modern" life-styles. The cultural differences are relative, and the degree of physical separation need not be very great to symbolize the difference. The kinds of cultural differences that are symbolized include both historic cultural traditions of the particular groups involved and the new models that guide their reinterpretation and reformulation of these traditions.

In a study of a Tamilian-dominant cultivating caste whose members have gone into industry as skilled mechanics and office clerks, Stephen Barnett found the "at-home culture" in an urban neighborhood that had evolved from an old village settlement. He suggests that they are "reformulating" their cultural traditions based on kingly and Brahmanical models in such a way as to incorporate industry and urban life by adopting the models of the Dravidian movement.

McKim Marriott has pointed out that, in the Mahārāṣṭrian town of Wai, which he has studied, "low artisans," whose places of work and residence are not physically separate, also "blend" rather than compartmentalize modern and traditional segments. In this town, the "high" professionals (lawyers, doctors, and teachers) do, however, compartmentalize both between office and household, which are usually separate, and within the household, where the areas for work, visitors, and the family are distinctly demarcated.

R. S. Khare has described in detail the way in which the home is compartmentalized into an intimate family area, a work area, and a visitor's area and has analyzed the home-office adjustments among the Kanya-kubja Brahmans of North India, who have gone chiefly into the professions and government service, in terms of compartmentalizing process which he calls "interjacency."

Michael Ames's study of two Jamshedpur factories finds compartmentalization within the factories and between the city and the village:

> The social relations in the "works" departments of the factories appeared more impersonal and "modernized" than the relations in the clerical departments; managers or supervisory personnel, who sometimes ran their offices like petty zamindars, would quickly switch to more professional, job-specific behavior when dealing with workers inside the factory. The most noticeable compartmentalization, however, was between Jamshedpur (work) and native place (home). It seemed that many of the workers considered their quarters in the company housing colonies as part of the working rather than home compartment. They preferred to hold ceremonies, births, confinements, etc., at home at their native places; but when it was necessary to use company or city quarters, all manner of ritual neutralization was permissible (e.g., the neutralization or remission of female pollution resulting from menstruation and childbirth, the abbreviation of ceremonies, the substitution of elements in ceremonies, etc.).

Ames's observations extend those of an earlier study by Martin Orans on Santāl tribals in industrial employment in Jamshedpur. Orans found that the degree of "modernization" varied directly with residential proximity to the city. He also found, however, that such proximity was not automatically followed by acculturation to Hinduism. Although the Santāls were adapting to industrial life, they were doing so by incorporating some of its features into a newly created Santāl "Great Tradition."

The Ames and Orans studies suggest that a company house is not a home and that the significant compartmentalization in these cases is between the village and the industrial-urban environment. Another study, by Raymond Owens, of small-scale industrial entrepreneurs in the Howrah District of Calcutta adds still another variable to these conclusions. Owens found that the most successful entrepreneurs came from a dominant cultivating peasant caste with some experience in skilled machine work. Maintaining their village base and unemcumbered by expensize overhead, these entrepreneurs have outdistanced their more educated upper-caste competitors. Owens's impression is of village-city compartmentalizing among the former, and urban household-factory compartmentalization among the latter. He also reports that the peasant-entrepreneurs are supporting efforts to promote a cultural model of caste identity that is different from that of upper castes but still Hindu in nature.

It seems plausible to me to assume that the lower castes also are trying to adapt modern and traditional segments of culture in a dynamic manner with the resources at their command. Their adaptations need not follow a general "law" of change any more than those of the upper or middle castes do. How far their adaptations make use of the strategies of compartmentalization, vicarious ritualization, ritual neutralization of the work sphere, *bhakti* movements, and the like, is a question that needs further research. I can refer here only to one recent study.

Pauline Mahar Kolenda found that the Sanskritization of an untouchable caste in Uttar Pradesh includes reinterpretations of the basic Hindu concepts of *karman* and *dharma:*

> As an aspect of the new Hinduism, many of the more thoughtful men took cognizance of Hindu religious concepts such as *karma*. They did not agree, however, that their caste position reflected *karma,* a deserved destiny. They concluded that their duty (*dharma*) was not to rest content with being sweepers. One could have a happy fate no matter what one's caste, they felt, and one's character was not faithfully portrayed in a traditional dirty occupation.[51]

Even among uneducated sweepers, Dr. Kolenda found understanding of the ideas of *karman* and transmigration and the use of these ideas to explain levels of poverty or prosperity. One uneducated young sweeper gave her the following explanation of his caste's present status:

> One's position in life reflects the deeds done in the past. If one did bad deeds, one is in a poor place. If one did better, one is in a good place. If one did some good deeds, he would be in man's form, but if he had also done some bad deeds, he would come to serve others. If we had done better, others would have served us. God does not create people as Rājpūts, Camārs, or Sweepers. He determines only whether they shall serve or be served. Some are made beggars; some are on a throne.[52]

Other low castes have turned in their adaptations to non-Hindu models—to Buddhist, Muslim, Christian, and purely secular ideologies. These adaptations do not necessarily involve new kinds of adaptive strategies; they may, however, involve some kinds of cultural models distinct from that of Sanskritic Hinduism.[53]

The above strategies of adaptation to urban and industrial life are not in themselves new. One need not do much research on the history of Indian civilization to find precedents for each of the adaptive strategies—Sanskritization, vicarious ritualization, contraction and consolidation of rites, structural adaptations of the joint family and the caste system, *bhakti* movements, changing interpretations of theological and philosophical doctrines, and even the ritual neutralization of the work sphere. Castes have always mixed in work, in religious festivals, and in cultural performances. It is likely that in artisan shops, bazaars, and markets, the "mixing" required for economic cooperation and exchange occurred, although there is little historical material. Max Weber noted the exemption of the workplace from ritual restrictions; he cited the ancient precept that "the hand of the workman is always clean in his work." The "caste mixings" in modern industry probably follow these old precedents; work-related caste mixings may always have coexisted alongside more caste-restricted conduct in the domestic and social spheres.

Another modern feature of industry that probably has important historical precedent is the departure of Brahmans from traditional occupations into agriculture, commerce, and other fields. Such departures are very old, as the distinction between *laukika* and *vaidika* Brahmans testifies.

On reflection, this prefiguring really should not surprise us: Indians have had to adapt to change throughout their history—change in residence, occupation, and political, economic, social, and ritual structures. The survival and growth of a rich civilization over a period of almost 5,000 years would not have been possible had it not also developed a number of flexible, adaptive strategies for coping with change. Sanskritization, for example, as M. N. Srinivas and N. K. Bose have pointed out, has operated for more than 2,500 years to absorb all sorts of foreign groups into a common social structure and cultural system. This and the other adaptive strategies have enabled Indians to maintain some of their cultural traditions under foreign rulers, in cities, in overseas empires, and in good times or bad. Indian cultural traditions have, to be sure, changed under the changing conditions; underlying continuities have also persisted. The rate of absorption of new or borrowed elements has never been so great as to swamp and destroy the underlying cultural continuities; it has been great enough to create special modes of adaptation to the new and the foreign.

Are we to conclude that it has all happened before, including "modernization"—that there is nothing new under the Indian sun? no real change? Such a conclusion would be congenial to some Indians' cosmic perspective and to the stereotype of India as an unchanging traditional society, but it does not seem to be justified. Many important changes *have* taken place in the history of Indian society and culture, and they have often been perceived and acknowledged, if not always welcomed, by orthodox Hindus. The Śaṅkarācārya who sees the erosion of Hinduism's "sociological foundations" in the diminishing attachment of Brahman families to their traditional disciplines certainly perceives and understands the cumulative pressures of social and economic change. Although he regrets the trend and tries to counter it, he does not deny its reality. Nor do the Madras industrial leaders deny the reality of the changes that have come to India since independence. They are emphatic, on the contrary, that these changes represent "progress" on balance and are irreversible, however insignificant and transitory they may appear from the perspective of the recurrent cycles of "ages" of creation and destruction or from the point of view of Absolute Being.

Of course, it would be easy enough to point out that modernization has introduced quantitative differences of scale—in numbers of people, areas settled, migrations, urban agglomerations, population densities, and the like. Increases in scale do not, however, necessarily bring with them basic changes in cultural and social structure; that they do so has to be proved in particular cases. With increasing population growth and movement, it probably becomes much more difficult to monitor and control the traditional social and ritual structure. In the case of the Madras industrialists, we find some evidence that the quantitative enlargement of the area of ritual neutrality in the work sphere of modern industry is creating a new status hierarchy that overlaps the old in one narrow area and otherwise diverges from it. Whether such a status hierarchy should be called a "secular" class system is, however, open to question, since from the points of view of Hindu industrial leaders, at least, industry retains much religious and ethical significance.

The combinations of adaptive strategies generated by urbanization and industrialization are not an especially decisive element of novelty. As we have seen, different individuals, families, castes, and other groups tend to adopt different combinations of adaptive strategies at different periods in their life histories to cope with different circumstances and opportunities. The question therefore remains: In what respect are the industrialists' adaptive strategies in the modern urban and industrial setting new and distinctive? And do these strategies transform the traditional system?

I am inclined to take the position that neither individual adaptive strategies nor particular combinations of them are distinctively new, but that such strategies are being applied to some novel elements and arenas as well as to traditional materials. One of the novel elements is the technology and products of the industrial age—automobiles, plastics, chemical fertilizers, electricity, printing, radio, movies, and television. We may call this the area of "technical modernization." The process of "technical modernization" need not always destroy the traditional culture and inevitably bring in a "modern" system of economic classes, nuclear families, and secular ideologies. In fact, a good deal of the "technical modernization" in India has strengthened aspects of the traditional system while also partially changing it. The same observation holds for the joint family, the caste system, temples, pilgrimages to shrine centers, and theological beliefs. Just as the use of neon lights in temples; of automobiles, railroads, and planes for pilgrimage; and of a public address system for discourses on the Upaniṣads, does not destroy these venerable institutions but may actually make them more popular, so may the institutions of joint family, caste, ritual, and belief be "technically modernized" in the urban and industrial centers without being totally transformed in the image of British society after the industrial revolution.

Some anthropologists and many sociologists will be uncomfortable with my analysis of the relation of Indian cultural traditions to industrial entrepreneurship in terms of adaptive strategies used by individual industrial leaders and their families. Such analysis, they would say, is too particularist and voluntarist. They would prefer an analysis that finds determinist "laws" to explain why the leaders choose particular kinds of strategies. Max Weber's "law of ritual" remains for them the model at which an analysis should aim, although they might prefer to replace his formulation with others in terms of general "laws" or "principles" of caste, kinship, cognitive structures, or a generic process of social mobility. A few recent studies have in fact attempted to formulate such general determinist "principles" or "laws."

To speak of "adaptive strategies" is not to deny the existence of constraints on adaptations. My analysis has not assumed that the industrial leaders are completely free to adopt any strategy whatever. On the contrary, it has attempted to identify a variety of constraints on the choice of strategies, including specific caste status, family composition and background, individual experience, training and ability, available opportunities, legal structure, public opinion, and others. It has also found that the industrialists and their families tend to develop a constellation of strategies organized in relation to one another into a single system, however particular and differentiated are the situations in which they function. In the light of the variety of constraints and the complexity of the situations, it is doubtful that one can find a single deterministic "principle" or "law" to explain functional adaptations of "the system." Those who have tried to formulate such general principles do so at a very abstract level of analysis from which most of the complexity of actual behavior has been omitted. They try, for example, to codify the rules of pollution in the *Dharmaśāstras,* or the general principles of caste and ritual hierarchy, or some general process of social mobility.[54] In most cases, these formulations are based on postulated definitions of abstract concepts and relations and on deductive reasoning from them. This is, of course, a legitimate and well-known procedure in scientific reasoning, usually called "the hypothetico-deductive" method. Both Weber's ideal-type constructions and more recent "model-building" make use of such a method. Two common pitfalls, however, imperil its use: The first is the tendency to reify the abstract postulated principles into concrete, causal forces, and the other is to translate the purely hypothetical relations into categorical generalizations. A more fruitful approach is to build up the generalizations from the intensive studies of the adaptive strategies used by individuals and families in different occupations, castes, sects, and regions.

The variety of adaptive strategies reported in recent studies suggests that the modernization of a traditional society and culture, such as India's, does not set off a uniform and linear cause-and-effect chain of reactions. Different groups participate in the modernization process according to their traditional backgrounds, present status and aspirations, their resources and opportunities, and their individual talents and motivations. Their specific adaptive strategies are a net product of their distinctive group and individual characteristics and of the general ritual and social structure within which they act.

The failure to understand the functional relation of adaptive strategies to modernization and the tendency to misinterpret this relationship as a temporal succession of mutually incompatible types of society derive from the overemphasis on *social mobility* as distinct from *cultural mobility.* While the adaptive strategies are frequently a means to social mobility, they are also an important means of maintaining or changing a cultural identity in terms of a Great Tradition. They are, in other words, a means of acquiring and affirming a status within a *cultural* as well as a social system. To say, therefore, that they are "culture-bound" is literally true, for they are bound to a particular set of historic cultural traditions that define model life-styles for different individuals and groups within the system. But the system is neither static nor homogeneous. It contains a variety of changing cultural models, as well as a variety of changing relations among them. The cultural models are drawn from indigenous Great and Little Traditions and from foreign sources. A concept of social mobility that abstracts from the variety and the cultural content of the models may tell us that Indians are "status-seekers" like other people, but it will leave out what is most important and distinctive about cultural and social mobility in India. It will certainly not tell us very much about how Indians are changing their cultural traditions as they incorporate modern industry, and how they are changing modern industry in order to maintain their cultural traditions. Indian modernization is not simply an "aping" of the West that destroys the traditional way of life, but rather a highly selective process of borrowing and innovation, which seeks to develop and incorporate useful, novel elements into a highly organized and continuing civilization.

## Appendix A: List of Companies

The following information about the companies in the study was obtained from directories, other published material, and personal interviews during the winter of 1964.

1. Standard Motor Products of India Ltd., 29 Mount Road, Madras 2
   Founded: 1948
   Managing Director: K. Gopalakrishna
   Managing Agents: Standard Motor Co. (India) Private Ltd.
   Capital: Authorized: Rs. 20,000,000
   Paid up: Rs. 11,575,000
   No. of employees: 1,750
2. Kothari & Sons, Oriental Buildings, Armenian Street, Madras 1
   Founded: 1918
   Partners: D. C. Kothari
   H. C. Kothari

Started as a firm of stock and share brokers, and by 1938 branched out into various industries. Firm has controlling interests in the companies listed below either in the capacity of managing agents or as associate companies of the managing agents. The firm also undertakes the publication of an annual directory, *Kothari's Economic Guide and Investment Handbook of India.* This publication gives detailed information, including the financial working of more than 3,000 public limited companies (corporations) in India. (A copy of this publication is available in the U. S. Department of Commerce, Washington, D.C.)

| | Capital (rupees) | | No. of |
|---|---|---|---|
| | Authorized | Paid Up | Employees |
| Kothari Textiles Ltd. | 20,000,000 | 8,520,000 | 2,600 |
| Mill No. 1 (1938) | | | |
| Mill No. 2 (1958) | | | |
| Managing Agents: Kothari & Sons | | | |
| Kothari Sugars & Chemicals Ltd. | 50,000,000 | 8,000,000 | 800 |
| Founded: 1960 | | | |
| Managing Agents: Kothari & Sons (Industries) Pvt. Ltd. | | | |
| Adoni Spinning & Weaving Co. Ltd. | 10,000,000 | 5,000,000 | 1,000 |
| Founded: 1954 | | | |

| | Capital (rupees) | | No. of |
|---|---|---|---|
| | Authorized | Paid Up | Employees |
| Managing Agents: Kothari & Sons | | | |
| Blue Mountain Estates and Industries Ltd. | 20,000,000 | 8,400,000 | 1,400 |
| Founded: 1943 | | | |
| Managing Agents: Kothari & Sons (Agencies) Private Ltd. | | | |
| Waterfall Estates Ltd. | 20,000,000 | 5,225,000 | 1,300 |
| Founded: 1943 | | | |
| Managing Agents: Kothari Mehta & Co. Pvt. Ltd. | | | |
| Balmadies Plantation Ltd. | 1,000,000 | 375,000 | 1,200 |
| Founded: 1943 | | | |
| Managing Agents: Planting Agencies Private Ltd. | | | |
| Madras Safe Deposit Co. Ltd. | 300,000 | 160,000 | 25 |
| Founded: 1936 | | | |
| Managing Agents: Kothari & Sons | | | |
| Investment Trust of India Ltd. | 10,000,000 | 10,000,000 | 10 |
| Founded: 1946 | | | |
| Managing Agents: Kothari Mehta & Co. (Private) Ltd. | | | |
| Kothari Coffee Curing Works | This is a subsidiary of the Waterfalls Estates Ltd. | | 100 |
| Founded: 1961 | | | |
| Kothari Fertilizer Factory | This is a subsidiary of the Blue Mountain Estates and Industries Ltd. | | 800 |
| Founded: 1962 | | | |

3. W. S. Insulators of India Ltd., "Dhun Building," 175/1 Mount Road, Madras 2

    Founded: 1961
    Chairman: C. S. Loganathan
    Managing Agents: W. S. Industries
    Capital: Authorized: Rs. 20,000,000
    Paid up: Rs. 900,000
    No. of employees: 45

4. India Cements Ltd., "Dhun Building," 175/1 Mount Road, Madras 2

Founded: 1946
Chairman: P. Suryanarayana
Managing Agents: Essen Private Ltd.
Capital: Authorized: Rs. 50,000,000
Paid Up: Rs. 38,350,000
No. of employees: 2,500

5. Chemicals & Plastics India Ltd., "Dhun Building," 175/1 Mount Road, Madras 2
Founded: 1956
Managing Agents: Ind Plast Private Ltd.
Capital: Authorized: Rs. 20,000,000
Paid up: —
No. of employees: 10

6. Murugappa & Sons, 11/12 North Beach Road, Madras 1
Founded: 1933
Partners: A. M. M. Murugappa Chettiar
A. M. M. Arunachalam
M. V. Arunachalam
M. V. Murugappan
M. V. Subbiah
M. A. Muragappan
M. A. Alagappan

The firm acts as organizers and promoters of industrial ventures. It has controlling interest in the following companies:

| | Capital (rupees) | | No. of |
|---|---|---|---|
| | Authorized | Paid Up | Employees |
| Tube Investments of India Ltd. Founded: 1949 Managing Directors: A. M. M. Muragappa Chettiar and A. M. M. Arunachalam (no managing agents) | 70,000,000 | 25,000,000 | 1,200 |
| Subsidiaries: | | | |
| T. I. Diamond Chain Ltd. Founded: 1960 Managing Director: A. M. M. Muragappa Chettiar (no managing agents) | 7,000,000 | 3,400,000 | 400 |

| | Capital (rupees) | | No. of |
|---|---|---|---|
| | Authorized | Paid Up | Employees |
| T. I. Miller Ltd.<br>Founded: 1960<br>Managing Director: A. M. M. Muragappa Chettiar<br>(no managing agents) | 7,000,000 | 1,737,600 | 200 |
| Carborundum Universal Ltd.<br>Founded: 1954<br>Managing Directors: A. M. M. Muragappa Chettiar and M. V. Arunachalam<br>(no managing agents) | 7,000,000 | 5,500,000 | 500 |
| Coromandel Engineering Co. Pvt. Ltd.<br>Founded: 1950<br>Managing Director: A. M. M. Muragappa Chettiar<br>(no managing agents) | 1,000,000 | 1,000,000 | 500 |

7. E. I. D.-Parry Ltd., "Dare House," Madras 1
   Founded: Private firm, 1786; corporation, 1947.
   Chairman & Managing Director: H. V. Iyengar
   Registered Office: London
   Head Office: Madras
   Capital: Authorized & paid up: £1,327,700
   No. of employees: 2,000
8. K. C. P. Limited, "Ramakrishna Buildings," 38 Mount Road, Madras 6
   Founded: 1941
   Chairman: V. Ramakrishna I.C.S. (Retd)
   Capital: Authorized: Rs. 30,000,000
   Paid up: Rs. 11,200,000
   No. of employees: 1,000
9. India Leather Corporation Private Ltd., "India Leather Mansions," 9 Davidson Street, Madras 1
   Founded: 1948

Managing Director: A. Nagappa Chettiar
Capital: Authorized & paid up: Rs. 10,000,000
No. of employees: 800

10. Easun Engineering Co. Ltd., 5-7 Second Line Beach, Madras 1
    Founded: 1939 (proprietory); 1948 (corporation)
    Chairman: K. R. Sundaram Iyer
    Capital: Authorized: Rs. 5,000,000
    Paid up: Rs. 2,080,000
    (no managing agents)
    No. of Employees: 700
11. Southern Structurals Ltd., GDC Building, 19 Cathedral Road, Madras 6
    Founded: 1956
    Chairman: V. P. Menon
    Managing Director: N. Ranganadhan
    Capital: Authorized: Rs. 10,000,000
    Paid up: Rs. 6,605,000
    No. of employees: 500
12. Madras Rubber Factory Ltd., "Dhun Building," 175/1 Mount Road, Madras 2
    Founded: 1960 as a private company, and converted into a corporation in 1961.
    Chairman: K. M. Cherian
    Managing Director: Mammen Mappillai
    Managing Agents: Young India Agencies Private Ltd.
    Capital: Authorized: Rs. 40,000,000
    Paid up: Rs. 14,020,000
    No. of employees: 1,400
13. Dr. Rajah Sir M. A. Muthiah Chettiar of Chettinad, "Chettinad House," Adyar, Madras 20, Chairman, Madura Mills Ltd., Madurai
    Founded: 1889
    Managing Agents: A & F Harvey Ltd., Madurai
    Capital: Authorized and paid up: Rs. 17,562,480
    No. of employees: 1,800
    Chairman, Indian Bank Ltd., Madras
    Founded: 1907
    Capital: Authorized: Rs. 10,000,000
    Paid up: Rs. 8,860,000
    No. of employees: 800

He is connected with various other industries in South India without any controlling interest.

14. T. V. Sundaram Iyengar & Sons Pvt. Ltd., "TVS Building," West Veli Street, Madurai
    Founded: 1929
    Chairman: T. S. Rajam
    Capital: Authorized: Rs. 10,000,000
    Paid up: Rs. 5,550,000
    No. of employees: 2,600

This is the parent firm of:
Sundaram Motors Pvt. Ltd., Madras 6
Authorized, Rs. 2,500,000; paid up, Rs. 2,000,000; employees, 600
Southern Roadways Pvt. Ltd., Madurai
Madras Auto Service Pvt. Ltd., Madras 6
Madras Motor and General Insurance Co., Ltd., Madras 6
Sundaram Finance Private Ltd., Madras 6
Sundaram Industries Pvt. Ltd., Madras 6
Wheels India Pvt. Ltd. Madras 6
Authorized, Rs. 20,000,000; paid up, Rs. 5,704,500; employees, 800
Sundaram-Clayton Ltd., Madras 6
Authorized, Rs. 9,000,000; paid up, Rs. 6,240,000; employees, 600

15. Simpson & Co. Ltd. 202/203 Mount Road, Madras 2
Founded: 1925
Chairman: M. V. Venkataraman
Holding Company: Amalgamations Ltd., Madras
Capital: Authorized: Rs. 25,000,000
Paid up: Rs. 7,500,000
No. of employees: 3,310

Coach-builders and light engineering specialists, and manufacturers and distributors of Perkins diesel engines.
The following are the subsidiary companies:
Addison & Co., Ltd., Madras
Authorized, Rs. 5,000,000; paid up, Rs. 2,000,000; employees, 500
Addison Paints & Chemicals Ltd., Madras
Authorized, Rs. 5,000,000; paid up, Rs. 2,500,000; employees, 620
Amco Batteries Pvt. Ltd., Bangalore
Authorized; Rs. 1,500,000; paid up, Rs. 1,500,000; employees, 1,000
Tractors and Farm Equipment Pvt. Ltd., Madras (Massey-Ferguson collaboration)
India Pistons Pvt. Ltd., Madras
Reichhold Chemicals India Pvt. Ltd., Madras
Authorized, Rs. 10,000,000; paid up, Rs. 3,075,000; employees, 500
Shardlow India Pvt. Ltd., Madras
Wheel & Rim Co. of India Pvt. Ltd., Madras

16. Shaik Mohamed Rowther & Company, KPV, 41 Linghi Chetty St., Madras 1
Steamship agents. One of the partners, Mr. K. S. G. Haja Shareef, in his capacity as a director in another company, was interested in obtaining collaboration for the manufacture of meters. He has succeeded in obtaining Japanese collaboration.

17. Essel Private Ltd., Kottayam, Kerala State
Managing agents of Travancore Cements Ltd., which was founded in 1946 in Kottayam, Kerala State, with an authorized capital of of Rs. 10,000,000, and a paid-up capital of Rs. 5,000,000. The chairman of both the companies is Mr. C. S. Loganathan. He is connected with various other industries in South India as a director or chairman, without any controlling interest.

18. Integral Coach Factory, Madras 23

General Manager: I. Hydari
Project started in 1952 and took shape in 1955.
No. of employees: 9,600

Public sector enterprise, an important production unit of Indian Railways.

## Appendix B: Table 4*

### Analysis of Backgrounds of Candidates Applying for Industrial Employment, 1963

| | 1959 to 1962 | Apprentice Machinist | Unskilled | Semiskilled | Skilled | Supervisory Staff (Technical and Administration) | Clerical Staff | Peon Attender Watchman etc. | Total |
|---|---|---|---|---|---|---|---|---|---|
| Total | 1322 | 44 | 88 | 218 | 273 | 33 | 86 | 41 | 783 |
| Age Group: | | | | | | | | | |
| 20 and below | 442 | 18 | 27 | 67 | 52 | 1 | 10 | 3 | 178 |
| 21–25 | 608 | 24 | 29 | 114 | 159 | 13 | 36 | 16 | 391 |
| 26–30 | 169 | 2 | 19 | 34 | 39 | 7 | 24 | 6 | 131 |
| 31–40 | 76 | — | 10 | 2 | 17 | 5 | 12 | 12 | 58 |
| 41–50 | 24 | — | 3 | 1 | 6 | 7 | 4 | 4 | 25 |
| Over 50 | 3 | — | — | — | — | — | — | — | — |
| Educational Qualification: | | | | | | | | | |
| Illiterate | 70 | — | 4 | — | — | — | — | — | 4 |
| Class I to Form I | 330 | — | 61 | — | 50 | — | — | 13 | 124 |
| Form II and III | 161 | 1 | 13 | 8 | 31 | 1 | — | 15 | 69 |
| Form IV and V | 125 | 25 | 5 | 101 | 85 | 1 | — | 5 | 222 |
| Form VI, S.S.L.C. | 532 | 15 | 5 | 93 | 98 | 14 | 43 | 8 | 276 |
| P.U.C., Inter | 66 | 1 | — | 11 | 7 | 5 | 18 | — | 42 |
| Graduate | 38 | 2 | — | 5 | 2 | 12 | 25 | — | 46 |
| Marital Status: | | | | | | | | | |
| Married | 299 | 1 | 44 | 26 | 61 | 16 | 22 | 26 | 196 |
| Bachelor | 1016 | 43 | 44 | 192 | 212 | 17 | 64 | 15 | 587 |
| Children living | 231 | — | 48 | 19 | 43 | 23 | 22 | 64 | 219 |
| District or State: | | | | | | | | | |
| Madras City | 815 | 32 | 61 | 72 | 139 | 14 | 18 | 18 | 354 |
| Chingleput, S. Arcot, N. Arcot | | 7 | 9 | 33 | 34 | 6 | 10 | 7 | 106 |

| | | | | | | | | | |
|---|---|---|---|---|---|---|---|---|---|
| Tanjore, Tiruccirāppaḷḷi | | — | 6 | 13 | 24 | 4 | 25 | 2 | 74 |
| Madurai, Tirunelvēli, Rāmnād, Kanyākumārī | 322 | 2 | 3 | 23 | 23 | 5 | 20 | 5 | 81 |
| Kōyamputtūr, Salem | | 1 | — | 6 | 5 | — | 3 | — | 15 |
| Andhra Pradesh | 44 | — | 5 | 48 | 24 | 1 | — | — | 78 |
| Kerala | 84 | 2 | 4 | 19 | 20 | 3 | 6 | 2 | 56 |
| Others | 37 | — | — | 4 | 4 | — | 4 | 7 | 19 |
| Community: | | | | | | | | | |
| Brahman | 274 | 10 | 4 | 27 | 29 | 13 | 54 | 5 | 142 |
| Non-Brahman | 761 | 24 | 50 | 128 | 173 | 15 | 24 | 30 | 444 |
| Harijan–Hindu and Christian | 177 | 6 | 28 | 50 | 44 | 1 | — | — | 129 |
| Christian | 87 | 4 | 5 | 7 | 18 | 4 | 8 | 6 | 52 |
| Muslim | 23 | — | 1 | 6 | 9 | — | — | — | 16 |
| Parents' Occupation: | | | | | | | | | |
| Landlord | 27 | — | — | 2 | 2 | — | 2 | — | 6 |
| Rural laborer, small landholder | 303 | 20 | 24 | 65 | 58 | 16 | 27 | 19 | 229 |
| Petty trader | 104 | 4 | 4 | 17 | 12 | 1 | 8 | 1 | 47 |
| Skilled worker | 313 | 5 | 34 | 49 | 83 | — | 3 | 13 | 187 |
| Unskilled worker, urban | 259 | 15 | 23 | 39 | 58 | — | — | 2 | 137 |
| Policeman, Sepoy | 34 | — | 1 | 1 | 4 | — | — | 1 | 7 |
| Clerk, teacher, musician, postmaster, etc. | 263 | — | 2 | 41 | 56 | 15 | 42 | 5 | 161 |
| Lawyer, engineer, registrar, Tahsīldār | 19 | — | — | 4 | — | 1 | 4 | — | 9 |
| Entry through relatives | 609 | 8 | 15 | 33 | 54 | 3 | 11 | 5 | 129 |

* See note 26, p. 378 below, for source.

## Notes

1. Weber, *Religion of India; idem, Sociology of Religion;* Bendix, *Max Weber;* K. William Kapp, *Hindu Culture, Economic Development, and Economic Planning in India* (Bombay: Asia Publishing House, 1963); Eisenstadt, *Protestant Ethic and Modernization;* and Myrdal, *Asian Drama.* For more critical reviews of the application of the Weber thesis to India, see Singer, "Religion and Social Change" (see note 44, Chapter 1, above); A. K. Singh, "Hindu Culture and Economic Development in India," *Conspectus,* Vol. 3, No. 1 (1967); and M. D. Morris, "Values as an Obstacle to Economic Growth in South Asia: An Historical Survey," *Journal of Economic History* 27, No. 4 (December, 1967): 588–607. Page numbers in parentheses give location of each citation in Weber, *Religion of India.*

2. Max Weber, *General Economic History,* trans. by Frank H. Knight (New York: Collier Books, Macmillan, 1961), p. 361.

3. Bendix, *Max Weber,* p. 206.

4. S. Playne, *Southern India* (London: The Foreign and Colonial Compiling and Publishing Company, 1914–15), p. 624.

5. Kalidas Bhattacharya, "The Status of the Individual in Indian Metaphysics," in Moore, ed., *Indian Mind;* Raghavan, "Some Leading Ideas" (see note 14, Chapter 2, above); M. T. P. Mahadevan, ed., *A Seminar on Saints* (Madras: Ganesh & Co., 1960); and Brown, *Man in Universe.*

6. Weber's "psychocultural" derivation of the "spirit of capitalism" from Calvinism will be found in Chapter 4, "Religious Foundations of Worldly Asceticism," and Chapter 5, "Asceticism and the Spirit of Capitalism," of Weber, *Protestant Ethic and Spirit of Capitalism.* His parallel "psychocultural" derivation of an other-worldly asceticism and irrational mysticism from Hinduism is scattered through Weber, *Religion of India,* and is summarized in Chapter 9, "The Orthodox Restoration in India," which closes with these lines: "Instead of a drive toward the rational accumulation of property and the evaluation of capital, Hinduism created irrational accumulation chances for magicians and soul shepherds, prebends for mystagogues and ritualistically or soteriologically oriented intellectual strata (page 328)."

Weber's dismissal of modern reform movements, such as the Brāhmo Samāj and Ārya Samāj, as "foreign to the basic Indian character" (page 328) and his judgment that Indian character could not possibly "rationalize life conduct" (page 325) are reminiscent of "national character" theories. His conception of "national character," however, did not emphasize racial or psychophysical dispositions, but "factors imprinted through education, and the objective elements of the respective interest situations" (page 339). In this respect, Weber's theory resembles the later "culture and personality" approach, although he gave more emphasis than that approach usually gives to the belief systems of adults in different social strata. His contrast of Asian and Occidental "characters" refers to the result of specific historical and cultural factors (pages 337–43). My quarrel is not with this approach, which I believe is sound, but with the particular application and the assumption that the "essential character" of a nation or a civilization does not change.

7. I have discussed this Hindu analogy with the "Protestant ethic" in "Cultural Values in India's Economic Development" (see note 44, Chapter 1, above); it has also been analyzed in Susanne Rudolph, "Self-control and Political Potency: Gandhi's Asceticism," *The American Scholar* 35, No. 1 (Winter, 1965–66): 79–97, and in Erikson, *Gandhi's Truth.* Weber noticed the analogy but thought it was confined to a few unimportant sects (*Religion in India,* pp. 317–18). Bellah has criticized the search for such analogies in Robert Bellah, "Reflections on the Protestant Ethic Analogy in Asia," *Journal of Social Issues* 19, No. 1 (January, 1963): 52–60.

8. Brown, *Man in Universe,* p. 93. See also W. Norman Brown, "Escape from Fate: A Hindu Paradox," in *Studies in Honor of Maurice Bloomfield* (New Haven, Conn.: Yale University Press, 1920).

9. Attempts to relate textual and contextual studies will be found in Marriott, "Little Communities" (see note 33, Chapter 2, above); Singer, ed., *TI;* and Singer, ed., *Krishna.* Some of the problems of method and theory posed by these kinds of study are examined in Redfield, "Social Organization of Tradition" (see note 1, Chapter 3, above); in Chapters 2, 3 and 7 of this volume; in Singer, "Social Anthropology and Comparative Study" (see note 2, Introduction to Part One, above); in F. G. Bailey,

"Two Villages in Orissa," in Max Gluckman, ed., *Closed Systems and Open Minds* (Chicago: Aldine Publishing Co., 1964); in Clifford Geertz, "Religion as a Cultural System," in Michael Banton, ed., *Anthropological Approaches to the Study of Religion* (New York: Praeger Publishers, 1966); and in Leach, ed., *Dialectic in Practical Religion.* Discussions in Indian anthropology of the relation of the scriptural *varṇa* classifications to local and regional caste rankings provide an important example of the text-context problem. Richard G. Fox, "*Varṇa* Schemes and Ideological Integration in Indian Society," *CSSH* 11, No. 1 (January, 1969): 27–45, is a good introduction to the subject. See also David Mandelbaum, "Structure and Process in South Asian Religion," *JAS* 23, (June, 1964): 5–20; Goody, ed., *Literacy in Traditional Societies;* and Spiro, *Buddhism and Society.*

10. Louis Dumont, "Hierarchy and Marriage Alliance in South Indian Kinship," Occasional Paper No. 12. The Royal Anthropological Institute of Great Britain and Ireland, 1957, and references; E. Kathleen Gough, "Brahman Kinship in a Tamil Village," *AA* 58, No. 5 (October, 1956): 826–63; *idem,* "The Modern Disintegration of Matrilineal Descent Groups," in D. Schneider and K. Gough, eds., *Matrilineal Kinship* (Berkeley and Los Angeles: University of California Press, 1961; Edmund R. Leach, *Pul Eliya: A Village in Ceylon* (Cambridge and New York: Cambridge University Press, 1961); J. Mencher, "The Nayars of South Malabar," in M. K. Nimkoff, ed., *Comparative Family Systems* (Boston: Houghton Mifflin, 1965); M. N. Srinivas, *Marriage and Family in Mysore* (Bombay: New Book Company, 1942); N. O. Yalman, "The Structure of the Sinhalese Kindred," *AA* 64 (1962): 548–75; and Yalman, *Under the Bo Tree.*

11. For example, Marion J. Levy and Lloyd Fallers, "The Family: Some Comparative Considerations," *AA* 61, No. 4 (August, 1959): 647–51; F. F. Furstenberg, "Industrialization and the American Family: A Look Backward," *American Sociological Review* 31, No. 3 (November, 1961): 312–22; Firth, "Family and Kinship in Industrial Society" (see note 6, Introduction to Part Four, above); Raymond Firth, *Two Studies of Kinship in London* (London: Athalone Press, 1956); D. M. Schneider, *American Kinship: A Cultural Account* (Englewood Cliffs, N.J.: Prentice-Hall, 1968); D. M. Schneider and G. C. Homans, "Kinship Terminology and the American Kinship System," *AA* 57, No. 6 (December, 1955): 1194–1208; E. Cumming and D. M. Schneider, "Sibling Solidarity: A Property of American Kinship," *AA* 63, No. 3 (June, 1961): 498–507; M. B. Sussman and L. B. Burcinal, "Kin Family Network," *Marriage and Family Living* 24, No. 3 (August, 1962): 231–40; and Edward M. Bruner, "Medan: The Role of Kinship in an Indonesian City," in Alexander Spohr, ed., *Pacific Port Towns and Cities* (Honolulu: Bishop Museum, 1963).

12. William J. Goode, *World Revolution and Family Patterns* (New York: Free Press of Glencoe, 1963); Nimkoff, ed., *Comparative Family Systems* (note 10, *supra*); Marion J. Levy, *Modernization and the Structure of Societies,* 2 vols. (Princeton, N.J.: Princeton University Press, 1966); and Moore and Feldman, eds., *Labor Commitment and Social Change* (see note 21, Chapter 4, above).

13. Levy, *Modernization and Structure of Societies,* p. 74.

14. Firth, "Family and Kinship in Industrial Society," p. 83.

15. Desai, *Some Aspects of Family in Mahuva.*

16. Among the contributions to the discussion are I. P. Desai, ed., "Symposium: Caste and Joint Family," *Sociological Bulletin* 4, No. 2 (September, 1955): 85–146; F. G. Bailey, "The Joint Family: A Framework for Discussion," *The Economic Weekly* 12 (1960): 345–52; K. M. Kapadia, "The Family in Transition," *Sociological Bulletin* 8, No. 2 (September, 1959): 68–99; H. Orenstein, "The Recent History of the Extended Family in India," *Social Problems* 8, No. 4 (Spring, 1961): 341–50; Bernard S. Cohn, "Chamar Family in a North Indian Village," *Economic Weekly* 13 (special issue, 1961): 1051–55; T. M. Madan, "The Hindu Joint Family," *Man* 62, Article No. 145 (June, 1962): 88–89; A. M. Shah, "Basic Terms and Concepts in the Study of Family in India," *Indian Economic and Social History Review* 1, No. 3 (January-March, 1964): 1–36; Pauline M. Kolenda, "Region, Caste, and Family Structure: A Comparative Study of the Indian Joint Family," in Singer and Cohn, eds., *Structure and Change;* and H. Gould, "Time Dimension and Structural Change in an Indian Kinship System," in Singer and Cohn, eds., *Structure and Change.*

Studies reflecting the new trend include Desai, *Some Aspects of Family in Mahuva;* Gore, *Urbanization and Family Change;* K. M. Kapadia, *Marriage and Family in India* (Madras: Oxford University Press, 1958); Karve, *Kinship Organization in India;* T. M.

Madan, *Family and Kinship: A Study of the Pandits of Rural Kashmir* (Bombay: Asia Publishing House, 1965); Mayer, *Caste and Kinship;* Orans, *The Santal;* and Ross, *Hindu Family in Urban Setting.*

17. W. H. R. Rivers, "The Genealogical Method of Anthropological Inquiry," *Sociological Review* 3, No. 1 (January, 1910): 1–12.

18. Berna, *Industrial Entrepreneurs in Madras State,* Table 11, p. 43.

19. *Madras Tercentenary Volume,* published for the Madras Tercentenary Celebration Committee (Madras: H. Milford, Oxford University Press, 1939); Henry Herbert Dodwell, *The Nabobs of Madras* (London: Williams & Norgate, Ltd., 1926); and Percival Spear, *The Nabobs* (London: Oxford University Press, 1963).

20. Ānanda Raṅga Piḷḷai, *The Private Diary of Ananda Ranga Pillai,* ed. by J. Frederick Price, 12 vols. (Madras: The Government Press, 1904; London and Bombay: H. Milford, Oxford University Press, 1939), 4:148–49.

21. Playne, *Southern India* (note 4, *supra*), pp. 131 ff.

22. *Ibid.*, p. 591.

23. Berna, *Industrial Entrepreneurs in Madras State,* Table 10.

24. A. Devasagayam, "A Survey of Dwellings and Living Conditions of Industrial Employees in Madras City," *Indian Journal of Social Work* 26, No. 1 (April, 1965): 69–86.

25. *Ibid.* For comparative data, see Lambert, *Workers, Factories and Social Change;* Morris, *Emergence of Industrial Labor Force;* and Sheth, *Social Framework of Indian Factory.*

26. *Simpson's Industrial Health Service, Madras, 1959–64* (Madras, 1964), p. 31.

27. Berna, *Industrial Entrepreneurs in Madras State.*

28. Srinivas, *Social Change in Modern India,* contains a recent discussion of the author's ideas about Sanskritization and Westernization, as well as a review of some of the literature. See also Bose, "Hindu Method of Tribal Absorption" (see note 17, Chapter 2), reprinted in *idem, Culture and Society;* Sinha, "Media and Hindu-Bhumij Interactions" (see note 33, Chapter 2); Singer and Cohn, eds., *Structure and Change;* and Silverberg, ed., *Social Mobility in Caste System.*

29. Devasagayam, "Survey of Dwellings."

30. Srinivas, *Social Change in Modern India;* Kopf, *British Orientalism;* Irschick, *Politics and Social Conflict;* and Shils, *The Indian Intellectual Between Tradition and Modernity.*

31. See Chapter 5 in this volume for additional discussion of these cultural classifications.

32. M. B. Emenau, review of La Meri, *The Gesture Language of the Hindu Dance,* in *JAOS* 62, No. 2 (1942): 148–50.

33. Chapter 4 of this volume discusses compartmentalization of medicine and its results. See also Charles Leslie, "Rhetoric of the Āyurvedic Revival in Modern India," *Man* 63 Article No. 80 (May, 1963): 72–73; *idem,* "Health Cultures in South Asia" (see note 14, Chapter 4, above); *idem,* "Professionalization of Āyurvedic and Unani Medicine," *Transactions of the New York Academy of Science,* Series II, 30 (1968): 559–72.

34. At one company, the following holidays were observed in 1964:

| Holiday | Month | Date |
|---|---|---|
| Pongal | January | 14, Wednesday |
| Republic Day | January | 26, Sunday |
| Telugu New Year's Day | March | 15, Sunday |
| Good Friday | March | 27, Friday |
| Tamil New Year's Day | April | 13, Monday |
| Independence Day | August | 15, Saturday |
| *Āvaṇiyaviṭṭam* | August | 23, Sunday |
| *Kṛṣṇajayantī* | August | 31, Monday |
| *Vināyakacaturthī* | September | 9, Wednesday |
| Mahatma Gandhi's birthday | October | 2, Friday |
| *Āyudhapūjā* | October | 14 or 15, Wednesday or Thursday |
| Dīpāvalī | November | 3, Tuesday |
| Christmas | December | 25, Friday |

35. See Devasagayam, "Survey of Dwellings."

36. See references in note 24, *supra,* for comparative data and A. Bope-Gamage and P. V. Veera Raghavan, *Status Images in Changing India* (Delhi: UNESCO Research Center, 1967).

37. Srinivas, *Coorgs,* pp. 106–7, and *idem, Social Change in Modern India,* p. 121. McKim Marriott has pointed out that upper castes frequently give pollution to lower castes, as in giving soiled clothes to the laundryman, in order to display superiority over them and to insult or cajole: "Most villagers, including Brahmans, prefer to remain ordinarily in a protected, impure state." Marriott, "Caste Ranking and Food Transactions" (see note 25, Chapter 7, above). See also Edward Harper, "Ritual Pollution as an Integrator of Caste and Religion," in Harper, ed., *Religion in South Asia;* R. S. Khare, "Ritual Purity and Pollution in Relation to Domestic Sanitation," *Eastern Anthropologist* 15, No. 2 (May-August, 1962): 125–39; and Mathur, *Caste and Ritual.*

38. See Chapter 5 above for descriptions of cultural performances in Madras City.

39. J. L. Martin, "Hindu Orthodoxy in a South Indian Village," *Journal of the American Academy of Religion,* Vol. 35, No. 4 (1969), describes one of these family temples.

40. Kane, *History of Dharma Śāstras* (see note 11, Chapter 4, above).

41. Raghavan, "Musicians and Patrons" (see note 11, Part Two, above); Thurston, *Castes and Tribes* (see note 20, Chapter 4, above), pp. 250–56; Shoji Ito, "A Note on the 'Business Combine' in India, with Special Reference to the Nattukotai Chettiars," *Developing Economies* 4, No. 3 (1966): 367–80; and Louis Dumont, "World Renunciation in Indian Religions," in Dumont and Pocock, eds., *Contributions to Indian Sociology* 4 (April, 1960): 33–62.

42. Piḷḷai, *Private Diary* (note 20, *supra*) 4:539.

43. *Ibid.*

44. For more details on joint family adaptation in industry, see under subheading "The Role of the Joint Family in Modern Industry" in this chapter.

45. Playne, *Southern India* (note 4, *supra*).

46. Eisenstadt, ed., *Protestant Ethic and Modernization,* introduction by S. N. Eisenstadt.

47. Playne, *Southern India.*

48. Weber, *Protestant Ethic and Spirit of Capitalism,* pp. 69–71. For a comparison of Indian and U.S. conditions, see J. Baranson, *Manufacturing Problems in India* (Syracuse, N.Y.: Syracuse University Press, 1967).

49. J. A. B. van Buitenen, "The Indian Hero as a Vidyādhara," in Singer, ed., *TI.*

50. See, e.g., Tandon, *Punjabi Century;* Kushwant Singh and Arun Joshi, *Sri Ram: A Biography* (Bombay: Asia Publishing House, 1968); Sheth, *Social Framework of Indian Factory;* Gore, *Urbanization and Family Change;* Hazelhurst, *Entrepreneurship and Merchant Castes;* and Gillion, *Ahmedabad.* Studies referred to by Barnett, Marriott, Ames, and Owens are not yet published. The quotations are from personal communications. R. S. Khare's study, "Home and Office: Some Trends of Modernization Among the Kanya-Kubja Brahmans," has been published in *CSSH* 13, No. 2 (April, 1971): 196–216. See Michael Ames, "Modernization and Social Structure," *Economic and Political Weekly* 4, No. 3 (special issue, July, 1969): 1217–24, and Tabe Noboru, *Indian Entrepreneurs at the Crossroads,* Institute of Developing Economies Occasional Papers, Series No. 8 (Tokyo: Institute of Developing Economies, 1970).

51. P. Mahar (Pauline Kolenda), "Changing Religious Practices of an Untouchable Caste," *EDCC* 8, No. 3 (April, 1960): 279–87.

52. P. Mahar Kolenda, "Religious Anxiety and Hindu Fate," in Harper, ed., *Religion in South Asia,* p. 74.

53. Bailey, *Caste and Economic Frontier;* Cohn, "Changing Status of Depressed Caste" (see note 32, Chapter 7, above); A. C. Mayer, "Some Hierarchical Aspects of Caste," *SWJA* 12, No. 2 (Summer, 1956): 117–44; David Pocock, "The Movement of Castes," *Man* 55, Article No. 79 (May, 1955): 71–72; S. Sinha, "Bhumij-Ksatriya Social Movement in South Mambhum," *Bulletin of the Department of Anthropology,* Calcutta University, Vol. 7, No. 2; G. Berreman, "Caste in India and the United States," *American Journal of Sociology* 66, No. 2 (September, 1960): 120–27; O. Lynch, "The Politics of Untouchability: A Case from Agra, India," in Singer and Cohn, eds., *Structure and Change;* Orans, *The Santal;* Hardgrave, *Nadars of Tamilnad;* E. B. Harper, "Social Conse-

quences of an Unsuccessful Low Caste Movement," in Silverberg, ed., *Social Mobility in Caste System;* W. L. Rowe, "The New Cauhans: A Caste Mobility Movement in North India," in *ibid.;* Mandelbaum, *Systems of Society;* and Beteille, *Caste, Class and Power.*

54. See, e.g., Dumont, *Homo Hierarchicus;* Lynch, "Politics of Untouchability" (note 53, *supra*); and H. Orenstein, "Toward a Grammar of Defilement in Hindu Sacred Law," in Singer and Cohn, eds., *Structure and Change.*

# PART FIVE / *BEYOND TRADITION AND MODERNITY*

# 9 / *Beyond Tradition and Modernity in Madras*

## Introduction

The study of the modernization of non-Western cultures has been dominated by the metaphor of the "take-off" introduced by economists and by an assumption of incompatibility between "modern" and "traditional" cultures. These interpretations of modernization are shared both by those who view it as a process of diffusing Western culture and by those who view it as an internal process of development that may require an external stimulus to "trigger" the take-off. On either view, modernization becomes a problem of suddenly transforming a traditional *type* of culture, society, and personality into a modern *type*. This view of modernization is supported, and perhaps suggested, by the classical nineteenth- and early-twentieth-century social science theory of traditional and modern societies as opposed types, a theory associated with the names of Marx, Weber, Durkheim, Maine, and Tönnies, among others.

While the history of English industrialization may have provided the stimulus for some of the more influential formulations of the dichotomy, extrapolations from this history of fixed uniform sequences of development in the transformation of traditional into modern societies have not been empirically confirmed by the later history of industrialization in Europe, Russia, Japan, China, India, and other countries. Later history has in particular cast doubt on the assumption that modernization is governed by the "inner logic" of an internal law of development, according to which a correlated set of traditional institutions is transformed into a set of modern institutions. While it is possible to explain divergences from this "law of development" by invoking such items as differences in culture, history and economic backwardness, the emulation of early arrivals, the increasing role of the state and of planning in development, and the differential strengths of traditionalism and modernism in transitional phases, such explanations "save the hypothesis" at the cost of rapidly multiplying *ad hoc* and accidental factors.

It is not surprising, therefore, to find that the recent literature on modernization shows a growing disaffection with the "modern versus traditional" typology of societies and cultures, and a search for new theories. At least, this typology is now increasingly recognized as a set of constructed ideal types and not as an empirical description of societies or a set of generalizations about them. Those who continue to use the modern-traditional contrast at an empirical level do so by mapping the statistical distributions of traits designated modern or traditional in different countries or by making lists of such traits for a single country. The implications of such lists and frequency distributions for a theory of modernization as a process of social and cultural change are at best opaque.[1]

Although no single comprehensive alternative theory has yet emerged to sweep the field, it seems to me likely that a new theory of modernization will articulate much more closely with a general theory of cultural change than does the classical theory of traditional and modern societies. It will not only go beyond the "traditional versus modern" dichotomy but will also transcend the bifurcations between cultural diffusion and cultural evolution and between "culture" and "society." Above all, it will be grounded on the comparative and historical studies of literate civilizations as well as of primitive and peasant cultures. It will look at the process of modernization as envisaged by those engaged in it, in their cultural categories, world view, and value system, as well as in the objective evidence of behavior and numerical magnitudes.

My own observations in India, and particularly in Madras City, over an extended period beginning in 1954 have led me to join the ranks of those disaffected with the classical theory of modern and traditional societies. The point of departure for these observations was Redfield's study of modernization in Yucatan, which to some extent derived from and empirically supported the classical theory. After World War II, when Redfield became interested in China, India, and the comparative study of civilizations, he began to explore in collaboration with historians of civilization the processes of cultural change in societies with literate Great Traditions. I was associated with him in these explorations and helped extend them to India. In my personal research I was particularly interested in exploring the question of what happens to the Great Tradition of Sanskritic Hinduism in a contemporary "heterogenetic" urban center such as Madras City. In this setting, is it secularized and replaced by a modernizing ideology or does it continue to play an important role in the modernizing process? And if the Great Tradition is still alive in the modern city, does this imply, as Eric Wolf suggests, that "perhaps there is always an interplay between traditionalizing and modernizing trends in any society"? [2] If there is such an interplay, what are its characteristic modes of operation and results?

I should like to draw on the Madras studies for answers to the above questions.[3] As will soon become apparent, these answers not only confirm the fruitfulness of Redfield's approach and so support Wolf's hypothesis, at least for India; they also point to the cultural ideology of "traditionalism" as one of the major instruments of modernization. Structural differentiation occurs in the process, although it does not take the form of a linear progression through evolutionary stages of development.

It may be that India is a special case. In some respects, it no doubt is distinctive. Its caste system and traditionalism are proverbial. Yet it also has the largest parliamentary government in the world, universal suffrage, a modern educational system, an extensive network of modern media of communication and transportation, growing industrialization, and was the first in Asia to have nuclear reactors. The coexistence of the traditional and the modern in India have not produced the "schism in the soul" predicted by classical theory. If India is a special case, it should be given special attention, for it may teach us something about the process of modernization in a historic civilization that has not been dreamed of in classical theory. Ronald Dore has recently written that India does not feel the strain between tradition and modernity so acutely as Japan or China "partly because of the syncretic tradition of Hindu culture, partly because a *modus vivendi* between the traditional and the modern cultures has had time to become established, and finally because India and the West are not in political conflict." [4] This seems to me a reasonable suggestion, but it presents a set of problems for inquiry, not a set of findings. In such an inquiry, we shall want to find out the nature of the *modus vivendi* between the traditional and the modern cultures, how it has come to be established, and what its relations are to the syncretic tradition of Hindu thought and to foreign influences. This chapter will deal with some of these questions and will return, in conclusion, to the question of whether the process of modernization in India is unique or can also be found in other civilizations.

## Tradition and Change in Indian Civilization: The Theory of Sanskritization

Indian society and culture are not "traditional" in the sense of the nineteenth-century stereotype that it is dominated by unchanging traditions and immemorial customs, nor even in the sense that many characteristic institutions, culture patterns, values, and beliefs have persisted in spite of the numerous changes that have occurred. The traditionalism of Indian civilization lies elsewhere—in its capacity to incorporate innovations into an expanding and changing structure of culture and society. This capacity is reflected in a series of adaptive mechanisms and processes for dealing with the novel, the foreign, the strange. The operation of the adaptive mechanisms makes possible a kind of "cultural metabolism" that ingests foreign cultural bodies, segregates them, breaks them down into usable forms, and eventually builds them into indigenous "cultural protoplasm." I should like to relate the processes observed in the modernization of a Great Tradition in contemporary Madras to the more generic processes of change in Indian civilization.

The most comprehensive and widely accepted anthropological theory of social and cultural change in Indian civilization is M. N. Srinivas's theory of Sanskritization. In a recent article, he defines it as "the process by which a 'low' caste or tribe or other group takes over the customs, ritual, beliefs, ideology and style of life of a high and, in particular, a 'twice-born' (*dvija*) caste." He continues:

> The Sanskritization of a group has usually the effect of improving its position in the local caste hierarchy. It normally presupposes either an improvement in the economic or political position of the group concerned or a higher group

> self-consciousness resulting from its contact with a source of the "Great Tradition" of Hinduism such as a pilgrim centre or monastery or proselytizing sect. . . . In the case of a group external to Hinduism, such as a tribe or immigrant ethnic body, Sanskritization resulted in drawing it into the Hindu fold, which necessarily involved its becoming a caste having regular relations with other local castes.[5]

Srinivas first stated and applied the theory in his monograph on the Coorgs of South India. Since then, there have been a number of criticisms and revisions of the theory, in which Srinivas has actively participated. Among the most important amendments are the following:

1. More than one *varṇa* model of the life styles and rank hierarchy of the twice-born castes is emulated in the process of Sanskritization. The models vary with region and with the locally dominant caste.[6]
2. Sanskritization is not only, and perhaps not even primarily, a process of social change; it is also a process of cultural change that occurs in the fields of language, literature, the arts, music, drama, religious law, medicine, science, and philosophy.[7]
3. The theory's account of the relationship of Sanskritization to Westernization and modernization has remained obscure and unstable. In his earlier formulation, Srinivas emphasized the manner in which Westernization leads to a strengthening of Sanskritization by providing improved communications and transportation. Later, taking account of the studies of Bernard Cohn, Harold Gould, and others, he stressed the way in which upper castes were modernizing and secularizing, while the middle and lower castes were Sanskritizing their life-styles. In his most recent statements, Srinivas is beginning to raise questions about the contradictions and oppositions between Sanskritization and modernization. Philip Mason's description of the over-all position is both a concise summary, and an indication of the need for more detailed specification of the relationship: "It is clear that the two processes of Sanskritization and Westernization are both at work, that they are often opposed but sometimes in alliance, that here one prevails and here another, here there is revolt against one and here against the other." [8]
4. Although Srinivas's theory of Sanskritization has proved a fruitful and powerful explanation of how Indian civilization has been able to incorporate foreign groups and cultural products into the caste system and the Great Tradition of Sanskritic Hinduism, it seems doubtful that it can account for all the major processes of change without radical revision. In particular, the theory seems unable to deal with those changes and social movements along paths to mobility that constitute alternatives to Sanskritization, for example, modern political organization and administration, or conversion to Christianity and Buddhism. The social and cultural mobility associated with the operation of Sanskritization in the past has resulted, according to Srinivas, in changes in positions within the caste system, but it has not brought about a significant change in the system. The non-Sanskritizing or de-Sanskritizing kinds of change and the efforts of some groups to reject affiliation with Sanskritic Hinduism and to

seek affiliation with other Great Traditions or modern creeds raise the question of change in the system.[9]

## Tradition and Innovation in Madras

The Madras studies help to answer some of these questions, in some respects supporting Srinivas's theory of Sanskritization and in others going beyond it. They show that the relationship of modernization (and of Westernization) to tradition is neither one of deep antagonism and struggle for dominance nor one of harmony and mutual support. It is rather a historical process in which the new and the foreign are culturally differentiated as such from the indigenous traditions, then tried out in a "neutral" area, and eventually selectively integrated into an "essential" core of indigenous traditions, which has itself changed in order to incorporate the new items.

In this process, the chief actors are not castes or religious communities as corporate groups but individuals and their families, generally making up a small fraction of a caste or community. The ways in which individuals and families relate their modernizing activities to their castes and religious communities are important but do not imply that modernization is best studied as an activity of special castes and communities. The "lagging emulation" theory, which sees lower and middle castes Sanskritizing their life-styles while upper castes are modernizing theirs, must be qualified by the finding that the upper-caste family and individual will simultaneously modernize and Sanskritize. They can do so because they tend to *compartmentalize* their lives, following a "modern" model in a ritually neutralized work sphere and a "traditional" one in their domestic and social life. Their Sanskritization is not the same in aim, means, or result as it is among the lower castes described by Srinivas. The upper castes do not aim to raise their ritual status through Sanskritization, since their status is already high. They are interested rather in not losing ritual status as they modernize. The means they use—*vicarious ritualization*—involves a lapse of personal ritual observance; justification of the omission, contraction, and consolidation of rites on the grounds of present circumstances; and a *reinterpretation* of traditional norms and beliefs. The main line of reinterpretation is that modern urban and industrial life brings and requires a shift from ritual to devotional, ecumenical religion, and that the "essential tenets" of Hinduism remain valid and relevant in the modern context even if the caste system should disappear.

Whether these lines of reinterpretation originate with religious leaders or with the modernizing families and individuals, they reassure the modernizers that they are still good Hindus. For most of the modernizers, the definition of a good Hindu is Sanskritic; a few have adopted an anti-Sanskritic model. The possibility and plausibility of this reassurance to those who are themselves active agents of modernization depend on certain adaptable general features of Hinduism and of Indian society. Some of these features are consciously recognized and appealed to, others are not always acknowledged but operate at a level of "cultural drift."

Among the consciously acknowledged features is the view that Hinduism comprises many different paths to salvation and enjoins different duties for different people according to their development and station in life. Within this conception, the paths of ritual observance, devotion, and ascetic withdrawal and meditation are all available options to those who are able to follow them. The householder, for example, can pursue his salvation without ascetic withdrawal by doing his daily work and fulfilling his social obligations to his family and society. An important practical corollary is that there is no single authoritarian hierarchy for the interpretation and enforcement of religious law. Pandits who specialize in matters of *Dharmaśāstra* say there is a rank order of "authorities," with revealed scriptures at the top (*śruti*), followed by remembered scriptures (*smṛti*); local and regional customs, if they are not in conflict with the scriptures; the opinion and practice of a learned and wise man; and individual conscience. In practice, this hierarchy permits a wide latitude for interpretation and enforcement; one may consult one's father and relatives, one's guru, a caste council, the head of one's sect, local and national leaders and officials, and public opinion. Industrial leaders in Madras City, for example, seem not to have any difficulty in finding spiritual authorities to assure them they are doing their moral duty and pursuing a path to salvation while following a career in industry.

A second general feature of Hinduism, one that supports its doctrinal pluralism and decentralized authority structure, is the notion that religious and philosophical truths have both a theoretical and a practical level of validity and application. Such doctrines as the eternally recurring cycles of world creation and destruction, the unreality and ephemeral nature of this world, and the unimportance of the ego are familiar to and even believed in by many of my "modern" Madras informants. These leaders are not thereby prevented from taking an active lead in practical life or from believing in the reality of the political and economic "progress" that India has achieved since independence; they are convinced that progress is irreversible and that they have made personal contributions to it through their own careers. When asked about the apparent contradictions between these convictions and the religious doctrines, they usually reply that the religious doctrines are valid at a different "level," a cosmic level, so there is no conflict. The same people, however, extend and apply other religious doctrines such as those of fate, rebirth, duty, and salvation to modern fields of practical activity. Their spiritual guides support them in both kinds of interpretation.

The extension of the doctrines of fate, rebirth, duty, and salvation to industry and to other modern innovations is more than a convenient rationalization. At least since the *Bhagavadgītā*, these doctrines have had an inherent relevance for social life and practical activity. This relevance is manifest in a third general feature of Hinduism, its scriptural model of social organization—the famous *varṇa* scheme of the four orders of society, Brahmans, Kṣatriyas, Vaiśyas, and Śūdras, and the fifth order of untouchables and outcastes. Anthropologists and historians are fond of pointing out that the model is a normative one and not an accurate description of the variety and movement of local castes and ethnic and occupational groups. Recognizing the validity of this point, Srinivas has nevertheless emphasized that the *varṇa* model has important validating and cohesive functions with respect to regional variations and mobility and that these functions are performed chiefly in the linking of Sanskritization to the economic and political mobility of castes who acquire wealth, power, and modern education. Sanskritization is thus the process whereby groups outside the system are brought into it and groups already in the system can achieve mobility within it.

In several other respects, the scriptural model of the *varṇas* is more open and dynamic than is usually recognized. As Max Weber and, more recently, Louis Dumont have noted, one can escape the constraints of the system by renouncing and becoming an ascetic or a saint.[10] This path presumably leads to withdrawal from worldly activities and social obligations, although the example of Gandhi, as of many holy men, shows that the withdrawal need not be complete and that it can have practical effects and stimulate social change.

The system is also open in the worldly sphere in permitting, even in the scriptural formulations, members of all *varṇas* to undertake occupations and activities that may be auxiliary to their traditional caste occupations or even departures from them. Historically, the fields of agriculture, trade, and government administration were open areas in this sense. Recent additions include the modern professions and the whole field of industry. While economic necessity is frequently cited as a reason for departures from the traditional division of labor prescribed in the *varṇa* scheme, regional variations in the interpretations of the scheme and the difficulties of fitting new types of occupations into it are also factors.

## The Cultural Metabolism of an Innovation

Granting that Sanskritic Hinduism has some features of flexibility, how are they used in the recurrent processes of cultural change? As a first approximation, we may take Sanskritization to represent a process of orthogenetic change and Westernization and modernization to represent heterogenetic change.[11] This definition is ultimately inadequate, however, since it does not explain the interrelations between the two kinds of process. In particular, it leaves unclear the question whether culturally alien innovations can be incorporated into the traditional system and how such incorporation would change that system. We have been prevented from giving adequate answers to these questions by the equation of the traditional with the indigeneous and of the modern with the foreign. The assumption has been that modernization is wholly a heterogenetic replacement of indigenous traditions by alien imports. Either one becomes modern by adopting a foreign culture or one remains traditional by clinging to an outmoded indigenous culture. Since Indian civilization during its long history has incorporated many foreign groups and cultural elements while maintaining a recognizable continuity, there must be something wrong with the equation "modern equals foreign" and the associated assumption that everything modern in India was introduced by Europeans or other foreigners.

A more adequate theory of the interrelationship between Sanskritization and modernization, and between orthogenetic and heterogenetic processes of change generally, is suggested by the study of the interactions between ritually neutral areas and ritually restricted areas. Some interactions can be directly observed or documented in the life histories of individuals and families over a short-run time perspective of two or three generations. Such interactions are expressed in the active movements of individuals and groups into cities, modern education, the professions, government service, and industry. The conflicts thus encountered are masked, mitigated, or resolved by a series of adaptive strategies that usually begin with a cognitive compartmentalization of the conflicting spheres of activity and are followed by mutual adjustments and modifications, the formation of new norms, and an eventual reintegration at a new level.

From the point of view of a longer-run, diachronic perspective, it is of interest to see whether the adjustments and adaptive strategies observed in contemporary Madras can be translated into recurrent processes of cultural change, and whether evidence can be found for their continued operation in social and cultural history. I believe it is possible to describe such recurrent processes in the form of a sequence of hypothetical phases and also to give some cultural-historical evidence for their operation.

### *Enclavement of Foreign Imports*

Items new to the culture—whether artifacts, activities, styles of life, or people—are perceived as new or foreign, named accordingly, and segregated ecologically in a special "enclave" with an appropriate symbolic designation. The early settlement of Europeans in Madras was within the Fort Saint George area and in a segregated quarter outside the fort called "White Town." The Indian settlement just to the north was called "Black Town." These were, of course, English designations, but the Indian prototype, in the form of segregated streets and quarters for different caste and occupational groups, is well known. The graphic description in the Tamil epic *Śilappadikāram* of the ancient city of Puhār, a port city probably located not very far from modern Madras and Pondicherry, includes both kinds of segregation, the foreign enclaves and the indigenous clustering of occupational and status groups:

> The riches of the Puhār shipowners made the kings of faraway lands envious. The most costly merchandise, the rarest foreign produce, reached the city by sea and caravans.
>
> The city spread wide, vast as the capital of the northern Kuru—beyond the Gāndhāra country—where dwell sages famous for their asceticism.
>
> The sunshine lighted up the open terraces, the harbor docks, the towers with their loopholes like the eyes of deer. In various quarters of the city the homes of wealthy Greeks were seen. Near the harbor seamen from far-off lands appeared at home. In the streets hawkers were selling unguents, bath powders, cooling oils, flowers, perfume, incense. Weavers brought their fine silks and all kinds of fabrics made of wool or cotton. There were special streets for

merchants of coral, sandalwood, myrrh, jewelry, faultless pearls, pure gold, and precious gems.

Each trade had its own street in the workers' quarter of the city.

At the center of the city were the wide royal street, the street of temple cars, the bazaar, and the main street, where rich merchants had their mansions with high towers. There was a street for priests, one for doctors, one for astrologers, one for peasants. In a wide passage lived the craftsmen who pierce gems and pearls for the jewelers. Nearby were those who make trinkets out of polished nacre and sea shells. In another quarter lived the coachmen, bards, dancers, astronomers, clowns, prostitutes, actresses, florists, betel-sellers, servants, oboe players, drummers, jugglers, and acrobats.

In wide fields near the town were encamped horsemen and their swift mounts, war elephants, chariot drivers, soldiers fearful to look upon. Near these were palaces of knights and princes. Between the quarters of the workers and the nobles lay an open square, large as a battlefield where two great armies might have met. There, under rows of trees, the sheds of a market were set up. The haggling of buyers and sellers could be heard there all day long.

The lovers crossed the main street, with its warehouses of merchandise from overseas. Then they came to the low-lying quarters near the sea, where flags, raised high toward the sky, seemed to be saying: "On these stretches of white sand can be found the goods that foreign merchants, leaving their own countries to stay among us, have brought here in great ships."

Near the shore lighthouses had been built to show ships the way to the harbor. Far away one could see the tiny lights of the fishing boats laying their nets in the deep sea. All night lamps were burning, the lamps of foreigners who talk strange tongues, and the lamps of the guards who watch over precious cargoes near the docks. Bordered by rows of aloes, the seashore was more enchanting even than the fields with their lotus ponds and streams. The lamps gave such abundant light that one could have found a single mustard seed had it fallen on the clear sand, spread evenly like fine flour.[12]

### *Ritual Neutralization of Foreign Enclaves*

For various reasons of curiosity or economic interest, individual groups of the indigenous population associate themselves with the foreigners and foreign imports as interpreters, brokers, servants, traders, and in other capacities. The association brings them into close contact with the innovations and innovators and gives them the opportunity for direct observation, emulation, and production of the new products and styles. At first, the terms of association are presumed to be influenced by the social code of the foreign group, however deviant it may be from the traditional code. Those who associate with the innovations and innovating groups do so at their own risk, and that risk may include ostracism by their own social group and other severe sanctions. The early servants of the East India Company and converts to Christianity probably found themselves in an uncomfortable, marginal position.

As the indigenous population that is economically and socially dependent on the innovations increases, as the new products are accepted and used by a larger group, and as those closely associated with their introduction prosper and strengthen their conformity to traditional norms in the domestic and religious sphere, there is a tendency to relax social attitudes toward the innovators and their associates and to recognize the particular innovational sphere as a neutral area to which scriptural and customary norms need not apply with the same rigor as in traditional spheres. In the neutral area, the cultural differences between the foreign and the indigenous tend to diminish, and new norms of behavior arise.

Industrial technology, enterprise, and employments have been undergoing just such a process of neutralization during the last hundred years. The modern professions of law, medicine, teaching, and the clerical and supervisory office work connected with government administration probably went through a similar process almost a hundred years earlier.

The recognition that some fields of activity are not the monopolistic preserve of any particular caste or religious group creates ritually neutral public areas open to all castes. Their ritual neutrality derives from three different sources:

1. The fact that the field of activity may be so recent an innovation that there has not been time to determine its relations to the traditional social code. This is true, for example, of television and electronic equipment, the manufacture, sale, and use of which is too recent to have received social and cultural definition.
2. The fact that different castes and groups with different norms of conduct interact in these public areas without severe social sanctions. It is not simply the intercaste mixing that is decisive but the *social recognition* that such mixing will not incur heavy social sanctions. In many villages today, a member of a clean caste cannot enter an untouchable settlement without being heavily polluted, and an untouchable cannot enter a Brahman street without being beaten. Yet on buses and streetcars, in shops, in offices and plants, in theaters and movie houses, and at political gatherings, members of these same castes mix freely, incurring only a mild form of pollution or hostility, if any.
3. As new techniques, products, and social relations are introduced and developed in ritually neutral public areas in relative freedom from the rigors of the traditional code, new norms governing such innovations also emerge. In this way, new standards of speech, dress, diet, belief, and conduct very different from the traditional standards are formed and become accepted in the neutral areas, without necessarily being accepted in other areas of domestic and social life.

An individual's daily passage between "ritually neutral" public areas and private domestic areas subject to traditional ritual restrictions does not result in traumatic and schizophrenic emotional reactions or lead to a dominance in his life of the public area over the private, or conversely. It results instead in an adaptive *modus vivendi* that I call "compartmentalization." He mentally categorizes the two areas as socially and culturally different in behavior, belief, and norms. By so doing, he reduces direct conflicts between the areas and gains the time and opportunity to try out innovations and develop adjustments in the religious and domestic sphere through vicarious ritualization and restructuring of observances and beliefs.

While the growth of urban centers and of industry has expanded the areas of ritual neutrality, such areas also exist on a smaller scale in village and small-town life—in agricultural work teams, shops, bazaars, public festivals, and processions. In fact, one can discern the basic matrix of ritual neutrality in the mildly impure "normal ritual status" in which every Hindu, according to Srinivas, finds himself as he goes about his daily affairs.[13] Urbanization and industrialization have brought the Hindu into new arenas where he can conduct his affairs with new materials and techniques. He is able to maintain a normal ritual status in his daily life because the new arenas, materials, and techniques have been socially recognized as areas of ritual neutrality.

Not all innovations in Indian society and culture have entered the system through the ritually neutral areas. Many innovations and changes have been made within the family, hereditary occupation, caste organization, or religious sect. These innovations, however, are seen as minor changes within a long-established structure of accepted cultural traditions. They are "orthogenetic" changes that attract little attention, except as appreciation for unusual performance. The innovations that originate in the ritually neutral areas, on the other hand, frequently appear to be alien to and in conflict with cultural traditions, and they require special treatment and selection before they can be reconciled or absorbed. They are the heterogenetic changes perceived and regarded as culturally foreign or strange, calling for special adaptive reactions and strategies. Enclavement, ritual neutralization, and compartmentalization are some of the adaptive strategies that have been developed in Indian civilization for introducing heterogenetic innovations. In the later phases of the process, which I shall describe, the strategies for incorporating orthogenetic innovations appear.

### *Foreign Imports Become a Typological Option in the Culture*

When an innovation along with its associated sphere is neutralized, it becomes available to a much larger group of producers and consumers among the indigenous population. Its extension does not yet mean assimilation of the innovation and the innovating group into the indigenous culture and society. It marks rather an intermediate step in that direction and is distinguished by classification of the import as a stylistic or typological variant among a set of options. Western-style clothes now manufactured and worn by Indians are still referred to as "European dress," modern medicine taught and practiced by Indians is designated as "allopathic" or "modern" medicine in contrast with the "homeopathic," "*Āyurvedic*," "Yunānī," and "Siddha" systems, which are all included in the category of "indigenous Indian medicine." Systems of dance, music, astrology, law, and philosophy have all been introduced in this way and have in many cases retained their distinct class names to designate variant styles long after all traces of foreign origin have disappeared.

Several features of this phase of innovation are especially noteworthy. The specific groups and historical contexts associated with the innovations are subordinated to a conception of them as cultural types and styles. As such, they are dissociated from racial, ethnic, and religious affiliation or historical origins and become available options to anyone in the society who is willing and able to use them. The adjective "European" applied to dress, cuisine, medicine, science, or education in India now refers to cultural styles followed by modern Indians; the materials, techniques, and personnel involved in their production are often all Indian. When European-owned and managed firms were Indianized after independence, the new Indian owners and managers continued many of their predecessors' practices—the use of the English language, European-style clothes, and industrial organization—because they believed that these cultural styles were still functionally useful.

A particularly striking cultural-historical example of the process of stylistic "typologizing" of foreigners and foreign innovations is the word *Yavana*. It has been documented in the history of Tamil language and literature by Kamil Zvelebil, whose conclusions I shall summarize.[14]

About three dozen references to *Yavanas* occur in old and medieval Tamil literature. Zvelebil finds that, in the earliest Tamil texts,

> the *Yavanas* are traders coming by sea from the West; slightly later, they are soldiers, bodyguards and guardians employed by Tamil kings; still later, some *Yavanas* settled down in the South, mostly as craftsmen and traders, and in some aspects their handiwork and craftsmanship seem to have been superior to native craftsmanship (this concerns mainly some kind of lamps and ear-rings). Ethnically, the term *Yavaṉar* referred probably to Greeks, Syrians, Jews, Southern Arabians, and East Africans, Romans and Byzantines; later, it covers also early Arabs and Muslims (cf. the related term cōṉakaṉ, cōṉakar used for some Muslim communities, especially in eastern Ceylon). One thing is certain: *Yavaṉar* came to denote all aliens coming to South India from the West, and the adjective *Yavana* means "foreign, alien/Western," just as the term cīṉar, "the Chinese," was used (in a somewhat more limited sense) for all aliens coming from the East.

In later medieval Tamil literature, references to *Yavana* artisans, villages (*yavaṉaccēri*), and works of art are frequent. The term *cēri* implies, according to Zvelebil, that these villages were outside the Tamil village or town proper. The term *cēri* is still used in Tamiḻnāḍu to refer to villages and settlements of untouchables as well as in a more generic sense. The *Yavana* craftsmen who settled in these villages worked in wood-engraving, wood carving, carpentry, sculpture.

But just as the meaning of *Yavana* referring to people was generalized and extended to any type of foreigner from the West, so the references to *Yavana* works of art and craftsman were generalized and extended to any *Yavana* style of art and craft whether made by foreigners or Indians. Zvelebil notes that "some types of products are mentioned so often, and in such a stereotyped manner, that it seems that the term *Yavana* refers not to their origin (made by *Yavanas*) but to the type, to the model." The term is used typologically—"especially [in] the two items *Yavana* (*pāvaiyaṉai*) *viḷakku,* 'the *Yavana* lamp (held by, or adorned by, or in the shape of, a statue),' and *yavaṉappēḻai, 'Yavana* chest, box.' Also, the term *yavaṉak kaiviṉai, "Yavana* craftsmanship,' is almost a cliché in early Tamil medieval texts. It just seems to refer to foreign, *Yavana*-like and/or foreign-like handiwork, craftsmanship."

*The Foreign Innovation Enters the Indigenous Sphere*

The typologizing of foreign groups and imports marks an acceptance of them as optional variants of indigenous groups and products but does not yet mean their acceptance as parts of the indigenous culture and society. "Indigenization" takes place in the succeeding phases of incorporation, during which the innovation is recognized as modern, but its foreign origins are forgotten or ignored. The ecological or symbolic foreign enclavement is dropped or loses its charge, leaving the innovation to mix freely in the indigenous culture and society, both "modern" and "traditional." Foreign loan-words, such as "thanks," "hotel," or "station," enter colloquial speech and are used without any self-consciousness about their foreign origin except on the part of the linguistic specialist. A great many literary and social forms, techniques, and technical products, which may have been foreign in origin, are now accepted as modern and Indian. The use of sewing machines, wristwatches, radios, telephones, bicycles and automobiles; eating from plates on tables while sitting on chairs; working for a college degree in a modern subject—all are now recognized as parts of a modern culture that is produced as well as consumed by Indians. Sometimes a special class of people is associated with these items as a modern class because it follows a style of life that uses the modern items or because it has the adaptability and desire to do so. The modern class frequently includes the better-educated and well-to-do groups living in urban centers, but one can find general recognition of the prestige and value of modern culture in the scale of dowries offered for husbands in different kinds of professions—the civil service and modern medicine get the highest—and in the popularity of wristwatches, transistor radios, and bicycles as wedding gifts even among poor villagers.

Modern culture is not confined to any one class but may be found distributed unequally among members of the same family, caste, or village. Children in college tend to be more modern than their parents, and husbands more modern than their wives. Brahmans have the reputation in Tamiḻnāḍu of being very modern and adaptable because they have acquired modern education and have gone into the professions, business, and industry, although they are also regarded as representatives of Sanskritic Hinduism and the Great Tradition.

Modernity, then, is a permanent layer or dimension of indigenous culture and not simply a collection of recent foreign imports or the fashionable life-style of a privileged class. When an innovation has entered this layer, it is no longer associated with strange and foreign groups, nor is it segregated from the rest of the indigenous culture. It may be recognized for its functional or aesthetic value as an innovation and acquire prestige and status on that account. In any case, it is differentiated from the traditional culture, from which it may be a departure and to which it may also offer a challenge. The challenge is usually not very deep or threatening, because, when it has reached this phase, the innovation of foreign origin has been desegregated and neutralized and appears as a freely available variant in the culture. In this phase, heterogenetic innovations are hardly distinguishable from orthogenetic innovations, except to the culture historian. When an hereditary image-maker in contemporary Madras finds and uses a finer grade of sand than his father used, or members of a Brahman family go into agriculture and trade; when a musician improvises on a classical *rāga,* or a Sanskrit scholar writes and produces a play in Sanskrit, these are orthogenetic innovations. They may even be admired for their originality, workmanship, resourcefulness, and taste, just as some of the heterogenetic innovations are. But the orthogenetic innovations have a different point of origin and a different career from the heterogenetic. Let us note some of the significant differences between a foreign innovation and an indigenous one.

Because an indigenous innovation emerges within the system and is not associated with the alien and the strange, it is not regarded as a threat to tradition and requires no special segregation and neutralization. It is permitted to develop on its own merits or demerits, so to speak; its eventual acceptance or rejection is not posed as a dilemma of either accepting or rejecting all the basic institutions, values, and beliefs of the traditional system. On the contrary, the cultural presumption is that the acceptance of such innovations will not change the traditional system in any essential way; they represent merely varying manifestations of the system. This presumption is given metaphysical expression in Śaṅkara's Vedānta philosophy of causation, which regards the cause as unchangeable, giving only an appearance of suffering change:

> The clay is spoken of as the only reality in all its transformations as the pot, the jug, or the plate. It is said that though there are so many diversities of appearance that one is called the plate, the other the pot, and the other the jug, yet these are only empty distinctions of name and form, for the only thing real in them is the earth which in its essence remains ever the same whether you call it the pot, plate, or jug. . . . All the various modes in which the clay appear are mere appearances, unreal, indefinable, and so illusory. . . . So in all world-phenomena the one truth is being, the Brahman, and all the phenomena that are being imposed on it are but illusory forms and names.[15]

The lady from contemporary Madras who insists that her sari is essentially a traditional one although it is made of modern material (nylon) and in the modern colors of pink and beige is echoing, perhaps unknowingly, Śaṅkara's philosophy of causation. That nylon happens to be a recent foreign innovation and that the colors are an indigenous departure from the dark greens, reds, and browns of the traditional South Indian sari does not matter in this philosophy. Both kinds of change are merely varying appearances of an unchanging eternal tradition.

### *The Foreign Import Becomes Traditional*

By the time a heterogenetic innovation has entered the layer of the modern and the indigenous culture, where it is no longer distinguished from an orthogenetic one, it may be said to have been accepted and incorporated into the culture. Yet the acceptance is not complete until the import is no longer regarded simply as modern but *also* as traditional. It may sound paradoxical to speak of a foreign import's becoming traditional, but this is precisely what happens in the final phase of incorporation. In this respect, there is an asymmetry between the curves of the orthogenetic and heterogenetic innovations, although both kinds may end up as traditional. The heterogenetic innovation follows a career, when accepted, from the foreign and recent to the modern, indigenous, and traditional. The orthogenetic innovation, on the other hand, follows a path from the indigenous traditional to the indigenous modern and back to the traditional.

For a foreign import or group to enter the hallowed realm of the traditional, it must become old, must conform to customary or scriptural norms, and must have an origin myth in which it is linked to a great traditional set of ancestors or precedents. These three requirements for traditional status are closely interrelated but not identical. To become old and ancient is to persist for many generations. A family, its property, an institution, an artifact that has persisted is called "traditional" (*paramparaiyāṉa,* from *paramparai:* generation). Such an old family also acquires a reputation for solidity and integrity. Its customs will be considered "civilized" and educated in "traditional culture" (*paḻanākarikam*). In the sense of social customs and social institutions, "traditional culture" (*paḻampaṉbu*) has a good and moral connotation *because* it is old and traditional. When a family's genealogy can be traced to the deities, sages, kings, and cultural heroes of the Epics and Purāṇas, it has established its claims both to antiquity and to moral righteousness. It is not necessary, however, to furnish a complete and scientific family history in order to establish these claims. Professional genealogists and bards are usually able to connect the four or five generations of a family's remembered genealogy to the epic and purānic dynasties. Sometimes genealogists and their families have maintained oral and written records of family genealogies from generation to generation. But it does not really matter whether the reconstructed genealogies that intervene between living memory and those in the scriptures are "scientific." The important thing is to have one's claim to an ancient affiliation socially recognized in the present, since such recognition is one of the major ways to validate one's status, change in status, or status aspirations.[16]

Not only families but also castes, tribes, villages and towns, temples, sects, and *maṭhas* have genealogies that go back to ancient scriptural origins. Artifacts and aspects of civilization, such as the dance, drama, and music, have scriptural genealogies to validate their status as traditional arts and crafts. Westerners are sometimes astonished and amused by the efforts of Indian traditionalists to find evidence in the Vedas and other scriptures for the airplane or nuclear fission or fusion. The effort is not really different in form and principle from the process of incorporating foreign groups into the caste system or raising the status of a lower caste through Sanskritization. The origin myth gives the foreign group or innovation a local habitation and a name within the structure of an Indian Great Tradition. In this way, its present acceptance into the society is culturally validated. To deny the alleged novelty of an innovation by asserting its antiquity is to recognize and accept it as an integral part of the indigenous culture. Archaization is, in this case, also a form of modernization.

## Plus Ça Change . . .

During the last 200 years, traditional Indian arts and crafts, social institutions, and religious practices and beliefs have undergone widespread and profound changes—in materials, techniques, methods of training, design, name, use, and status. Yet most of my Madras informants do not look upon these changes as a process of modernization that transforms items of traditional culture into items of a modern culture. They see some of these changes as leading to neglect, corruption, and even destruction and disappearance of tradition but not to modernizing transformations. The tradition-minded among them participate in efforts to reconstruct, revive, and restore the fading cultural traditions, but they certainly do not regard this as an effort at modernization.

Their attitude creates an apparent mystery about the process of cultural modernization and is very often misinterpreted as resistance to real change and innovation. The mystery is quickly cleared up if we recall that it is people who modernize and not depersonalized cultural artifacts. Individuals, families, and communities can and do modernize, by entering modern occupations, using modern artifacts or adopting a modern life-style. These individuals or groups are considered modern (*muṟpōkku,* from *muṉ* = forward, plus *pōkku* = movement) in the sense of being psychologically adaptable or progressive. Modern occupations, artifacts, and life-styles are not the outcome of a linear transformation of traditional occupations, artifacts, and life-styles. They are produced by orthogenetic or heterogenetic innovations, that is, by the endless variety of nonessential modifications in a susbtratum of cultural traditions, by the recurrent novelties in the births and declines of such traditions through the ages, as in the "eternal renewal" of life in the green shoot of rice and in the newborn infant,* and by the acceptance into the culture of neutralized and desegregated foreign imports. Accordingly, one can classify most items in the cultural universe as either "modern" (*pudunākarikam*) or "traditional" (*paḻanākarikam, paḻampaṉbu*), some items as mixtures of both (the pink nylon sari), and some as neither "modern" nor "traditional" (television), because they are such recent innovations (*puttampudiya, paccaippudiya*) (brand new, green, fresh-new) that they have not yet been processed and classified. If modernization can be defined as a process in which innovations are incorporated into the

* In Tamil *pudidu,* "that which is new or wonderful," also refers to the first sheaves of a rice crop; *pudidu ākkutal* means "to modernize, to make new." *Pudumai, pudinadu, pudai* are words for "newness, novelty," "anything new," "novelty," respectively. *Puduppaḻakkam,* "new habit, usage, fashion," does not mean a renovated old habit or usage but that something not previously habitual or a matter of usage has become so. To "traditionalize, make old" is expressed by *pāṉmai ākkutal* and *paḻamai ākkutal.* Linguistic information from K. Zvelebil, *A Dravidian Etymological Dictionary* by Burrow and Emeneau, Kokilam Subbiah.

indigenous culture, it does not follow that the process automatically transforms the traditional culture into modern culture.

Indians recognize innovation and novelty in many forms, yet look on modernization as a cultural process of "traditionalization," in which the new is turned into something old, and not as a cultural process that makes something new out of that which is old. It seems likely that the asymmetry in the conception of modernization is based on the observation of growth and aging in nature. Young plants, animals, and infants do grow old, but old ones do not grow young. At the same time, this world view recognizes that culture is different from nature, that it can be acquired by man as a member of society in each generation. People are not considered culturally modern or traditional because of racial or even ethnic criteria but because of their life-styles and the artifacts they use. Different psychological aptitudes for change and new learning are recognized among individuals and groups, but these differences are not necessarily linked to biological traits. They are accepted as observed differences in psychological adaptability. Even the most traditional-minded can learn modern ways if they are adaptable. Brahmans, for example, may explain their psychological abilities in terms of family inheritance, but they are also widely considered by non-Brahmans to be very adaptable to modern conditions.

## New Model for a Great Tradition

The different phases in the incorporation of a foreign innovation into a traditional society and culture represent the "normal" cultural metabolism involved. Not every import or innovation goes through every phase. Some may be rejected or arrested at a particular phase, some may skip phases and be directly archaized.

Some foreign imports or groups may meet with extreme resistance and hostility because they become symbols of threats to the indigenous society and culture. The alleged lard-greased cartridges of the 1857 mutiny and the more recent vegetable cooking oils, such as Dalda, are symbols of this kind and for a short period may become targets for xenophobic emotions. Selected items of traditional culture may similarly become symbols of an indigenous Great Tradition and of Little Traditions and rallying points for movements of cultural nationalism. Gandhi's use of the spinning wheel, the movements for cow protection, and the revival of indigenous medicine are examples.

The process of selecting symbols of a tradition and of an antitradition is a highly complex and creative one. Much of it goes on at the unconscious level of "cultural drift" that pushes the growth of cultural traditions in one direction rather than another. Some of it, however, is a product of deliberate planning and cultural policy by cultural policymakers.[17]

The success of a cultural policy that aims to revive or restore selected indigenous traditions is not always easy to evaluate. Gandhi's campaign for weaving hand-spun Khādī, for example, did not succeed in replacing factory looms with the ancient spinning wheel. Yet it does seem to have succeeded in dramatizing concern for cottage industries, the dignity of hand labor, and village underemployment, while providing a symbol for a self-respecting cultural identity in a successful mass political movement. From this point of view, one might argue that the *carkhā* (spinning wheel) really articulated in an archaic idiom the voice of Congress and of the sewing machine.

Many of the revivalist and restorationist movements and their associated symbols turn out to have this Janus-like character—traditional from the front and modern from the back. In this respect, their traditional face serves the same function as the archaizing of a modern innovation—it puts a seal of legitimacy and acceptance on an imported foreign institution or product, just as the lion-headed capital from an Aśoka pillar was chosen to be the official seal and emblem of a modern democratic government in independent India.

Cultural movements and policies that select specific items of foreign and indigenous cultures around which to build a cultural identity for a modernization program are not confined in India to the movement for cultural nationalism and political independence. Such movements have been organized by tribes, castes, religions, communities, sects, and political and linguistic groups as vehicles of change. In general, these movements aim to validate an actual or proposed change by claiming great antiquity for the proposal, a familial or spiritual line of genealogical descent from the ancestral origins, and conformity to accepted cultural norms and values. In practical effect, a traditionalizating validation implies that the proposal for change is restorationist, that is, it aims to restore an original status that for some reason has been lost or forgotten.

A particularly interesting example of such a cultural movement is the Dravidian movement in Tamiḻnāḍu, which not only seeks to validate modernizing changes with archaic models but also attempts to construct an alternative model of a Great Tradition. The model depicts a Dravidian civilization with a complete culture that preceded the Aryan civilization of Sanskritic Hinduism. The Dravidian culture is represented as independent of the Aryan, self-sufficient, and different in language, literature, architecture, sculpture, dance, music, religion, philosophy, and social structure. Sanskritic Hinduism is portrayed as a foreign intrusion into India, especially into South India, where it was brought by Brahman custodians who imposed it on the indigenous Dravidian culture and population. The proposed policy of the Dravidian movement is to "de-Sanskritize" and "de-Brahmanize" South Indian culture and society and restore the original Dravidian civilization. Their restoration program has included attempts to remove Sanskrit, Hindi, and other "foreign" elements from Tamil language and literature, the smashing of idols and images, the simplifying of rites and ceremonies by not using Brahman priests and rituals, the reinterpretation of the *Rāmāyaṇa,* the Purāṇas, and the Vedas to reveal Brahman "oppression" of and "calumny" against the Dravidians, and attacks on Brahmans and the "superstitious" beliefs and practices of Sanskritic Hinduism. On the social side, the movement has advocated later marriage and widow remarriage; a quota system for Brahmans in education, government administration, and politics; the rejection of the *varṇa* classification; and the use of Tamil as the medium of instruction in schools and universities.

While the Dravidian movement has found support for its reinterpretations of South Indian history in the rediscovery and translations of such ancient Tamil classics as the *Śilappadikāram,* the *Tolkāppiyam,* the Saṅgam Anthologies, and the *Tirukkuṟaḷ,* its significance does not lie in its contributions to Tamil or comparative Dravidian studies. These studies, which were given a great impetus in the nineteenth century by such Western scholars as C. V. Beschi, R. Caldwell, and G. U. Pope, as well as by some Brahman and non-Brahman scholars, are now becoming a part of the world of international scholarship and culture in the same way in which Sanskrit language and literature, or Latin and Greek, have been made available to a world audience. The significance of the Dravidian movement lies rather in its use of such studies and of the modern techniques of propaganda and political organization to propagate a cultural ideology and model of a Dravidian Great Tradition and to make it the cultural basis for a successful political party, the Dravidian Progressive Federation, DMK, which is now in power in Tamiḻnāḍu.[18]

Although the cultural ideology of the Dravidian movement has declared Brahmans and various aspects of Sanskritic Hinduism "the foreign enemy," it nevertheless incorporates many foreign imports. E. V. Ramaswami Naicker, the founding father of the Dravidian movement, told me that a trip to Europe in the early 1930's was the source of many of his ideas and organizational techniques. During the trip, he had discovered Lenin's communism, Mussolini's fascism, Bertrand Russell's rationalism, and Robert Ingersoll's atheism; in each of them he said he had found something useful. It is also clear by now, although perhaps not transparently so, why this radical innovator should have become the leader of a restorationist movement.

As a cultural phenomenon, the Dravidian movement has followed a pattern familiar from the wider cultural history of India and of many other countries. Archaeological, historical, linguistic, and literary studies inspire a vision of a classical golden age. The post-classical middle period between the golden age and the present is viewed as a decline caused by foreign intrusions. A renaissance aiming to rediscover and emulate the classics of the golden age generally also becomes a vehicle for purification and repression of the "degraded" traditions of the middle period and for modernizing reforms.

The Dravidian ideological view of Tamil cultural history reflects this pattern. According to Zvelebil, the ideology posits a scheme of five successive ages:[19]

1. A classical golden age of the Saṅgam period of the third and fourth centuries A.D.
2. A dark age under the influence of Aryan Buddhism and Jainism
3. An age of inimical Aryanization beginning with the *bhakti* movements of the Pallava period of the sixth century (Kambaṉ's ninth-century translation of the *Rāmāyaṇa* is given as a typical representative of literature of this age.)

4. An age of decadence and ruin that develops in the late medieval period as a result of Sanskritization and the "corruption" of Tamil language and literature
5. A Tamil renaissance and restoration of the golden age models, bebeginning around the eighteenth century

Although the Dravidian movement suggests that the rejection of a foreign import involves processes of cultural metabolism similar to those involved in the acceptance of such an import, it nevertheless represents an extreme case of the process, since the "foreign import" that is being rejected is not a recent innovation but the long-established Great Tradition of Sanskritic Hinduism. The Dravidian ideology justifies the rejection on the grounds that it is necessary in order to restore the "pure" Tamil Great Tradition that has been "corrupted" by foreign influences. In practice, such a restoration would involve the re-evaluation and elimination of the entire Tamil linguistic, literary, and cultural heritage, which begins with the *bhakti* literature of the sixth and seventh century and which has undergone much creative development since then. Whatever the merits of this view of Tamil cultural history, it cannot be taken as an accurate historical account of the nature and development of Sanskritic Hinduism in South India. It represents rather a cultural ideology whose function and meaning are to be found in contemporary political, economic, and social conflicts, not in historical precedent. The Dravidian portrayal of Sanskritic Hinduism is a very simplified one in whch a few elements are highlighted to symbolize the whole tradition.

Cultural differences among peoples are not absolute facts of nature or biology but derive their importance from the manner in which they are perceived, evaluated, symbolized, and acted upon. They are, in other words, cultural facts, expressions of world views and values, shot through with the subjectivity, relativity, and volatility of such facts. This anthropological dictum applies to the Aryan-Dravidian opposition. The Sanskritic tradition at first came into South India from the North in a gradual and limited way. As early as the third and fourth centuries A.D., during the Saṅgam period, clear distinctions were already being made, according to Zvelebil, between *vaḍa* (northern, Aryan, Sanskritic) and *teṉ* (southern, Dravidian, Tamil). The distinctions were not, however, regarded as antagonistic. But with the massive Sanskritization of Tamil culture during the Pallava period and later, the Aryan-Dravidian distinction expresses hostility and opposition to various aspects of Brahmanism and Sanskritic Hinduism.

In historical Tamil linguistics and literature, the distinction between indigenous culture and foreign culture was expressed in Old Tamil, according to Zvelebil, by the contrasting terms *akam* and *puṟam*. This pair of terms, which is also of basic importance in the ancient Tamil poetics of the *Tolkāppiyam,* links the cultural difference between the indigenous and foreign to the difference between what is "inside" and belongs to the family, household, and village, and what is "outside" and belongs to a public world. In ancient classical Tamil poetic, the *akam-puṟam* contrast represents a classification of two kinds of poetry—love poetry of an ideal "interior landscape" and "public" poetry "placed in a real society and given a context of real history." [20]

This ancient contrast seems to attach no great importance to the difference between a foreigner or strange object that comes from another village or province and one that comes from another country. Both are foreign in the sense that they do not belong to the "inner world" of kin and household. The distinction between the two kinds of foreigners, on the other hand, is sharply drawn in medieval and modern Tamil and is probably related to cultural and political nationalism. In modern Tamil, the distinction between indigenous culture and foreign culture is expressed by the terms *contam,* "what is ours, our own" (from a Sanskrit loan word *svānta-*), and *ayal* "alien, foreign," "what does not belong to us" (a Dravidian word). On the surface, the new pair seem similar to the ancient usage, but *ayal* refers to the sum total of *non-Tamil* features, so the line between indigenous and foreign is now drawn at the level of an entire culture—Tamil versus non-Tamil, Dravidian versus non-Dravidian, Indian versus non-Indian—rather than at the level of family, household, and village. The older usage is continued in such words as *a̱riyādava̱n,* "he who is not known by the village," "stranger," and in the compartmentalizing tendencies of modern Madras people, but the usage has been overshadowed by expressions that connote regional and national Great Traditional cultures.

While the ancient Tamil contrast between one's own culture and alien, foreign culture, in terms of *akam* and *pu̱ram,* seems much closer to the outlook of a primitive or folk̩ mentality, in other respects, it was more universalistic than the later distinctions, as the following remarkable *pu̱ram* poem testifies:

Kaṇiya̱n Pūṇku̱ṉṟa̱n

Every town's a home town,
every man a kinsman.
Good and evil do not come
from others;
pain and relief of pain
come of themselves
Dying is not new.
We do not rejoice
that living is sweet,
nor in anger
call it bitter.

Wise men
have shown that lives
are but logs in a raft
rushing in a torrent
sounding over rocks
after a lightening storm.

So
we're not amazed by great men
we do not scorn the little.[21]

## IS INDIA'S MODERNIZATION UNIQUE?

The account I have sketched of the adaptive mechanisms that India has developed for incorporating or rejecting innovations would tend to support those who characterize India as essentially "traditionalistic." The usual connotations of this characterization, however, are not supported by this account. The traditionalism of Indian civilization is *not* opposed to innovation and change, to modernity, to the foreign and the strange. Traditional India is not a monolithic and immovable accumulation of immemorial customs and beliefs blocking the road to progress. India's traditionalism is rather a built-in adaptive mechanism for making changes. Essentially, it is a series of processes for incorporating innovations into the culture and validating them. The processes include enclavement, neutralization, compartmentalization, vicarious ritualization, typological stylization, reinterpretation, archaization, and, undoubtedly, others. The validation culminates when a change can be related to the traditional layer of the culture. This requirement does not really impose a very narrow constraint on the innovating process. The traditional layer contains such a rich reservoir of oral and written myth, legends, histories, and genealogies that the professional genealogists and mythographers, as well as the amateurs, have no difficulty in finding ancient precedents for modern changes. Since, moreover, there is no single "official" definition and interpretation of "the tradition," ample latitude exists for commentators and interpreters to adapt it to changing needs and circumstances.

The fluidity and relativity in the definition of tradition is given philosophic sanction in Indian systems of thought whether or not those systems acknowledge the reality of novelty and change. Even Śaṅkara's Advaitavedānta, whose doctrine of causation recognizes changes only as illusory appearances of an unchanging Being, allows for several different paths to truth and salvation, as well as for choice among the paths according to individual temperament, capacity, education, degree of spiritual development, and other factors. Other systems of thought, such as that of the Sāṅkhya school, developed a theory of causation (the *pariṇāma*) holding that "the effect is a product of a real change in the cause through the action and combination of the elements of diversity in it." [22]

A contemporary Indian scholar writing on Indian theories of knowledge denies that these theories elevate memory as the only valid or the most important form of cognition: "Most thinkers hold that novelty should also be regarded as a necessary character of knowledge worthy of the name. So memory (which is a reproduction of knowledge acquired in the past through perception or any other sources) is not regarded as a separate kind of valid cognition." Other thinkers regard memory as a substantive source of knowledge about "the pastness of an experience or its object—information which could not be obtained from any other source without its aid." [23]

Given the variety and flexibility in Indian conceptions of tradition, one can see how easy it would be for Indians to accept all sorts of innovations and changes by traditionalizing them. One looks for changes not in a self-conscious ideology of progress and innovation but in the ways in which "structural amnesia" and "patterned memory" operate to select from the rich storehouse of tradition each group's or each cultural product's genealogical links to its remote ancestors. In the process, traditionalization is not simply a blind handing-down of meaningless and functionless "survivals" but rather a creative incorporation of *contemporary* events and innovations into the living and changing structure of tradition.

It is often said that flexibility exists in Indian civilization at the level of tolerance for a wide range of beliefs but is not to be found at the level of conduct, which is rigidly prescribed and proscribed. The distinction, which has played so important a part in the Western liberal tradition, does not quite describe the Indian situation, for the question is not the actual behavior of some individual or group, but the normative structure within which the behavior occurs. At the level of Indian civilization's normative structure, its culture, the variety of alternative paths of conduct is as great as the variety of systems of thought. Flexibility in interpreting and applying these normative structures to individuals and groups in particular circumstances is equally great in the two cases.

When a group wishes to change its position in the structure, it must change not only its own and others' behavior but its thought as well. Frequently it may be more difficult to change its thought than its behavior. One of the general psychological mechanisms involved in such changes is the acting out of some role with which the actor has identified in order to change his own and others' beliefs, attitudes, and sentiments. In Srinivas's Sanskritization, the identification is with a claimed position in the *varṇa* structure, and the acting out includes a set of beliefs as well as behavior. In the Dravidian movement, the identification is with a whole Tamil Great Tradition, and the acting out includes the disestablishment of the Great Tradition of Sanskritic Hinduism as well as the restoraration of the Dravidian traditions. In the Rādhā-Krishna *bhajanas,* the identification is with Krishna and the milkmaid *gopīs* of the *Bhāgavatapurāṇa,* and the acting out is the singing and dancing, which represent Krishna's "sports" with the milkmaids. In all these cases, the success of the identification and of the acting out can be measured only by the actor's subjective conviction that he has attained the state he is seeking and by social recognition of that attainment.

The identifications with and acting out of social roles not only operate at the levels of both thought and conduct; they also simultaneously express an individual's decision *to affirm* some aspect of his cultural traditions through the selection of myths and rituals that are the vehicles of the identification and the acting out, and *to change* another aspect of it by giving the myth and ritual a contemporary relevance. The dual set of tensions between affirmation and innovation, between thought and behavior, was eloquently expressed in the description a Krishna devotee in Madras gave me of his search for salvation and brotherhood in the Rādhā-Krishna *bhajanas.*

In his account, behavioral gestures, such as mutual prostrations, are the vehicle for an expression of the innovative ideal of equality in the ritual context, while the devotee's thinking and ordinary behavior continue to express inequality and a belief in superiority and inferiority. Traditional hierarchical thought and innovative equalitarian behavior will be harmonized when, "by constant practice, their minds imbibe equality as their bodies express it. . . . The two then act alike and there is correlation between them." [24] The underlying social and psychological theory here is reminiscent of the James-Lange theory of emotions and George Herbert Mead's theory of role-taking.

India's traditionalizing cultural metabolism is probably not unique, although it may have a distinctive rate and style. The comparative cultural study of how different societies deal with innovation and change is too underdeveloped to permit precise comparisons. The old dichotomy of traditional and modern societies and the alleged linear laws of development that inexorably transform traditional into modern types of society have not been supported by the highly differentiated picture beginning to emerge from recent research. In particular, the theory has not been able to give an adequate explanation of the mixtures of tradition and modernity that are to be found in India, Indonesia, Japan, China, and many other countries. To place these cases on a linear graph of transition to modernity is a plausible interpretation consistent with the general theory. But the construction of such a graph requires the addition of so many special variables in order to take account of differences in history, culture, leadership, degree of underdevelopment, and the like and to explain the differences in degree of transition, that a simpler theory seems called for. The transition interpretation, moreover, does not take seriously the possibility that the mixture of tradition and modernity may reflect important long-run interactions and adjustments, that it may be a "permanent transition," as Clifford Geertz suggests in the case of Indonesia, and not simply a prelude to "take-off" or a mismanaged modernization program.[25]

The Indian case points to an alternative possible interpretation, and it should be further explored, especially as societies with Great Traditions modernize. Perhaps such exploration will reveal, as I believe it does in the case of India, that the cultural problem that modernization presents to these societies is neither one of blindly imitating some Western model of development nor one of reaching through internal transformations the modern rung on a universal ladder of social evolution. The problem is of the same general kind that these societies have had to solve again and again in their history in order to survive and maintain any culture at all, namely, how to adapt to change and innovation, whether it originates abroad or inside the country. If the process of modernization is studied comparatively in terms of strategies that different cultures and civilizations have developed to cope with change, we shall see that modernization does not pose a new dilemma of either rejecting one's traditional culture as a whole in order to replace it with modern culture or rejecting modern culture in its entirety in order to preserve one's traditions. The problem faced by traditional societies is how to continue their normal cultural metabolism, that is, how to continue converting the events of history into assimilable cultural traditions.

The application of this approach to the modernization of cultural traditions in India suggests that the processes of cultural intake and assimilation operate with artifacts, technical processes, idea systems, and social institutions, as well as with social groups. Innovations are introduced into the system, tried and tested, and accepted or rejected in somewhat the same manner as are human newcomers. While there are many differences of detail in the process, depending on the cultural field in which the innovation occurs; on whether it has been brought in by members of a particular foreign group or has been introduced by natives who have traveled and studied abroad; and on whether it has originated within the indigenous culture or outside of it, the reactions to, and eventual selection and incorporation of, an innovation probably follow the sequence of phases that I have outlined.

Max Weber makes some interesting comparative observations on the process of cultural innovation, especially in the economic field. I do not now refer to Weber's well-known theory of how the Protestant ethic was converted into a "this-worldly asceticism" and so became a motive force for technical and economic innovation. The Protestant ethic is, in any case, supposedly absent in India, according to Weber. I have in mind rather his more marginal discussion of how "guest people" and "pariah people" may be sources of economic innovation.[26]

Weber's discussion is provocative and provides a good starting point for an analysis of the sources and phases of cultural innovation, especially if considered in the more general context of institutionalized hospitality to strangers and cultural attitudes toward the new and strange. Weber's treatment unfortunately is brief and emphasizes rather the low ritual status occupied by guest and pariah peoples and some of the transitional stages by which groups outside the caste system are brought into the system by conforming to its norms or by which low-caste groups rise in the rank order by emulating the higher castes. Although he describes these groups as providing indispensable trade, services, crafts, and industry that the local population cannot or will not provide, he does not stress their role as importers and innovators, nor does he trace the career and assimilation of the innovations within the system. His analysis concentrates on the "enclavement" phase of innovation and restricts that phase primarily to the acquisition of a particular ritual status in the caste system. Weber narrowed his analysis because of his assumption that "Hinduism is primarily ritualism" and his interpretation of that ritualism in terms of unconditional and unchanging ritual obligations (*dharma*) inherited by each caste.[27]

In spite of his unrealistically rigid conception of Hinduism and the caste system, Weber also cites evidence, drawn chiefly from the census reports, of the adaptability and mobility of different groups as well as of the system as a whole. Ritual barriers, he finds, have not stopped everyday economic transactions in the past.[28]

He finds contemporary trends destructive of the ritual system:

> Today, the Hindu caste order is profoundly shaken. Especially in the district of Calcutta, old Europe's major gateway to India, many norms have practically lost their force. The railroads, the taverns, the changing occupational stratification, the concentration of labor through imported industry, colleges, etc.,

> have all contributed their part. The "commuters to London," that is, those who studied in Europe and maintained voluntary social intercourse with Europeans, were outcastes up to the last generation; but more and more this pattern is disappearing. And it has been impossible to introduce caste coaches on the railroads in the fashion of the American railroad cars or station waiting room which segregate "white" from "colored" in the southern states. All caste relations have been shaken, and the stratum of intellectuals bred by the English are here, as elsewhere, bearers of a specific nationalism. They will greatly strengthen this slow and irresistible process. For the time being, however, the caste structure still stands quite firmly.[29]

Weber regarded such departures from the ritual law as temporary European intrusions into the Hindu system. He thought that the system and the "Hindu character" would reassert themselves when the Europeans withdrew:

> When, today, the penetration of Indian society by capitalistic interests is already so extensive that they can no longer be eliminated, it is still possible for some eminent English students of the land to argue on good grounds that the removal of the thin conquering strata of Europeans and the Pax Britannica enforced by them would open wide the life and death struggle of inimical castes, confessions, and tribes; the old feudal robber romanticism of the Indian Middle Ages would again break forth.[30]

Weber obviously was not able to reconcile the evidence of change within the system with his conception of it as governed by a fundamental ritual law that prevents change. He concluded, contrary to the evidence he had presented, that the result of the system's great adaptive and assimilative powers would not be a changed system but the continued expression of its unchanging "spirit." While he recognized traditionalization and archaization as forms of legitimation, he does not seem to have appreciated their roles as sources of change. In particular, he underestimated the extent to which changes originating outside the system (heterogenetic changes) are selectively incorporated into it through the mechanisms of compartmentalization and neutralization. His discussion of the role of the Jews as a pariah people in the economic life of Europe should have alerted him to the importance of these mechanisms as the proving ground for innovation and for the formation of new cultural norms within the system. He missed this insight because he saw compartmentalization only in terms of a "double standard of morals" as between strangers and one's own community, rather than as an encounter between *different* cultural standards, which is not "ethically indifferent" but which gradually neutralizes and reduces the differences and may even produce an integration of the alien and the indigenous standards into a new positive ethical code or ecumenical religion.

The degree of conflict between two different cultural standards depends in part on how the parties to the encounter perceive and react to the differences. Ecological enclavement of a foreign group or of returnees from abroad is one expression of such perception and reaction and may be linked to a deliberate cultural policy toward foreigners. European colonial powers in Asia, for example, frequently did create enclaves for Europeans even where there was no need for extraterritoriality. In Indonesia, as Geertz has shown, the "dual economy" and the "dual society" were in part creations of Dutch policy. The neutralization of the conflicts in cultural standards encountered in these enclaves and the cognitive compartmentalizing, which reduce the conflicts for the participants, may develop in partial independence of any deliberate cultural policy. Such enclavement seems to have occurred in the bazaar area of Modjokuto, the Indonesian town studied by Geertz, and in the industrial plants in and around Madras City.[31]

Judging from the Madras example, as well as from other recent studies by cultural anthropologists, cultural geographers, and cultural historians (such as Clifford Geertz, Paul Wheately, T. G. McGee, and Rhoads Murphey), the cultural processes associated with Westernization and modernization are not unilateral diffusions of elements of Western culture into traditional societies, nor do they originate with European colonialism. They are processes endemic in the history of those societies and represent a kind of cultural metabolism, which regulates for each society a distinctive balance between cultural continuity and cultural innovation.

When I first became interested in Madras City in 1954, it was in the context of a general theory of the cultural role of cities in the comparative history of civilizations. Madras appeared at that time to be playing the heterogenetic role of a former colonial city, that is, it seemed to be serving as a "head-link" for Westernization and modernization through its commercial, administrative, educational, and transportational functions. The research question that interested me then was how to relate contemporary and limited field observations in Madras City to the wider context of Indian civilization. I formulated the question in the short-hand operational form of "what happens to the Great Tradition of Sanskritic Hinduism in a metropolitan center."

It was something of a surprise to find, on closer familiarity with Madras, that much of "Sanskritic Hinduism" remained alive in this heterogenetic center and that they were also many movements for cultural revival and restoration. This was not a complete surprise, since Robert Redfield and I had concluded in our paper, "The Cultural Role of Cities," that "the progressive spirit of Asia and Africa is not simply a decision to walk the road of progressive convictions that we have traversed, but rather in significant part an effort of the so-called backward peoples to recover from their disruptive encounters with the West by returning to the sacred centers of their indigenous civilizations." The paper also suggested that these encounters be viewed not as cases of "simple diffusion or spread of urban influence from a city," but rather as "a cultural interaction which takes place against a background of ancient civilization with its own complex and changing pattern of urbanization now coming into contact with a newer and different civilization and giving rise to results that conform to neither.[32]

As we take a fresh look at these former colonial cities in the perspective of cultural history, we shall find further evidence, I believe, not only of efforts in the postcolonial period to recover the orthogenetic Great Traditions but also of efforts to continue the ancient heterogenetic roles as harbors for foreign imports and indigenous innovations, for heresy and reform. Both roles will be found in Madras today and in the past. Their operation and interrelationship can best be understood as a sequence of phases in the selection and incorporation of foreign and domestic innovations into the modern and traditional cultural layers of an indigenous civilization.

As modes of adaptation to foreigners and to foreign imports, enclavement and the associated adaptive strategies have been practiced in all these civilizations for many hundreds of years before the coming of European colonialism. The Europeans, and later the Americans, brought in products, peoples, and national flags new to those civilizations. They also brought out many innovations that were new to the West. This exchange of cultural novelties has been going on for a long time, as the ancient references to Europe's luxury trade with the Orient indicate.[33] The trade has left its own record in the many loan words in European languages for pepper, cinnamon, nutmeg, cloves, gold, diamonds, pearls, precious stones, ivory, silks, and cottons. The record continues to grow with the entry into English of such Indian words as *sitar, tabla, yoga, swami, ashram, ahimsa, satyagraha,* and many others. The cultural processes for dealing with the reception and assimilation of novelties within each civilization have also been developed as distinctive aspects of its own historic growth and transformations. To assume that the processes originate with the modern European intrusions is simply "temporal ethnocentrism."[34]

J. H. Plumb, the historian, has recently published a set of lectures on *The Death of the Past* in which Comte's law of intellectual progress is brought up to date with great eloquence, erudition, and sophistication. The progress of rationalism and science, Plumb argues, has made obsolete the religious-metaphysical interpretation of the past as a sanction for the present or as a source for divining a millennial manifest or hidden destiny:

> Men and women today are not conditioned in their daily lives to a world that is tied to an imperceptibly changing past, in which the patterns of work, the relationship between fathers and children, or even between the social classes, possess the sanctity of tradition. Life is change, uncertainty, and only the present can have validity and that, maybe, not for long. The consequence, of course, is to accept a similar attitude in ideas of conduct, in the concepts of social structure or family life. They can be judged by what they do, but lack validity because they have been. So we are witnessing the dissolution of the conditions which tied man to his past and gave him his Janus face.[35]

The past is dead, long live the present. And scientific history, "which [is] so deeply concerned with the past, has, in a sense, helped to destroy it as a social force, as a synthesizing and comprehensive statement of human destiny."[36]

But the scientific historian can no more than Comte give up his saving remnant of a religious-metaphysical view of man's past and future, albeit a universal and rationalistic "religion of humanity."

> Any historian who is not blindly prejudiced cannot but admit that the ordinary man and woman, unless they should be caught up in a murderous field of war, are capable of securing a richer life than their ancestors. (There is more food in the world, more opportunity of advancement, greater areas of liberty in ideas and in living than the world has ever known: art, music, literature can be enjoyed by tens of millions, not tens of thousands. This has been achieved not by clinging to conservative tradition or by relying on instinct or emotion, but by the application of human ingenuity, no matter what the underlying motive might be.) The great extension of rationalism has been a cause and a consequence of this development. In field after field, rationalism has proved its worth. It still has vast areas left to conquer in politics and social organization which may prove beyond its capacity, owing to the aggressive instincts built so deeply into man's nature. Nevertheless, the historian must stress the success, as well as point out the failure. Here is a message of the past which is as clear as, but far more true than, the message wrung from it by our ancestors. The past can be used to sanctify not authority nor morality but those qualities of the human mind which have raised us from the forest and swamp to the city, to build a qualified confidence in man's capacity to order his life and to stress the virtues of intellect, of rational behavior. And this past is neither pagan nor Christian, it belongs to no nation and no class, it is universal; it is human in the widest sense of that term.[37]

If my analysis of the traditionalization of innovations in India has any validity, then Plumb's announcement of the death of the past may be premature and exaggerated. For this analysis suggests that life is always "change and uncertainty" and that it derives meaning and validity not from "scientific history" but from the cultural philosophy—the world view and value system—of a society. The fact that one society's cultural philosophy bestows meaning and validity on incessant change and the present, and another's bestows it on the traditional past, does not enable us easily to decide which is the "scientifically true" cultural philosophy. It may be as great a myth for one society to assume that it can get along without any traditions, except "the tradition of the new," as it is for another to assume that all change is eternal recurrence of an ancestral past.

Myths or no, these two contrasting cultural philosophies lead to contrasting attitudes toward modernization. The interesting comparative cultural problem is not especially the nature of these contrasts in cultural philosophy or in attitudes toward modernization but the complementary questions: How does a society with a traditionalistic cultural philosophy deal with change and innovation? And how does a society whose cultural philosophy attaches supreme value to progress deal with tradition? The answers to these questions will probably show greater affinity between the traditionalistic and progressive cultural philosophies at the living, contextual level than is apparent at the textual level. For India, at least, the contextual approach suggests that its traditionalistic cultural philosophy, which Weber has called the "theodicy of the caste system," is capable of becoming a theodicy for a changing industrial system.

For Madras industrial leaders, the "great transformation" is taking place within two or three generations as they assimilate their innovative industrial roles to the traditional structures of joint family, caste, ritual, and belief. They do this not by rejecting the existence and value of novelty or their cultural traditions but by making a series of adaptive adjustments both in industry and in the traditional structures. In the long-run cosmic time perspective of Hindu cosmology, innovations and adjustments may look like the ephemeral appearances of an absolute reality, or the recurring disorders of a Kali age. In the short-run time perspective of human life and cultural history, however, the changes are very real and progressive even to a devout Hindu. To traditionalize them is to seek legitimacy and meaning for them in an accepted world view and value system.

## Notes

1. See R. Bendix, "Tradition and Modernity Reconsidered," *CSSH* 9, No. 3 (April; 1967): 292–346, for an excellent historical and critical review; see also Edward Shils, "Tradition and Liberty: Antinomy and Interdependence," *Ethics* 48, No. 3 (April, 1958): 163–65; *idem,* "Political Development in the New States," *CSSH* 2, No. 3 (April, 1960): 265–92, and No. 4 (July, 1960): 379–411; B. F. Hoselitz, "Tradition and Economic Growth," in Ralph Braibanti and J. J. Spengler, eds., *Tradition, Values, and Socio-economic Development* (Durham, N.C.: Duke University Press, 1961); Sylvia Thrupp, "Tradition and Development: A Choice of Views," *CSSH* 6, No. 1 (October, 1963): 84–92; and *idem,* "A Skirmish with Tradition" (unpublished ms.).

2. E. R. Wolf, "Understanding Civilizations," *CSSH* 9, No. 4 (July, 1967): 446–65. See also Redfield, *Primitive World and Its Transformations; idem, Peasant Society and Culture;* and Redfield and Singer, "Cultural Role of Cities" (see note 3, Introduction to Part One, above).

3. See Chapters 3, 4, 5, 6, and 8, above.

4. Ronald Dore, "Modernization," in *International Encyclopedia of Social Sciences* (see note 7, Chapter 6, above), 10:407.

5. M. N. Srinivas, "The Cohesive Role of Sanskritization," in Mason, ed., *India and Ceylon;* Srinivas, *Social Change in Modern India; idem,* "Sanskritization and Westernization" (see note 21, Chapter 2, above); and *idem, Coorgs.*

6. See Srinivas, *Social Change in Modern India,* pp. 6 ff., and articles by Srinivas, Rowe, Lynch, and Marriott in Singer and Cohn, eds., *Structure and Change.*

7. Raghavan, "Variety and Integration" (see note 19, Chapter 2); Singer, ed., *TI;* Staal, "Sanskrit and Sanskritization" (see note 21, Chapter 7); and van Buitenen, "Archaism of Bhāgavata Purāṇa" (see note 23, Chapter 7).

8. Mason, ed., *India and Ceylon.*

9. Bailey, *Caste and Economic Frontier;* Orans, *The Santal;* Hardgrave, *Nadars of Tamilnad;* Lynch, *Politics of Untouchability;* Silverberg, ed., *Social Mobility in Caste System;* and David L. Pocock, "Sociologies; Urban and Rural," in Dumont and Pocock, eds., *Contributions to Indian Sociology* 4 (April, 1960): 63 ff.

10. Dumont, "World Renunciation" (see note 41, Chapter 8, above). For the relation of Gandhi's asceticism to social reform, see Singer, "Cultural Values" (note 44, Chapter 1, above); Rudolph and Rudolph, *Modernity of Tradition,* Part Two; and Erikson, *Gandhi's Truth.*

11. For the distinction between "orthogenetic" and "heterogenetic" changes, see Redfield and Singer, "Cultural Role of Cities" (note 3, Introduction to Part One, above).

12. Prince Ilango Adigal, *Shilappadikaram* (*The Ankle Bracelet*), trans. by A. Daniélou (London: George Allen & Unwin Ltd., 1967), p. 30. Ramanujan has suggested that Puhār and Madurai as described in the *Śilappadikāram* are literary representations of, respectively, heterogenetic and orthogenetic cities. See A. K. Ramanujan, "Toward an Anthology of City Images," in Fox, ed., *Urban India.*

13. For Srinivas's account of "normal ritual status," see Srinivas, *Social Change in Modern India,* p. 121, and *idem, Coorgs,* pp. 106–7.

14. The material on *yavana* has been kindly made available to me by my colleague Kamil Zvelebil. See Zvelebil, "The Yavanas in Old Tamil Literature," *Archiv Orientalni*

24 (Prague, 1956): 401–9. Ramanujan has called my attention to a linguistic process similar to ritual neutralization that is also called "neutralization." He believes that linguistic neutralization plays an analogously important role in the formation of new colloquial standards of speech from literary and colloquial Tamil. See A. K. Ramanujan, "The Structure of Variation: A Study in Caste Dialects," in Singer and Cohn, eds., *Structure and Change.*

15. Surendra Nath Dasgupta, *A History of Indian Philosophy* (Cambridge: Cambridge University Press, 1922). I am also indebted to J. F. Staal for this reference to the Śaṅkara theory. See Staal, "Sanskrit and Sanskritization" (note 21, Chapter 7, above). p. 269.

16. For a field study of how a living caste of genealogists and mythographers records genealogies and relates them to mythical ancestors, see Shah and Shroff, "Vahīvañcā Bāroṭs of Gujarat" (note 23, Chapter 2, above), and the foreword by M. N. Srinivas in Singer, ed., *TI.* See also Weber, *Religion of India,* pp. 9–11; Sinha, "State Formation and Rajput Myth" (note 20, Chapter 7, above); Hitchcock, "Idea of Martial Rajput" (note 24, Chapter 2, above); S. Hivale, *The Pardhans of the Upper Narbada Valley* (Oxford: Oxford University Press, 1946); Cohn, "Pasts of Indian Village" (note 5, Introduction to Part Four); and Fürer-Haimendorf, "Historical Value of Bardic Literature" (note 40, Chapter 7, above).

17. For cultural policy and policy-makers, see Chapter 3, above; Marriott, "Cultural Policy in New States" (note 5, Introduction to Part Four); and Redfield, *Little Community,* pp. 106–8.

18. For the history of the Ḍravidian movement, see Hardgrave, *Dravidian Movement;* Irschick, *Politics and Social Conflict,* esp. Chapter 8; L. Rudolph, "Urban Life and Populist Radicalism: Dravidian Politics in Madras," *JAS* 20, No. 3 (May, 1961): 283–97; R. L. Hardgrave, Jr., "Religion, Politics and the DMK," in Donald E. Smith, ed., *South Asian Politics and Religion* (Princeton, N.J.: Princeton University Press, 1966); and Zvelebil, *Smile of Murugan,* esp. Chapter 18, "Tamil Renaissance."

19. K. Zvelebil, in a personal communication. For another interpretation, see A. L. Basham, "Some Reflections on Dravidians and Aryans," *Bulletin of the Institute of Traditional Cultures* (Madras, 1963).

20. The information on historical Tamil usage has been obtained from K. Zvelebil. For ancient Tamil poetry and poetics, see Ramanujan, *Interior Landscape,* and Zvelebil, *Smile of Murugan.*

21. Dasgupta, *History of Indian Philosophy* 1:53 and 466–68. For a contemporary Madras interpretation of Advaitavedānta in terms of the different paths, see Raghavan, "Some Leading Ideas" (note 14, Chapter 2, above).

22. Translated by A. K. Ramanujan, reprinted with translator's permission.

23. D. M. Datta, "Epistemological Methods in Indian Philosophy," in Moore, ed., *Indian Mind,* pp. 119–20.

24. See Chapter 6, page 231 above.

25. Geertz, *Social History of Indonesian Town,* esp. p. 152.

26. Weber, *Religion of India,* pp. 11–20; see also his *Sociology of Religion,* pp. 108–17, on the Jews as "pariah people."

27. Weber, *Religion of India,* p. 112. See Chapter 8, above.

28. *Ibid.,* pp. 111–12. On the relation of European medieval religious law to the taking of interest, see B. Nelson, *The Idea of Usury: From Tribal Brotherhood to Universal Otherhood,* 2d ed. (Chicago: University of Chicago Press, 1969).

29. Weber, *Religion of India,* p. 30.

30. *Ibid.*

31. Clifford Geertz, *Agricultural Involution* (Berkeley and Los Angeles: University of California Press, 1963), p. 61; *idem, Social History of Indonesian Town,* p. 54; and *idem, Peddlers and Princes* (Chicago: University of Chicago Press, 1963), p. 139. In this passage, Geertz uses "compartmentalized" and "compartmentalization" to refer to three processes that I have called "enclavement" (the "sharp social and cultural segregation of both traders and trading"), "ritual neutralization" (trading develops as an "interstitial pursuit, one to which the values of the wider society are held by common agreement not to apply"), and "compartmentalization" in the sense that the "nearly total insulation of commercial behavior from the general nexus of cultural activities" provides a "preserve for the exercise of economic rationality independently of non-economic

constraints." Geertz also sees a normative ethical code developing from the combined operation of these processes, at least in the situation of the bazaar economy, if not at the level of more complex industrial organization.

Geertz's development of the "compartmentalization" theory is, so far as I know, independent of mine. My own interest in the concept was first aroused by the widely noted observation of modern Indians who adhered to traditional practices and beliefs, and the usual interpretations of this situation as somehow paradoxical, anomalous, and contradictory. When I found that most Indians I met did not experience the coexistence of the modern and traditional as a cultural contradiction or even a conflict, it seemed to me that the compartmentalization theory offered a better explanation than the theory of modern and traditional societies as mutually exclusive types with mixed cases interpreted as transitional from the traditional to the modern.

The compartmentalization theory is implicit in Shils, *Intellectual Between Tradition and Modernity;* R. S. Khare has applied it explicitly to an analysis of the home-office adjustments of the Kanya-Kubja Brahmans in "Home and Office" see note 50, Chapter 8, above).

An extended effort to apply the classical dichotomous theory of modern and traditional societies will be found in Myrdal, *Asian Drama,* esp. Prologue and Part I in Vol. 1. On the psychology of compartmentalization, see Alex Inkeles, "Making Modern Men," *The American Journal of Sociology* 75, No. 2 (September, 1969): 208–25. See also McGee, *Southeast Asian City,* and R. Murphey, "Traditionalism and Colonialism: Changing Urban Roles in Asia," *JAS* 29, No. 1 (November, 1969): 67–84.

32. Redfield and Singer, "Cultural Role of Cities" (note 2, *supra*), pp. 69–70.

33. On the luxury trade with the Orient, see W. M. Wheeler, *Rome Beyond the Imperial Frontiers* (London: Bell, 1954); Wheatley, *Golden Khersonese;* and Chapter 1 of this volume.

34. Sylvia Thrupp has introduced the phrase "temporal ethnocentrism" in this sense. See her "Skirmish with Tradition" (note 1, *supra*).

35. Plumb, *Death of the Past,* pp. 58–59.

36. *Ibid.,* p. 136.

37. *Ibid.,* pp. 140–41.

# *Selected Bibliography*

ARCHER, W. G. *The Loves of Krishna*. New York: Grove Press, 1958.

BAILEY, FREDERICK G. *Caste and the Economic Frontier*. Manchester: Manchester University Press; New York: The Humanities Press, 1957.

———. *Tribe, Caste and Nation*. Manchester: Manchester University Press, 1960.

BALA RATNAM, L. K., ed. *Anthropology on the March*. Madras: Book Center, 1963.

BARY, WILLIAM THEODORE DE, *et al. Sources of Indian Tradition*. New York: Columbia University Press, 1958.

BASHAM, ARTHUR L. *The Wonder that Was India: A Survey of the History and Culture of the Indian Subcontinent Before the Coming of the Muslims*. 3d ed. New York: Taplinger, 1968.

BEALS, ALAN R. *Gopalpur: A South Indian Village*. New York: Holt, Rinehart & Winston, 1962.

BENDIX, REINHARD. *Max Weber: An Intellectual Portrait*. New York: Doubleday, Anchor Books, 1960.

BETEILLE, ANDRÉ. *Caste, Class and Power: Changing Patterns of Stratifiication in a Tanjore Village*. Berkeley and Los Angeles: University of California Press, 1965.

BHARATI, A. *The Tantric Tradition*. New York: Hilary House Publishers Ltd., 1965.

BOSE, NIRMAL K. *Culture and Society in India*. Bombay: Asia Publishing House, 1967.

BROWN, W. NORMAN. *Man in the Universe: Cultural Continuities in India*. Berkeley and Los Angeles: University of California Press, 1966.

COHN, BERNARD S. *India: The Social Anthropology of a Civilization*. Englewood Cliffs, N.J.: Prentice-Hall, 1971.

DERRETT, J. DUNCAN. *Religion, Law and the State in India*. New York: The Free Press of Glencoe, 1968.

DESAI, I. P. *Some Aspects of Family in Mahuva*. New York: Asia Publishing House, 1964.

DIEHL, C. G. *Instrument and Purpose*. Lund, Sweden: C. W. K. Gleerup, 1956.

DIMOCK, EDWARD C. *The Place of the Hidden Moon: Erotic Mysticism in the Vaiṣṇava-Sahajiyā Cult of Bengal.* Chicago: University of Chicago Press, 1966.

DUBE, SHYAMA. *India's Changing Villages.* New York: The Humanities Press; London: Routledge & Kegan Paul, 1958.

DUMONT, LOUIS. *Homo Hierarchicus: The Caste System and Its Implications.* Chicago: University of Chicago Press, 1970.

———. *Religion, Politics and History in India.* The Hague: Mouton & Co., 1970.

———. *Une Sous-caste de l'Inde du Sud.* The Hague: Mouton & Co., 1957.

DUMONT, LOUIS, and DAVID POCOCK, eds. *Contributions to Indian Sociology.* 5 vols. The Hague: Mouton & Co., 1957–61.

EISENSTADT, SHMUEL N., ed. *The Protestant Ethic and Modernization.* New York: Basic Books, 1968.

EPSTEIN, T. S. *Economic Development and Social Change in South India.* New York: The Humanities Press; Manchester, University of Manchester Press, 1962.

ERIKSON, ERIK. *Gandhi's Truth.* New York: Norton, 1969.

FAIRBANK, JOHN K., ed. *Chinese Thought and Institutions.* Chicago: University of Chicago Press, 1967.

FARQUHAR, J. N. *A Primer of Hinduism.* London and New York: Oxford University Press, 1912.

FOX, RICHARD G. *From Zamindar to Ballot Box.* Ithaca: Cornell University Press, 1969.

———, ed. *Urban India: Society, Space and Image.* Durham, N.C.: Duke University Press, 1970.

GEERTZ, CLIFFORD. *Islam Observed: Religious Development in Morocco and Indonesia.* New Haven, Conn.: Yale University Press, 1968.

———. *The Religion of Java.* Glencoe, Ill.: The Free Press, 1960.

———. *The Social History of an Indonesian Town.* Cambridge, Mass.: The MIT Press, 1965.

———, ed. *Old Societies and New States.* Glencoe, Ill.: The Free Press, 1963.

GHURYE, GOVIND S. *Indian Sādhus.* 2d ed. New York: The Humanities Press, 1964.

GHURYE, KUMUD G. *Preservation of Learned Tradition in India.* Bombay: Popular Book Depot, 1950.

GILLION, KENNETH L. *Ahmedabad: A Study in Indian Urban History.* Berkeley and Los Angeles: University of California Press, 1968.

GLUCKMAN, MAX, ed. *Closed Systems and Open Minds.* Chicago: Aldine Publishing Co., 1964.

GOODY, JACK, ed. *Literacy in Traditional Societies.* Cambridge: Cambridge University Press, 1968.

GORE, M. S. *Urbanization and Family Change.* Bombay: Popular Prakashar, 1968.

GRUNEBAUM, GUSTAVE E. VON, ed. *Modern Islam: The Search for Cultural Identity.* Berkeley and Los Angeles: University of California Press, 1962.

———, ed. *Unity and Variety in Muslim Civilization.* Chicago: University of Chicago Press, 1955.

Guiteras-Holmes, Calixta. *Perils of the Soul: The World View of a Tzotzil Indian.* Glencoe, Ill.: The Free Press, 1961.

Hardgrave, Robert L. *The Dravidian Movement.* Bombay: Popular Prakashar; New York: The Humanities Press, 1968.

———. *The Nadars of Tamilnad: The Political Culture of a Community in Change.* Berkeley and Los Angeles: University of California Press, 1969.

Harper, Edward B., ed. *Religion in South Asia.* Seattle: University of Washington Press, 1964.

Hay, Stephen N. *Asian Ideas of East and West.* Cambridge: Harvard University Press, 1970.

Hazlehurst, Leighton W. *Entrepreneurship and the Merchant Castes in a Punjabi City.* Durham, N.C.: Duke University Program in Comparative Studies on Southern Asia, 1966.

Hoijer, Harry, ed. *Language in Culture.* Chicago: University of Chicago Press, 1954.

Irschick, Eugene F. *Politics and Social Conflict in South India: The Non-Brahman Movement and Tamil Separatism.* Berkeley and Los Angeles: University of California Press, 1969.

Karve, D. D., and Ellen E. McDonald. *The New Brahmans: Five Maharashtrian Families.* Berkeley and Los Angeles: University of California Press, 1963.

Karve, Irawati. *Kinship Organization in India.* Poona: n.p., 1953; rev. ed., New York: Asia Publishing House, 1965.

Khare, R. S. *The Changing Brahmans: Association and Elites Among the Kanya-Kubjas of North India.* Chicago: University of Chicago Press, 1970.

Kopf, David. *British Orientalism and the Bengal Renaissance: The Dynamics of Indian Modernization.* Berkeley and Los Angeles: University of California Press, 1969.

Kothari, Rajni. *Politics in India.* New Delhi: Orient Longman, 1970.

Kramrisch, Stella. *The Art of India.* London: The Phaidon Press, 1954.

———. *The Hindu Temple,* 2 vols., Calcutta: University of Calcutta, 1946.

Kroeber, Alfred L. *An Anthropologist Looks at History.* Ed. by Theodora K. Kroeber, foreword by Milton B. Singer. Berkeley and Los Angeles: University of California Press, 1963.

Lambert, Richard D. *Workers, Factories and Social Change in India.* Princeton, N.J.: Princeton University Press, 1963.

Leach, Edmund R. *Dialectic in Practical Religion.* Cambridge: Cambridge University Press, 1968.

———, ed. *Aspects of Caste in South India, Ceylon and North West Pakistan.* Cambridge: Cambridge University Press, 1960.

Leslie, Charles. *Now We Are Civilized: A Study of the World View of the Zatopec Indians of Mitla, Oaxaca.* Detroit: Wayne State University Press, 1960.

Lewis, Oscar, with asst. of Victor Barnouw. *Village Life in Northern India: Studies in a Delhi Village.* Urbana: University of Illinois Press, 1958.

LYNCH, OWEN M. *The Politics of Untouchability: Social Mobility and Social Change in a City of India.* New York: Columbia University Press, 1970.

MCGEE, T. G. *The Southeast Asian City: A Social Geography of the Primate Cities of Southeast Asia.* New York: Praeger Publishers, 1967.

MANDELBAUM, DAVID G. *Society in India.* 2 vols. Berkeley and Los Angeles: University of California Press, 1970.

MARRIOTT, MCKIM, ed. *Village India: Studies in the Little Community.* Chicago: University of Chicago Press, 1955.

MASON, PHILIP, ed. *India and Ceylon: Unity and Diversity.* London and New York: Oxford University Press, 1967.

MATHUR, K. S. *Caste and Ritual in a Malwa Village.* Bombay: Asia Publishing House, 1964.

MAYER, A., MCKIM MARRIOTT, and RICHARD L. PARK, eds. *Pilot Project: India.* Berkeley and Los Angeles: University of California Press, 1958.

MAYER, ADRIAN C. *Caste and Kinship in Central India.* Berkeley and Los Angeles: University of California Press, 1960.

MOORE, CHARLES A., ed. *The Indian Mind: Essentials of Indian Philosophy and Culture.* Honolulu: East-West Center Press, 1967.

MOREHOUSE, WARD, ed. *Understanding Science and Technology in India and Pakistan.* New York: Foreign Area Materials Center, 1967.

MORRIS, MORRIS D. *The Emergence of an Industrial Labor Force in India: A Study of the Bombay Cotton Mills, 1854–1947.* Berkeley and Los Angeles: University of California Press, 1965.

MUKERJEE, RADHAKAMAL. *The Lord of the Autumn Moons.* Bombay: Asia Publishing House, 1957.

MYRDAL, GUNNAR. *Asian Drama: An Inquiry into the Poverty of Nations.* New York: Pantheon, 1968.

NEHRU, JAWAHARLAL. *Discovery of India.* New York: John Day Co., 1946.

NILAKANTA SASTRI, K. A. *History of South India.* London: Oxford University Press, 1958.

NIVISON, DAVID S., and ARTHUR WRIGHT. *Confucianism in Action.* Stanford, Calif.: Stanford University Press, 1953.

ORANS, MARTIN. *The Santal: A Tribe in Search of a Great Tradition.* Detroit: Wayne State University Press, 1965.

PHILIPS, C. H., ed. *Historians of India, Pakistan and Ceylon.* London and New York: Oxford University Press, 1961.

———, ed. *Politics and Society in India.* London: George Allen & Unwin, 1963.

PLUMB, J. H. *The Death of the Past.* Boston: Houghton Mifflin, 1970.

RADHAKRISHNAN, SARVEPALLI. *Hindu View of Life.* London: Oxford University Press, 1926; New York: Macmillan, 1939.

RAGHAVAN, V. *The Great Integrators: The Saint-Singers of India.* Delhi: Government of India, 1964.

———. *The Indian Heritage.* Bangalore: The Indian Institute of Culture, 1956.

RAGHAVAN, V., and C. RAMANUJACHURI. *The Spiritual Heritage of Tyagaraja.* Madras: The Ramakrishna Mission Students' Home, 1957.

RAMANUJAN, A. K. *The Interior Landscape: Love Poems from a Classical Tamil Anthology*. Bloomington: Indiana University Press, 1967.

REDFIELD, ROBERT. *The Folk Culture of the Yucatan*. Chicago: University of Chicago Press, 1941.

———. *Human Nature and the Study of Society*. Ed. by MARGARET PARK REDFIELD. Chicago: University of Chicago Press, 1962.

———. *The Little Community: Viewpoints for the Study of the Human Whole*. Chicago: University of Chicago Press, 1955.

———. *Peasant Society and Culture: An Anthropological Approach to Civilization*. Chicago: University of Chicago Press, 1956.

———. *The Primitive World and Its Transformations*. Ithaca, N.Y.: Cornell University Press, 1953.

RENOU, L., and J. FILLIOZAT. *L'Inde Classique*. 2 vols. 1, Paris: Payot, 1947; 2, Hanoi: n.p., 1953.

ROSS, AILEEN D. *The Hindu Family in Its Urban Setting*. Toronto: University of Toronto Press, 1961.

RUDOLPH, LLOYD I., and SUSANNE H. RUDOLPH. *The Modernity of Tradition: Political Development in India*. Chicago: University of Chicago Press, 1967.

SARADANANDA, SWAMI. *Sri Rama Krishna: The Great Master*. 2d rev. ed. Madras: Sri Ramakrishna Math, n.d.

SHETH, N. R. *The Social Framework of an Indian Factory*. Manchester: Manchester University Press, 1968; New York: The Humanities Press, 1969.

SHILS, EDWARD. *The Indian Intellectual Between Tradition and Modernity: The Indian Situation*. The Hague: Mouton & Co., 1961; New York: Har-Row Torchbooks, 1970.

SILVERBERG, JAMES, ed. *Social Mobility in the Caste System of India: An Interdisciplinary Symposium*. The Hague: Mouton & Co., 1960; New York: The Humanities Press, 1968.

SINGER, MILTON B., ed. *Introducing India in Liberal Education*. Chicago: University fo Chicago Press, 1957.

———, ed. *Introduction to the Civilization of India: Changing Dimensions of Indian Society and Culture*. Chicago: University of Chicago Press, 1957.

———, ed. *Krishna: Myths, Rites and Attitudes*. Honolulu: East-West Center Press, 1966; Chicago: University of Chicago Press, Phoenix, 1969.

———, ed. *South and Southeast Asian Studies at the University of Chicago*. Chicago: Committee on Southern Asian Studies, 1966.

———, ed. *Traditional India: Structure and Change*. Philadelphia: American Folklore Society, 1958, 1959.

SINGER, MILTON B., and BERNARD S. COHN, eds. *Structure and Change in Indian Society*. Chicago: Aldine Publishing Company, 1968.

SMITH, DONALD E., ed. *South Asian Politics and Religion*. Princeton, N.J.: Princeton University Press, 1966.

SPEAR, PERCIVAL. *India, A Modern History*. Ann Arbor: The University of Michigan Press, 1961.

SPIRO, MELFORD E. *Buddhism and Society: A Great Tradition and Its Burmese Vicissitudes*. New York: Harper & Row, 1970.

SRINIVAS, MYSORE N. *Caste in Modern India and Other Essays*. Bombay: Asia Publishing House, 1962.

———. *Religion and Society Among the Coorgs of South India*. London and New York: Oxford University Press, 1952.

———. *Social Change in Modern India*. Berkeley and Los Angeles: University of California Press, 1968.

———, ed. *India's Villages*. West Bengal: Government Press, 1955.

STAAL, J. F. *Nambudiri Vedic Recitations*. The Hague: Mouton & Co., 1961.

TANDON, PRAKASH. *Punjabi Century, 1857–1947*. London: Chatto & Windus, 1961; paper, Berkeley and Los Angeles: University of California Press, 1968.

TURNER, VICTOR W. *The Ritual Process: Structure and Anti-Structure*. Chicago: Aldine Publishing Co., 1969.

VAN BUITENEN, J. A. B. *The Pravargya, An Ancient Indian Iconic Ritual Described and Annotated*. Poona: Deccan College, 1968.

VIDYARTHI, LALITA P. *The Sacred Gayawal*. Bombay: Asia Publishing House, 1961.

WAGLEY, CHARLES. *The Latin American Tradition*. New York: Columbia University Press, 1968.

WEBER, MAX. *The Protestant Ethic and the Spirit of Capitalism*. New York: Charles Scribner's Sons, 1930.

———. *The Religion of India: The Sociology of Hinduism and Buddhism*. Glencoe, Ill.: The Free Press, 1958.

———. *The Sociology of Religion*. Trans. by EPHRAIM FISCHOFFS. Boston: Beacon Press, 1964.

WEINER, MYRON. *Party Building in a New Nation. The Indian National Congress*. Chicago: University of Chicago Press, 1967.

WHEATLEY, PAUL. *The Golden Khersonese: Studies in the Historical Geography of the Malay Peninsula Before A.D. 1500*. Kuala Lumpur: University of Malaya Press, 1961.

———. *The Pivot of the Four Quarters, A Preliminary Enquiry into the Origins and Character of the Ancient Chinese City*. Chicago: Aldine Publishing Co., 1971.

WISER, WILLIAM H., and CHARLOTTE V. WISER. *Behind Mud Walls, 1930–1960*. Berkeley and Los Angeles: University of California Press, 1963.

WRIGHT, ARTHUR F., ed. *Studies in Chinese Thought*. Chicago: University of Chicago Press, 1953.

YALMAN, NUR O. *Under the Bo Tree: Studies in Caste, Kinship and Marriage in the Interior of Ceylon*. Berkeley and Los Angeles: University of California Press, 1967.

ZVELEBIL, KAMIL. *The Smile of Murugan: A History of Tamil Literature* (ms.).

# Index